LARRY COHEN

The Stuff of Gods and Monsters

Praise for Michael Doyle and
Larry Cohen: The Stuff Of Gods And Monsters

"Michael Doyle is not only one of the best writers I've ever known, he's one of the best interviewers. *Larry Cohen: The Stuff of Gods and Monsters* is a vital look at one of genre filmmaking's more important, and less appreciated, artists. A wonderfully-written, well-researched, and completely captivating portrait of a consistently brilliant auteur, this book is an absolute must-have for anyone who loves genre movies, filmmaking tales or in-depth character studies."

– Dave Alexander, Editor-in-chief of *Rue Morgue* magazine

"Larry Cohen is a truly independent American filmmaker whose remarkable body of work continues to entertain and astonish. Michael Doyle's book, *Larry Cohen: The Stuff of Gods and Monsters*, provides new insights into this unique and always surprising filmmaker."

– John Landis, director of *The Blues Brothers* and *An American Werewolf in London*

"For those of us who love the works of Larry Cohen, this is the most revealing and informative material ever published about him. And if by some chance you don't know about Larry's remarkable career, take this opportunity to learn how one maverick writer/director/producer has been able to survive and flourish in the ever changing madhouse of show biz."

– Joe Dante, director of *The Howling*, *Gremlins* and *The 'Burbs*

"With *Larry Cohen: The Stuff of Gods and Monsters*, Michael Doyle has delivered an essential and profoundly illuminating volume on one of American cinema's most idiosyncratic and unheralded talents."

– John Hancock, director of *Bang the Drum Slowly*, *Weeds* and *Prancer*

LARRY COHEN

The Stuff of Gods and Monsters

by Michael Doyle

BearManor Media
2016

Larry Cohen: The Stuff of Gods and Monsters

© 2016 Michael Doyle

All Rights Reserved.
Reproduction in whole or in part without the author's permission is strictly forbidden.

For information, address:

BearManor Media
P. O. Box 71426
Albany, GA 31708

bearmanormedia.com

Typesetting and layout by John Teehan

Published in the USA by BearManor Media

ISBN—1-59393-850-0
978-1-59393-850-5

*This is for my two lovely little monsters,
Poppy Mae & Milo Jack*

Table of Contents

Acknowledgements ix

Foreword by Laurene Landon xi

Introduction by Mick Garris... 1

Youth (1941-1958).. 5

The Television Years... 27

Screenplays: Part I (1966-1986)... 67

Bone (1971) 91

Black Caesar (1972)... 107

Hell up in Harlem (1973)... 123

It's Alive (1974).. 139

God Told Me To (1976) 159

The Private Files of J. Edgar Hoover (1977).................... 179

Photo Section I 207

It Lives Again (1978).. 227

Full Moon High (1981).. 241

See China and Die (1981) 257

Intermission: *I, the Jury* (1982)... 265

Q – The Winged Serpent (1982).. 275

Perfect Strangers (1984) 295

Special Effects (1984) 309

The Stuff (1985) 325

Screenplays: Part II (1987-1996) 345

Intermission: *Deadly Illusion* (1987) 367

It's Alive III: Island of the Alive (1987) 373

A Return to Salem's Lot (1987) 389

Maniac Cop Trilogy (1988-1993) 405

Wicked Stepmother (1989) 423

Photo Section II 441

Intermission: *The Heavy* (1990) 457

The Ambulance (1991) 463

As Good As Dead (1995) 481

Original Gangstas (1996) 489

Screenplays: Part III (1996-2011) 507

Masters of Horror: Pick Me Up (2005) 529

On Writing 545

Methodology, Movies & Madness 563

Notes 581

Credits 639

Bibliography 675

About the Author 679

Index 681

Acknowledgments

A **WRITER,** whose name presently deserts me, once remarked that no book is ever written alone. The one you now hold in your hands is certainly no exception.

Of those helpful individuals who assisted me in realizing it, my profound thanks go first and foremost to Mr. Larry Cohen for his unwavering enthusiasm and patience with this project. The myriad interviews that comprise *Larry Cohen: The Stuff of Gods and Monsters* were conducted from June 2011 to September 2014, and involved several additional phone calls during that period in order to corroborate facts and add further details and depth to existing answers.

Throughout this endeavour, Larry always gave generously of his time as my innumerable questions demanded a seemingly effortless feat of memory on his part. Needless to say, this book would not have been possible without his full co-operation and support. Let me also submit for the record that ever since I first saw *It's Alive* as a traumatised eight-year-old—peeping through my fingers as Frank Davis discovers his newborn baby has decimated the entire maternity staff—Larry's movies have been a constant source of entertainment and enlightenment for me. I thank him again for the countless hours of pleasure they—and our many long conversations—have given me.

I would also like to express my sincere gratitude to Laurene ("nobody knows Larry Cohen like I know Larry Cohen") Landon for furnishing this volume with a deeply heartfelt foreword, and for giving me some personal insights into Larry and his work. The same goes for Mick Garris, a man who is truly deserving of his reputation as the nicest guy in Hollywood, for providing me with a wonderful introduction. Aside from being a passionate director and writer, Mick is also an eloquent voice and erstwhile advocate for all that is great about the horror genre.

In addition, I would like to extend my appreciation to Dave Alexander and Rodrigo Gudino of *Rue Morgue* magazine for kindly giving me something else to do whilst toiling on this book. I also offer similar sentiments to Ben Ohmart and John Teehan for their quiet but consistent encouragement, and Dale Warner for his invaluable technical assistance with digitizing photographs, stills and illustrations, all of which came courtesy of Larry Cohen, Steve Neill, and Mick Garris (cheers, guys!)

My deepest love and thanks everywhere and at all times to my wife, Siân, whose unfailing belief in me is the source of all my strength. Not only did you lend a hand in tracking down rare copies of movies, television shows, books, periodicals, and other elusive research materials, you also plied me with copious cups of soul-restoring tea. And big love to my beautiful children, Poppy and Milo, for distracting their Daddy both when it was necessary and when it wasn't.

I am also indebted to my parents, John and Christine Doyle, my siblings Steven and Sarah (who have both survived their childhoods reasonably intact despite having me for an older brother), and my parents-in-law, Howard and Daryl Morgan, for all their love and support over the years.

Finally, I would like to take this opportunity to remember my beloved grandparents, Evan Idris Evans (1925-2001) and Evelyn May Evans (1923-2008), as this book owes its very existence to their contagious love and passion for cinema. Thank you both for always allowing me to watch horror movies like *It's Alive*, *Q – The Winged Serpent* and *The Stuff* on any day that ended in a Y, and for letting me burn out a succession of your video recorders with barely a complaining word.

– Michael Doyle
November 14, 2014

Foreword

A Few Thoughts on Larry

MOST PEOPLE CONVERSANT WITH THE SATIRICAL allegories of a Larry Cohen film are well aware that in every movie he has made there is a thematic echo or accompanying social commentary. It may be subliminal or subversive, but it is there.

I first met Larry during the filming of *Full Moon High*, when my then agent, Beverly Hecht, sent me to see him for a small role. After speaking with him for maybe half an hour and witnessing his joyful sprit (not to mention how handsome he was) I became more and more intimidated. He was in the process of firing the lead actress and asked me if I wanted to star in the film. Being Polish, blonde, and a moron, out of sheer terror I lied and said I couldn't star in his film due to an audition.

There was no audition!

Larry is arguably one of the most distinctive twentieth century film-makers and one of the few who has been consistent as a writer for over fifty years. He is the most convivial and jocular man one could ever hope to encounter—which I sincerely hope people will remember—and to lose him will undoubtedly be the darkest day of my life; the absence of light in my heart. He has been my best friend and confidante for over thirty-seven years and I have always felt that we are one soul intertwined in two bodies.

I sometimes wish Larry had authored more comedies as his humour by far eclipses his fame as a suspense/thriller/horror director and word-smith. He has so many fans it is simply mind-boggling, but, despite that fact, Larry is still the most insecure and humble mortal on God's earth.

Larry Cohen is not one in a million; he is one in a lifetime. No one comes close. Everywhere I go, there's no one who compares. It's like climbing to the top, then falling down the stairs.

– Laurene Landon
June 20, 2014

[Laurene Landon is an actress and model, who has worked on many Larry Cohen productions including *I the Jury*; *It's Alive III: Island of the Alive*; *The Stuff*; *A Return To Salem's Lot*; *Maniac Cop*; *Maniac Cop 2*; *Wicked Stepmother*; *The Ambulance*; and *Masters of Horror: Pick Me Up*. She has also appeared in *Roller Boogie* (1979); *All the Marbles* (1981); *Airplane II: The Sequel* (1982); *Hundra* (1983); *Yellow Hair and the Fortress of Gold* (1984); *America 3000* (1986); and *Day Out of Days* (2014).]

Introduction

CohenVision

I THOUGHT THAT THE BRILLIANT *It's Alive* was my introduction to the unique filmic mind of Larry Cohen, but I was wrong.

A child of the 1960s, I was brought up by the family Magnavox television, and Cohen's footprint was stamped large and indelibly there. *Branded*, a Western starring Chuck Connors, whose theme song still remains seared into my musical memory, was created by the same man who has brought us mutant babies, hermaphrodite gods, killer desserts, and maniacal undead policemen. So was *The Invaders*, the classic paranoid science fiction series about insidious aliens with rigid pinkies who are secretly infiltrating American society. Cohen's other writing credits from this period include some of the best episodes of the Emmy-festooned, high falutin' legal drama, *The Defenders*, which was the *Law and Order* juggernaut of its day.

These shows might have been huge successes, and maybe even drew audiences in far greater numbers than his iconoclastic feature films, but the man achieved fame and glory for his movies—all of them independently produced and each possessing a singular style and undefined sanity that could only have come from one director. Larry Cohen's cinematic vision is truly one of a kind and often not of this earth. His sense of storytelling logic is his own and, though eccentric might be a gentle term, its brilliance and audaciousness sets him apart from all others.

It's Alive was made (or acquired) by Warner Bros. in 1974, the same year that studio took William Friedkin's *The Exorcist*. This whacked-out ecological baby monster thriller, featuring one of a very young Rick Baker's earliest monster creations, rolled through America—market by market, drive-in by drive-in—and was a huge, if quiet, success. Though I later caught up with earlier work by the Maestro—including Cohen's trenchant directorial debut, the uncompromising and unforgettable racial drama *Bone*—it was this picture with its notable tagline ("There's only one thing wrong with the Davis baby…it's alive!") that pricked up my ears.

But it was Cohen's next movie—known at the time that I saw it as *God Told Me To*—that completely blew me away. The film, with its committed and excellent cast including Tony Lo Bianco, Sandy Dennis, Richard Lynch, and Silvia Sydney, among others, was a stunningly original science fiction horror story and drama of religious doubt that was like nothing I had ever seen before. It was played completely straight and was an incredibly powerful indictment of blind faith and religious fervour—mostly through Catholicism—that was written and directed by a Jew. It's deep, it's perceptive, it's brilliant, and it's out of its fucking mind!

I had just started writing about genre films at that time—it was 1976—and had to interview the guy who had made this amazing movie. So, I contacted him through New World Pictures and met him where he was editing *The Private Files of J. Edgar Hoover* in a little cutting room on Santa Monica Boulevard in Hollywood. That was my first meeting with Larry Cohen, and I was amazed to find that this auteur of remarkable lunatic cinema was a kind, normal, really funny former Borscht belt comedian who had discovered a new life in the world of horror films.

It is rare indeed to find an original voice in film, rarer still to find it in the world of horror. Practically by definition, horror movies are self-referential and deal in the tropes and techniques of decades of scaring audiences. But Larry's films are like no others. Aside from his wildly original themes, his characters are richly drawn. They are not just flawed but are sometimes downright off their rockers—like Michael Moriarty's likable low-life criminal Jimmy Quinn in *Q - The Winged Serpent*, the tale of Quetzalcoatl, a flying dragon-lizard god that nests in the Chrysler Building in Manhattan. There is also the charmingly demented Mo Rutherford in *The Stuff* (Moriarty again), an industrial saboteur who pits his considerable wits against an implacable and remorselessly homicidal ice cream dessert.

But it is not just the wild tales and brilliant performances that make Cohen's idiosyncratic work so legendary; it's how he makes them as well.

This is the ultimate guerrilla filmmaker we're talking about here. The director who, during the making of *God Told Me To* (also known as *Demon* and I have the one-sheet to prove it) brought his crew—without permits or anything—to the St. Patrick's Day parade in New York City with dozens, maybe even hundreds, of New York cops marching and participating, and without telling anybody what he was doing then started a shoot-out between characters from the film in the midst of all of this real-life action! A very young Andy Kaufman—before he became legendary for his masterly audience-baffling stand-up comedy—played one of those cops, and I ran into him at a movie theater not long after that. I asked him about the experience and he just said, in the most angelic way, that he wasn't sure about it as he was new to movies then.

Similarly, there was gunfire, mayhem, and mischief aplenty on the streets of New York during the shooting of *Black Caesar*, *Hell up in Harlem* and *Q - The Winged Serpent*, and again, all done without the necessary permits! No one but the members of the production were informed of what was actually going on, and if you watch those movies a little more closely, you'll notice that the terror, confusion, and concern you read on the faces of many actual bystanders is quite genuine.

It is about time that there was a book that chronicled the remarkable life and work of one of our most unique and under-appreciated filmmakers. I was thrilled to be able to bring Larry back behind the camera for his 2005 *Masters of Horror* film, *Pick Me Up*, which showed he was still in peak visionary condition, even when the script (and this one was written by David J. Schow) was not his own. And now his work has finally been chronicled here and laid out for your inspection.

Larry Cohen is a filmmaker whose canon has to be seen to be believed but, once seen, can never be forgotten.

– Mick Garris
October 20, 2014

[Mick Garris is a writer, producer, and director, and is responsible for such acclaimed films and mini-series as *Psycho IV: The Beginning* (1990); *Sleepwalkers* (1992); *The Stand* (1994); *The Shining* (1997); *Quicksilver Highway* (1997); *Riding the Bullet* (2004); *Desperation* (2006); and *Bag of Bones* (2011). He is also the creator and executive producer of Showtime's *Masters of Horror*, directing a film in each of its two seasons, *Chocolate* (2005) and *Valerie on the Stairs* (2006).]

"Though this be madness, yet there is method in it."
—Polonius, *Hamlet*, Act 2, scene 2

"If I had all the freedom, time and money to do what I wanted, I'd still do things my own way because I can only be me. Only I can make the kinds of pictures that I make."
—Larry Cohen

"To a new world of gods and monsters!"
—Dr. Septimus Pretorius, *The Bride of Frankenstein*

Youth (1941–1958)

MICHAEL DOYLE: Conflicting sources claim that you were born on July 15, either in the year 1938 or 1941, in Kingston, New York, and that your family later moved to the Riverdale section of the Bronx. Is any of this accurate?

LARRY COHEN: No, not entirely. I was not born in Kingston and neither did I move with my family to the Riverdale neighbourhood. That information is all wrong. I was born in 1941 and grew up in Manhattan and I've never even been in Kingston. My folks did move to Riverdale, but I was no longer living at home with them anymore. I had already moved out by the time they'd arrived there. Before that, we had been living in the Washington Heights section of New York City in uptown Manhattan.

What was your neighbourhood like?

Washington Heights was a very nice neighbourhood. There was a huge park there called Fort Tryon Park, and at the top of the park was a reconstructed church called The Cloisters that the Rockefellers had shipped over from Europe and reassembled back in the 1930s. It looked just like a medieval castle and had drawbridges and all kinds of turrets. My friends and I used to play Robin Hood there and games like that. We would be duelling with each other and excitedly running around the parapets and it was a truly wonderful, magical place. The park was great during the wintertime and there would be sleigh-riding through the snow. In the summertime, it would be beautifully lush and green and I enjoyed that place very much. I actually made my first 8mm movie in Fort Tryon Park.

What was that first film about?

It was about Russian spies and I actually shot it on the very same day that Stalin died.[1] The whole idea of the story was that Russian spies were using the park as a place to drop off top secret microfilm. This one defecting Russian spy wants to destroy the microfilm but he is captured. He has the microfilm rolled up in the barrel of his gun, so he wants his enemies to shoot him as they will inadvertently destroy the microfilm when he is killed. That was the gimmick of the movie. It was a real Larry Cohen story even though I was only ten years old when I made it. I used my father's 8mm camera, and you had to wind it up and it ran for about forty-five seconds or a minute before you had to wind it again. All the cuts were done inside the camera. I'd do a master shot then cut in for a close-up; followed by another master shot, another close-up, an over-the-shoulder shot, and so on. When the picture came back after being sent away to be processed, the whole movie was right there with all the different cuts and angles. Then, a couple of years after I made this film, the most remarkable thing happened: the FBI arrested a man named Rudolf Abel, who was the number one spy for the Soviets in the United States. Abel was the spy ringleader and, after he was captured, it turned out that he was actually using Fort Tryon Park as the drop-place to pick up secret microfilm from other spies—just like in my movie! I was amazed at this coincidence. Unfortunately, today, I don't have a copy of my first little film and I don't even remember what it was called.

Did you make any other 8mm movies around this time?

As a matter of fact, that was probably the only one I made that was completed. I got friends from school to be in it and gave them comic books as a salary. I literally paid them off in comic books! [Chuckles] The film wasn't scripted as I would simply tell the kids exactly what to do and say. Of course, it was also a silent movie. 8mm movies had no sound in those days and so you'd have to place a title card in there every once in a while to illustrate the dialogue and action.

Was yours a happy childhood?

I thought so. We didn't have a lot of money but I always had enough to go to the movies. I used to carry packages for the customers at the local grocery stores and supermarkets. I would wait out in front and if I saw a woman coming out with a big bundle of groceries, I'd ask if I could carry her bags home for her. When my good deed was done, she would then give me a quarter. If I'd managed to collect 25¢ or 50¢, I could then go to the movies. I would also collect empty soda bottles as in those days they gave you back a deposit on them. So, I would bring the bottles in and collect enough dough to go to the theater. That was my main preoccupation as a child—going to the movies. If I could, I'd sit through the movie twice because in those days it was all double features. I'd watch the movies a couple of times and it was great. I guess that I was subconsciously studying them; trying to figure out how these wonderful stories and images were put together, but I always had a good time at the theater.

What are some of your earliest memories of cinema?

Well, my mother said that the first picture I ever saw was *The Wizard of Oz*, but I don't remember that occasion. She also told me that the first time she took me to the movies there was some kind of skiing movie playing with Ann Sheridan.[2] When I entered the theater, there was a scene where these people were skiing downhill and all that motion scared the hell out of me! I suddenly started screaming and Mom had to take me out of the theater. She then waited a while and took me back again to watch *The Wizard of Oz*. Apparently, I managed to sit through that without panicking but, again, I don't remember it. I started going to the movies when I was four or five years old. The first film I think I actually saw on my own—unaccompanied by an adult—was a Bob Hope picture. My mother put me in the theater and came back later and got me. I do recall seeing movies like *The Adventures of Robin Hood* with Errol Flynn and all those kinds of swashbuckling action pictures. I particularly liked that kind of stuff. Growing up, I always loved the Warner Bros. movies the best as they were the quickest moving pictures with a lot of hardboiled characters and fast-talking dialogue. They always featured actors that I liked, Humphrey Bogart, Edward G. Robinson, and James Cagney, performers with considerable screen presence who really made the dialogue stand out. Also those pictures often featured the distinctive music of Max Steiner[3] and I always loved them.

I imagine there were a lot of theaters in your neighbourhood.

Oh, I think we had about six theaters. We had the Loews Inwood and then there was the Alpine Theatre, which was the smaller theater that ran the pictures a week later. Those movies usually played the RKO Coliseum on

181st Street which was a bit of a walk, but not so bad. Also on 181st Street they had the Heights Theatre which ran foreign films like *The Wages of Fear* and *Rififi*, and also British films. Then, there was the Lane Theatre and the Gem Theatre which played revivals. So you could go there and see Boris Karloff in *Frankenstein* and Bela Lugosi in *Dracula*, as well as a lot of the classic movies that they re-ran. There was also the Dyckman Theatre, which was a little bit further away, and the Loews 175th Street Theatre. These were all movie theaters that carried double features and they changed the picture every week, sometimes twice a week. In the old days, the movie would open on a Wednesday—that would be the big star picture featuring somebody like Clark Gable or Errol Flynn—and that would run from Wednesday through to Sunday. Believe it or not, as of the Monday, they would then take the A-picture out of the theater and would put in a B-picture like a *Boston Blackie*[4] movie, or a *Frankenstein* movie, or a *Charlie Chan* movie, or a Western with Gene Autry and Roy Rogers. They would be the Monday and Tuesday movies and would play for just two days. Then, on the Wednesday, they would open the A-picture again. It was very infrequent that they ever carried a film over more than one week. It would have to be a big, successful picture to play more than seven days. Usually it would only play for five days, so if you wanted to see the movie you had from Wednesday until Sunday to catch it. It would then move to a second-run theater which played the pictures that had played the previous week at the first-run theater. Many of these movies had also played downtown for a couple of weeks at the major Broadway theaters but when they came uptown to the local theaters, they only played for five days. So, theoretically, you could easily see four pictures a week—two main features and two second features.

Was cinema more than a means of escape for you?

Oh sure, absolutely. Movies were a means of escape, but they were also something that I was passionately interested in. Remember, there was no television back in those days. This was quite a while before television really got started and movies were the main source of entertainment for people during World War II. For me, movies were like discovering whole new worlds of excitement and adventure.

What were some of the first films that really had a profound or formative effect on you as a child?

All of them! I'm not kidding. Every movie I saw as a child meant something to me. When I look back now at the kinds of movies I enjoyed as a kid, I realize that a lot of my favorite pictures were directed by Michael Curtiz.[5] He was just one of those unique filmmakers who seemed to be adept at every genre he ever tried his hand at. Curtiz made gangster pictures, musicals, melodramas, Westerns, action films. He could make any kind of movie you wanted to see. If you look at pictures as diverse as *Casablanca*, *The Sea Hawk*, *Mildred Pierce* and *Yankee Doodle Dandy*, they are all very different films. Curtiz made several movies with Errol Flynn and, being an Errol Flynn obsessive, I also loved *Captain Blood* and, again, *The Adventures of Robin Hood*. So, the whole experience of seeing movies at that age was profoundly formative for me. I really enjoyed going to the theater and would watch the movies more than once. In fact, I would have been there all night long if the managers hadn't have come down and said, "You've got to go home, son. It's getting to be nighttime and your parents will be wondering where you are." Of course, they weren't. My parents were just as happy that I was out of the house, frankly! [Laughs] Later on, when I was a little older, I would visit the sets of movies that were being shot in New York City. If I heard that a movie was being made nearby, I'd make my way over to wherever they were and watch them shoot. I saw Martin Ritt directing Sidney Poitier on the set of *Edge of the City*. Then, I discovered that Sidney Lumet was shooting *That Kind of Woman* with Sophia Loren in locations around New York and I went to that set, too. I was also present when Alfred Hitchcock shot the Grand Central Station scenes in *North By Northwest*. I followed Hitchcock around various locations in New York just to watch him work. I actually played a little joke one day: Hitchcock had filled Grand Central Station with a lot of extras and at one point, over the loudspeakers, I started paging John Robie, who was the character Cary Grant played in *To Catch a Thief*, and Huntley Haverstock, who was the character Joel McCrea played in *Foreign Correspondent*, to "please pick up the telephone." I thought it would be fun and a way for Hitchcock to notice me, but he showed no reaction or recognition to those names whatsoever. He was so totally immersed and concentrated on directing his film, I'm sure he never heard a thing. But it was thrilling to me, being physically in the presence of these great moviemakers.

Do you think it is an advantage for a filmmaker to have seen more films or possibly even a disadvantage?

Today, with television, cable, and Netflix, there are thousands of movies available simply at the push of a button. People literally have the entire history of the motion picture industry at their fingertips. You can see almost every movie ever made and most of them for free. I think that's an incredible educational advantage over previous filmmakers, particularly those of my generation who never enjoyed that level of unprecedented access to movies when we were first starting out. In America, you can get Netflix for $7.95 a month and view thousands of films. That's quite amazing when you think about it and is something that people take for granted today. I sometimes look at the technological developments in home video and entertainment formats and say to myself, "I wasted my childhood!" I spent my entire youth paying to look at all of these movies and now I can see them all for nothing! And in my own home! I mean, this is really my childhood dream come true. I used to lie in bed at night as a kid and dream about such a thing happening. I'd think, "Oh, wouldn't it be wonderful if there was a big movie screen on my wall, so that I could look at movies in my own bedroom." I used to have this recurring dream that there was a hole in the floor of my apartment that led to a movie theater downstairs. I could simply look through this hole and see all the movies that were endlessly playing there—for free! It was a beautiful dream. Of course, I can now see every available movie on a screen on the wall of my home. The dream has finally become a reality. It's interesting, but I don't know what this luxury will do to the minds of the kids today or how it will impact on them. I'm very concerned that audiences are now becoming stupider as time goes on. I don't see any educational benefits or gains for potential filmmakers if they don't search out the classics. If all they are consuming is movies with car chases and big explosions and special effects, cinema is doomed! Any modern film that makes demands of the viewer's intelligence and concentration is now frankly an oddity. Whereas, back in my youth, movies were simply better, that's all.

What did your parents do for a living?

My mother managed the house. In those days, women stayed at home and took care of the kids. My father was in real estate. He managed apartment buildings, but his hobby was photography. He was a very gifted photographer and took all of his own pictures. He would blow them up, touch them up and mount them. He submitted his photos to various places and won a lot of awards. He was a brilliant photographer, and would have been very successful as a professional, but he chose not to pursue it as a career. In his way of thinking, you weren't supposed to earn your living doing anything that you enjoyed or liked. He believed, as many of his generation did, that your job should make you miserable every day of your life. My father had a job that made him miserable every day and he saved all of his happy times for his photography. When I saw the way he lived, I was determined not to follow in his footsteps. I was going to do what I wanted to do with my life. I was going to get satisfaction out of something that I really liked doing. Of course, your parents are always likely to give you a negative response when you tell them you want to go into show business. I mean, nobody else in the family was in show business, so it was completely alien to them. They believed it was not something I could ever make a living out of doing. They thought you could never succeed as a writer or a comedian or a filmmaker, and that I'd simply be wasting my time and energy in the attempt. As a matter of fact, it didn't take me much time to get started selling scripts. By the time I was twenty-one, I was already selling scripts. I was out of college and was really rolling along. Actually, I believe I was even in college when I first started selling scripts.

You just said that "nobody else in the family was in show-business," but I understand that your grandfather was a Vaudeville performer.

Yes, that's true, he was. I'd heard from members of the family that my grandfather had apparently been in Vaudeville and, before that, had also been a minstrel in travelling shows back at the turn of the century. He and his brother were eccentric banjo players. They would tell jokes, perform comedy skits, and there would be various acts of dancing and music. In the minstrel shows, they'd both be in blackface and would perform as the end men, Mr. Bones and Mr. Tambo. At the time, I'm sure the minstrel shows were already beginning to wane as a popular entertainment form for people, but my grandfather later played in Vaudeville on a bill that included Jimmy Durante.[6] He toured the west extensively, moving from place to place. He once performed in a saloon that was owned by Frank James, Jesse James' brother. When his mother was on her deathbed, she made my grandfather promise that he would give up show business and do something else. So, he placed his banjo in a closet and never played it again for the rest of his life. He had made this solemn and rather strange promise and he intended to keep it. All through my childhood this instrument was just sitting in the closet, gathering dust. As a kid, I kept trying to get Grandpa to play the banjo for me. I must have asked him a million times, but he never once took it out of the closet. I suppose it brought him some pain to think about those days and he didn't want to revisit old memories. All of this had happened to him by the time he was twenty-one. Then, for the rest of his days, he lived a rather conventional existence, running a men's furnishings store on 125th Street. He made his living that way and never showed any inclination towards returning to show business. In fact, when my mother once expressed an interest in becoming an actress, she was strongly discouraged from doing so. I guess it wasn't regarded as a suitable profession. When I think about all this now, it's certainly very odd that my grandfather did blackface performances. I mean, the fact that my father would end up managing buildings in Harlem and I actually went to school in Harlem. Who would have believed it? On top of that, I later ended up making several Black movies such as *Black Caesar*, *Hell up in Harlem* and *Original Gangstas*. I don't know. It's peculiar how these traditions just seem to occur. It was never planned that way, but that's how it all worked out.

Did you enjoy a good relationship with your mother and father?

It was alright. It certainly got better as time went on, particularly my relationship with my father. He mellowed as he got older, but he was an unhappy man. He was unhappy with his work and was basically dissatisfied with his life, really. I think my father felt that family was a trap. He believed himself fortunate not to have been drafted in World War II because he had a kid. But the Army could have actually provided him with a great opportunity as they might have made him a military photographer. He could have had some great life experiences, that's if he hadn't got himself killed, of course! I think my father would have enjoyed going to Europe or Asia, visiting these historic places and taking pictures. I think it would have reinvigorated him. As it was, he stayed at home. My Dad was one of the few people who didn't go in the Army and didn't make any money out of it either. Most of the people who got out of military service during World War II made money because they were at home and took advantage of the economy and everything, but not my father. I was determined not to waste any talent that I might have or fail to seize any opportunities that were presented to me. In a way, I felt sorry for my father, too. I had sympathy for this man who basically had to support other people. My father had to go out to work every single day and bring home money to feed my mother, me, and eventually, my sister. I felt bad that this entire burden was placed solely on his shoulders and he had to do something for a living that gave him no pleasure.

Do you see any echoes of your parents in any of the characters in your work? Do they reappear in any of your films in some form or another?

No, not at all. I don't see any connection between them and the work that I do. I haven't drawn upon them to create certain characters in my movies. Well, actually, I once wrote a play that we performed in New York called *Washington Heights* and that was about the family and my childhood.

Do you know how your parents met?

They met at a dance and, apparently, on their very first date, they went to see a horror film. It was *The Invisible Man*, directed by James Whale and starring Claude Rains. Looking back, maybe that's what first influenced me and set me on this path. Maybe it was the fact my parents went to see that movie on their very first date that inspired me to direct horror films. [Chuckles] I don't know.

You said that your father felt "trapped," but was theirs a happy marriage?

It was relatively happy, yes. My parents lived in a very different time when people rarely got divorced. In fact, back then, you couldn't even get a divorce. The Catholic Church had such a lock on the political arm of the Government in New York State you couldn't secure a divorce in New York City. The only way you could get one was on the grounds of infidelity and, of course, you had to prove it. People used to hire what they called "co-respondents," which was a person who would testify in court that they were having an affair with you, even if they weren't! This was so someone could go to the judge and say, "My wife has been unfaithful and I want a divorce." They literally faked infidelity in order to end the marriage. If you didn't have the money to hire lawyers and co-respondents, it was almost impossible to get a divorce. People just didn't have that kind of money, so they would simply have to endure and suffer the marriage for the rest of their lives. But my parents didn't have that problem as their marriage was a relatively harmonious one.

Did your family practice any particular type of religion?

No, we were not religious at all. We were Jewish, but we didn't practice Judaism. I've never been particularly interested in organized religion. I've never thought that anybody should be telling people what God wants them to do. They have no way of knowing anything about it and it's presumptuous of them to take on the role of interpreting God's will. I say, "Leave God alone and maybe He will leave you alone." I never got into religion, but I do like to celebrate Christmas. I've always liked having a Christmas tree and I like giving and receiving presents. I enjoy having a good old *Jingle Bells* kind of Christmas. Of course, that really has nothing to do with religion.

Did you have any literary passions during childhood? What were you reading?

I read books like *The Hardy Boys Mysteries* and several of the classics like *Treasure Island*, things like that. I actually memorised half of *Treasure Island* so that I could recite it by heart. I often liked to do a trick at a party where I would go to a shelf and pick out a copy of *Treasure Island* as if I didn't know it was going to be there. I would briefly glance at the book, then close it and suddenly start reciting it aloud. Everybody would just be amazed! [Laughs] I also used to collect comic books. In fact, I had a fabulous comic book collection that would probably now be worth more money than my father earned during his entire lifetime. Unfortunately, when I was away at camp one summer, my parents threw them all out. I came back home and saw that my entire cabinet was empty. When I queried them about this, they said, "Well, they were gathering dust and you are getting too old for them anyway." These were all first editions of Batman, Superman, and Captain Marvel. It was a truly terrific collection and would have been worth tens of thousands of dollars, perhaps more. Of course, I can't guarantee that if my parents had not thrown my comics out, I would have eventually thrown them out myself. I mean, who could have ever imagined they would now be worth as much as they are?

Many of your contemporaries, such as George A. Romero and John Carpenter, enjoyed the EC Comics like *Tales from the Crypt* as kids. Were you also a fan?

I remember those horror comics, but I wasn't as passionate about them as perhaps those other guys were. I used to like a series of comic books that are a little obscure today called *Crime Does Not Pay*. These were comics that were very realistic as opposed to the rotting corpses and monsters of *Tales from the Crypt*. As a kid, I liked comic books that were more firmly based in reality, rather than ones that were about superheroes or the supernatural, although I liked them, too. You won't find the *Crime Does Not Pay* comic books around much anymore, but some collectors might have them. I think the publisher actually ended up murdering his wife and, naturally, that was the end of the *Crime Does Not Pay* comics. Obviously crime really does not pay! But they were very good comics and somehow my tastes always ran back to them. They were more grown-up, intelligent, and sophisticated than most comics and contained intricate stories and interesting characters.

You actually drew your own comics in your youth, didn't you?

Yeah, that was one of my principal hobbies as a boy. I would sit down and draw a sixty-four-page comic book with six panels on each page. I would really go to town on them. I would do a lot of detailed artwork and develop elaborate storylines that had complex dialogue and plotting. I did a bunch of these comic books and would sometimes even color them. Unfortunately, today, I don't have those either. They are all gone now. Back in those days, I basically had to bribe people to read them. I used to give the other kids in the neighbourhood a free comic book—if they would read my comic book. I also used to put on little shows at my house and I'd invite the kids in the neighbourhood to come over. I had this slide machine and would put the slides up and have puppets and stuff. Again, I would have to bribe the kids to come over by giving them comic books, so it was a truly captive audience! My father would say, "Ah, you don't have any friends! Nobody will have anything to do with you unless you give them a comic book." That really made me feel good! [Chuckles] He once asked me why I didn't have any friends come over to our house, and I said, "Well, Dad, because every time I do you embarrass me in front of them. That's the reason."

You must have been a precocious child.

Well, I guess I was the kind of kid who lived inside his own head to some extent. I was very creative with my free time and I liked to dream up movies and stories. When you're a child, you do seem to be more in tune with your imagination and imaginative life. You're not so self-conscious as you can be when you grow older. I think a lot of adults seem to lose the magic of childhood. Naturally, that's because you have to get a job and get married and have children of your own. Then your dreams and desires change into something else with the new responsibilities you have. Your fantasy life, or the way your express yourself through creativity, can be reduced or abandoned. That was certainly true in my day, but maybe now things have changed. Today, it seems to be more acceptable for an adult to be a fan or a nerd and celebrate their interests and passions. You can be more childish and childlike now and nobody persecutes you for it. But yeah, I had a big imagination as a kid. I used to draw the comics and I would also create my own little radio shows. I got a tape recorder as a present and I started going into my bedroom and creating these programs—acting out all the parts and adding background music and everything. Like the comic books and the 8mm films, it was a way to get what was inside my head out into the real world.

What about your musical tastes? Growing up, what were you listening to?

I listened to whatever was popular at the time. I didn't have any avant-garde tastes. As time went on, I got into The Beatles and all those rock and roll performers. Back in my early days, I particularly liked Big Band music. I also liked Latin American music because I used to go to dances in Manhattan on weekends. There would be Tito Puente[7] or some other live band playing Latin music. When I worked at various weekend resorts and summer resorts up in the Catskills Mountains, they were very favorable to Latin American dance music. So, I did shows up there, doing comedy routines, emceeing shows, and working weekends. A singer and I would tour different hotels and do two or three shows, and I thought at the time that I wanted to be a comedian. But then I found out later on that I really didn't like it. I didn't like working at night. I didn't like being occupied every single evening, performing, because I couldn't have any kind of social life. All you could do is have some poor girl waiting around all night—waiting for you to get finished with your act so you could go have a drink together. I wouldn't be through until one o'clock in the morning, so it was not something that I liked to do. When I later went to the City College of New York, I started putting on regular variety shows every Thursday afternoon, or every other Thursday afternoon, for an audience. We would do a complete review and have comedy sketches and a monologue.

Did you enjoy that experience?

Oh, yeah. I was acting like I *was* on television! Seriously, I had the crazy impression I was doing my own network television programme and had to devise a whole new show every week. So, we'd have singers and performers, and people who worked with me. We'd do our skits and for a while it was a lot of fun but, unfortunately, I didn't like the kind of person it was making me. I was too full of myself, too oblivious of other individuals and what they might be feeling. I just didn't see other people when they were talking to me. I didn't know who they were and, frankly, I didn't care. I was so self-centred I would do anything for a laugh. In my own mind, I was like a big comedy star or movie star. No, it wasn't right. I didn't like the kind of person I was becoming, so I just stopped doing the shows. I didn't want to do that anymore.

What did you want to do?

Well, around this time, I had the idea that I wanted to become a writer instead. I suddenly switched into that gear, writing teleplays for New York TV programmes, and I put the comedy performing firmly behind me. I mean, I was good at comedy and felt I had a gift for writing and performing as it came very easily to me. As a kid, I was always the clown of the class at school. All the time, I would thrive on trying to get the other children to laugh. That usually drove the teachers crazy, but I always had to be the star. I would also frequent this coffeehouse in Manhattan called Hansen's Drugstore where all the comedians would go. I used to go down there after high school and hang out on the corner and sell the comedians jokes. I would receive $10 for each joke, which seemed like a lot of dough back then. I wasn't exactly making a fortune, but that didn't matter because I was having a lot of fun. The only downside was that sometimes the comedians wouldn't pay me for my jokes, which I didn't think was fair. I kept harassing them for my money and, on one occasion, this comedian and his manager threatened to throw me out of an eleventh floor window if I asked them for my money again. That wasn't very nice of them, but, hey, what can you do?

When you went to the City College of New York you majored in film, correct?

Yes. This was in the late 1950s, just before I started selling television scripts. CCNY didn't have a regular film course in theatrical motion pictures. The course they offered was in documentary filmmaking, so I took that. I learned a lot about various aspects of filmmaking while I was attending there. I learned how to load the Cine-Kodak Special 16mm Camera; I learned how to shoot; I learned a little about camera lenses; and I learned quite a lot about how to edit film.

Were there any famous teachers instructing you at CCNY?

Actually, the best teacher we had was Gene Milford, who taught the editing class. Milford was a fabulous editor, who had cut a number of great movies for Elia Kazan, including *On the Waterfront* and *A Face in the Crowd*. He was Kazan's principal editor and was also a wonderful teacher, too, as you can imagine. I learned a lot about editing from Milford. He was about the only one teaching at CCNY who was a notable filmmaker. Oh, there was also a celebrated surrealist filmmaker named Hans Richter, whom you may have heard of.[8] He became chairman of the documentary department. Most people considered Richter's work to be awful and pretentious, but he seemed to enjoy quite a lot of attention and acclaim from his admirers.

What about your fellow alumni? Did anyone else in your class go on to be successful in the industry?

Let me think. [Pause] No, not really. I can't think of anyone else. I think I was the only one. Of course, if they had moved forward and were successful in the documentary industry I wouldn't know much about it, because I've never been steeped in the documentary world. Somebody might have been successful in that area as an editor or something. I do know that some of the guys who worked with me in my comedy shows became notable in different fields. For instance, one of them was Vic Ziegel, who later became a famous sports writer and columnist for the *New York Post* and the *New York Daily News*. Another guy was Paul Kagan who founded Paul Kagan Industries, which is one of the leading media research companies for motion pictures and television in the world. Paul's really made a big fortune for himself.

Did any famous filmmakers come to lecture you?

Otto Preminger[9] once came to speak with us, but he only stayed for five minutes—literally! The students asked him all kinds of stupid questions and then one kid suddenly jumped up and claimed he was Preminger's nephew. That's all poor Otto had to hear. A moment later, he was out of there.

Did you run any film clubs in college or organize any screenings?

Oh, there were screenings all the time. They were showing everything from the famous silent Hollywood movies by filmmakers like D.W. Griffith all the way to some of the acclaimed foreign pictures by Ingmar Bergman, Rene Clair, and Akira Kurosawa. They screened some extraordinary movies at the school and it was truly revelatory. I mean, these films were unavailable anywhere else because of course there was no home video back then. Very often I would duck out of school early and go downtown to the Broadway theatres, where they had first-run movies and sometimes a stage show. In those days, they would often screen a movie and afterwards there would be a live performance onstage. I saw some incredible people perform like Danny Kaye, Jack Benny, and Abbott and Costello—they all appeared in person onstage! The movie would run and then they would come out and put on a show for forty-five minutes or an hour. Then the movie would come on again. I would sit through the picture a couple of times, just so I could see the stage show all over again. What was wonderful about that time was they didn't throw you out after a screening. The movies were continuous and people just walked in whenever they got there. Nobody actually came in at the beginning of the movie. They simply showed up at the theater, bought their ticket and an usher with a flashlight took them to their seat. Subsequent to that, I actually worked as an usher at the Roxy Theatre for a part-time job, so I was showing people to their seats, too. I didn't particularly like wearing that stupid usher's uniform, I must say. I sometimes felt like an idiot.

Was it a struggle getting money together during your college years?

Well, CCNY was free. It was $15 a term for a registration fee. $15 for two terms was just $30 a year, so I went to college for four years for the princely sum of $120. That's all my education cost me. Despite that, my father still wasn't particularly happy about paying for the school books I needed. I remember he said to me, "Hey, you got books last year." I said, "Dad, this is for a different class. Different classes require different books." Anyway, I finally squeezed the money out of him and eventually graduated college. By that time, I was already writing scripts anyway.

Did you make any short films at college?

We made a film called *Coney Never Closes*. It was about a little girl who goes down to Coney Island and it's all a mess as, at the time, Coney Island was more or less abandoned. All the rides in the amusement parks were shut down and were just rotting and rusting away. As this little girl wanders through the decimated ruins, in her imagination all the rides and attractions suddenly come alive again. It was a cute little movie. I don't know where that one went either. That has sadly been lost, too. I really made no effort to salvage all these films.

What was the budget and shooting schedule for *Coney Never Closes*?

There was no budget! They simply gave us the cameras, then they gave us the film, and then we went off and made our picture. That's all there was.

How did your fellow students and the faculty react to the film when it was first screened for them?

I think it received a fairly average response. I mean, it was nothing extraordinary. Nobody declared, "This is the work of a future Orson Welles!"

Did you make any other short films during your college years?

That's the only one I can remember, but I did edit some other people's films, stuff like that. They would give us the raw footage and we had to cut it together, but I believe we only got to make one film of our own. The college provided us with the equipment and the other students in the class were assigned to be our support crew. Then, we would perform that duty for the other students and be their support crew when they went off to shoot their movies. That's how it worked.

In 1958, I believe you worked part-time as a pageboy at NBC.

That's right. I then became an NBC pageboy, working on different television shows, ushering the audience into the studio and providing services for the performers. One time, I remember actually meeting Bob Hope in the elevator at NBC. As we were standing there I said to him, "Well, Packy East, what are you doing here?" Now, Packy East was the name Hope boxed under as a kid and he thought it was amusing that I'd called him that. He then invited me to a screening that very same night of his new picture, *Paris Holiday*, in which he co-starred with the French comedian, Fernandel. It's one of the worst movies Bob Hope ever made, I might add. It's just dreadful! Hope asked me if I would bring some of the other NBC pages and guidettes to provide an audience, so I brought a whole bunch of people with me and we all went to the theater. I can remember saying to myself, "Okay, this is my big chance. I'm now going to get to write for Bob Hope! I'll ingratiate myself to him and show him how clever I am. He'll be so impressed." When we all entered the screening room, Bob Hope was there. He got up and made the usual speech that everybody always makes when they run a rough cut of a picture: "Ladies and gentlemen, you will notice in the movie you are about to see that the color isn't right and the sound is off, and some of the cutting is all confused, but you've got to remember"—and he was about to say that it was a work print—when I suddenly yelled out, "It's a Bob Hope movie!" Well, everybody in the room laughed, except for Bob Hope. Right there, at that very moment, was the end of my possibly writing for Bob Hope. [Laughs] I had to be the clown of the class again, but Bob Hope didn't like anybody being funnier than him.

What other memories do you have of the NBC Studios back in those days?

Before I was a pageboy, I would actually sneak into the NBC Studios. I would usually glide confidently past the pageboy in the lobby, who would often be the only security staff on duty, with a script under my arm as if I belonged there. I would really look like I was going some place for an important meeting. The truth was I was only just out of high school, but if they ever tried to stop me I would just say, "That's okay," and keep on walking to the elevator. [Laughs] Nobody ever queried me about exactly what was "okay" and I don't know what the hell I would have told them if they had. The only guy who ever gave me any problems was a floor manager, who was always chasing me around the studio. He was very suspicious of me and was consistently trying to get me thrown out of there. That guy was actually Dominick Dunne, who would later become a very famous writer.¹⁰ In later years, I would always remind Dominick about it whenever I ran into him.

You obviously had a tremendous amount of confidence, guile, and bravery at such a youthful age.

I guess, but you have to venture out and try these things if you want to get anywhere in life. I was a determined kid and I wanted to find a way into the business. After managing to successfully infiltrate NBC Studios once or twice, I started going down there every week. I'd ride up to the ninth floor then sneak down the fire stairs to the eighth floor to avoid security, and then I'd find myself on the stage where they were rehearsing shows like *The Philco Television Playhouse* or *Robert Montgomery Presents*. This was the kind of crazy stuff I did, but it was a lot of fun. I would just spend the entire day hanging out with the cast and crew. I became such a regular face people began to assume that I actually worked there. Nobody ever questioned whether or not I belonged. Can you imagine trying to pull a stunt like that today? You wouldn't get anywhere near a stage, it just wouldn't happen. But I saw great shows being shot that had fabulous actors in them. I was present at the shooting of *Marty*, which had been scripted by Paddy Chayefsky and starred Rod Steiger in the title role. This was a couple of years before they made *Marty* into a movie, which then won an Academy Award for Best Picture. Ernest Borgnine also won a Best Actor Oscar playing the part that Steiger had originated, but I was there when they shot the original. I was also there when Eva Saint-Marie and E. G. Marshall were doing another of Chayefsky's scripts, *Middle of the Night*, and when Robert Montgomery did *Appointment in Samara*, which was a play set during The Great Depression. I also saw Ginger Rogers and Trevor Howard performing in *Brief Encounter*.¹¹ I actually got talking with Howard, who was a pretty nice guy and very approachable. It was a fascinating time for me and I learnt a lot of invaluable stuff about the staging, blocking and performing of live television shows.

Was it at this stage of your life that you decided to commit to being a writer?

Well, I instinctively knew that I could write because I'd been writing those comic books as a kid. When I was finishing up college, I tore out a page from the telephone directory which had a list of all the production companies in New York City. I then went around to every office and told them I wanted to work. When they asked me what I wanted to do, I told them that I wanted to be a writer. I finally found a guy named Alfred Levy, who was the president of a company called Talent Associates. He happened to be sitting by the elevator in front of an electric fan—it was the summertime and they didn't have air-conditioning—as I walked into their building. When I came into the vestibule and approached the receptionist, I announced that I was looking for a job. She was so nasty to me, so vile and insulting, that as I walked back to the elevator this man got up, came over to me and said, "Son, I'm the president of the company and I want to apologize for her behavior." He then took me over to the side, sat me down and asked, "What would you like to do?" I said, "Well, sir, I'd like to write." He said, "What have you written?" I said, "Nothing." So Levy then gave me a script and said, "Okay, this is what a script looks like. Call me if you have any questions." So, I went home—this was on a Friday—sat down and started writing and on the following Monday morning I was back there with a completed script. Levy then came out and couldn't quite believe that I had written an entire script over the weekend. I thanked him and said that I would call in to see him again the following week, but Levy said, "No, if you've written a script over the weekend I can certainly read it tonight." So, I called him the next day, and he invited me in. He said, "I'm afraid this is all wrong. It's not what we are looking for, but it is very well-written and has great dialogue. Why don't you try something else?" He then gave me another subject to write about and I later wrote five or six scripts for them—for nothing—before they finally paid me to write something. But I knew that if I kept going back I'd wear them down and eventually they'd give me a job. Once you get your foot in the door you don't want to meekly remove it and just walk away.

What was this first paid script that you wrote for Talent Associates about?

It was called *Too Young to Go Steady* and was a half-hour teenage comedy. It was supposed to have starred Tuesday Weld and Don Ameche, but the show never got on the air. I received $500, which I then brought home to show my family. My father was continually berating me, saying that I was never going to earn any money. When I pulled out the cheque for $500 and showed it to him, it was probably the saddest day of his life! [Laughs] It broke his heart, because it meant that I was now on the road to success.

I mean, my father wanted me to be a success but, on the other hand, he also wanted to be right. As I said, the general consensus back then was that people were not supposed to make a living doing something that they liked to do. What I did find amusing was the fact that some people thought I'd secured the writing job simply because I'd been working as an NBC pageboy. Of course, that had nothing to do with it at all. Sure, I took the job as an NBC pageboy to hopefully make some contacts and be around certain influential people, but I worked my ass off—often for free—until people felt guilty enough to pay me for my writing.

Moving on, I'd like to talk about your—

[Interrupting] Hey, wait a minute! I've gone through puberty with you, but we've left out the most important thing about that period of my life—girls! Undoubtedly, my primary interest at that time, aside from writing scripts, was acquiring girlfriends.

So, you enjoyed an active social life during this time?

Oh, yeah. I was something of a celebrity because I'd been doing these variety shows. I remember doing this one show at CCNY and it was a big one. Some star failed to show up and I had to fill in for her. So I performed for thirty minutes and I was really great that night. I was just at my absolute best and I'd written a lot of original jokes. After the show, when everybody had left the theater, I was sitting on the edge of the stage and was kind of stunned by my own success. All of a sudden I was alone and the big crowd had gone. Then I looked up and there was this very tall, very beautiful girl standing in front of me. She said, "I really loved your act, blah-blah-blah, who are you?" This girl had been a guest star of the show and had appeared in a successful Broadway musical called *Li'l Abner*[12] playing the character of Stupefyin' Jones. They had invited her to come there and make a personal appearance and this gorgeous, stupefying girl was none other than Julie Newmar. She said to me, "Why don't you come down and we'll have dinner one night." She then gave me her phone number, and I couldn't believe that this stunning actress was interested in me, but she was. I took Julie out quite a few times and we had a nice time. I do remember that she was sharing a dressing room with Tina Louise, who was another beautiful actress who later became famous for *Gilligan's Island*. So, I'd go in there and these two beautiful girls would be undressing and I'd be sitting there, watching them. It was great! [Chuckles] I dated Julie all through the period where she did *The Marriage-Go-Round* on Broadway with Charles Boyer and Claudette Colbert, and I saw her off and on for quite a few years. Then, she went to Hollywood to do the movie version of *The Marriage-Go-Round* with Susan Hayward and James Mason, and I didn't see her anymore after that. Later on, she played Catwoman in the television series of *Batman* and made a Western called *McKenna's Gold* with Gregory Peck in which she played an Indian girl. For a moment, Julie became a Hollywood star, but then she didn't do anything at all. That's the familiar history of a lot of people in Hollywood. They appear in a few things then you never see them again. I don't think life has treated Julie very kindly since, but there was a movie made about three female impersonators who go to Hollywood to meet Julie Newmar. The title escapes me right now . . . .

To Wong Foo, Thanks for Everything! Julie Newmar.

That's the one! Yeah, that was about as famous as Julie became in her later career. One thing I do remember about her is that she had very bad eyesight. If she didn't have her glasses on she wouldn't recognize you. You could pass her on the street and she wouldn't even know you were there. You would mistakenly believe that you had fallen out with her and she was ignoring you. I've always found that tall girls have very bad eyesight for some reason. I actually ran into Julie a number of years ago at a party and she pretended not to know me. That actually happens a lot with these women as time goes by. They want to try to erase their past. Sometimes actresses have been through a number of marriages and relationships, and everything starts to blur. They don't know who they've slept with or who they haven't slept with, but I think Julie did remember me. She just didn't want to get into it at that moment.

Stuart Gordon[13] recently told me about another celebrity story from your early days that you once relayed to him. It concerned an amusing and rather strange encounter you had with Stanley Kubrick when you were a young man.

Yeah, it was rather strange. This is my Stanley Kubrick story: one day, many years ago when Kubrick's film *Lolita* had just opened at the Loews State Theater, I was walking down Broadway.[14] I don't know how acquainted you are with downtown New York City, but there used to be a big newspaper stand on an island in the middle of Times Square where you could buy out of town papers. As I was walking across the street nearby, I saw a man leaning into a garbage can and rifling intently through the trash. He was unshaven and shabbily dressed, and looked much like a bum. I recognized him instantly as being Stanley Kubrick as, a few years earlier I had briefly wandered onto the set of *Spartacus* when I was working at Universal. Although I'd never talked to him, I did happen to notice that every time Kubrick gave a direction on the soundstage Kirk Douglas would grab him by the arm and drag him off to have a private conversation. Kubrick would then come back and revise the directions he had just given! Anyway, here was Kubrick, going through the garbage cans in Times Square and pulling out newspapers, so I walked over to him. His head was literally buried deep in the garbage can when I arrived. After a moment I said, "Looking for your reviews?" Without even looking up Kubrick calmly said, "Yeah, I've already got *The Chicago Tribune*, but I'm still looking for *The San Francisco Examiner*." He just kept rummaging through the garbage cans as if there was nothing unusual about what he was doing. We then had a whole conversation as if we knew each other and had been together the whole day. Looking back now, it was very peculiar that we were so comfortable. Finally, Kubrick found what he wanted, straightened himself up, and said, "I'm going to go over there and stand in front of the theater and watch people buy tickets. That always makes me feel good." I said, "Well, can I come with you?" He said, "Sure, let's go over there." So we both walked over to Loews State, which was just down the block, and stood in front of the theater for about twenty minutes and watched the patrons buy tickets. As we did this, we schmoozed for a while about movies and the movie business. Then we said our goodbyes, went our separate ways, and that was it. I never saw Kubrick again. It was incredible to see somebody hungrily pouring through garbage cans like that, but it was indeed Stanley Kubrick. Actually, I can remember avoiding shaking hands with Kubrick as we parted company. I mean, who knows what kind of foul waste was gathering down there?

The Television Years

In 1958, when you weren't even twenty years old, you sold your first two teleplays to *Kraft Mystery Theater*. What were those scripts?

The first script was called "The Eighty Seventh Precinct," and I was paid $1,500 for it. I was not allowed to sell any scripts until I was twenty-one. I was seventeen at the time, so I lied and said I was twenty-one. That was the only way to get jobs. "The Eighty Seventh Precinct" was an original based on the characters created by Ed McBain in one of his first *87th Precinct* novels. In fact, it might have been the very first. McBain later wrote forty of them in the series and they were very popular. The company had optioned the rights to do an original work based on his characters, so I don't think I adapted the novel. I believe I just took the characters and fashioned an original script out of it and that was my very first credit as a writer. My teleplay, which was shot live from the Brooklyn Studio, concerned a woman who is constantly telephoning the police to report a burglar that is breaking into her house. The cops ignore her calls, and then eventually she is found murdered in her home. It was great because I had worked as a pageboy on the *Kraft* show and all the pageboys loved doing it. We'd always go into the studio and eat all the food that was used in the commercials after the show went off the air. That was just one of the little perks of the job. After "The Eighty Seventh Precinct" was telecast, I quit the NBC page staff and really focused on my writing. I remember that the local New York newspapers picked up on this first success and printed stories with the headline: "Pageboy Writes Teleplay." I even got my picture in there, which was great.

What was the second script?

It was called "Night Cry" and that was also performed live. It was based on a book by William L. Stuart, which had previously been made into a movie by Otto Preminger called *Where the Sidewalk Ends* starring Dana

Andrews and Gene Tierney, and was also done as a radio play on *Suspense* with Ray Milland.[1] It was about a cop who commits a murder and then attempts to cover it up. The company that produced the television version, Town Associates, didn't know that "Night Cry" had been made into a movie before. When I informed them of this fact, they told me I was wrong. I didn't want to argue with them, so I just let it go, but I knew it had been made into a film previously. Sure enough, when I saw the picture again, the credits read "Based on the book *Night Cry* by William L. Stewart," so I was indeed correct. Although *Where the Sidewalk Ends* was directed by Otto Preminger, it wasn't a very good movie. I actually thought my TV version was much better.

Who starred in "Night Cry"?

Jack Klugman played the lead and he was good. There was also a small supporting role of this sleazy informer who attempts to blackmail a cop. That part was played by an unknown actor named Peter Falk. "Night Cry" was actually Peter's first television appearance. He was only on screen for about six minutes, but he completely stole the show. He was that good! He just leapt off the screen at you with this tremendous energy and presence. Peter loved the dialogue and as soon as the show was over, the phone suddenly started ringing in the control room. It was newspaper people from all over the country, calling up, wanting to know who the actor in that scene was. Peter actually got a big column written by Jack O'Brien in *The New York Journal American* subsequent to that. I remember he called me up one day and said, "Larry, I never got to see the show because it was live. Do you perhaps have a copy of it?" I then invited Peter to come into the office at Talent Associates and I ran him what they call a kinescope, which was a film copy of what was on the screen. Peter sat there with a pad and wrote down everything he had done. It turned out that he was about to audition for The Actor's Studio and was going to perform a scene from "Night Cry." A couple of days later, Peter called me up again and said The Actor's Studio had turned him down after his audition. So, Peter Falk was rejected by The Actor's Studio performing my scene. However, it also turned out that the producer of the film *Murder, Inc.* was looking to cast somebody for one of the major roles. He'd seen Peter in "Night Cry" and immediately hired him for the movie. Peter basically played the same character that he'd played on my show and even wore the same suit, shirt and hat. He later earned an Academy Award nomination for Best Supporting Actor and is by far the best thing in the picture. Of course, for the next thirty years, Peter basically played the same character in *Columbo* but he was a very fine actor. After "Night Cry" was telecast, both Peter and Jack Klugman got hired to play the kidnappers in *The Kidnapping of Jackie Gleason*,[2] so the impact of my show was considerable.

What was it like being involved in live television and mounting dramatic works?

Oh, it was great. When I first started out doing live television back in New York, the writer was always included in every step of the process. You had to be present because changes were constantly being made to the shows. The writer came to the first reading of the play with the cast and then attended the rehearsals. The writer was also always there on the day of production, because the show had a couple of run-throughs, and then after each run-through the show would either be too short or too long. This meant that you would either have to write an additional scene, or extend an existing one, or you would have to cut something from the script. After the run-throughs, there would be the dress rehearsal and further changes would be made after that. Finally, the show would go out live on the air and the writer would be sitting in the control room throughout the whole of this procedure. So, the writer was always around and you really felt like you were a vital and active part of the production as it moved along. Live TV was great for that reason. It was an incredibly dynamic and creative environment to be immersed in, particularly for me as I was so young.

As your early career in television progressed, and the medium itself began to evolve, was the writer always as valued and involved?

No. As soon as they went to film television, or "tape" as it's often called, that was the end of the writer's participation. It all changed so quickly. Soon, everything was being done at the exclusion of the writer, and we were no longer welcomed in anymore as an integral part of the process. That was a shame because I enjoyed being deeply involved in live television. It's actually enormously beneficial for the whole production if the writer is constantly available, but in many cases a lot of writers don't want to be there for various reasons. Today, making television is a lot like making movies. A movie shoots for thirty or forty days, and the writer doesn't want to be up at seven o'clock in the morning everyday and be at the command of the director or producer. They don't want to be standing around watching everybody do their jobs, whilst they are rarely being called upon to make changes. Very often, there is nothing for the writer to do, and the weather may be poor on location, and the hours very difficult. I think if you asked most writers to come out on the set everyday, they would probably want extra money for taking the trouble. That's the way a lot of writers are. I wouldn't be that way, but I do understand that view. I think, for the most part, writers feel that being on a set is a waste of time. Not every writer, but many of them. Also, if their work is being tampered with, it can be a very painful place to be. But in the days of live television, there was more of a sense that you were directly connected with the whole operation of creating something. You were firmly on the inside looking out and you were all working together. That was wonderful.

What prompted you to move to Hollywood in late 1959?

I decided to try my luck on the West Coast because, after my first couple of shows were on the air, nothing was really happening for me. I just had no luck at all. I was rejected everywhere and it was rather a depressing time. I was actually collecting unemployment insurance and was living on something like $52 a week. I was repeatedly being turned down, and people kept asking me, "When is your next show coming on? When can we see it?" The truth was I had absolutely no idea. I then had this troubling thought that I would have to go back to being a pageboy again. I was determined that was never going to happen. It would have just been too embarrassing for me, particularly after tasting a little success. So, I went to California and got into doing live television remakes of old movies. One of the things we did was a version of *Meet Me in St. Louis*, which had Walter Pidgeon, Jane Powell, Tab Hunter, Ed Wynn, and Patty Duke in the cast. I don't mind telling you that it was a poor imitation of the Vincente Minnelli original with Judy Garland, but I was happy to be working.

How did you find Hollywood at this early stage of your career?

Exciting, intoxicating, but also a little difficult. I had never been there before, so it was a new experience for me. Hollywood was full of beautiful girls and sunshine. It was like this wonderland, but it was also a tough place to find work. I was staying at the Montecito Hotel, which was frequented by a lot of writers and actors from New York. It had a private swimming pool, and you'd meet a lot of interesting people there. The actor Martin Balsam was staying while he was shooting *Psycho* with Hitchcock. He seemed to take great pleasure in telling me the ending one day when we were sitting out by the pool. Naturally, that ruined the picture for me. Brendan Behan[3] was also staying at the Montecito and we became pals for a time. Brendan was a great guy, drunk most of the time, but always jovial. He was quite a character. I do remember that one day he was driving up from Hollywood Boulevard in a car with his wife when he turned to wave at me and crashed into a tree! Another time Brendan approached me and said, "They want to throw me out of the hotel. They claim that every time I come out of the swimming pool, I take my bathing trunks off and my robe is hanging open and everyone can see my genitals. I don't know what the matter is with these people. Over in Ireland, even the priests go swimming naked!" [Laughs]

Was the Montecito Hotel affordable?

The rent was only $150 a month, which was pretty good, and it was a great place to be. I was comfortable, hobnobbing with all these fascinating people. Sidney Pollack[4] was living at the Montecito as he was working as an assistant director to John Frankenheimer at the time; Mel Brooks was also there, as was Percy Kilbride, a famous character actor who played Pa Kettle in the popular *Ma and Pa Kettle* films. Percy really was a remarkable old guy. He must have been in his late seventies back then, but he'd be in the pool most days in his bathing cap and would effortlessly swim fifty laps as we all looked on in amazement. All the time I was out in Hollywood, I was having a good time, but I still wasn't selling anything. But I was determined to experience Hollywood moviemaking and learn as much as I could about the business. Like I had done at NBC, I decided to gatecrash the studios and hang out with the stars. One day, I wandered onto the set of *The Sins of Rachel Cade*, which was shooting at Warner Bros. with Angie Dickinson, Peter Finch, and Roger Moore. The director was Gordon Douglas[5] and I was just watching him work. I couldn't quite believe that I was on a real Hollywood soundstage, but there I was drifting around, soaking it all in. Nobody had any idea who I was, but the crew all assumed that I was employed by the studio in some capacity. The cameraman on *The Sins of Rachel Cade* was Peverell Marley.[6] At one point, Marley was conferring with Douglas about how they were going to block the next scene. I quietly strolled up beside them to listen and when they'd finally finished talking, Douglas suddenly turned to me and said, "Is that okay with you?" [Laughs] He knew very well that I had infiltrated the studio and had no reason for being there, but he let me be. I don't know. I couldn't help myself.

In 1960, whilst in L.A., you wrote for the Western anthology series, *Zane Grey Theater*, delivering a script called "Killer Instinct."

Well, after not being able to get a lot of work in Hollywood, I returned to New York. As soon as I got back there, I immediately got a phone call from my agent, who was a terrible agent by the way, telling me that the *Zane Grey Theater* wanted to buy a story I'd submitted for $350. Unfortunately, they did not want me to write the teleplay and were looking to put another writer on it. The story was called "Member of the Posse" and was about a marshal who swears in a bunch of deputies in order to hunt down some bad guys. After a while, these deputies all want to go home but the marshal refuses to let them. He keeps the posse as virtual prisoners and makes them face death when they don't want to. It was intended to be a parable of the Vietnam War, where President Johnson had sent all these American guys over to a dangerous, foreign land and wouldn't let them come home. So, anyway, I didn't get to write "Member of the Posse" and it ended up being re-titled as "Killer Instinct." It was a pretty lousy show, which starred Wendell Corey as the marshal. I don't remember who wrote it, but whoever it was, he didn't do much of a job.[7] It kind of broke my heart that I had been in Hollywood all that time and didn't really sell anything. But when I came back to New York, things quickly picked up and I started selling some things.

One of the scripts you sold whilst in New York was "False Face," a disturbing episode of the anthology show *Way Out*, hosted by the celebrated Welsh author Roald Dahl. Since "False Face" was first broadcast on May 26, 1961, it seems to have attained legendary status, hasn't it?

Yeah, it really has. "False Face" has been described as the most memorable segment of *Way Out*, although the series was only on the air for seventeen weeks. Of course Roald Dahl was a famous writer, responsible for *Charlie and the Chocolate Factory* and many other books. His job as the host was kind of a take-off on Hitchcock's role in *Alfred Hitchcock Presents*, where he would introduce these strange and scary stories each week.[8] "False Face" was about a horror actor who is playing the part of Quasimodo in a play of *The Hunchback of Notre Dame*. He copies his stage makeup on the deformed face of an unfortunate derelict he has picked up. The play has a successful opening night, but afterwards the actor discovers to his horror that he can't remove the makeup and it's stuck on his face permanently. He then tracks down the derelict to a nearby flophouse, but finds that the homeless man is dead and now has the actor's face. It was a very good episode with a nice, macabre twist. Dick Smith did the makeup on "False Face" and it proved to be very influential for a generation of young makeup artists who watched that show. Again, everybody who saw "False Face" said it was the best segment of *Way Out* that was ever done. Personally, I agree with them! [Chuckles] But it is a classic bit of television. You know, I never met Roald Dahl when we were working on the show, but he did visit my house once when I held a party. Several years after *Way Out* was cancelled, somebody brought him over to my place one evening and we talked. Dahl had no idea that I had written anything for *Way Out*, but that was the one and only time I ever met him. I do remember feeling thrilled when I caught the telecast of "False Face" and heard Dahl's British accent say in his introduction, "And tonight's show is by Larry Cohen." After everything that had happened in Hollywood, that really made me feel good.

How did your career move forward after *Way Out*?

I then went back to Hollywood again and picked up a very good agent by the name of Peter Sabiston. Peter was with me for about twenty-five or thirty years and got me a lot of jobs. I started picking up work on TV shows in California and, subsequently, got jobs in New York on things like *The Defenders*, which was basically a courtroom drama which concerned a father and son team of lawyers who were involved in a variety of difficult legal cases, and *The Nurses* and *Espionage*. All of a sudden I was making a lot of money and was constantly working on various things. It's hard to remember the exact chronology of these shows, but around this time I wrote an episode of *Checkmate*, which was a show about a detective agency on CBS, and an episode of *Sam Benedict*, which was a legal drama on NBC starring Edmund O'Brien as an attorney. I also wrote an episode of *Arrest and Trial*, which was a ninety-minute crime show on ABC that starred Ben Gazzara as a cop in Los Angeles. *The Nurses* was a film show that was produced by Herbert Brodkin, who was also producing *The Defenders* at the same time. I actually started off writing for *The Defenders* and wrote seven or eight episodes of that show. Since they were also doing *The Nurses*, I wrote three episodes of that show, as well, and those episodes are very good ones, too. I thought *The Nurses* had some social relevance and addressed some fairly sensitive issues of the time, but there were certain limits we adhered to. Sometimes, in my eagerness to do something I felt was important and potentially very good, I was pushing at what was acceptable and what was not. One episode I wrote, "Party Girl", originally had a woman character in it that had recently had her breast removed. This was deemed to be too much and so I changed it to her having a leg amputated. That was still fairly strong stuff for the age in which it was made, but not as powerful as my first idea. I also wrote an episode called "Night Sounds" which dealt with one of the nurses being harassed and molested by a patient. That was changed a little, too, but it was still a very good episode. So, I was now being kept quite busy around this time and producing work that I felt was good and was even breaking some new ground.

I know that around this time you joined the Army. By my reckoning this would be sometime around 1962, correct?

It might be, yeah. I was in a reserve unit and I was called up on active duty and shipped down to a small Army base in Virginia, near Williamsburg. As fate would have it, I arrived there around Christmas, just as the Army were preparing to do their annual Christmas pageant. The chaplain, who was a Protestant chaplain, got me to write the Christmas show, which I was happy to do. When the chaplain discovered I could write a little, he decided to keep me on to write the radio program. David Carradine was also stationed at Fort Eustis, Virginia, at the same time I was, and we became very close friends. I was writing the radio program and David was painting the murals. We were both supposed to be stevedores, but we were working for the chaplain. We didn't mind because it was a lot better than some of the other tasks we could have been doing there. I was happy to end up with the chaplain because I had access to a typewriter and the freedom to write stuff. It was great. Officially, I may have been a stevedore but there was really nothing for the recruits to do when they were called to service. It could all get pretty mind-numbing because each and every day we would be expected to load and unload the very same ship. It was incredibly boring, very monotonous work, and I don't like to do monotonous work. No, I was fine writing the little radio show in the chaplain's office. I could just sit in there and write my scripts. I thought my time in the Army was very enjoyable and I was still able to be creative. David and I did a play together called *Once Upon a Mattress*, which had been a famous Broadway musical based on the Hans Christian Anderson fairy tale, *The Princess and the Pea*. We did a tour of it around some of the Army bases and had several military personnel playing the various parts. It was fun.

How did your Army service affect your television writing career?

Well, I actually wrote my first episode of *The Defenders* whilst I was in the Army and mailed the treatment in to the producers. It was called "Kill or Be Killed" which was about a man who commits a crime as he is being transported to Sing Sing prison. My mother called me and said that the makers of *The Defenders* were trying to reach me. Apparently, they took a liking to what I'd done and allowed me to write the show. Of course, now certain people wanted to meet with me which was a potential problem because here I was in the Army. This inevitably meant that I would have to go AWOL if I was going to convene with these people. I had to go AWOL on Fridays, so I could get into New York City and meet with the producers. They were well aware of the situation and would always schedule my meetings for Friday afternoons. I remember I would get on a plane in the morning and fly into Manhattan from Virginia. I then had my meetings, spent the weekend in New York, before flying back to Virginia on the Sunday night. It was too close for comfort at times, but I never got caught. Not once.

You also wrote "The Golden Thirty" for *The United States Steel Hour*, which I understand had some autobiographical content.

That's correct. "The Golden Thirty" was an autobiographical play about a boy who wants to become a comedian. I was played in it by—of all people—Keir Dullea of *2001: A Space Odyssey* fame. I thought that was pretty unlikely casting to be honest with you, but Keir was a nice fellow. Nancy Kovack was the leading lady and she ended up marrying Zubin Mehta, the famous conductor, and quit acting altogether. The comedian Henny Youngman was also in it, playing the aging comedian who steals the boy's jokes. I was originally hoping that we'd get Jack Carson for the role, because Carson had the comedic qualities that I felt were necessary for that character, but he could act, as well. But Youngman did a very good job and really captured that sense of desperation and sadness that some comedians have, particularly when they get older. You used to see some old comics who'd been churning out the same tired routine for decades, night after night, year after year, always the same material. That was the life and that sadness was pretty endemic and very depressing. So, "The Golden Thirty" has a lot of truth in it, and I think it was Youngman's only dramatic role on television. I really enjoyed doing that show because it had a lot of familiar, personal elements in it about my life. That one was also done live.

You contributed two episodes of *The Fugitive*, "Escape into Black" in 1964 and "Scapegoat" in 1965. What was it like working on that show for producer Quinn Martin's company?

I didn't much like working for them, but I thought "Escape into Black" was one of *The Fugitive*'s very best shows. It was a very clever story in which Richard Kimble, who, of course, is wrongfully wanted for the murder of his wife, has temporary amnesia. He starts to believe that he really did kill his wife and now thinks that the police are entirely justified in their pursuit of him. Kimble decides to surrender himself to the authorities and take his punishment. He calls up Lieutenant Gerard, the cop who has been relentlessly chasing him, and agrees to meet with him. Then, as Kimble travels on the train to meet with Gerard, he remembers the train wreck which allowed him to escape from custody on his way to the death-house. He suddenly realizes that he is indeed innocent and he has to get away. I thought "Escape into Black" was an excellent show. It was different from a lot of the other episodes in what it did with Kimble's character and his situation. It also gave Gerard a little something extra. I mean, after Kimble confesses on the phone that he is guilty of murdering his own wife, Gerard believes all the more intensely that this guy should be brought to justice. So, it gave the lieutenant an added conviction to get his man as the series continued. I don't remember anything about "Scapegoat." I have no recollection of having written that episode. That might even be a mistake on somebody's part.

I believe you only furnished the story for "Scapegoat."

Well, if that's the case, I don't even know if I got paid or not. I don't really remember much about it at all. You know, Quinn Martin and I were not the best of friends to say the least. I first met him when I had written "Kill or Be Killed" for *The Defenders*. He'd caught the show on its original telecast and he contacted me to talk about it. He said, "How did you know what we did in our pilot?" I didn't know what the hell he was talking about. I said, "I'm not sure I understand you. What pilot are you talking about?" He said, "We just made a pilot for a show called *The Fugitive* and the first sequence in your episode was identical to the one in our pilot. You see a convict being taken to Sing Sing prison on a train and there's a train wreck and the guy escapes. It's the same situation with your show. How can that be?" Well, I couldn't give him an answer to that because I hadn't seen the pilot for *The Fugitive*. I told Quinn Martin that I thought it was just a coincidence but he couldn't accept that. He always felt something mysterious and treacherous must have happened, but I certainly wasn't a party to it. In my dealings with Martin, I didn't always feel that he enjoyed having me around very much. I did invite him over to my house one time for a party, and he was a decent companion for the evening, but when it came to business he was a very different proposition. He was an incredibly uptight guy who wanted to control everything, but he didn't really know that much to tell you the truth. He had a good staff of smart people working under him who did most of his thinking for him. I don't think he really knew that much about creativity, he just didn't want anybody else around him to have any authority. So, Martin presided over a bunch of subordinates who worked with him for years and then, after he stopped making shows, most of them retired. I was glad to have written the one episode of *The Fugitive* because I liked the characters and I liked the show. But after having done that one episode, I was more than happy to move on and not have to worry about it anymore.

That same year, in early 1964, you also wrote "Medal for a Turned Coat," an acclaimed episode of the aforementioned *Espionage*. That was about a German officer, who travels to England during World War II to negotiate a peace settlement after Hitler is supposedly assassinated by the Nazis.

I was very happy with "Medal for a Turned Coat." That script was a play on the idea of the "Good German," which, to some people, may have once seemed a highly improbable thing. But I wanted to write about an honorable man surrounded by all this destructive evil that was the Nazi machine. "Medal for a Turned Coat" had a few flashbacks in it, which I liked. I thought it gave the episode a certain poignancy. Again, Herbert Brodkin was a producer on *Espionage* and I was greatly satisfied with the way it turned out. That episode was directed by David Greene and he did a beautiful job. It was a good script that deserved a good director and a good cast, and it certainly got them. Fritz Weaver and several other distinguished actors were in the piece, people whose names I can't quite recall right now.[9] It was an intriguing idea in the way it dealt with the themes of trust and mistrust, good and evil, condemnation, and redemption, and how the chaos of war colors our perceptions of the enemy and his true intentions. Around this point in my writing career, I became fascinated with the dramatic potential inherent in treason, betrayal, and subterfuge. I revisited the theme of treason a number of times in my work, particularly in *The Defenders*.

Let's go back to *The Defenders*, which is one of the most famous TV shows of its era. Originally, the father and son characters had appeared in *Studio One in Hollywood* played by Ralph Bellamy and William Shatner. Was there ever any possibility that Bellamy and Shatner would resume their roles in the series?

I really have no idea. When they turned *The Defenders* into a television series, they recast those parts with E. G. Marshall and Robert Reed playing the leads. I was not involved in that decision as I came in a little later. In fact, by the time I was working on *The Defenders* it was already a huge hit and had won the Emmy Award for Best Series. In those days, they used to make thirty-two episodes in a year, so they desperately needed scripts. Thirty-two episodes is a lot of television to produce in just twelve months, particularly when you consider that nowadays they do around eighteen episodes a year. I was fortunate enough that when I sent in my story idea for "Kill or Be Killed," the producers liked it very much and let me write the script for it. The director assigned to my first episode was actually Sydney Pollack. He was only a television director back in those days, long before he became an Academy Award-winning filmmaker. Sydney didn't like Brodkin and he didn't like the company. He came in from California and he quickly went right back there. Sydney did not enjoy the experience of working for them because they treated him like he was a nobody. Meanwhile, he had been directing a lot of television in California so he didn't need them. I think he left rather abruptly, even before finishing the show. On the last day, Sydney just took off in the afternoon and left the assistant director to finish the job.

Did you work closely with the series creator, Reginald Rose?

Yes, and Reginald Rose was very nice to me. He respected my work and didn't try to change it. He was always complimentary and encouraging, a positive, nurturing presence. His associate, David Shaw, who was the story editor on *The Defenders*, was equally helpful. They were both very kind to me and really helped my career tremendously. They were two smart guys and I had a lot of respect for them.

What were your favorites of the episodes you wrote for *The Defenders*?

I liked "The Traitor," which was a very well-received episode. It shared a lot of similarities with "Medal for a Turned Coat" and, coincidentally, was also directed by David Greene. "The Traitor" was about a Russian spy living in the United States and posing as an American who gets put on trial for treason. I also liked "The Secret," which co-starred Martin Landau and was also very well-received. That was about an American nuclear scientist who refuses to give up his discovery to the U.S. Government. He is put on trial by the Government, who claim that his mind belongs to them. I later turned that story into a stage play called *Nature of the Crime* that I did off-Broadway. Another of my *Defenders* episodes that I like is "May Day! May Day!" That was about a military person, an admiral, in a nuclear submarine. He wants to usurp the Government and start World War III, and is tried for sedition. That was yet another story about treason. I did a bunch of them and I actually referred to them as the "Treason Trilogy." I love dealing with the same recurring themes in my work, but in different ways. Back then, rather than just doing individual episodes of television shows, I was consciously trying to create a body of work which had some relationship to each other. That was not always easy as some of these shows differed greatly from each other in their specifics. I also thought that "The Go-Between" with Arthur Hill and "The Unwritten Law" with Kim Hunter and Jessica Walter, were both very good episodes, as well. So, there were quite a number of strong ones that I wrote for *The Defenders*, and they all got me a lot of positive attention. In fact, I don't think I have a distinct favorite out of any of them. I like them all.

The Defenders ran for four seasons before being cancelled in 1965, the same year that you created the Western series Branded. Was there any overlap in terms of your writing commitments between these shows?

No. I was back in California at that point, and I wanted to see if I could get my own show on the air. I had generated some heat because I was now well-known as a writer for *The Defenders*, which was the #1 TV show in the country. I wanted to cash-in on the good reactions that people were having to my work.

Branded debuted on January 24, 1965, as a replacement for the NBC sitcom, *The Bill Dana Show*, which had been cancelled. What inspired you to create the show?

Well, there had been a lot of blacklisting in America in the preceding years. The House of Un-American Activities Committee had attempted to identify communist sympathisers and influences in the motion picture industry and vanquish them. As a result of this, many people's reputations had been destroyed. They could no longer work and lived in disgrace. They couldn't clear their names after they had been accused of being communists and were considered disloyal and dangerous. These individuals were accused of being subversives, because they had once been the member of a liberal organization or a communist-related organization. None of them were spies or anything, they were well-meaning people. Sometimes they were stupid, but they certainly weren't trying to overthrow the Government. They were just citizens who believed in civil rights and other forms of progressive politics, and the only way they could express themselves was through leftwing organizations. But suddenly, because of these affiliations, they couldn't work anymore in Hollywood and were blacklisted. I began to think about that terrible situation and the inevitable effects it caused. I realized that it would be impossible to do a television show about that contemporary period, but maybe if I disguised the story as a historical Western I could address some of these things directly. So, that's exactly what I did. *Branded* was basically about a blacklisted cowboy, a United States Cavalry captain who has been unjustly accused of cowardice. He is unfairly stripped of his rank and ordered to leave the fort in shame, never to return. It would have been unthinkable to have dealt with this subject literally in the 1960s, but by taking the blacklist and dramatising it in an acceptable manner—and in a popular form like the Western—it was possible. So, I thought I'd do a Western show about somebody whose reputation had been destroyed and that taint and those accusations followed him around wherever he went.

You once famously described the hero of *Branded*, Captain Jason McCord, as "the tallest underdog in the whole West."

Yeah, he certainly was. Chuck Connors, who played McCord, was a big guy, and we were lucky to have him for the role. As soon as Chuck had signed on to do *Branded*, we were immediately scheduled on NBC for Sunday nights at 8:30 and that was a great time period for a show. *Branded* was preceded by *Walt Disney Presents* and was followed by *Bonanza*, so it was sandwiched between these two huge hits, two of the biggest shows on NBC. Without even shooting a pilot, *Branded* was on the air and that was pretty remarkable. In fact, it was pretty much unheard of. Everybody was astonished that I'd managed to get this show on television, and shown in a primetime slot like that, without ever shooting a pilot. That made me a big hero in Hollywood.

Were you friendly with Chuck Connors?

For a while. Then, one day, when we were both sitting around talking and having lunch, I told him that *Branded* was really about a blacklisted cowboy. The moment those words left my lips it was the end of the friendship. Chuck was a right-wing conservative guy, and when he heard my revelation about the show, he thought he'd fallen into the hands of a communist! After that, we didn't have very much to do with each other. I do remember that before that incident occurred we were shooting the first episode of *Branded* out in Utah. In the middle of the night, when everybody else was asleep, Chuck suddenly knocked on my door. He was wearing these long cavalry boots that came up to his knees and he asked me if I would go back to his room and help him take them off. I immediately thought, "Uh-oh, this is suspicious! I do not want to go back to this guy's room! It's the middle of the night and he's a lot bigger and taller than me!" I didn't know if he had any romantic inclinations but I thought to myself, "This is the worst thing that could possibly happen! I finally get my own show on television and the star makes a pass at me!" [Laughs] Eventually, I agreed to go back to Chuck's room with him. When we got there I teetered down and began trying to pull his boots off. He said, "No, you've got to turn around and put my foot between your legs. Pull on the boots and I'll push on your ass with my other foot." I thought to myself, "Oh Jesus, this is a classic! I should have brought my wife with me." Anyway, I pulled and pulled on the boots and then, after one mighty last effort, the boot came loose and Chuck suddenly went flying back off the chair and hit his head on the coffee table. He was just lying there on the floor, unmoving, and for a few horrifying moments I thought I'd actually killed him. All I could think was, "The show isn't even on the air yet and I've just killed the star! I've really fucked everything up!" But after a few minutes Chuck regained consciousness and slowly got back up. I said, "Hey, this story is going to look great in *TV Guide*." Chuck suddenly flashed me a look like he thought I really meant it. Despite that incident, we still remained on good terms, until that fateful day at lunch when I told him the origin of *Branded*. Once I intimated that the show had something to do with the unfortunate blacklisting of people, which I'm sure Chuck was very much in favor of, by the way, it marked the immediate termination of our friendship.

What was the significance of McCord's broken sword in your mind and his insistence that he always carry it around with him?

In the other series Chuck had starred in, *The Rifleman*, his character always carried a Winchester rifle. I felt we needed to give McCord his own weapon, something unusual that was uniquely his own. Of course, the sword is an ancient weapon and perhaps a more honorable one than a gun. The half-sword also seemed like it was integral to the story as it directly symbolised the memory of McCord's disgrace. He had been unfairly accused and is wrongly despised, and is trying to shed this image of cowardice and dishonor. The sword gets broken in the opening sequence of every episode when the officer strips McCord of his rank and snaps the weapon over his knee in front of him. We shot the court-martial sequence in Kanab, Utah, and not in Hollywood. The reason being if we did it in Utah, we could secure a lot more extras and wouldn't have to use members of the Screen Actors Guild. It was as simple as that, really. Incidentally, the actor playing the officer had been a big movie star at one time. His name was John Howard and he'd played Bulldog Drummond in five or six films, some of them alongside John Barrymore. Howard had also played Ronald Coleman's brother in Frank Capra's *Lost Horizon* and had been Katherine Hepburn's fiancée in *The Philadelphia Story*. He was a terrific actor.

What were the events that led to your creative control of *Branded* being rescinded at the end of the first season?

That was directly a result of my falling out with Chuck. I wasn't kidding earlier. As soon as Chuck heard that his character was really a blacklisted cowboy, boy, he seriously wanted to get rid of me! It took a while for that to happen but, eventually, they did replace me. I was happy to be done with the show at that point, too. When it all started turning sour, they had other writers come in and start fussing around with my scripts, making changes after I was finished with them. Subsequently, there were script assignments given out that I didn't know about and I finally realized it had become a deeply unpleasant situation just showing up to work every day. So, I left. I mean, I don't think the other writers on the show did a very good job. I don't think they fully explored the potential inherent in the character and his story. *Branded* could have been a lot better, actually. They brought in another producer and he had a penchant for hiring old movie actors. Not that I had a big problem with that, but it was obvious to me that the overall quality of the show was beginning to plummet. When that happens a show is doomed.

I understand that Connors' erratic behavior was also partially responsible for the demise of *Branded*. Is this true?

The truth is Chuck did become increasingly more arrogant and difficult to deal with as time went on. Frankly, I think success must have gone to his head. He began to agitate the sponsors, Proctor and Gamble, and then finally alienate them altogether until they were just furious with him. They would ask Chuck to make personal appearances at various sponsored events, dinners and publicity opportunities, and he made it very difficult for everybody. I guess he thought that because the ratings for *Branded* were so good he was invulnerable, but that was certainly not the case. The sponsors owned that time period and NBC had nothing to do with it. It was Proctor and Gamble's 8:30 slot and they made the decision to cancel *Branded*. Connors' behavior was tantamount to committing suicide as far as the show was concerned. You don't provoke your sponsors. You just don't do that. I mean, *Branded* was consistently in the Top 10 shows, or floating around just outside the Top 10, but it ended up getting cancelled after two successful seasons. That was a shame because there were many more stories to tell, more adventures for the character to enjoy, but it was all gone. I think *Branded* could have run for five or six years if certain individuals had been a little more focused, friendly and harmonious. All it would have taken is a little attitude adjustment and it could have continued moving forward.

Was Connors ever contrite in later years?

Well, in the years that followed, Chuck's career waned and he did become a lot more friendly and approachable. He had another television series on the air after *Branded* called *Cowboy in Africa*, but that was cancelled after just one season. Then, several years later, an event was held at what used to be the old Republic Studios. It was a dinner to celebrate all the great Republic Westerns that they used to do. They honored people like Gene Autry and Tex Ritter, and invited everybody that had ever been associated with Westerns. Chuck and I were seated together and we had a friendly evening. We started talking about the past and Chuck actually told me that he regretted his behavior on *Branded*, and wished things had turned out differently. He said, "If I'd just treated the sponsor a little better we could have had a few more seasons." What could I say to that? I completely agreed with him. He then said, "Hey, do you remember that day when I tried to ride you down on the Western street at Paramount and you didn't run? I galloped that horse right at you and you just stood your ground and didn't move. Boy, I had a lot of respect for you after that." I said, "Well, to tell you the truth, Chuck, I was so terrified I was frozen in position!" [Laughs] I certainly hadn't forgotten that day either.

Am I to believe Connors attempted to ride you down with his horse merely because he thought you were a Commie?

What happened was I was walking down the Western street—the very same Western street that was used in *Bonanza* and other Western shows— and there was Chuck sitting on his horse. He saw me, turned the horse around, and suddenly started galloping in my direction. I didn't move and he didn't stop, but finally he pulled the reins up right in front of me. I'm not exaggerating when I say I could feel the snorting of the horse's hot breath on my face—it was that close! Chuck glowered down at me and said, "I thought you were going to run." I just looked up at him nervously, not knowing what to say. That incident occurred towards the end of our relationship and pretty soon after that I was gone. If he was attempting to run me off the show, he was trying to do it literally as well as creatively! [Chuckles] Anyway, he did more or less apologize about it that night we were reunited and that was good. The last time I actually saw Chuck was at The Magic Castle where I was having lunch one day. He looked a little old and a little tired, but he seemed very glad to see me and we had another nice little reunion. The next thing I heard Chuck had died. That's the way things work out sometimes in this business. You have conflicts with people, you have words and bitter disagreements, and everything ends on a poor note. Then, years later, you see them and it's like nothing ever happened. They suddenly forget that they behaved poorly towards you and are as friendly as can be. That has happened to me several times in my relationships in Hollywood, but there is no sense in holding grudges. I mean, sometimes I've wanted to kill people I was so angry with them, but then a few years later ended up working with them again.

You mentioned that *Branded* was always in and around the Top 10 shows. Did the ratings ever dip over the course of its two seasons and forty-eight episodes?

The ratings may have gone down a little bit over time, but it was certainly the best ratings that Proctor and Gamble had ever achieved in that time period. When *Branded* was eventually cancelled, they replaced it with a comedy show that was a total disaster.[10] The new show didn't get half the ratings that *Branded* had earned, which I'm sure did not go unnoticed. So, it was a big mistake on Procter and Gamble's part to end *Branded* because they quickly lost half of their audience.

Back in the mid-1960s, a lot of shows were moving to the hour-long format. Do you think *Branded* would have succeeded better as an hour-long show?

I don't know. Of course, *Branded* was a thirty-minute show going up against *The Ed Sullivan Show* on CBS and *The FBI* on ABC, which were both one-hour shows. Both *Ed Sullivan* and *The FBI* started at eight o'clock, and it was an intensely competitive time period. Despite that, we more than held our own. It's hard to believe that back in those days there were so many dramatic shows on television that were just half an hour long. They could tell a story in under twenty-six minutes and sustain a show with the budget for thirty minutes, but in those days things were much cheaper to make. There were many, many dramatic half-hour series on the air including police shows, Westerns and comedies; comedy shows having always been thirty minutes long. Comedies were cheaper to produce because they usually had only one set and not that much production. Even when we did shows like *Blue Light*, which was a World War II spy show on ABC, it was supposed to be set in Nazi Germany during the 1940s. That show involved period costumes, period cars, and period sets, and everything had to be geared towards realistically presenting a story that was set in the past and in a foreign country. The production values had to be quite high and it was only a half-hour show. It's amazing that we could actually do shows like that. Today, there isn't a single half-hour dramatic show on television—not one!

Why do you think *Branded* struck such a chord with audiences and continues to be fondly remembered to this day?

One of the reasons is undoubtedly its theme song, which I was instrumental in creating, by the way. It just seemed to resonate and linger in viewers' minds for years afterwards. People would always be able to recall the lyrics: "Branded—marked with a coward's shame." The music immediately evoked memories of the show, it was so distinctive. You know, the Coen Brothers made a movie some years ago called *The Big Lebowski*, which starred Jeff Bridges and John Goodman, in which they repeatedly talk about *Branded*. They are discussing television shows and one of them brings up *Branded*. The other one remembers the theme song and together they sing it. After doing that, they decide to go see the creator of *Branded*. This is really in the movie! They want to find the guy who wrote all the episodes of *Branded* and created the show. I suppose that this gentleman is supposed to be me. Anyway, off they go and eventually find the guy and they discover that he has an iron lung and is paralysed! [Laughs] And his name isn't Larry Cohen, but he's supposed to be the fabled creator of *Branded*. They take this soldier in to see him, to pay homage to him. It was supposed to be funny and it was certainly very amusing to me, anyway. There's even a scene where Bridges is drunkenly singing the *Branded* theme song in the back of the police car, which is great. *The Big Lebowski* had been out for ten years before I saw it. I didn't know anything about the movie and its references to *Branded* until somebody mentioned it to me at a party. I thought, "Hey, I better see this film." When I did, I was like, "Oh my god, there I am!" It was terrific. I had actually worked with the Coen Brothers on John Landis' film, *Spies Like Us*, back in the 1980s.[11] John had asked a lot of directors to come in and play bit parts, people like Sam Raimi, Michael Apted, and myself. The Coen Brothers worked with me on the same scene on the same day, as did the musician BB King and a bunch of other guys. So, we did spend a little time together and we may have even talked about *Branded*. I don't really remember. Somehow or other that show stuck with them, as it has with a lot of people over the years, and they celebrated it in their movie.

You just mentioned *Blue Light*, a spy show you co-created in the wake of the success of *Branded*, but it ran for just sixteen episodes in 1966.

Yeah, it wasn't on the air for long. I became involved with *Blue Light* when Robert Goulet's company paid me to write the pilot. They had some development money and engaged me to write something for Goulet to star in. Walter Grauman had the idea of doing a series set during World War II, but I devised the story and the characters. They were all mine, but Grauman received a co-creator credit on the show, which was okay with me. *Blue Light* was about an American journalist, who pretends to go over and join the Nazis. Instead, he is actually a double agent working for the United States against Hitler's Germany. I thought Goulet could play the lead part of the spy who is passing information back to the Allied Forces on what the Nazis are doing. The company then sold the project to NBC and it became a pretty good show. I thought the scripts for *Blue Light* were excellent. I wrote most of the episodes. Unfortunately, audiences did not take to Robert Goulet as a dramatic actor, even though he was good in the series. I mean, the main problem with Goulet was you couldn't mess him up. If you were doing an action scene and you threw him off the back of a moving truck into a dirt road, Goulet would get back up on his feet and still look like he was suavely strolling into the Academy Awards ceremony! It was virtually impossible to ever remove the glossy, manicured look he had. Viewers just couldn't accept him in the role, even though he was a solid actor.

Despite its quality, *Blue Light* did not fare well in the ratings did it?

No, it didn't do well in the ratings at all. I think the whole idea of wartime spies and espionage may have been too obscure a subject for the general audience to digest at that time. It was 1966, the same year that the *Bat-*

man TV series became a big hit with kids. *Batman* offered people a stupid mix of colorful action and comic satire, but a more serious show like *Blue Light* didn't really click with them. Actually, very few shows with a World War II background have ever been successful on television.

Some episodes were edited into a ninety-minute movie called *I Deal in Danger*.

Yeah, that was my idea. I suggested we take the first four episodes of *Blue Light*, which were all connected, and cut them together to make a movie. So, that's exactly what we did. *I Deal in Danger* played in theaters and I went to see it at the New Amsterdam Theatre on 42nd Street in New York City. It's now a beautiful Broadway theater where they mount gorgeous first-rate productions of things like *The Lion King*, but back in the 1960s, it was something of a grind house. When I saw *I Deal in Danger* there, the theater was crowded, and I can remember sitting next to this incredibly huge guy. He was about six feet eight inches, an enormous hulk of a man, and his feet were pushed over into my section of the seating. All of a sudden, *I Deal in Danger* came on and this guy started grunting and grumbling to himself. Within minutes, his grumbles had exploded into shouting and he yelled at the screen: "Godammit, I seen this on television! I paid to get in here and I already seen this on TV!" I was cringing in my seat because, as I say, this was all my idea. No doubt if this guy had discovered that fact, he would have probably reached down and strangled me to death! [Laughs] You know, that place was such a tough theater the usher, who was a uniformed security guard, would walk down the aisle with a baseball bat in his hands. I'm not kidding. He was ready to use it on anybody who started acting up. Can you believe that? Oh, that was one tough theater, but I did manage to get out of there alive.

Did *I Deal in Danger* do well theatrically?

No. 20th Century Fox put it out as a co-feature with other pictures. In those days, they had double features and it was the double feature with something else. They did the same thing with *Broken Sabre*, which was a three-episode compilation of *Branded* that was also released theatrically. They actually did two of them. There was another three-parter from *Branded* called *The Mission* that they put out, which was something I wrote. It was perfectly acceptable to do these compilations back then as there was no home video or Netflix. Of course, today, the modern audience would never accept such a thing. Nobody would ever go see them.

You continued with the World War II setting by contributing an episode to *The Rat Patrol* entitled "The Blind Man's Buff Raid."

That came about after I got a call from a friend of mine named Stanley Shpetner, who was producing *The Rat Patrol*. The show was set during the North African campaign the allies fought in World War II, so it took place in the desert with the allied forces driving around the terrain in jeeps, firing submachine guns at the Germans. I really wrote "The Blind Man's Bluff Raid" as a favor to be honest with you. I got hold of a secretary and dictated the entire half-hour teleplay to her over at the Goldwyn Studios, right from beginning to end. A couple of days later, I received the script and was reading it, and I immediately noticed that the secretary had rewritten my teleplay herself. She had altered some of the scenes and the dialogue, and made everything much sharper and better. I told her that she had improved my work considerably and that she clearly had some talent. That was certainly one of those rare instances where a little interference paid off handsomely. It usually doesn't, you know. Usually when a script is compromised it's ruined, but not in this case. She did a very good job. *The Rat Patrol* ran on ABC for a couple of seasons but, again, it was that ambivalence audiences had towards World War II shows that probably sealed its fate.

What was *Coronet Blue*?

Coronet Blue was a show I created for Herbert Brodkin's producing company, which eventually ended up on CBS. Brodkin had a deal with CBS and he sold them the series. It was actually done before *Blue Light*, but may have been shown afterwards.

I understand that *Coronet Blue* was filmed in 1965 but not broadcast until 1967.

Yeah, that sounds about right. *Coronet Blue* was a series that starred Frank Converse as an American guy who discovers that he is not American. He is found floating in the river one day and is pulled out of the water. He's been shot and is suffering from amnesia. The only words that he is able to recall are "Coronet Blue." He doesn't know who he is and nobody recognizes him. They can't find any match to his fingerprints and he has no knowledge or memory of his past. It turns out, as the show progresses and he unravels certain clues, that he is actually a Russian posing as an American. He attended the Russian school for spies and has taken on the persona of an American citizen and successfully infiltrated America. That is why nobody knows him. When he tried to defect, the spy organization known as Coronet Blue shot him and threw his body in the river. But he has survived this attempt on his life, so they now want to come back and finish the job. That was the basic story and it's the exact same plot as *The Bourne Identity*, which came later. I don't know if Robert Ludlum saw my series and decided to turn it into a book, or he saw *Coronet Blue* on TV and it just stuck in his subconscious, but people often do acquire somebody else's ideas subconsciously as well as consciously. I'm not accusing Ludlum of anything, but the similarities are rather striking. It's also interesting that there is a similar show being screened right now on TV called *The Americans*.[12] Of course, many years earlier, I got there first with *Coronet Blue*, before any of these things were ever dreamed up.

It is generally thought that *Coronet Blue* was an offshoot of your *Defenders* episode, "The Traitor." Was that indeed the case?

No. I mean, yes, there was a similarity between them, because "The Traitor" was about a Russian spy who is posing as an American and is put on trail for treason. It is finally revealed that he is not in fact a traitor, he is actually a spy, and again, that was one of my best shows for *The Defenders*. I can definitely see the connection between "The Traitor" and *Coronet Blue*, but it was not derived from that episode.

What caused the delay in the show's broadcast?

Well, by the time CBS eventually put *Coronet Blue* on, Jim Aubrey, the executive who'd originally bought it, had been fired. A new administration then came in that wasn't too sympathetic to anything that Aubrey had purchased. So, we didn't last very long. We only made thirteen episodes of *Coronet Blue* and were on the air for just a few weeks. When Aubrey was removed at CBS, the shows that he had ordered basically sat on the shelf until they were finally played in the summer as a summer replacement show. So, *Coronet Blue* did play, but it didn't go on until the summer. Today, a lot of shows are put on in the summer and sometimes they premiere a new series during the summer and it's very successful. So, there is nothing wrong with being on at that time of year. However, at the time they put *Coronet Blue* on, the contracts for the actors who were in the leads had expired. This meant there was no way to continue the series anyway, because they had all moved on to something else.

You've previously stated that Herbert Brodkin turned *Coronet Blue* into an anthology show.

That's more or less right. They didn't know how to do a hardboiled action show. That was not their genre. Brodkin's company were more interested in doing things like *The Nurses* and *The Defenders,* more intellectually stimulating shows in which the action was demoted in favor of the characters and story. They were not into doing a suspense show like *The Fugitive,* for example, and so *Coronet Blue* was not the kind of television they were usually associated with. They tried to bend and reshape *Coronet Blue* into something that they wanted it to be. They played down certain ideas and aspects of the show until it just wasn't recognizable anymore. Whatever *Coronet Blue* had started out as, it was no longer the same thing. You just had this guy stumbling from one episode to another without any real connective element between them. After that, I'm afraid the show just didn't work anymore.

I understand that you apparently "suggested" the Civil War drama series *Custer* in 1967. What exactly was the extent of your involvement with that show?

Basically, *Custer* was a settlement on a lawsuit. I had told the idea to some executives and then they went ahead and did the show without me. So, I had to go and make claims against them and they finally agreed to pay me a royalty and give me a credit on the show. I really didn't have anything specifically to do with the actual making of the episodes; I just watched a few of them. I didn't watch all of them, either. The series had good supporting actors and character actors in it, but the guy who played Custer was never heard of again.[13] He simply evaporated into thin air. *Custer* could have been a great show, but it just wasn't. That's really all there is to say about it.

We'll move on to *The Invaders*, one of the iconic science fiction series of the 1960s. How did the idea for that show come about?

ABC invited me to come in and pitch some ideas, and I pitched them *The Invaders*. I just made it up, you know? I had always liked the original versions of *Invaders from Mars* and *Invasion of the Body Snatchers*, where you had these alien creatures arriving on Earth and taking on human form. In those movies, it was difficult to distinguish the humans from the aliens, and that was a scary idea. So, I came up with the similar concept of this man, David Vincent, who discovers that alien beings from another world have invaded the Earth and are hiding out amongst the human race. ABC went for the idea right away and made a commitment to do the show immediately. *The Invaders* was originally envisioned to be two half-hour shows a week, like a serial with dramatic cliffhangers. Each episode would end with our hero in jeopardy and viewers would have to tune in to the next episode to see how he got out of the situation. Now, at that time, there had been no nighttime TV serials like *Peyton Place,* and so the idea of whether that would be successful was doubtful in the minds of the executives. So, they decided that they wouldn't do *The Invaders* as a serial, but as a regular one-hour show. Shortly after that, they decided to bring in Quinn Martin's company to produce it, as he had enjoyed a lot of success with *The Untouchables* and *The Fugitive*. Quinn Martin was one of the major suppliers for ABC, and he came in subsequent to my writing the pilot.

To what extent did you have creative control over *The Invaders*?

I wrote thirteen or fifteen storylines for them, and they took most of them and used them in the series. I didn't take credit for any of them, but that was basically it. *The Invaders* was bought when the pilot wasn't even finished. They were only a couple of weeks into shooting the show and it was already confirmed that it would be on the air. Everybody said that it was the best pilot ever done. They just loved it and they programmed the show right away, so I had achieved what I had set out to do—I had got another series on. Amazingly, I had now managed to get *Branded, Coronet Blue,* and *The Invaders* on the air and, in all three cases, there was no pilot finished at the time. That really was incredible. Back then, nobody else had a track record like that in television—getting three shows bought based mostly on the scripts without having a pilot. I consider that to be the major achievement here, actually getting the shows on. I must tell you that once they were on, I was always looking for a light at the end of the tunnel. I would be restlessly thinking, *How am I going to get out of this? How can I move on with my career and do what I really want to do?* My objective was to make movies. That's what I really wanted to do.

So, who was creatively in charge of *The Invaders*?

The producer, Alan A. Armer, who is deceased now.[14] Alan was okay, but he never came up with a truly original idea in his life. Like most producers, he could effectively recycle ideas. A lot of producers don't have any affinity for, or ability to, come up with something that is new. Alan eventually quit the business and taught television at a university. I don't know this for a fact, but I heard that Quinn Martin ended up kind of stabbing Alan in the back. Alan had produced many shows for Martin over a long period of time, and I think when it came time to share the profits, or whatever the situation was, Quinn Martin would not give him a fair shake. Alan was so disillusioned by this that he gave up the business. I don't know whether that story is true or not, but I think it's what must have happened. Alan just walked away from television completely. He could have continued to work, but he just threw his hands up and said he didn't want to be part of it anymore.

What would you have changed if you had secured creative control?

Firstly, I would have insisted that there be fewer Invaders, that's for sure! Every other person in the show seemed to be an alien. Roy Thinnes, who played David Vincent, would sometimes end up killing ten or twelve of them in a single episode and the aliens would always die so easily. He would just be knocking them off right and left, and that ensured that there was no real suspense or fear. I would have made the aliens much tougher and harder to kill. I mean, the Invaders were so vulnerable to Vincent— and there were so many of them—it negated the threat. There needed to be fewer of them. The whole basis of my original concept was that you had to guess which one of these people would turn out to be an alien. The Invaders had managed to successfully infiltrate our society and they weren't meant to be that easy to spot. That idea was intended to generate paranoia and suspicion because here was this subversive group, much like what we have today with Al-Qaeda and other terrorist organizations, hiding within our society, ready to suddenly reveal themselves and attack us. You don't know who they are or where they are going to show up next. That was part of the fun. Unfortunately, they took all of that uncertainty and unease out of the show by having numerous Invaders popping up everywhere.

What did you think of the special effects created for *The Invaders*?

I thought the special effects were quite repetitive and tiresome. Every time Vincent killed an alien it would glow red and burn up before vanishing, each and every one of them, over and over again. There was never any variation to the Invaders' deaths and no attempt was made to find a clever way of depicting the actual process of the burning up. If the aliens had to burn up each time they perished, I would've had them burning up the furniture, the floor, or the walls. Wherever they happened to be at that moment, the surroundings would have also caught fire, and that would have been more spectacular and threatening. As it was, they just went *poof* and were gone! After you saw that three or four times, so what? Show us something new! I also thought the alien spaceship was kind of hokey. It should have been more awe-inspiring. What can I tell you? Ultimately, *The Invaders* was executed with a lack of imagination.

Is there anything else you would have done to remedy the show?

Oh, there would have been several things. I've always thought that David Vincent needed to have more of a sense of humour. He was a little too stiff and serious at times when he needed to be a far more engaging hero. The audience really had to go along with Vincent when he was fighting the aliens, so that when he was in serious jeopardy it would be a matter of concern for them. I also felt that Vincent should eventually have more believers to assist him in his conflicts with the Invaders, so there was more of a team situation. I mean, Vincent did have his believers. He had people who sympathised with him, like Kent Smith, who played a millionaire industrialist that was supposed to be helping him, but he was a rather ineffectual character. Those who believed never did anything to help Vincent or to progress the story. The series could have developed much further and gone much deeper. For example, the U.S. Government could have gotten in on it and there could have been a war against the alien infiltration. That would have given *The Invaders* so much more to play with, an even greater scope. None of these suggestions are rocket science. It could have all been very easy and simple to do, but it just didn't happen.

What inspired the notion of the aliens having a "mutated" little finger?

It really came from Alfred Hitchcock's *The Thirty-Nine Steps*. I believe the villain in that movie is actually missing a pinkie, or a part of his pinkie. Robert Donat, who plays the hero, is looking for this super-spy and one of the things he must note is that this individual is missing a portion of his little finger. I thought, *Oh, pinkies-Hitchcock, Hitchcock-pinkies! Now what distinguishing feature would Hitchcock give these aliens? I know, he'd give them a deformed pinkie! That's what!* Besides, I always saw British people drinking tea with an extended pinkie and I always found that somehow suspicious. I always wanted to grab that damn thing! [Laughs]

Some critics have interpreted that distinguishing feature, and the aliens' secret underground society, as a sly commentary on the homosexual community.

Well, there was something rather effete about a pinkie, you know? Some people have read a lot of gay subtext into my work, such as in *God Told Me To*. The respected critic Robin Wood[15], who was himself gay and I think saw gayness in everything, read a homosexual meaning into the story of *God Told Me To*, the character of the hermaphrodite alien, and into some of the other things I had written. I will admit that I did deal with gay themes in television way before anybody else did on shows like *Sam Benedict* with Edmund O'Brien and Eddie Albert. I wrote an episode called "Accomplice," which was about two gay guys who are both charged with murder. Each of the accused had a lawyer, one was represented by O'Brien, the other by Albert, and both attorneys were attempting to get their client to turn on the other. The accused men were obviously gay lovers, and one was White and one was Black which made "Accomplice" even more controversial and politically charged. NBC aired that episode at 7:30 p.m., but they didn't know what the hell they were putting on. They had no idea what those characters were really talking about and what their relationship to each other was. I sneaked it right by them. At any rate, if people do interpret a gay subtext into things like *God Told Me To* and *The Invaders*, I certainly don't mind. People often do read different meanings and elements into my work and it just means that they are watching things very carefully. That's a good thing.

You have previously complained that the "Red Scare" subtext of *The Invaders* was neither recognized nor welcomed by the producers and actors on the show.

No, they didn't understand any of that. I don't know about the actors per se, as I didn't deal directly with them on a day-to-day basis. I've since become very friendly with Roy Thinnes, but back in those days, I didn't know Roy that well. But yes, there was a reluctance or a refusal to engage with some of the themes and ideas I wanted to explore. *The Invaders* was definitely a show of its era. It related to the fraught times we were living in and the paranoia about communist infiltration in America. There was this palpable fear that a communist was hiding under every rock and that the Government was completely infested with them. People thought the country was going to be overthrown from within by spies and that the American way of life would come to an abrupt end. It was also a fact that the British Government was completely infiltrated by communist spies. Kim Philby and Donald MacLean were at the higher echelons of British intelligence and they were communist spies. Both Philby and MacLean fled to Russia and that's where they lived for the rest of their lives. This meant that everything America knew and shared with the British fell right into the hands of the Russians. It's probably true that we were infiltrated as well, although we didn't want to admit it. You only have to look at the situation with Alger Hiss. Hiss was one of the top advisors at The White House and was accused of being a Soviet spy. It was this atmosphere of paranoia and communist witch-hunting that made me want to write *The Invaders*. The manner in which David Vincent was going about trying to unearth aliens who have permeated our society was mirroring America's search for communists who had insinuated themselves into our society. Just like *Branded* was a way to comment on the blacklist, *The Invaders* was a way to explore the political climate and deal with the idea of an unseen enemy in our midst. I thought the subtext was obvious, but to some people involved with the show it clearly wasn't.

At what point did you learn that *The Invaders* had been cancelled?

Uh, I don't remember. I really don't. I believe I just read about it in the trade papers, *The Hollywood Reporter* and *Variety*. I was so removed from the show at that point; I really had nothing to do with it by the time it was cancelled. I thought for sure that it was going to be cancelled anyway, because it wasn't very good anymore. You must understand, there are some people in television who don't want to hear anything from anybody else. They don't want suggestions from anybody, particularly, in this case, from the guy who had actually created the show. The problem with the business is that it's all about personalities. It isn't just the creative work; it's the people involved and their irrepressible egos. Everybody wants to protect their ego and their position. They want to be in a place of authority and they feel threatened when that authority is challenged in any way. If you come up with a good idea, it threatens them. So, this was a time of great change for me personally. I wanted to get away from all of that argumentation and make my own movies. Television was too difficult and restricting, and there were other problems, too. Another unpleasant thing you have to deal with is people trying to take credit for your work and ideas. They'll say things like, "Oh yeah, he did that, but he didn't really do the show." They try to wrestle the credit away from you simply because they can. There is no way that you can really protect yourself, other than to write, produce, and direct the show yourself. If you can do all that, there can be no question of authorship. Nobody can claim to have anything to do with it.

How exactly was this period one of change for you?

Around the time of *The Invaders*, I had been offered a daytime serial by ABC. They wanted to do a teenage soap opera in the afternoon for the kids when they came home from school. They already had a rock show, an *American Bandstand* kind of show that they were putting on in the afternoons.[16] Their thinking was that they would follow the rock show up with another offering that would appeal directly to teenagers. They were going to call this project *Never Too Young* and they wanted my company to deliver it. Basically, ABC wanted to turn me into a supplier like Aaron Spelling and Quinn Martin. They brought me in for a meeting and we discussed it, but it soon became apparent that I had a choice to make: I was either going to follow the road that would take me into being a producer of television shows, or I was going to continue my work as a writer and someday become a director of movies.

And you chose movies over television?

Well, not immediately. I chose to do the show, but I didn't really put much heart into it. I didn't like *Never Too Young* and writing teenage dialogue was not something that I really wanted to do. ABC later scheduled the show at one or two o'clock in the afternoon. I told them, "How can you schedule a teenage show at that time of day? The kids don't get home from school until three o'clock. It should be on at four o'clock so they can actually see it. You are programming this show at a time that excludes its target audience." They said, "No, that is the time period we are giving it." I knew at that moment *Never Too Young* was doomed. The only good thing I did on that show was to hire Patrice Wymore to play the mother. Patrice had been a contract star at Warner Bros. and had done a few movies. She had married Errol Flynn; in fact, she was Flynn's last wife. I was absolutely crazy about Errol Flynn movies, and as soon as Patrice walked in, I gave her the job right away. Everybody in the casting department was aghast that I'd just awarded her the part. They said, "What are you doing? We are supposed to be interviewing people here?" I said, "I've made my choice. I'm the producer and I'm hiring her." So, Patrice came to work and she did a fine job. Unfortunately, the Internal Revenue Service showed up and took her salary every week to pay for Errol Flynn's back-taxes. Of course Flynn was dead by this time, but it didn't matter. Patrice was stuck with his back taxes because she had been his wife when he died. So, the IRS ruthlessly came after her every single week, which was very sad. That's really the only memory I have of *Never Too Young*. Some of the episodes are at the Paley Museum of Television, but it wasn't much of a show. It was on for a year and after a while I kind of abandoned it and turned the show over to other people. I didn't want to be a showrunner, or producer, or supplier of TV shows. So, that was a time when I entered a crossroads and made some big decisions about my career. I wanted to be a movie director and I started following that road.

Although you did indeed spend the 1970s making features, you continued to dip your toe in episodic television, furnishing several stories for *Columbo* in its first few seasons. How did you get roped into contributing to the show?

I was friendly with Richard Levinson and William Link, who were the creators of *Columbo*. They kept pestering me to help them out and write some episodes for the show and, finally, I relented. I gave them a story which was eventually made into a show called "Murder by the Book." That was actually one of the first episodes of *Columbo* ever telecast and perhaps one of the most memorable.[17] I gave the story to Levinson and Link and they brought in a story editor named Steven Bochco to write the script. Bochco got the credit for my work and also received an Emmy Award for his trouble![17] Tragically enough, to compound matters, "Murder By the Book" was directed by Steven Spielberg. I've never forgiven myself for giving that story away. Never! It was a mistake. Peter Falk heard about what had happened and he demanded that Levinson and Link hire me to write some more episodes of *Columbo*. So, they both came back to me and asked if I wanted to do some more shows. I said, "Well, I'm going to live in London for a year, but this is what I'll do: if you'll pay me X amount of dollars I'll mail you some storylines. Either you use them or you don't, but I'm not attending any meetings or doing any rewrites. I'll provide some storylines, you shoot them, and you pay me. That's it." I then went to London with my family for a year as planned and we lived at No. 9 Chapel Street, off Belgrave Square. We had a wonderful time there and, over that period, I occasionally sent Levinson and Link stories for *Columbo*. They shot three or four of them and that was it, really.

I recently discovered your name connected with developing the 1972 pilot for an unsold mystery-comedy series called *Call Holme*. It starred Arte Johnson as a private eye, who is a master of disguise. Did you have anything to do with it?

I've never heard of it. That has nothing to do with me. Never even heard of it.

How strange. I do know that you were heavily involved with the series *Cool Million* which went into production that same year.

Yeah, I created *Cool Million*. It was a series at NBC that was produced by Universal and starred James Farentino.[18] I wrote a two-hour movie for television, which is called "The Mask of Marcella." That was the pilot, and the series got on the air. *Cool Million* was on what they call the "Mystery Wheel," which meant it rotated with other ninety-minute shows in the same time-slot: *Columbo*, *McCloud*, and Rock Hudson's show, *McMillan & Wife*. Of course, *Columbo* was the real heavyweight of the package, but *Cool Million* wasn't bad. It was about a former CIA agent, who now runs his own detective agency. He has a private jet and only handles major big-time cases. His deal is that he receives a million dollars from his clients for each case that he solves. However, if he fails to solve the crime then he gets nothing. That was the central conceit of the show. Unfortunately, Farentino—who is a good actor—didn't exude the class and sophistication required for the role. You had to believe that this guy enjoyed a lavish lifestyle and would be able to secure a million dollars for each successful case. Farentino was more like the private eye who had a crowded little office on the second floor of some dingy building and got $25 an hour. He didn't seem like the kind of man who owned a private jet. You needed somebody like Roger Moore or Cary Grant to play the part; that was the sort of actors it was written for. Farentino did his best, but if a role is cast wrong at the start you can never make a show work later on.

Your next script for television, *Man on the Outside*, was filmed in 1973 but not broadcast until June 29, 1975. Why was that?

Man on the Outside was really the two-hour pilot for a television series and was about a retired police captain played by Lorne Greene, whose son becomes a private detective. When the son is murdered, the father takes over the detective agency and tries to solve his murder. At the end of the movie, having solved the crime and rescued his grandson who has been kidnapped by the mob, the elderly cop decides that he will come out of retirement and stay in the private detective business. That movie of the week was spun-off into a television series called *Griff*, again starring Lorne Greene, on ABC. The network had been interested in the show based on the strength of the script and the prospect of Lorne Greene playing the lead. Lorne was a successful TV star, but we had to wait for six months to make sure that he wouldn't be picked up for another season of *Bonanza*. I had suggested that we try and get another actor of a similar, or perhaps even greater, stature than Lorne Greene, but instead we waited. Once it was finally established that Greene was available, a considerable amount of time had passed and another series suddenly appeared on CBS called *Barnaby Jones*.[20] Our first episode and the pilot of *Barnaby Jones* were virtually identical. Both guys were retired police captains; both had a son who they felt was wrong to be a private detective; the son was then murdered and both Griff and Barnaby Jones investigate the deaths and both have a grieving daughter-in-law. There were just too many glaring similarities for it to be a simple case of coincidence.

What do you think happened?

Basically, I think the idea was stolen by Quinn Martin. Martin did *Barnaby Jones* in the exact same format as *Griff* with hardly any variations. With *Barnaby Jones* being broadcast before we were on the air, it had stolen our thunder. This was even after *TV Guide Magazine* had said that *Man on the Outside* was a pilot for *Barnaby Jones*. All of this happened because old Quinn Martin stole the idea when he heard what I was doing. He copied it and got it out—only instead of Lorne Greene he had Buddy Ebsen, a very gifted actor, as the lead. Ebsen was, of course, very good in his part, better than Greene was in *Griff*, but that wasn't the point. *Barnaby Jones* ran for seven or eight years and was a huge success. We then had to change the format of *Griff* because *Barnaby Jones* had got on the air first. We did that so it would at least be different, but it took all of the guts out of our show. It wasn't even worth putting *Griff* on because there was nothing left of it after *Barnaby Jones* had stolen everything. We didn't receive any credit or money for it either. So, that's just another example of something getting stolen which has happened to me periodically over the years. If you've been around as long as I have and written so much, inevitably, things do get stolen, and *Griff* was stolen! What makes it particularly tough to take is, sadly, it was due to a friend of mine. He was a partner with me on several projects and knew about my script. I told him my idea and the next thing I know he was working for Quinn Martin and directing a hundred episodes of *Barnaby Jones*. I don't know this for a fact, but I have a sneaky suspicion that my friend had something to do with the theft.

Did you ever confront your friend?

No, there was no point. It was all over and there was nothing I could do about it. I mean, what can you do? In this business you have to be careful of your friends as well as your adversaries. Sometimes your friends are your adversaries.

In 1978, you wrote a little seen pilot for CBS called *Sparrow*.

Yes, and we actually did that pilot twice. *Sparrow* was another show about a private investigator, who operates a detective agency in New Orleans. It was produced by Herbert B. Leonard, who was the producer of *Naked City*, a truly wonderful and important police drama series that began airing on ABC in the late 1950s. Before we embarked on *Sparrow*, I'd anticipated that Leonard would be a brilliant producer, but it soon transpired that he wasn't. I quickly discovered that *Naked City* was actually the brainchild of the writers, Stirling Silliphant and Howard Rodman, rather than Leonard, who didn't really know anything. I mean, the lead role of the detective in *Sparrow* was cast very badly.[21] When we shot the first version of the pilot, it became obvious that this actor just wasn't right for the part. He didn't have any panache or presence, and it just didn't work. All of a sudden, they came back and said, "CBS still thinks this show has merit, so they want to mount another pilot." I was very agreeable to that suggestion, but then Leonard did something that I thought was remarkably inept. As they prepared to re-shoot the pilot, who does he secure for the lead role? Only the very same actor who was no good the first time around! I couldn't believe it. Leonard actually hired this same guy again and he wasn't any better the second time around! What can I tell you? *Sparrow* was a clever idea and it could have been a successful series. Unfortunately, it didn't turn out that way. Once again, I got some money for it and I tried my best, but I didn't have control over the situation.

Leaping ahead nearly twenty years, your next episodic television work was the critically acclaimed "Dirty Socks" episode of *NYPD Blue* which appeared in the second season. How did you come to write for the show?

I knew the creator of the show, David Milch, socially. David asked me if I would write an episode of *NYPD Blue,* and so as a favor to him, I did. "Dirty Socks" was a terrific episode, too. I sent Milch the script and he called me up, and said, "We've moved your episode ahead of two other shows and we're building the sets right now. We're actually going to start shooting it next week." Milch invited me to the set and he was very complimentary towards me. He then invited me to view the first cut of the episode, and later welcomed me into his house to see the telecast. Afterwards, he even took us out for dinner. Milch then called me up and said, "You are not going to believe this, but our ratings are the highest they've ever been for your episode. There was also a bigger response on the Internet for this show than anything we've had on previously. It's a great show and you did a wonderful job." Naturally, I was thrilled to hear this. I was thinking about what Milch had told me and the positive reaction the episode had received. I called him back a few days later and said, "Hey, why don't we do a sequel to my episode since it went over so well? We could take the characters I created and use them in another story?" Milch said, "Uh, I've already written it." I said, "What? You've already written it? Why didn't you ask me to write it?" Well, there was really no answer for that. Milch had done his own spin-off episode using some of the same characters again. He had gone in a different direction, something I also had a good idea for. He just went ahead and did it without asking me or giving me an opportunity to write it myself. I should add that Milch's episode was lousy, too, by the way. It was nowhere near as good as "Dirty Socks" and it went right into the ground. Anyway, that was the end of my association with *NYPD Blue*. Well, almost. There was one character I had created in my episode that went on to become a continuing character in the series. He was a gay guy who worked in the police station as a receptionist or aide.[22] When they used him each week for the rest of the series, they had to pay me a royalty. So, I got paid every week on *NYPD Blue* for about two years, solely based on the appearances of that one character.

Why do you think Milch wrote a sequel to "Dirty Socks" without you?

Ego. He couldn't stand the fact that the show I'd done had been so successful. Milch was the head writer on *NYPD Blue* and he wanted to prove that he could probably write it better than me. So, he went ahead and wrote the episode himself instead of asking me to come back and do it. Again, it is like I told you, ego is always the problem on all of these shows. The show will always come second to preserving and bolstering people's egos, every single time. Why, you might ask? Because it's always about themselves. They must always make themselves look good.

Am I to believe that you yourself are without ego?

In television? No. But as far as my movies are concerned, I don't work with anybody else, so I don't need an ego. I do it all myself—everything—so I don't have to be better than anybody. I don't have to compete. I supervise every element of my films from the casting to the editing. But television is something else entirely. You can't enjoy that kind of freedom for the most part. The only thing I could have ever required anybody to do for me when I was making my movies would be to change the typewriter ribbon when I was writing the script. It was not like that in television. You were always competing, always striving not to be crushed beneath these enormous egos.

What do you consider to be the best of the television scripts you have written?

My best TV scripts were the ones I wrote for Herbert Brodkin Productions in New York—*The Defenders* and *The Nurses*. They were both wonderful shows and they are also on exhibit at the Paley Museum of Television. I'm still thrilled to watch them today because they have such good quality writing and beautifully-judged performances. Admittedly, the production values are minimal. Brodkin was very stingy with the money, but he did spend his cash on good writers and good actors. Those shows were just fabulous and I'm still very proud of them. Actually, I think they rate with the very best in television. Although I did write a few things for *Arrest and Trial*, *Sam Benedict* and a couple of other shows out in California, that work was mainly inferior to what I'd been doing in New York. Ultimately, this was a prelude to what I really wanted to do—write my own movies. Frankly, if things in television had worked out differently; if I had assumed the autonomous position that writers and showrunners enjoy today and I had stuck with television and accepted ABC's offer to become a supplier, no doubt my whole career would have been very different. I would never have made the movies that I made, but it all worked out for the best. I just didn't want to go to an office every day and deal with producers, co-producers, executive producers, story editors, network executives, and suffer meetings and endure all the changes and memos. I did not want to contend with all that.

You were ready for a new challenge?

I was ready. That was my ambition in life—to make movies. I've been involved in a lot of television series and one of the things I must say, to my credit or disservice, is that I get tired of writing the same thing week after week. I'm really not interested in doing the same show time after time, which is exactly what series television offers you. You are merely doing variations on the same characters every week, and I always got tired of it after six months or a year. I always wanted to move on and do something else, stretch myself creatively. Again, I really wanted to go make my own movies—write, produce, and direct them—and be in full and absolute control. If I learned anything during my television experience, it was that you can make a lot of money but you really don't have any control. You constantly have to make compromises with people, and you are constantly arguing and fighting them to get what you want, and you never do quite get what you want. But when you are writing screenplays, it always seems like you are painting on a much bigger canvas, at least that's what it seemed like to me back in the late 1960s. I was going through some changes. I wanted to try different things. There was more room to experiment and push ideas in film, and there seemed to be a wider range of subjects you could take on. Television just couldn't give me that. Certainly not back then.

Screenplays: Part I (1966-1986)

You sold your first feature film screenplay whilst you were still writing for television. What was it and how did that opportunity present itself?

The first one I sold was *The Return of the Magnificent Seven* to the Mirisch Company and United Artists. I talked to Walter Mirisch,[1] who was the head of the company, and he called me in. Walter said that he wanted to do a weekly TV series based on *The Magnificent Seven*, which had been one of their pictures. I said, "Don't waste such a great property, when you could do a film sequel to the original picture and have a big box office hit." Actually, the first movie wasn't much of a hit in the United States as it was very badly released. It only became popular over the years after television reruns. I felt the time was right for a sequel, and so Walter called Yul Brynner and Brynner said that he would do it. Walter then came back to me and said, "Okay, if we're going to do it your way, you write it." So, I got the job of writing the feature and I wrote a very good script, I think. In fact, Walter later said the screenplay was much better than the movie he made. That's generally the case, anyway. In most instances, the pictures were never as good as the original scripts they were derived from.

Did *The Return of the Magnificent Seven* move into production quickly?

It lingered on for a while and then finally they got it put together. We met with various directors for the project, and throughout this period, Yul Brynner remained committed to it. I remember that one director who came through was Irvin Kershner, who later went on to do *The Em-

pire Strikes Back. I believe that Kershner had been a teacher at USC film school, and George Lucas was actually one of his students. Several years later, when Lucas was looking for somebody to direct *The Empire Strikes Back*, he gave the job to his old teacher. I don't think Kershner had much to do with the planning or the ideas for the movie. He was just a traffic cop, because Lucas didn't want to direct anymore after *Star Wars*. Anyway, Irvin was a nice man, but was very rabbinical. We had a meeting with Walter Mirisch, and started going through the script, and Irvin seemed to have a question for every single page we turned. He had to analyse every element of the picture and this went on and on. Finally, Kershner looked up at us and said, "Why do there have to be seven?"

[Laughs] Seriously?

This was *The Return of the Magnificent Seven* and he asked why there had to be *seven*! I looked over at Walter and Walter looked at me, and at that very moment we both knew that Kershner was the wrong director for this project. So, we went on and on and continued looking for somebody, until finally we ended up with Burt Kennedy.[2] Now Burt had directed a lot of what I would call "inferior" Westerns. Honestly, between Burt Kennedy and Andrew McLaglen,[3] both of these men had succeeded in completely destroying the Western as an American motion picture staple. There had been many, many Westerns made over the years—every year there had been Westerns like crazy—but all of a sudden after Kennedy and McLaglen had got through directing some of them, there were no more Westerns anymore. They basically killed the genre, in my opinion. I mean, Kennedy was okay, but he was a very slow-moving director who would just creep along. He also made the mistake of cutting out roughly twenty-five percent of my story so that it didn't really make sense anymore. All the developments of the story had been removed. There were no longer any twists and it became more of a linear piece.

What exactly was lost?

Oh, many things, a lot of scenes and little touches that really gave it some depth and detail. For instance, my story concerned these poor Mexicans, who were kidnapped from their village and forced to become slave laborers for a vicious Mexican general. The idea was that this general wants to construct a church out in the desert that will stand as a monument to his deceased sons who have all perished whilst defending their country against its enemies. The Magnificent Seven then show up and chase the general away, freeing the enslaved people so they can now return to their homes. I then had a nice touch in the story where the Mexicans decide to remain and willingly build the church. This is because they want something lasting in their lives, something that is their own. The Magnificent Seven join the Mexicans in their efforts to build this place of worship, setting aside their guns for probably the first time in their lives. They are now creators rather than killers, but this proves to be only a temporary thing as the general returns and blows up the newly-built church. The script was full of little details and twists like that, but Kennedy only shot half of my story. There was some other stuff lost, too. I just can't recall all of it right now.

Did you have any other issues with *The Return of the Magnificent Seven*?

I had several problems with it. Artistically, the sequel was nowhere near the achievement the original was, but it was more successful financially. They had secured the budget from Spain as a co-production. This had saved money, but meant they had to fill the cast with Spanish actors. Now *The Magnificent Seven* had featured several terrific young stars, people like Steve McQueen and James Coburn, who later emerged as important actors in movies, but *The Return* had a very meager cast. Naturally, Yul Brynner and Warren Oates were very good, but the rest of the people were second-rate. Then, later, Walter Mirisch came to me and said, "We can't use Elmer Bernstein's music because it's been used for a car commercial on television." I said, "Walter, if you don't use Bernstein's score then don't make the picture. There simply is no *Return of the Magnificent Seven* without that music." Once again, Mirisch listened to me and he re-used the original score—re-orchestrated, of course. Believe it or not, the sequel actually got Bernstein an Academy Award nomination—for the exact same music that had been used previously! Crazily enough, he had not received any kind of Academy recognition at all for the original film. It was all thanks to me.

Some sources list you as the writer of Joseph Adler's 1969 horror film, *Scream, Baby, Scream*. Apparently, it's about a psychotic artist who kidnaps models and slices up their faces to create mutant models.

I'm not the one responsible for writing that. No, those sources are incorrect. I've never even heard of *Scream, Baby, Scream*. Obviously, a different Larry Cohen is guilty of creating that movie. There are more than one of us in the business.[4]

Another early screenplay you wrote was the thriller *Daddy's Gone A-Hunting*, which eventually found its way into the hands of the acknowledged master of suspense himself, Alfred Hitchcock. How exactly did that happen?

Well, the idea for *Daddy's Gone A-Hunting* concerned this disturbed young man, who comes back to stalk the estranged young woman who has aborted his child and moved on with her life. He tries to get his revenge on her by getting the girl to abort the child she now carries, which has been fathered by another man, thus killing her new baby. I relayed this story to a gentleman named Mike Ludmer, who was head of the script department at Universal. Mike liked the idea a lot and suggested it would make a wonderful movie for Hitchcock. [Gasps] Gosh, I thought I was dreaming! I mean, Hitchcock was one of my heroes. I adored his movies and still do. Ludmer then arranged for me to meet with Hitchcock at the St. Regis Hotel in New York. They also sent along a Universal representative, who sat there and said nothing. He was there just to keep me company, I guess. I got to meet Hitchcock in his suite, the usual suite that he used at the St. Regis Hotel, which was his favorite and was actually reproduced in his movie, *Topaz*. I arrived there, and Hitchcock was very cordial, warm, and friendly. He talked to me for three and a half hours. The first three hours was Hitchcock just regaling me with stories about the movies he made, the scenes he shot, the scenes he never shot. He spoke about all the incredible people he had worked with and shared anecdotes from his career in England and then later in Hollywood. It was obvious that he liked to talk and I certainly liked listening to him. It was a fascinating conversation and he was just delightful. Then, after Hitchcock had talked for three hours straight, he suddenly stopped and said, "Well, how about you tell me your story?" So, for the remaining half hour, I told him about *Daddy's Gone A-Hunting*.

What was Hitchcock's reaction to the story?

He loved it. He said, "That's a wonderful story, so full of suspense. How shall we get started? Shall we go into first draft immediately?" Oh, it was just wonderful to hear Hitchcock say these things to me. After I left the hotel, I phoned him up about an hour later and said, "You know, I think we really should go right into script because the story is so well-developed." Hitchcock said, "Yes, I agree. I'll see you back in L.A." I then started telling everyone I knew that I was working with Alfred Hitchcock and what a thrill it was! I arrived back in L.A., and Mike Ludmer called me. He said, "Hitch has changed his mind." [Sighs] I said, "What happened?" Mike said, "Ed Henry talked him out of it." Now Ed Henry was a studio executive at Universal, who was known around the lot as "Dr. No." He got that name because he screwed up every project he ever involved himself in. He was a complete negative force. If anything good came along, Ed Henry always fucked it up! Henry had managed to get to Hitchcock and tell him that he shouldn't do *Daddy's Gone A-Hunting*. At that time, Hitchcock was under the influence of the Universal executives to a very high degree. They really messed around with all of his pictures. Everything he later did over there at Universal was terrible, stuff like *Torn Curtain* and *Topaz*. Fortunately, he was able to go over to England and do *Frenzy*, which was the only good picture Hitchcock made in the last ten years of his career. I mean, *Family Plot* was certainly passable, but *Frenzy* was good.

What happened to *Daddy's Gone A-Hunting* after Hitchcock's departure?

Well, after they had talked him out of doing this wonderful script, my friend Lorenzo Semple Jr.[5] and I decided we would sit down and write *Daddy's Gone A-Hunting* on spec. The idea was that after we wrote it, we'd then give it to Hitchcock to see what he would say after he read the completed screenplay. In just ten days, we had written the entire script, typed it up, and sent it to Hitchcock. His response was: "It's wonderful, but you haven't left anything for me to do." You see, Hitchcock liked to be heavily involved in the development of his projects, and we had made the perfect Hitchcock movie without Hitchcock. When he read it, he didn't have any input to offer because everything was already there. I then received a call from Joan Harrison, who had been Hitchcock's secretary in England and later became his associate producer. Eventually, she became his producer and co-writer on a couple of pictures and, later on, produced the *Alfred Hitchcock Presents* TV series. Joan called me up and said, "I've heard about this script you've written and I'd like to produce it." So, I met her for lunch at The Brown Derby, and Joan agreed that it was the perfect

Hitchcock movie. She wanted to do it herself, and I was inclined to give her the script, but then we got an offer from Mark Robson and a company called National General for a couple of hundred thousand dollars. That was a lot of money in those days, and Robson was a very good director. He had previously made some excellent films like *Champion*, *Home of the Brave*, *The Harder They Fall*, *Ryan's Express*, *Peyton Place* . . . .

And *Isle of the Dead*, of course.

Yeah, he did some pictures with Val Lewton at the beginning of his career. Robson had worked with people like Frank Sinatra, Humphrey Bogart, William Holden, and Kirk Douglas. He had also directed Ingrid Bergman in *The Inn of the Sixth Happiness* and Grace Kelly in *The Bridges at Toko-Ri*, so he was undoubtedly an A-class director. In fact, around this time, Robson had just made *Valley of the Dolls,* which had made a lot of money, so he was fairly hot. Since they were offering all that money and Mark Robson, we sold them the script, which I was later very sorry about. I'm sure Joan Harrison would have made a better picture out of *Daddy's Gone A-Hunting* than Robson eventually did. Robson seemed to be hopelessly confused by the story, and he also cast the leading actors poorly. After working with so many great movie stars on his previous pictures, there was a distinct absence of them on this picture. Hitchcock had told me that he wanted John Phillip Law and Sandy Dennis for the two leads, and they would have both been wonderful. Unfortunately, Robson later cast Carol White as the leading girl.[6] White was actually the mistress of the head of National General Pictures, so that's how she got the part. Not that she was a terrible actress—she wasn't—she simply came across like a second-string Julie Christie. For the leading guy, Robson had discovered this terrible actor, who went on to do nothing of importance in his career.[7] These decisions more or less ruined the picture. *Daddy's Gone A-Hunting* was also shot rather flatly and was badly thought-out, so what can I say? I mean, it did some business and got some good reviews, but both Lorenzo and I were very disappointed in the film. Ultimately, this frustrating experience was one of the things which led me to decide that I should direct my own scripts in the future.

Did you ever meet Hitchcock again after that first conference in New York?

Yeah, I met with him again some years later. We spent a long afternoon together at his office in Studio City and I saw him at the premiere of *Family Plot*. I also encouraged Hitchcock to do *Frenzy*, but it was a totally different *Frenzy* from the film that he eventually made in England. This version of *Frenzy* had an entirely different story, different characters, and a different plot. They only shared the same title.

You are obviously referring to Hitchcock's legendary unmade film, *Kaleidoscope*, which was rejected by Universal executives in the late 1960s because it was deemed to be too horrific and sexually explicit. I do know that Hitchcock filmed some test scenes for *Kaleidoscope*, but what do you recall of the project?

Well, Hitchcock had told me the whole story whilst we'd had our meeting at the St. Regis Hotel. It was about a famous Broadway actress, whose son is a sex fiend and serial killer. He is slaughtering all these women in a series of violent and brutal sex murders. I do remember Hitchcock telling me he wanted John Phillip Law to play the part of the serial killer. He was pretty eager to work with him. I also had the feeling that Hitchcock wanted to get Ingrid Bergman back for the role of the stage actress. He wanted Bergman to play this character and have the mother and son together in a morbid thriller. I'm sure the finished film would have bore some relationship to *Psycho* with that element of the story. Hitchcock had all kinds of various plot-lines and detailed storyboards done on it, and he even had the climax all worked out. There was going to be this extended chase sequence on the Mothball Fleet, which was located in upstate New York. They had anchored a bunch of old ships there that had been abandoned after World War II, and I'm sure it would have been an interesting place to shoot a movie. At the end of this version of *Frenzy*, a female victim has been taken onboard one of the ships, stripped naked and is about to be slaughtered by the psychopathic son. She manages to escape and the killer chases her across the ship and up the vessel's smokestack. Obviously, the imagery of a naked girl climbing a phallic-looking smokestack is very sexual and maybe that's one of the many things that put Universal off the project. Ultimately, the studio talked Hitchcock out of doing this incarnation of *Frenzy*. They did not want him to make that film, but I thought it would have made a fascinating movie.

I remember hearing that Universal's refusal to make *Kaleidoscope* was the first time anybody had said no to Hitchcock in over twenty years.

I don't know if that's true because Hitchcock had always been subject to the influence of studio executives and producers. I was trying to get him to resurrect *Frenzy*, but he could sense that Universal did not want to proceed with the project. Hitchcock seemed particularly intimidated by Lew Wasserman[8] and I think his confidence was stripped away—bit by bit—to the point where he no longer believed as strongly in his own abilities as he once did. What can you say? Hitchcock had enjoyed great commercial success and became a rich man, but along the way he had ended his association with Bernard Herrmann as some of the Universal executives preferred that he work with Henry Mancini instead. This was unfortunate because the Hitchcock-Herrmann collaboration had been remarkably productive. But Hitchcock had allowed his mind to be poisoned by the studio executives and his creativity was diminished as a result. He should have stood his ground, but Hitchcock would always run away when there was any opposition. He was very averse to having personal confrontations with people. I remember Mike Ludmer actually telling me: "Now don't be surprised that Hitch has changed his mind. He never likes to say no to people in person. That's why we don't like him having meetings with writers, because he always encourages them and then we have to disappoint them later." Maybe that was the case with *Daddy's Gone A-Hunting*, but he did seem awfully enthusiastic about the project and excited about doing it. I was certainly disappointed that it didn't happen with Hitchcock as director.

Did you ever confront Hitchcock directly?

I actually went out to the lot one day—right after that happened—to confront him about it. I arrived at Hitchcock's bungalow at Universal and this little old British lady, who was his assistant secretary, said, "I'm afraid Mr. Hitchcock isn't here." I then walked across the street and ran into my agent. As I was standing there, talking to him, I noticed that Farley Granger was walking down the Universal Street. I watched as Granger strolled up to the back of Hitchcock's bungalow, where there was a private door, and knocked on it. A moment later, Hitchcock himself opens the door and I could actually hear their conversation. Hitchcock said, "Oh Farley, what are you doing here?" Granger replied, "Well, I'm just doing some television." "Oh, Farley, we must have lunch this week!" "Yes, Hitch, I'd really like that." And this went on and on, with Hitchcock giving Granger a song and dance about the possibility of their having lunch together later that week. Only I knew for a fact that Hitchcock was going away the very next day to his place up in Northern California for Thanksgiving holidays. He wasn't going to be there to make that dinner, but he was feeding Farley a nice line of bullshit. Anyway, Granger went away and I immediately approached the very same door and knocked on it. The door opened and standing there was the same old British lady again that had chased me away earlier! She then growled, "Didn't I tell you that Mr. Hitchcock isn't here?" [Laughs] I mean, what can you do?

Despite your grievances and the missed opportunity with Hitchcock, at the very least you did succeed in selling *Daddy's Gone A-Hunting*.

That's true. In fact, when Mark Robson first bought the project I actually remember thinking, *Oh well, this has all worked out for the best.* The sad thing about Hitchcock is that he treated his writers so poorly. You could be sure that you wouldn't receive any credit or would be fired from your own script. Hitchcock was constantly replacing writers, but he sometimes treated them royally and invited them into his home and plied them with fine wine. One day, he would be an extremely cordial and convivial host, but then two days later, the studio would suddenly notify the writer that they were fired. So, that was just the way he was. Leon Uris, who had authored *Topaz*, told me that he had enjoyed a wonderful relationship with Hitchcock, but then one day was notified that he was fired. Uris couldn't get Hitchcock on the phone after receiving the news and that was that. Even John Michael Hayes, who had written several pictures for Hitchcock, felt he had been shabbily treated by him.[9] Hitchcock simply turned his back on Hayes, and again, that was that. Peggy Robertson had been Hitchcock's assistant for twenty-five years and is depicted in several movies that have been made about Hitchcock, including the one that recently starred Anthony Hopkins.[10] Despite their long working relationship, even she suffered his ill treatment. Although Robertson had remained incredibly loyal throughout a lengthy period, one day she unexpectedly received a termination notice from Universal. She got two weeks pay and that was the end of her association with Hitchcock, without as much as a goodbye or a thank you. There was no severance, no gift, no parting words; it was simply the end, and that was that. So, Hitchcock had no real affection or sense of loyalty for the people who worked for him. I can only assume that if my services had not been terminated before I'd even started writing *Daddy's Gone A-Hunting*, somewhere along the line I would have probably been canned also. Hitchcock wasn't especially generous to writers, or to anyone else who could possibly lay claim to any credit for the work. Ironically, over the following years, I probably had a better relationship with Hitchcock having not sold him the script than if I had sold it to him.

What else comes to mind when you think about the times you spent with Hitchcock?

Well, you always have an image or an expectation in your mind of who or what a famous person is going to be before you meet them, particularly somebody with such a recognizable and iconic presence as Hitchcock. But he was a very engaging and garrulous man, and he quickly put me at ease. One other thing I do remember about him is that whenever we met he would always gesture with his hands when he spoke. Hitchcock would often walk around the room, emphasising his words with the most delicate and expressive movements of his hands. He had very interesting hands, actually. Another thing I remember about him was his handshake. He had a very firm handshake. It's funny, the things you notice and recall about people, but Hitchcock had these big fingers and thumbs and I've always thought they would have been the perfect hands for a strangler. [Cohen makes choking noises] I could just imagine those hands closing around some poor victim's throat—ugh! Maybe he would have ended up strangling me if we had worked together! [Laughs] But for a large man advancing in his years, Hitchcock was incredibly graceful and light on his feet. Of course, in the years that followed, his health deteriorated and he wasn't quite as graceful.

Did you ever mention to Hitchcock the failed practical joke you had attempted at Grand Central Station during the making of *North By Northwest*?

Yeah, but it didn't get much of a reaction out of him. I thought it was a cute little joke, but he had absolutely no memory of it.

When did you last see Hitchcock? Was it at the premiere of *Family Plot*?

Yes, it was. We chatted for a while and it was nice. He died about four years later. I was over in Venice at the time, so I wasn't around for that. By then Hitchcock had left the studio, gone home, and more or less drank himself to death. He'd enjoyed a long and successful career that had lasted more years than many of his contemporaries. In fact, most of the directors who worked in his era were finished by the time they reached their sixties, whereas Hitchcock managed to stay on until he was well into his seventies. If you examine the careers and history of a lot of big directors, you'll notice that many of them stop making movies when they reach their sixties. Not only do you lose your stamina and drive when you get older, perceptions of you and your work can often change. It gets harder to make your movies. Directors in their sixties often stop making pictures of any importance and their careers are well behind them, not in front of them. Besides Hitchcock, John Huston was probably the only one who made good films late into his career. Huston had a couple of strong movies towards the end, such as *Prizzi's Honor* and *The Dead*, but most of the other great directors—even people like Billy Wilder—their careers just fell apart. Wilder couldn't even get distribution on one of his final pictures, *Fedora*, with William Holden.

Your next produced screenplay was the 1970 Western *El Condor* starring Jim Brown and Lee Van Cleef.

[Interrupting] Please, I should also mention one more thing about *Daddy's Gone A-Hunting*: there's this wonderful Korean filmmaker who directed *Oldboy*. Do you know who I'm talking about?

Park Chan-wook.

That's him. Park Chan-wook was in the United States recently making a picture at 20th Century Fox.[11] He contacted me and said he wanted to take me to lunch. So, we had lunch together and he didn't speak much English, but he had an interpreter with him. He told me how much he loved all of my films and was a big fan. He then asked me if I had anything that he could direct, so I pulled out the old script of *Daddy's Gone A-Hunting* and gave it to him. He immediately fell in love with it and wanted to do it. So, his agents took him to Warner Bros., the company that now owns the rights to *Daddy's Gone A-Hunting*, and proposed that Park Chan-wook do a remake of the film. Unfortunately, Warner Bros. didn't go along with it and they made no effort to help get this project made. At the very least, Park did love the script and thought he could have made a good picture out of it. It would have probably been much better than the original. Maybe one day somebody else will come along and do a remake of the picture. We'll wait and see. Okay, you asked me about *El Condor*?

Yes, how did that movie happen for you?

Well, that was an interesting thing. National General, the company that had bought *Daddy's Gone A-Hunting*, called me up and said, "Listen, we've got a project in Spain that we're trying to make, a Western called *El Condor*. We've built a huge fort and we've also built a town, but we've decided that we hate the script!" [Laughs] Can you imagine that? They had all these big sets, but they had no satisfactory screenplay. The company wondered if I wanted to go over to Spain, look at the scenery and the sets that had already been constructed, to see if I could write a script that could utilize them. I said, "I've never heard of this before—writing a screenplay to fit scenery—but if you pay me enough money I'll do it. My wife and I want to go first class all the way." So, they gave us this tremendous deal, and we did indeed travel first class to Almería, Spain, where the Clint Eastwood spaghetti Westerns and *Lawrence of Arabia* had been previously shot. The producer of *El Condor* was Andre de Toth, a very famous old director himself.[12] The director of *El Condor* was John Guillermin, who would go on to make *The Towering Inferno* and several other big movies.

Including the notorious 1976 remake of *King Kong*.

Oh yeah, and that movie finished him! Anyway, Guillermin was an Englishman and had been in the RAF. He was a thin, wiry, tough, little guy, and de Toth was this big, thick Hungarian, who was also very tough. Now I was something of a hero over there because I was coming to save the production. They were all sitting around not knowing if they would get the chance to make the picture. It all depended on whether or not my script was any good. So, everybody was literally following my wife, Janelle, and I around all of the time. They were treating us like royalty and gave us the most beautiful suite. We also got $1,500 a week per diem, which was a lot of money back then. We didn't have to touch the per diem because every night either Guillermin or de Toth would take us out for dinner. They were all vying for our attention, so everybody kept being more lavish and generous in their treatment of us. They even organized a banquet for me and it was splendid. Despite this generosity, if anybody saw me swimming down at the beach they wanted to know why I wasn't upstairs, writing. Everybody was desperate to get started on the picture and was eager to read my pages. So, I wrote them a script that they liked, and Jim Brown and Lee Van Cleef were quickly cast, and everybody was happy. They gave me a big statue of a knight in shining armour that read: "To the liberator of *El Condor*." Finally, on our last day, everybody saw us off on a boat when we left for Morocco. They even had fireworks on the pier and it was the best that I've ever been treated on any movie in my life.

Was that the end of your involvement with *El Condor*?

No. When I got back to Los Angeles, the executives at National General called me and said, "We've got a big problem. Lee Van Cleef won't get on the plane. He doesn't like the script and believes this movie is going to destroy his career. He won't do the picture." Apparently, an Italian producer named Alberto Grimaldi, who had produced several of the Spaghetti Westerns Van Cleef had previously appeared in, such as *The Good, The Bad and The Ugly*, had read my script and thought it was disastrous. He warned Van Cleef not to do *El Condor* as his character was ridiculous and could potentially ruin him. I then said to one of the executives, "Well, can I meet with Lee and discuss this?" They said, "Okay, we'll arrange a meeting for you in a coffee shop." So, I went there and met with Van Cleef, and at first he was extremely hostile. He said, "This film is going to damage me because people will laugh at me in this part." I said, "But Lee, it's a comedic role. The audience is supposed to laugh at you. This is your chance to do some comedy in a movie." He looked at me and said, "You mean this is meant to be funny?" I said, "Of course it's supposed to be funny. Didn't anybody tell you that? It's meant to be like Humphrey Bogart's character in *The African Queen*—a broken down bum. This is a great opportunity for you to try something different." Van Cleef's hard face suddenly softened into a smile and he said, "Oh, that's wonderful! I know what I'll do—I'll play it without my toupee!" I said, "That's a fabulous idea!" He then got on the plane the very next day and was never happier. That was probably the very first time that I knew I could direct actors. By the time we finished that meeting, I had turned Van Cleef around completely. I realized that all I had to do was talk to actors in a decent fashion and fill them with confidence and self-belief. If you speak to actors intelligently they will respond.

What was John Guillermin like?

Guillermin was kind of an aggressive guy. I do remember that he liked to drive extremely fast. He was an excellent driver, but he always scared the hell out of everybody in the car. He would speed around the curved, narrow roads of the Costa del Sol, which were hardly wide enough for two vehicles to pass in opposite directions at the same time. I think that if anything had ever been travelling from the opposite direction you and I would not be having this conversation. Guillermin's wife would be sitting in the car, screaming at him to slow down, but that would only make him step on the gas more. I don't know what he was trying to prove, but it was a miracle that we all weren't killed. I did not like to travel in a car with that guy.

Did Guillermin and de Toth enjoy a good relationship?

No, they didn't get along at all. Guillermin kept saying to me, "Andre wants me to quit so he can take over and direct the picture." It was well-known that Andre had previously produced a movie called *Play Dirty* for the French director René Clément. It had starred Michael Caine, and Andre had succeeded in driving Clément off the picture. As soon as Clément resigned, Andre took over the directing of *Play Dirty*. Apparently, Andre was trying to do the same thing with Guillermin by forcing him to quit *El Condor*, but Guillermin proved to be a much tougher proposition. They were both at each other's throats all the time and eventually got into a huge fistfight in the office one day, which I was not witness to. I had gone back to America by that time so I wasn't there to intercede in any way, but they had this terrible row that became violent. They would have these endless discussions about what color uniforms the Mexican Army should wear. Guillermin would say, [speaks in a cut-glass English accent] "Andre, I wish to acquire the red uniforms for the film." Andre would then reply, [speaks in a harsh Hungarian accent] "No, John, you must have the blue uniforms! The blue uniforms are the best uniforms!" Guillermin would then say, "No, Andre, I'm afraid you don't understand. I'm directing this film and I wish to have the red uniforms." "No, John! You don't know what you are talking about! We must have the blue uniforms!" "No, no, no, Andre. Please order the red uniforms from London"—which was where the costume house was located. Naturally, as soon as Guillermin left the room, Andre picked up the phone and said, "Send the blue uniforms!" When the blue uniforms arrived in Spain—by the hundreds—what could Guillermin do? It was too late to change anything. It was the exact same situation when Guillermin found out that Andre was going off with the second unit and shooting scenes from the screenplay. He did this without telling Guillermin that these scenes were being shot. I mean, Andre was doing anything he could to provoke the guy. I'm sure he agitated Guillermin to the point where they were both literally punching each other out.

Did de Toth often make strange or controversial decisions during shooting?

Well, here's another thing he did: I said to him, "Andre, suppose we have a tribe of Indians in the movie that live in the desert. They are emaciated Indians who are starving to death. They are eating insects and gila monsters—anything they can get their hands on. I want them to be the most seedy, rugged, dusty Indians you have ever seen." Andre said, [speaks again in a harsh Hungarian accent] "I like that idea! The chief should be a very frail and skinny old man, but he fights like the Devil himself!" I said, "Yeah, but don't give me any Hollywood Indians. And for god's sake, don't get me a cigar store Indian like Iron Eyes Cody." If you don't already know, there was an actor named Iron Eyes Cody who looked like Tonto in *The Lone Ranger*. He had appeared in many Westerns playing Indians. I think he was actually Italian, but he did look like an Indian. After telling Andre I didn't want Iron Eyes Cody, about three weeks later he walks up to me and says, "I've hired the chief! He is on his way!" I said, "That's great. Who did you get?" He goes, "Iron Eyes Cody!" I said, "Wait a minute, Andre, I wasted half an hour of my life asking you not to hire Iron Eyes Cody." He said, "Yes, but he will work as technical advisor." I said, "What the hell does he know about Indians? He was born in Brooklyn for Christ's sake!" [Laughs] Anyway, that was that. You simply couldn't do anything with Andre.

Do you like *El Condor*?

I don't know. Andre actually let me re-cut it. When he first came in with the film and previewed it in Hollywood, I looked at it and said, "Andre, you have got to make some cuts to this picture. There is some stuff that is really laughable and there is other stuff that simply does not work." I gave him a list of about six cuts to do in the movie, and he followed my suggestions exactly and made all the changes that I'd requested. Whatever *El Condor* is, be it good or bad, a lot of it is because of the suggestions I made. I don't think it's a bad picture at all. I think it's a rather enjoyable film.

After *El Condor*, you wrote the suspenseful 1971 television movie, *In Broad Daylight*. The story concerned a blind man, who discovers his wife is cheating on him with his best friend and devises a plot to murder her and frame him.

Uh-huh, and I thought that was a highly original idea. *In Broad Daylight* starred Richard Boone and Suzanne Pleshette, and it turned out pretty well. They were doing Movies of the Week for television, and I came up with this idea of a blind man who commits a murder. That one thought was basically the genesis of the story. We convinced ABC to finance the script and it wasn't a bad movie except for one thing: the casting of Richard Boone. Boone is a wonderful actor, but the character he plays in the movie is supposed to be a blind stage actor who pretends he can see in order to kill his philandering wife. To successfully commit this murder, he has to put on a disguise so he won't be recognized when he goes to the place where he hopes to execute the crime. Even though he can't see, he knows this location by heart and can find his way there. The important aspect of the plan is that he is wearing a successful disguise, but unfortunately it was impossible to disguise Richard Boone's face. He had such a huge, craggy face there was almost no way you could conceal his distinctive features. So, the whole concept didn't work as far as I was concerned.

It's still an intriguing idea if it could be executed with some plausibility.

It's funny you should say that, because a couple of years ago I got a call from the producer Marty Erlichman, who is also the manager of Barbara Streisand. Somehow, Erlichman had seen this old TV movie and wanted to do a feature film remake of *In Broad Daylight* starring the blind opera singer, Andrea Bocelli. His idea was that Bocelli would play a blind opera star who commits a murder. Erlichman felt that Bocelli would be perfect for the lead role. I said, "Yeah, that sounds great. Let's get the rights back and I'll be happy to do it." Unfortunately, the project fell apart because people became convinced that Bocelli really couldn't carry the part off. They felt he could certainly sing, but he really couldn't act. Bocelli is really quite wonderful but he keeps his eyes closed all the time. It might have been slightly disconcerting for an audience to have a leading man in a film who never opens his eyes.

The executive producer of *In Broad Daylight* was Aaron Spelling, one of the giants of American broadcasting. What was he like to work with?

I didn't work with Aaron Spelling at all. I had nothing to do with him. I only met Spelling on one occasion when we had a meeting about some television projects. I suggested a series idea to him called *Mod Squad* which was about a bunch of young cops who go undercover in high schools to try and uncover crime amongst teenagers and drug dealers, things like that. I gave Spelling my idea for *Mod Squad* and he never said a word about it and actually changed the subject. A few months later, he announced a new television series on ABC called *The Mod Squad*, which was about three young people recruited to work as undercover cops. I'm convinced that he stole the idea from me. So, that was my one and only experience with Aaron Spelling.

In 1974, shortly after completing work on *It's Alive* and *Hell up in Harlem*, you wrote the well-received Western *Shoot-Out in a One-Dog Town*.

That was another TV movie, which starred Richard Crenna and Stephanie Powers. It was originally called *Bank,* but was later re-titled *Shoot-Out in a One-Dog Town*. My script was rewritten by another writer who did receive credit. The thing I liked about that movie was it had all these wonderful character actors in it that had appeared in Westerns—people like Jack Elam[13] and others that you've seen in cowboy pictures for years.[14] Most of the time you don't know their names, but you recognize their faces. They are the usual stock villains in Westerns and they were all in this one picture. It wasn't a bad idea and it wasn't a bad movie, but it wasn't a good one either. *Shoot-Out in a One-Dog Town* was about a gang of bad guys who want to rob this payroll. The people with the payroll arrive in a small one-horse town and discover there's a little bank located there. The banker, who is played by Crenna, has just installed a big safe into his building. He receives the cash from the people who were carrying it, who I guess have been killed or wounded, and deposits the payroll in the safe. Then, the vicious outlaws show up and, naturally, they want the money. This means that the banker must now decide whether he is going to give up the cash or try to keep it. The dilemma is that if he gives up the money, it is not only the end of the bank but the end of the town, too. The only way to establish a thriving town is to demonstrate that there is some law and social order in place, some modicum of normal, civilised behavior that is securely fixed. If the bank collapses, that will all be lost, and there will be nothing. The town will just dry up, die, and blow away. So the banker tries to resist giving the villains the dough. In the end, he blows up the bank with himself stored inside the safe with the money. The bad guys all come into the bank and the building blows up all around them. Nobody survives except for the banker nestled in the safe. [Chuckles] I thought that was good.

The film has been routinely compared to Fred Zimmerman's *High Noon*.

Yeah, but *High Noon* is every other Western! Zimmerman's film was nothing but the last ten minutes of all the other Westerns you've ever seen, comfortably stretched out to an hour and a half. It basically shows you that the bad guys are coming into town and the sheriff is going to have to face them alone because nobody wants to help him. Isn't that the standard plot of most Westerns? What Zimmerman succeeded in doing was making that one idea last the whole ninety minutes. There's nothing particularly original in *High Noon*, but at the time it was released people took it to be some kind of political statement about conformity in America and the communist witch hunts. They felt it was a comment on individuals being ostracized and abandoned by their friends. It was certainly pertinent for the time in which it was made.

In 1980, you provided the story for William Richert's black comedy, *The American Success Company* based on your script *The Ringer*. It starred Jeff Bridges as a wealthy but disillusioned husband who assumes a separate second identity as a would-be criminal in order to get back at his wife and his boss who have routinely humiliated him. Can you talk about the history of this project?

That was a really great script, which William Richert ruined. He really made a huge mess of it. The original idea was that the wife would fall in love with Jeff Bridges' alter ego. She then plans to knock off her husband so she can live happily ever after with his double. Of course, the husband has created this second identity in order to rob the bank he works in and blame the double for the crime. Unfortunately, Richert abandoned much of my script and exchanged it for some puerile nonsense that was embarrassing to watch. I also thought that Jeff Bridges was the wrong choice for the husband. To be honest with you, I was just happy to get the damn thing made. I'd been through so many false starts with that movie. At one time, we were going to do it with Rock Hudson and Vanessa Redgrave playing the leads, but that didn't work out. Then I went to England for a while and got Peter Sellers to agree to star in it. Sellers was on his downers at the time, so his agent, Dennis Selinger, gave him to me for just $100,000. I then came back to Hollywood, and I couldn't get anybody to make the movie with Peter Sellers for $100,000. People kept telling me, "Oh, Sellers is all washed up! He's made three unreleased movies and is just poison. We wouldn't take Sellers if you gave him to us for free." So, I had to go back to the agent and say, "Look, I haven't got $100,000 for Peter, but I'll give it to you out of my own pocket." Selinger was then kind enough to get me out of the deal, so I didn't have Sellers anymore. Then, as fate would have it, a few months later *The Return of the Pink Panther* was released and was a huge hit. Suddenly, Sellers was back on top again and those very same people who had turned him down with me were now giving him millions of dollars to be in movies. That's just the way it works out sometimes.

Didn't you also approach Michael Caine for the lead role?

Yes, that's right. Another time we talked to Michael Caine about doing the film, but nothing came of that either. I think Caine would have been great in that role and would have really brought a lightness to it. Unfortunately, it wasn't meant to be. It was pretty incredible, really. I mean, we went through a roster of famous names but never got the picture made with any of them. Eventually, I just sold the damn thing and they finally put Jeff Bridges in it. Again, I think he was wrong for the part. They actually shot *The American Success Company* over in Germany because that's where the money came from. The rest of the cast was very offbeat, including Bianca Jagger making one of her only motion picture appearances in the role of the prostitute. The sex scenes between her and Bridges where you have this clock timing him, oh, it was just terrible! William Richert cast his girlfriend as the female lead[15] and then proceeded to fuck around with the script. Richert changed almost everything and it was just a shambles, frankly. I think if *The American Success Company* is ever described as being awful, it is still being vastly overrated. It's a terrible picture.

The American Success Company plays like a satire on capitalism and anticipates the greed and excesses of the Reagan years that would eventually flourish in the 1980s. Did you see that coming when you wrote the story?

Of course, that was what *The American Success Company* was about, for sure, but I don't know if it was specifically about the Reagan Administration or was anticipating what the 1980s would bring in terms of our values. I mean, there is no question that greed and selfishness and exploitation was rampart in every administration in the United States. They are all crooks, including Barack Obama, unfortunately. The inspiration for it came about simply because of my desire to write a comedy script.

The film also seems to be satirising the American hero. Why did you feel you wanted to attack that as you seemed to have celebrated machismo as a virtue in *Return of the Magnificent Seven*, *Branded*, and *Shoot-Out in a One-Dog Town*?

Well, in regards to the Westerns, you had to feature the traditional strong American hero, but I would argue that in *Shoot-Out in a One-Dog Town* the hero was more of an anti-hero. He was not a gunfighter, a marshal, or a sheriff; he was a banker. He was certainly not the typical tough guy you see in movies. In fact, he was the kind of character usually portrayed in Westerns as a meek and cowardly individual. Any picture you ever see where there is a banker, that character is never a heroic, dependable, and resolute figure. In that movie, the banker was all of those things, so in a way *Shoot-Out in a One-Dog Town* is an even earlier example of my subverting the traditional American hero. I don't know if the hero of *The American Success Company* subverts or satirizes the American hero—or American manliness, whatever it is—but firstly it should have succeeded as a story. Otherwise, everything else becomes redundant. I must say that despite my misgivings about the casting of Jeff Bridges, he is a terrific actor. I met Bridges a year or so ago, and I think he actually agreed with me that it was one of his worst performances. The film just didn't work for me at all. Not on any level you'd care to discuss.

In 1983, you furnished the story for *Women of San Quentin*, which followed the story of a young female prison guard, whose first assignment is one of the toughest prisons in America. How did this project come about?

Well, interestingly, I had actually gone up to San Quentin to research a different project, but when I arrived there, I discovered that women were working as guards in a men's penitentiary. I could never have imagined that would ever be possible, but there they were. I said to this one rather pretty girl, "Why would a woman want to work in a men's prison?" She replied, "Why would a man want to work in a men's prison?" I thought about that and quickly realized it was a pretty damn good answer! [Laughs] So, I came back and sold the idea to television, but they then rewrote it and changed it from the story I'd originally conceived. Basically, I had little to do with the actual film. It was just the basic plot that was mine, which is why I received story credit.

You are also credited with devising the story for Ron Cohen's disastrous 1984 crime caper, *Scandalous*, which co-starred John Gielgud and purported to be "A comedy about adultery, blackmail, murder—and indoor sports."

Scandalous certainly claimed to be a comedy of some kind, but I'm not so sure. It seemed pretty flat and tepid to me, and didn't qualify as a comedy at all. It was based on a stage play I had done in New York and in London.[16] Eventually, I wrote a screenplay based on the play and sold it. Then, after acquiring the script, the company once again did me the favor of changing everything around and screwing everything up! I thought *Scandalous* was an utterly dismal movie, at least on a par with *The American Success Company*. If you have an actor as distinguished as John Gielgud in your cast, you should at least give him some material that is worthy of his talent. I don't think anybody liked that film, including its director.

In 1985, shortly after the release of *The Stuff*, you had a number of intriguing projects in various stages of development, some of which were never realized. Two interesting projects that were announced around this time were *Crack in the Mirror* and *Master of Suspense*. Were these film scripts?

No, they weren't. *Crack in the Mirror* was an idea for a television series, but it never got anywhere. I don't believe I ever wrote a script; it only existed as a treatment. It was sort of a fantasy/science fiction piece that concerned two elements of reality, one that existed on one side of a mirror and one that existed on the other side of the mirror. Basically, you could literally step through the glass and enter this other world. *Master of Suspense* was an idea for another TV series I had that concerned a famous movie director, who, quite naturally, directs suspense movies, and a young would-be director, who has sneaked onto the lot and allied himself with this famous filmmaker. The older director was intended to be a takeoff on Alfred Hitchcock, and the would-be director was supposed to be a takeoff on Steven Spielberg. Together, these two characters would go off and solve real life mysteries. Unfortunately, that project didn't get anywhere either.

Did the idea for *Master of Suspense* later mutate into your acclaimed feature film screenplay, *The Man Who Loved Hitchcock*?

Yes, it did. *The Man Who Loved Hitchcock* was the same thing again: Hitchcock and a young would-be director trying to solve a bunch of mystery murders that have been stolen from Hitchcock's files. The murder ideas that he himself has dreamed up are now actually being carried out by somebody. Joining Hitchcock and this young fellow in their investigation is Bernard Herrmann, who appears as a character in it also, and the three of them set out to find the killer. *The Man Who Loved Hitchcock* was a terrific script and a lot of fun. Bernard Herrmann's wife, Norma, said it was wonderful; she absolutely loved it. Another person who adored it was Norman Lloyd. He had been Hitchcock's sidekick and had co-produced the *Alfred Hitchcock Presents* TV series. He'd also acted in a number of Hitchcock's films, famously playing the part of the Nazi spy in *Saboteur* who falls off the Statute of Liberty. Norman said that I had captured Hitchcock perfectly. Norman's wife, who also read my script, agreed with him. They both thought that I'd done a marvellous job of recreating the reality of Hitchcock in a fictional story. Recently, there have been a couple of Hitchcock movies made that have tried to paint him as some kind of sexual psychopath or deviant,[17] but that is not what my script was about.

Did you have any ideas for casting?

Oh, sure. We had the great Peter Ustinov in line to play Hitchcock. I thought that he was just about perfect casting in my mind. If any actor could bring off that part, it would be him. When I met Peter at the Beverly Hills Hotel, he wasted no time in telling me he was crazy for the script. He just loved it! Peter said that he hated reading screenplays, but this was one of the best he'd ever read. He and his wife both agreed. Peter was going to do the picture, and I was thrilled at the prospect of working with him. We tried to raise finance for *The Man Who Loved Hitchcock* at the Cannes Film Festival, but we just didn't get enough money to go forward right away. We kept trying and trying, but then Peter got sick and he died. So, sadly, that was that. Before Peter was onboard the project, I did get a brief commitment from Robert Morley[18] who was interested in playing the role. I do remember that Morley wanted Eli Wallach to play Bernard Herrmann alongside him. For a while, we flirted with that idea but, to be honest with you, I liked Peter Ustinov much better than Robert Morley. Peter was very friendly, enthusiastic, and congenial, and Morley was always a little bit distant and haughty. One day Morley said to me, "I met Hitchcock only once and I did not care for the man." I suddenly thought to myself, *Hmmm, maybe this guy should not be playing this part!* [Chuckles] Oh, but Peter Ustinov was a delight. He was a pretty remarkable man altogether. Peter was a great writer himself and had also directed movies and theater plays. To hear his approval of the material made the whole thing worthwhile for me. Even though the project never got made, I felt it was an invaluable experience just hearing the nice things he had to say about it. I feel privileged just having met him, actually. Maybe someday *The Man Who Loved Hitchcock* will get made. That's the thing with all these great unmade scripts; you just sit around and wait and hope for the best. That's all you can ever do.

Bone (1971)

After more than a decade of writing for television, you saw your chance for creative freedom and expression in low-budget cinema. Can you talk about what motivated those feelings and how you made the transition into movies?

Well, by making my own low-budget movies, I could finally make every decision myself. That was the single motivating factor here. I could cast every part, frame every shot, edit every frame, and hire the crew and composer. That was my goal and that's exactly what I did. My ambition was never to be the showrunner of a television series and stick with it for perhaps four or five years. I was going to be a movie director. Television was built on compromises and conflicts and concessions. You can't survive intellectually, artistically, or spiritually when you are endlessly warring against people to maintain your artistic vision. It will simply destroy you. I wanted to do creative work, and I didn't want anybody telling me what to do. I knew that I would make mistakes when I was doing movies, but that the movies would always be my own and I would learn from every mistake. I wanted total control, and that's how you get total control in filmmaking—you make low-budget pictures. The only people who have absolute control in movies are people at the very pinnacle of the business, who are consistently producing huge hits. You can have a Steven Spielberg type of situation, where you can do anything that you want to do; or you can dwell at the lower end of the business, where you make pictures for such a low figure nobody ever bothers you. Nobody ever demands to look at the dailies. Nobody ever hounds you or bombards you with notes, suggestions, and directives. You simply make your pictures, and they release them. After my years in television, that was the place I wanted to be and that was the place I eventually went with *Bone*.

Can you talk about the genesis of *Bone*, your first feature film as director?

I was looking for a film I could do as my first directorial effort that required a small cast and a limited number of locations. That way, I would only have to worry about getting performances out of the actors and wouldn't have many problems with the geography of physically moving the equipment and crew from one place to another. I eventually settled on something that I could actually shoot in my own house, and that something became *Bone*. I always wanted to do a story about racism in America, which I thought was a tremendous problem, and still is. At that time—it was 1970—I settled on the rather inflammatory idea of a Black criminal who breaks into the home of a supposedly affluent White family. So, that's how it all started and then I worked backwards, thinking in terms of the characters and developing their individual fantasies. The Black man's fantasy was the co-operative and willing White housewife. The White housewife's fantasy was the complacent Black man, who is basically going to come into the house as a dominant figure, but then gradually become a passive figure in her hands, which is exactly what happens. The husband's fantasy is the young girl he is going to pick up on the street. The young girl's fantasy is the older molester, who bothered her when she was a child in the movie theater. Everybody's collective fantasy is the couple's son, who is in prison on a drug wrap in a foreign country. The idea was that the son is actually fantasising the entire film in his head from his cell, and all the characters are becoming the fantasies of the other characters in the piece. So, it was quite a complicated theme, but I think we made it work.

Were you deliberately choosing such incendiary material as a way of announcing yourself as a filmmaker in the loudest possible way?

Yes. I thought if people got what I was doing; the outrageousness of it, *Bone* would be a picture that would get some attention. The tough thing with a small movie, particularly back then, when there was hardly any independent film industry at all, was what do you do with a picture like this once you get it finished? Where is it going to play? Will it get distributed so that people can actually see it? How do you attract their attention and what will the reaction be? Of course, I think *Bone* was so volatile as a picture and the material so hot; I may have gone a little too far in the direction of being provocative. Racism and race relations are such dangerous issues to deal with in cinema. Such a controversial subject matter might have scared off a lot of people, despite the fact they may have thought *Bone* was a very well-directed and acted film.

How did the financing for the film come together?

Well, I had estimated that I would need at least $85,000 to get *Bone* started. After talking to various people, I went to a very kind gentleman named Nick Vanoff, who'd made a lot of money on television shows such as *The Hollywood Palace* and the Country and Western series, *Hee Haw*. Nick had a lot of money, and he wanted to get involved in the movie business, so I approached him for financing. I told him that if he didn't recoup his investment I would write him a free screenplay. At that time, I had a pretty good track record as a screenwriter and was getting good money for writing scripts, so it was my intention to help compensate Nick for any losses. He agreed and gave me the advance money to shoot *Bone,* which I used for principal photography. But then I still didn't have enough money to pay the laboratories and equipment houses that had given me credit. So, I had to get completion money, and money to finish the editing, music, and get the answer print out of the lab. Only then could I go out into the world and try to sell the film. Incidentally, after *Bone* was released and didn't do so well, Nick never requested that I write the free script that I had promised him. He never asked for it.

How did you find Yaphet Kotto for the titular role?

I saw Yaphet in *The Liberation of Lord Byron Jones*[1] which dealt with racism in the American South, and was directed by William Wyler. It was actually one of Wyler's last films. Yaphet played this huge powerful Black man, who, at the end of the movie, takes this vicious sheriff and literally feeds him into a threshing machine so that he comes out squared-up in messy bails like stacks of hay. Yaphet was incredibly dangerous in that picture and physically imposing. I thought, *This is the guy for me!* He was my first choice and, thankfully, I got him. Even if I'd had $30 million to make the picture I'd still have wanted Yaphet to play Bone, regardless. He was electrifying.

Was Kotto comfortable with delivering dialogue like this to the White middle class husband of a White middle class wife: "I'm gonna bang

the hell out of her and cut her throat with your own gold letter opener?"

Yaphet seemed very comfortable with the material. He understood that *Bone* was supposed to have a humorous aspect to it. He also fell right into the improvisations we did. The only thing that made him uncomfortable was the fact that the entire crew was White. In those days, there were very few Black people working as skilled technicians on a movie. It was a small crew anyway and consisted mainly of older people like my director of photography, George Folsey. George had been a cameraman with MGM for many, many years, and had received sixteen Oscar nominations for movies like *Meet Me in St. Louis, Ziegfeld Follies,* and *Green Dolphin Street*. He had also been the photographer on the first two Marx Brothers pictures, and had worked with great stars like Clarke Gable, Judy Garland, and Lana Turner. I mean, George had photographed everybody! Now, here he was, working as my first cameraman. George's son, George Folsey, Jr., was the camera operator and editor of *Bone*, and went on to have a successful career as a producer on most of John Landis' pictures, such as *The Blues Brothers* and *An American Werewolf in London*. George Folsey, Sr. had actually retired by the time I made *Bone*, but I lured him back to work. I also called up a number of his old crew people who had joined him in retirement. They were all tired of just sitting around the house all day or going to the golf course, so they came out of retirement and worked on the picture. I had a fantastic crew on *Bone* and each of them had vast experience of working on high-budget movies. These were all older, White people and Yaphet was the only Black person associated with the film. One day, Yaphet told me he was a little uncomfortable about that but there wasn't very much I could do about it.

What can you tell me about your first aborted attempt at making *Bone*?

Before I secured the services of George Folsey, Sr., I had gathered a bunch of friends together, who were in the movie business making low-budget pictures. I had decided that we would shoot *Bone* in 16mm. We shot for three days, and when those three days were over, I looked at what we had and realized that it simply wasn't good enough. If I was going to take this very good script and make a good movie out of it, I needed to do things the proper way. This meant shooting the film in 35mm with the best possible equipment and technicians that were available and affordable. So, we abandoned the 16mm version and recast the part of the housewife, who was originally played by Pippa Scott.[2] Pippa is a perfectly good actress, but her performance didn't have the comedic edge that I wanted. Joyce Van Pattern, her replacement, clearly had that comedic ability. Joyce's speaking voice and her whole attitude lent itself to the humorous aspects of the picture and Pippa just didn't have that. Pippa was the only cast member that was changed before we got the money from Nick Vanoff and went back and started all over again. However, all that unused material appears on the Blue Underground DVD release of *Bone* for those who are interested in seeing it.

How did the rest of the principal players come together?

Andrew Duggan was a personal friend of mine, who had acted in "The Captive," one of my episodes of *The Defenders*. He was also someone I saw socially in Los Angeles on a regular basis. I thought Andy was a wonderful actor, who never got to do the parts that he was capable of doing. He always played authority figures like a general, or the President, or some corporate executive, which never allowed him to display the sheer breadth of his talent and comedic ability. What happens in Hollywood is that people often get typecast in a certain kind of part. They may work all the time and make a nice living, but pretty soon the limitations of what they are called upon to do wears them down and the actor becomes a walking, talking cliché. I thought that Andy deserved better than that, so I wanted him to play the husband from the very beginning. For the part of The Girl who befriends Andy's character, I had originally auditioned Susan Sarandon. She was very good and, in fact, I would have given her the part if—and it sounds rather odd to say this—my German Shepherd dog had not disagreed. That dog was the most placid animal that ever lived and never acted aggressively with anybody. But as soon as Susan Sarandon entered my house, that dog went out of her mind! She would not stop barking and trying to attack Susan. I had to lock the dog in the back and she never stopped barking all the time Susan was in the house. I figured that something must be wrong with this girl. I mean, why would my dog hate her so much? So, I didn't give her the part. You could even say that my dog cost me the chance to have Susan Sarandon in my first movie.

How did Jeannie Berlin come to your attention for the role?

We were on a talent hunt for someone to play The Girl and Joyce Van Patten suggested Jeannie, who was the daughter of Elaine May.[3] Joyce mentioned that Jeannie had the same qualities that her mother had. I then interviewed Jeannie and liked what I heard (I particularly liked her voice) and gave her the part. She did a good job, and the very next picture Jeannie did after *Bone* was *The Heartbreak Kid*, which earned her an Oscar nomination. As a matter of fact, Elaine May, who was directing *The Heartbreak Kid*, flew out to Hollywood to see me so she could view the scenes that Jeannie had done in *Bone*. She was trying to get Jeannie the lead in *The Heartbreak Kid*, but certain people didn't want to hire her because they didn't know her work. Elaine was trying to put her daughter in the movie and she asked me if I would make a copy of the scenes Jeannie was in and send them to the New York office so she could show them to the producers. I did this at my own expense, and, sure enough, they liked what they saw, and Jeannie got the part. I felt good that I was able to help Jeannie move on with her career, but then she was later interviewed in *Newsweek* magazine and asked about her work in *Bone*. She said, "Oh, that's something I'd rather not talk about." I don't know why Jeannie said that. I'm sure she regretted it later on, but at that particular time Jeannie was going through a period of unfortunate arrogance. After she did *The Heartbreak Kid* and received the Oscar nomination, Jeannie got the opportunity to star in a picture at Paramount called *Shelia Levine is Dead and Living in New York* which was based on a best-selling book.[4] Apparently, she was a monster during the making of that film and attempted to run the whole show, alienating a lot of people in the process. She showed no respect for anybody and suddenly thought she was Barbara Streisand. The picture was a huge flop and Jeannie basically managed to sabotage her career as after that nobody would go near her. All the people she had been abusive to were very happy when that movie was a total failure. I gave Jeannie her start. Unfortunately, she gave herself a finish.

Did you ever see her again?

About a year or two after *Shelia Levine* failed at the box office, I got a call from her in the middle of the night. She sounded all doped-up and was asking if she could come over to my house and take a shower. I couldn't understand it, but Jeannie said she had been living on the street for ten days. I had kids and I didn't want her in the house in that state. I certainly didn't want to invite her over in the middle of the night to take a shower after the way she had behaved. I wasn't feeling particularly sympathetic to her anyway. After that, I didn't hear from Jeannie again for several years. Then I ran into her at the Mayflower Hotel, when I was shooting a picture in New York.[5] Jeannie was going in to interview with Martin Scorsese for a role in *The King of Comedy*.[6] She called me up later and said, "I didn't get the part. Somebody called Sandra Bernhard got the job." I thought that was rather ironic since I had also helped Sandra get her start in the business. Sandra used to be my first wife's manicurist and wanted to be a comedian. I actually got the owner of The Improvisation Club to give Sandra her first chance to go on stage as a performer. She's always been grateful and friendly about that, so it was funny that the part Jeannie was hoping to get went to somebody else I had also helped. I've seen Jeannie since then and have taken her to lunch. We are both on a very friendly basis now, which is nice.

Did you storyboard *Bone* extensively, as a lot of first time directors are inclined to do?

I've never storyboarded any movie that I've made—ever! It would be the last thing in my mind to do and that's odd because of the detailed sixty-four-page comic books I conceived and drew as a kid. I was quite accustomed to illustrating an entire story, but, interestingly, it never once occurred to me to draw one of my movies out. This was the case even with regards to some of the more complicated movies I've done, like *Q - The Winged Serpent* and *The Stuff*, which both involved a lot of special effects.

How fast were you shooting *Bone*?

I don't remember how many set-ups I did on an average day. I never think about anything like that. I never count my shots. I just stage the action and then cover it and try to do some innovative camera angles in the scene. I wouldn't have been able to tell you how many set-ups I had done the previous day even if you'd asked me when I was shooting the picture. I never think about it. Of course, when you do a studio picture that's all they talk about. They ask you, "Where is your shot list? How many set-ups are you going to do?" That's why I don't do studio pictures. That's not my style of working. I just like to make it all up as I'm shooting.

What was the thinking behind having Bill [Andrew Duggan] make sales pitches to camera in a junkyard crammed with the bloody corpses of accident victims?

At the time I was writing the script, it was very prevalent to have all these pitchmen coming on television at night selling used cars. Most of the late night movies on TV were sponsored by pitchmen, and Los Angeles was the automobile capital of America. I had to find an occupation for this character and decided to make him a car salesman. It seemed like an interesting idea and a means of integrating some of these familiar commercials into the narrative of the picture but do it in a way that maintained the dreamlike fantasy aspects of the piece.

The scene where Bone attempts to rape Bernadette [Joyce Van Patten] is still quite shocking. What was the atmosphere like on set when you shot that scene?

It was nothing that was particularly provocative. I mean, we knew we were going to do that scene and we just did it. Joyce was a good sport about it and got into the action. Obviously, the whole crew were standing around and there was nothing intimate about the situation. I think the most shocked of anybody on the crew was good old George Folsey and his cohorts from MGM. They were all between seventy-five and eighty years old, and these elderly gentlemen were not used to seeing a Black man mauling a White woman like that. It was certainly nothing that they had ever anticipated shooting in a movie, but they did their job. Nobody in the crew ever said anything to me, but I do think they were a little shocked by it. They were probably thinking, *What have I got myself into here?*

What was the audience reaction to that scene?

It was exactly what we expected: they were shocked. We put funny lines of dialogue in there, the funny, absurd things that Bone said to the housewife as he was trying to attack her, that I think counterbalanced the scene. At one point he says, "I'm just a big Black buck doing what's expected of him." Bone is basically saying that he is adhering to the common thoughts, misconceptions and expectations of the Black man. I thought that while he was saying that line, it took the edge off the intensity and seriousness of what was happening in the scene.

The press-book for *Bone* presented an "advance think-piece" claiming that the film "is the first time in motion pictures that the subject of a Black rapist has been explored in detail." Exactly what myths were you trying to explode?

I have always felt that the whole core of racism has a sexual basis. White people have always been afraid that the Black man is more potent than the White man. They are afraid that the Black man is a more ferocious lover, that the Black man is superior physically to the White man at sex just as he usually is in sports. In athletics, there is no question that Black people are more advanced over White people in terms of their speed and power. That's why most of the great basketball players, football players, and runners are Black. There's no denying it. So, if that superiority would correlate to sex, then the Black man would be a more sexually potent person and the White woman's idealised fantasy figure. That is the primary reason that White people would fear Black people and try to subjugate them. It would be the root of racism.

Is that the significance of Bone's speech about "The Nigger Mystique"?

That was Bone articulating these ideas. There is a perpetual fantasy that is being projected about Black people: that they are more dangerous, more formidable, and, again, more sexually potent and active than White people. They were considered more of a sexual threat but then, as time passed, people became more rational and somebody like Sidney Poitier emerged. Poitier became the acceptable image of the Black man rather than the negative image of some violent, immoral figure. He was intelligent, articulate, and attractive, and was sort of a homogenised Black man. He was the #1 movie star and assisted in relegating the old stereotypical image of the Black shoeshine boy, or the Black porter, or the Black criminal that White people had created. That image faded into the background and a new kind of Black man came along, who was now compatible with White people and didn't have to be feared. Bone does not look like a contemporary Black man. He looks like a Black man from the 1930s and '40s because that was the old image that was feared: the big Black buck. Usually, that image of the Black man has a packet of camel cigarettes stuffed in his shirt pocket and that's exactly what some people imagine and expect to see. That is not the Black man of Sidney Poitier or Bill Cosby. This is a different kind of Black man. This isn't even the Black man of the rock and roll era that produced figures like Jimi Hendrix that White people have often found attractive and entertaining. No, Bone was the old-fashioned Black man that had just stepped off the plantation. So many times, White people would see a Black man walking towards them and they would cross the street. The very sight of a Black person on a lonely street would be enough to frighten them. I tend to say that even today things are not so very different.

What was the most pertinent lesson you learned in making *Bone*?

That, again, having total control is what it is all about. I didn't have anybody looking over my shoulder telling me what to do, or making any suggestions. I had the freedom to do whatever I wanted to do. I thought, *Yeah, this is the way I want to make movies. I don't want to make movies the way I wrote screenplays, where everybody weighs in with their opinion and you have to do rewrites and make changes that pretty soon end up destroying—or at the very least diluting—what I set out to do.* Here, I was making a movie which I wrote, directed, produced, controlling every aspect of the production. So, I realized very early on that this was the way I wanted to make my films and I more or less did it that way for the rest of my career. I was totally spoiled by my first directing experience on *Bone*.

Was the finished film in any way different from the original script?

We added a few things while we were shooting and there were some improvisations with the actors, but it was more or less pretty close to the script. I never went back and compared the completed film with my script. I can't recall which lines of dialogue were dropped or which moments were added. When it came to putting the movie together in editing, whatever we got, we got, and that was it. Editing a movie is like writing a movie in a way, in that you are taking elements and moments of the story and are molding and restructuring them in order to find your movie. We didn't eliminate anything important and pretty much included everything we shot. We just tightened it up a little bit.

Speaking of the editing, I noticed there are a lot of quick cuts in the movie.

I figured that a movie which is, for the most part, shot inside one house with very few extraneous locations, meant I needed to energise the picture and move it along visually. Another reason that there are also a lot of cuts is that I was trying to control the performances. I would speed the performances up by taking out pauses. This helped to create moments of overlapping dialogue that lent the scenes more urgency and kept the pace going as quickly as possible. I could do that by cutting and trimming the scenes, which gave the impression that the actors were performing faster than they actually were. Sometimes I look at the picture now and I think there are too many cuts. On my later movies, I found that some stuff—particularly comedy—works better in two shots or a master shot rather than in a series of quick cuts and close-ups. At the time I was working on *Bone*, it was my first film and I was trying to do something different. I was experimenting with various things, but I still think it looks good today. In fact, I was delighted with the DVD of *Bone* put out several years ago. The quality of the transfer and the rich vibrancy of the colors look just great. It really brings out George Folsey's terrific photography, which in some scenes almost looks three-dimensional. Yaphet comes out looking particularly beautiful. The tone of his skin, the blue-black quality of his skin, looks just remarkable.

The suggestion that Bone is an imaginary presence is reinforced with his mysterious disappearance at the end of the film.

That's right. He was the wife's fantasy figure, but he may have also been both the wife and the husband's fantasy figure. The Black criminal is a fantasy figure of middle class and upper class White people, and the character of Bone embodies that fear. What they feared above all else was the intrusion of a Black man into the sanctity and sanctuary of their homes; allowing this bogeyman to assault their wives and ransack their property. It was a very common bug-a-boo, a popular fantasy-fear. The housewife may have also wanted to destroy her husband and used the figure of Bone to perform that service. Bone simply allowed her to basically kill her husband before vanishing. What is also interesting about that last scene where you see Joyce Van Patten sitting in the sand, blaming this Black man for the crime she herself has committed, is how similar it is to the final scene in *Last Tango in Paris*. In that movie, you have the young Parisian girl, who concocts this whole fantasy story around Marlon Brando's character whom she has just killed.[7] The girl claims that he is a complete stranger that has attacked her, ignoring the fact that she was using him for sex up in this apartment. The girl fantasises this lie to justify the murder in preparation for the arrival of the police and rehearses her story directly to camera, just as Joyce does in *Bone*. Those final scenes are exactly the same, but it's my understanding that *Bone* was made before *Last Tango in Paris*.

Tell me about your efforts to sell *Bone*.

I had to find a distributor, so I took the picture all over Hollywood and New York. That wasn't easy because I only had a work print of the film. It was ten reels of picture and ten reels of matching track, which meant there were twenty reels that had to be transported from one place to the other. I was the only one who could do it and, frankly, I was the only one I would trust with the reels. If I'd lost that print it would have been the end of me, so I personally escorted it around. It was difficult lugging all of this stuff around from office building to office building, screening room to screening room. I was often mistaken for some kind of delivery boy and doormen would try to send me around to the service entrance. But I managed to get the film to all the screenings and showed it to Columbia Pictures. That screening was supervised by Bosley Crowther, who was a notable critic for the *New York Times* that I greatly admired. Crowther liked my movie, but Columbia weren't interested in buying it. I then showed *Bone* to David Brown at Warner Bros. He said, "Oh, I'm afraid I have a meeting scheduled for today, so I won't be able to stay for the duration of the picture." I immediately knew that was his excuse to get up and leave the screening if he didn't like what he saw. Then there was a moment in the film where Bone is pulling books off shelves and he picks one up that happens to be *The Confessions of Nat Turner* by William Styron. That moment intrigued Brown because as it turned out, he had purchased the rights to Styron's book when he was over at 20th Century Fox. It was merely a coincidence, but it kept him in his seat. So, Brown watched the whole of the film, but he was concerned about certain elements of *Bone* that he felt were controversial and difficult. So, Brown passed on the movie, too. I then hauled the twenty reels back over to New York and screened the picture for Joseph E. Levine, who had produced *The Graduate* and *Carnal Knowledge* for Mike Nichols. In fact, Levine asked to see *Bone* again and, after the second screening, he compared my work with that of Nichols, which, of course, was a great compliment. He then said, "Kid, let me be honest with you: if you had walked in here a year or so ago I would have tied you to that chair! Unfortunately, I'm having problems with financing at the moment, so I don't have the money to buy your picture or pay for prints and advertising." And that was it. Our hopes were dashed again. All of this was a little frustrating as Levine had told us to wait and give him another look at the movie—despite his knowing that he was in no position to buy it. Incidentally, I would always insist on staying in the screening room and supervising the exhibition of the film.

Is that practice unusual?

Most of the executives had never heard of a filmmaker being present at the screening of their movie. They don't ever want you to be there and the simple reason for that is because they can take phone calls, or talk during the screening, or even switch reels without you knowing. They can't do that when the director is sitting in the same room as them. But I wouldn't show the picture if they wouldn't allow me to be present. I would announce that I was going to leave with my movie and they would always acquiesce and I'd be invited to stay for the screening. Generally, the reactions to *Bone* were quite good, but people were scared of the racism aspect of it and the sex scene between a Black man and a White woman. A lot of the dialogue, which was highly inflammatory, also concerned them.

What can you tell me about your dealings with the infamous producer and distributor Jack H. Harris and how he became interested in acquiring *Bone*?

Well, firstly, let me say that Jack Harris is an extremely nice man, and I've kept up a very friendly relationship with him over the years.[8] Jack is a lovely guy, but he knows absolutely nothing about movies! [Chuckles] Jack made some money with *The Blob* and he still continues to make money with *The Blob*. He did put out a number of other exploitation movies, but he was certainly not a class-A distributor. However, of all the people I showed *Bone* to, Jack was the only one who stood up when the lights came on and said, "I want your picture. How much money do you need?" He stepped right up and bought it. Of course, he bought it for all the wrong reasons because he thought he could sell *Bone* as a blaxploitation movie like *Shaft* or *Superfly*. He was completely wrong about that as *Bone* was not that kind of picture. It was a comedy, but he tried to sell it as a drama. When I tried to explain this to him, he said, "Well, I'm not going to stand in the aisle and tell the audience when to laugh." I said, "Jack, that's not the point. When you advertise a picture as a drama and people come in and discover it's actually a comedy they are not going to be happy. If they order vanilla ice cream and you give them chocolate ice cream, they won't swallow it. People have to buy a ticket to see a movie they want to see. You can't deceive them and show them something that they didn't expect." Jack did not understand that. He kept trying to sell *Bone* first as a blaxploitation movie, then later he changed the title to *Housewife* and tried to put it out as a sex film. I asked Jack where he got that title from and he replied, "Well, there is a housewife in the film." I mean, he was just going in the wrong direction.

I've seen the lurid print ads that Harris sanctioned that exclaim: "White meat, black bone—what a dish!"

Yeah, it was very embarrassing, but the ad campaign in England was even worse! I went over there and met with the British distributors and explained what Jack had done. They politely listened and were incredibly sympathetic. They seemed to be so intelligent, but of course, a sophisticated British accent can fool you into mistakenly believing that you are dealing with someone who knows what they are doing. Unfortunately, that was not the case because these people were equally stupid. They put the picture out over there as *Dial Rat for Terror*! [Sighs] It couldn't have been a worse or more inappropriate title for a picture that was supposed to be a comedy. They just didn't get it either. I felt there was an audience out there for *Bone*. I mean, Jack held a preview at a rather disreputable theater called the World Theater. It was located on Hollywood Boulevard and was a third-run theater that is long gone now. I told Jack that the audience at the theater would not be the audience for *Bone* as there was only one Black man in the film. Of course, he wouldn't listen and said, "Let's just arrange the preview and see what happens." So, we did and, to my surprise, the picture played wonderfully. It was a predominantly Black audience and they all laughed in the right places and understood the subtleties and nuances of the film. That was probably the first time that I really felt confident about the movie. I knew it was good but I now realized that it could really work for an audience. Jack then arranged a second screening over at a theater in Westwood, which was a more upscale and fashionable theater. *Bone* went over well again—this time with a White audience—so I really knew we had something cooking. But when Jack started with the wrong title and the wrong ad campaign, we were hobbling the picture before it really had a chance to fly.

What was the response from critics?

Some of the critics, like Judith Crist in New York, liked the picture very much. We got a lot of good reviews but, naturally, Jack wasn't going to go out and spend money taking ads out to reproduce positive critical quotes. That was not the way he distributed the picture. Good notices really mean nothing if you don't make use of them, but of course it costs money to exploit good reviews. You have to be able to take ads out and spend a good deal of revenue to try and promote all the audiences to come into the theater. A picture like *Bone* required that quality of distribution, but that's not what happened. We did finally find a home for the movie on home video many years later. Since it has been released on DVD, *Bone* has enjoyed fabulous reviews. It's earned four-star ratings, been picture of the week in various magazines and publications, and received a great deal of attention. So, the movie has finally found an audience after all this time and that's wonderful. I always knew that someday people would discover *Bone*. If the picture had been received the way I hoped it would back at the time of its original release, I believe it would have changed my entire career.

Changed it how exactly?

If *Bone* had been appreciated artistically within the circles I hoped it would, I think I may have gotten a chance to make a more esoteric type of film. Instead, I was immediately invited to do a blaxploitation picture because Yaphet Kotto was so good people thought, *Oh, this guy can really direct Black actors*—as if there was a difference between directing White and Black actors. So, I got to make *Black Caesar* and *Hell up in Harlem* and made a lot of money. I enjoyed some success, but those were not the kinds of movies I would have gotten had *Bone* been better received. I always felt that I would get a chance to do the kind of quality pictures that Mike Nichols did like *Carnal Knowledge*. You know, it's odd when you look back at the direction your career has gone in, but as long as you get a chance to continue making movies life goes on. Again, I don't think I could ever have been a studio director anyway. I wouldn't have been comfortable or happy in such a restrictive system where you experience all kinds of supervision and collaboration. They say that making movies is a collaborative process, but I'm not a good collaborator. I like to do everything. I like to be in charge of every aspect. Again, I just want people to do everything that I tell them to do.

Bone still has important things to say about race relations in the United States, but how do you feel about the film today?

I feel that *Bone* is just as uncomfortable and difficult for audiences to deal with now as it was when it was first made. The picture played at an arthouse in Chicago about five years ago and the management of the theater said that the Black people who attended the screening enjoyed the movie, but a lot of the White people were offended by it. Remember, this was more than thirty-five years after the film was first released! People in America think that the racial situation has changed because we now have a Black president, but there is still a lot of racial unrest out there. Every once in a while, something fiercely divisive, like the O. J. Simpson trial, suddenly arrives and stirs up all those old tensions and hatreds again. It is the same thing with anti-Semitism. People will often say, "Oh, that's old, that's all over with!" But it's still very much out there, simmering under the surface. Sometimes a lot of the shadowy side of life in our country is brushed away or ignored. We think the sun is shining in America and that kind of unpleasantness is gone, but it may not be so. The darkness is still there and you can't be too surprised when racism and anti-Semitism becomes visible again because it never goes away. It's always there and for as long as human beings continue to exist it probably always will be.

Black Caesar (1972)

How did *Black Caesar* become your second directorial offering?

It started when I was approached by the manager of Sammy Davis, Jr. to write a picture for him. Sammy was tired of playing second fiddle to Frank Sinatra and Dean Martin and wanted to be the hero or leading part in his own movie. They were offering to pay me $10,000 to write a treatment, and so I started to think of some ideas. I realized that Sammy was a little guy, like Edward G. Robinson and James Cagney were little guys, but both Robinson and Cagney still had a formidable screen presence. I particularly remembered and liked Robinson in *Little Caesar*. I thought we could do our own movie about a Black gangster in Harlem and call it *Black Caesar*. I then wrote a treatment and delivered it to them, but they never paid me the $10,000. Sammy's manager came back and said, "Sammy is in trouble with the IRS and his taxes. He hasn't got any money and he can't pay you." So, what was I going to do, sue Sammy Davis Jr. for $10,000? No, I just took the treatment back and decided to keep it. Then I got a call from Samuel Arkoff[1] at American International Pictures, who was starting to make some blaxploitation movies like *Coffy* and *Foxy Brown*, stuff like that. Sam basically said, "Listen, we're looking for some action pictures that can star Black actors. I saw that movie you made with Yaphet Kotto and thought you did a very good job directing him. Do you have anything?" I said, "Well, you've come to the right place because it just so happens that I've got a treatment downstairs in the car that might interest you." So, I ran down, got the treatment out of my trunk, brought it back up to Sam, and we made a deal within fifteen minutes. We then made the picture for something like half a million dollars.

It's interesting that you selected a gangster vehicle for Sammy Davis, Jr. considering the rumours that he and other members of The Rat Pack reputedly had Mafia connections.

Sammy and all those guys claimed to have Mafia connections, but that was because they all played in nightclubs. In those days, all of the nightclubs in Las Vegas were owned by the Mafia. That's how people like Sammy and Frank Sinatra formed those relationships, but they were never really "in with the mob" in any serious or meaningful way. The mobsters enjoyed their music and seeing them perform and just liked to hang out with them. That's really as far as it went.

How did you find Fred Williamson for the lead role of Tommy Gibbs?

Fred had just made a successful picture called—believe it or not—*The Legend of Nigger Charley*, which had stirred up some controversy.[2] I mean, who ever heard of a title like *The Legend of Nigger Charley*? Anyway, he had this movie out and it was a hit, which meant that Fred was now considered a viable Black star. Somebody I knew was friendly with Fred's manager and they arranged for us to meet. We had a cup of coffee together and we hit it off immediately. Fred was acceptable to AIP and so he was cast in the movie and became the Black Caesar.

Did you change or remodel the character at all after casting Williamson?

No, not really, except that Fred was a very attractive, good-looking guy as opposed to Sammy who was a little bit more of a character—certainly not a sex symbol. Fred was a very handsome leading man and we played off of that. He had a fabulous wardrobe and really looked great and imposing in the part.

Whereas other contemporary efforts such as *Shaft* updated the forties model of the private eye melodrama, *Black Caesar* follows the conventional mechanics of the traditional Hollywood gangster film, particularly *Scarface* and *Little Caesar*.

I was definitely attracted to stories like *Scarface*, *Little Caesar*, and *The Public Enemy* because those were the kinds of films I enjoyed as a kid— the Cagney, Robinson, and Humphrey Bogart films. I loved Warner Bros.

movies very much, and this was my chance to do my own Warner Bros. gangster movie in what was, at that time, modern dress. *Black Caesar* followed the same established pattern of the old gangster films where you saw the rise of the gangster and then his eventual collapse and destruction. In every other contemporary blaxploitation picture that was being made in the early 1970s, the Black hero was always utterly infallible. He dispensed violence and defeated everybody and usually ran off with a lot of White women. There was no downfall for any of those characters, and I didn't find that particularly interesting. So, this was a completely different story because it didn't fit the cliché of the typical blaxploitation movie with its Black superhero. Tommy was a vulnerable character with a lot of flaws and insecurities. He was betrayed by the people he loved and eventually ended up back in the slums where he began. He was not impervious and all-powerful. I thought we made a legitimate film in *Black Caesar* rather than a cliché-ridden blaxploitation movie that people were used to seeing back then.

You have previously stated that certain people had no desire to follow you into the slum areas where you shot the film for fear of being accosted. Did you encounter any problems during the shoot?

Well, we were making a non-union movie. We couldn't afford to pay for Teamsters and for the expensive New York unions that were around in those days. Shooting in New York was prohibitively expensive and we couldn't afford any of that. So, when they found out that we were there, the Teamsters and the union people came around to harass us and stop us from shooting. We then drove up to Harlem, and when we eventually reached 125th Street, the Teamsters and the union people immediately turned around and went back. They were not going to follow us into Harlem. Frankly, they were scared to go up there. We weren't scared to go up there because we were going to make our movie. We felt perfectly safe, but then the local gangsters in Harlem came around and wanted to shake us down for money. There had been a movie shot up there previously with Anthony Quinn called *Across 110th Street* that was a big studio picture.[3] They had arrived in Harlem with all the trailers, the portable toilets, and dressing rooms, but discovered that they had to pay off the gangsters in order to be allowed to shoot. So, when we got there, they also came around to see us, but we had hardly any equipment and only a small crew. The tough guys immediately said, "You can't shoot here. This is our neighbourhood and you have to pay us." I didn't have any money to give them, and so I said, "Hey, you gentlemen look great. Can you act? We're looking for guys to play Fred Williamson's henchmen in the movie and you guys would be fantastic." The next thing I know, I'd hired all of them to be in the movie. These gangsters loved the experience of shooting a film and the prospect of seeing themselves up on the big screen. We even put these guys on the poster. In fact, when we opened the picture at the Cinerama Theatre on Broadway, all these gangsters were standing around in front of the theater signing autographs! So we never had any trouble in Harlem. Anything we wanted, we got. On one occasion I happened to mention that we needed something that looked like heroin for a particular scene. The next thing I know, they had arrived back on the set with a real bag of heroin. I quickly said, "Get that out of here now!" That was the last thing I needed.

Tommy refers to himself in such derogatory terms as "nigger," "jig," and "jungle bunny." Were you concerned at all about using that kind of language?

No, because that was the language that the Black people used up there on the streets. That is exactly how they talked. They literally referred to themselves that way all the time. Of course, they didn't like outsiders referring to them with those words, but it was the accepted vernacular of the street.

It is also a way for Tommy to knowingly disarm his White adversaries.

Yeah, I understand what you mean. There's the scene when Tommy is talking to the White Mafia guys where he clearly does that. Fred had no problem saying those lines and there was no problem with any of the other actors either. Everybody seemed to be comfortable with it. I know that today, in our era of political correctness, people get very uptight if they hear The N Word. Dick Gregory, who was one of the first Black comedians, actually called his autobiography *Nigger*.[4] He was quoted as saying that, "Every time people use the word 'nigger' they will be advertising my book." In those days, it was totally acceptable to use that term—not as a means of attacking someone in real life, but within the framework of a dramatic form. It was used not only by me but by many other writers, including Black writers who wrote Broadway plays, off-Broadway plays, and movies. The people who made *The Legend of Nigger Charley* obviously had no problem using that word in the title of their picture.

At one point, Grossfield [Patrick McAllister], the first of Tommy's White Mafioso victims, coldly declares: "Nobody likes to lose like the Negro—they are born losers."

Yeah, but that was his point of view. Back in those days, that comment was a perfectly valid one from the perspective of the Mafia and the mob bosses. They felt that Black people were there just to be victimised. Cardoza gives Tommy his big break but then, later on, he himself is victimised by Tommy. It's his time to lose.

Do you think the ear-cutting scene in any way influenced *Reservoir Dogs*?

I suppose so, yeah. It's quite possible that it could have done. I know that Quentin Tarantino is a big fan of all those blaxploitation movies.

Tommy commits these acts of violence without remorse. He rapes his own girlfriend and seeks power and money at any cost. In spite of this, Fred Williamson still makes him an engaging, even sympathetic character.

I think that's true. All of the actors who played gangsters in the movies, whether it was Paul Muni, Robinson, Bogart, and particularly Cagney, they always seemed to make this apparently heartless character appear terrifically attractive. Even though the gangster was violent and vicious and cruel, audiences still liked them. People seem to gravitate towards the bad guys, but also those kinds of characters can be star-making parts for actors. I mean, in *Kiss of Death* Richard Widmark plays a crazed, cackling killer who throws a disabled lady in a wheelchair down a flight of stairs, and he became a big star! In fact, more stars have been made playing villains than probably any other characters. Robert Mitchum was at his best in *Cape Fear* playing an absolutely unrepentant psychopath who is terrorising Gregory Peck's family. It was one of Mitchum's best performances and it was also the part he most liked playing. He once told me that he would much rather play a bad guy than a good guy.

Do you think *Black Caesar* in any way articulates the Black experience as it was for certain people in the early 1970s, or were you principally concerned with simply making a commercial entertainment?

Black Caesar was always intended to be an entertaining action picture, but it did have a lot to say about the relationships between Blacks and Whites during that period. Like *Bone*, it was another exploration of racial conflicts in our country and the manner in which racism was so deeply embedded in the psyche of American life. Interestingly, I did find out later that a lot of what happens in the movie turned out to be actually true. There was a lot of illicit activity occurring between the police and the underworld in terms of pay-offs—particularly in the drug trade. At the beginning of the film, we see Tommy as a twelve-year-old boy being used to make a pay-off to the police. I later found out that in reality criminals were in fact using children as couriers to deliver drugs and money. I did not know that when I wrote the scene, but it turned out that my instincts were absolutely correct. I was right on the nose there.

Did you experience any negativity from members of the Black community in regard to the portrayal of the Black characters in the film?

The only problem we had was when we previewed *Black Caesar* at the Pantages Theatre in Hollywood. The movie went over just great but then, at the end, when we came to the final scene where Tommy is killed by a gang of Black teenagers, the audience did not like that at all. Some of the people in the theater, and in the lobby, objected and started screaming and hollering. They basically said, "Black people would not do that to each other!" Of course, they were completely wrong about that as the largest number of crime victims in the Black community are Black people who have been killed by other Black people. There was no question that they were, and still are, being incredibly violent towards each other. There are drive-by shootings out here in Los Angeles all the time and the victims are almost always Black kids. Even though in films like *The Public Enemy* and *Little Caesar* you see the gangster getting killed at the end, I felt the Black audiences did not want to see their gangster suffer the same fate. They wanted Tommy to live.

That reaction must have concerned you.

Yes, it did. I called up Sam Arkoff and told him that the preview audience did not like the ending. He said, "Well, I told you not to kill him." I said, "Okay, you were right and I was wrong. Now we have to do something about it." Sam said, "The picture opens in five days at three major theaters in New York. There's nothing you can do about the ending now." I said, "Yes, there is. I'll go back to New York and I'll cut the last scene of Tommy getting killed out of the picture before the movie opens." Sam said, "If that's what you think should be done, then do it." So I visited the first theater in New York and introduced myself as the director of *Black Caesar*. I then went upstairs to see the projectionist in the booth and physically cut out the last scene and tacked on the closing credits. I then travelled to the next theater and did the same thing, before moving on to the third theater and repeating it again. The projectionists had never met an actual director before. They were overwhelmed by the experience of having somebody come up to the projection room and literally re-cut the movie in front of them. *Black Caesar* opened later that very same day—just a few hours later—and was a huge hit. I mean, *Bone* was a good movie but it didn't do any business. *Black Caesar* was my first hit and there were lines right around the block and it was such a success that they were opening the theater at nine o'clock in the morning and running shows right through until four o'clock the following morning. They raised the prices (and this was in the wintertime in New York, when it was seven degrees outside and was a freezing cold February) but people still lined up in the streets, waiting for the next show to begin. I kept driving by the theaters, looking at the crowds that had gathered to see my movie. I thought, *Wow, this is fantastic!* After that, I really believed that every movie I made subsequently would be a hit, but of course, life doesn't always work out that way. Sometimes you are wrong.

Why did you restore the original ending for the home video release?

I didn't restore it. What happened was this: when they were preparing the DVD release of *Black Caesar*, they went back to the original negative which had never had the ending removed. So, as I'd always intended, Tommy died at the climax, murdered by the street gang. I was much happier with that conclusion as I thought it was better and stronger. Although we had removed that ending from the domestic release, it was accidentally left in the foreign release, which, like the home video release, was also made from the original negative. By the time they put *Black Caesar* out on DVD,

I think attitudes had changed considerably. People were now more willing to accept a bleak ending, so audiences were not as furious and condemning as they were at the time of the film's American theatrical release.

Can you relay to me a telling anecdote about the shooting of *Black Caesar*?

In the course of making this picture, there were a lot of stunts that had be done, like when Fred Williamson had to throw himself out of a moving taxicab and onto the sidewalk. I would say, "Okay, Fred, we are going around the corner here. I want you to open the door and then throw yourself out of the cab." He'd look at me and say, "You do it first!" So, then I would say, "Okay, I'm going to show you there is nothing to be worried about." Then I would go and throw myself out of the moving taxicab and onto the curb. I'd get up, brush myself down, and say, "See? There's nothing to it." Then I'd calmly walk around the corner and start screaming in agony, but I'd never show Fred that I was in pain. Fred would say, "Yeah, you're right. There's nothing to it." Then he would do it, get up on his feet, walk away and start wincing in pain, too! [Chuckles] Neither of us wanted to show the other one that we couldn't do something. Anything that Fred had to do in the movie I had to do it first.

It sounds like it was an eventful shoot.

Oh, it was. Those who worked on *Black Caesar* were just amazed at what we were getting away with each day. We stole all kinds of shots in New York City and were literally chasing people through the streets with guns. That whole sequence we shot in front of Tiffany's on Fifth Avenue, with Tommy getting shot by an assassin and collapsing on the street, was filmed with hidden cameras. Everybody thought that situation was real, that a guy was actually lying in the street, seriously wounded. People were stopping and trying to help Fred at one point because they thought he really was injured. I mean, here was this nicely dressed man lying on the street with blood on him and they believed that something terrible must have happened. They had no idea whatsoever that they were in the middle of a movie and this was a complete fantasy. In fact, if you watch the film again, you will notice how the people react to what is happening. It's pretty incredible, but we stole that whole sequence. We would shoot the scene on the street and then we'd go away for half an hour until all the spectators had drifted away. Then we would go back and do it again, shooting the action from a different angle. It was interesting seeing what reactions we would get from people as they saw these events unfold. I was like a mystical figure to the crew because they did everything I asked them to do. They figured, *Hey, this guy can do no wrong—he owns New York City!* [Laughs] I mean, we were actually driving taxi cabs on the sidewalks and running through the streets with guns. If we did that today we would all be arrested or shot down by the cops as suspected terrorists. It would be impossible to do that now. Nobody will ever do anything quite like that again.

How did you go about staging the poolside massacre sequence where Tommy annihilates the Cardoza Brothers in California?

We shot that entire sequence at my house using the roof and my swimming pool. We threw all of those people into the pool along with all this fake blood as well. We had to drain all of the water out afterwards and fill the pool back up again. That ended up costing me a lot of money. We could never have done that to somebody else's swimming pool so we had to do it to mine, I guess. Anyway, that scene worked out okay so it was all worth it.

What are your memories of working with Gloria Hendry who plays Tommy's girlfriend, Helen?

Gloria was and still is a lovely person. I see her occasionally around town and she still looks great. She remembers the experience of making *Black Caesar* as being a positive one and she was treated well. I think it was one of her best opportunities as an actress and led to her getting the part in the James Bond movie, *Live and Let Die*, as well as a lot of other work at the time. I had no trouble with any of the actors on the picture. Everyone was extremely cooperative and did everything I asked them to do. It was a pleasure working with people like Gloria, Val Avery, and Art Lund.

As McKinney, the bent cop who torments Tommy, Lund makes an impressive adversary for Williamson, doesn't he?

Oh, Art was great. He had once been a very famous singer. I believe Art had played with Benny Goodman and other bands, and had also performed in Broadway musicals. He had enjoyed a lot of success, but then came to Hollywood to be an actor and appeared in films like Martin Ritt's *The Molly*

Maguires.⁵ Art was not only a good actor, he was a very big man with a tremendous physical presence. He was six foot four, and had these huge hands, and I knew he would make a formidable opponent for Fred. I mean, Fred is a big guy, but Art was even bigger than him! He had that White Scandinavian look to him that seemed like the perfect counterpoint to Fred's Blackness. It made their confrontation all the more visually dramatic as it seemed like they were coming from two entirely different worlds. I was very pleased with Art's performance and used him again in *The Private Files of J. Edgar Hoover* and *Island of the Alive*. He was wonderful.

The most ferocious scene in the film is when Tommy blackens McKinney's face with boot polish and makes him sing "Mammy" before killing him. That was a far more savage comment on racism in America than anything found in *Bone*.

I was tremendously happy with that scene because it really had operatic pretensions. It was written in the script and was always very, very strong. We just decided to go ahead and do it. I thought it turned out to not only be the most powerful scene in the film, but one of the most powerful scenes in cinema actually, certainly during that period. I mean, it was pretty hot stuff back then to have a Black man blacken the face of his White adversary and then make him sing like Al Jolson before killing him. The 1960s had only just ended with all the civil unrest and the assassinations of Martin Luther King and Bobby Kennedy, but we still went all the way with that scene. There was never a problem with anybody on the movie objecting to what we were doing. I think they knew it was something special. Fred and Art really got into it and they loved playing the scene because they saw that it worked. They realized that it had so much expiation of anger and fury; that the Black man was finally turning the tables on the White man. I thought Fred's acting was fabulous and that scene was probably the best thing he ever did. We played it with the American flag clearly visible in the background as it really said a lot about racism in America and its inevitable consequences.

It is certainly a bold statement.

Yeah, and still a very valid one. It's interesting that in America we had all of these race riots and unrest happen to us about twenty or thirty years ago and now you guys in the UK are only just starting to get it. I noticed that the same thing happened in England recently with the riots that took place in London.⁶ I think the disturbances all started in the Black communities and spread to the White communities and people were looting the stores and stealing stuff and getting away with it. Then everybody else decided to join in, too, but it all started because a Black boy got shot by the police and the Black community felt compelled to rise up in anger and protest. Some used it as an excuse to vent their rage and it's always some individual incident that occurs, which then becomes an excuse for people to release their fury and frustration—whether that anger is directly linked to race relations or some other grievance that people have. One incident can trigger it all and explode into violence and death.

Unlike Joe [Philip Royce], who wants to invest money in community projects and improve living conditions in the ghetto, Tommy is only interested in acquiring more money and power. He is not interested in social reform.

I suppose that Tommy's neglect of his community and his pursuit of wealth and power is why he gets his comeuppance at the end of the movie. In the traditional gangster pictures like *The Public Enemy* and *Little Caesar*, such behavior inevitably results in the gangster taking a fall. I guess that the truest relationship Tommy had with anybody was with Joe, who had been his very close friend from childhood. Tommy ended up breaking off with Joe after he discovers he has been having an affair with his woman, but then Joe gets killed and he feels terribly guilty about that. In the cut version of *Black Caesar*, the last thing Tommy actually says is Joe's name. He looks up at the window of the old building they once lived in and says, "Joe," and that was the end of the film. Of course, in the complete version, the teenagers then come out of nowhere and murder Tommy to steal his wristwatch, but the last thing he is thinking of before he dies is his friendship with Joe. I guess that's our rosebud! [Chuckles]

How did James Brown become involved with scoring *Black Caesar*?

I wanted a name to score the movie, a composer that really meant something in terms of Black music. First we approached Stevie Wonder and screened the film for him. It's hard to believe that we actually screened the picture for a blind man, but that's what we did. Stevie came to the screening room with his assistant, who sat next to him and explained exactly what was going on. Stevie listened carefully to the movie, but he thought it was just too violent for him and so he passed on doing it. Our second choice was James Brown. He agreed and went ahead and did a fabulous score. James later adopted the name "The Godfather of Soul" directly from this picture. The full title of our movie was *Black Caesar: The Godfather of Harlem* and after James did our score, he advertised himself as "James Brown: The Godfather of Soul," which he continued to use for the rest of his career. Our picture really brought him back to people's attention and the album was a big success. I think it really helped to turn his career around.

How exactly did you and Brown work together?

I gave James a copy of *Black Caesar* to work from. The only problem I ever had with him was that when he had to score a three-minute scene, he wrote five minutes of music; and when he had to score a five-minute scene, he wrote nine minutes of music. I said, "James, this music is supposed to fit this scene exactly." He said, "Well, then you've got more than you need." I said, "That's not the way it works. You are not supposed to have more than you need. You are supposed to score the action perfectly." Unfortunately, that's not what he did. James then did the exact same thing on *Slaughter's Big Rip-Off*.[7] He had been hired by AIP on the strength of his score for *Black Caesar*, but had delivered all of this music to the makers of that movie and they didn't know what to do with it, because it didn't fit. When I was in that same situation with him on *Black Caesar*, I just went into the editing room and re-cut the music myself and made it work. The people on *Slaughter's Big Rip-Off* didn't have me to fix their problem for them, so they panicked and went crazy. That is why AIP wouldn't hire James Brown again when we did the sequel, *Hell up in Harlem*. That was the issue they had. It wasn't that James didn't do good music; it was because his score did not time-out to be properly inserted into the movie. That necessitated me having to rework it all, but I'm glad I did because it turned out fine. It just took a little more time and effort on my part. I had no intention of getting upset and panicking like they did on the other picture. I just made it work.

Was Brown upset at not landing the gig to score *Hell up in Harlem*?

James wanted to score the sequel, but American International was not going to let that happen because his previous efforts were deemed unsatisfactory. When *Hell up in Harlem* was finished, I begged them to use him again, but they wouldn't do it. I told James's manager, Charles Bobbitt, "They will not hire him again. The only way we can do this is if James will write and record the music on spec. If they like what they hear I'm sure AIP will use it, because they can have no doubts about his ability to deliver." Bobbitt called me back the next day and simply said, "The man accepts the challenge!" I couldn't believe that a big star like James Brown would be willing to do that, but he readily agreed. So, we gave James a print of the movie, and he went out with his band and back-up singers and created the entire score for *Hell up in Harlem*—for free! He then delivered us the completed tapes and I played them for AIP, but they were absolutely intransigent. They were still furious about the previous problems they had experienced with James on *Slaughter's Big Rip-Off*. In fact, I think they were actually suing him. So, they refused to use James Brown and I went back to Bobbitt and said, "I'm sorry. I think the music is terrific but they just won't budge on the matter." He said, "Hey, no problem. You did your best for us and we appreciate it. We'll use the music someplace else." They then took that music and released it as an album called *The Payback* and it turned out to be the most successful album of James Brown's entire career! The score he originally recorded for my movie has since featured in films like *Lock, Stock and Two Smoking Barrels* and a lot of other big pictures and is instantly recognizable. Every time I hear it I say, "Oh my god, that music was written for *Hell up in Harlem*!" Unfortunately, it is now associated with other director's movies and not mine.

Who came up with the ad slogan for *Black Caesar*—"The cat with the .45 claws!"

Not me! [Chuckles] AIP had their own advertising people, and they didn't usually ask you to approve their work. I mean, you do have an approval in your contract but that approval really means nothing if they have finished the advertising and it's already been printed-up. They did what they wanted to do, and I couldn't stop that slogan being used, regardless of what my opinion was. I thought it was terrible, but the picture did tremendous business, so maybe it was a good slogan as far as the audience they were aiming the film at was concerned. No doubt, also calling the picture *Black Caesar: The Godfather of Harlem* sold a lot of tickets, too, because it was riding on the recent success of *The Godfather*. That was a source of some embarrassment for me because Mario Puzo, the author of *The Godfather*, was a personal friend of mine. I had known Mario for years and his kids used to stay at my house when they came to California. I do remember that one day Mario walked in and just stared at the poster for *Black Caesar* that was hanging on my wall. He then turned and looked right at me. I was so embarrassed because I had clearly made the Black *Godfather*!

How was *Black Caesar* received by AIP and then later by critics?

American International loved the picture. They certainly got much more than they paid for, that's for sure. I don't think they expected it to be as good or as spectacular as it was for the money that it cost. As for the critical reaction to *Black Caesar*, it was probably like the critical reaction to all blaxploitation movies: it was pretty much dismissed by the reviewers. That didn't really matter. Nobody cared because people were lining up at the box office to see the film. I actually think *Black Caesar* was more positively reviewed than the average blaxploitation movie because no critic ever really took that genre very seriously anyway.

What did you make of the other major blaxploitation films of the era such as *Shaft*, *Superfly*, and *Foxy Brown*?

Shaft and *Superfly* were pretty good movies, and I guess *Foxy Brown* was okay, although it was a little disgusting. *Foxy Brown* was a simple revenge movie where the main protagonist went out and killed everybody who had screwed her over. None of those films had much depth to them and, in fact, those three pictures you mentioned are probably the only blaxploitation movies I ever saw. I'm not even sure if I saw *Foxy Brown* on its original release. I may have seen it later on television or on video. Frankly, I didn't go to the theater to see those kinds of films. I certainly enjoyed making them, but most of those pictures were so bad I had no desire to sit through them. Let's face it, what killed the blaxploitation picture was that they made so many awful movies it couldn't possibly survive as a commercially viable genre. Of course, filmmakers then started combining Black stars with White stars in later movies like *48 hrs* and *Lethal Weapon*, teaming Eddie Murphy with Nick Nolte and Mel Gibson with Danny Glover. This meant that both the White and Black audiences could now go to the theater together to see this new combination. That development effectively signalled the end of the exclusive blaxploitation movie as we once knew it. It was pretty much dead—at least until I made *Original Gangstas* many years later and deliberately re-teamed a lot of the old blaxploitation stars.

Has there been any interest in remaking *Black Caesar*?

Yeah, there's talk about a remake all the time. Nothing has happened yet, but every once in a while somebody will run the idea past me. I guess there's already been a remake in all but name. A few years ago, Denzel Washington appeared in *American Gangster*, which is basically a big-budget remake of *Black Caesar*.[8] If you saw that movie, you'd realize it was the same damn story! Washington even looks like Fred Williamson and is dressed up in the same suit, the same hat, everything. That film was simply taking *Black Caesar* and remaking it under a different title, even though they claimed the story was based on the life of an actual person. It's certainly possible that it was, but it was still uncomfortably close to my movie. I think *Black Caesar* is better than *American Gangster*. Even though they spent fifty times more money than we did to make it, they didn't have the "shoeshine scene" in their film where he blackens the White guy's face. That scene alone is better than anything found in *American Gangster*. That one scene transcends their whole picture.

Hell up in Harlem (1973)

***Hell up in Harlem* has the look and feel of a film that has been rushed into production. Was that indeed the case?**

Yeah, it was. American International Pictures demanded a sequel be made because of the commercial success of *Black Caesar*. They obviously wanted to cash-in on the first picture after it did so well at the box office. They wanted a sequel immediately and I had no choice but to make the second movie, because if I didn't do it they would have simply given the project to somebody else. I did not want that to happen. I wanted to control and maintain the story and the characters, so I agreed to do the picture. My original title for the film was *Black Caesar's Sweet Revenge*, but AIP were convinced that title would confuse certain members of the audience, who might think they were watching *Black Caesar* all over again on a re-release. So, we went with *Hell up in Harlem*, which I thought was a rather good title. The unfortunate thing was that the picture had to be made so quickly.

With such a swift turnaround, is it safe to assume that you were unable to develop any other ideas for the sequel?

Oh, I pretty much went with the first idea I had and that's exactly what I wrote. AIP wanted the sequel so quickly that I didn't have time to perfect the script as much as I would have liked. Before I knew it, we were shooting the sequel and I had to kind of wing the whole picture. I didn't really have enough time to prepare *Hell up in Harlem* and, frankly, I don't know what other ideas I could have had. I immediately knew that I wanted to do a story where Tommy's father comes back, gets into the gang, and evolves into a gangster himself before the father and son part ways. I also knew that I wanted to kill off Gloria Hendry's character and introduce Tommy's son, continuing that father-son dynamic. There are some very good scenes between Tommy and his father, and I was interested in the development of that relationship. I also thought that Mr. DiAngelo, the crooked district attorney, who was the villain of the piece, was interesting. I actually intended to kill that character off fairly early in the film, but Gerald Gordon, who played DiAngelo, was so good in the part I wrote more scenes for him and turned his death scene—which I'd already shot—into a dream sequence. I didn't want to waste one foot of film, and I liked the moment where Big Papa murders DiAngelo in the street, so I used it. Some of the other stuff in the movie was certainly more disjointed and uneven, because I just shot action scenes and had to somehow slot them into the story. Again, to be perfectly honest with you, we were kind of making it all up as we were going along.

I agree that *Hell up in Harlem* is "disjointed" and often has a loose, freewheeling quality. It's clearly padded with several disparate sequences—the "Florida Keys" episode perhaps being the most glaring of all.

Yeah, that's really what I'm talking about. You have these guys swimming onto the shore of some unnamed island off the Florida Keys and there's some gunplay and fighting. If I had cut that entire sequence out of *Hell up in Harlem*, it wouldn't have mattered because it doesn't really have anything to do with the central story. I did scenes like that because I could do them, and I had fun doing them. My reasoning behind the island invasion sequence was that I felt we needed a big action scene somewhere that was the equivalent of the swimming pool massacre in *Black Caesar*. So, we shot that sequence out in Malibu and had a bunch of underwater cameramen and frogmen. We also had a lot of people in the picture that were relatives, friends, and associates. Everybody wanted to be in the movie, and I'd say to them, "Okay, come on out and we'll shoot you." Actually, one of the boys who gets killed in that sequence is Eugene Puzo, the son of Mario Puzo. I thought it would be fun to have Mario's son in the picture and then kill him off. The girl in the bikini who you see doing a little martial arts was Mindy Miller, who was actually dating Fred Williamson at the time. I even had my agent, Peter Sabiston, in there. I also killed Peter in *Black Caesar*, too. In fact, whenever he was around I would grab him, put him in a costume, and usually kill him off! [Laughs] Not that my doing that ever reflected my feelings and respect for Peter; he just died very well.

Would you agree that the Florida Keys sequence is also rather odd in some ways?

Yeah, it is a little odd, and I do still question my motivations for doing it. When I look at *Hell up in Harlem* now, I realize that we either had too many friends or we just killed too many people in the movie. It would have been a lot better if we had shortened that sequence and actually murdered a lot less people. At the time, I liked the idea of these Black maids infiltrating this property and then suddenly pulling out guns and laying waste to people as Tommy and his guys invade the island. I should also say that, frankly, I don't think Fred Williamson could swim, although he would never admit it! All we see in the film is Fred coming up on shore in the wet suit. He looks great, but I don't think he actually did any swimming during that sequence. Fred would never dream of telling you he couldn't swim, but I'm pretty sure he couldn't. It probably wouldn't be good for any action movie star to admit such a thing.

Tommy's father is a righteous, repentant man in *Black Caesar*, who returns to build a new relationship with his estranged son after "selling cosmetics in the South." However, in *Hell up in Harlem*, he is suddenly transformed into the ruthless gangster Big Papa Gibbs. Do you think his transition is a little extreme based on the evidence of the first film?

Well, that character's transformation does not occur overnight. DiAngelo tries to kill him, and so he becomes a fugitive, who is attempting to stay alive. His son takes him into his organization and effectively trains him to be a gangster. Over time, the father evolves into Big Papa, but that process isn't immediate. You may remember that in *The Godfather*, Michael Corleone is first introduced as a nice, square kid, who comes back from the Marine Corps after the war. He wants nothing to do with the family business but, over a fairly short time, he then evolves into the leader of the organization—the Godfather himself—after committing a murder. I was trying to do a similar thing with Tommy's father. Although he becomes a gangster and is engaged in criminal activities, I still think Big Papa retains his sense of decency and is a moral man, it's just that his moral compass is maybe a little skewed. Of course, tragically, he then dies and it's a credit to Julius W. Harris, who played Tommy's father in both pictures, that his death is so affecting. I must say that I loved working with Julius. He did a great job, and later appeared in *Full Moon High* and *Maniac Cop 3*. I saw Julius regularly over the years, and he was a gentleman and a fine actor. All I had to do was pick up the phone and he would be there for me, ready to work. That is the kind of actor I like. Julius would never ask what he was supposed to be doing or what was happening. He simply showed up and did whatever was required. He always gave his best, and I appreciated that. In fact, I always enjoyed having Julius around. When we were shooting in New York, we took him out to nightclubs and stuff like that, and we always had a good time with him socially. He was a great guy that is sadly no longer with us.[1]

What were the challenges you faced in shooting *Hell up in Harlem*?

There were several challenges, actually, the first being the small problem of Tommy dying at the end of *Black Caesar*. Of course, in the American theatrical release, we had removed the sequence in which he dies but, as I told you, in the foreign and home video versions, Tommy is killed by the street gang. So, we had to somehow restore him back to life. This was a relatively easy thing to do as there was no way for the audience to know for certain that Tommy was dead. He'd been severely beaten by the gang members, but I thought he was such a physically tough and determined guy he could survive it and stumble away to fight another day. A far more serious challenge was the fact that Fred Williamson was not always available for shooting. He was making a picture at Universal called *That Man Bolt*[2] and he was very busy. It turned out that Fred would only be available on Saturdays and Sundays. We were actually shooting *It's Alive* during the week from Monday to Friday, which meant we had to shoot *Hell up in Harlem* on the weekends. So, we were literally working seven days a week and usually with most of the same crew members. I was working both them and myself to death, but we did eventually get enough scenes with Fred. I then had to go to New York with Fred's double and shoot all the scenes with a stand-in. This guy looked like Fred from the back, but when Fred finally saw the finished film, he was very unhappy and complained that the guy's ass was too big! [Laughs] Anyway, we shot the scenes and then I came back to California and shot the reverse shots with Fred—all the close-ups of Tommy. It was incredible to think that we were shooting a movie where the lead actor wasn't present for a large portion of the shoot, but we did.

All things considered, those shots of the double in New York and the inserts with Fred in Los Angeles cut together surprisingly well.

Yeah, they did. It could have been disastrous, but I knew exactly what I was doing. When Fred saw *Hell up in Harlem* a couple of times, he swore that he was actually present at the time the New York scenes were being shot. I had to keep saying, "No, Fred, that's not you, that's the double. You were never there." No matter how many times I repeated this fact to him, Fred refused to believe it. He kept insisting that it was him and eventually I just had to let it go. I figured that if I could fool the actor himself into believing that he was physically present in those shots, the audience would certainly believe it, too.

You clearly enjoyed an interesting relationship with Williamson during the course of shooting both films.

Oh, it was—and continues to be—an interesting relationship. I think Fred actually wore some of his costumes from *That Man Bolt* in my movie. I got a kick out of the fact that Universal was helping us out, even though they didn't know about it! But things were always lively when you were working with Fred. As I said, when we were making *Black Caesar*, Fred would not perform a single stunt or action that had a degree of risk to it without asking me to do it first. This situation also continued into the shooting of *Hell up in Harlem,* as well. When we got Fred back to New York, we shot the scenes where Tommy runs through the airport and has the shootout with the people in the coal yard. During the coal yard scene, there is a point where Tommy gets buried in a big pile of coal. When we wanted to shoot that stunt, naturally, Fred wouldn't do it. Just as he had done on *Black Caesar*, he looked at me and said, "You do it first." So I had to have this machine literally scoop me up, carry me along, and then bury me in this pile of coal. When I climbed out of the coal, I was blacker than Fred was! We actually took a picture of us together, playfully comparing the colors of our skin. After I did that stunt, Fred did the shot.

What do you recall about shooting the airport chase sequence?

The chase sequence was shot at JFK Airport. While we were there, I suddenly heard a voice calling out, "Hi boys, what are you shooting?" I turned around and standing right in front of me is none other than Lew Wasserman, the president of MCA Universal. Now, I'll remind you, Fred was under contract at this point with Universal and was supposed to be back in California filming *That Man Bolt*. He was certainly not meant to be in New York making our movie. Here was the head of the studio standing a few feet from me with his wife, asking what was going on. Oh, Jesus! It was a pretty surreal moment, but I had to think quickly. After a few seconds I said, "Mr. Wasserman, how would you like to be in the movie? You could play a gang-lord. Yeah, you are a gang-lord at the airport and you spot this guy getting on the plane and blah-blah-blah." Wasserman immediately shook his head and said, "No, I can't do that." But I kept going, "Sure you can! Come on, Mr. Wasserman, you'd be great in this part." He was already backing away from me as I was talking, so the ploy was obviously working. Wasserman and his wife turned and quickly fled down the hall and no more questions were asked. That soon got rid of him! After that, we went back to California and shot the other half of the chase. So, that sequence begins in New York's JFK Airport and actually ends up in the LAX Airport in California.

Was shooting at LAX any less perilous?

Here's the thing: when we arrived at LAX, we were supposed to shoot the big fight that takes place on the conveyor belt. We literally just turned up there with the crew and actors and didn't have any permits or anything. We were standing at the turntable where all the luggage was coming down and literally just started shooting the scene. The two actors just threw themselves onto the turntable and started fighting amongst the luggage. A gun came out and people were just standing there waiting for their bags, watching this struggle take place. They couldn't quite believe what they were seeing. I then cried out to Tony King, who was playing one of the bad guys, "Hey, Tony! See the ramp going up to the airfield where the luggage is coming down? Run up there now!" So, Tony ran up the ramp, and Fred ran after him, and I ran after Fred, and the crew ran after me! [Laughs] We then all arrived up on the airfield and were actually running amongst the airplanes. It was insane! Again, we had no permission from anyone to do this. It was completely crazy. If we attempted something even remotely like that today we would either be shot on sight or jailed for at least five years. Of course, this was a different time in history when there were no terrorist threats in America. I'm sure that nobody present at LAX that day thought for one moment that we had the guts to shoot there without the proper permits. People just stood there looking at us, figuring, "Well, if somebody is doing all this with a camera crew then the proper authorities must have been informed and given their blessing." When I think about it today, I can hardly believe what we did. Once again I got away with it, but I would never try something like that a second time. Never again!

It must have been a logistical nightmare trying to arrange the shooting schedules for both *Hell up in Harlem* and *It's Alive*?

We knew that we were shooting *It's Alive* five days a week in Los Angeles. We also knew we would be shooting the L.A. portion of *Hell up in Harlem* on Saturdays and Sundays. That was understood. The main difficulty for me was making sure that it all fit together so that the stuff we shot in L.A. would fit seamlessly with the stuff we shot in New York. The reverse shots would have to match the other angles that Fred was absent for in which the double was used. If not, it would be very bad for us. I had to know exactly what every angle and cut was going to look like and where the cuts would be. I had all of that information stored in my brain. As usual, I had no shooting schedule and no boards prepared. Despite what they teach you at film school, I've never used boards or shot lists. I had both pictures worked out in my head, but that meant that nobody else on the crew knew what was going on except me. That was just fine with me. It simply meant that I could exercise full control of the situation and get everything done. The less people knew the more control I had.

Did that approach end up complicating the process somewhat?

No. In my experience, filmmaking is a simple process that can often be needlessly complicated by others. During the editing of *Hell up in Harlem* and *It's Alive*, I was using the same editor, Peter Honess, for both pictures. I think poor Peter was sometimes a little confused about what film he was actually cutting! [Chuckles] Three days a week, we would work on one movie in the editing room, and two days a week, we would work on the other. Peter was never quite sure what was going on, but it didn't make any difference because he didn't have to know. I told Peter where to put all the cuts. All he had to do was listen to my instructions. I think Peter learned some things about editing from me, but he eventually became a major editor. He cut a lot of big pictures, such as *L.A. Confidential*, for which he received an Academy Award nomination, as well as a number of *Harry Potter* movies. Another talented editor I worked with back in those days was Chris Lebenzon. Chris went on to edit some of the biggest pictures ever made, like *Top Gun,* and later teamed up with Tim Burton and cut all of his pictures, including *Charlie and the Chocolate Factory* and *Alice in Wonderland*. Chris started editing with me as an assistant, and I was the first to let him do some cutting. I always gave him the exact instructions of where the cuts should go, and I think Chris, like Peter, also learned a lot from me about what you can fake and cheat during editing. I'm pleased that both of those guys have done so well with their careers. When we were cutting *Hell up in Harlem*, Peter and I had to play around with a few things and discover what this movie was going to be; how we could best structure the film, and find the right emphasis on each scene. It wasn't easy cutting two films at the same time, but it didn't really matter to me. It all worked out in the end.

One location you utilized in New York was the Harlem Hospital where Tommy is taken to treat the wounds he sustained at the climax of *Black Caesar*. Did you have any problems securing permission to shoot there?

No, none at all. The hospital sequence was all shot using Fred's double and we inserted the close-ups of Fred in pain that had been shot back in L.A. It worked rather nicely. I do remember that when the two guys grabbed Tommy out of the vehicle and dragged him towards the emergency room, there was a big glass door situated there. The double's head was down low as we obviously did not want anybody to see his face. Unfortunately, these two actors then managed to walk the double right into the glass door and it shattered! There was glass flying all over the place and Fred's double got cut a little bit and was bleeding. I think he even needed a couple of stitches. Fortunately, we were in the emergency room of a hospital, so we didn't have to take him very far to receive medical attention. We quickly bandaged him up and just kept on shooting. That was the first mishap of the day, but of course this was a working hospital and here we were running around the corridors with guns, having the time of our lives. Patients and staff were hastily ducking back into their rooms, wondering what the hell was going on. I really only wrote that scene because somebody told me they could get me Harlem Hospital for the film. I was informed that we could go there in the early afternoon and so I thought, *Oh, great! Now we'll have Tommy taken to a hospital!* We literally grabbed our stuff, ran right over there and started shooting immediately. If we had not secured the Harlem Hospital, I guess Tommy would have been taken to a warehouse or a cellar to get patched up.

Did any of the cast of *Black Caesar* require any coaxing to return for *Hell up in Harlem*?

Not that I recall. Fred, Julius, Gloria, they all came back, as did D'Urville Martin, who played the Reverend Rufus. D'Urville was quite a character. He was more trouble than anybody! He was this feisty little guy that would occasionally give me a problem. I do remember that one day he was whining about something and I said, "Hey D'Urville, would you please lie down on the ground there? I want to get a quick shot of your character lying down." So, he got down on the ground, and we set the camera up, and I took a shot of him. D'Urville then got back on his feet and asked, "What was that all about?" I said, "Well, basically, you just died. If you give me any more trouble on this picture I'm going to kill you off with that shot. Do you understand?" After that, he never gave me another problem. I find that ploy often works when you are dealing with difficult actors. [Chuckles] But no, D'Urville was a lot of fun. I enjoyed our times together. Sadly, he's also departed now. He died at quite a young age and that was very unfortunate.[3] We also had some new additions to the cast, not only Gerald Gordon and Tony King but Margaret Avery, who plays Tommy's love interest in the film. Margaret was a terrific actress. Several years after *Hell up in Harlem*, she went on to play one of the leads in Steven Spielberg's *The Color Purple*. She was the beautiful woman who moved in with Whoopi Goldberg's character and they fell in love and had a lesbian affair. Margaret had a great part in that picture and I really thought that *The Color Purple* would graduate her to A-class movies. I expected her to get a lot of high-profile jobs, but unfortunately that doesn't seem to have happened.

What else comes to mind when you recall location shooting in New York?

Well, you literally never knew what was going to happen next. We went all over the city—all over Harlem and Manhattan—and found the locations and simply shot the scenes there. In most cases, we hadn't previously scouted these areas or made any attempt to secure permits. We simply went there, and if I saw some place I liked, I'd simply say, "Okay, this is it! Let's go!" Then we'd stop, get out, and shoot there. Most productions arrive at a location and have a period of preparation. They bring all these trucks, portable dressing rooms, portable toilets, and by the time they get through unloading and setting up their equipment, they've already lost half a day before they've shot anything. In those days, we used to just leap out of the cars, set up the cameras, shoot the scenes, and move on—and that was it! What was most interesting to me is that usually these locations that we chose, often almost instantaneously, would turn out to be great. Again, I never knew what was going to happen next. Everybody would urgently say to me, "Larry, what if we have some terrible disaster here? What if nothing works out? Are we really going to go to Coney Island and shoot on the beach? How do you know if they will allow us to do that?" I said, "I don't know, but why worry about it? If I'm not worrying, then you shouldn't worry. We are going to do this and we'll be gone before anybody knows we were even there." And we did go there, and we did shoot our scenes, and it didn't really take that long. And, just as I'd promised, as soon as we were finished, we were gone. There is certainly a high risk to that kind of guerrilla filmmaking, but that's just the way I operated.

Much of the film's third act is consumed by Tommy's mission of vengeance after the murder of his father, resulting in a number of violent set-pieces.

Yeah, but I don't think the violence is too excessive, not when you compare it with what you see now in action movies. Directors like Quentin Tarantino, Tony Scott, and James Cameron have made far more violent films than me. If you look at a picture, like *The Terminator*, you have Arnold Schwarzenegger blowing away dozens of police officers right and left. That is far more brutal when you weigh it against the violence in *Hell up in Harlem*. In most of these movies, it's usually cops getting killed by the bad guys in a hail of bullets. Police officers seem particularly expendable for some reason. Everything descends into a bloodbath, or a series of explosions and car-wrecks. That is what the action genre is built upon. Even though Tommy does embark on this mission of revenge and starts killing people, I think *Hell up in Harlem* is fairly mild by today's standards. The violence in modern action cinema has—I won't say evolved because that's not the right word—but in terms of intensity and realism it has certainly continued an upward trajectory in becoming far more explicit. Everything is louder and louder [raises his voice] and louder! The death toll has gotten a little higher, and the explosions have gotten a little bigger, but very few of these pictures address the causes and effects and consequences of violence in any meaningful way.

Does Tommy's spearing of the bad guy with a beach umbrella address the subject of cinematic violence in any meaningful way?

Oh, I don't know. If we're talking about the violence in *Hell up in Harlem*, that scene is actually one of the things I don't like about the movie. I don't like the moment where you see the guy getting stabbed in the chest as he's lying on the beach. I tried to put a visual effect in there of the blood spurting out of his chest. Unfortunately, it looks like a cartoon. I should have cut that out, but it's still in the picture. That effect takes you out of the reality of the moment. The violence is too fake-looking to be truly effective or gratuitous. That's the only big technical flaw in the film as far as I'm concerned. It would have been better to have thrown some fake blood on the guy and have it be a physical effect. The violence would have been more potent, I think.

To what extent would you say *Hell up in Harlem* is conscious of the causes and effects of violence when compared with *Black Caesar*?

It's difficult to say. I mean, Tommy commits violent acts in *Black Caesar*, but then he ends up becoming a victim of violence himself in the uncut ending. In *Hell up in Harlem*, Tommy is trying to avenge the death of his father and appears somewhat more justified in his actions—somewhat. In other words, the violence is prompted by the behavior of others rather than being instigated by Tommy himself. Maybe that's the difference, I don't know, but these films are full of violent men doing violent things. They occupy a violent world and sometimes the only way to survive a violent world is to commit acts of violence.

At one point in the sequel, you try to approximate the ferocious power of McKinney's humiliating death in *Black Caesar* by having Tommy lynch DiAngelo at the end. Do you think you succeeded in matching it?

No, frankly. The "shoeshine scene" in *Black Caesar* is much, much better. I'm sure I did consciously attempt to do something in *Hell up in Harlem* that was the equivalent of it, but we didn't succeed. DiAngelo had to be dispatched in a dramatically satisfying way, but I don't think we even approached the ruthlessness and visceral power of Tommy blackening McKinney's face with shoe-polish. Seeing a Black man utterly degrade and destroy a White man in such a devastating way was never going to be matched by Tommy simply stringing the villain up in a tree, although, of course, lynching was a common way for racists to callously murder Black people in years gone by. So, the anger is naturally still there in that ending, but not the subversive savagery. Personally, I don't think anybody can top the "shoeshine scene" in *Black Caesar*. For me, it's one of the great sequences in film in terms of paying off a villain and giving him his comeuppance. It's so grandly over-the-top, there was no way we were ever going to better it.

So you think *Hell up in Harlem* compares unfavorably with *Black Caesar*?

It doesn't quite measure up to *Black Caesar*, and, again, that's probably because I didn't have enough time to properly prepare it. I actually think *Hell up in Harlem* is one of my poorest films. Of course, another unfortunate thing was the whole situation where we couldn't use James Brown's wonderful score for the movie. That was very disappointing. The score we had for *Hell up in Harlem* was composed by Fonce Mizell and Freddie Perren. Freddie is most famous for writing the song "I Will Survive" for Gloria Gaynor. What they gave me was okay, but what James wrote was far superior and would have improved the film. A great score is like salt to food—it improves the overall taste. *Hell up in Harlem* is certainly a more conventional blaxploitation gangster picture. I mean, we were not really moving away from the formula we established in *Black Caesar*. We were not trying to do something experimental or unusual. It was a straight, down-the-line action film.

So you were celebrating the gangster and action genres rather than stripping away the metaphorical trimmings and accoutrements? You weren't subverting the conventions as you have done in some of your other films?

I guess we were celebrating them, but *Hell up in Harlem* is what it is. It was made during the full flowering of blaxploitation, the Golden Age. I like to invest my pictures with some political and social commentary, but there simply wasn't enough time to really give the sequel as much depth and shading as I would have liked. But I would argue that in *Black Caesar* Tommy is not the conventional blaxploitation hero. He is haunted by his childhood experiences, his poverty, the abuse he suffered at the hands of McKinney. He gains revenge on McKinney in the "shoeshine scene," but then he becomes a victim of the very poverty he has escaped. His origins reclaim him and he is in effect killed by those he has left behind—the kids who are still wallowing in poverty. He has tried to play the White man's game and live the White man's life, but he has failed and his failure costs him his life. The unfortunate thing for Tommy is that after he has acquired all this money and power, he has no place left to go but down. He's conquered his poverty and his low social status, but he has not conquered the demons that exist within him. He has not conquered himself or resolved his personal relationships. That's a very complex scenario, wouldn't you say?

I would indeed, but that's not the trajectory that the sequel takes is it?

No, but I think *Hell up in Harlem* is probably a far more seductive movie than *Black Caesar*—seductive in terms of following the genre. Do you know what I mean? Even in its darker moments, the sequel is a little more forgiving and there's a concentration on having more actions scenes. What can I say? Maybe it was celebratory in that way. We had a lot of great action scenes and I think the picture ultimately settles for the demands of the genre, but those are probably the best action scenes I've ever directed. Yeah, there was far less complexity and subtlety on other levels but some of the character development was good. In spite of his flaws, Tommy is in some ways a more typical hero in *Hell up in Harlem*. He gains his revenge without punishment, survives the criminal lifestyle and slips away to a potential new life with his son.

Yes, one very noticeable thing is that the climax of *Hell up in Harlem* is far more upbeat than *Black Caesar*.

Oh, absolutely, particularly if you had seen the uncut ending of *Black Caesar*. That was a pretty grim and difficult climax.

Were you concerned that the ending of the sequel threatened to descend into mawkish melodrama?

Well, we had to find an ending for the picture and that was it. I don't have a problem with melodramatic and sentimental endings if they have been earned. I thought we had been building towards this conclusion as we went through the film, so it was somewhat authentic. It also had the cyclical element of the father and son reunited that I liked. I mean, *Hell up in Harlem* is really the story of a father and a son, and it ends with Tommy promising his boy that they will get out of town and start a new and better life together. In some ways, it's a reconciliation of the father and the son after Big Papa's death. The family is united again and that relationship lives on through them, so it's a very hopeful ending. I think that's a fairly unusual and unexpected conclusion for a gangster picture. The sequel reduces the power of *Black Caesar's* climax, because we now see that Tommy has survived his beating by the gang, but that was an inevitable consequence of making the movie. There was nothing anybody could do about that. But at the time *Hell up in Harlem* was released, audiences wouldn't have known anything about the downbeat ending anyway.

Although the on-screen caption that concludes the film states that Tommy and his son have vanished, "never to be heard of again," I always felt that the climax was set up for another sequel. Did you ever consider making one?

We did talk about making a third movie, but it was never anything concrete. I certainly didn't conceive of any strong ideas about what the story should be, although it probably would have concerned Tommy returning to New York with his son at some point in the future. I don't remember any details about it because in truth I didn't really want to do a third movie. I had already done two Black gangster films and it was now time to move onto different projects and tell other stories. So, there was no third *Black Caesar* movie but, interestingly, we did talk a few years ago about doing a project with Snoop Dog, which was kind of a loose remake of *Black Caesar*. It was more or less the same plot with a few nice variations: a boy grows up and doesn't realize that he is the son of the famous gangster who once ruled Harlem. He comes back to New York but cannot understand why people are constantly trying to kill him. Of course, he gradually figures it out and learns of his ancestry. The kid then becomes every incarnation of his father and starts ruling the gang. The idea had some potential but we never really got very far with it, because nobody was particularly interested in Snoop Dog playing a dramatic lead in a movie. So, the project just dropped away.

That's too bad.

No, it's not. I'd really had enough of all that. No more gangster pictures for me!

After embracing *Black Caesar*, what did Arkoff and AIP think of the sequel?

They were very happy with *Hell up in Harlem*, particularly when it did a lot of good business again. Some of the reviews were surprisingly good, but the picture wasn't as profitable theatrically as *Black Caesar*. However, later on, it did tremendously well on video. I think *Hell up in Harlem* has actually done better business on video than *Black Caesar* ever did, despite it being the inferior film. *Hell up in Harlem* is still respected and various people have done takeoffs on it. There were some filmmakers who used the *Hell up in Harlem* title as the prototype for a documentary done on all the blaxploitation movies.[4] Its always mentioned as one of the most enduring and successful of that genre and that period. There are a lot of people who like it but, again, I wouldn't advertise it as one of my best works.

It's Alive (1974)

How was the idea for *It's Alive* born?

The story was born out of real life tragedy. The early 1970s saw a lot of changes in the relationships between parents and their children. Many people watched their kids growing up and began to see their personalities, appearance and habits change to such a degree the parents didn't recognize them anymore. It was impossible for them to relate to their offspring in any meaningful way as they once did. Their children had now grown their hair long and were listening to this strange new music; they took drugs and had sex outside of marriage; they even talked differently. These kids also had a set of values that were vastly different from those of the previous generation. Inevitably, this not only caused parents to feel alienated from their children, it caused parents to be afraid of them because they didn't understand the way these young people were now living their lives. Their children had suddenly turned into total strangers in the house and that was deeply unsettling. Some parents didn't know how to deal with this situation. I'd read an article in the newspaper which described how one father had actually murdered his son because he'd felt so threatened by him. His child had been on drugs and I started to think about the fear these parents had of their own flesh and blood. The idea of killing one's own child seems completely foreign to most people but I started thinking, *Well, what if there was a normal happy family that suddenly had a monster born into their midst? What would happen? How would they deal with it?* That's when the ideas for the movie started to come together.

But why a monster baby specifically?

I had seen infants lying in their cribs crying and having violent fits of anger. I mean, when you think about it, a baby is pure id without any restrictions. What I suddenly noticed was the intensity of a baby's anger when they are uncomfortable about something or require nourishment. When you watch them raging, their faces turn red and they go completely crazy. I then asked myself, *What if that baby could get out of its crib? What if it possessed considerable strength and agility from birth? What if it had sharp claws and fangs?* I realized that such a thing would be extremely dangerous and furious, and would really come after you. That idea fascinated me and I thought, *Yeah, what could possibly be more terrifying than a monster baby?* You see, filmmakers are always making the monsters in their movies big, but I realized that people are actually more afraid of the small things. They are terrified of rats and bugs and snakes and spiders. The whole concept of a monster baby that was physically capable of moving around and killing people had not been done before. I knew that if the story was done right, it could be very frightening.

What kind of reactions did you get when you first pitched a movie about a homicidal mutant baby?

It's Alive was a spec script, so there was never any problem about the film's premise or subject matter. However, when we delivered the picture six months later the same executive who had bought it was no longer with Warner Bros. New people were in place and they were just appalled that somebody had walked into their studio with a movie about a monster baby. They thought it was in extremely bad taste and did not want to be associated with the film. They certainly didn't think that anybody would want to see a movie with a premise like that. I liken the situation to being a waiter at a restaurant: they bring food out of the kitchen and the waiter delivers it to the table only to discover that new people are suddenly sitting there, saying, "We didn't order that." I actually said to the new management, "Hey, what's the problem here? You guys just had a huge success with a movie called *The Exorcist*, which features a young girl masturbating with a crucifix! Is that in good taste?" That observation made absolutely no impression on them. They were just looking to denigrate any project that had been initiated by the previous administration. It was all political, that's all. We had to wait until those executives were replaced, but it actually took a couple of years for those people to get out of there. Then, when a new administration came in that had no axe to grind, we went back with the picture. So, the negative reactions and comments only came after *It's Alive* was completed, not before.

The opening titles sequence with its drifting, pulsing lights strikes me as suggesting the beginnings of life, but maybe not life as we recognize it.

Yeah, that was sort of the idea. We did a similar thing in *God Told Me To* also, where we had this semen-like substance floating across the universe. We shot the title sequence for *It's Alive* ourselves because I don't like to farm out the titles to a company. Many of the big motion pictures over the years have employed somebody like Saul Bass to do the titles for them.[1] Bass devised many of the titles for movies back in the 1960s and '70s. You would just tell him what the movie was about and he would come up with the title sequence for you. I did not want to do that. I wanted to make every frame of the picture my own, so I insisted on making the titles myself. What I did was gather about four or five people over at my house and we all went down to the basement, which is huge. We then had ladders and positioned people on them in different spots. We gave each person a flashlight and pumped some smoke into the room before turning off all the lights. We then stopped, changed positions, and repeated the exact same procedure we had done before with the flashlights coming on in a different area. We repeated this process again and again and again. We then took the footage we had shot and multiple-printed those different takes and that became the titles sequence.

It very quickly establishes the appropriate mood, doesn't it?

It does, but Bernard Herrmann's music helps a lot, of course. As we were working on the title sequence, he was over in England creating a musical score for the film. Benny was working on the theme for the main titles, but he didn't know what the titles sequence was going to be. He just told me to give him something for an overture in order to give the audience some kind of indication of what picture they were about to see. He said, "I'll write something for ninety seconds so give me ninety seconds worth of titles." Benny didn't actually see the titles sequence until the recording session in London. By that time he had already recorded the main title before I'd arrived. I then brought the film over to the recording stage and we put it up and Benny played back the title music he had recorded just the day before. Amazingly, all the beats came at the right places. As the flashlights came on the orchestral beats were simultaneous and it was as if they had been scored directly to picture. The coincidence was remarkable and Benny was very impressed, as was I. We were both totally surprised and delighted that it had matched up so perfectly. That happy accident was probably what bonded us together. Benny and I became close friends after that and spent a lot of time together in the following years until his death.

Why did you decide to keep the birth of the mutant baby and its subsequent decimation of the entire maternity staff in the delivery room, off-screen?

Basically, I thought that seeing the aftermath of what happened in there was far more disturbing and scary than actually seeing those events occur.

Nowadays that sequence would have been shown in a very overt way.

It's interesting that you should say that because as we were preparing the recent remake of *It's Alive*, I actually included a scene in the delivery room when I rewrote my original script. What happens is the father comes in with a video camera—as fathers often do now in America—to videotape the birth. When the baby is born, naturally, all hell breaks loose, and you see this video camera go skittering across the floor. Then you get various snatches of what is happening as the camera is getting kicked around by the feet of frantic people. You see bodies fall into frame and get glimpses of something moving—a quick flash of the monster here and there. All of this action was being viewed through the discarded video camera and that was the central conceit of the sequence. When the remake happened, that scene was never shot, but it's the way I planned it in the script. In the original *It's Alive*, the monster only appeared every once in a while. In fact, it hardly ever appeared on screen at all.

I think that is one of the film's strengths and I don't say that to denigrate the excellent work of special makeup effects artist, Rick Baker.[2]

No, Rick did some great work on *It's Alive* and the monster effects looked great. I just decided not to show the monster much, but instead show its point-of-view. It was all done with suggestion, with low-angle point-of-view shots, moving shadows, and shots of its claws. I think that was more effective and frightening than blatantly showing something and allowing the audience to get a good look at it. It was always important to make the monster baby a believable and frightening presence. There was always the danger inherent in the absurdity of having a baby as the monster in a movie. If the audience saw it crawling around, they might have thought it looked hokey and laughable and that would have killed us. Steven Spielberg used that same approach in *Jaws*. You see the shark's point-of-view for the first half of the movie as it glides through the water attacking its victims. That approach really helps to heighten the suspense and terror. Steven understood, as did I, that sometimes what the audience doesn't see is far more terrifying than what they do see. You can't compete with people's imaginations because imagination is not restricted by time, money, and technology. In their own minds, that monster can be as big and as scary as they want it to be. Once you fully reveal it, you reduce the monster to the piece of rubber that it actually is and the illusion is destroyed. Once the reality is gone for the audience you can't get it back, and then you've lost them.

Tell me about your dealings with Baker and the creation of the mutant baby.

I first met Rick through John Landis, whom I've known since 1970. Rick had fashioned the gorilla suit for John's film *Schlock*[3] and was already an accomplished artist. George Folsey, Jr. was also a friend of Rick's, and had brought him onto *Bone*. Rick ended up doing all the makeup on the dead bodies that were inside the automobiles in the opening sequence. He then worked for me on *Black Caesar* and *Hell up in Harlem*, creating the various bullet wounds and injuries, including the effect in *Black Caesar* where Fred Williamson cuts off somebody's ear and drops it in a plate of spaghetti. When it came time to do *It's Alive*, Rick and I sat down and I drew a picture of what I thought the monster should look like. I wanted it to a monstrous version of the baby you see at the end of Stanley Kubrick's *2001: A Space Odyssey*. So we gave it large eyes, sharp teeth, and an enormous forehead with the protruding veins, but we still didn't make it an entirely unappealing creature. I wanted it to be something that would be enjoyable to look at, much like Boris Karloff's Monster in *Frankenstein* is enjoyable to look at even though it's still frightening. After I drew the monster baby, Rick went off and did his own rendering of it, which was pretty much derivative of what I had shown him. He then sculpted it, painted it, and made the creature, and I was very impressed by his work. The monster baby was probably one of Rick's first big monster creations in movies and he ended up working on all three *It's Alive* pictures. Of course, he's now gone on to reach the very top of his profession and has won countless Academy Awards.

John P. Ryan gives a remarkable performance as Frank Davis, the father of the mutant baby. He firmly anchors the story in reality.

John was a wonderful actor. I actually taught him how to do the Walter Brennan[4] impersonation he does early in the film. [Cohen speaks like Walter Brennan] "Sure, I can do the talking like Walter Brennan myself. All you do is you pick it up and you do it like that and go dancing out on the prairie, that's right!" John and I had gone to CCNY together, and then, a few years later, I saw him on Broadway with Irene Papas in *Medea*. Oddly enough, *Medea* is not too far away from *It's Alive*; it's an ancient Greek tragedy about a woman who slaughters her children. Anyway, I went backstage to see John and said, "I'm making a movie that you might like to be in." I handed him the script and that was it. He agreed to do it and we made the picture. John's performance is fantastic. He really added believability and compassion to the movie, which is exactly what I wanted. *It's Alive* is really a dramatic movie about people and not just a straight horror movie, or monster movie. Unfortunately, several years later, John was involved in a serious helicopter accident whilst shooting a movie.[5] He was supposed to be in a scene located in a helicopter, but John was very hesitant to do it. The director finally convinced him and John reluctantly got inside the helicopter. They flew up in the air, but then the chopper suddenly dropped out of the sky and crashed down to the ground. Everybody in the helicopter was killed, except for John. He was very badly hurt and had to endure a lot of surgeries. I think he got something like a million dollars in compensation, but more or less retired from acting after that. John got to be very religious as he got older. He had been ill for a long time and, sadly, died about two or three years ago.

You've never been afraid to mix moments of raw emotion with elements of horror, particularly in the *It's Alive* trilogy. What's the secret of not letting the pathos negate the scares and atmosphere you are attempting to construct?

The first and most important thing is that you have a valid premise that has some kind of relationship with reality. Just doing a film about a giant tarantula that is running around eating people doesn't give you much of an opportunity to do that. When you have a subject that deals with the interrelationships of people and the misunderstandings they have, and the pain they cause each other, and the guilt they feel, then you have something meaningful to write about. *It's Alive* was the extremely painful story of a family in crisis. It paralleled the real-life agonies that a lot of families experienced when they had a thalidomide child or some other kind of unfortunate birth where the kid just didn't turn out right. I mean, you still hear about parents who have had children with mental and physical disabilities, and they always blame themselves for what is happening. The parents feel it's their fault; it's all because of something they did; and they suffer for it. The characters in *It's Alive* are also experiencing a lot of suffering. When I made the three *It's Alive* pictures, I was dealing with a lot of truths about how parents feel about their children. They can feel responsible and guilty, and this idea also extends to their children's actions. In reality, even the parents of somebody who goes out and commits a bunch of murders is dealing with that same kind of pain. Whether their kids are serial killers, kidnappers, or whatever, all of these people who are committing awful crimes have parents, too. How do they feel about raising a child that has become a monster and killed people? How do they deal with the tremendous guilt they must feel about bringing a person into the world that has done such harm? There was a certain basic truth underlining the whole of *It's Alive,* and when you deal with something as powerful as that, then you are off and running. You can now write a screenplay that has some veracity. It's not just about the horrors and the scares revolving around some kind of giant spider or giant rabbit that is running around nibbling at people. So, many of the horror pictures back in the 1950s were like that.

The horror films and monster movies that are firmly rooted in a recognizable reality are often the most profoundly disturbing.

Yes, of course, and it's the relationship of that monster to the normal people, or the so-called normal people. Sometimes the so-called normal people are pretty monstrous themselves. Even when you go back to the great classic movies like *Frankenstein,* you have the guilt of Dr. Frankenstein for having created this creature out of the assorted parts of dead people. He's brought this thing to life and somehow he is responsible for it. I guess that theme of responsibility and guilt is made even clearer in Mary Shelley's original novel than it was in many of the movies of *Frankenstein* that have been made. The novel was not so much a horror novel, or a genre piece, as it was a legitimate piece of writing with great ideas.

Interestingly, at one point, Frank confesses to confusing the identities of Frankenstein the creator with his creation.

What I'm saying in that scene is Frank is now thought of by people as being akin to the monster. He is seen as the creator of the creature, much like Dr. Frankenstein is the creator of the Monster. The creature has become known as "The Davis Baby" or "The Davis Monster," and he is the father of the monster. So, his identity has suddenly become entwined with it and always will be. He's got this inescapable connection to the monster which, of course, is what we all have with our children. As in *Frankenstein*, the monster has now taken his creator's name and Frank is trying to get out of the situation he finds himself in. That is why he is cooperating with the police and is so intent on killing this creature and getting it out of his world. However, in the end, we see that when Frank has to deal with it directly, he can't help but feel emotionally tied to the monster. He then desperately tries to save his child and that is what gives his character an emotional arc.

The climax, which sees Frank finally confront his offspring down in the storm drains of Los Angeles, is unexpectedly moving. In my imagination—and I may be wrong about this—I get the impression that the cries of the baby in that final scene are less monstrous and more human.

I think we did subtly alter the sound effects of the baby, yes. I believe we tried to make those wails softer, more human-sounding. You know, for most of the movie, the monster is relating to people who it perceives to be its enemy. At the end, it is relating to somebody who it perceives to be its parent. So, of course the creature has a different, more appealing sound to it. It recognizes that its father is now here and they are both reunited, if only for a very short time.

Many view the ending of *It's Alive* as a conscious nod to the classic 1954 film, *Them!*[6] Is that indeed the case?

Well, I can tell you that back in the 1950s, I did see *Them!* I was just a kid at the time, but I was actually the first one in line the day that film opened in New York. For some reason, I desperately wanted to see that picture and was there for the very first show. It's my understanding that they created the storm drains in *Them!* on a soundstage, but we actually shot *It's Alive* down in the real storm drains of Los Angeles. Everything was there for us to shoot, except we knew that if it started to rain the drains would fill up very quickly and we would have to get the hell out of there. Fortunately, it didn't rain, so we were okay, but everybody was working in water up to their ankles. There were a lot of electrical cables, lights, and other equipment, so it was dangerous to be walking and running around with all that electricity. Somebody could have been electrocuted. Luckily, we got through it without anybody getting hurt.

You've voluntarily revealed in previous interviews that your pet dog is actually tucked under the blanket in John Ryan's arms when Frank emerges from the storm drains.

Yeah. [Chuckles] We had to have something moving around under the blanket for the moment John flees from the storm drains and is confronted by all these cops who want to kill the monster. To get the desired movement, we wrapped my dog—a Pekinese dog—up in the blanket. Actually, it was my daughter's dog. It's funny how putting a dog under a blanket and telling everybody that it's a monster seems to work. The audience's imagination then does the rest. I personally like the idea that you can use virtually nothing to scare people and create a certain effect. Of course, it's easy enough with CGI and the millions of dollars that people spend on movies to create things. But to be able to create something out of nothing—out of sheer imagination—is fun and deeply satisfying. If you look carefully at that scene again, you can see part of the dog sticking out from under the blanket in some shots. I deliberately made some of the dog visible so that you could see it. I wanted to tell people about it, so they could go back and watch the movie again and see it for themselves. I mean, if you are not specifically looking for that you would never see it.

You earlier mentioned the great Bernard Herrmann. How did he become involved with the film?

Bernard Herrmann was my favorite composer, and so when it came time for me to hire a composer for *It's Alive*, Benny was of course my first choice. He had scored *Citizen Kane*, *The Devil and Daniel Webster*, *The Day the*

Earth Stood Still, *Psycho*, *Vertigo*, *North by Northwest*, and so many other great films. I was very excited at the prospect of maybe employing him to do the score for *It's Alive*, and I knew that he had recently done the music for Brian De Palma's *Sisters* and was apparently approachable. When I asked Warner Bros. to contact him, they came back and said that he wasn't available as he was doing *The Exorcist* for William Friedkin. Then he and Friedkin had a falling out and Benny walked off the picture. What happened was Benny had gone to New York to see *The Exorcist* and after the lights came up Friedkin said to him, "I want you to write me a better score than you did for *Citizen Kane*." To which Benny replied, "Well, why didn't you make a better picture than *Citizen Kane*?" Friedkin, having no sense of humour, reacted poorly. The two of them then got into an argument and that was the end of their association. I was suddenly advised that Bernard Herrmann was available, and so I asked Warner Bros. to approach him and make him an offer, which they did. Benny agreed to look at my film and so I sent him a black and white dupe, a rough cut, of *It's Alive*. He called me up and said that he and his wife had liked the picture, and that he would write the score for it. We then closed the deal and I said, "Do the music your way. Do whatever you feel is right. I'm not going to make any suggestions. I would just like to see what you come up with. I'll come over to England if you want me to, but if you prefer that I didn't come over, that's okay, too. Just do whatever you want." I think he liked that attitude, but he did eventually ask me to come over for the recording sessions which were held inside Cripplegate Church in London. This was the same historic church where John Milton was buried and Oliver Cromwell was married. Benny chose that place to record the music because of the organ they had in there. I remember the resonance of that organ would make the whole church tremble when it was played. This was around Christmas, and I do recall that it was freezing as there was a power shortage in England at the time. Benny had brought a generator into the church in an attempt to heat the place, but we all had overcoats and scarves on.

Were you concerned at all about Herrmann's notorious reputation for being short-tempered with his directors?

No. I had no difficulties with him whatsoever, except for one small altercation over the telephone. There was a scene in the movie where a cartoon was playing on the television set, and I asked Benny if he could write a little music to accompany the cartoon. He suddenly exploded and said,

"I don't write music for cartoons! Get yourself another composer!" I then said, "Okay, don't write music for the cartoon. I'll just use sound effects, it's no big deal." He calmed down, and that was the end of the argument, and we continued on. Other than that incident, I had no problems with him and, as I say, we became very close friends. He liked me and I think he liked my wife at the time, Janelle, too. I remember the first time we met him, we picked him up from his house in a chauffeur-driven car to go to the recording session for *It's Alive*. His wife, Norma, kissed him goodbye, and Benny got in the car with us. As we were heading down the street, Janelle said, "Oh Mr. Herrmann, you have a lovely daughter." Benny looked at her for a moment and said, "That's my wife. Ah, the world's oldest composer with the world's youngest wife!" Then we all started laughing and after that we became good friends.

Herrmann clearly had a sense of humour as he labeled one of the music cues for *It's Alive* "The Milkman Goeth."

Yeah, that's the scene where the milkman gets killed by the monster. You know, Benny always had this reputation for being a very acerbic person. Yes, he would insult people, but that was just his sense of humour. If you insulted him back, or laughed and got the joke, he was just fine. If your feelings were hurt and you sulked and looked unhappy then, naturally, you were not going to be his friend. All you had to do was take the remark as it was intended—which most people couldn't—and then you could get close to him. Benny would open up to you and after that you couldn't do anything wrong in his eyes. As a matter of fact, Benny's wife wrote me a letter just a few months ago. We were corresponding as Norma still lives in England. She wrote, "To my memory, you are the only person that Benny never got angry with." That was certainly a compliment. I mean, out of all the people he knew, I was the only one he didn't lose his temper with, and he actually had a couple of good reasons to get angry with me. I remember one time I went over to his house and he started playing me his opera *Wuthering Heights*. We sat down in the living room and Benny put the records on. Now this opera was very, very long and about half way through it I fell asleep right in front of him—while he was playing me his music! Later, when I woke up, Benny said, "Uh, I think we've had enough of this." He then simply got up, took the record off and didn't get mad, which he could have. He could have gotten furious if he'd wanted to, but he didn't. He just didn't ever want to get angry with me. We got along fine and would have dinner at least twice a week when I lived in London. Our friendship aside, I would also say that my working association with Benny was one of the most creatively satisfying of my entire career. I only wish it could have continued further on my subsequent movies and that he was still here with us.

What do you remember about the final days you spent with him?

Well, Benny came over to Los Angeles to do the music for Martin Scorsese's *Taxi Driver* and, on the last day of recording, he finished the score. Actually, they had a few more cues they planned on doing the very next day, but Benny suddenly said, "No, let's finish it up tonight." So, they stayed a little while longer and completed the score. Then he and Norma came over to the Goldwyn Studios, and I was there with my wife. We ran *God Told Me To* for Benny in the screening room because he was going to compose the music for the film. In fact, *God Told Me To* was the last movie he ever saw. After the screening, Benny took us out to dinner at a restaurant and we discussed the film. He was making notes and had already worked out in his mind what he wanted to do with the music. Unfortunately, that night, there had been a fire in the restaurant's kitchen and there wasn't much food left in the place. They did eventually serve us dinner, but the menu was rather truncated and the meal wasn't very good. Anyway, we enjoyed each other's company, and afterwards we drove Benny back to the Universal Sheridan Hotel where he was staying. Oddly enough, Benny always said that he never wanted to go back on the Universal lot after his break-up with Hitchcock on *Torn Curtain*. Of course, Universal had been instrumental in coming between Benny and Hitchcock, and ending their successful association. Despite all that history here Benny was again, a few years down the line, spending the night on the lot overlooking the sound-stages and Hitchcock's bungalow. That evening we kissed Benny and Norma goodnight, and they went upstairs and we drove back home. The following morning, I got a call from Martin Scorsese's girlfriend. Apparently, she and Marty had gone over to Universal to have breakfast with Benny, only to discover that he'd died in his sleep during the night. [Sighs] Well, I couldn't believe it. We rushed back over there and the composer John Williams also showed up. We went inside and saw Benny and he was lying in bed, looking very peaceful. We then took Norma back to our house and that's where she stayed for a week or ten days afterwards, before returning to London. All the condolences and the reception after the funeral were held at my house. Benny had died the day before Christmas Day and so Norma had Christmas dinner with us. She drew a picture of everyone sitting at the table and she drew Benny into the picture, too, as if he was sitting right there with us. I still have that picture and I treasure it.

What do you recall of the funeral?

Benny's funeral was conducted by a funeral home here in Los Angeles. The most memorable thing about the service for me was as we were all sitting there, I turned around and looked to the back of the chapel and standing there, at the very last row, was François Truffaut.[7] I said to Norma, "Truffaut is back there." So we both got up and walked to the back and she spoke to Truffaut in French. I then invited him to come back to the house after the service for the memorial party we were going to hold in memory of Benny. Truffaut said that he couldn't come because he had his car waiting outside to take him back to the airport. We then learned that Truffaut had flown in from Paris and come directly from the airport to the service. His car was waiting to take him back to the airport again. He had actually flown all the way from Paris on a round trip just to attend the funeral and say goodbye. I thought that was certainly a great tribute to Benny. A lot of other wonderful people attended the funeral: Marty Scorsese, Brian De Palma, Robert De Niro, Norman Lloyd, and a number of venerable composers also came. They had set up a stereo to play Benny's music, but it was this terrible piece of equipment. No doubt if Benny had still been alive, he would have probably smashed it with his cane! [Laughs] He certainly wouldn't have wanted his music played on that contraption; the sound was just awful. But the oddest thing about the funeral was that Benny wasn't even in the coffin. His body had already been transported to New York City to be buried in Brooklyn in the family plot. He had his daughter in the New York area, so the body was quietly shipped back there and our service was conducted to an empty coffin. So he wasn't actually present at the time of his own funeral.

Despite their well-documented falling out, did Hitchcock come to the service to pay his respects?

No. Hitchcock was not there but his assistant, Peggy Robertson, did come. She claimed that Hitchcock was out of the country. I don't know if Hitchcock was out of the country or not, but that was the excuse given for why he didn't show up. Actually, it was me who called Hitchcock's office at Universal and spoke with Peggy on the phone. I told her that Benny had died in case Hitchcock wanted to pay a condolence call or something, but he sent his condolences through her and she came to the service. Then, after the funeral, everybody came back to my house for the reception. I remember the Rabbi who was officiating wanted to have what they call a *minyan*, which is a Jewish prayer for the dead. However, you need ten Jewish men to perform the ceremony and we didn't have ten Jews in the place. So, instead we got Scorsese, De Palma, and De Niro and put yarmulkes on their heads. They joined us in the living room, and we all stood in a circle to perform the minyan and started praying. I remember De Niro actually came over to me and said, "What should I do here?" I said, "Well, just keep nodding your head. No matter what the Rabbi says keep shaking your head, that's all you have to do." So, I actually got to direct one of the greatest actors of our time in a Jewish ceremony. I only wish I had taken a photograph of it. I mean, here were all these Italians, standing there in my house with yarmulkes on their heads, saying farewell to Bernard Herrmann. It was quite a sight.

What can you tell me about the marketing campaign devised for *It's Alive*?

The first ad campaign—the one that was created after the picture was first delivered to Warner Bros.—was severely damaged by the fact that the studio really didn't want the movie. As I said, the people who had bought *It's Alive* from me had all been fired and a new management were in their place. When the picture came in, they devised an ad campaign which did not reveal that the movie was about a monster baby. The first ads showed a dead woman on the ground and simply read: "Whatever it is—it's alive!" I didn't know exactly what that was supposed to mean and I doubted very much that anybody else would either. Warner Bros. then went out and tested *It's Alive* in San Diego and it didn't do very well. So, they only made something like fifty prints of the movie and decided to give it a minimal release. I flew into Chicago from London to attend the opening and the local Warner Bros. executive was very sympathetic to me. At one point I said to him, "Can I change the marquee outside the theater?" He said, "Do whatever you want." So I went outside and put up a marquee which read: "It was born three days ago and it's killed seven people. *It's Alive* and its parents are human!" Then, I found a baby carriage and put a tape recording inside there of the baby growling. I had my wife wheel that carriage around the downtown area of Chicago with the sound of this growling baby coming out and a sign hanging on it saying: "See it at the Woods Theatre!"

And what was the response?

The response was terrific! People just flocked to see the picture. The second week did more business than the first week, and the third week did more business than the second week. By the time the picture had played, it had out-grossed the Clint Eastwood movie, *Thunderbolt and Lightfoot*, which had preceded it. So, we did some very good business, but that didn't seem to make any impression on the Warner Bros. people in Los Angeles. It just didn't matter to them. Nor did it matter that *It's Alive* had won a prize at the Avoriaz Film Festival over in France—with Roman Polanski as chairman and François Sagan, Édouard Molinaro, and Claude Chabrol all members of a very auspicious jury.[8] That didn't mean anything to the crowd back in Hollywood. Then, *It's Alive* became the second-highest-grossing picture in the history of Warner Bros. in Singapore, which was a pretty decent market in the East. In fact, the only picture that ever out-grossed *It's Alive* there was *My Fair Lady*. Nobody ever thought for one moment that my movie would have garnered such accolades and good box office in places like Singapore and France, but the Americans did not want to play the picture. *It's Alive* then hung around for three years, playing as double features and triple-features in some places and at drive-ins. That's when the new administration came into Warner Bros., and I contacted them and asked if they would take a look at the film. They agreed, and after seeing it, said, "Hey, this is a very scary movie." They immediately checked out where the picture had been distributed, then came back to me and said, "We are going to give this picture another shot." And I must say they certainly did. Warner Bros. organized a brand new release, and made 1,000 new prints, and came up with a big ad campaign. *It's Alive* then went out again and went on to become the #1 box office hit in America. It was incredible. Now, this was three years after it had originally played! I mean, that could never happen today because the picture would come out on DVD ninety days after it played theatrically and that would have been the end of it. There would have been no opportunity to revive the picture theatrically, and certainly not as spectacularly as that. The millions of dollars it generated would never have come in. So, *It's*

Alive really was a complete once in a lifetime phenomenon in the history of the movie business.

What kind of business did the film do?

The picture did about $38 million, and that's in 1970s money. Nowadays, taking into consideration today's box office as the prices are triple of what they were back then, you've got a movie that is making between $120-130 million. So, it was a big hit for Warner Bros. and earned me a lot of money. I ended up becoming a millionaire out of that picture and it became a source of revenue for me for many, many years. I was able to buy a brownstone in New York with that cash and it was all because I'd kept pushing and fighting for the picture to be released again. I had faith in *It's Alive* when everybody else thought, "Hey, this guy must be crazy! What's he doing pestering Warner Bros.?" At one time, the studio was so fed up with me, they actually said, "If you give us $100,000 we'll give you the picture back. How does that sound? Give us the money and we'll give you the film and you can turn around and do whatever you want with it." So, I went around with my hat in my hand to American International and several other places, saying, "Please buy this picture!" They all said, "If Warner Bros. couldn't make a hit out of this movie, why do you think we can?" I finally found a company in New York called Bryanston that had put out *The Texas Chainsaw Massacre*. They said they would give me the $100,000 for the picture. So, I then went back to Warner Bros. and said, "Okay, you've got a deal." Then, a week later, Bryanston reneged on the deal. I had to go back to Warner Bros. again and tell them I couldn't take the $100,000. Bryanston later turned out to be a Mafia-owned organization, and, eventually, they were investigated and went out of business. I don't know if anybody went to jail—that I don't know—but it would have been a disaster if they had taken *It's Alive*. I probably wouldn't have collected a nickel if they had bought it. At the time the deal fell through, I was despondent, but it turned out to be the best thing that could have ever happened to me. Just a year and a half later, all those management people at the studio were gone. I was then dealing with a new bunch of people headed by Terry Semel, who eventually became the chairman of the board at Warner Bros. He was the one who had the foresight to put *It's Alive* out again and pick up all that money that was laying there waiting to be earned if the film was released properly. Once it was released properly, the picture went through the roof. For a while it seemed like an exercise in futility, but finally it came out the way I wanted and hoped it would. We managed to make a success out of the picture.

Were you concerned, even at this premature stage of your career, that the immense success of *It's Alive* might typecast you in the public and industry's minds as a horror director? I know that George Romero and Wes Craven have felt confined in the genre after enjoying early successes with horror movies.

Frankly, at that point, I was just happy to get any type of movie made whether it was a horror film or anything else. I was never afraid of being viewed as a horror director. I just wanted to make movies and that's exactly what I did. It's always been tough to get a movie approved and into production, so if that was the kind of picture that people wanted from me, I was more than happy to deliver it. Nobody ever forced me to go out and write these stories. I wrote them because I wanted to write them. That was as true of *It's Alive* as it was of my next film, *God Told Me To*. It was also true of a spec script like *Black Caesar* and even in meeting the demands of creating a sequel in *Hell up in Harlem*. Although they weren't horror movies, I did what I wanted and always had the choice. In fact, I never really considered the *It's Alive* films to be strictly horror movies. I always thought they were defined as much by the strong performances of the cast, the rich personal stories of the characters and other dramatic elements, than by any of the horror that was depicted or suggested.

***It's Alive* is often read as an anti-abortion tract, but there are some who view it as a pro-abortion film. Would you like to clarify your intentions?**

What I think or don't think, or what I intended or did not intend, isn't important. *It's Alive* is whatever you want it to be. Whatever feelings or beliefs or attitudes you have are merely reinforced when you see the film. So, it works both ways. That is why I thought the picture was okay, because if *It's Alive* had been staunchly pro-abortion or staunchly anti-abortion it would have quickly turned off a large portion of the audience. As it was, it worked for everybody. The movie allows the audience to decide for themselves and that's the way movies should be. Once you fall heavily on one side of an argument, everything becomes too literal. That's less interesting dramatically because the drama comes from the doubt and the debate. It's the ambivalence that draws out the viewer's feelings and lays them bare. If you take that away and just make a strong statement about something, the film is diminished.

What was the extent of your involvement in the 2008 remake of *It's Alive* other than delivering an early draft of the script?

I was not involved. I merely sold Millennium Films the rights and took the money. Yes, I gave them a script, but that script was completely ignored. My story was pretty similar to the original, only it was modernized slightly. I built up the part of the baby's brother, who was now a high school student, and had some switches where the various events and action occurred. The climax was going to take place in an abandoned swimming pool in the basement of the high school. It was a very good script and contained some interesting touches, strong scares and good dramatics. All of that was absent in the finished film. The remake didn't have the drama or the emotion of the original; it had nothing! They threw away what I had written and devised a completely different story, which was dreadful, and shot the movie in Bulgaria. Their problems were then compounded by lousy sets and terrible performances. The remake was an absolute piece of unadulterated garbage, and I would certainly not advise anybody to see it. Even the producer of the movie, Avi Lerner, approached me on the street in Beverly Hills and apologized for making such a terrible film out of my property. He said, "I'm sorry, we really fucked that one up." What can you say? The only positive things are that hardly anyone saw it and I did get to keep the money. I also have the rights to make another *It's Alive* picture in time, so there is always the possibility that we'll get around to doing another one again in the future. Of course, it's going to be a while before we can live down the disgrace of this last effort, but it could happen. It's just a shame that they did such a terrible job. It could have been good but, sadly, it wasn't.

Interestingly, there have been a whole series of new issues and scientific advancements in pregnancies since the original *It's Alive* was made that could be integrated into a remake.

Oh yeah, there is all that stuff. Think about the concerns we now have as a society about pregnancy, about DNA, about cloning, about how science has impacted on our lives, and the way we have babies. A lot has happened since the 1970s. People have information and choices they can make nowadays that would have seemed like pure science fiction not so long ago. There are tests that can be performed, which reveal certain defects in the foetus that were not available to parents back when we were making *It's Alive*. If there were, perhaps the monster baby would have been terminated before it could have even been born.

But then we wouldn't have the movie.

Exactly! I suppose *It's Alive* is a film of its time—as any film is really—but it can also be a film for all times. I mean, people will always be having babies and sometimes those babies will come out wrong. It's just the science and the technology that evolves and changes. The joys and despairs of parenthood will always be the same.

God Told Me To (1976)

It's been suggested that only someone with their own production company could ever hope to make a film as brave and compellingly eccentric as *God Told Me To*.

Well, that's probably the case for most of my movies. [Chuckles]

Was it an especially difficult project to secure funding for?

I don't remember it being unusually difficult. I mean, it was always difficult getting the money to make every film, but then someone would always turn up to help out. In most instances, I would give them a budget that was way below what they thought I could make the picture for. The financers would then think they were taking advantage of me by underfinancing the picture—meaning you would often have to lay out a lot of money on your own. I usually found some way to make the movie within the budget they gave me, so I wasn't spending my own money and might even make a little on it, too. *God Told Me To* was financed by Edgar Scherick and Daniel Blatt, who were two producers of some note. Scherick had produced *The Heartbreak Kid* and *The Taking of Pelham 123*. He had formerly been head of the ABC Television Network and had bought a number of shows from me. Blatt had originally been Scherick's lawyer and then later branched out on his own, producing movies like *The Howling* and *Cujo*. These two guys had managed to find this tax shelter group located in Georgia, who had given them the money to make *God Told Me To*. I never knew who or what this group were, but I was very happy that they'd been found. Scherick and Blatt then became the executive producers but, later on, when *God Told Me To* was finished, they both saw it and asked me to take their names off the picture. I said, "Okay, but this means I have to make the titles all over again and it's going to cost $600." They said, "We'll pay the $600!" So, they actually paid to have their names removed from the movie and, in my opinion, it's the best picture that either one of them has ever been associated with.

What inspired the central concept of the film—that apparent acts of random violence are being willed and guided by a messianic hermaphrodite alien?

If you read *The Bible,* it will certainly tell you what started the idea. There is no character—fictional or real—in the whole of literature as violent as God. Who else fucked up the entire human race and drowned everybody? I mean, come on! The violence that God has perpetrated on the very creatures that He created is infinitely more vicious and horrifying than anything you can possibly imagine. Consider what a fearsome creature God must be. If you get to Heaven, it must be terrifying to live in the shadow of this dictator. There has never been a dictator in recorded history that is as diabolical and vengeful as God is, and so this is a formidable creature indeed. Nobody has ever created a character in horror that is as extreme as God is.

I presume that Erich von Däniken's book *Chariots of the Gods?*[1] was another influence on the writing of the script?

Absolutely. The idea that the Earth was originally populated by an ancient extraterrestrial intelligence seems very feasible to me. It's not outside the realm of possibility to consider that aliens may have come to our planet in prehistoric times and mated with the inhabitants of the Earth. I don't know if they were Cro-Magnons or whatever, but they were certainly some lower, less developed form of the human race. These aliens may have helped create human beings as we know them today with their high intellect and imagination, bestowing upon them the power to envision and create technology. So, I think we must at least accept the possibility that we are the product of an alien insemination that occurred long ago. Certainly, there was a major jump in our evolution at some point.

America has enjoyed a strong fascination with UFOs and alien abductions since the days of Roswell. Why do you think that is?

People are always interested in things that are beyond the scope of their reality, like religion and extraterrestrial visitations. It's that strong desire and need in each of us to know the unknowable. I've always enjoyed an interest in the possible existence of alien life and had dealt with the subject before in *The Invaders*. People always like a mystery, a conspiracy, and *God Told Me To* allowed me to combine the alien concept with the religious concept, and explore two areas that are increasingly baffling and fascinating at the same time.

How much has religion played a part in your own life?

Very little. I don't believe in an organized anything. I do believe in a higher power of some kind, but I don't think it looks like a human being. I certainly don't think it looks like an old man with a beard and some kind of angry face that is looking down on us from above. If anything, in one of my more recent scripts, I depicted God as a creature who has created the human race for His own entertainment. We are all just articles of amusement for Him, something for God to pass His time observing. We're like the TV show God watches to whittle away eternity, to enjoy Himself as He sees the horrendous things that we are doing to each other every day. God only created human beings and gave us free will so that we could go out and screw everything up. We're all just fictional characters devised by God, but we don't ever realize this.

Was the film motivated by your lack of spiritual faith?

No, I don't think so. It was motivated by a need to tell this particular story, that's all.

But you just said that you don't believe in "an organized anything" and that view is evident in *God Told Me To* as it is in the *It's Alive* trilogy and *The Stuff*. You don't appear to have much faith in institutions and organized systems, whether they be the Government, the media, the military, or the church.

Well, all you have to do is look at the newspapers you read. Every week somebody in power is exposed as being a complete creep. Our leaders all lead double lives. They are not the idealistic and benevolent characters that they would like us to believe they are. They have all got a mistress or a boyfriend on the side, or are stealing money, or are doing something else that is entirely dishonest and unjust. There are so many phoneys and fakes around, to believe in anything with a strong degree of faith is extremely difficult. Every time you turn around there is a company that is exposed as having covered up the defects in their automobiles or the chemicals in their products that are poisoning people. When I was a kid during the war, I remember they used to announce that Camel, Lucky Strikes, and Phillip Morris were all sending 500,000 cigarettes to our boys in uniform—every week—in the Pacific and in Europe. They were only sending them cigarettes for the purpose of addicting an entire generation of young men, so that when they came back from World War II, they would be addicted to smoking. The cigarette companies actually killed more American boys than the Germans and the Japanese combined. That's what they did! It was a premeditated interest in addicting them by giving them free cigarettes and they just did it, regardless of the consequences. So, what can you say about people who would do such things? It's that kind of behavior which gives you a contempt for authority, but that's the way it is. You just have to learn what the world is all about. You see the poor guys on Memorial Day lying in their graves having died for their country. You inevitably ask, "Hey, what happened? How come all of our enemies are now our friends and all our friends are now our enemies? And how was it that you were unlucky enough to have been caught in the middle of all this and be dead? What did you die for? Who decided that you should die?" There is a lot of pain and sadness and dishonesty in the world as a direct result of organized systems—governments, religions, the military, whatever it is. The decisions they make and enforce cause immense pain, confusion and death. Of course, it's my job to put all of this into the movies.

One of the most disturbing moments in *God Told Me To* is when the father, who has just slaughtered his entire family, calmly describes to the Detective how he tricked his young daughter out of a locked bathroom in order to execute her.

Yeah, right. He says, "Come on out of the bathroom, honey." It's probably the father's sense of tranquillity that makes that scene so disturbing—the way Robert Drivas, who plays that character, delivers it. He recounts this hideous, unforgivable act he's committed so calmly and vividly, it becomes far more effective than actually showing him killing his loved ones.

A lot of directors would have showed the deaths onscreen simply for the shock value, but it's far more powerful when you don't show the violence. It kind of lingers in the audience's imagination, the utter horror of it. I didn't copy that situation from any real transcript or case, but that's the kind of thinking that goes into these people who end up murdering their families. A week doesn't go by out here in L.A. that we don't have a story in the newspapers saying that somewhere in the country somebody has executed their family. Sometimes they knock off the whole family, including the kids, and then usually end up shooting themselves. That is real horror because it's the horror that cuts the deepest and rings most true. People clearly recognize that these terrible incidents do actually occur.

You worked for the first time with Paul Glickman, who would be your cinematographer on a number of projects over the next decade. How did you become aware of him?

I don't remember exactly how Paul Glickman came into my life, but I do know that one day I summoned him and when he showed up with his crew, he made quite an impression. Paul was wearing a big leather hat and a pair of torn jeans with his ass hanging out! [Chuckles] He had this beard and looked like a hippy. Paul was kind of a wild guy, which meant he was perfect to work with me. As a matter of fact, Paul and I have become very friendly again and actually spent some time together just recently in Chicago. When we were shooting *God Told Me To*, I told Paul that I wanted the whole picture to be shot with a handheld camera. Even though there was no reason for everything to be shot that way, I wanted that candid feeling. I wanted that sense of immediacy that would make the film look like a hard documentary, like a street movie about crime in the inner city.

The pseudo-documentary feel of *God Told Me To* with its handheld camera, jagged editing, and naturalistic performances is very affecting.

Yeah, and applying those techniques to a genre film was fairly revolutionary at the time. I mean, you just didn't see that back in the 1970s. Of course, the hard documentary look has been duplicated in several movies and television shows that have appeared since. It's really taken for granted today. You just accept it now because a handheld camera and naturalistic performances can lend anything a documentary reality, even when you have a totally preposterous story. Back then, I wanted to explore the elements of horror and fantasy in *God Told Me To* in a very serious and realistic fashion, and use the camera and performance as a means of making the audience believe that these apparently fantastical things were real.

The film is a science fiction/horror/police procedural and is a prime example of your ability to mix and match various genres. How conscious were you of combining assorted tropes and elements in *God Told Me To*?

Well, firstly, I should say that I think *God Told Me To* inspired *The X-Files*.[2] It came way, way before *The X-Files*, but the way our movie took science fiction and horror and played them directly against the intense reality of a police procedural was definitely an approach that hadn't been done before. So, we were breaking some new ground there, I think. But I don't consciously mix and match genres. I just sit down and write these conceits and then make the picture. When I'm writing, I'm not into self-analysis too much. I never think about why I'm doing something, or if two very different elements will work together or not. It's just a part of the story that is unravelling and usually I'm just making it all up as I go along.

As is the case with most of your movies, the cast is very strong. I think Tony Lo Bianco is particularly good as Detective Peter Nicholas.

Originally, the part of the Detective was played by Robert Forster. Robert did act in the picture for a couple of days, but we didn't get along and so I let him go. I then had to find a new lead actor and remembered Tony Lo Bianco, who had played the lead in my off-Broadway play, *The Nature of the Crime*. I had also seen Tony in *The Honeymoon Killers*[3] and thought he was great in that picture. He did such a fine job for me on the play that after I'd dispensed with Bob Forster's services, I knew Tony was the right choice for the Detective. So, he quickly stepped in.

What exactly was the problem with Forster, his performance or his attitude?

The problem with Forster was his chewing gum! I kept telling him, "Hey, this character is possibly a demigod and gods don't chew gum!" So, Bob would take the gum out of his mouth, or would at least pretend to. A few minutes later, I would see his jaw working again and he'd still be chewing gum. I wasn't going to put up with that for very long. I said, "Look, if you keep doing that you are going to chew yourself out of this movie." A short time later, we agreed that it would be better for the both of us if we went our own separate ways, and that's exactly what happened. I should also add that, all these years later, Bob has now become a very good personal friend. Back in those days we didn't get along, but we get along great now.

What about Sandy Dennis who plays the detective's estranged wife? Was she good to work with?

Yes, very good. Sandy was a pretty big star and a wonderful actress. She had won the Academy Award for *Who's Afraid of Virginia Woolf?* and had starred in *Up the Down Staircase* and a lot of other great movies. She had also won a Tony Award for *Any Wednesday* and, frankly, I was lucky to get her for the film. Sandy really brought a sombre intensity to the role and was really into it. She was doing theater in New York at the time and sometimes when actors are doing stage work they are also willing to do a movie, too, because the theater doesn't really pay that well. Actors can augment their earnings by trying to fit a movie in and I'm always happy to adjust my schedule to accommodate them. That way, they will be able to do their matinees on Wednesdays and Fridays and finish shooting in time to get to the theater every night. Sandy only had to work on the film for a few days, so there was never a problem.

The "St. Patrick's Day Parade" sequence is extremely impressive for such a low-budget production. How did that come about?

There was no way to do that sequence except to shoot it during the actual St. Patrick's Day Parade in New York. I could never have staged the parade again, so it was a complete one-shot deal. Many years later, they had a similar scene in *The Dark Knight* where The Joker wreaks havoc in the middle of a police parade. What I find interesting is that for such a big-budget movie, their sequence was much smaller than the one we did—certainly in terms of the number of cops they used. We had 5,000 cops in our sequence and utilized the real parade. The only way for us to possibly do that was to somehow infiltrate the event itself and put our very own actor into the parade. That actor turned out to be Andy Kaufman, who was a complete unknown at the time but went on to become a great comedy star. Andy played the cop who suddenly pulls out the gun as he marches along and goes berserk. Of course, we had no permission and no permits to place our actor in the parade, but I thought we could at least attempt it and see what happens.

How did you actually cover the event?

I had three camera crews because everybody had to work on foot. Once the parade started, it wasn't going to stop for us, so we had to keep shooting as it was in motion. That meant that one unit would have to shoot and finish up, before running on ahead a couple of blocks. They would then have to quickly get set up to pick the parade up as it marched by again. The second unit would then take over and would shoot for a while, before they, too, would run further ahead and prepare to shoot again, unless they went up on a rooftop to catch an overhead shot. Everything had to be co-ordinated and executed with a tremendous amount of speed and precision. I guess that because we were in the middle of this parade, brandishing all these cameras, everybody just assumed that we had obtained permission. Nobody else would have ever dared walk into the midst of 5,000 cops and start shooting illegally. When you are usually shooting without a permit in New York City and you see cops, you just flee in the opposite direction as quickly as possible. Here we were right in the middle of them—surrounded on all sides by policemen—and we were going to have people getting shot at and crazy things like that. It was really absurd. I think the fact that the cameras were present meant the police knew that there was a movie going on. They didn't get scared or react when they saw somebody with a gun in their hand, because there was a camera only a few feet in front of them calmly filming everything. Actually, the cops all cooperated quite a bit. After we shot that day, I came out to California and contacted the Irish-American organizations here and asked them if they would like to march again. They said they would as they only got the opportunity to do it once every year. I said, "Well, here's your chance to do it again. All you have to do is show up in downtown Los Angeles at a specific location on Saturday morning." They arrived at the agreed time with all their people, their musical instruments, their marching band, their drum majorettes, and everybody else who was willing and available. We then restaged the St. Patrick's Day Parade in L.A. and put Andy Kaufman back in there. We shot some more footage of chaos ensuing with blood-squibs going off and people falling down and fleeing in all directions as musical instruments were being scattered. Then we matched the L.A. shots with the footage we filmed in New York and made an integral sequence out of it. Incredibly, this did not cost me any money because all the Irish-American people came free of charge. They even arrived in buses that they had arranged for themselves. All we had to do was shoot them.

How did Andy Kaufman become involved with the film?

Well, I had first seen Andy at The Improvisation Club in New York. He came in to do his act and was just breaking into the business at this point. I knew immediately that Andy had something special about him. I thought he was so remarkable I just had to talk to him after his performance. I approached him and said, "I'm making this movie called *God Told Me To* and I'd like to put you in it. I know you've never done a picture before, but I'd like to able to say that I was the director who gave you your first movie role." When he heard what the movie was about and what I planned on doing, Andy realized that he had finally met somebody who was crazier than he was! [Laughs] Everybody thought that Andy was rather deranged—and he was—but I was even more deranged! No one could have imagined that we could pirate a scene during the St. Patrick's Day Parade in the midst of thousands of police. You would have to be crazy, and I think Andy appreciated that. When he agreed to do the movie, I said, "Okay, first we have to get you a policeman's uniform. Tell me the size of your shirt and jacket." He said, "I don't know. I wear my father's old clothes." I looked at him and figured that he was about my size, so we got him a policeman's uniform and went down to Fifth Avenue. We got him dressed in one of the luncheonettes that was right off the street and, when the time was right, calmly walked him into the parade. Of course, Andy utters just one line of dialogue during the scene. We didn't have any sound recording equipment with us, so there was no means to record his voice. As his character lay on the ground, dying, Andy just mouthed the words: "God told me to." Later on, when we did the mix, I recorded that line myself but when Andy saw the finished film, he said, "How did you get my voice?" I said, "Andy, that's not your voice, it's mine." He said, "No, I know my own voice when I hear it. That's my voice! How did you do that?" I tried to explain to him that we didn't have any microphones with us when we shot the scene, but he kept insisting that it was his voice in the movie. Andy was just perplexed about how I was able to do that and almost every time we spoke afterwards he'd always bring it up.

So you and Kaufman remained friends?

Oh, yes. As a matter of fact, I was constantly talking with him on the phone about us doing another picture together. Andy hadn't had a lot of success as a movie actor, but he had become popular in clubs and on television in *Taxi*.[4] I'd written a script called *Miracles in Brooklyn* and Andy was going to play five or six different characters in the picture. It was a comedy in the style of Mel Brooks and was about three miracles that take place in Brooklyn, New York. It was a very funny script and would have been a nice showcase for Andy's talents. He would call me up and say, "What's happening with the financing? When are we starting? I'm anxious to get moving with this." I would then update him on any developments. Of course, all the time he was talking to me and expressing his excitement, he was sitting in a wheelchair and dying of cancer, and he knew it. He knew there was never going to be any chance of him ever doing a movie with anybody, but he constantly kept talking to me about the project. He was very ill at the time, but I would never have known that from our enthusiastic phone conversations. Perhaps he was just trying to convince himself, but it was all self-delusional. Andy was in no condition to work. Then somebody called me and said that Andy had died. I couldn't believe it, because we had been making all these plans to do another picture together and now it was never going to happen.

Richard Lynch[5] plays Bernard, the shimmering alien. How did you locate him for the role?

I had seen Richard in a couple of pictures including *Scarecrow*, a road movie about two drifters played by Al Pacino and Gene Hackman, that had been released two or three years before we shot *God Told Me To*. Richard had played this very dangerous psychopathic villain that the drifters encounter. At one point in the film, Richard's character brutally beats Pacino almost to death. I thought Richard had a very interesting look and presence about him. He had this weird threatening quality in his performances that I felt would work perfectly for the alien. When I contacted him, he was living in New York and had never actually worked in California. He agreed to do *God Told Me To*, and I was happy about that. One day, I remember we were shooting the confrontation between the alien and the Detective in this deserted tenement building in Manhattan. Unfortunately, we didn't have any dressing rooms available for the actors. All we had were these various dilapidated rooms or apartments where they could change clothes. I walked into one of these rooms as Richard was changing and saw that he was stripped down to the waist. As I looked at him, I suddenly noticed that his entire body was covered in thick, crisscrossing scars. Apparently, he had set fire to himself during a binge of some kind—I guess he might have been high on drugs at the time—but whatever happened, Richard had immolated himself. Thankfully, he had survived this traumatic event, but the scar tissue grew back all over his body. The alien chest that you see in the movie with that large, peculiar, vaginal indentation in the center of it, is actually Richard Lynch as he really was. There was no makeup applied to his torso at all for that scene. I looked at Richard's scars and said, "Hey, would you mind showing that body of yours as the body of the alien?" He simply said, "Yeah, no problem," and we just did it.

How were the ethereal alien effects achieved?

Paul Glickman had assured me that he could achieve the alien effects in-camera using only the lights. This meant that we didn't have to do them in post-production, which I found rather appealing. Paul put a special gel over the lights and increased the light so that Richard would be over-exposed and pick up a strong, bright, almost angelic glow. When Tony Lo Bianco was in the same frame as him, Tony was lit normally and Richard was over-lit, so that he would be over-exposed. The color that was added to the lights gave Richard that yellowish, shimmering, unearthly luminosity. So those effects were all done right there on the set and they worked out pretty well.

What led you to doing some of the special effects shots at Pinewood Studios in England?

In those days, it was much less expensive to shoot in England. You could probably shoot there for about, I don't know, a fifth of what it would cost to shoot in Hollywood. I also liked England. I had enjoyed living over there and being with Bernard Herrmann during the scoring of *It's Alive*. I had gotten friendly with Benny's friends and that gave me another good reason to visit London. I thought I could combine the shooting with having a nice trip—along with the added bonus of saving a lot of money. So, I went to Pinewood and worked with some of the same special effects technicians who had worked on several classic movies of the past, going back as far as Alexander Korda's *The Thief of Baghdad*. One gentleman there was Les Bowie, a legendary special effects guy from the British cinema.[6] All of these guys were pretty old and they were a delight to work with. It was a lot of fun being with them. I always like to work with experienced old timers who have enjoyed a rich history in the motion picture business. You always end up learning a great deal from them. I had loved working with the great George Folsey, Sr. on *Bone*, and here I was with all these other great artists at Pinewood, getting the opportunity to watch them work and listening to all their stories. The only problem with Pinewood was that the soundstage was not heated and everybody was working with overcoats on. We were all freezing to death and that wasn't particularly pleasant, I must say, but everything else was wonderful. The British crew even voted to give me an extra thirty minutes of overtime. In the English cinema, the crew has to vote as to whether or not they will work an extra thirty minutes for you. If one person on the crew doesn't agree—just one—then you can't have the overtime. Fortunately, everybody agreed and I got the extra thirty minutes. [Pause] Whatever that meant anyway.

God Told Me To is augmented with stock footage, is it not?

Yeah. It features in the flashback sequence where Sylvia Sydney tells the Detective the story about when she was kidnapped as a young woman by the aliens and brought onboard their spaceship to be inseminated. Unfortunately, I had bought some stock footage that turned out to be from a British science fiction television series called *Space: 1999*.[7] It had starred Martin Landau, but I had never seen nor even heard about the existence of this show. All I knew is that I had found some suitable stock footage of a spaceship and was able to incorporate it into the footage I'd shot at Pinewood. I simply didn't have the money to go ahead and create new flying spaceships for that sequence. However, I didn't realize just how many people were going to recognize that damn thing from the TV show. *Space: 1999* wasn't that popular in America, but just about everybody who sees *God Told Me To* brings up that spaceship's appearance. Actually, it doesn't really bother me that much. In fact, it wouldn't have made much difference whether I'd bought pre-existing stock footage or hired some special effects house to create new shots. Either way, you would not be fully realizing the scene yourself, you'd be farming it out to somebody else. When their work is completed, they hand it over and you then edit those effects shots into your movie. This is exactly what happens on most science fiction films. The director doesn't actually direct the scenes involving a lot of visual effects. They are mostly done by Industrial Light & Magic, or some other outfit, who literally create the sequence for you. That means that some of the key stuff in the movie is not done—and, occasionally, not even supervised—by the director. As I always say, I like to do everything myself. I wasn't capable of spending the money to create a flying spaceship scene, so instead I just bought one. If I had paid for George Lucas's company to devise those effects shots for me, it still wouldn't bear any closer relationship to my work—and perhaps my ideas—than what we currently have in the picture.

During the final confrontation, Bernard offers to bear Peter's child in order to create another god-like hybrid. Do you think that was a fairly radical concept for 1970s horror and science fiction cinema?

I imagine so. I had not heard of anything remotely like that before in movies. But you must understand that I'm not an avid reader of science fiction novels, so there might have already been a lot of books written which had a similar concept to *God Told Me To*. I do find it interesting that Robin Wood, amongst other critics, felt that the whole picture had some kind of homosexual theme. In his analysis, Wood felt that the central idea of *God Told Me To* was concerned with the rise of homosexuality and how it will overtake society. I'm often amused by the different analyses people have of the movies I've made, some of which I understand and some of which I have difficulty comprehending myself. In general, the whole idea of the mating between the Detective and the alien came from the fact that Richard Lynch literally had this big crevice in his chest that looked like a vagina. That was it, really. I saw that and said, "Well, here's something new we can do." It's fascinating how certain ideas can emerge out of the making of a film that you might not have considered or planned before you started shooting. We'd already established that the alien was the product of a virgin birth. That tied in directly with the religious concept of a virgin birth, and the fact that the alien's sexual identity was indeterminable. So, these new additions to the story followed in good logic.

Speaking with you, I get the strong sense that such serendipitous events as this have played a considerable part in your filmmaking process.

That's the mystical quality of making movies, particularly when you don't have the authority of a studio behind or above you. If you are not required to seek approval for every single event or idea that occurs, you can go out there and watch as your film starts to magically come to life. These fortunate things that happen can sometimes be incorporated into the picture, but only if you have the freedom to do so. You don't want to be writing a memo or placing a phone call to the studio every time an interesting idea comes to you; or you want to get an extra shot of a car driving along, or a sunset, or a dog barking, whatever it is, and you are required to get permission from somebody. That just makes the whole process tedious and restrictive.

In the movie, Peter often seems to experience great emotional conflicts between his lifestyle and his faith, would you agree?

He has conflicts, guilt, shame, but he doesn't hide his faith. His girlfriend, played by Deborah Raffin, knows that he is a devout Catholic and she asks him in an early scene, "Where is all the pleasure that this faith is supposed to give you?" He is conning her into thinking that he is going to get a divorce from his wife, but he has no intention of getting a divorce because that would be against his faith. Peter is so devoutly wrapped up in his beliefs he feels a powerful attraction to the religious aspects of his life. But, of course, it's not that exactly. It's actually the fact that he's not quite human, that he's partially alien, which makes him different from everybody else. It isn't God that he's close to, that he's continually drawn to; it's this alien force. It's confusing him and he comes to deal with it later on in the picture.

Yes, the final revelation is that Peter—like Bernard—is an alien hybrid himself.

Yeah, and that also ties-in with elements of the superhero story. For example, Superman is an alien who was raised by human parents, but he is clearly not of this world. Like Peter, Superman has to deal with the fact that he is very different from other people. Consider if a being such as Superman actually existed and had grown up from childhood in America possessing super-strength, x-ray vision and the ability to fly and leap tall buildings in a single bound. He would be growing up in a largely Christian society where he would be exposed to the story of Jesus Christ. Superman may then very well come to the conclusion that he himself must be God. I mean, he has all these superior powers that other human beings do not have and that must mean he is the embodiment of God like Jesus Christ. So, it seems pretty logical that Superman might mistake himself for God as he has been following the mythology of Christianity. Now, when I used the word 'mythology,' I'm not discounting Christianity as being fictitious. I simply have no idea what the true facts of existence are, or what the true facts of God are, or the true facts of the true religion, if there is such a thing. I tend to think that there is no orthodoxy. Nobody can speak for God. Nobody knows what God wants or what the truth of creation is. Yet some people have an effrontery to put themselves in the position where they will tell you what God wants, and what God demands of you, and what you have to do in order to please God. Every society seems to have this religious aspect to it and some are even dominated by it. Everybody is so worried about what God wants that they make a miserable life for themselves. But in keeping with the mythology, if I may use that word again, that we have of Jesus being born of normal people but having God-like qualities, I thought the Superman analogy was fitting. If anybody who had superpowers grew up in that environment, they would inevitably come to the conclusion that they must be divine. That's exactly what happens with this alien. Bernard truly believes he is God and makes other people believe that he is God, but he's not. He's just an alien. [Pause] If the word "just" can actually be applied to something as unique as an alien.

After the untimely death of Bernard Herrmann, where did your search for a composer then take you? It's been reported that Miklós Rózsa was your next choice but that he refused the job by quipping, "God told me not to."

It wasn't Miklós Rózsa who said that; it was actually Sam Arkoff. When I tried to get Sam to distribute the picture he said, "God told me not to do it," which I thought was cute. [Laughs] I don't believe I contacted Miklós Rózsa until I made my next film, *The Private Files of J. Edgar Hoover*, as I thought that was a more appropriate project for him. I would've loved to have had Rózsa score *God Told Me To*, but Bernard Herrmann had an agent over in England, who was a very nice lady, and she also represented an English composer named Frank Cordell. She said, "I'm so desperately sorry that we've lost Benny, but if you need somebody else to take over you should consider Frank Cordell. He is a wonderful composer and I think he'd love to do your film." Frank had earned an Academy Award nomination for his score for *Cromwell*. I had actually heard the music for

Cromwell and liked it very much. I thought Frank could do a good job and he did. I remember telling him that I wanted a "Herrmann-esque" score. I also told him about Benny recording the music for *It's Alive* in Cripplegate Church. Frank then recorded the music to *God Told Me To* there also, as the acoustics in that church are simply wonderful.

How did New World Pictures acquire *God Told Me To*?

Actually, I didn't have very much to do with that. It was Mr. Scherick and Mr. Blatt who were looking for distribution for the movie. Of course, at the time, New World Pictures was Roger Corman's company, but Roger had absolutely nothing to do with the making of *God Told Me To*. It was a finished film and he merely bought it for domestic release—and paid quite a lot of money, too. Roger was famous for acquiring movies for next to nothing, but in this case he did pay quite a hefty sum. It was probably one of his highest acquisition payments ever, but then he took *God Told Me To* and made a miserable job of distributing it. Roger just didn't understand the movie. We later opened the film in a couple of cities with a very unpleasant ad campaign which basically said, "The leaders of all organized religions have forbidden their constituents to see this movie," and all that stuff. It was an incredibly negative campaign. I didn't really understand what Roger expected to get from it. They should have sold *God Told Me To* as a scary movie and a thriller, but instead they sold it as some kind of picture that was going to offend everybody.

Where did the film open?

New World originally opened the picture in Texas for some unknown reason. I mean, why they opened it somewhere in the Bible Belt I do not know. The people down in Texas are more religious than, for example, the people in New York or Chicago, where you might get a more liberal audience. When they opened it in Texas, *God Told Me To* didn't do well and Roger immediately called this meeting. I went in to see him, and this was the one and only time I met with Roger on this picture. When I got there, Roger told me that he wanted to change the title of the movie. He said, "*God Told Me To* is not a good title. We have to come up with a new one." I said, "Okay, why don't we call the picture *Alien*? I mean, this guy is an alien from another planet, so I think that title will work." Roger said, "No, you can't call a movie *Alien* because everybody is going to think it's about wetbacks sneaking over from Mexico." I said, "Roger, I think *Alien* is a great title," but he wouldn't listen. We ended up calling it *Demon* and, of course, just a couple of years later, Ridley Scott's *Alien* was released and quickly became one of the most recognizable and seminal titles in the history of horror and science fiction. So, I guess Roger was wrong about that one, wasn't he? [Chuckles] You know, as far as I was concerned, he was wrong about everything. Roger really messed up the release of the picture, but eventually we did open at the Cinerama Theatre on Broadway at a first-run theater. So, the movie did play theatrically and it did get its shot. Unfortunately, it just didn't have the right ad campaign or the right TV spot either. The TV spot was certainly not very good. Oddly enough, it was edited by Joe Dante who, at the time, was working for Roger in the trailer department at New World. Joe actually cut the trailer, and, in fact, that's how I first met him.

Some believe that *God Told Me To* is in the public domain. Is it?

No, it isn't, but you're right, a lot of people think it is. There has been a considerable amount of confusion about this, but the copyright has been renewed and we do have a secure copyright on the picture. However, we did have a problem with a chain of drugstores here in the United States that were distributing a low-budget version of the picture on DVD without licensing it. Some company had mistakenly sold them the idea that *God Told Me To* was a public domain film, and so we had to take legal action against them. The drugstore then ceased distributing the film, but what happened next was they sent me all their copies of the movie. I mean, literally thousands of DVDs arrived at my house! My entire basement is filled with DVDs of *God Told Me To* which the drugstore chain decided to send to me because they didn't know what else to do with them. Now, on every occasion I attend a screening or something, I try to give out as many free copies as possible so I can get them out of my house.

Is it true that Gaspar Noé[8] met with you in 2010 in order to discuss the possibility of his doing a remake?

Yes, that's true. Gaspar Noé was in New York and he called me up and asked if he could come see me. We met in a little coffee shop up on the West Side and talked for about an hour and a half. Noé claimed that he was trying to get the money from some company in France. It might have been Wild Bunch. Then, he left, and I've never heard from him again. He hadn't written a script or anything, but based on what he said, I was just going to supply him with the rights to *God Told Me To* and then he was going to make his own movie. I did see a number of the films that Noé has made. He gave me a few copies of his work to look at and I did watch them.

What did you think of them?

I don't know. Frankly, I thought his movies were a little vulgar and sexually explicit. Apparently, Gaspar Noé has a big following so I should be honored that he wants to remake *God Told Me To*. I've seen blurbs that have been in certain columns announcing that he wanted to do the picture. But, as I say, I never heard from him again after that one meeting and nothing has ever come of it.

God Told Me To **appears to be one of your most under-appreciated works. Personally, I think it stands as one of the great horror films of the 1970s.**

A lot of people say that *God Told Me To* is their personal favorite out of all my films. Oliver Stone once approached me and told me that it was one of his favorite movies. In fact, I get more requests from film festivals all over the world for that picture than any other film I've made. Recently, we ran it at the Vienna Film Festival, where I ran fifteen of my pictures, and of all the movies that were shown the poorest audience reaction was to *God Told Me To*. The audience was offended by the picture. In Vienna, people are intensely religious, and I think that film upset their religious sensibilities. Everything else went over great, but that particular movie did not. The response was very mixed, and I felt that I'd offended people by my apparent dismissal of religion and, yeah, okay, maybe so. *God Told Me To* is very much like *Bone* in that what you bring to the theater when you come in involves what you take out of the picture when you leave. Your feelings about racism are revealed when you see *Bone* and your feelings about religion are revealed when you see *God Told Me To*. You know, our perceptions of art are always colored by our own beliefs and it's the same with all art, be it movies, novels, paintings, whatever. Let's say you visit a gallery or a museum to look at some paintings: depending on whom you are, what your upbringing is, and what your faith happens to be, all of those things are going to greatly affect and determine how you respond to the paintings that you see. Some people will see obscenity in those paintings; others will see value and humanity and will view them as great works of art. That's both fascinating and frustrating at the same time, but then all people are different.

The Private Files of J. Edgar Hoover (1977)

Why exactly did you want to make a film about J. Edgar Hoover?

That's a very important question. Many people asked me how I could dare make a picture about Hoover, particularly after what he had done to the people out here in Hollywood for such a long time. They asked me if I realized just how terrified this town was of the guy and what he stood for; how the blacklist had destroyed the careers of so many people in the motion picture business and in television, as well. Hoover had been dead for just two years when I first started making the picture, and I was warned by everybody not to deal with this subject as it could have terrible repercussions. That's probably why I wanted to make the picture most of all—because everyone told me not to do it! [Chuckles] I just thought I'd be my usual stubborn self and do something that everybody insisted I should not do. I mean, the FBI was a sacrosanct organization that was seemingly beyond reproach. It was the finest investigative agency in the world—integrity personified—but of course, upon closer examination, there were considerable flaws in it. The FBI had demonstrated a lot of monstrous behavior and had inflicted a lot of cruelty and pain on people, some of it unnecessarily. I suddenly thought, *Well, I can do the same thing with the FBI that I did with a baby in* It's Alive. *I can show the devilish side of this apparently honest organization and make the first FBI movie without the express authorisation and supervision of the Bureau itself.* You must understand that up until the time I made *The Private Files of J. Edgar Hoover*, nobody had ever made an FBI movie without the FBI's approval, and without having an FBI agent present on the set. This was obviously done to check and approve everything. All the pictures made about the FBI back then were basically public relations movies for the Bureau like *The FBI Story* with James Stewart.[1] That was certainly a public relations movie in which every element of the story was greatly sanitized. I was going to make a more realistic and honest film. It would be an entirely different—and probably a very dangerous—undertaking but, perversely, I liked the idea of doing something dangerous.

You've said that you structured the script as "a post-mortem of Hoover's life and career." Why take that approach?

With Hoover having only recently died, it seemed rather appropriate. When a person dies and you read their obituary, it's basically a summing up of their entire life—all their major achievements and disgraces framed in a few sentences. A number of movie biographies follow that same structure, such as *Lawrence of Arabia*. That film begins with Lawrence getting killed on a motorcycle, then we see the funeral before we flashback into his life story. Naturally, when you do a movie based on someone's life, you examine not only the details of their personality and career, their public and professional and private relationships, but also their morality and philosophy. You try to include all these things and retain a balance and objectivity, but above everything you want to make the picture entertaining. You don't want it to be too factual and dry, because it then plays like you are hanging the story on familiar historic events rather than trying to get at the heart of this person. You have the dramatic imperative, but you also have a responsibility to the truth. What are the facts here? Who was this guy? What did he do? What things shaped him? The structure of looking back and contemplating the past also added a certain poignancy that I liked. So, I was really just trying to write a complex portrait of a complex man within a complex structure.

How did you raise financing for such a potentially controversial project?

I didn't, actually. I went to Washington DC with cast and crew, and I didn't have any financing confirmed. The first week I was there, I was directing the picture and, at the same time, was also on the phone trying to raise money. I figured I could lay out enough cash to get us there for the first week and then, after that, I would have to get money from someplace. Finally, I got money from Samuel Arkoff at American International Pictures based on the actors I had assembled. I told Sam that the cast included no less than four Academy Award-winners. He didn't know exactly which ones, but I did hire Dan Dailey to play Hoover's long time associate, Clyde Tolson. I also remembered some of the old FBI movies I saw as a kid starring Lloyd Nolan as an FBI agent, things like *The House on 92nd Street*,[2] *The Street with No Name*[3] and *Walk East on Beacon*.[4] I was very lucky to get Lloyd to play the Attorney General Harlan Stone in the film, the guy who appointed Hoover as acting head of the Bureau, which led to Hoover becoming Director a short time afterwards. I really sold Lloyd to Sam. I insisted, "You simply can't make an FBI movie without Lloyd Nolan! It can't be done!" But when it came to casting the lead, Sam originally believed that Rod Steiger was going to play Hoover. Naturally, I didn't tell him otherwise.

What was Arkoff's reaction when he eventually learned that Hoover was being portrayed by Broderick Crawford?

Well, Broderick Crawford had also won an Academy Award[5], but I think Sam had his heart set on Rod Steiger. But Crawford was better than Steiger would have been. Actually, my first choice for the role was Albert Finney. When I'd originally written the script and was over in England, I was trying hard to get Finney to do it. I thought he could play Hoover when he was young and, with the aid of some makeup, when he was old. Finney also had that same kind of punched-in nose that Hoover had. So, I approached his assistant and he read the script. His assistant then recommended it to Finney, but Finney had too many other commitments, and for big money, too. I couldn't afford to compete with that kind of price, and so we didn't get him. I had anticipated that Finney would have been attracted to the part and he would have been great. As it was, when he got older, he ended up playing Winston Churchill instead.[6]

How extensively did you research Hoover's life when writing the screenplay?

I read everything that was available on Hoover including many, many books that were critical. I also engaged a man named John Crewdson, who was *The New York Times* reporter assigned to cover the FBI and was later a Pulitzer Prize-winner. Crewdson knew the FBI intimately and he also knew all the inroads to the right people. He knew how to get me face-to-face with many of the individuals who had worked under Hoover, some of whom liked Hoover, some of whom didn't. We spent nearly two years off and on interviewing people, compiling notes, and finding out stuff. Over the course of this time, we came up with a couple of front page stories that *The New York Times* carried on the FBI, based on revelations that we had uncovered ourselves whilst researching the movie. I felt that was a very satisfactory result—above and beyond the making of the picture—as we had made some news. We even stayed at the homes of several FBI agents and their families. We got close to them and found out even more information that we could use in the film. I mean, we not only discovered the existence of the Security Index, which was a list of people who were going to be arrested, we also uncovered the identity of Deep Throat. Of course, as most of us already know, Deep Throat was the informant who gave Woodward and Bernstein the information that resulted in Watergate and the eventual resignation of President Richard Nixon. The identity of Deep Throat had become a big secret over the years, but I knew it was a top-ranking executive at the FBI. In fact, he was the #1 executive at the Bureau. It was supposedly a top secret and there were all kinds of speculation going on for thirty years as to who this person might be. In our film, we stated very clearly that the information came from the FBI and we also put in a headline at the end of the picture: "Mark Felt Denies He is Deep Throat." That was about as close as I could get to giving out the information because we knew exactly who it was! I couldn't say that Felt was Deep Throat or I would have been the subject of a lawsuit. But we did say that Felt "denies" he is Deep Throat; it's right there in print on the screen and nobody ever paid any attention to it! Nobody wanted to! *The Washington Post* was the newspaper that Woodward and Bernstein worked for, and which really exposed the Watergate story. They went to a great deal of trouble to discredit *The Private Files of J. Edgar Hoover* when it opened in Washington. They wrote two reviews of the movie—the first a creative review, the second a political review—in which they attempted to make the picture seem like it was badly researched. The fact was they knew we were too close to the truth. We had actually unearthed something that everybody else had decided to completely overlook.

Did any part of you fear that machinations would be put in place against you by various individuals or parties when this information was featured in the film?

I don't know. I do know that the whole FBI involvement in Watergate was not much different from the usual tactics they had employed over the years under Hoover. They often leaked information to friendly newspapers and columnists such as Walter Winchell.[7] The leaking of information was one of Hoover's most potent weapons and this situation was no different really. Watergate happened because Mark Felt who, let's not forget, was the #1 man in the FBI after Hoover died and Clyde Tolson retired. Felt had moved into the top position. He wasn't merely an FBI executive; he was the head of the organization. Then, Nixon appointed a kind of political appointee to run the FBI, and L. Patrick Gray came in as acting director, but he was a complete incompetent. Gray knew nothing about the Bureau and had no experience with the FBI. He didn't even know many of the people working there. He was basically a figurehead, and his job was to destroy certain documents that Nixon wanted removed from the files. So, Felt ran the FBI and was the guy making all the decisions. So, when I said that the information which brought Watergate about came from Deep Throat, I was absolutely correct. It was the #1 guy who was responsible. That's where it came from; there's no question about it. The only thing that's never really been examined—and it's mentioned in the picture—is solving the riddle of why Nixon didn't erase the tapes that incriminated him.

Why didn't Nixon destroy those tapes?

Well, that's the burning question isn't it? The degaussing of those tapes could have been done in just a few minutes. They were all kept in a room in the Executive Office building and could have been easily erased. Nixon could have claimed executive privilege, preventing any action being taken against him, and that would have been the end of Watergate, but he didn't do that! Again, the question is why? In my movie, we suggested that Hoover had duplicated some of the tapes. The tapes were readily available to the Secret Service and many of those agents in the Secret Service were former FBI Agents. So, Hoover had access to those tapes, and if Nixon believed that the tapes had been duplicated, then he couldn't take the chance of erasing them and then have them turn up again later. That would have made him look even worse and is the secret of why Nixon's tapes were not destroyed. That's never been examined, and for what reason? Well, because nobody wants to pay attention to anything that's in a movie. There are those that take the position of thinking, *How can a movie actually break news and have a journalistic approach that beats the newspapers and television media to the scoop?* But the fact remains that we did. We really were way ahead of everyone. After *The Private Files of J. Edgar Hoover* came out, Senator Frank Church organized a senate subcommittee, which spent $4 million conducting hearings about the FBI. There was not one thing uncovered by those inquiries that had not already been revealed in our film or through our research.

You spoke with William Sullivan, who, at one time, was the third-ranking official at the FBI behind Hoover and Tolson. Was it he who first revealed to you that Mark Felt was Deep Throat?

More or less, yes. Sullivan considered Felt to be an enemy. Sullivan had been removed from the FBI because he was doing too many favors for Nixon. He was vying to be appointed as the new director of the FBI and he really thought that he was going to get the job. In the movie, Sullivan is more or less the character that Jose Ferrer plays. Sullivan looked like he was going to succeed Hoover—if Hoover was to be relieved of his position. When Hoover found out what Sullivan was doing, he fired him, locked his office, and sealed his files. Naturally, Sullivan, who was rather a nice man if you knew him personally, had a lot of scores to settle with Hoover, Felt, and Tolson. That meant he was a more than willing supplier of information to me. I visited Sullivan at his house in Sugar Hill, New Hampshire, and stayed with him for a few days. He let us sleep in his son's room and, during that time, gave us a lot of fascinating stuff. Not too long afterwards, Sullivan was killed behind his house when he was mistaken for a deer and shot by a hunter.

Do you think that Sullivan's death in November 1977 was indeed an accident?

I have no idea. I couldn't speculate on it. It was just unfortunate that he was shot in an apparent freak accident. As I say, Sullivan provided me with some intriguing information. It was Sullivan that informed us about the existence of the Security Index and the Nixon tapes, and he also gave us almost all the backdrop on Watergate. I put a lot of what he shared with us directly in the movie. Sullivan also revealed to me that he was responsible for writing the letter to Martin Luther King suggesting that Dr. King commit suicide. Sullivan actually mailed that letter from Florida to hide its origin. He told me that he wasn't ashamed of having done it, too. He sent the letter down to Florida, and then they mailed it from there. Hoover had an enormous grudge against Martin Luther King and had been secretly recording Dr. King's sexual activities in hotels around the country. Hoover felt that King was what he called "a tomcat"—someone who had a penchant for White women and was not at all like the image he presented of himself as the benevolent clergyman and Noble Prize-winner. Hoover was appalled at what he heard on those recordings, particularly some of the comments that were made by King. This included one that was made during the funeral of President Kennedy in 1963. Hoover had actually recorded King and his friends watching the funeral on television. At the moment Mrs. Kennedy approached the casket and kneeled down to kiss it, Dr. King apparently remarked, "Well, that's the last time she'll go down on him." When Hoover heard that comment, that was *it*! These were highly unfortunate circumstances, and it doesn't mean that Dr. King was not a tremendous political leader and a great spiritual leader of his people. It's just that, like President Kennedy and many other political figures, he had a sexually impulsive side to his nature that he couldn't control.

Despite what we now know of Martin Luther King's private life, did you encounter any resistance from his supporters during or after the film was made? Was anybody displeased with his rather unflattering portrayal?

No, I never heard from anybody. As you know, over the years I've made a lot of movies with Black actors, and I never heard a single comment or complaint from anybody regarding the portrayal of Dr. King in the picture. Not from one person.

Was there anything you discovered about Hoover's life or administration that you decided not to put in the movie for any reason?

No, not really. I certainly never found any evidence of a homosexual aspect to Hoover's life or character. There were a lot of accusations and rumours that had persisted for forty years concerning Hoover and Clyde Tolson, and whether or not they were lovers and had a physical relationship. I saw absolutely no evidence of anything like that.[8] We actually shot at Tolson's apartment, which was located twenty-five minutes away from Hoover's house. We also shot inside and outside of Hoover's home in Rock Creek Park, just outside of Washington. If you had seen Hoover's home, you would realize that there wasn't one gay aspect to the whole premises. When you visit the homes of gay people, they usually have a wonderful sense of style and preparation. From that standpoint alone, there was absolutely nothing in Hoover's house that indicated he was homosexual. Seriously, walking in there was like walking into your grandparents' house. It was full of old, musty stuff and nothing was up-to-date or repaired. I remember Hoover had a Marilyn Monroe calendar hanging over the bar and when I went over to look at one of his leather chairs, I picked up the doyley that was draped on the back and there was a crack in the leather. It was the same with the other furniture; I lifted up one cushion and underneath there was a visible tear. It was obvious to me that this was an old man's house and not a gay old man's house.

What about the lingering rumours of Hoover's transvestism?

The story about Hoover's cross-dressing is another total lie. It was claimed in a book by Anthony Summers, a British writer, whose previous credits included a biography of Marilyn Monroe. Summers had to put something in his book in order to sell it, so he filled it with regurgitated information from other books. There was one section consisting of maybe ten or fifteen pages that contained this woman's ridiculous testimony that she had attended a party at the Waldorf Astoria where Hoover had appeared in ladies clothing. This woman was an alcoholic, who had once been in jail on Riker's Island for committing perjury. Her story is staggering in its insanity and there is absolutely no corroboration of it. To think that J. Edgar Hoover, the most infinitely private and guarded person one could imagine, would appear in a public place in that condition is ludicrous. That woman was a complete liar and a fraud. Any historian who has written a book since that time which has touched on Hoover's life, discounts all of this nonsense. It's a stupid story that makes no sense whatsoever.

And yet this myth continues to endure.

Yeah, and was recently regurgitated again in *J. Edgar*, Clint Eastwood's biopic of Hoover. There is a scene where Hoover, played by Leonardo DiCaprio, puts on his mother's dress and gazes at himself in the mirror. After Summers' book was first published, the cross-dressing story was picked up by comedians and they started doing jokes about Hoover dressing in women's clothes. It became a running gag, an untruth that was being repeated and reasserted until it was accepted as the truth. Even President Clinton made a remark at a correspondence ball, where he mentioned that he still hadn't managed to find someone "to fill J. Edgar Hoover's pumps." I think Clinton soon regretted having made that joke because it wasn't long afterwards when the whole Monica Lewinsky case was exposed. I'm sure that certain elements in the FBI had a lot to do with breaking that story and sending Paula Tripp out to milk Lewinsky for information about her affair with the President. That intelligence could then be made public to humiliate and possibly destroy Clinton. Personally, I believe the reason it was exposed was because Clinton had made that joke about Hoover.

Other than circling around any affirmative statement that Felt was Deep Throat, did you leave anything else out that you feared would result in litigation?

Well, there were attorneys at American International Pictures who actually reviewed the movie and asked me to be careful. They didn't want to get into a court action over this picture. But, again, nobody ever made any attempt to divert or thwart my efforts to make a movie about Hoover, not before, during, or after I made it. However, when we first arrived in Washington DC with the actors, every place we went and asked for permission to shoot at we were denied. After a day or two, I was wondering how we were ever going to make this film. Some people would initially give us permission, only to call back half an hour later and say they had suddenly changed their minds. They had obviously found out it was a movie about Hoover and the FBI, and they did not want to get involved. It looked like we were going to be in a tough place for those first few days, but then we shot at the Mayflower Hotel in Washington. The Mayflower's publicity man got a story in the newspapers about Broderick Crawford and Dan Dailey appearing in this movie that was being shot in Washington. The article and accompanying photographs made a pretty big splash in the papers and the very next day we received a call from The White House. It was from President Gerald Ford and Betty Ford inviting Dailey and Crawford to have lunch at The White House with them and Henry Kissinger. I quickly closed down the production, so the actors could go to The White House and have lunch with the President. It turned out that Mrs. Ford used to be a dancer and she really loved Dan Dailey. Dan had appeared in all these great 20th Century Fox musicals—usually opposite Betty Grable—and was this old-fashioned hoofer. Mrs. Ford really wanted to meet him, and so when Crawford and Daily went to The White

House, I immediately got on the phone and started calling people up. I would say, "We'd like to shoot at the FBI Training Academy at Quantico, but we can't shoot tomorrow because the stars are having lunch at The White House with the President of the United States. Would it be possible for us to shoot there sometime later in the week?" Then they would put me on hold and come back five minutes later and say, "What day would you like to come?" [Laughs] Then I would call the next location and say the same thing, and then call the next location, and the next one, and by the end of the week we had permission to shoot at every place we wanted to go. It was all thanks to Betty Ford.

How important to you was that sense of authenticity in terms of the locations?

I would have still made *The Private Files of J. Edgar Hoover* if those locations were not made available to us, but I'm proud of the fact that we filmed at the actual locations, some of which don't even exist anymore. Seeing places like the Justice Department Building and the Quantico Training Academy gives the film a unique sense of realism, I feel. For example, the empty office that you see at the beginning of the movie was actually Hoover's real office. That is exactly what it looked like when we got there. They had pulled out all the furniture and everything, and it was actually a strange feeling being in that room. When Clint Eastwood made *J. Edgar*, he had to fabricate everything—exteriors and interiors—but we worked in the real environments. Also Broderick Crawford looked just like Hoover, whereas Leonardo DiCaprio had to have extensive makeup on him to approximate Hoover's appearance. As a matter of fact, when we were over at Hoover's house in Rock Creek Park, we shot a scene with Crawford and Daily as Hoover and Tolson. Both men had to step out of the house and say some dialogue on the lawn before walking up the street. As we were shooting, an elderly neighbour came out of his house from across the way to see what all the commotion was about. Now, what this old man saw from a short distance away was two dead men come strolling out of Hoover's house! The shock of suddenly seeing them again brought on a heart attack and this poor guy just collapsed. He was taken away by an ambulance but, thankfully, he survived. In a way, that unfortunate event confirmed to me how well we had cast the movie.

Did you obtain permission to shoot at Hoover's house?

No, we hadn't cleared it with anybody. We just walked up to the door and rang the bell. I remember that Hoover's little maid, Annie,[9] answered and I said, "Hello, we're here to shoot the movie with Broderick Crawford and Dan Dailey playing Mr. Hoover and Mr. Tolson." Her face immediately brightened and she said, "Oh, they're both wonderful! They look just like them." The next thing I knew, we were shooting inside Hoover's home. It was incredible. We shot everything we needed in one day and just got the hell out of there. I'm certain that if we had asked for permission we would never have obtained it. I actually got to go through Hoover's house and look around. I went into his bedroom, inspected his possessions, looked through his closets—and there were no dresses! [Chuckles] What I found fascinating was the fact that Hoover was dead, but all of his clothes were still hanging neatly in the closets. At this point, they hadn't decided what they were going to do with the house. Eventually, half of it was left to The Boys Club of America and the house was sold.

Were you at all tempted to take anything out of the house as a memento?

No, I wouldn't do something like that. I do remember that the house contained all kinds of stuff that had been sent to Hoover by people from all around the country. For example, women had embroidered the FBI seal on blankets. In fact, everything in there seemed like an object that someone had sent him as a gift. It would be some rinky-dink thing that had the FBI emblem or the American flag on it. Hoover had received all kinds of nonsense items and they were sitting all over the house or were hanging on the walls. There really wasn't anything of true value in there. I mean, when Hoover died, he left an estate of maybe $500,000 and that included the house in Rock Creek Park, which was possibly worth $300,000. So, he probably left a couple of hundred thousand in securities and stuff. When you consider that this man sat at the very top of the heap for forty-eight years and had only accumulated a minimal amount of money during a period when taxes were very low in the United States, it's very interesting. All of the authority and fame he had at his disposal; all the books he had written, and everything else he could have acquired in that time, suggests to me that Hoover really was an honest man. To have all of that power for so long and then end up with such a modest estate, it really wasn't much. If anybody wanted to cast aspersions on him for doing anything improper, it really wouldn't apply. This guy did not procure a lot of money and material goods. He just lived for the FBI.

Broderick Crawford had previously played an FBI agent in *Down Three Dark Streets*,[10] but I understand that he had actually met Hoover at one time.

Yes, Crawford did mention to me that he'd once met Hoover, many years before. I have no idea under what circumstances they met. I do know that when Hoover went to New York, he would always frequent places like The Stork Club, and those were venues where actors often congregated. I'm sure that somewhere along the line, he and Crawford did cross paths. Actually, Lloyd Nolan had also met Hoover because Lloyd had done all of those FBI movies. Lloyd told me that Hoover was very pleasant and he'd enjoyed meeting him. Other than that, there was no special recollection.

Did Crawford research his role?

I don't think so. Before we started shooting, I showed Crawford all the photographs I had of Hoover and I talked to him extensively about the character. The best piece of direction I gave Crawford was to tell him that Hoover was so all-encompassing and powerful at the FBI he never really had to raise his voice. I knew that Crawford had a very melodious voice, but he very often ruined it by shouting and bellowing. I had seen previous pictures he'd made where he was almost constantly yelling. I thought he'd repeatedly done himself a great disservice by getting too excited, too loud, and too boisterous in his roles. Crawford had this beautiful speaking voice when he didn't yell and I wanted him to keep that voice calm and soft to illustrate how in control Hoover was. I only had to tell Crawford this once and never had to repeat myself. He immediately got what I was saying. Then, towards the end of the shoot, I said, "Broderick, remember when I told you never to holler? Well, in this next scene, you can let it all out!" That was actually one of the last scenes in the picture where Hoover yells at his staff to see if they can copy the Nixon tapes. It's the only time that Crawford really lets go and I felt that contained approach worked much better.

What were some of the other difficulties you encountered making the film?

Well, we were about ten days from starting the picture when I received a phone call informing me that Dan Dailey's medical exam had been a negative. It was apparently discovered that Dan had a bad heart and it would not be possible to insure him. We were applying for cast insurance and I had a lot of older actors in the picture like Dan, Broderick, and Jose Ferrer. So, I had a big decision to make. I should have replaced Dan, but I couldn't tell him that he'd failed the medical exam. I just didn't have the heart to say he was not insurable. I was contemplating what I should do, but then I told the insurance company to cancel the application for the insurance. If they would not insure Dan Dailey, I wasn't going to insure any other member of the cast either. I decided to keep my premium and take my chances. I think it was unheard of to make a picture without cast insurance, particularly with so many elderly actors. But this was my production and I was able to do what I wanted. I never did tell Dan that he had failed the medical exam and, as it turned out, I was very lucky that I decided to keep him. If it wasn't for Dan, we would never have received an invitation to The White House and, as a direct result of that, would never have secured access to all of those locations we shot at. It turned out that my act of generosity paid off spectacularly and it really became a blessing for us.

Rip Torn plays Agent Dwight Webb, a fictional character you devised to be Hoover's adversary. How did you find working with Torn?

I've always thought that Rip was a terrific actor. I still do, but he did have a reputation at the time for being difficult. I remember he came to the Jefferson Hotel in Washington DC, where we were all staying, and immediately picked a fight with me. I mean, we hadn't even shot anything at this point and he was already complaining angrily about something. He was behaving in such a volatile manner, I said, "Rip, why don't you simply go back home? Just vacate your room, go back to New York, and I'll replace you with somebody else." He then growled, "Well, maybe you'd like to go outside in the street and settle this?" I said, "Okay, if that's what you want to do, let's go outside." So, we both proceeded to walk through the lobby doors of the hotel and just before we got outside, he stopped and said, "Look, Larry, I just want to be in the movie. I just want to do my part." I said, "Rip, if that's what you want to do, you can stay. Let's just work together on this." After that incident, he was extremely co-operative. In fact, at the end of the production when we were running out of money, Rip came to me and said, "Larry, you don't have to pay me. All you have to do is give me my car-fare and I'll come to work. I'll finish the picture for free." That was incredibly nice of him. I won't forget that.

Was it all smooth sailing after that?

The only problem that occurred with Rip after that concerned his hairpiece. Actually, it was two hairpieces that he would stick to the sides of his forehead. When we would arrive at various locations, Rip would sometimes hide his hairpieces. He refused to let them fall into the hands of the makeup people because he didn't entrust them to anyone. Rip would wander off and conceal the hairpieces somewhere, but unfortunately, he would then forget exactly where he had hidden them. So, when it came time for us to leave the location, we would have to go out and search for Rip's hair. This became something of a running joke. On one occasion, Rip left his hair behind at the Pimlico Race Course where we had been shooting. We had to send the limousine driver back to find his hair and bring it to him. Another time, Rip claimed that back in New York somebody had broken into his car and stolen his toupee. I said, "Rip, why would somebody break into your car and steal your hair? It just doesn't make any sense!" He said, "Well, I guess we can't shoot today." I said, "Oh yes, we can. [Cohen shouts loudly] Somebody get me a baseball cap!" We then found one and Rip played the entire scene with a baseball cap on. Actually, that scene didn't end up in the finished film anyway, but we sure did make him work that day! [Laughs] I don't know why Rip would tell me a story that his hair had been stolen, but there was no doubt about it, he was obsessed—bordering on psychotic—when it came to his hairpieces. He was always afraid that somebody was going to steal them and, eventually, somebody did break into his car and take his hairpieces, which of course confirmed his worst fears. So, maybe there was some truth to this madness after all.

Despite his obsession, were you happy with Torn's performance in the film?

Oh, absolutely. He always does good work. You know, you just had to deal with Rip. Every morning I usually had to go to his apartment in New York and pick him up in my limo. I'd bring him to work and then take him back home at night. Rip lived in downtown Manhattan and the doorbell had a sign on it that read 'Torn Page.' This was because Rip's wife was the actress Geraldine Page and that's actually what it said on the doorbell—'Torn Page!' [Chuckles] But we both got along fine. Years later, I ran into Rip and his son, Tony, at a restaurant when I was shooting *Wicked Stepmother* outside on the street. Rip told me that Tony wanted to be an actor and he asked if I knew any way of getting his boy into the Screen Actors Guild. So, I sat down and immediately started writing a little scene for Rip's son to play, then said, "Okay, let's go outside." We went out onto the street and quickly shot the scene I'd written, which featured Tony playing the street drifter. Tony also gets to say a little line and that got him his SAG card. I remember Rip said, "Larry, you are the only person in Hollywood who would do something like that." Frankly, I had to agree to him. A few years after this, I ran into Rip again in the theater district in Manhattan. Now, he'd always been pestering me to obtain his FBI file for him. I would keep saying, "Rip, I have no means of getting you your FBI file." He said, "C'mon, Larry, I know you are in with the FBI. You would never have been able to make *The Private Files of J. Edgar Hoover* if you weren't connected with the Bureau. You can get me my FBI file, I know you can." I said, "Look, I really can't help you." I ran into him again a few years later and, by this time, I knew that the Freedom of Information Act had meant a lot of people now had access to their files. So, I asked Rip if he'd succeeded in obtaining his file. He then proceeded to tell me that he had, but he was very disappointed that there was nothing in it. I think Rip really believed that he was a major subversive. Apparently, the FBI didn't agree.

Another intriguing performer you hired was the criminally underrated Michael Parks, who plays Robert F. Kennedy. I've always enjoyed his work.

Yeah, he's a splendid actor. I really enjoyed working with Michael. I got him on Rip's recommendation, actually. At first I was a little reluctant to cast him because I'd heard he was a lot of trouble. Despite that, I eventually hired Michael for the role of Bobby Kennedy and he came down to Washington and was no trouble at all. He was just fine and worked very hard. I've always felt that Michael should have been a big star in movies. He certainly had that potential. I know that at one time people thought he was going to be another James Dean. Unfortunately, Michael just didn't get the right movies at the beginning of his career. He had played Adam in John Huston's religious epic, *The Bible*, but it just didn't quite happen for him. He ended up having a TV series called *Then Came Bronson*[11] and that was successful for a few years. But then I guess his career just drifted off. Now he works for Quentin Tarantino quite often and has developed into an excellent character actor. Michael is sometimes so good he is unrecognisable in the parts he plays. You don't even know that it's him. In fact, I think his Bobby Kennedy is the best that has ever been done in movies. There have been a lot of depictions of RFK, but nobody has ever come close to Michael's portrayal. It's very easy to veer into an impersonation when you do that kind of iconic role, but Michael seemed to capture the reality and humanity of Kennedy. The actor who played Bobby in Clint Eastwood's movie was just completely wrong for the part; he was terrible! That scene with Bobby in *J. Edgar* was taken almost exactly from my movie—nearly word for word—but it was very badly played. I couldn't imagine how and why they spent so much money and made such a weak picture.

How did you navigate the considerable problem of making an ambitious period film on such a low-budget?

Firstly, I got the idea to look up some of the vintage car clubs and discovered that there was one in nearby Maryland, right across the way from Washington DC. This club had quite an extensive collection of vintage cars of all makes and models, so I called them up on the phone. I asked them, "How would you people like to be in a movie?" They got very excited about this and said, "Yeah, that'd be great! Hey, we have cars from the 1930s and the 1940s. Not only that, we also have all the authentic costumes of the periods. We usually dress our families up in these costumes and take them to various fairs and events. In fact, we can not only bring the cars in for you, we can bring people dressed in period costumes—all for free!" Oh, that was just what I was waiting to hear, because "free" really was the key word on this picture. True to their word, they all came into Washington on a specific day. It was a parade of about thirty or forty antique cars and it really was something to see. But the question then quickly became: "How are we going to run these vehicles up and down Pennsylvania Avenue in front of The White House and up to the capital? Not only that, but how can we prevent the period cars from being mixed in with all the contemporary cars on the street?" The only course of action available to us was to close off Pennsylvania Avenue, the main thoroughfare from the White House to the capital. Fortunately for us, they have a lot of parades in Washington. In the event of any parade or the passing-by of some dignitary, they have these big wooden barricades that are piled up on the side-street or in an alley. Of course, the idea of closing off Pennsylvania Avenue to allow all these cars to drive through there seemed incredibly risky. Several of the crew were very nervous about attempting such a crazy thing. I simply kept on smiling reassuredly at them, saying, "Well, let's just do it and see what happens." So, the crew went ahead and barricaded the street and we did indeed close off Pennsylvania Avenue. Then we quickly brought the vintage cars in and shot the scenes. As we were doing this, somebody came to me and said, "You do know there are parking meters in the street, right? They didn't have any parking meters back in those days." I said, "Yes, that's true. We have got to get rid of them." This person asked, "How are we going to do that?" I said, "It's very simple: take two people and stand them in front of those parking meters. Then take three people and stand them in front of those parking meters. We'll have clusters of people on the street and they will all be blocking the parking meters from view and nobody will see them." And that's exactly what we did. We shot all our scenes and got away with it. Actually, I do recall that as we were doing all this, the Washington DC police force came driving by. They saw us standing there with the entire street shut down and all these vintage cars crowding the area, and the cops just waved out the windows at us! [Laughs] We then politely waved back and they just kept on going. It was incredible. Nobody thought for a minute that anyone would have the nerve to do such an outrageous thing without a permit. To this day, I have no idea how we managed to get away with it.

I understand that your unwavering pursuit of authenticity also led you to The Justice Department Building.

That's right. We later went over to The Justice Department Building to shoot another sequence that was meant to be set during the 1940s. We placed the vintage cars on the street, but then I noticed that the building didn't look exactly right. There were all these modern air conditioners located prominently in the windows. Now, I should also mention that we were shooting in the middle of a very hot summer. Despite this, I said to one of my crew, "Go into the Justice Department Building and tell everybody that they have to take the air conditioners out of the windows." This guy just stared at me and said, "What are you talking about? It's ninety-eight degrees!" I said, "Look, just tell them we are making a movie and that everybody has to remove the air conditioners out of their windows." He said, "Larry, you're crazy! This is the Justice Department Building! Nobody is going to do that for you—especially in this heat!" I said, "Just go ahead and do it." So, this guy reluctantly ventured inside and, I swear to god, the next thing I see all the air conditioners are being pulled out of the windows. I thought, *This is ridiculous! I just tell people to do something and they do it!* I suddenly felt this tremendous sense of power and authority, probably the same feeling Hoover himself had when he was in charge of the FBI. I suddenly thought, *Hey, this is amazing! I can do anything I want here!* Sometimes, as a director, you just can't seem to lose and that was certainly one of those intoxicating moments.

It's my understanding that there are several people featured in the film who were real-life acquaintances of Hoover.

That's correct. The barber in the barber scene is the actual person who always cut Hoover's hair. Also the waiter in the Mayflower Hotel, the Black gentleman who Hoover called "Castro" because he may have been Cuban, was the actual waiter who waited on him every day at the restaurant. Hoover always ate lunch at the Mayflower. He always had the same table and almost always ordered the same meal. Every day the waiter would come to him and say, "I've got a surprise for you today, Mr. Hoover." Then the waiter would proceed to bring in the exact same meal that he brought Hoover every other day.

A disturbing moment occurs when Hoover candidly reveals to a horrified waiter who is attending to him, private details of the man's family life. Was that in any way true?

Oh yes, that's all true. Hoover extensively researched everybody who had anything to do with him. I'm sure he checked on the barber, the waiter, and any other person who had regular contact with him. I believe that the incident with the waiter is supposed to have occurred at The Stork Club. Of course, it's not been verified that Hoover actually recited Rudyard Kipling's poetry to the waiter. I made that bit up, but that was indeed his favorite poem.[12] For that reason, I put it into the scene.

There are other moments in the film where it is tempting to wonder if they actually happened or you were merely adopting a dramatic license. For instance, there is the amusing scene where RFK drops into Hoover's office and finds the FBI director asleep on his couch.

That incident was documented. That supposedly really happened. Now, of course, I don't know if the dialogue they say in that scene is the exact words that were spoken, or if indeed anything at all was actually said during that moment, but it's true that Bobby Kennedy did drop in at Hoover's office and caught him taking a nap.

What about Hoover's "Negro fly-swatter"? Was there really such a person charged with this duty?

Yes, that's also documented. The moment when the man takes a swipe at Hoover's shoulder with the fly-swatter is quoted as having actually occurred. Another scene that's also supposedly based on a real life incident is when Hoover encounters the young FBI agent carrying a copy of *Playboy*. Hoover gives him a copy of his book, *Masters of Deceit*, and transfers him to Knoxville, Tennessee, to "improve his mind."

A moment that is unnervingly prescient is when the armed hijacker says to Dwight Webb: "When we get this plane up in the air I'm gonna have him crash this mother into The White House."

Or the Pentagon, which of course, they did do many years later. Again, that scene was based on actual fact. There was a guy who once hijacked a plane in the Washington Airport and planned to crash it into one of the executive buildings. So, it wasn't actually an unheard of thing—somebody attempting to use a plane as a destructive weapon like that. Apparently, it never dawned on too many people that such a terrible thing could become a reality; that is until the events of 9/11 occurred.

Another contentious moment is when Hoover is seen getting his vicarious thrills from listening to the tape of some political figure having illicit sex with a woman.

Well, the tape features a minor political figure, a member of some radical group; a student for democratic action, something like that. Interestingly, that same scene was done by Clint Eastwood in his film; he also had Hoover listening to a tape of somebody having sex. I thought our scene was much better.

What was the length of your first initial cut of the film?

It was maybe ten or twelve minutes longer than what you finally saw. We lost just a couple of additional scenes with Jose Ferrer, and also a scene at the beginning that featured Hoover's mother. That was about it, I think. I cut them out because Miklós Rózsa made some suggestions about trimming down the length of the picture. I listened to him because, after all, this man had won a couple of Academy Awards and had scored some of the greatest movies ever made for directors like Billy Wilder, William Wyler and others. Rózsa's opinions were always worth listening to.

You arranged a formal screening of *The Private Files of J. Edgar Hoover* for a largely political audience at the Kennedy Center. How was it received?

Actually, I did not attend that screening. It was scheduled for the day before Christmas Day, and I decided not to leave my family and go to Washington DC. It was snowing and you could get into the city, but there was the distinct possibility that you wouldn't be able to get back out again. I wasn't going to miss celebrating Christmas with my loved ones back in California, even if it was for my movie. So, I didn't go and, as it turned out, that was just as well. It was a real mistake to screen the picture at the Kennedy Center. First of all, if you are going to do anything in Washington DC, you have to adopt a particular stance or point of view. Basically, you either have to be a Republican or a Democrat. You can't make a politically neutral film like *The Private Files of J. Edgar Hoover* in which both the Republicans and the Democrats come off badly. I mean, Nixon doesn't come off well in the movie, and neither do the Kennedys or Lyndon Johnson. Even President Roosevelt doesn't come out smelling of roses. What I found fascinating was those people who could tolerate criticism of other politicians, couldn't stand any kind of criticism whatsoever of Roosevelt. In fact, Arthur M. Schlesinger, Jr., the celebrated historian and intellectual, praised Broderick Crawford's performance but deplored our unflattering treatment of Roosevelt. However, the fact remains that everything we put in there was factual. Unfortunately, it was not the kind of stuff that certain people liked or wanted to see. The Republicans didn't appreciate what they saw and neither did the Democrats, which meant that we had no advocates on our side. Everybody was unanimously pissed off at the movie. So, previewing the picture in a political city like Washington DC was not a smart idea because there are too many factions. Also, as I told you, *The Washington Post* was really out to get us, too, because we were too close to the facts about Watergate.

I noticed that you've listed some of the film's positive reviews on your website.

Well, *The Private Files of J. Edgar Hoover* was well-received by critics—particularly those in England. Sadly, in America, it was an entirely different story, but if you had read the English reviews you would have thought this picture was *Lawrence of Arabia*! I mean, the notices were just incredible. All the big critics loved it. Some of them said that the movie should be seen more than once and that it was an astonishing piece of work. It played at The Screen on the Hill for seven or eight weeks and had a very nice engagement. Then, the BBC played the picture twice, and so we did remarkably well in England. A lot of people saw it, and I attended a screening at the London Film Festival. Actually, I was dismayed to discover that they were not going to run *The Private Files of J. Edgar Hoover* at the National Film Theatre. I was informed that they were going to run the picture at ten o'clock on a Sunday morning at the Odeon in Leicester Square. I didn't realize at the time that the Odeon was the biggest theater in London, but the idea of showing the movie on a Sunday morning was very disappointing. I mean, British people are church-goers and I doubted very much that anybody would be in attendance at that particular time on that particular day. But when I arrived at the Odeon, I saw that there were lines of people stretching right around the block. It was like Radio City Music Hall: the theater was completely full. In fact, there was no place for me to sit! [Laughs] I had to go sit up on the balcony in the last row. I can remember looking down at the audience and marvelling at the number of people that had turned out. The picture then began and the reaction to it was fabulous. After it finished, I went up on stage and the applause was deafening. That led to the movie playing at The Screen on the Hill and I was amazed at the response it got there, too.

Did any notable British filmmakers attend any of these screenings?

Well, here's an interesting thing that happened: when I arrived at the film festival, they had organized a luncheon at the London Film Theater. I was invited to attend, and when I arrived there, somebody led me to my table. I was then introduced to my dinner companion, the person with whom I'd be sitting, and I was astonished to discover it was none other than Elia Kazan! [Gasps] Oh, you could have floored me! As soon as I saw him, my legs were shaking. I mean, this was the greatest director of them all! I got to sit beside him and we spent the whole afternoon talking about movies. But what movie does Kazan want to talk about? He doesn't want to talk about *On the Waterfront* or *A Streetcar Named Desire* or *Gentleman's Agreement* or *East of Eden*; he wants to talk about *The Private Files of J. Edgar Hoover*! I wanted to ask him questions about his career—questions I'd always wanted answers to—about the great movies he made, about working with Brando, all that stuff. But all Kazan wanted to discuss was my film. He wanted to know how I made the picture, how I did this, how I got away with that, how I even had the nerve to make it. Of course, Kazan had been blacklisted himself and ended up testifying before the House of Un-American Activities Committee. Although he had suffered a terrible period with the blacklist, eventually he did testify against people and did name names. This was very controversial, as a number of people suffered terribly during this time, but Kazan was able to have a tremendous career afterwards. As Kazan said in his book, he had the biggest period in his career after he testified. In later years, Kazan was still regarded as a villain by some people. In fact, when the Academy wanted to give him an honorary Oscar, there was a lot of talk in Hollywood that he wasn't deserving of such an award as he had testified several decades earlier at a time when careers and reputations had been destroyed. He did eventually get the honorary Oscar and it did prove to be divisive in Hollywood.[13] Anyway, Kazan had a lot to talk to me about regarding the blacklist and we had a wonderful lunch together. It's an afternoon that I'll certainly never forget. I just remember Kazan repeatedly expressing his amazement to me that I'd had the balls to make a movie about J. Edgar Hoover.

Why do you think *The Private Files of J. Edgar Hoover* failed to generate as much of an enthusiastic response in the United States as it did in England?

The studio did not want to spend a lot of money advertising the picture because they didn't know if it was going to do any business. They thought *The Private Files of J. Edgar Hoover* was too political and too historical, so they didn't play it much. Even after we'd finished the film, I remember Sam Arkoff saying to me, "You know, this really isn't our kind of picture over at American International. If you want to try and sell it to somebody else, you can. We'll give you the picture back and you can sell it at another studio." So, I showed the film to Warner Bros. and they almost bought it, but in the end they didn't. I next showed it to MGM, and they were very enthusiastic. The chairman of the board at MGM came in, looked at it, and when the screening was over, said, "Kid, we're not in the movie business; we're in the gambling business. We have all these casinos in Las Vegas and we rely heavily upon the FBI. If you think we are going to piss the Bureau off with this movie, you've got another thing coming. God bless you, son. You made a good movie, but we're not going to distribute this picture." Universal also felt the same way. At the time, they were in the process of negotiating to buy some national parks from the United States Government and they did not want to get mixed up with anything that could possibly irritate them or the FBI. It seemed to me that a lot of people liked my movie, but nobody wanted to stick their neck out for it. AIP had put up the money, so they got the picture back. They then sold it to a tax shelter and that put the film into profits right away. So, I came out of it with a profit before the movie had even played. Unfortunately, when the picture opened, they didn't play it that widely. Of course, they didn't have to because they'd already made their money back. That's the problem with these things—once the company make their money back and are in profits, they don't feel the need to make an effort to sell your picture. They don't want to take a chance because the advertising costs are so high. Believe it or not, I eventually made about $300,000 profit on *The Private Files of J. Edgar Hoover,* even though it hardly played in America.

What can you tell me about Broderick Crawford's appearance as guest host of *Saturday Night Live* on March 19th, 1977?

I actually helped to organize that. After we went to New York and did a public relations announcement for the movie at the Waldorf Astoria, we took a room there and had cocktails and invited the press. Broderick arrived in an old vintage car, and there was a photo op, and then he made a little speech. We got a number of articles, including a big half-page in the Sunday *New York Times*, and the people at *Saturday Night Live* saw it. They called up and asked if Crawford would appear as the guest host on the show. Crawford agreed, and went to do it, and I went back to California. Shortly afterwards, I received this desperate phone call from the *Saturday Night Live* people, saying, "Hey, you got us into this, now you've got to help us! We can't control Crawford! He keeps disappearing all the time and ending up in the local bar. He's been drinking a lot and we have to constantly keep an eye on him. We've got John Belushi staying with him for an hour, then Dan Aykroyd staying with him for an hour, then

Bill Murray, then Gilda Radner. We assign different people to be with him all the time. We dare not leave him alone, but somehow he always manages to slip away! Can you come here and get him under control?" [Laughs] So, I arrived in New York and went to Rockefeller Plaza. I hung out with Crawford and kept an eye on him, but, as always, he did his usual thing and disappeared frequently. I said to the people at *Saturday Night Live*: "Look, Broderick will drink and carouse around all week long, but when the show goes out live on Saturday night, he'll be absolutely perfect. Believe me when I say he's always totally focused and professional. He'll know every line of dialogue and will remember every piece of blocking, but you people will all be so nervous you'll be falling apart. You'll blow all of your lines worrying about him, but he'll be just fine." And you know what? That's exactly what happened! When the show went out live on the air, Crawford was fine but everybody else was tense and nervous. In fact, at one point, they were doing a take-off on Crawford's famous TV series from the 1950s, *Highway Patrol*, and John Belushi inadvertently dropped his gun on the floor.[14] Crawford suddenly yelled, "Pick it up!" Belushi then ran over, picked up the gun and Crawford covered for him.

Did you get involved with the episode in any way?

Oh, yeah. In fact, I sat around and actually wrote endings for all the sketches. *Saturday Night Live* had some funny sketches, but they usually didn't have an ending and could meander. The writers didn't always find a way to get out of them. So, I sat down and wrote all the endings for the different sketches and gave them to the associate producer, Jean Doumanian. Jean informed the writing staff that she had written the endings. She told me that if she had indicated that I had written them, the staff would have been very upset. The writers were very protective of their work and their noses would be put out of joint if they knew I'd written the stuff. They actually did use most of my material on the show and it was great being around comics like Belushi, Aykroyd, and Murray. I do remember that the last sketch of the show featured Crawford playing Hoover and Aykroyd playing Nixon. Hoover is in his bedroom at night when Nixon breaks in. At the very end of the sketch, I put in a moment where Hoover climbs into bed and pulls a teddy bear out from under the covers. He then wraps his arms around it, closes his eyes and says, "Goodnight, Clyde."

Wasn't there a danger that such a joke was endorsing one of the myths about Hoover that you profess to reject?

Well, yeah, I guess so, but if you want to get a laugh sometimes you have to descend into the depths of bad taste!

On October 29th, 2011, you published a memo on your website, which criticized Clint Eastwood's *J. Edgar* for its perceived inaccuracies. Having reiterated some of them here, it's safe to assume you have no regrets about doing that.

None whatsoever. *J. Edgar* was just an awful movie, a terrible smear on a man's life and reputation. The guy who wrote that screenplay was a perfectly nice gay fellow[15], but he just wrote the gay man's version of J. Edgar Hoover, that's all. He had no real information at his disposal, so he just made it all up. None of that stuff ever happened. None of those scenes ever occurred in reality. Everything in that picture is his fantasy. If you want to see a gay man's fantasy of Hoover, then *J. Edgar* is the movie for you because that's exactly what it is. I actually tried to contact Clint Eastwood, whom I'd worked with years before on a project called *The Hostiles*. For two years in a row, Clint had optioned that script, which we hoped to do with John Wayne. Clint and I had worked together so nicely I thought he would be open to discussing his Hoover project with me. I talked to his producer, but Clint would never agree to meet with me. I did get a chance to read the first draft of the *J. Edgar* script and sent him some notes on it. They told me they were going to make some adjustments, but naturally, they didn't. They just shot the first draft—shot everything that I'd told them was all wrong. Of course, I had no right to tell them what to do and I wasn't trying to. I was simply trying to offer them some advice and additional information that they might have been able to incorporate into the picture. This was mostly regarding the revelations that had come out over the years, particularly the Deep Throat thing and the copying of the Nixon tapes. I thought that would have made some interesting news for Clint's movie, but instead nobody would talk to me about it.

Would you agree that if we labored to identify the glaring factual errors in most Hollywood biographies, it would be a long and illustrious list?

I don't think I have the years left me to undertake such a task! Hollywood has a wonderful way of establishing falsehoods and inaccuracies about history. These falsehoods are continually perpetuated and then become accepted as truths by some members of the audience who don't know any different. Quentin Tarantino and I were once having drinks together and discussing his movie, *Inglorious Basterds*. I said, "Quentin, fifteen years from now, kids are going to be telling each other that Adolf Hitler was killed in a movie theater in Paris by a bunch of Jewish guerrillas." Seriously, that is what people are going to believe because they know so little about history. The kids of today have no background knowledge at all about the events that have shaped this nation and other nations. In fact, they don't want to know anything about history. Some of them have never heard of the Korean War and—if we're lucky—they may have heard about World War II. I've met kids who don't know anything about Vietnam either, or any other historical subject of value and importance. I'm sure that a great deal of them believed everything they saw in *Inglorious Basterds* and that Hitler did indeed meet his end in those crazy circumstances.

You've listed your problems with *J. Edgar*, but what do you think are the deficiencies in your movie?

Well, I wish we'd had a little more money. I wish we'd been able to have a little more production, but what we sacrificed in terms of production values we more than compensated for with integrity and accuracy. We told the story as it really was—the true story. In fact, I consider *The Private Files of J. Edgar Hoover* to be the definitive movie about Hoover. It is utterly superfluous that Clint Eastwood's picture probably cost twenty-five times as much. The fact of the matter is we made the best picture about Hoover and Broderick Crawford is the best on-screen Hoover there's ever been, and probably ever will be. I'm extremely proud of the film and of the reviews we got over in England. I only wish we had gotten that same kind of positive attention in America. I mean, some American critics said it was the best FBI movie ever made, and Robin Wood also stated that it was the best political film ever made. Again, not a lot of people saw *The Private Files of J. Edgar Hoover*, and it doesn't play on television or cable that much. However, it is out on DVD, and pictures do have a way of being rediscovered by audiences. I thought that when Clint's movie came out, it would renew interest in my film, but *J. Edgar* was so badly received critically, and did so poorly at the box office, it didn't do anything for my picture either.

Hoover's career stretches over so many defining passages of twentieth century America from Prohibition, World War II, McCarthyism and anti-communism, to the Kennedy assassinations, the Civil Rights movement, and Vietnam. But what is the current attitude towards Hoover in America? How is he seen?

I don't think he is seen at all. There isn't much talk about Hoover anymore. He only seems to reside in the past as some relic. Back in the 1940s, '50s and 60s, even well into the 1970s, Hoover symbolised something significant for the American people. If you mentioned his name or showed someone a photograph of him, everybody knew exactly who he was: the unmistakable bulldog face, the tough grizzled manner, the crisp suit, all that stuff. Today, the whole FBI has been so diluted that there is no personal image to the Bureau anymore. Hoover *was* the image of the FBI, but nowadays you don't even know who the FBI director is and you couldn't care less. There's none of that singular personification of the Bureau in any one individual. The FBI is as faceless as most organizations are. So, I don't believe that anyone is currently thinking about Hoover. I don't think anybody went to see Clint's picture, because nobody was interested anymore, certainly not in their tired depiction of him as some sort of sissy. That portrayal bears no resemblance to Hoover's true character.

Do you think you judged Hoover evenly in your film?

I think we gave him a fair shake. You know, in our everyday dealings with people, we rarely encounter somebody who is either totally good or totally evil. I'm sure there are such individuals in the world, but they are rare. Most human beings are a mixture of both good and bad. Sometimes we perform generous deeds and sometimes we commit hideous acts. The idea with *The Private Files of J. Edgar Hoover* was to tell both sides of the story and try to be completely objective about everything, as much as you can be objective when you're making a movie. I wanted to explore that conflict and show Hoover's good side and bad side. During his administration, Hoover was a tough guy who inflicted a considerable amount of pain and damage on a lot of people, but he also did a lot of good, too. He succeeded in keeping the FBI free from the politicians and took pains to remove the Bureau from any political influence or affiliation. It was important to him that neither the Democrats nor the Republicans assumed control of his organization. So, he was tough on the Right and the Left. He was tough on the Civil Rights Movement and the Ku Klux Klan. He was tough on all the various elements and factions that he considered threats to America. Hoover may have been misguided—and perhaps even callous—in many cases, but his intentions were mostly to protect his country. That's what I strived to show in the movie.

Over the course of researching, writing, and shooting *The Private Files of J. Edgar Hoover*, did your feelings towards the man change?

This is my own feeling on Hoover: what it all boiled down to in the end was that he was merely a frail old man trying to hold onto his job. You can easily get under the skin of a person like that and understand their fears and desires. I think a character like that ultimately becomes a tragic figure. In fact, anybody who starts a company and builds it up into a great success can relate to a situation where they eventually have to deal with the stockholders or new people coming in, trying to take over and kick you out. That scenario has happened to so many people in various fields and organizations. It happened in the movie business to moguls like Louis B. Meyer at MGM and Darryl F. Zanuck at 20th Century Fox. Almost everybody who founded these movie companies in Hollywood ended up getting deposed and removed from the very studio they had more or less given birth to. It was the same story with Hoover as old age and poor health eventually claimed him, as it does each of us. When you consider that this man single-handedly built the FBI up into this powerful and influential force—from *nothing*—it really is quite some achievement. But then, finally, Hoover had to deal with the knowledge that he'd reached the end of the road. He knew that certain people were trying to take it all away from him and that his power was dwindling. When you consider all that, it becomes very easy to sympathise with him and his vulnerabilities and fallibilities. This is what makes us human and it's what made Hoover human, too. But here's one final irony: no newspaper writer has ever dealt with the fact that Nixon could never have been removed from office if his Vice-President, Spiro Agnew, had not been removed first. Nobody wanted Agnew to become President of the United States, but the information that brought Agnew down came from Mark Felt. This means that Felt, Hoover's surrogate, actually ensured the fall of the Nixon administration. So, even after his death and with others now running his organisation, the FBI was still carrying out Hoover's orders as he lay in his grave.

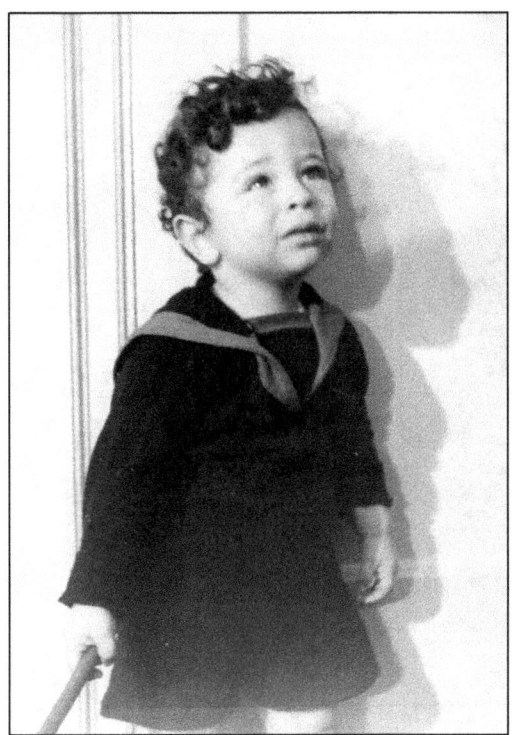

Little Lawrence G. Cohen as a toddler in Washington Hiegths. Photo courtesy of Larry Cohen.

Cohen poses pensively on his trike. Photo courtesy of Larry Cohen.

A teenage Cohen emcees a variety show at City College in 1957 during his stint as a standup comedian. Photo courtesy of Larry Cohen.

Cohen out on the town with his first wife, Janelle Webb Cohen, mother of his daughters Jill and Melissa. Photo courtesy of Larry Cohen.

Photo Section I • 209

Cohen makes two new friends on the set of "False Face," his classic episode of *Way Out*. Photo courtesy of Larry Cohen.

A twenty-year-old Cohen confers with Henny Youngman during the shooting of "The Golden Thirty." Photo courtesy of Larry Cohen.

Cohen chats with Sydney Pollack on the set of *The Defenders* episode "Kill or Be Killed" in 1963. Photo courtesy of Larry Cohen.

Cohen on location in Utah with Chuck Connors during the making of *Branded*. Photo courtesy of Larry Cohen.

Cohen discusses his teleplay with actor Robert Goulet and producer Buck Houghton on the set of *Blue Light*. Photo courtesy of Larry Cohen.

Yaphet Kotto, Joyce Van Patten and Andrew Duggan enact the class struggle in Beverly Hills in Cohen's controversial debut film *Bone*. Photo courtesy of Larry Cohen.

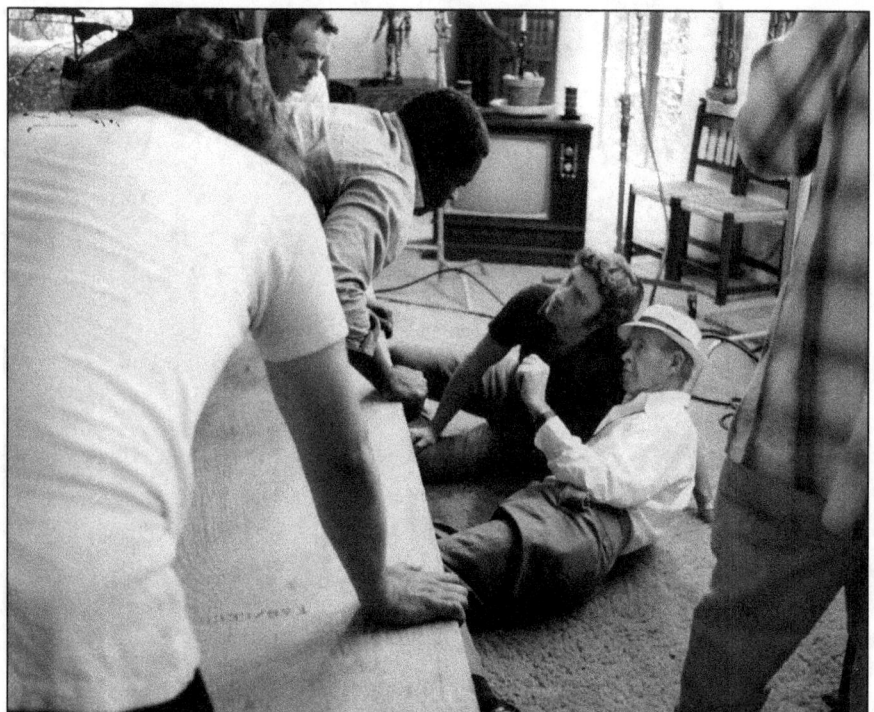

The next Mike Nichols? Cinematographer George Folsey, Sr. discusses camera angles with Cohen during the shooting of *Bone*. Photo courtesy of Larry Cohen.

Dangerous dudes with 'tude: Cohen and the gangsters of *Black Caesar*.
Photo courtesy of Larry Cohen.

Photo Section I • 213

Cohen directs the poolside massacre sequence in *Black Caesar*, lensed at his own home in Coldwater Canyon. Photo courtesy of Larry Cohen.

Cohen, shortly after demonstrating to Fred Williamson the proper way to execute a stunt in a coal yard during the shooting of *Hell up in Harlem*. Photo courtesy of Larry Cohen.

Cohen lines up a shot on location for *It's Alive*. Photo courtesy of Larry Cohen.

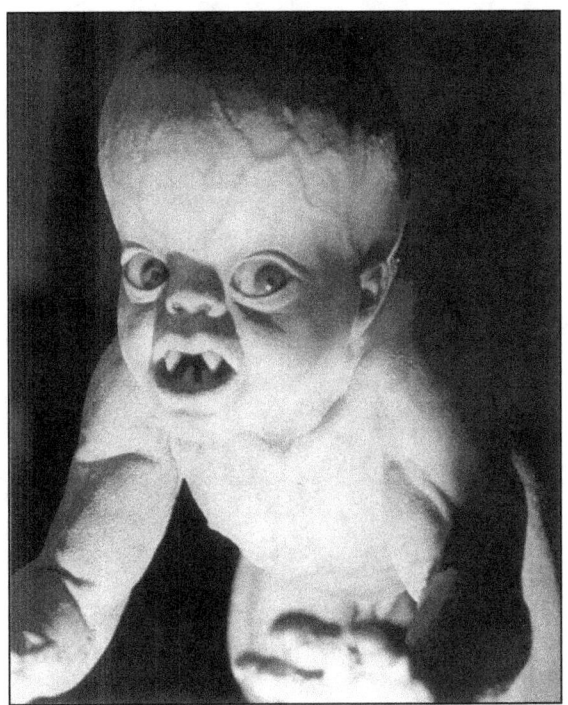

"Pure id without any restrictions": The Davis Monster from *It's Alive*. Photo courtesy of Larry Cohen.

Cohen and actress Sharon Farrell spend some quality time with The Davis Monster on the set of *It's Alive*. Photo courtesy of Larry Cohen.

Bernard Herrmann talks with Cohen during the scoring sessions for *It's Alive* at Cripplegate Church, London. Photo courtesy of Larry Cohen.

Janelle Webb Cohen, Larry Cohen, and Bernard Herrmann share a joke despite the biting cold at Cripplegate Church. Photo courtesy of Larry Cohen.

God and monster: Richard Lynch as the messianic hermaphrodite alien of *God Told Me To*. Photo courtesy of Larry Cohen.

Deborah Raffin, Tony Lo Bianco, and Cohen during the shooting of *God Told Me To*. Photo courtesy of Larry Cohen.

Cohen directs Sylvia Sydney on the set of God Told Me To, as cinematographer Paul Glickman looks on. Photo courtesy of Larry Cohen.

"The best Hoover there's ever been in movies": The imperious Broderick Crawford as the legendary FBI Director in The Private Files of J. Edgar Hoover. Photo courtesy of Larry Cohen.

Broderick Crawford consults with Cohen on the set of *The Private Files of J. Edgar Hoover*. Photo courtesy of Larry Cohen.

Cohen prepares a scene with Broderick Crawford for *The Private Files of J. Edgar Hoover*. Photo courtesy of Larry Cohen.

Cohen on location for *The Private Files of J. Edgar Hoover*. Photo courtesy of Larry Cohen.

Cohen with Miklós Rózsa, as the composer conducts the London Philharmonic Orchestra during the scoring sessions for *The Private Files of J. Edgar Hoover*. Photo courtesy of Larry Cohen.

Cohen directing from a crane during the filming of *It Lives Again*.
Photo courtesy of Larry Cohen.

A rare photograph of the werewolf mask, fibreglass under-skull, feet, and claws created by makeup artist Steve Neill for *Full Moon High*. Photo courtesy of Steve Neill

Cohen encourages Alan Arkin to ham it up as they rehearse a scene for *Full Moon High*. Photo courtesy of Larry Cohen.

Laurene Landon as Velda on the set of *I, the Jury* in 1981. Photo courtesy of Larry Cohen.

Cohen with Richard Roundtree, David Carradine, and Michael Moriarty on the set of *Q – The Winged Serpent*. Photo courtesy of Larry Cohen.

Cohen attempts to get Michael Moriarty into the spirit of things during the making of *Q – The Winged Serpent*. Photo courtesy of Larry Cohen.

Cohen reviews his script with Michael Moriarty and David Carradine on the set of *Q – The Winged Serpent*. Photo courtesy of Larry Cohen.

Cohen directs an unsettled David Carradine on the set of Q – *The Winged Serpent*.
Photo courtesy of Larry Cohen.

It Lives Again (1978)

Do you think the spectacular commercial success of *It's Alive* meant there was a certain inevitability to the siring of a sequel in the form of *It Lives Again*?

Oh, absolutely. Well, that's the movie business. That's what a successful picture does: it breeds and multiplies! [Chuckles] When *It's Alive* came out and was a huge hit, and was sitting at #1 in the box office charts and making a fortune, Warner Bros. immediately came to me and said they wanted a sequel. I agreed to do one and I went away and wrote the script. The studio then gave me the go-ahead to make *It Lives Again,* and we started shooting the picture right away. So, it all happened very fast and I had no reservations about doing a sequel to *It's Alive*. I wasn't concerned in any way about the possibility of doing some damage to the original. I was happy to be making another movie and thought I could do a little variation on *It's Alive*. I wanted to create something interesting that held an equal amount of dramatic weight as the first picture, and also had some social commentary and metaphorical value.

Do horror films without a metaphor have any value?

I'm sure that some of them do, but I would imagine only very few. I'm certain they do hold value for those viewers who will tolerate a lack of serious subject matter or thematic depth and exchange it for mindless entertainment. Of course, people often read metaphors into stories that aren't always present or intended. That's okay, too. At least it means they are paying attention.

Is the central metaphor of *It Lives Again* more latent than manifest when compared to *It's Alive*?

I think it's still there at the same level for the audience member, who wants to look a little deeper and engage with all of that stuff. *It Lives Again* is probably more of a continuation of the same ideas and themes found in *It's Alive*, but expanded slightly to include other things: other characters, other situations, and of course other monsters. *It's Alive* is a little more interior than *It Lives Again*, in that the focus of the original is primarily centred on the Davis family. *It Lives Again* still has a young family at its heart, but I wanted to explore what the wider effects and consequences the monster babies would have on society as more and more of these creatures were being born every day. Those new elements to the story probably invite other meanings, but I didn't want to pitch the second movie too close to the first one.

You didn't want to repeat yourself?

No, because there would have been no point in doing that. It wouldn't be interesting for the audience and it certainly wouldn't be creatively satisfying for me, although it would have probably been a lot easier to just regurgitate exactly what had come before. When you are doing a sequel, you have to push the story further and explore some new areas and I think *It Lives Again* succeeds in doing that. It's very progressive. There must always be a strong creative incentive for making a sequel that moves beyond simply making a little more dough, although the money is always nice, of course.

The usual approach with sequels to monster movies is to either make the monsters physically bigger and more imposing, or, as in the case of James Cameron's *Aliens*, to increase their numbers.

Well, the ad campaign for *It Lives Again* basically stated "Now there are three of them . . . ." and we saw three cribs instead of one. For the sequel, Rick Baker created two males and a female, whereas we only had one monster baby in the first film. I liked the idea in *It's Alive* that this rather small, lonesome creature was creating such havoc, death, and fear in a big city. As I said, the idea with *It Lives Again* was that there were now more women giving birth to these monsters and it was becoming a more widespread problem—an epidemic. Naturally, you have to raise the stakes somewhat in a sequel because you don't want to give the audience a duplicate version of the original film. But you also don't want to change things beyond recognition because some people won't find those familiar aspects that they may have found appealing the first time around. That's always the tricky part of doing a sequel. You have to play around with the characters and the story, and, of course, with the monsters. Rick's work was so good, there was always a temptation to reveal more of it and have the monsters doing a variety of different things they didn't do in the first film. But I still kept them mostly off-screen or shot them in a way that made them somewhat elusive.

Yes, the monsters are occasionally reflected in glass, or shot out-of-focus, or are situated in the shadows, or partially obscured behind the bars of their cage.

Yeah, and I also re-used the double-image point-of-view shots that had worked so well in *It's Alive*. I thought they were particularly effective in generating suspense and tension. You'll also notice that I reference Val Lewton's *Cat People*[1] in the scene where one character takes a swim alone at night, and once again that's my swimming pool, as something is crawling about in the darkness. In *Cat People*, the girl is in a darkened pool and hears something, but you don't see the creature moving around in the shadows. You still get a strong indication of its presence and movement, and I always thought that scene was very scary. I wanted to create that same kind of fear in my sequence, and so that was my very sincere tribute to Val Lewton. I think Lewton was the greatest exponent of the rather unfashionable idea that often what you don't see is far more unsettling and effective than what you do see.

***It Lives Again* begins with Frank Davis gate-crashing a baby shower as he calmly confronts the unwitting parents with the news that their unborn child is a mutant. In your mind, how has Frank's character developed from the first film?**

I see Frank as making a natural progression from the closing events of *It's Alive*, where we last saw him failing to save his son from the cops. In the sequel, Frank is now intent on warning and helping other parents who are about to experience the same tragedy that befell his own family. He is an advocate of their rights and is dedicated to doing what he thinks is the right thing: shielding and nurturing the monster babies from those who would do them harm, namely the authorities. Some of the more perceptive and thoughtful critics commented that *It Lives Again* was one of the first horror films to reverse and subvert the standard premise of most monster movies. What I mean is in the vast majority of horror films, the authorities are always trying to find the monster and destroy it. *It Lives Again* features characters like Frank, who are working to save the monster and protect it from doing harm to others and to itself. I think that was a highly unusual and revolutionary approach to take with the material. You just didn't see that concept being executed in other horror movies, and I was delighted that some of the critics recognized that.

The expectant parents are played by Frederic Forest and Kathleen Lloyd—

[Interrupting] Two very good actors. They really brought that sense of desperate tragedy, which was crucial to the story working. I needed two solid actors to play those parts because the audience had to invest in them, as they had done with John P. Ryan and Sharon Farrell in *It's Alive*. Without that strong emotional center, the events of the film are not nearly as affecting and disturbing. It all plays very naturally, I think. I mean, the relationship between Frederic and Kathleen is fraught with tension and stress, as any relationship would be in that kind of situation. Their lives are changed irrevocably, just as the Davis family were forever changed by their experiences in *It's Alive*.

As Forest says when Lloyd pines for the normalcy of their previous life, "We are not going to be the same people anymore."

Exactly. There is also the generational issue between Kathleen's character and her own mother who plants a bug on her and betrays her whereabouts to the FBI. This tension exists between them, as it so often does in relationships between mothers and daughters, sometimes with disastrous results and a terrible cost. Kathleen must then later betray her own child as she has been betrayed, which gives the story and the characters some very credible layers. It all kind of comes full circle, the sins of the parents coming down on the children. Again, that situation is very authentic and we can identify with these people's emotional lives.

Were Forest and Lloyd two actors you admired before making *It Lives Again*?

Yeah, particularly Frederic Forest. I had seen him in Francis Ford Coppola's *The Conversation* and I liked that movie and his performance in it. Frederic worked with Coppola several times more after *It Lives Again*, in *Apocalypse Now* and *One From the Heart*. He was Coppola's favorite actor for a time and also starred in the title role of *Hammett*, a film about Dashiell Hammett, the author of *The Maltese Falcon* and other hardboiled detective books. Frederic was also originally supposed to be in one of *The Godfather* movies, too. He told me that, unfortunately, he had done another gangster picture shortly before *The Godfather* and that had negated his chances of being in Coppola's historic film.[2] I don't know if it was the part that Robert De Niro ended up getting, but of course, De Niro won an Academy Award for that role. As for Kathleen Lloyd, I seem to remember that she was somewhat reluctant to do a horror film. That's my memory of it, anyway.

Which is interesting, as Lloyd had only recently appeared in Elliot Silverstein's *The Car* (1977), the year before *It Lives Again* was made.

Yeah, and maybe that's what it was all about. I don't know. Kathleen had just done the movie about a killer car, but at that time she had also recently appeared opposite Jack Nicholson and Marlon Brando in *The Missouri Breaks*.[3] She more than held her own in that film, playing alongside such heavyweight talents as Nicholson and Brando, who were both basically trying to act each other off the screen in that picture. I don't know what Kathleen's problem with horror movies was. They are just a lot of fun, kind of an antidote to reality. I think Kathleen was maybe a little dubious about revisiting the horror genre again so swiftly, but she gave a terrific performance in *It Lives Again* and was committed to the picture. Frankly, I always thought that Kathleen had the potential to be a big movie star and she was being viewed by some as "the new Jane Fonda." Unfortunately, it just didn't happen for her. That's an old story in Hollywood, but you never can tell what will happen in this business. That is part of the inexhaustible mystery of cinema and stardom: nobody knows anything. If they did, we'd all be able to reproduce that magic every single time.

So, who decides whether somebody becomes a star or is relegated to character actor status and supporting roles? Or is it all just random chance?

Well, that's the $64,000 question, isn't it? Sometimes talent isn't enough and you really need luck. Sometimes it's the audience that decides who becomes a star and who doesn't. I mean, people either flock in their droves to see a picture, or they don't and it bombs. That actor can then become poison in some studio executives' minds. Even when a movie sometimes hits big or has a lot of visibility, it still doesn't mean that the lead actor is going to become a big star. I think it's also important that if an actor has a big hit they must have another big movie to follow it. I don't think that ever happened for Kathleen. I don't believe *The Missouri Breaks* was a massive hit and neither was *The Car* or *It Lives Again*. Here's another example: many years after we did *It Lives Again*, I made *Original Gangstas* with Pam Grier. Pam went on to do *Jackie Brown* with Quentin Tarantino as her next film, which was probably the biggest movie she ever did. Unfortunately, I don't think there was a follow-up to that picture for her. It wasn't like she got a lot of big movies with starring roles afterwards. Unlike what happened to John Travolta, who became a huge star again after appearing in *Pulp Fiction*, nothing really happened for Pam Grier or Robert Forster for that matter. They didn't become stars as you would define a true movie star.

Forster did get the Oscar nomination for *Jackie Brown*.

Yeah, but it didn't do him any good. For years after, Bob just went back to doing B-movies again. It was the same thing with David Carradine after *Kill Bill*. You would have thought that after his performance, David would have gotten some A-class movies. I mean, he was the "Bill" in *Kill Bill*, after all, and was very good in that picture. When I spoke to David after the film came out, he said, "Aw, they are still just offering me the same kind of crap I was doing before!" Unfortunately, David always took every job that was ever offered to him, so he very quickly sank back down into the lower echelons of filmmaking again, you know, the real cheap exploitation pictures that hardly ever play in the theaters anymore and get dumped onto DVD and Blu-ray. Some of these films were never released at all, so it was kind of sad to see that opportunity just drift away for David.

Another unmistakable face in *It Lives Again* is that of Eddie Constantine who plays Dr. Forrest, a sympathiser to the monsters' cause.

People are always surprised when Eddie Constantine suddenly turns up in the movie. They don't see that coming. I was delighted to have Eddie play a part in *It Lives Again* as he was an accomplished B-picture actor. He was a very distinctive-looking guy and had this wonderfully rugged face. He was a big international star, particularly in France, and was famous for playing the role of a detective named Lemmy Caution[4] in a series of well-received pictures. He had worked with Jean-Luc Goddard on *Alphaville* which is still considered to be one of the great movies of world cinema.[5] Eddie had this interesting screen presence that I liked. By the time we were making *It Lives Again*, his greatest successes were well behind him. He had returned to the United States and was now looking to re-establish himself as an actor. I met Eddie at a party at the Beverly Hills Hotel, immediately liked him, and invited him to my home. I introduced him to my wife's sister and he actually ended up marrying her and becoming my brother-in-law. I thought I could help Eddie revive his career, and so I cast him in *It Lives Again*. When Eddie was here in America he wasn't getting any jobs, so I thought I'd give him a job in my movie. Eddie has one of those faces that people instantly recognize. I remember that one day I was over in France with him and we were both walking along the Champs-Élysées in Paris. All these people suddenly started shouting out Eddie's name and swarmed around him. Everybody—*everybody*—mobbed him and couldn't wait to say hello to him. I found it slightly ironic that Eddie couldn't get a job, but everybody knew exactly who he was and enjoyed his movies. People just loved him. He and my wife's sister later got divorced and Eddie eventually returned to France, but I was very happy to have known him.

Where did you shoot the film?

We shot *It Lives Again* in eighteen days in Tucson, Arizona, and also back in Los Angeles. We also shot part of the movie at my house, which doubled as the private children's school which has been converted into a secret sanctuary for the monsters. Some of the interiors were also shot in the basement of the Harold Lloyd estate up off Benedict Canyon, which I believe was up for rent at the time. I must say that the days we spent shooting in Tucson were absolutely wonderful. The people there were incredibly warm and friendly. I loved Tucson and I think Tucson loved us back. It's always good when a movie company arrives in a town or city, because it always boosts the local economy. Tucson had offered us the use of their town, their citizens, and their entire police force. The city was basically willing to give me anything that I required. The level of cooperation and compliance they showed us was incredible, it really was. Naturally, the temptation was to take everything they offered and more, but I do think the allure of doing that actually hurt the movie in one or two scenes.

Which scenes in particular are you referring to?

Well, there are far too many cops in some of the scenes, particularly the sequence where the parents arrive at the hospital for the birth of the baby and you have all these cops with guns storming the delivery room. Although we had established in *It's Alive* how incredibly dangerous and violent the monster baby was, it still seemed a little absurd and excessive to have as many cops as we did. We had them patrolling the place with firearms and support vehicles with flashing lights. It was frankly ludicrous, but the authorities were willing to put the entire city at our disposal and I wasn't going to argue with them. I've often found that when you arrive in a town with a crew and are making a picture, the townsfolk will pretty much give you anything you want. There's just something about the whole moviemaking process that people find exciting, magical, and important. They suddenly feel compelled to give you anything you need or ask for, simply because a little stardust has gotten in their eyes.

You had to fire your original director of photography as you were apparently in daily conflict with each other. What exactly caused these disputes to arise?

Well, it was a very unfortunate thing that ultimately turned into a very fortunate thing. It's true that I didn't get along with some of the crew I was working with in Tucson. They didn't appreciate my way of working—the loose, improvisational approach that has served me well on a lot of movies. The first cameraman I hired for *It Lives Again* was the kind of DP that wanted everything rigorously planned ahead of time, with no room for spontaneity and exploration. He wanted shot lists and everything, and I just couldn't give it to him. I asked him to hang in there with me and just go along with what we were doing, but he was extremely resistant. I had my own methods and he clearly found them intolerable. He started getting very irritable and uncomfortable, and was openly criticizing me in front of the whole crew. He simply couldn't align himself with my improvisational style, and so he left the production. That put me in the calamitous situation of having nobody to shoot the film. I remember that this was on a Tuesday and I desperately needed a new cameraman or else disaster was imminent. I immediately got on the phone and called Daniel Pearl, whom I'd recently met and was impressed with. Daniel had shot *The Texas Chainsaw Massacre* for Tobe Hooper and was an excellent DP. I asked Daniel: "Is there any way you can get here for tomorrow morning by eight o'clock?" I said this more in hope than expectation but, incredibly, he and his crew arrived later that night in Tucson and really saved my ass. It could have been catastrophic, but it all worked out. We were then able to continue shooting and I enjoyed working with Daniel very much. It was the beginning of a very successful working relationship that continued on several of my movies.

Frank theorizes that the mutant babies are the beginning of a new superhuman strain of humanity "that will finally eclipse our own." He believes that they could be the next evolutionary step in our development, "a way in which the human race can survive the pollutions of the planet."

I think it's only natural that if these monsters were actually born into our world, we would speculate about their origin and purpose. Where did they come from? Why were they born? Was it by accident or design? We would immediately suspect that they were the unfortunate product of pollution, or some unknown disease or contagion. If they were a natural part of our evolution as human beings, I doubt they would arrive so suddenly and dramatically, as these things often take many thousands of years to establish themselves. But it makes sense to me that Frank would consider them as a new strain of humanity and the inevitable result of the terrible pollutants that affect the earth, air, and water. People would need to find some way of surviving any impending environmental disaster and it would probably have to begin with a genetic transformation in our DNA. We would have to change to suit our new surroundings. Of course, it's also interesting and disturbing to think that this new strain of humanity will supplant us, in the manner in which humans replaced the Cro-Magnons and Neanderthals. Will this strain be a more intelligent form of the human race or will it simply be a more durable one designed to survive the new, poisoned world we are creating? It's probably better just to put these questions out there and let the audience decide and debate them. I just make these movies.

So, you didn't feel compelled to give the mutant babies some kind of origin?

No. I just thought it would be more interesting to offer some loose, grasping explanation. It's just a theory Frank has, one of many theories that would probably be offered as the authorities fumbled to discover what the hell these creatures were.

The mutants have a built-in homing device and can form a telepathic link that allows them to locate their blood relations. Where did that idea come from?

I just thought it was another intriguing—and perhaps inevitable—development of these monsters and their continuing evolution. It's also something that is hinted at in the first film when the monster baby comes back and meets his brother; and is made clearer in the second film when the creature homes in on its parents. There have been reports of family members and blood relations having psychic links to each other. I've heard of several cases where twins have felt their sibling's pain from miles away. They may be separated by a city or a state, sometimes even by oceans, but they still experience the same physical symptoms and agonies.

What was the general response to *It Lives Again*?

It's funny you should ask that question, because I was reminiscing with someone about the response to the movie just a few days ago. I'll never forget the night we organized a sneak preview of *It Lives Again* at a theater on Hollywood Boulevard. I remember it was held on a Wednesday and Ted Ashley, who was the head of the studio at this point, and a bunch of other executives were in attendance. That screening was incredible. In fact, it was too incredible, if you can understand me. We ran the picture and the audience went crazy for it. They were screaming and hollering and leaping out of their seats. They were reacting to the movie in a way that I hoped an audience would: they were scared and were clearly having a good time. They were responding to such a strong extent that the executives became increasingly convinced that I had placed "ringers" in the crowd! Afterwards, as we walked out of the theater, Ted Ashley accused me of having peppered the audience with people who were going to react strongly for his benefit. I said, "Ted, there isn't one single person in this audience that has anything to do with me. I didn't bring anybody here tonight except myself. All those people in there were honestly enjoying the film." He said, "Well, if you didn't put people in that audience you should have." Again, I protested my innocence but he didn't believe me. None of them would accept the fact that those were genuine responses. They continued to claim that I knew all of these people and I continued to insist to the contrary. I don't know. The executives thought that the entire screening was an elaborate set-up designed to engineer a false response that would impress them. What can you do?

Is that a common practice in Hollywood?

Using ringers? Well, I was later informed that this was in fact the standard practice during some preview screenings. Filmmakers would often bring in people to cheer and scream loudly in order to generate a positive reception for their movie. It was impossible for me to convince the Warner Bros. executives that I had not rigged that screening. Looking back, I think the crowd that night were serious horror movie fans and were relishing the whole experience, as only horror movie fans can. The horror crowd can really create a great atmosphere, particularly if the movie is playing well and they are warming to it. It was just unfortunate, that's all. But that screening is certainly one of the oddest little evenings I've spent in my career.

You've already indicated that *It Lives Again* did not repeat the remarkable box office success of *It's Alive*.

No, *It Lives Again* was nowhere near the financial success that *It's Alive* was. I knew that matching that kind of unique success was going to be difficult and, lo and behold, that was pretty much the case. But I do like *It Lives Again*. I think it's pretty good. I do know that at the time it was to hit theaters, Warner Bros. were about to release *Superman*. Of course, *Superman* was going to be this giant blockbuster with Marlon Brando and Gene Hackman. You have to remember just what a huge deal that movie was back then, and so *It Lives Again* pretty much got pushed aside. All of the studio's interest and resources were focused firmly on *Superman* and that was that. Of course, why shouldn't they put all their energies into *Superman*? Warner Bros. had hundreds of millions of dollars tied up in that picture and it was certainly where their hearts were lying. Everybody wanted to see *Superman* and I wanted to see it, too. *It Lives Again* was just small potatoes in comparison. I also don't think *It Lives Again* was properly promoted and the picture suffered for it. The studio didn't spend the necessary money promoting it and, ultimately, the box office receipts reflected that.

Did you complain to the powers-that-be about it?

Well, Warner Bros. did an ad campaign that was based on a suggestion that I'd made. I'd conceived this idea that we could show a child's birthday cake with these monster claw marks tearing through it. The studio followed my concept, but they didn't do a good job of executing it. I mean, you couldn't really tell what it was. It just looked like a complete mishmash, when it should have revealed exactly what the movie was about. We should have built upon the great reputation and interest in *It's Alive*. By the time I'd objected to what had been done, they had already gone to press. They had printed all the posters and the ad campaign, and that was that. There was no going back. What they often did in these deals at the studios is they would give the producer a consultancy on any ad campaign. In other words it was the same old story: you retained consultancy rights which basically meant that after they had completed the ad campaign and it was finished, you couldn't do anything about it! They would merely show it to you and you got to give them your opinion. Of course, your opinion didn't really matter as it was far too late to change anything. That's the consultancy clause in the contract. It's absolutely meaningless. It's a fucking insult, actually. By the time Warner Bros. came out with the ads for *It Lives Again*, it was far too late. In those kinds of situations you were often stuck with something that was totally inappropriate or bafflingly obscure or just plain stupid. I mean, this was a horror film! It wasn't that difficult to come up with something that could have resonated with the public.

I'd imagine that it would be easier to devise an ad campaign for *It's Alive* and *It Lives Again*, than say *The Private Files of J. Edgar Hoover*.

Oh, definitely. Horror is a distinctive genre, like the Western and science fiction genres, and they follow a certain method and mood. You only had to glance at the ad campaign for *The Exorcist* or *The Omen* to know they were horror films. I mean, black often seems to be the color when advertising a horror movie as it gives the graphics a threatening feeling. *The Private Files of J. Edgar Hoover* was a political film and was a difficult sell because that genre is not as well defined or as popular as horror. Audiences have a grasp of what appears to be scary but when you fuck around with that approach, there's a good chance that you are sending the wrong message about what your movie is. This isn't rocket science, you know? It's all very simple. *It Lives Again* was a horror movie and it needed a good ad campaign to lure people into the theater. That's all.

Why exactly do you think that horror movies are "an antidote to reality?"

I think all movies are in some ways an antidote to reality—not just horror movies. They are an escape from the boredom, the repetition and the predictability of real life.

Wes Craven once famously declared that horror movies were "The boot camp for the psyche." I was wondering what active purpose you think horror films like *It Lives Again* serve in society beyond being grim entertainment?

I think people have fun watching horror films. They are pure fantasy when compared with the many things that actually exist which are threatening to human beings. As a species, we innately realize that we are finite and there is so much fear that people have, the fear of violence, disease, war, poverty, whatever it is. Those are all very disturbing things for people to deal with because they are real and can kill you. Horror films allow you to be afraid of things that you are sure don't exist. So, you say, "Oh, I can be afraid of this and still have a good time because it's just like a ride at an amusement park." You understand that you can't really be hurt by this movie. There aren't really monster babies like in *It Lives Again*, or creatures like the Alien in *Alien*, that can destroy you. It's all make-believe and there is some safety in knowing that we can be scared of them because it's just a harmless release of energy and adrenaline in a controlled environment, the movie theater or your own home. It's just like when you tell children stories about Hansel and Gretel and the witch, or Jack the Giant Killer. Now, it's okay to scare kids with things that don't really exist, but if you were to scare children with something that is very common and familiar, it would really terrify them. For example, if you were to inform the kids that the babysitter is going to kill them, that's very different to telling them there is a witch in the woods that is going to boil them in a pot or put them in an oven. I mean, you certainly wouldn't want to tell them that their schoolteacher is going to kill them because that would really freak them out! It's just too close to home. So, it's the varying degrees of reality and unreality, the familiar and the unfamiliar, mixed up with the fact that people do like to be scared, that makes horror movies work. I think Wes Craven is suggesting that watching horror films is a cathartic process for some people and maybe he's right. I'm sure they are, but it's mostly about the amusement audiences derive from watching them. Beyond that, I really don't know.

Full Moon High (1981)

Full Moon High is almost a transitional work for you in that comedic elements will now be ever-present in your movies, sometimes to the detriment of the scares and atmosphere. Is that fair to say?

Yeah, I'd agree, definitely. Looking back, I guess I was going through my happy period back then. I was enjoying myself during that time, but that might have been coincidental with my divorce. After I broke up with my first wife, who is a truly wonderful person, by the way, and no harm to her, but afterwards I was out playing around and being a kid again. I was chasing after girls and reclaiming that kind of life. At the same time this was happening, my movies started to get more fun-like and comedic. Even when there were opportunities to exploit the seriousness and darkness of a particular theme or subject, I still found a way to somehow make the story more upbeat. It was just my happy state of mind. I mean, one of the principal reasons I'm a director is that I get to chase after all these great-looking actresses!

Well, some observers have interpreted the werewolf myth as an unleashing of repressed and beastly sexual desires.

Gosh! [Laughs] Well, I was right on the nose again then, wasn't I?

So, the film simply grew out of this newfound frivolity and optimism?

I guess so. I went to American International Pictures and said, "Look, I think I can make a comedy out of *I Was a Teenage Werewolf*," which was a horror film they had made in the 1950s starring Michael Landon. Since AIP owned that movie and thought my proposal to do a comedic version was a good idea, they let me use the same premise of having a teenage werewolf attending high school. I resisted using the title *I Was a Teenage Werewolf*—which I could have done—and decided to call it *Full Moon High*. After that, I could go out and do whatever I wanted with the idea, which was great for me because I wanted to attempt some comedy—some broad comedy—and this project gave me the opportunity to try something different.

And were you happy with the results?

I think *Full Moon High* is probably one of my lesser films, but I still enjoyed the picture and had a good time making it. It really has a warm spot in my heart. I liked working with the cast, particularly Adam Arkin, who played the werewolf. When I cast Adam, he was on Broadway playing Nathan Detroit in *Guys and Dolls*. He had great charm and comic delivery, but for some reason he never became a big star. He's worked continuously over the years and is now directing himself, mostly in television. Adam gives a very likable performance, but at one time I was also considering Jay Leno for the part if Adam proved unavailable. But I'm glad it worked out with Adam. There are a lot of big laughs in the picture, like when the guy is trying to shoot the werewolf but accidentally shoots the cameraman. It's very broad stuff, but it was fun to do. I like seeing *Full Moon High* with an audience because they laugh and have a good time, and the movie also has something to say.

Why exactly is it a "lesser" film for you?

The picture has its flaws, but then most of them do. Its intentions were never serious. There is commentary in there but you have to search for it. You have this kid, who is the werewolf, coming back to his hometown after being away for twenty years. He still looks the same, like a teenager, but all of his friends and the people he knew are now middle-aged. He is a literal monster and transforms at each full moon, but they have all turned into monsters of one kind or another also. Age has monsterized everybody and I think one of the main points or sub-themes of the picture is that's exactly what happens to you. As we grow older, life has its negative effects and ends up turning you into something you once weren't. Physically, people look horrible and they learn how to act horribly, too. Along with their looks, these characters have lost their hopes and dreams which have not come true. They must accept that their life has not worked out the way they wanted it to and that their existence is a perversion of what they had originally envisioned it would be. They are locked in an unhappy marriage; they are stuck in a job that they never really wanted; they have children that they don't like. So, it's turned out to be a miserable world for them, and the kid who is the werewolf comes back and—aside from being a monster—he's probably better off than the rest of them because he hasn't changed at all. Everything has frozen in time for him and so the disappointments and disenchantments of middle age have still not arrived. He just goes around and bites people, that's all!

Those are some fairly meaningful themes you are addressing for what purports to be just a knockabout horror-comedy.

Oh, absolutely, but that's why I did it. Just to make a comedy of stupidity wouldn't have interested me unless there was some serious subtext to it. We talked before about that strong sense of alienation and people killing their own blood relations because of it, and it's more or less the same thing here. Life in America had changed a lot since the 1960s, and some of the values we once held dear as a country no longer have the same validity. As time has gone by, a lot of things have changed in our perceptions of ourselves and other people; in our ideals, our politics and our attitudes. So, there is a lot of room there to explore ideas and satirize some of these things in the movies.

The film was financed with tax shelter money, correct?

Well, the tax shelter came in later. First, we made the movie and then they sold it to the tax shelter. Back in those days, almost all the movies that AIP were making were made with tax shelter money. Frankly, I haven't got the slightest idea how tax shelter money works and why! I just know that they had the picture and it was their right to do whatever they wanted with it. They were the financial officers who controlled the purse strings. As long as they didn't bother me as far as what the content was and the editing and the production, and simply let me do what I wanted to do, I didn't bother them regarding the financial aspects of the project.

1981 has come to be known as "the year of the werewolf." Interestingly, *Full Moon High* was made before *The Howling*, *An American Werewolf in London* and *Wolfen* but was released after them.

Yeah, that's right. I guess there were all kinds of werewolf movies appearing that year, but I don't remember the chronological order they came in. It's all a blur now, but that was just one of those things that sometimes happen. It still happens. You get a lot of the same kinds of movies released at the same time. That year was the time for werewolves.

What exactly did you make of the competition?

I thought *The Howling* was very good. It's a pretty scary picture with great special effects and good performances. *An American Werewolf in London* certainly has some good sections to it, and again the effects are wonderful, but I don't think it's quite as strong as *The Howling*. I didn't think *Wolfen* worked very well at all. It was the weakest and most confused of the three movies.

Was it at all frustrating for you to suddenly have several movies appear almost simultaneously that were dealing with the werewolf theme?

It was just coincidence that there was a rash of werewolf movies being made around the same time, so I wasn't frustrated by that. I actually paid very little attention to those other films. In fact, just a few years later, another werewolf picture came out called *Teen Wolf* that had far greater similarities with *Full Moon High*.[1] As I say, it isn't unusual that you get a lot of the same kinds of things in movies and that is also happening right now, too. There are just a plethora of vampires, werewolves, and aliens—on television and in movies—that are coming out of your ears. We see them over and over and over again, and, of course, there are always the zombies! [Sighs] There are zombies galore now, and I'm getting sick and tired of them. What we need is some new monsters. Filmmakers have got to come up with a new monster every once in a while to reinvigorate the genre. I mean, *The Mummy* movies[2] that were made several years ago had nothing to do with mummies as I remembered them back in the 1930s and '40s. They were just these big, sprawling action pictures with great special effects, but there was no real connection with the mummy franchise from the old Universal pictures. They didn't have the same atmosphere and scares because we've seen them all before. We really do need some new monsters, or at least a fresh take on the old ones, because I'm sick to death of sombre, pale-faced people with blood dripping down their cheeks. It's all getting very tiresome.

Ed McMahon plays the werewolf's CIA commie-hating patriot father, who believes in conspiracies and has constructed a bomb shelter in his house. How did McMahon come to be drawn to the project?

Ed McMahon was the co-host of *The Johnny Carson Show*, one of the most popular shows on television. I thought that since he was already recognizable and favored by audiences, his involvement might help the television distribution of *Full Moon High*, which is a big part of the money that comes in from a film. Ed was a familiar name, but he was also an actor who had performed in a number of films.[3] I instinctively knew that he could do a good job playing the part of the werewolf's father, and that instinct was proved correct. He was a very pleasant fellow, and I had a good time working with him. I remember that one day, I told Ed that he reminded me of another actor that had been in movies years before called Paul Douglas.[4] Well, it turned out that this was the greatest compliment I could have possibly paid Ed because he then proceeded to tell me that Paul Douglas was his all-time hero. He was absolutely thrilled that I had likened him to Douglas, and happily—just by coincidence—I had said the right thing.

I like the line McMahon delivers a moment before enjoying the Romanian women: "Okay, my lovelies, let's see what communist infiltration is all about!"

[Chuckles] Yeah, I just made that line up. It was cute. I thought it was a pretty cute picture altogether, actually. *Full Moon High* was kind of an adorable movie.

There are some neat low-tech touches in there, such as the toy airplane moving stiffly over the map to illustrate the journey to Romania.

That was a takeoff on all those hokey devices they used to use in old movies whenever anybody travelled from one location to another. It just seemed to be in keeping with the whole feel of the picture. There's a sweetness to it, don't you think?

Yes, I do. Another neat transitional device is the changing pictures of the American Presidents on the wall illustrating the elapsing of twenty years until finally we end up with the image of a Black woman. Who was that lady?

She was my housekeeper, Bette Adams. I dressed her up in a nice little suit, and took a picture, and put her in a movie, implying, of course, that she would become the first female Black President. I was pretty close, wasn't I? Nearly thirty years later, we did eventually end up with a Black President after all.

What doubled for the brief exterior shots of Romania in the film?

That was stock footage. I used to buy stock footage from the stock footage libraries, usually at MGM. They always had an amazing amount of stuff that you could utilize, so I would go there in the hope of finding something good. Sometimes I would pick out the stock footage first and then select the appropriate scenes so that the shots would fit in later. I wasn't the only director that used to do that. I remember on one occasion when I went out to look for stock footage, I noticed that certain pages had been removed from the library catalogues—pages that had literally been stolen out of the books. I went to the librarian and said, "Look, these shots that I'm looking for are not here, even though I know they should be." The librarian said, "Oh, it was Francis Coppola and his people that did it! They came in here and took that footage for *The Godfather*." It turns out that whilst working on *The Godfather*, Coppola had made sure that nobody else could reuse the stock footage shots he had selected by tearing the pages out of the catalogues. This obviously meant that nobody else would ever be able to locate and order the same shots that he had used. I actually managed to find and use some of those same stock footage shots in *Black Caesar*, so some of the material that is in *The Godfather* is also in my movie, too. If it was good enough for Francis Coppola then it was certainly good enough for me. But the footage we used in *Full Moon High* was not authentic shots of Romania. I don't know what they were or where they came from, but they seemed to resemble Romania—or at least the Romania of my imagination—and fit in rather nicely.

The late Elizabeth Hartman gives a charming performance as the neurotic Miss Montgomery, a teacher at Full Moon High.

Yes, she was lovely. Elizabeth had been a big star at one time and had received an Oscar nomination for a movie she had done with Sydney Poitier.[5] She had also starred opposite Clint Eastwood in *The Beguiled*[6] and was the lead in several other movies and had enjoyed a nice career.

Unfortunately, for some reason she had experienced an emotional breakdown. I remember her agent called me up and said, "If you want to do a good deed, could you possibly find a part in your film for Elizabeth Hartman? She's just got out of the hospital after having a mental breakdown and she needs a job." I said, "Well, it just so happens that I've got a good part for her and I will give her the job." Her agent said, "That's great, but one thing: she can't drive. You'll have to pick her up every day and bring her to the set and then take her back home every night." I said, "That's no problem, we can arrange that." So, we gave Elizabeth the part, and she was a delight to work with. She was a rather delicate and fragile lady, but was very cooperative and I had a good time with her. Then, tragically, a few years later, she killed herself. Apparently, she jumped out of the window of some building and fell to her death. I saw no evidence that such a thing was going to happen during the making of *Full Moon High*, but she was very shy and quiet. She probably had some terrible emotional trauma in her life. I don't know what it was and I never tried to find out. I just tried to make every day a pleasant one for her. I always made sure to compliment Elizabeth on her work and give her as much support as I could. She did a good job, but she was vulnerable—very vulnerable. I would have certainly used her again in another of my movies if I could have found the right part for her.

What about Alan Arkin, who plays Dr. Jacob Brand?

Originally, before we hired Alan Arkin, the other people I was considering for that part were Bob Newhart[7] and Don Rickles.[8] They were both successful television actors, but I thought we'd be better off hiring Arkin because he was a legitimate movie star. Of course, Alan was also the father of Adam Arkin. One day I said to Adam, "Do you think your dad would like to be in the movie? I was thinking he could play the part of the doctor. Tell him we'll give him a Rolls Royce as payment." Adam came back later and said, "My father liked the script and said he would do the film. But he doesn't want a Rolls Royce; he wants two Mercedes." So, I called Sam Arkoff and said, "Alan Arkin has just finished doing a hit movie called *The In-Laws*. He's a popular A-picture actor and we can get him in *Full Moon High* for the cost of two Mercedes." Now, back in those days, a Mercedes was priced at something like $26,000. But as soon as I was given the okay, we agreed to buy Alan the two Mercedes, and he committed to doing the picture. During the shoot, he was very pleasant and we both got along fine. Alan bounced off every idea I suggested to him in terms of the improvisations and he was a very creative actor. He completed the film and, as promised, we gave him the two cars. Several years later, I ran into Adam Arkin and asked him if his father still owned the two Mercedes. Adam told me that Alan still had one of them, but that he'd given the second car to his friend. I don't know who that friend was, but it must have been a pretty good friend to receive a car as a gift. Then, about three years ago, I actually ran into Alan Arkin in a supermarket and started a conversation with him. I happened to mention the two cars and suddenly he flew into a tremendous rage! He started screaming at me in front of some friends that I had with me. It was really rather embarrassing. Alan insisted that he'd never received any cars from me and didn't know what I was talking about. He was infuriated and screamed, "Don't ever say that again—that you gave me a car! You never ever gave me a car! I don't know what the hell you are talking about!" [Exhales] Well, I didn't know what to say to him, because I had run into Alan previously and he had openly acknowledged the cars. He knew very well we had given him two Mercedes, and his son knew it, also. The only reason I could think that prompted such an outburst was that the woman standing next to Alan was his wife, and whoever he'd given the other Mercedes to, she didn't know about it. Anyway, I quickly decided to drop the entire matter. I didn't want to wreck his marriage, but he certainly did embarrass me in front of the people I was with. I mean, just moments before I had said to them, "Oh, there's Alan Arkin. I once directed him in a film; he's a friend of mine. Let's have a word with him." Then, to walk over and have him react like that, so viciously; I'm not kidding, I really thought he was going to attack me! At any rate, I certainly won't be mentioning it to his face again. However, the fact of the matter remains that Alan Arkin did indeed receive two Mercedes for appearing in *Full Moon High*.

At the time *Full Moon High* went into production, the flourishing technology of special makeup effects was being embraced by filmmakers such as John Carpenter, David Cronenberg, John Landis, and Joe Dante.

Well, any new or developing technology is going to be embraced by filmmakers. That's just the way it works. The field of makeup effects was really moving ahead in leaps and bounds at that time through the efforts of people like Dick Smith and Rick Baker. The popularity and proliferation of special effects really happened after *The Exorcist* and *Star Wars*. Suddenly, a lot of effects were being used in movies.

And in some cases dictating the content and narrative of films.

Oh, dominating them I'd say. A lot of movies, then and now, were full of special effects and were almost an excuse for them. I think the 1980s was a time when effects really began to take over. Movies started becoming cinematic spectacle rather than any truly meaningful experience. Some of those pictures contained very few interesting characters and very little story. They merely paraded the effects. *Full Moon High* was almost taking a step back from all that. I guess it was a little more restrained and old-fashioned in a way, but that was okay.

In keeping with the admittedly low-tech approach on *Full Moon High*, you decided to employ jump cuts for the werewolf transformation instead of the traditional lap-dissolves favored by some filmmakers in the 1940s. Why is that?

I never liked those old lap-dissolves in werewolf movies as they were always so obviously done. They would put makeup on the actor, sit him down in position, shoot him, then put a little more makeup on, and shoot him again, and slowly this transformation would occur. That didn't work for me because they would never get the actor back in the exact position, so when they dissolved between shots the eyes, nose, or mouth never quite matched up. To me, that looked crummy and destroyed the illusion. During our discussions on *Full Moon High*, I thought it would look better if I had the werewolf writhing around in motion and then tried to sneak the cuts in there as the transformation was taking place. I don't know if we got away with it or not, but I much preferred that energetic approach as opposed to using static lap-dissolves. Having the actor simply lying there absolutely still as this horrifying metamorphosis is happening to him just seemed ridiculous to me. Today, they have "morphing," which allows a person to turn into a werewolf in one fluid shot without a cut, but CGI still doesn't improve on the makeup effects in *The Howling* and *An American Werewolf in London*. Those movies may be more than thirty years old now, but the work of Rick Baker has a reality and a texture to it that digital effects can't duplicate. Actually, I think the very best werewolf transformations ever done were in *The Howling*, where it was all done live on the set with prosthetics.⁹ Seeing that movie for the first time and watching this guy's head literally stretch and grow fur and fangs was amazing. You can't beat that.

There are what seems like conscious nods to other horror films in *Full Moon High*, not only to *The Wolf Man* but *Carrie* and *Psycho*.

I'm not entirely averse to referencing other director's movies in my own work when and if I think it's appropriate. I know some filmmakers do that a lot, but you can lose a little of what makes your movie uniquely your own if you do it too often. You are playing to some other director's sensibilities and style, rather than your own ideas. I mostly strive for originality, but I thought the subject matter and general tone of *Full Moon High* allowed for those moments. So, we did a takeoff of *Carrie* in the cemetery scene and a takeoff of *Psycho* with the girl in the shower and all that. Those are two seminal films in the world of horror and I thought the fans would immediately recognize and appreciate the connotation of it all. Those pictures were hugely popular and influential, and I greatly admired them.

An inventive moment occurs when the man at the disco inadvertently creates a new dance craze whilst trying to convince the other revellers that a werewolf is on the loose.

I don't know where that idea came from, but it seems to work in the scene. It was one of those moments of inspiration. If something gets a laugh in the right place and works then you keep it—if you're smart! So, I just threw that in there. That scene is probably a good example of why I couldn't work in regular, traditional motion pictures at the studios. Let's face it, I'm a one-man show. I'm producing these pictures, and writing and directing them, and I can make up anything I want and insert it in as I go along. I have nobody that I have to get approval from and nothing I have to run by someone. I'm totally spoiled. I don't want to go on about this, but when you are in a situation where you have to get approval for everything you do and there are all these people on your back telling you what the schedule is, and how much time you have left to shoot, and whether or not you are on budget or over budget or under budget—no way! You then have people reporting back to the front office and looking at dailies, and that's too much like factory labor for me. My movies are my own and I supervise every element of them. The only person I don't supervise is the composer. I'm not going to tell Bernard Herrmann or Miklós Rózsa what to do and I don't want to. Aside from that, everybody else doesn't exist.

Most filmmakers would concede that filmmaking is a collaborative process.

Not me. I mean, I don't even like to have a production manager on my movies. I usually pay my production manager and ask him not to come to the set, because I want to do all that. I must be in absolute control of every aspect of production and not have to deal with anybody else. I don't want to boss anybody or push anybody around. I just don't want anybody else to be there. Don't misunderstand me: none of this affects the atmosphere or vibe I try to create on a set. I like a happy and productive atmosphere on my sets, and that was certainly the atmosphere I tried to create on *Full Moon High*. I make movies in a very enjoyable way that cultivates a real sense of freedom, elation, and creativity. Most of the actors who've worked on my pictures have never worked in a situation like this before, where one person has all the power and makes all the decisions and calls all the shots. They are sometimes amazed to see that I can basically do anything I want to do. So, if I want to make up a new scene, or get a new location, I just do it. That's it. I doubt that a moment like that dance scene in *Full Moon High* would survive the studio process and that's a shame.

Do you have any interesting anecdotes regarding the shooting of *Full Moon High* that you would like to share?

The funniest thing that happened was when we were shooting at the John Burrows High School in Burbank, California. I remember one day the fire department suddenly walked in wearing their shiny hats and uniforms. The fire chief strode over to me and said, "You can't shoot here because you don't have a permit." I said, "Well, we've been paying $1,500 a day to this high school for the privilege of filming here." He said, "I'm afraid that's not enough. You need a permit from the City of Burbank." I said, "Nobody at the high school told me that we needed a permit. Can't we go over and get the permit from the necessary authorities?" He said, "Yes, but it's going to take a week to get it approved." I was absolutely horrified by that. I said, "You mean I can't shoot my movie for an entire week? I've got all these actors and crew standing around here and I'm paying them big money. Look, we've already got the set lit and the camera is in position and everything." The fire chief just shook his head, "No, it doesn't matter. I'm afraid you can't shoot here. You'll just have to take all the lights down and vacate the premises immediately." Oh, I could hardly breathe! I literally had my head in my hands at this point. I thought, "Jesus, this is an unmitigated disaster! How am I going to get out of this mess? What am I going to do? All the risks I've taken in my career, all the crazy stunts I've gotten away with, and now everything unravels so tamely?" Then, at the very moment I was contemplating all this, our production manager—who was standing right next to me—suddenly collapsed to the floor and went into an epileptic seizure. We were all just standing there in shock, looking down at the guy as he's writhing and convulsing on the floor. Now, the fire department were accompanied by the emergency guys and the medics came running in and heaved our production manager onto a stretcher. We were just staring open-mouthed as they strapped him down, carried him outside to their vehicle, and sped off to the hospital. Meanwhile we were all still standing there in silence, just looking at each other. The fire chief then walked over to me, tapped me on the shoulder, and said, "Go shoot your movie." And that was it! The fire department simply turned around and left and didn't bother us anymore. We quickly continued shooting the scene and everything was beautiful again. But I just couldn't believe what had happened. It was as if the production manager had suffered his epileptic fit right on cue. I mean, that was certainly the one time when I didn't have any way of getting out of the situation. I was completely pinned to the wall and couldn't figure out what my next move would be. I was thinking, "How am I going to outwit these firemen? What do I have to do to finish this picture?" Then—and precisely then—the production manager drops and the whole situation changes almost in an instant. I thought, "God is now my production manager!" [Laughs] It was crazy. I can't think of a more bizarre story than that one.

Who drew the cartoon family portrait that is glimpsed at the end of the film?

That's a good question. [Pause] You know, I have a copy of that portrait on my wall, but I don't remember who drew it. It might have been one of the cartoonists from *Mad* magazine. It looks like a Mort Drucker, but I don't think it was him.[10] Maybe it was one of Drucker's disciples.

Is it true that you encountered some distribution problems with *Full Moon High*? I know the film was delayed.

Well, AIP distributed the film, and one of the problems we encountered was they had sold *Full Moon High* to the tax shelter, just as they had done previously with *The Private Files of J. Edgar Hoover*. So, they had made a profit on the movie before it had even played anywhere. With the picture already in profit before it was finished, they didn't have to play the movie to make money. In fact, if they risked too much money on advertising and putting the film into theaters they would have stood a chance of losing money, whereas if they did nothing, they would end up making money. They had to distribute *Full Moon High* in a token fashion to satisfy the requirements of the government. To qualify as a tax shelter, the picture had to actually play, but they didn't have to play it that much in order to make money. It was a rather confusing scenario, but there you have it. The film went into profit and the studio made some money. I've been receiving cheques and making dough off *Full Moon High* for thirty years, even though it didn't really get a wide release. So, not only do I have a warm spot for the picture in my heart, every time I receive a cheque I get a warm spot in my wallet, too! [Chuckles]

Although *Full Moon High* is not one of your most accomplished efforts, it does seem to be one of your most fondly remembered films.

Everybody liked *Full Moon High*. Audiences just warmed to that movie and still do. It's constantly playing in the United States on cable and the DVD is out, so what can you say? After all these years, its still getting seen by people and that makes me very happy because a lot of films get lost along the way. I don't remember what kind of reviews it got from the critics at the time of its release, but it did receive a few positive notices. I do recall that one critic thought it was "second-rate Mel Brooks." It probably was, but I didn't mind being a second-rate Mel Brooks. It's interesting that you should mention distribution problems because I was just talking to Mel on the phone the other day. He was commiserating with me about how much trouble he's having even trying to put the financing together for a picture. Mel said, "Nobody wants to put up the money anymore. All the financing has dried up." Not only is he having difficulty financing projects as a director, he's having difficulties also as a producer. As you may know, Mel has produced movies such as *The Elephant Man* and *The Fly*. So, even though he is an older filmmaker, he could still produce, but nobody seems to want to give him any money. Now, I totally understand what that's like because it's tough for us all. The business has changed so much it's hard to really get a movie out there in the theaters. You know, I've been through the valleys like this before when things were slow. But then you sell something and it picks up again and you make another movie. You can't get discouraged by it. I *don't* get discouraged by it. It's just one of those things you have to go through and there's always a light at the end of the tunnel. Making movies, or tying to make movies, is not always as bad as some people make it out to be. It always looks depressing if the answer is no, but then somebody eventually says yes and all is right with the world again.

Speaking of Mel Brooks, one of his most cherished players, Kenneth Mars, appears as the football coach. Were you a fan of his?

Oh, I was a big fan. Kenneth was a great guy. He had terrific humour and charm about him. He was a very inventive comedic actor. In Mel's film *The Producers*, Kenneth famously played the Nazi who wrote the play "Springtime for Hitler"—a terrific performance. He'd also appeared in *Young Frankenstein* for Mel and was fantastic in both movies. In fact, Kenneth was fantastic in everything he ever did. He was a wonderful talent, and I was very sad to hear that he recently passed.[11] When we were making *Full Moon High*, Kenneth was always willing to try anything and was brimming with energy and enthusiasm. He was a dream to work with, actually. That whole cast was a dream. I couldn't have been happier with them. That's why I always look back on the experience of making *Full Moon High* with such affection.

Is it harder doing improvisations in a comedy than it is in a horror or science fiction film, particularly if you aren't working with a seasoned comedic actor?

Some actors do have better comedic timing than others, that's true. When you are improvising in a dramatic movie, even the mistakes can prove beneficial. It's funny how it sometimes works, but if the actors are fumbling for something, it can lend their performance a reality that you just don't get if they are simply delivering the lines as written. But comedy is slightly different and requires certain skills. You can fail more easily because humour can mean very different things to different people.

Did the famous quote by Edmund Gwenn "Dying is easy, comedy is hard" apply in your experience of making of *Full Moon High*?[12]

Well, firstly, let me just say there are various arguments about who actually said that quote. Edwin Booth[13] has been quoted as saying it. A lot of other people have been quoted as saying it. Somebody then suggested it was Edmund Gwenn, but it's been attributed to all these various individuals and improperly I would say. I don't even know if the statement itself is actually true. Secondly, I don't think that a comedy like *Full Moon High* is hard to make, but how a comedy plays to an audience may be a different issue entirely. When you make a dramatic film and it plays in the theater, you are not required to have a dramatic response from the people who are watching it. The audience just sits in their seats and watches the movie. However, when you make a comedy film, you are called upon to get an audible response from the audience every minute or so. If you are sitting in the theater watching a comedy and you don't hear anyone laughing, the audience quickly becomes aware that the picture is dying. That's why I think comedy can sometimes be harder. It's not the making of it as much as the reaction to it. If a comedy picture doesn't work, then you truly do die, and what a painful and miserable death it is. So, I would like to offer my own little twist on that famous quote: "Comedy is easy, but when the comedy dies in the theater it's very, very hard!"

See China and Die (1981)

Shortly after completing *Full Moon High*, you wrote and directed the little-seen TV movie *See China and Die*. How did that project get started?

See China and Die was originally a pilot for NBC. It was intended to be a series called *Momma the Detective* that would star Ester Rolle, a well-known television comedy star, who had appeared in the CBS show *Good Times*.[1] Ester was ripe to have another series, as she was extremely popular with audiences. *Momma the Detective* was an attempt to get her back into television again with a show that I would create, write, and direct. Regrettably, our series didn't get on the air.

What was it about?

It was about a Black maid named Momma Sykes, who loves reading detective fiction and whose son is actually a detective. She works as a housekeeper at a luxurious tower block for the richest people in Manhattan. Although her clients are incredibly wealthy, this maid is much smarter than the people she works for. She knows all about the rich tenants—their secrets and affairs and indiscretions—every nefarious thing they ever do. She knows something about everybody, but nobody knows anything about her. None of the people who employ her even know where she lives, which is usually the case with employers of household help. The thread of the mystery is that one of her clients is murdered shortly after returning from a trip to China. This film was set right after the Chinese Government had allowed tourism into their country. Unfortunately, he saw something over there which has caused him to be killed. The police begin to investigate the murder, but the maid then decides to solve the crime herself. Obviously, if the pilot had gone to series the maid would have investigated various crimes in each subsequent episode. *Momma the De-*

tective was similar in that respect to *Murder, She Wrote,* which appeared several years later. Both shows feature a woman who solves crimes in each episode and there is a parade of guest stars appearing every week in supporting roles. That was the idea anyway.

As much as I know these kinds of questions annoy you, may I enquire what the budget for the pilot was?

Sure, but I don't remember exactly. I think it was somewhere around a million dollars.

Did you have high hopes for *Momma the Detective*?

Yeah, I thought it was a good idea. When we got a deal with NBC to make it, *Momma the Detective* was supposed to be an hour-long pilot, and that would have been the title of the series had NBC continued with it. But I decided to make a ninety-minute version out of it and that eventually became *See China and Die*. My reasoning was that if I was going to make the hour-long pilot, I might as well make a ninety-minute version, so that it could be made as a theatrical movie, or as a TV movie, I could then sell into syndication. The fact is there's nothing more useless than an unsold one-hour pilot because there is no place to play it. A one-hour pilot has no value whatsoever as you can't market them in any way. I was able to make the ninety-minute version for the same money as the sixty-minute pilot, and we did indeed succeed in selling it into syndication. When I did the feature, I had to come up with a different title, and so *Momma the Detective* then became *See China and Die*, and has played many times on different cable stations under that title. So, we were able to make some money off the project in the backend after the show wasn't picked up. The hour-long version was telecast on NBC, but by the time it was on the network had already decided not to make the series.

Why?

Unfortunately, NBC had received two or three complaint letters—and I mean just two or three—from various Black organizations. They had apparently objected to a Black woman being depicted as a maid as they felt that idea was repellent. Yes, the character of Momma Sykes was a menial servant, but we strongly indicated that she was much cleverer than all the rich people she worked for. For example, there's a scene I like where Momma Sykes asks this tax expert, played by Fritz Weaver, to help with her taxes, but she soon demonstrates that she knows more than he does about income tax. There were a number of scenes like that, moments where she revealed just how smart she was. Of course, on top of everything, she successfully solves the murders and wins the day, but none of this seemed to matter. Certain people still felt that this kind of portrayal was demeaning and derogatory, and should not be seen on television. They failed to appreciate that this formidable woman was actually extremely intelligent, talented, and resourceful, despite her apparent low status and occupation. That was really the whole point of the story: Momma was far, far better than what she appeared to be or the manner in which she was perceived by others. Anyway, these isolated complaints were all NBC needed to hear. They quickly decided that they weren't going to put the show on the air, and so, ultimately, *Momma the Detective* was an exercise in futility.

Who informed you about the negative letters that were coming into the network?

I believe it was the agents who represented the project. Look, all it took back then was for two or three letters to filter in from some organization and that was it! Who knows if that particular organization was representing no more than two or three people? If they have a letterhead on their letter the whole network trembles and suddenly falls apart. At any rate, I don't think NBC even looked at the pilot when it came in.

Interestingly, Ester Rolle had previously played the housekeeper, Florida Evans, in the CBS sitcom *Maude* and, as you said, had continued with the role in its spin-off show, *Good Times*. She'd also played a maid in *Summer for my German Soldier* for which she won an Emmy.

Yeah, that's right, Ester had played maids before. What can I tell you?

Despite that, her performance in *See China and Die* has been likened to the "maid-mammy" characters of Hattie McDaniel, who famously played maids in *Gone with the Wind*, *Judge Priest*, *Alice Adams*, *George Washington Slept Here*, and *The Golden West*. How do you feel about accusations that you were deliberately styling the character of Momma Sykes on McDaniel's work?

I deny them, because that's not accurate. Momma Sykes was much more intelligent and sophisticated than the maids that had been depicted in previous films and television shows. The servants in most of those movies you mentioned were either situated during slavery or on the fringes of slavery. What was objectionable about those characters was that they always seemed happy to be slaves, whereas Momma Sykes was extremely independent. Not only was she smarter than the people she worked for, she knew that she was smarter than the people she worked for. Eventually, the people she worked for realized she was smarter than them, too! In a curious way, *See China and Die* was an outgrowth of *Black Caesar* and *Hell up in Harlem*. We had a couple of scenes in those movies where the household help suddenly pulled out guns and shot the people they were working for. *See China and Die* was kind of a sanitized, tone-downed version of that idea. What I found interesting is that the household help are almost invisible in rich homes because they are there all the time. They see and know everything, but the employers see and know nothing of the household help. They don't know where the help live, or how many kids they have, or what their background is. So, there is an interesting split that exists between them and I thought I could exploit that division dramatically.

Did you secure all of your first choices for the project?

Oh yeah, we had a wonderful cast. The British actress Jean Marsh from *Upstairs, Downstairs* was in it. She was in New York at the time and was available, so we cast her. We also hired Paul Dooley[2], who is a great character actor, and Frank Converse, who had played the lead in *Coronet Blue*. I brought back Andy Duggan, who, as you know, had been in a lot of my movies, and Fritz Weaver, who had appeared in "Medal for a Turncoat." Fritz was always a very pleasant man and a true professional, and he does comedy so well. The same can be said about Paul Dooley. Paul has been in a lot of movies and is a lovely guy. I ran into him just recently and asked how he was doing. It turns out that he's doing great as his wife wrote the book for the musical, *Wicked*, one of the biggest musicals on Broadway and on tour. In every country in the world, they are doing productions of *Wicked*, and since Paul's wife wrote the book, she gets three and a half percent of all ticket sales worldwide. You can only imagine how many millions of dollars are flooding into Paul Dooley's bank account—next to his wife, of course—so he is a very happy man. I also hired Kene Holliday to play Momma's detective son. Kene was a nice fellow, but I don't know whatever happened to him.[3] There was also an interesting Spanish actor in the cast who played a small supporting role.[4] He was actually a Puerto Rican playwright, who had written *Short Eyes*, a very famous off-Broadway play about a gay prisoner in jail. So, we had some very compelling actors in the piece, and they were all extremely cooperative. They simply came in and did their jobs, which is all you can ask for. The great thing about dealing with talented people like Jean Marsh and Fritz Weaver is you don't have to tell them what to do. They already know their business.

What about the late Ester Rolle? What was she like to work with?

Oh, Ester was delightful. I loved working with her. She was absolutely as cute as can be. She was very funny and we'd often kid around together.

In one scene, a man in an oriental mask chases Momma Sykes out to the end of a pier. She then knocks him off the dock by continually rocking the boardwalk back and forth with her own weight.

Yes, well, there is no denying that Ester was a very heavy woman. I tried to make use of that by having her character use her weight to shake the narrow boardwalk. I thought that was a very funny bit.

Was Rolle ever concerned that the joke was being made at her expense?

No, not at all. She thought it was great. I actually made that up when we found the location. The pier was there and I said, "Okay, let's write this into the script." We just used it and devised that whole scene with Momma knocking the guy into the water. That's another good example of always using a location to its utmost advantage.

How did Rolle feel about the negative reaction from a few complaining viewers? Did she ever object to the screenplay and her maid character in any way?

No, absolutely not. Ester was delighted with the idea and that's why she signed on. As I say, she was a very popular TV star. Ester could have had her pick of what project she wanted to do next, but she thought *Momma the Detective* was going to be a successful series. I think Ester was just as appalled as I was when the network treated it so badly. But you know, most TV pilots don't get on. I mean, at the time we made *Momma the Detective* NBC had sanctioned something like forty pilots but only a few new series were actually made. When you weigh that situation up, the odds are always stacked heavily against you when making a TV pilot and the venture often ends in disappointment. Even if the network does put the show on sometimes they schedule it during a time period that is absolutely ridiculous and self-defeating. When that happens, you can't get a rating because you are up against some established blockbuster hit that is going to bury you. Television is extremely difficult, but thanks to cable and the fact that there are now forty different stations airing shows rather than three or four, you do have a better chance. Also, with the instant recording we have at our disposal today, people can now record a show and see it later at their behest. They can get it on demand and that adds a lot to the viewing possibilities.

Why did you choose to set the story in New York?

I was living in New York at the time. I had a townhouse on 79th Street, and I was really enjoying the city. More than that, I always enjoy shooting movies in New York, and I thought it would be the perfect place to set this particular story. I always used to describe New York City as "my backlot" as I was so familiar with it. We shot some scenes around Rockefeller Centre and the Radio City Music Hall, and also around the Diamond District of the city. 47th Street is where the diamond merchants all sell their wares and is located between Fifth Avenue and Sixth Avenue in midtown Manhattan. It famously featured in *Marathon Man*[5] during the scene where Laurence Olivier, who plays a Nazi war criminal, knifes an elderly Holocaust survivor who recognizes him in the midst of this bustling street. We used that same area when we shot a chase sequence, which was a lot of fun to do. What was interesting about the film was we had a full union crew of about fifty or sixty people. Obviously, I couldn't shoot that chase scene in the Diamond District with so many crew people, so I knowingly sent them to a different location. Basically, I lied! [Chuckles] I sent them to a fictitious location and I only took five or six people with me. We went over to the Diamond District, shot the sequence, and left the rest of my crew abandoned someplace else until we got finished. We later went over and joined them, but I guess I was resorting to my old ways, even though we had a very big crew on that particular picture. The fact that *See China and Die* was originally an NBC pilot meant we simply had to carry a full load of crew people.

What is the extent of your own interest in detective fiction and mysteries? Are you a fan of that brand of literature?

Not particularly, no. I find that most mystery books and thrillers start off rather well, but when they attempt to tie the story up at the end they are usually rather disappointing. A lot of these books run out of steam and stutter to an unremarkable and inane conclusion in the last couple of chapters. As a reader you often say to yourself, "Why did I read 400 pages to get to *this*?" It would have been much more valuable if I had spent that time writing something myself. Very often, when I'm reading a book, after a few chapters I'll say, "I can do better than this!" I then put the book down and do that exact thing. I have a lot of unfinished books.

Are you a fan of Agatha Christie?

I've read a lot of Agatha Christie's books because they are very short. They are good to read on an airplane, something like that. I like her classic ones such as *Ten Little Indians*[6] and, of course, I love the movie adaptation of *Witness for the Prosecution*[7] very much. As a matter of fact, the mystery at the heart of *See China and Die* is resolved—in the classic tradition—during a dinner scene. We did a thing like Agatha Christie does in her Hercule Poirot books, where we assembled all the suspects together in one place for the final revelation. In this case, since Momma Sykes was a housekeeper and a cook, she invites everybody over for a big meal and they all sit around the table as she serves them. During the course of the meal, she cleverly exposes the killer and then brings out the dessert, which was a Baked Alaska. All the suspects who were innocent then blow out the candles, and that was the end of the film. I thought the mystery elements of *See China and Die* were very successful and that the resolution paid off well.

Do you think the comedic elements were as successful?

Oh yeah, I thought so. I thought the picture was a lot of fun. When we screened it for people in New York, we had a lot of laughs and I think the audience really seemed to enjoy the comedic aspects. I believe I only screened *See China and Die* for a theater audience once, but it played very nicely. Actually, in general, I thought it was rather cute but I certainly wouldn't call it one of my major achievements.

Do you think *See China and Die* looks and plays like a TV movie?

Yeah, it was rather television-ny. I don't know what the rule about that is but if you have an unmade pilot, or an un-bought pilot, it doesn't get on the air unless it is feature-length. If you've made a two-hour pilot or a ninety-minute pilot, you can always release it as a feature, despite the fact that it has the look and feel of a TV movie. Usually the dead giveaway that a film is a TV movie is every fifteen minutes or so—for no reason at all—there is a fade-out punctuated with a bland musical sting followed by a fade-in. Obviously, this is where the commercials were situated when it was originally telecast. When I shot *See China and Die*, I didn't have those fade-outs and fade-ins, because I instinctively knew that it would make it look like the generic TV movies we usually saw back then. I find all that business unnecessary anyway, because whenever the audience saw and heard those cues it was obvious that they were looking at a TV movie. I did not want that.

***See China and Die* is one of your rarest films and hasn't been awarded any kind of official DVD release.**

Well, after the one-hour version was aired on NBC and I sold the show into syndication, it played on syndicated TV for a while. I've heard of one person who actually sells copies of *See China and Die*, but, yeah, it is very hard to find. I have a VHS copy here in my house, and I also have a 35mm print somewhere upstairs. I haven't run that print in a long time, so god knows what it looks like now after more than thirty years. It would be good to have a DVD release of the picture—if there was any interest in it. To be honest with you, I don't know how many people would be interested in buying that particular movie. But it is worth repeating that for an unsold television pilot, which are hardly ever seen again if they die a death, it was very good. At least this one got some visibility and we still made something out of it. There were quite a number of good things in *See China and Die* as a film but, unfortunately, it wasn't appreciated. If I had not made that ninety-minute version, it would have probably suffered the same fate that most pilots suffer: it would have completely disappeared without trace.

Intermission: *I, the Jury* (1982)

Let's talk about *I, the Jury* which you began shooting in 1981 before being fired from the production and replaced by Richard T. Heffron.[1]

Well, *I, the Jury* was a picture that I started making in New York for a company called American Cinema. It was based on the novel by Mickey Spillane[2], and starred Armand Assante as Mike Hammer, the famous private eye. We also put together a great supporting cast for the movie, which included Barbara Carrera, Paul Sorvino, and Laurene Landon, but it wasn't one of my own productions and I had a lot of problems with the producers. Basically, we just couldn't get along because they didn't know what they were doing. I found out that they wouldn't be able to pay a lot of the vendors in New York that I had dealt with over the years—the laboratories and equipment houses that I had used on other films—and we had to lie about it. I had good credit with these companies, and so when I learned that the people I was working for were not going to be able to pay them, I was horrified that the vendors would think it was all my fault. So, I called them up and told them to be sure to collect their money right away or they might not get paid at all. When the producers learned about what I had done, they fired me. At the time, I was pretty devastated by that decision. I mean, it's not a pleasant feeling being fired off a movie. You can feel very alone and isolated and vulnerable. I had optioned the novel of *I, the Jury*, and put the whole project together. Of course, these producers had then come in with the money but, unfortunately, they just didn't have a clue. It was a very disappointing experience, but I couldn't just stand back and allow them to take advantage of the people who had been kind enough to give me credit in the past. I figured that if I didn't do something about it, I would never be able to make another picture in New York again. I would be blamed for the fact that these vendors got stiffed on their equipment and services, and my reputation and good standing would be in ruins. I just couldn't let that happen.

How long into shooting was it before you were fired?

It was just under a week. I think it was six days. Then, afterwards, the movie descended into total chaos and the company went bankrupt. The picture ended up costing $11 million and it still looked rather cheap. 20th Century Fox then bought *I, the Jury* in a bankruptcy sale, so it didn't really end well for anybody.

It's been reported that Mickey Spillane was displeased that you were mounting a second theatrical version of *I, the Jury* as he was shooting his own loose reworking of the novel as *Margin for Murder*, a TV movie for CBS. Were you aware of this?

No. Mickey Spillane didn't have the rights to *I, the Jury* anyway. He sold the rights. I bought the rights from Sir John Wolf over in England, who was the son-in-law of Victor Saville,[3] the man who had made the first *I, the Jury* movie. It was a 3D movie and it was terrible—a real dog! Anyway, Saville's estate owned the rights to the book. Spillane did not have a say in the matter anymore and I think he was unhappy because he didn't get any money out of the remake. He may not have received a cent, but we did succeed in reviving interest in the character of Mike Hammer by doing the movie. Spillane was then able to do a TV movie based on the character and that later spun off into a series starring Stacy Keach, which was on for several years. Later on, they had another series with Stacy Keach, so there were two Mike Hammer series made. I mean, the character was as dead as a doornail until I optioned the rights for *I, the Jury*. In fact, I only paid $50,000 for the rights, so it was a very good deal. Spillane would not have been too happy because he didn't get anything out of that deal himself.

Is it true that the Victor Saville estate also sold you the rights to two other Spillane properties, as well as *I, the Jury*?

No. I had a right to go back and option two more properties, which I believe were *My Gun is Quick* and *Kiss Me Deadly*, but I didn't. I only acquired *I, the Jury*. I knew that *I, the Jury* was a very popular book. In fact, I'd read somewhere that it was the most popular detective novel ever written in terms of sales.

I've read that Spillane rejected your invitation to help promote *I, the Jury* when you initially approached him about it before shooting began. Is this accurate?

I never approached Spillane, so I wasn't rejected about anything because I never approached him. He was not part of the equation.

Did you ever meet Spillane?

No, never.

That's interesting, because it's my understanding that he was apparently delighted that you were fired from *I, the Jury* by the "money men."

I had no idea about that. I don't understand why Mickey Spillane would be delighted that I was fired. I had never even talked to the man or had any connection with him. He would have had no knowledge of the internal workings of the project or the reasons for why I was fired. I hope he didn't blame me for the fact he wasn't getting any money. I simply didn't have anything to do with him. I just bought the rights from the Victor Saville estate and went ahead and put the picture together. I had no intention of harming Spillane in any way or dealing him any dirt. It was just the way it was, that's all. He wasn't entitled to any money and he didn't receive any.

Do you think Spillane's attitude may have also partly stemmed from the fact that you abandoned much of his original novel?

Oh, I didn't follow his novel at all except for a few key things. If you read Spillane's book and then my screenplay, you will see that I changed a lot of it. That practice is by no means unusual when I have adapted books into screenplays. I did retain the opening scene with the murder of the one-armed man and also the climax with the woman psychiatrist, who is played in the movie by Barbara Carrera. I included her character because the last scene of the book in which Hammer shoots the psychiatrist and says "It was easy" is a very famous one. I simply had to include it. That's a rather iconic quote from *I, the Jury* and has even been quoted in Paddy

Chayefsky's movie, *Marty*. There's a scene where the guys are all sitting around, talking about a book they've read and what a great writer Mickey Spillane is. One of Marty's buddies describes the last scene in the book, the famous "It was easy" scene. So, I had to keep that in and I had to retain the fact that Hammer's friend was murdered and he is trying to solve and avenge the crime. There were probably other things in there, too, but the rest of the script was really me. I just used the book as a starting point to express my own ideas about the story and the characters.

Spillane hated your screenplay, so he must have read it at some point.

Again, I have no idea. Stop asking me questions about Mickey Spillane because I really don't know anything.

How did you approach the character of Mike Hammer?

I wanted to subvert the character of Hammer, try to see what would make a guy like that really tick. Who is this man? Why does he do the things he does? I saw Hammer as something of a psychopath himself. He had a psychopathic quality to him, only he doesn't know this. I don't know how many psychopaths literally pause for a moment and think, "Boy, I'm a real nut," you know? People just behave as they naturally do. But Hammer was a sadist who enjoyed inflicting pain on people. My idea was that his dealings with the psychiatrist would have revealed some disturbing aspects of his life and character to him, things that Hammer would not have wanted to confront. I mean, Hammer is a macho guy, sleeping with all these women and punching people out and everything, and he suddenly learns from her what all his hang-ups really are. One of the things I played with in my script was the subtle suggestion that there was the possibility of a homosexual relationship between Hammer and his best friend who has been murdered. The psychiatrist reveals to Hammer in a medical report that his close friend was gay and was in love with him. This comes as devastating news to Hammer, who, let's not forget, is a tough guy who lets his fists, and not his feelings, do the talking. This aspect of the story was there for those viewers who wished to read into it. That inference is mostly missing from the movie you see now, but that was an interesting subversion of Spillane's Hammer. Also, with a lot of these kinds of stories, you are playing with the idea that it takes a bad man to catch a bad man. Hammer has those same psychopathic tendencies as the criminals and he is going around killing people in cold blood. You don't do things like that unless you are a little crazy in the head. That's very much in keeping with the modern portrayal of heroes in films and in television. Today, there are no more heroes—only anti-heroes.

What prompted you to make Hammer a Vietnam War veteran?

I thought that if Hammer was of the age he was in the movie, he would have probably been in Vietnam. We were doing *I, the Jury* as a contemporary film rather than as a period piece. There was really no point in doing the picture as a period piece because, ultimately, what value would it have had? It was better to update the story and the characters, and bring in new elements like the Central Intelligence Authority and mind treatments, and so on. I came up with the idea that the Government were using psychopaths to commit political crimes and murders, and were using a sex clinic as a front to locate suitable candidates that could be successfully programmed. As it turns out, we weren't that far off in terms of what the Government was trying to do with psychopathic people—programming and training them to be ruthless killers. Again, I wanted to play with the idea that Hammer was not that different from the psychopath that is programmed to commit sex crimes. Hammer is a vicious killer, too.

There were several films made throughout the 1980s that featured characters who were Vietnam veterans battling to preserve their own dignity, sanity, and destructive urges upon returning to civilian life. Of course, *First Blood* and its sequels immediately come to mind. What did you make of these portrayals?

Those movies usually depict veterans as being like human weapons: time bombs that are ready to detonate and turn on all those who mess with them. Hammer is very different to Rambo because he has more layers of depth and subtlety. He is on a mission of revenge for his dead friend. It's often said that a lot of veterans returned from Vietnam as damaged men, but I'm sure a percentage of them were already damaged before they went and their problems were exacerbated by the rigors of combat. I'm sure some men were traumatised by what they had witnessed and experienced, and some turned to drugs and alcohol as a means of escape. Of course, a lot of civilians do that, too. They don't need combat experience to have a reason to get wasted. But in my script, I made Hammer an ex-alcoholic who is struggling to hold his life together. He is constantly eating candy bars as a substitute and carries them in his pockets, ready to pull one out and gobble it down. He's an addict on the edge and he can topple off at any moment. None of his alcoholism is really played up in the finished film. There's the scene in *First Blood* where Jack Starrett plays the cop who is brutalizing Sylvester Stallone at the police station and Rambo goes crazy. Originally, I had a sequence in *I, the Jury* where the CIA capture Hammer and forcibly put some Scotch down his throat. It would have been a tremendous scene—very emotionally-charged and powerful—but, no, that had to go, too! They changed the whisky to Hammer having to endure some electric shocks. That may have seemed a more painful form of torture, but it's weaker, certainly dramatically. It was just too obvious for me and really lacked something. By using the whisky, Hammer's tormentors would have been forcing him to confront his own addiction. He would have had to summon all of his courage and willpower not to guzzle the liquor down. All of that was lost, along with the suggestion that Hammer may have wanted to surrender to his demons on one level. It's not unreasonable to suggest that he wanted to be forced to drink because that removed all his guilt and culpability. That was very interesting stuff and would have given the picture a lot more depth.

As you have already remarked, Hammer is somewhat psychotic and is incredibly violent in the finished film. How much of that was your doing?

The violence was all in the script. Everything that's in there was all in the script. Actually, they followed my script pretty well. I did have problems with the style of the film and the casting of some of the parts, but, in general, they followed my script. Everything Hammer did was in there: pouring cement over the guy; closing the cab door on the mobster's coat so that when the vehicle pulls away he's dragged across the street. That was all in the script.

What about Hammer driving the Japanese cook's face down into the burning hibachi grill?

Oh yeah, that was in there, too. I thought that moment was very poorly realized in the movie. It was just too abrupt and had no build-up. There was no rationalisation to it. All of a sudden, it just happens and plays like a brutal act of arbitrary violence. I mean, how is it that the cook just happens to be there? And how come he tries to slash the other person in the restaurant? There was just no build-up for how it was shot.

You have also gone on record as objecting to the orgy scene being intercut with the twins being stabbed to death.

I certainly objected to the way it was shot, but I didn't necessarily object to the concept itself. I just thought it was very shabbily done.

At the time of the film's release, you complained that Richard T. Heffron had inserted "obscene" sequences into *I, the Jury* and that you had originally wanted to make a "lighter, James Bond" sort of film. Is this true?

Well, I didn't say that, or I didn't mean that. I meant that *I, the Jury* should have been a slicker, glossier movie and not look quite as cheap as it did. I mean, the whole reason I got into this was because I'd read a review by Bosley Crowther in *The New York Times* when *Dr. No* opened. Crowther had likened James Bond to Mike Hammer and wrote, "This character owes a lot to Mickey Spillane." I thought, "Oh, if we could just make some Mike Hammer movies—and make them big and expensive-looking—we could do a whole series of them. We could have a continuing character that is similar to James Bond." Honestly, we could have done a number of big-budget pictures, but each picture would've had to have been beautifully done and made better than the previous one. You know, up until that time, Hollywood was making sequels and trying to make the picture at half the price of the preceding instalment. They would simply reuse the title, like they did with *The Return of the Magnificent Seven*. So, the idea was that each successive Mike Hammer picture would be bigger and more expensive than the last one. It would have more action and more quality to it, like the James Bond movies did. They kept elevating the production values, stunts, gags, and storylines, transforming Bond into this spectacularly successful and enduring franchise. With the Mike Hammer thing, they were just "cheaping-out" as they say.

The realization of Velda, Hammer's devoted secretary, has been described as one of the truest onscreen portrayals of the character.

Well, Laurene Landon was terrific in the role, and she got all the best reviews for the picture. Gene Siskel and Roger Ebert both loved her and thought she was going to be a big star. Laurene did a great job and she looked beautiful, even though she was a blonde and Velda was usually portrayed as a brunette. Frankly, Laurene stole every scene she was in. I think Armand Assante was a little upset with her because she was taller than him. On top of that, when they both went to the firing range to practice their shooting Laurene could also outshoot him. Assante wasn't too friendly to her throughout the course of filming. Anyway, Laurene did a good job, and she would have probably been a big star if she hadn't have gone off to Spain to do *Yellow Hair*[4] and *Hundra*, two sword and sorcery movies. That took two years out of her career. By the time she got back, all the momentum she had generated was gone. Laurene did play the leads in both those pictures but, unfortunately, it took the wind out of her sails. I always say that in Hollywood, you have to follow up every successful movie with another successful movie—one on top of the other—to become a box office star.

Did they use any of the scenes you had shot in the finished film?

No. The producers threw all out of the footage I'd shot and started all over again with the new director. I had started shooting *I, the Jury* in Panavision and they later changed the visual format to 1:85. So, my scenes were obviously not compatible or useable with the new stuff that they had shot, so it all had to go. They did one scene at the beginning where Hammer is in bed with the girl and he's talking to her husband on the phone. The husband has actually hired Hammer to follow the girl and Hammer is reporting back to the husband on his wife's doings as he's screwing her. All of that was shot in widescreen Panavision and the rest of the picture was shot in 1:85, so they changed the whole process of shooting after I was gone. They also recast one or two of the parts—replacing actors I had shot—with some very poor people.

How did you learn that your screenplay was being altered and certain scenes you had written were being excised altogether?

Laurene Landon and I were in a relationship at the time, so I viewed a copy of her script. I soon noticed that several changes had been made, and certainly not for the better! Laurene was also being told by certain people not to show me the new scenes that were being written. That was a little tough to take, but hey, what can you do about it? I was off the picture by then and that was it. My script had a lot of Larry Cohen touches and innovations, some that were unfortunately lost or executed rather poorly during shooting.

What kinds of things were changed?

Oh, I don't know. At the end of the film you see now, Hammer presents the woman psychiatrist with a box of flowers that actually contains his dead friend's prosthetic arm. I had nothing to do with that. All the endings I had in mind culminated with Hammer shooting the woman psychiatrist. That was always the last scene. I also wrote another scene in my version of the script where Hammer takes the prosthetic arm and viciously beats the bad guy to death with it. In effect, the villain has been killed by the fake arm of the very man he murdered. I thought that was a very clever touch and it would have made a terrific scene. As a matter of fact, I think it would have been comparable to the shoeshine scene in *Black Caesar*. It could have had that same kind of power, you know? Unfortunately, that was not in the picture.

Do you think Armand Assante was miscast in the role of Mike Hammer?

I don't think he was miscast; it was just that he wasn't good enough. I mean, Assante was okay for the part, but I did have somebody else in mind for Hammer at one point. When I was casting *I, the Jury*, I was reading various actors for the role of the villain and in walked a young actor that I immediately liked. I said to this guy, "Don't read the villain. Read the Mike Hammer part," which he proceeded to do. He was very good but, unfortunately, Armand had already been cast. I told this guy, "Look, you were great. In fact, you are a lot better than Armand Assante. I wish I could put you in the part, but it's too late now. Armand already has a contract and the wardrobe." This young man thanked me and we said our goodbyes and that was that. A few years later, I went to the Golden Globes in Los Angeles and this same young man approached me. I didn't know who he was, but he said, "I just wanted to thank you because you were the person who gave me the most encouragement back in New York." I smiled, thanked him, and he walked away. My sister was with me and she immediately said, "Do you know who that was?" I said, "I know he's an actor. I remember reading him once." She said, "Larry, that's Bruce Willis. He's got the hottest new show on TV. It's called *Moonlighting*."[5] Of course, within a very short time, Bruce Willis went on to make *Die Hard* and became a huge movie star. It was nice that he came over and said that to me. I think if we'd had Bruce in *I, the Jury* it would have been a far more successful picture.

He would have been an interesting choice for Hammer.

If Bruce had played that part, we would have made five Mike Hammer movies. He would have given it just the right touch and the thing would have taken off and been a big success. I don't think I would have been fired either if Bruce had been on the picture. Basically, I think one of the reasons I was fired was because of Armand Assante's lusting after Laurene Landon. Armand was well aware that Laurene and I were an item at the time. He was trying to get rid of me, so that he would have a clear path to Laurene. So, I think he worked with the producers and got me fired. I don't think that would have happened with Bruce, but you never can tell. Anyway, that's what happened and that's the way it was.

It's certainly no exaggeration to say that over the years you have been a highly vocal and unrepentant critic of *I, the Jury*.

Yeah, I have, but I must admit that the picture is a little better than I originally thought it was. I actually ran it last year and thought, "Well, it's not quite as bad as I remember." I mean, it's still bad, just not as bad as my memory told me it was. At the time, the whole experience of *I, the Jury* was depressing and a little weird, frankly. I mean, what can you do? My reaction was to simply refuse to let it get me down for too long. But I had such high hopes and expectations for the movie and all of them had been quickly dashed. I viewed *I, the Jury* as a missed opportunity to do something great, but it was all gone. Suddenly, I was out on the street with no movie and I needed something else to do. That's when *Q* came along.

Q – *The Winged Serpent* (1982)

Q – *The Winged Serpent* remains one of the films that your admirers like the most. After your dismissal from *I, the Jury*, I understand that the beginnings of this project were rather fraught and hasty?

You could say that. [Chuckles] After they fired me, the producers of *I, the Jury* thought I was going to leave New York immediately and return to California, but I certainly had no intention of doing that. After a few days spent alone in my hotel room feeling depressed, I suddenly decided that I was going to make another picture right away. I thought that if I didn't do something quickly, the stink over my dismissal would hang around and people would perhaps be second-guessing me, or thinking I was no longer employable or something. I already had the script for *Q – The Winged Serpent* sitting idly in my closet. I'd written it about six months earlier and devised this story about an enormous flying dinosaur terrorising a modern metropolis. I was now determined that I would make this little monster movie instead and show everybody that I wasn't beaten down. I didn't have any financing arranged or any actors in place, nothing like that. Actually, the very first thing I did was to hire a helicopter pilot and cameraman, and start shooting the aerial photography in the skies above New York City. So, only a matter of days after I was fired from *I, the Jury*, I was already shooting *Q*. I only did two days of pre-production!

How did you assemble the cast so quickly?

It all happened very, very fast. I was having lunch with a young actress at a restaurant opposite Lincoln Centre, when I noticed that Michael Moriarty was sitting at the next table. I'd always admired Moriarty's work, and started telling this actress what a wonderful performer he was. I mentioned some of the outstanding performances he had given in television and in film, and the various awards he had collected. I glanced over and noticed that Moriarty was looking over at me, listening to our conversation. He smiled and, a few moments later, I went over to introduce myself. We struck up a conversation and I mentioned that I had a script called Q that might contain a good part for him. Moriarty shook my hand and agreed to read it. The very next day he called me, saying he would do the picture and wanted to play the part of Jimmy Quinn, the small-time crook. Shortly after this, I got Candy Clark involved to play Jimmy's girlfriend. A few years earlier, Candy had been Oscar-nominated for her role in *American Graffiti* and, at the time I was readying Q, she was appearing in the off-Broadway play, *Two White Chicks*. I also asked Richard Roundtree to come in from California to play one of the cops, and after those actors were in place, I contacted my old army buddy David Carradine, who was attending the Cannes Film Festival. I thought he would be a good choice to play the detective who is investigating the mysterious deaths that are occurring in the city. I told David, "I'm doing this new picture and we start shooting in a couple of days. Michael Moriarty and Candy Clark are in it, and I've got a good part for you." Naturally, he asked me what it was all about and I said, "Look, just come back and do the picture. You'll love this part, I promise." David then agreed to be in it and flew back to the States from France. We were shooting the scene where Moriarty auditions for the job of a jazz singer and is playing the scat piano, when David literally arrived at the bar from the airport. He was actually wearing the same suit that he wears in that scene. I do remember that he was very nervous that first day. David really didn't know what he had gotten himself into. He was asking me all these questions, but I remember just telling him to enter the room, sit at the bar, and engage the bartender in conversation. It's that little exchange where the bartender asks the detective if he's found the window cleaner's head yet, and he replies, "No, but it'll turn up." Now, David didn't know anything about the character he was playing, or what scene we were shooting, or even what the whole movie was about! I don't believe he had ever allowed himself to be placed in such a vulnerable situation like that before in his career. Fortunately, he trusted me, but moments after we finished shooting that scene, David was so nervous and upset he immediately went outside and threw up in the street.

Meanwhile, as you commenced with the shooting of Q, the production of *I, the Jury* was also moving forward with its new director.

That's right. In fact, as we began work on Q, everybody congregated at the Mayflower Hotel in New York, which was also where the cast and crew of *I, the Jury* were staying. They were all astonished when they saw me leaving for work in the morning at the same time they were with a bunch of new actors. They couldn't believe that I was already making another movie within three or four days of being fired. On any given day, I had a crew of twelve people on Q as opposed to the hundred crew-people that were working on *I, the Jury*. Despite this, we finished shooting Q in eighteen days, but they continued on for about thirty days until they eventually ran out of money and filed for bankruptcy. That's when *I, the Jury* was sold to Fox in auction and, oddly enough, about eight months later, both pictures opened on the exact same day in New York. Q opened at the Rivoli Theatre and *I, the Jury* opened two blocks away at the National Theatre. Their picture cost ten times as much as ours, but we ended up doing three times as much business as they did. We also received better reviews. So, it all worked out very happily for me in the end, but it would never have happened if I hadn't been fired. I guess adversity can sometimes become triumph.

An intriguing aspect of Q is the promotion of low-life career criminal Jimmy Quinn from what would have ordinarily been seen as a secondary character to leading anti-hero status. This is at the expense of the cops who are usually the main protagonists in a genre film.

The cops would not have been very interesting characters because they only have one element to them: find the monster and kill it. You've already seen that approach a million times before in countless horror movies. This is exactly what the cops always do. Firstly, they don't believe that whatever it is out there killing people actually exists. Secondly, when they are finally convinced that the monster is real, they simply go out and attempt to destroy it. That's the familiar generic pattern we all recognize and it's almost a given. I thought it would be far more intriguing to move into the story from a different angle and tell it from the point of view of this kooky criminal who wants to be a jazz singer. He becomes the guy who discovers the location of the monster's lair in the Chrysler Building and decides to blackmail the city into signing away a million dollars to him. He also demands immunity from his crimes—a "Nixon-type pardon," as he puts it. Quinn is basically a nobody, who wants to become a somebody. He tries to make use of this monster for his own devices, and I thought that was a very unusual and original story that hadn't been told before. Also, it would demonstrate that people sometimes have an opportunity to exploit a situation and make a success of themselves at the expense of everyone else's tragedy. Quinn didn't have any compunction about doing that. He wasn't what you would call a conventional good guy, but he wasn't a total scumbag either. He was kind of like this blundering child-man; an entertaining, endearing loser that I think people liked.

Quinn is indeed a richly complex creation. He has greed and stupidity, but also a profound humanity that immediately reels you in.

Absolutely. Part of that character was arrived at in the writing, but a huge part of it was a mixture of Moriarty's brilliance and some good fortune. On the first day of shooting, I discovered that Michael could play the piano. I noticed he was wearing a walkman and I asked him what he was listening to. He said, "Oh, just some songs that I wrote." When I heard them, I said, "Wait a minute, do you play the piano?" He goes, "Sure." That immediately got my imagination working. I said, "Why don't we make this guy an aspiring jazz singer and piano player? Yeah, he wants to try and break into nightclub performing but nobody will give him a chance. He's frustrated by his lack of success and decides to join in on this robbery. If he'd gotten the job, he would never have gone out and committed the crime and none of this monster business would have ever happened to him." Moriarty quickly warmed to that idea. So, our next move was to quickly locate a nightclub or bar that had a piano in it and was open during the day. We found a bar in the East Village, and the next day we shot the scene with Moriarty playing scat-piano as Candy and David look on. Michael had prepared the song he plays in that scene and he loved the fact it wasn't in the script. That addition helped to give his character a little more depth and shading, but it was a completely fortuitous thing. Of course, Moriarty's performance is simply extraordinary.

Personally, I think it's one of the best performances ever to grace a horror film.

Oh, I agree with you, it's remarkable. Moriarty's performance has drawn incredible praise from some incredible people. I was talking with Steven Spielberg at an event and he told me how much he loved Michael in *Q*. I was surprised that Steven had seen the picture, but he apparently caught it one night on cable. He asked me, "How did you get that performance out of Michael Moriarty? I've never seen him do anything like that before." I explained to him the way we worked, and he seemed very impressed. That was a major compliment, but I find that Steven is very apt to compliment people and make them feel good about their work. He tries to say something nice as he knows how much it will mean coming from him.

Q marked the first of five collaborations you have enjoyed with Moriarty who is a fascinating actor. What continually draws you to him?

Number one, he's an exceptional talent and, number two, he's accustomed to my improvisational style of working. You can't give most actors new lines of dialogue on the set that are not written in the script, because they can't pull them off in the moment. When they are right there acting in the scene and the camera is rolling, you can't suddenly start feeding them new stuff to do and say without them getting terribly confused. But Moriarty is so much in character, and his concentration is so intense, that if you give him new directions he can implement them immediately. When we were working on Q—and on all the other films we've done together—I would often call out lines to him right in the middle of a scene. I would just yell things like, "Say this, say that," and he would integrate them effortlessly into his performance. Then, in editing, I'd just cut my voice out of the soundtrack so you didn't hear me coaching him. I can talk him through scenes and give him new stuff just at the very moment it comes into my head. Moriarty can pick this material right up and put it directly into the scene like an improvisation. I can't tell you how many other actors I've tried that with who have gotten totally befuddled. They just can't do it. But Moriarty is amazing in his ability to just wing it and collaborate with me throughout the whole picture. Michael has earned a reputation in the business for being "difficult," but I always kept him interested and entertained. There was always new material going into the scenes, and he is an actor who—if he grows bored with the project—will give you less of a performance. But if you can keep him hyped-up and stimulated about what is going on, then he's happy and churning out his best work.

Despite the outrageous speed with which Q happened, were there any other actors that you considered for the principal roles?

Actually, yes, there were. I had seen a young comic named Eddie Murphy perform at The Improv in New York and was very impressed with his act. You could see right away that this kid was going to be a star, and I thought he'd be an interesting choice to play Moriarty's character. This was just before Eddie broke out big with *48 Hrs* and *Trading Places*. Nothing ever came of it, and Moriarty may have already been cast by this point, but Eddie could have done it. Of course, I don't think Eddie could have played that part any better than Moriarty. No actor, not even Jack Nicholson or Al Pacino, could have done that. Michael just had this magic about him. Every sound, every gesture, every movement of his body was perfect. Moriarty completely inhabited that part and delivered an Oscar-worthy performance. I was happy with all my casting choices for *Q*, but I later felt that Bruce Willis would have been good for the part of the detective that Carradine played. This was before Bruce became a huge star. As I told you, I'd wanted Bruce to play Mike Hammer in *I, the Jury* but Armand Assante had already been cast. When it came time to make *Q*, I should have cast Bruce as the detective, but David Carradine was a name at the time and was being used to sell the picture, particularly in foreign markets. So, I went with David, although for the longevity of the film, it would have obviously been better to have used Bruce in that part. It certainly would have looked better on the DVD jacket all these years later. Can you imagine it? "Eddie Murphy and Bruce Willis in *Q*!" It would have been an interesting combination, that's for sure. Naturally, I would never have been able to secure Sam Arkoff's money if I'd cast two unknowns as the leads. Sam wanted recognizable names in the picture, and Eddie and Bruce had not done any real movies at the time. Back then, nobody had really heard of them.

Why did you settle on using the Mesoamerican deity Quetzalcoatl as a suitable monster for a monster movie?

I thought Quetzalcoatl would be an interesting monster to put in a movie. If you read any books about the history of Mexico you will come upon the worship of Quetzalcoatl. When the Spanish first came and conquered Mexico, they discovered chambers in these Aztec pyramids where human sacrifices had been made. These ceremonies usually involved the removal of the human heart and the Spaniards found thousands and thousands of human skulls all stacked up inside these pyramids. These remains had all been sacrifices made to an ancient God named Quetzalcoatl—The

Plumed Serpent. I learned of this and realized that they had a fierce devotion towards this deity and were killing people in order to appease it. That's exactly where I got the motivation of the priest who invokes Quetzalcoatl and brings it back from the netherworld in which it exists.

Carradine's Detective Shepherd theorizes that, "This thing has been prayed into existence." However, there is a subtle suggestion that Quetzalcoatl is almost summoned to New York by the city's violence and inequity.

Oh, that may be so, but I think I was approaching the idea more from an architectural standpoint. I mean, New York would seem to be the perfect city for a giant bird to visit. If Quetzalcoatl were to see those images of the New York skyline with all its towers and skyscrapers, it would look like some kind of ancient city where you might come to worship. All those structures and edifices could potentially hold some sort of religious significance, if you didn't know that they actually represented big business and industry. You might think that it was a holy place where the towers were actually temples or pyramids: monuments to some ancient god. New York City would be the perfect place for a monster-bird to come and maybe do a little eating! [Laughs] I mean, what other reason would he need? Several people have asked me how and why Quetzalcoatl chose to nest in New York. Originally, I did conceive a scene where some Mexicans jump out of a truck and place a giant egg up in the Chrysler Building, but I decided not to do it. I didn't feel that we needed to know exactly why the monster was there. The most important thing was that it *was* there. I genuinely feel that some element of mystery in a movie is a good thing. The audience don't always have to know the reasoning behind every single thing. But some people won't hesitate to crucify you if they think something like that is just the product of bad writing.

Interestingly, Shepherd also says: "It wouldn't be the first time in history a monster was mistaken for a god. I guess that's why I have to kill it. If you can kill it, it's not a god, just a good old-fashioned monster."

Sounds great, doesn't it? You know, if Quetzalcoatl is a god, then it's as cruel and unforgiving and destructive as any other god. The one thing it isn't is absent! I mean, it's really here—indiscriminately snatching people off rooftops and eating them. In my mind, a god and a monster can be one and the same thing. It depends on your point of view, I guess. Both can dispassionately destroy you and both can take on many forms. There have been monstrous people like Hitler, who have cultivated a god-like image, but are finally revealed to be very vulnerable and very human.

The gritty realism of the locations and naturalistic performances are heavily contrasted with the exploitative elements of Q and the primitive-looking stop-motion monster. Was that always your intention?

The idea was always to take the *Naked City* aspect that had served me on *God Told Me To* and combine it with the monster movie concepts. Again, it's that mixing of horror with the police drama and the depiction of street-life in New York City. I liked the idea that the locations were real and gritty, because that helped to ground the more fantastic elements of the story in reality. It also helped the actors, too, I think. Instead of having the picture shot in a studio, it was filmed in real places with real things and that allows you to do some interesting pieces of business. When you are shooting on a real location, you will always discover actual objects around you that you would never find in a fictitious environment where everything has to be designed or brought in to dress the set. Sometimes you'll be out at a location and discover something that has been scribbled on the walls or some defect in the construction of a building, that you can put into the scene that makes it seem more realistic and immediate. In fact, we intentionally looked for various places in New York where the structures, patterns and backgrounds had a visible Aztec element or influence to them.[1] This was in keeping with the idea that Quetzalcoatl was drawn to the city by its architecture. Why spend money replicating reality on a set when you can venture out onto the streets and capture reality itself? You can't build that stuff on a low budget. So, I prefer to work in actual locations rather than trying to create things artificially as there is no substitute for the real thing—even in a monster movie!

What about the realization of Quetzalcoatl itself?

We had some very good people that were animating the monster: Randy Cook[2] and David Allen.[3] Randy was the chief guy on *Q* and later worked for Peter Jackson over in New Zealand on *The Lord of the Rings* trilogy. He even appeared at the end of Jackson's *King Kong*, playing a pilot flying one of the planes that is firing its guns at Kong on the Empire State Building.

As for Dave, he was later nominated for an Academy Award for his excellent work on *Young Sherlock Holmes*. Sadly, Dave died several years ago, but both he and Randy were very talented artists that I suppose emerged out of the Ray Harryhausen[4] School of stop-motion animation. I thought for the money that was available to them to create the monster, they did a very good job. It turned out okay, but to be honest with you, I didn't want the monster to be in the movie too much anyway. I always considered it to be secondary to the characters. It's the characters that make the picture work, not the monster.

I've always found the stop-motion animation in *Q* to be a lot of fun and firmly in keeping with the spirit of the film.

The monster does have a quaint charm to it, that's true. Back then, there was no CGI and that's just how you realized something like that on film. In fact, all the special effects people were brought onto the picture after the shooting was over. All the aerial helicopter photography had been shot first, as well as all the stuff at the Chrysler Building, and none of it had been storyboarded. The special effects guys were not happy with the way I approached things. They kept complaining, "This is not how it's done: we follow a certain procedure and carefully plan the special effects in advance. We like to storyboard and prepare everything and do it right." I said, "Well, it's a little too late for that. The movie is already shot and we've got all the elements. I know exactly where I want the monster to be in the action. It may not be normal procedure for you, but that's the way it is." They said, "You can't matte the monster into a moving camera shot. The camera has got to be stationary." I said, "But it isn't stationary and you are just going to have to make it work!" And you know what? They went out and discovered that they could make it work. I mean, everybody has their own rules about how to do things, but when you tell them that they have to come up with a new set of rules they just do it. Randy and Dave did a very nice job and I was happy with the efforts of the special effects crew on *Q*. We also did some bluescreen shots, like the moment the monster suddenly sticks its head through one of the openings in the Chrysler Building and startles Carradine and Jim Dixon. All of that stuff was shot in the backyard of my house one night.

Tell me more about the impressive aerial photography that depicts Quetzalcoatl's point-of-view as it roams the skies in search of prey.

Well, I think those sequences are some of the very best aerial photography that has ever been shot in New York City. When I started getting that footage on the very first day of shooting, I hired Al Cerullo. I was well aware that Al was the premier helicopter pilot for movies and had shot all of the stuff for *Superman*. As we flew about, I directed Al exactly where I wanted us to go. As great a pilot as Al was, it was still a hair-raising ride! We were moving between all those skyscrapers, going in and out and circling all around. It was particularly terrifying when we shot footage at night because we wouldn't be able to really see the buildings. All we could make out were the little lights at the pinnacles of the structures. It was the only warning that we were hurtling straight into the top of one of these buildings. Fortunately, Al had a lot of experience of flying around New York and he knew where everything was. Still, we could have easily been killed as something can always go terribly wrong. Every time I watch *Q*, it makes me sad when I see the shot where the camera is flying towards the Twin Towers. It almost flies between them but, in reality, we got as close as we possibly could and then zoomed-in with the camera so that it looked like we'd soared between the two structures. Of course, the Twin Towers are now gone because of the 9/11 terrorist attacks and it always affects me when I see them in the movie.

There are some practical effects in the film, namely the oversized claw that is seen grabbing Quetzalcoatl's unfortunate victims. Who created that claw?

We hired some Asian gentlemen in New York who built that for us. We only used the big claw a few times: once in the swimming pool sequence where the monster grabs the guy and another time on the roof when Richard Roundtree's character is killed. The claw was suspended on some kind of crane and was lowered down into shot. It was fixed so that it would open and close, but in order for the talons to lift anybody up we had to secure the actor in there. This meant we had to cut between the time the claw came down into the frame and the time it seized the victim and lifted them back up. We needed that time to stop and wire the actor into the claw itself. You may have noticed there is always a quick cutaway in there of somebody reacting to the monster's attack. By the time we cut back to the victim, the actor is already attached to the claw and is simply lifted up and away. I thought those scenes worked rather well. We actually built a significant portion of the monster to be viewed on-screen, but I instantly knew that it wasn't going to work. I had no desire to follow in the unfortunate footsteps of Dino de Laurentiis and his awful remake of *King Kong*. On that picture they created an artificial model that was laughable. So, we quickly decided to restrict ourselves to just seeing the monster's claw. The fact is we had a small crew. We didn't have a lot of money to realize what were some very ambitious effects. We simply had to make everything work with the minimum of preparation.

Why choose the Chrysler Building as the location of the monster's nest?

The Chrysler Building wasn't originally specified in the script. It was just written as a skyscraper because I didn't want to be committed to a building that I might not be able to deliver. My thinking was the original *King Kong* had made the Empire State Building famous, so I wanted to do the same thing for the Chrysler Building and give them their big monster. In fact, when we did decide that we wanted to shoot there, the management of the Chrysler Building actually turned us down the first four or five times we approached them. I kept sending my people back again and again, offering them more money each time. Finally, they agreed to let us use it. I believe they were experiencing some financial difficulties at the time and warmly welcomed the $18,000 we paid them for the privilege of filming there. I was very happy because that was the building I always wanted for the movie. It's a beautiful construction and you may have noticed that it has this peculiar bird-like quality to it. The whole exterior facade of the Chrysler Building looks like feathers and has these bird-like gargoyles, engravings and motifs all around and inside the structure. My reasoning was that if a giant bird was going to pick one place to nest, this would naturally be it.

Were the management of the Chrysler Building present during shooting?

No, we were mostly left alone. They never even viewed a copy of the script. The management didn't know what the hell we were doing, although they did insist that we only shot on the top floor. I went up all eighty-eight floors, and, of course, as soon I saw the ladders going up even further I just had to explore. The only way you could get up to the very top of the building was by using these narrow, rickety ladders that you climbed hand over fist. You'd reach a level and then realize that you could go up even higher still; then you would get on a third ladder and that would go all the way up. After that, you were inside the pinnacle and could literally feel the building swaying from side to side in the wind. It was an amazing experience. We were now on a level that was not open to the public, but I knew this was where I wanted to shoot the movie. It wasn't an observation deck or anything—nobody ever went up there—we hadn't received permission to shoot this high up. So, I tried to get as much footage as I could on the first day. I knew that if we were discovered, I wouldn't get a second day's shoot. By the time they did find out about it, we were pretty much finished there. The management said that if we insisted on shooting on this unauthorised level, we'd have to insure ourselves for a couple more million dollars, which we then did. I remember Dennis Rief, our insurance broker, wrote the policy on the roof whilst the management looked on. It was a dangerous place to be. No question. I should also mention that the needle at the top of the Chrysler Building doesn't have any glass in it. All those openings you see in the film are not covered, so it would in fact be possible for a bird to fly in and nest there. The tops of most other skyscrapers are completely enclosed, but when you get to the summit of the Chrysler Building there's nothing there. It's basically a windswept platform eighty-eight stories above the street. That makes it a difficult place to shoot because there are no guard rails or gates to prevent you from just falling out and hurtling thousands of feet to the ground below.

What safety precautions did you take?

[Chuckles] Well, we actually hired a stuntman, whose main job was to walk around behind me at all times on the platform and hold onto my belt. People were concerned that since my mind was occupied with the details and distractions of directing the various scenes, I might inadvertently fall to my death through one of these openings. As you can imagine, for everybody on the crew it was quite terrifying. I think people were a little nervous about going up there—including me—but I tried my best not to let anybody know that I was scared. I just led the way. Of course, I never anticipated that anybody would actually follow me up there, but I think this crew of macho guys didn't want to lose face. I really had my doubts that I could get them to accompany me with all the lights and equipment, and shoot on that dangerous perch. On one occasion, we actually had a power failure and the entire level was plunged into total darkness. I suddenly shouted, "Everybody freeze! Don't move! Do not take one step!" One small step in any direction could have been fatal. There was no way we could climb back down, so we just stood there in the dark for about twenty minutes and looked down below at the city lights. Finally, the crew worked out what the problem was with the cabling and the lights came back on again. But that was a very tense twenty minutes we spent there. Very tense!

Was there anything in the screenplay that you weren't able to realize?

No, and interestingly enough, we ended up developing more gags and more sequences than I'd ever imagined in the script. When we got to the top of the Chrysler Building, I saw there was reconstruction work going on. I noticed that the steeplejacks, who were trained to work on skyscrapers, had placed these metal baskets all around the pinnacle. The steeplejacks would stand in these baskets as they were doing their repair work and since the baskets were hanging down on all sides of the building, I thought it would be great to put guys in there with machine guns and have them shoot at the monster as it flew by. Nobody else was ever going to have the guts to stand in those baskets, so we hired the steeplejacks because they were accustomed to being up so high. We put them in police uniforms, gave them machine guns and they climbed in the baskets. Then we had a helicopter circling the structure, filming them, and these steeplejacks were firing off blanks. Unfortunately, in the daylight, you couldn't really see the flashes of gunfire coming from the machine guns, so we had to put them in later. Another potential problem that had escaped our attention was as the steeplejacks were firing the guns out of the baskets, cartridge shells were continually being ejected from the weapons and were raining down eighty-eight stories to the streets below. Fortunately, a series of canopies had been erected around the lower floors and they collected all the shells before they hit the street. Frankly, that could have been disastrous for us and resulted in somebody being seriously hurt or killed.

That's another example of God being your production manager.

Well, we didn't escape entirely unscathed. A nearby television station heard the sound of our gunfire which had carried down to the streets. They reported on the news that the sound of machine guns being fired was coming from the top of the Chrysler Building. Then somebody mistakenly believed that the United Nations Building was coming under attack. The *New York Daily News* quickly sent some photographers over—their building was close by—to see what we were doing. The next day they put a big headline in their paper: "Hollywood film crew terrorizes New York City!" It was ridiculous! The article urged that something be done about Hollywood film crews arriving in New York and terrifying their citizens. Then, the *New York Post* had a similar headline that implied we were spreading panic throughout the city. We didn't terrify anybody! I actually had a camera crew down on the street to shoot the reactions of the people, but there were no reactions. Nobody was afraid or ran away, they were simply curious. In fact, some of the shots you see in Q of people running away from the monster in terror were lifted from *God Told Me To*. We even hired some off-duty cops as extras, who showed up in their uniforms, but it didn't matter as we were still considered dangerous. The *Daily News* had published a lie and it was a damaging lie. The Mayor of New York then became involved and various people were trying to ascertain blame so they could cover their own asses by denying they'd granted us the necessary permits to fire our machine guns. It appeared that certain individuals were afflicted with sudden memory loss. The person in charge of the Motion Picture Division had also been criticised for what we did. She actually called me up and said, "Finish your picture, but you can't shoot any more scenes on the streets. No more gunfire or chase scenes. Just finish your movie and get out of there."[5]

There is more gore in Q than in most of your other films with decapitations, severed limbs and the open flaying of victims being explicitly shown.

Some people were disturbed by the gore, but originally there was an awful lot of comedy in the movie. When Sam Arkoff became involved with Q, he wanted more moments of horror in the picture. We had already started shooting when I went to Sam and said that I needed some money to finish the film. Back then, Sam had just sold American International Pictures and was looking for another project to be involved with. Now people like Sam—who was a good-natured fellow—also love to get you in a situation where you really need them. That way, they can sock it to you in the deal. When you're already shooting a movie and need more money, you are in a vulnerable position. Sam realized this and soon took the foreign rights to Q. However, he did give me the money I needed to complete the picture.

Afterwards, Sam wanted to sell Q as a horror film and insisted on more gory moments like the faces being skinned, the chests being cut open with knives, and the decomposed bodies. So, I gave Sam what he wanted. Interestingly, the amount of gore and blood you can now view on TV in shows like *CSI* makes Q look fairly tame in comparison.

Do you have any other amusing stories from the shoot?

Let me think about that. [Pause] Oh, here's one: the turret of the Chrysler Building wasn't large enough to maintain the monster's nest, and so we needed a bigger area. Our solution was to rent an abandoned police headquarters situated in Little Italy, downtown Manhattan. It was deserted at the time and there was nothing in there except for guard-dogs and rats. We went up to the top of the police headquarters turret and discovered that it matched our requirements. The same Asian gentlemen who had built the monster's claw then came in and brought real twigs and branches, and actually constructed the monster's oversized nest. The nest was very complicated to build. Its branches were carefully weaved together to make it look like a real nest. When it was in place, we brought in the huge artificial egg and placed it in there. We then put up the lights, and our camera-man, Fred Murphy, shot the sequence. When we were finished, I told everybody to wrap-out and they started removing all the lights, and the dressing, and the large egg. Unfortunately, the crew did not remove the nest. They figured that nobody was ever going to climb up into the turret of this abandoned building again, so they left the nest where it was and walked away. I didn't actually know about this because I was long gone by then. About four months later, somebody decided to transform this building into very expensive condominiums. In scouting the premises, they had ventured up into the turret and suddenly discovered this huge nest. The next thing that happened was the *New York Times* published this small article on the front page saying that anthropologists were flying into the city from all over the world. Apparently, a gigantic nest had been found in the roof of the former New York Police Department headquarters. Experts were coming in to examine it as the nest had clearly been constructed by a mysterious and unusually large animal. I quickly realized exactly what they were talking about. To be honest, I thought the whole thing was very amusing, but I never said or did anything about it.

What about the title card that is seen at the end of some versions of *Q*— but not on others such as the 2003 DVD release—which states that Quinn has been awarded the million dollars he was promised by the authorities?

Firstly, I thought this guy was pretty adorable, and it would be great to see him come out on top. So, I put in the title card at the end saying, "Jimmy Quinn sued the city of New York and got $1 million tax free." I felt the audience would be happy to see this small-time crook finally make it big. Without that ending card, the movie really gives Quinn his one moment of notoriety and importance before allowing him to disappear into obscurity again. Secondly, I don't know why the title card is on some prints of *Q* and not on others. It could be that the title card only appeared on the CRI, which is the duplicate negative, and maybe the version you saw was from the original negative that was in the vault. They very seldom take the original negative out of the vault and use it. They use all the prints from the duplicate negative, which is safer, because if any damage does occur they still have the pristine original negative. In some instances, when companies have been making copies for home video in later years, they may have gone back to the vault and got the original negative and made the video and DVD copies from those. That is possibly why the DVD release doesn't have the title card on it at the end. I don't know.

For the record, which is your preferred ending—with or without the card?

I prefer the ending with the title card. I think it gives the picture a little laugh at the climax. Originally, Quinn was going to be killed by the Aztec priest at the end and sacrificed in honor of Quetzalcoatl. It was supposed to be a coming together of the various threads of the story, but Moriarty played that character so beautifully and made him so damn lovable and kooky and delightful, I just couldn't do it. It would have been a mistake for Quinn to die and conclude the movie on such a serious downer. So, we shot that little scene in the hotel room where Quinn tells the religious fanatic that he won't consent to his own sacrifice. He just says, "Fuck you," and then the detective bursts in and saves him. I'm very glad we did that scene. I think the picture works much better with Jimmy alive and well at the end.

What's the story with your efforts to get *Q* distributed?

We showed the picture to a lot of different places and everybody responded positively. At one point, Universal were very close to buying Q. In fact, Bob Rehme, who was the head of Universal at the time, really liked the picture. We actually ran the film three or four times for Rehme and he even visited us when we were shooting at the Chrysler Building. I was convinced Universal would buy the movie but then, for some unknown reason, one of the executives didn't like Q and Rehme was talked out of it. We then took the film to MGM, who were very enthusiastic about it. They were going to give us $5 million and buy the picture. This was on the Friday but, over the course of that same weekend, the head of distribution got fired and the deal was lost. It was just incredibly bad timing, that's all. If that person had held onto their job for another week, MGM would have bought the picture. We would then have made a huge profit up front because the movie had only cost $1 million to make. Q was eventually bought by United Artists, who gave it a decent distribution. I was pleased that Q was opening at the Rivoli because that was a terrific New York theater—the same theater where *Jaws* had opened. It did very good business and Q was the #1 box office film in New York City when it opened. I also think the movie played on 42nd Street at the New Amsterdam, where it broke house records. So, Q did very nicely, but it would have probably done even better if Universal had taken it as they would have been a better releasing company for the film. Anyway, it doesn't matter now as I was pleased with the way Q was put out. We also had some beautiful full-page ads they took out in the newspaper and there was also the television advertising. I also thought that the poster art for Q was impressive. They commissioned a wonderful piece of art that was rendered by the famed illustrator who had done the poster for *Conan the Barbarian*.[6] United Artists couldn't really sell Q any other way than they did. You had to have the New York skyscrapers clearly visible and, of course, you had to have the monster in there somewhere. I liked the image of Quetzalcoatl carrying this girl off in its claws accompanied by the slogan: "New York is famous for good eating." I came up with that. I thought that line gave you a good indication of what the tone of the movie was. Upon seeing the poster, I felt people would clearly understand that Q was a horror film with a comedic aspect to it.

In his review, Roger Ebert writes of an encounter between Sam Arkoff and critic Rex Reed. After seeing Q, Reed is reported to have said, "Who would have thought it? Amongst all that dreck was a wonderful performance by Moriarty."

[Interrupting] And then Sam is supposed to have said, "The dreck—or crap—was my idea," something like that. Yeah, I know all about that. Actually, a lot of people still remember that quote. I thought the whole picture worked well as it was, but Sam didn't have any creative input into *Q*, other than to say he wanted more horror. He was never specific about anything. He just wanted it to be more overtly violent and horrific to counter the comedy. Sam was afraid that we wouldn't attract the horror audience at all. Personally, I think you have to be careful about walking that line with these kinds of films. If people come to see a horror movie like *Q* and you give them a comedy, they are not going to like the picture. If you advertise the movie as a horror film, you better damn well give them some horror or you are in trouble. If you make a horror picture and you want it to be a success, you have got to scare the audience. If they don't scream then you are not going to have a hit. I mean, the audience did scream to some degree watching *Q* as we had a few shocks and scares in there, but it was not to the same extent as *It's Alive*. Now that film really did scare them!

Ebert also posed a difficult question: "How did Quetzalcoatl get pregnant?"

Well, that must have happened back in Mexico! That's all I can say about that. [Laughs] You know, the big-budget American version of *Godzilla* made by Roland Emmerich and Dean Devlin basically stole from *Q*. I noticed that in none of the previous *Godzilla* movies did Godzilla ever lay any eggs. In fact, I always thought that Godzilla was a male monster. In Emmerich and Devlin's version, Godzilla lays eggs in Madison Square Garden and, at the end of the picture, the last shot of *Godzilla* was the very same last shot as *Q*. You see another egg, which cracks open just before we cut to black and the credits roll. So, it's rather obvious that they lifted that exact scene from *Q*. I mean, the basic idea of this monster coming to New York to lays its eggs is taken directly from *Q*. I remember that the Academy of Science Fiction and Horror had an awards dinner and I actually ran into Dean Devlin there. I walked over to him and said, "I hear you are doing *Godzilla*. I guess we both have a monster in New York now." As soon as that sentence left my mouth, Dean turned and ran away! I was literally left standing there, wondering why he hadn't responded to me. Then I saw *Godzilla* and realized they had stolen some of the concept of our picture. Fortunately, I didn't sue them or anything because later on I did a picture with Dean called *Cellular*. I was smart enough to not make a big deal out of it and just let it go.

Finally, we should return to the late David Carradine.[7] What are your present thoughts on him?

As you know, David had been an old friend of mine. We had shared a lot of good times together in the Army and then, when he got out of the service, we maintained our close friendship. I was with him on the opening night of his Broadway show, *The Royal Hunt of the Sun*,[8] in which David played the Inca Chief. I was also with him all through his *Kung Fu*[9] period throughout the 1970s, when he famously played the character of Grasshopper. And, as I say, when it came time to make Q, David agreed to do the picture without ever once seeing the script. That would never have happened if our friendship had not been so strong.

Your collaboration with Carradine on *Q* was so fruitful, I'm wondering why you never worked together again?

Unfortunately, later on in life, David and I had a falling out. I actually did try to make another picture with him called *The Heavy*. We went down to shoot it in New Mexico, but David was drunk most of the time. He was very obnoxious and was giving everybody a hard time, so I fired him. We then closed the picture down, and that was pretty much the end of our friendship. Later on, he apologized and wrote me a letter. He said he was sorry and missed our friendship. He asked me to come up to Canada and direct some episodes of the recently resurrected *Kung Fu* series that he was making, which I declined to do. David then came to my house and apologized in person, and we tried to put our differences behind us. We also met for a drink in the Valley and had a nice time together. However, the last time I saw David he was again very unpleasant. I ran into him at a screening on the Paramount lot, and, for some reason, he was extremely nasty that day. He was there with his brother, Bobby Carradine, and was showing off for him.[10] I said, "David, I don't understand this. I thought you got over all that and we were friends again." He said, "Times change." And that was it. Sadly, that was the last time I saw him. The next thing I heard he was dead. [Pause] What can you say? Ours was a strange relationship. David was a restless, troubled person. I never went to a home of his where there wasn't a piece of paper tacked to the door saying: "This property has been seized by the Internal Revenue Division." Every place David ever went he was pursued relentlessly by the tax people. When I think about him, which I sometimes do, my feeling is that David was never really happy unless he was living in a state of absolute chaos.

Perfect Strangers (1984)

How did *Perfect Strangers* come about?

The germ of the idea came when I thought it would be interesting to make a picture that was more or less told through the eyes of a two-year-old child. Of course, there had been other movies made about little children witnessing crimes like *The Window*[1] with Bobby Driscoll, but that concerned an eight- or nine-year-old boy and was different from what *Perfect Strangers* would eventually become. I always try to present myself with an interesting obstacle when I'm writing a movie. I enjoy the difficulties of setting an entire movie in a phone booth or, in the case of *Perfect Strangers*, meeting the challenge of making a picture with a non-speaking actor. I don't think anybody had ever done a film with a non-speaking two-year-old boy in a principal part. Naturally, after dreaming up this approach, I then had to sit down and come up with the whole story and the surrounding characters. I conceived this idea that the little boy had witnessed a brutal crime in which the killer has murdered a man in cold blood. The killer then learns that this child is the only witness to his crime, and so he ingratiates himself with the boy's mother in an effort to determine if the child recognizes him and can identify him to the police. As he goes about this, the killer begins a romantic relationship with the mother, but she has her own her acrimonious relationship with her ex-husband—the father of her child. As the killer gets closer to the family, he is left conflicted when his criminal associates demand that he murders the child and disposes of the only person who can potentially incriminate him and the criminal organization that employs him. I must say that there was no real planning in advance as to what the story would eventually become. The script for *Perfect Strangers* just seemed to work itself out, as these scripts often do. Many of the finer details, such as the mother's relationship with the ex-husband and her association with the liberation and lesbian groups for women, came a little later.

I find it interesting that you chose to make two contemporary Hitchcockian thrillers in *Perfect Strangers* and *Special Effects*—back-to-back—that take place in New York City. What compelled that decision?

To be honest, what determined everything was the fact that I was able to secure the financing for both pictures at the same time. The entire enterprise was based on the agreement that I would make *Perfect Strangers* and *Special Effects* in New York with the same crew—without stopping. John Daly, the head of Hemdale Films, who bankrolled both films, suggested that we could make two pictures back-to-back. The first film would be *Perfect Strangers*, which was released in foreign markets as *Blind Alleys*, and the second would be *Special Effects*. So, we basically shot both of these movies as if they were one movie. As soon as we finished one picture, we segued straight into the second. I didn't have any additional preparation time or anything. We were able to keep the crew on and not have a start-up course again. We had the exact same unit in place, which ensured a smooth and comfortable transition. One of the most interesting things about both movies was that *Perfect Strangers* cost just $200,000 and *Special Effects* cost just $300,000. That included paying everybody's salary and covering the cost of the music—everything! There were no deferments. Everything was made within the allotted budgets.

Anne Carlisle was an interesting choice for the role of Sally, the little boy's mother. How did she drift onto your radar?

I had seen Anne in a non-union film called *Liquid Sky*[2], in which she had played both the male and female leads. It was a rather bizarre and brave little movie that had been made by a Russian director. Anne was great in it and I thought she had a highly androgynous appeal about her that was very unusual. I knew she would be a wacky and unexpected choice for the role of the mother, and I jumped on the fact that I could kind of build this character around her. Anne's ambisexual personality certainly came into play in the film and I thought she gave a very good performance. Another reason why I cast Anne was she wasn't a member of the Screen Actors Guild. We only used non-SAG actors for both *Perfect Strangers* and *Special Effects*. This meant that I was able to make both films more economically because I didn't have to deal with the union. All the members of the cast were Broadway or off-Broadway actors, but they hadn't made enough films to become members of SAG. They were all New York actors, and many of them, including Anne, had appeared in underground movies.

Carlisle seemed to specialise in playing sexually ambiguous characters, another one being the transvestite who is felt-up by Paul Hogan in *Crocodile Dundee*.

Yeah, and after *Crocodile Dundee,* she kind of disappeared. I haven't seen her since, so I don't know whatever became of the poor girl. Anne was a very good actress and was very co-operative. We had a lot of fun together and I thought she might enjoy a nice career in movies, but, like so many people, she just vanished afterwards. I was also interested in finding out whatever became of Mathew Stockley, who played the little boy. Of course, he would be an adult today, but I wonder if he has any recollection of having been in this movie? After we finished *Perfect Strangers*, I arranged a screening and Matthew's parents brought him along so he could see the movie. I watched him during the course of the screening. In fact, I think I had a camera on him to see if he had any reaction to seeing himself onscreen. To tell you the truth, there was no reaction whatsoever. I was quite disappointed. I thought that maybe he would have some kind of response to seeing himself in all these scenes, but he never reacted at all, not once. He just sat there and stared at it.

Another New York actor you hired was Brad Rijn, who plays Johnny, the hitman dispatched to kill Sally's child. What can you tell me about him?

Before doing *Perfect Strangers,* Brad had appeared in Susan Seidelman's first picture, *Smithereens.* He played a guy who drives to New York and lives in his van, and begins a relationship with this young woman in the lower Manhattan area. I thought Brad was very good in that part and had an interesting mix of strength and vulnerability, and I managed to locate him and get him involved in my movie. Brad is good in *Perfect Strangers*, but he's another actor who has made very few films. I immediately hired him again on *Special Effects,* and he got good reviews in *The New York Times.* He later made brief appearances in *The Stuff* and *A Return to Salem's Lot* for me, but then disappeared completely and was never seen again. I don't know what happened to Brad's film career, or his life for that matter. I can't tell you whatever became of him. Some of the people in my pictures just seem to disappear into the fog and are never heard of again. What can I say?

Dare I say it's the curse of Larry Cohen!

I don't know. I really don't. These were all solid actors, who responded very well to direction. They did exceedingly good jobs for me. At that time, Anne and Brad had some decent films under their belt that they could show people. I envisioned them both continuing to move forward after *Perfect Strangers*, acquiring agents and building their careers. Unfortunately, that's not what happened. It's a mystery to me.

In your mind, what is the significance of Johnny spray painting his shadow on the walls of the city?

There was an artist who was doing spray paintings in and around New York City, and I gradually became aware of his images.[3] I contacted this guy and obtained his permission to use his spray paintings in the movie. Of course, we did pay him for the privilege. I thought it was a wacky, crazy thing for Johnny to do and it demonstrated his mental aberration. Johnny is almost like a ghost. Nobody seems to quite know him. The cops don't have much information on him which makes him an ideal hitman. I also thought the spray paintings were a leitmotif to the picture that fitted in nicely with the song we used. I also asked my ex-wife, Janelle, to write a few songs for the film because she was a good songwriter.[4] I told her what the picture was about, and she wrote them specifically for the movie. I think those lyrics add something to *Perfect Strangers*. They comment on the action in a very subtle but meaningful way. The whole idea of Johnny recreating his image that way was meant to illustrate the fact that he considered himself to be no ordinary criminal. The audience could clearly see that he was severely disturbed. Well, I guess if you insist on going around killing people then you must be severely disturbed! But I liked the idea of him spray painting his own shadow on the walls of the city. It's as if he is attempting to leave his mark but, conversely, it's also like he isn't even there. Johnny is a shadow, a non-entity. I felt it certainly added something to that character and to the film.

The Canadian actor Stephen Lack turns up as Lt. Burns, the cop investigating the murder Johnny has committed. Lack is famous for working with David Cronenberg on *Scanners* and *Dead Ringers*. How did he get cast in the role?

His name came up as a possibility, and, apparently, Stephen was also not in the Screen Actors Guild. I approached him about playing the part, and he agreed to do it. We then built that role up a little bit and made him a gay detective, which was highly unusual back in those days, particularly having a gay character in any kind of authority role. Stephen wasn't suitable to play a tough, hardboiled detective, so I changed his character. I wanted to create something that would not only fit him better as an actor, but also give the detective a little more texture. I was also very happy to have any actor in my movie that had appeared in David Cronenberg's movies.

Lack has often been criticised in the past for his acting abilities, particularly for his performance in *Scanners*.

Well, David Cronenberg obviously liked Stephen because he's worked for him more than once. I've become friendly with David in recent years and he's a very nice fellow. We enjoy each other's company and conversation. If Stephen Lack was good enough for David, then he was good enough for me.

I liked the idea of Johnny using the plot of *E.T. the Extra Terrestrial* as a way of illustrating to Matthew why he shouldn't betray him to the cops.

I like that scene, too. *E.T.* was hugely popular at the time, but we didn't show any images from the movie or any photographs of the alien itself as we didn't have a license to do so. I did tell Steven Spielberg that I was doing the scene and he said he didn't mind. Actually, I may have told Steven that I'd already done it, not that I was going to do it. He said it was okay and, again, we didn't violate any copyright because we didn't show anything. I would've liked to have shown a picture of E.T. itself to sell the idea of what Johnny was doing, but I didn't want to get into a copyright situation.

Out of curiosity, are you an admirer of Spielberg's film?

Oh, I love *E.T.*! I thought it was a wonderful picture, absolutely wonderful. Every time I see it I end up crying! [Laughs] I always say to myself, "Okay, this time I'm not going to cry over this stupid puppet," and then, naturally, I end up crying again. Maybe it's the music that does it, I don't know.

Little Matthew's reaction shots in his scenes with Brad Rijn often seem quite genuine and appropriate. How did you achieve them?

It may be hard for you to believe, but before every scene I would sit down and try to explain it to Matthew. As I was talking, he would always stare blankly at me. I'd tell him what he was supposed to do and then we would shoot the scene and he would just do it! I don't know why or how this happened, or what power I had over him, or what actual recognition the kid had of what I was saying. I would simply relay to him what was required and he would simply do it. For example, if he was required to walk into a room and open a refrigerator, he would do it. If he was required to walk down a hall and duck into a closet, again, he would do it. It was remarkable. I mean, the crew were looking at me as if I was some kind of mesmerist or something. [Laughs] The kid's parents would always be on set, hiding somewhere when we were doing a shot. I would say to Matthew, "Go to your Mom." He would then go to wherever his Mom was hiding. Then I would call out, "Okay, now go to your Dad!" He would then turn around and walk to his Dad, who would be hiding behind a couch or something. That's basically how we did it. We moved him around by using his parents as destination points. If some kind of reaction was needed in the scene, I would say, "Okay, Matthew, see these photos? I want you to go through them and when you find this picture that looks like so-and-so, stop and really look at it." And, incredibly, he would do it. Before we did this everybody was standing around saying, "This director must be crazy if he thinks he can tell this kid what to do!" But every time—*every time*—he would do what I asked of him. They tell you never to work with children, but I just had a magic working for me on that film. That's why I felt that when we finally showed *Perfect Strangers* to Matthew, he would look at it and have some kind of reaction to the movie. But there was nothing visible that I could detect.

Did the shooting of *Perfect Strangers* pass without incident?

I do remember that one day we were shooting in an apartment and I had always told Matthew's parents to keep an eye on him. I said, "You must watch your son at all times, because we have cables everywhere and heavy lights and it's dangerous." I thought I had stressed this to them, but I suddenly looked down at the far end of a corridor and glimpsed Matthew walking along by himself. He had wandered off alone and I watched as he made a right turn into this room. I ran down the hall after him and got to the doorway in time to see he had picked up a cable and was pulling on it. Now this cable was attached to a heavy, scalding hot light, that was positioned on a stand, that was now starting to fall! I raced into the room and grabbed the light by the pole just before it toppled over and struck him. Oh Jesus, I just shuddered! [Exhales] I mean, it was such a close call. If I had got there even ten seconds later, Matthew would have been badly hurt—perhaps even killed. Of course, that would have been the end of *Perfect Strangers* and quite possibly the end of little Matthew, as well. Frankly, it was a miracle that I even saw him. I had a million things on my mind in that one moment, but I just happened to spy him strolling away. Afterwards I said to his parents, "Where the hell were you? What were you doing? How could you let him wander off like that?" I'm just thankful I was there in time, because that could have been a disastrous and devastating experience for all concerned.

I actually have a question about children being placed in harm's way: you staged scenes in *Perfect Strangers*, and in some of your previous films, that dramatise children in jeopardy. This device is occasionally used by filmmakers to bluntly heighten suspense and fear, is it not?

It is, but I don't feature children in my films strictly to generate a stronger reaction from the audience. I mean, there are children in our world and I'm constantly in contact with them. I also have a bunch of children myself and, as a parent, I can relate to the fear that exists in the audience when they see a child in jeopardy. But I don't really show any violence towards children in my movies. Other than *Perfect Strangers*, which films of mine have featured children in jeopardy?

Both *The Stuff* and *A Return to Salem's Lot* feature a child in jeopardy. *God Told Me To* also touches on the most terrible violence against minors. Then there's the inversion of that idea in the *It's Alive* trilogy which depict children as monstrous.

Yeah, but when the father in *God Told Me To* murders his own children you never see that happen. Yes, they talk about it, but it's not used as a means to construct suspense about whether the children are going to survive or not. It's a post-mortem thing, an after-the-fact kind of situation, where he is describing how he murdered his family. I see your point, but I don't see any connection between them. As you say, the *It's Alive* baby is an aggressor, but he is acting in self-defence. The baby immediately feels threatened, so I suppose you could argue that he was in jeopardy from birth. He was merely protecting himself by killing everybody in the delivery room, who would have probably killed him because he was born a monster. Maybe you could say that. I will admit that towards the end of *Perfect Strangers*, you do feel that the little boy is certainly in jeopardy. I'll concede that we do play with that idea.

The confrontation between Sally and her ex-partner, Fred [John Woehrle], on the street appears to have been filmed live before an unsuspecting audience. Was this indeed the case?

Yes, it was. If you look closely at that scene, you will see me standing in there amongst the crowd, trying to keep certain people from attacking John Woehrle! People really thought that the husband had run off with this child and that the mother was catching up with him and desperately required assistance. People were trying to intervene and help. As a matter of fact, they wanted to start beating up this poor actor! I had to get in the middle of everyone and keep repeating over and over again, "It's just a movie! It's just a movie! It's not real! Don't get involved!" I really believe that if I hadn't hastily told all those witnesses to back off, John would have been battered pretty badly by that crowd. We had the cameras hidden in different areas around Lower Manhattan, which was absolutely teeming with people at that time of day. I got the exact reaction that I was looking for from passers-by. I anticipated beforehand that staging such a dramatic confrontation on the street would provoke some individuals to intercede, but I didn't want the situation to escalate to the point where John got punched out.

Early in the film Sally's feminist friend, Malda, played by Ann Magnuson, talks about "feminist homicide" and how the kitchen—a place that is often viewed as a prison of domesticity for women—is also a potential armoury filled with weapons that can be used against violent men.

That little conversation sets up the ending where Sally kills Johnny with the kitchen knife. I thought that was good writing and I enjoyed putting that in. Of course, women do often kill their abusive husbands and partners using household implements as weapons. I suppose I made *Perfect Strangers* just to have that shot at the end of the film where Johnny comes back to Sally's apartment and she has the kitchen knife behind her back. She doesn't know if her child has been murdered or not and suspects that she may now be next. Sally opens the door and, thinking her son is dead, stabs Johnny and he falls forward. Then you see the little kid is standing behind him—perfectly safe—and is framed in the doorway. That was a good moment, I thought. I remember telling Matthew to hold his position and not move: "Just stay where you are!" And I'll be damned if he didn't do it! So, it was a perfect shot, my favorite shot in the whole picture. There aren't many times in your career where you can say that you made a movie just for one shot, but that was the case right there. That's *the* shot! I thought it was a classic shot, actually. Incidentally, unlike Anne and Brad, I should add that Ann Magnuson actually went on to have a fairly good career in films after *Perfect Strangers*.[5] She later appeared in a number of well-received pictures and was the only one who came out of that movie and did anything noteworthy.

Why did you include the feminist angle in the story?

Well, there was a lot of activism going on at the time. There was actually a feminist parade that had been organized in New York when we were shooting and I thought we could include it in the picture. There were many women in the movie who were lesbians, and we filmed the "Take Back the Night" parade, which is partly-straight, partly-lesbian, and partly-gay. We shot that sequence in Washington Square because I wanted to take the environment of Lower Manhattan as it was in those days and really capture it on film. I think *Perfect Strangers* succeeded in doing that. It really does authentically incorporate the milieu and atmosphere of that place and time. Also I wanted to give Anne's character a point of view, rather than have her simply be defined as a mother—a single mother— and an ex-wife. I wanted to give her a personality and a cause, allowing her thoughts that existed outside of her daily domestic routine. So, I made her an activist who worked in a recycled clothes store, and amongst her friends were many lesbians and fellow activists.

It's never made clear in *Perfect Strangers* whether or not Sally is a lesbian or bi-sexual character, or if she is merely sympathetic to their movement.

I think she's a borderline lesbian. I felt that made the character more interesting and offbeat. It also gave *Perfect Strangers* more depth as a movie and furnished the story with more layers of interest. I mean, the mother doesn't really like men to begin with, but then she lowers her guard and allows this guy to come into her life and her bed, and, of course, he is a murderer. So, she has made another bad choice, although I've always thought that Sally's ex-husband was also a tragic character in his own way. I can understand his position and point of view, too, as much as I understand the mother's disenchantments with men. In reality, Anne Carlisle was a lesbian and it was very difficult for her to do the love scene with Brad Rijn. We actually had to get Anne a bottle of brandy so that she could get drunk. After that, she was able to bring herself to do it. However, Anne's girlfriend, who actually plays the German-accented lesbian in the film, was very unhappy about her doing the love scene with Brad. In fact, she got very angry with Anne and they actually had a big spat over it.

I see the film being moderately concerned with veneers and surfaces under which other things lie. You have Johnny playing at being a family man when in reality he is a killer; you have Fred, who seems a little unhinged and angry, but who is finally revealed to be a decent guy who cares for his son; and you also have Moletti the gangster who has a respectable front as a hair-dresser.

I think that's a good analogy and it's partially true. *Perfect Strangers* is about a lot of things, but that sense of subterfuge is certainly part of it. Of course, I am interested in exploring the social masks that we wear. That's really an inherent part of drama: discovering who people really are; removing the masks they put on and revealing their true faces. People are never really what you know and believe them to be. I've come to realize that everybody's life is a performance: an act or a character they choose to adopt. It's almost like the clothing that we decide to wear, or the manner in which we style our hair and fix our makeup, all helps to form the image we present to society. It's really not who we are. Behind that veneer, when we are alone and the doors are closed and we look in the mirror, we see a different person staring back. We see a person that we don't want anybody to know about, someone with their own private fears and doubts and desires. We very seldom expose our true faces, even to those who are closest to us. Our wives, husbands and children never truly know who we are and sometimes they only find out the truth of someone's life after they are dead. They may go through a person's papers and belongings and discover things they hadn't expected to find. Maybe the deceased had a secret life or identity, or a secret side to themselves. It's fascinating because that's probably true of most people.

The scene where Johnny visits Moletti's barbershop is quite unnerving.

It's uncomfortable because the gangster is laying down the law. He's telling Johnny he must tie-up the loose end he's left dangling by murdering this kid, and he holds the scissors dangerously close to Johnny's nostrils as he does so. I thought the actor who played the gangster had an interesting voice.[6] He had this threatening little rumble to his voice, which I think also contributed to the underlying tension in that scene. I don't remember where that actor came from or where he went, but I thought he was very good. Sadly, he wasn't very good at cutting hair. He was supposed to be playing this tough, dangerous guy but he was a little nervous. He was afraid to trim Brad's hair in case he made a mess of it! [Laughs] We shot that scene in a real barber's shop in Lower Manhattan. In fact, all of the locations in the movie were real locations. I was happy with all the actors playing the villains, particularly the big, blond heavy that grabs Brad in the cemetery.[7] That guy was like six-foot five; he was just enormous, and had these huge hands. I mean, Brad was a big guy, but that fellow dwarfed Brad. I thought he was a suitably threatening reminder to Johnny that if he didn't do what he was told, this guy would be the enforcer. He would then take Johnny's place in the organization and that would be that.

Perfect Strangers closes with a shot of three spray painted silhouettes on a wall instead of one: a male adult, a female adult, and a child. Why?

That shot was meant to illustrate the dream that Johnny had. All through the movie, he has been spray painting a single figure on the walls to signify his own isolated existence. He's a shadow, but the more Johnny gets involved with this woman's life, the more he is exposed to other people: her ex-husband, her friends, the detective. At the end, we suddenly see that at some point he has painted a trio. In his heart, he had fallen in love with this mother and her child, and he wanted to form a family with them. He wanted them to be a unit together, so that he would no longer be alone. That shadowy image is as close as he will ever get. Sadly, he is dead now and the mother has killed the one that she loved. He loved her, too, and he didn't mean to hurt the boy, so it's a very tragic and bleak ending. I think we do feel some sympathy for Johnny despite the fact he is a killer. We do like him.

It's hard not to like an assassin who insists on saying "I'm sorry" to each and every one of his victims.

Johnny is trapped by the circumstances of his life and his commitment to the codes of the criminal organization he works for. Does he have a compulsion to kill, or is it just his job? Can he let the criminal life go? Will the criminal life permit him to go?

How did you find working with John Daly and the Hemdale Film Corporation?

John Daly was an extremely intelligent, tasteful, and notorious guy. I sold him about five different projects over the years, and they all got made, including *Best Seller*. Daly was the kind of guy you could go into a meeting with and in five minutes he'd give you a commentary on your script that was astute, concise, and insightful. Many studio executives can't tell you anything because they don't know anything. They often bullshit you, trying to make it appear that they know something when all they are giving you are these inane observations. Daly could cut through everything and very quickly tell you exactly what you needed to know. You would be in and out of any meeting with him because he was so incredibly bright. Unfortunately, he was also a terrible crook. Every time you dealt with him, you got swindled out of your money. He took advantage of people to such a degree that finally nobody would do business with him anymore, not just me but other people in Hollywood. Although Daly had produced Oscar-winning pictures like *Platoon* and *The Last Emperor*, it eventually came to the point where nobody wanted to touch a John Daly project.[8] He finally found it impossible to get pictures made and eventually lost Hemdale and pretty much everything else. He then directed his own movie, but couldn't get it distributed.[9] Daly tried to distribute it himself and probably lost the remainder of his money in the attempt.

I remember that towards the end of his life, I took him out to lunch at The Polo Lounge at The Beverly Hills Hotel. I bought him this expensive lunch and tried to be nice to him, even though he'd cheated me out of the back-end money on all of the pictures we had made together. At the time, I actually felt great because now it was Daly who was down in the dumps. I could still afford to take him out, ply him with food, and celebrate the fact that I'd managed to survive and he hadn't. After all the dirty tricks he'd played on me, I was so furious with Daly I sometimes wanted to kill the guy! I'm not kidding. He'd taken serious advantage of me, but, in the end, he'd received his comeuppance. Despite everything, I was amazed to discover that I actually felt sorry for him. In fact, he died soon after that lunch. I didn't poison him or anything, but I probably had thought of poisoning him many times. Daly was a talented man but, unfortunately, he couldn't control his greed. He had been raised in the slums of London and I think he had been a boxer at one time. That fighting spirit must have served him well because he fought his way to the very top, finally owning his own independent film company and tasting stunning success. Daly had originally started Hemdale with the actor David Hemmings, but had apparently cheated Hemmings out of his share of the company; kicking him out and assuming full control, even though he was the "Hem" in Hemdale. I don't think there was anybody who dealt with John Daly who didn't have something bad to say about him. The joke around town was that if Daly was ever murdered there would be so many suspects, the police wouldn't know where to look or what to do about it. They'd have to bring all of Hollywood in for questioning. I guess Daly never forgot his beginnings. He was a crook to start with and remained one all his life, but he was certainly a talented crook.

What kind of business did *Perfect Strangers* do?

It didn't do that well. *Perfect Strangers* only received a token release by New Line Pictures. John Daly had sold it to some kind of tax shelter company and, like others had done with *The Private Files of J. Edgar Hoover* and *Full Moon High*, was able to write off the cost of the film as tax deductions. This meant that *Perfect Strangers,* and my next film, *Special Effects,* only had to play a certain number of theaters to qualify for the tax shelter. Daly had sold them off in such a way that the impetus was not to make money in theaters, only to fulfil the commitment to the tax shelter. It was a very familiar story again. Naturally, they didn't make enough prints and they didn't spend a lot of money on advertising, so both movies quickly disappeared. You can't put movies like *Perfect Strangers* and *Special Effects* out and simply expect audiences to discover them. You have to actively promote them on television and in print, and both movies were not advertised and more or less suffered the same fate. What's interesting is that the critical reaction to *Perfect Strangers* was pretty good. Many people say it's one of my best pictures and I always knew that one day both *Perfect Strangers* and *Special Effects* would find an audience. They are both out on DVD and have played here and there on cable and Netflix, places like that. So, they have ended up enjoying a nice afterlife and I'm happy about that. Better late than never, I guess.

Special Effects (1984)

Am I right in my understanding that you originally wrote the script for *Special Effects* in the late 1960s, before *Bone*?

Yes, that's true. It was actually the first screenplay that I wrote for myself to direct and was intended to be my debut film. It was originally called *The Cutting Room* and was about a manipulative director, who makes a movie about a murder that he himself has committed—blurring the lines between fantasy and reality, and sucking several people around him into this disturbing project. Unfortunately, we never put the movie together at the time. There were a few people interested in it, but it finally just fell away. I had always kept that script in a drawer as something good that was waiting to happen at the right time. When John Daly said we could make *Perfect Strangers* and *Special Effects* back-to-back, that was the opportunity I was looking for. I took *The Cutting Room* out, re-titled it *Special Effects*, and that became the second film of the two-picture deal.

Why exactly did *The Cutting Room* not become your debut film?

It was partly due to the notorious Polanski murders, which took place near the end of the 1960s. Sharon Tate—Roman Polanski's wife—her unborn child, and several other notable people, were brutally murdered by members of the Manson Family. I felt that horrifying and tragic event drained all of the interesting humour out of my whole idea. It made *The Cutting Room* seem too harsh and painful, so I chose not to pursue the project at the time. I thought people would be repulsed by the movie coming out so soon after the killings as that crime did affect Hollywood tremendously. A lot of people out here in the motion picture business were very emotionally wrought over those murders and the fact they took place right in the center of the city, amidst all of their beautiful homes. I think my script just cut too close to the bone. I mean, that case involved a famous director in Polanski and a beautiful young actress in Tate, and the way she was mercilessly murdered like that—no, it would have just been extremely unpalatable and insensitive. I remember there were all these terrible stories that were floating about that maybe Polanski had something to do with the killings as he was such a weird guy. Of course, all of those rumours were completely untrue and unfounded, but they added to the disturbing and paranoid atmosphere that was brewing in Hollywood. People wanted to know who was responsible so they could sleep at night without having a gun tucked under their pillows. Then, the real culprits were eventually found and the community could stop worrying about who might be next. Anyway, back then, with that climate, I shied away from doing *The Cutting Room* because of the intense feelings that existed. The timing just wasn't right.

Did the script undergo any revisions during the intervening years?

Originally, the script was set in Hollywood, but we ended up doing it in New York City. That was the only major revision. I thought it was perfectly valid to transport the story to New York as so many directors like Martin Scorsese, Woody Allen, and Sidney Lumet were headquartered there. A whole breed of filmmaker preferred to use New York as their home base and make their pictures out of the city. There was an entire New York film industry, and I felt the story would be just as relevant in New York as it would be in California. Actually, it worked out better as we were able to find that fabulous house that was owned by the renowned painter, Lowell Nesbitt.[1] Nesbitt had this beautiful three story townhouse in Lower Manhattan that had an indoor swimming pool and a Jacuzzi at the foot of the bed. It had all these bizarre furnishings and paintings on the wall, and all the leitmotif of flowers everywhere. In fact, Nesbitt's artworks often involved flowers, and so every direction you looked there were paintings and sculptures of flowers. This detail later inspired a line that I added to the script, where the detective investigating the death of the young woman asks Chris Neville, the director, why he has such an obsession with flowers. Neville replies, "Because they are so beautiful and they die so quickly." So, this new environment we'd discovered ran perfectly into the character of Neville and into the themes of the story, too. We were very fortunate to find that unique location in New York. We would never have found a house like that in California.

Was the film always intended as a ferocious satire of the film business?

Well, naturally, we did attack the hypocrisy and cruelty of the film business, but we weren't the first to do that. I thought we did an apropos job of showing what can happen when somebody is a success in the business and then suddenly isn't anymore. I mean, during the interim period between the time I first wrote the script and the time we made the picture, a good many well-known and celebrated directors had fallen by the wayside and were no longer able to get work. These were people who had won Academy Awards, like Michael Cimino.[2] He had won the Oscar for *The Deer Hunter* and was one of the hottest directors in the business, and then, suddenly, after making *Heaven's Gate*, he was no longer employable. Nobody wanted anything to do with him and he was pretty much destroyed. That's more or less the same situation with Chris Neville in *Special Effects*. He's persona non grata in the industry after directing a big-budget disaster and nobody wants to be associated with him anymore. There are tainted directors in the film business like that, people who've had very bright but very brief careers, such as the English fellow who made *Chariots of Fire*.[3] He was a hot director for a while and then made a bomb and disappeared completely. So, there have been Academy Award-winning filmmakers whose careers have quickly evaporated and, frankly, I don't know what they do for the rest of their lives. They must direct commercials or rock videos, something like that.

The opening credits play over audio excerpts from a spiky press conference in which Chris Neville [Eric Bogosian] rolls off an array of witty retorts to assembled journalists. Are those actual questions you've fielded during junkets?

No, I made all of that up. I wanted to put in relevant comments that would be paid off by the movie itself as it went along. At one point, a journalist asks Neville who his favorite director is and he says, "Abraham Zapruder." Of course, Zapruder was the bystander who shot the 8mm footage of John F. Kennedy being assassinated in the Dallas motorcade in 1963.

Interestingly, Neville is later seen running the footage of Lee Harvey Oswald's assassination at the hands of Jack Ruby on a Moviola.

Yeah, we had the footage of Oswald being shot by Ruby and then Neville asks the young starlet played by Zoë Tamerlis, whom he has lured back to his house and is about to murder, "Is this real or is this fake? Can you tell the difference?" He is trying to bridge what separates reality and fantasy filmmaking. In running that footage back and forth Neville has command over it. He runs it forward, Oswald dies. He runs it back, Oswald lives. It's a way of controlling reality; a means of having power over life and death. I guess in some way Neville is also predicting the future of the film business. A lot of the movies that are made now attempt to blur the lines between reality and fantasy by trying to resemble actual documentary footage. Filmmakers deliberately degrade the quality of their images and deteriorate the sound in an effort to present a fictitious situation as a factual film, home movie, or newsreel. You have these horror films that are purported to be recovered footage that have the intentional look of amateurish photography. They are meant to be showing us the footage that the victims supposedly shot themselves before they were murdered. This approach was popularised by *The Blair Witch Project* and has continued on through many, many movies made since. The idea of taking fantasy and making it look like reality is something that Neville would appreciate. It is what he himself is trying to do with his movie. He is incorporating an actual murder into a fictitious film about the murder; when in fact viewers would be watching the actual murder taking place onscreen and would be thinking it was merely fantasy.

This idea of constructing a representation of reality, or instigating an indistinctness between fantasy and reality, is encapsulated by Neville's comment to Detective Delroy [Kevin O'Connor]: "People assume that special effects means taking models, miniatures; tricking them up, making them look real. I'm taking reality and making it look like make-believe. That's a special effect, too."

That's exactly what I'm saying, and it means what it says. The taking of an entirely fake situation and presenting it as real is now a very common approach for a lot of successful movies, but I kind of predicted that idea in *Special Effects*. That's what Neville considered to be a special effect. But in addition to that, I would like to point out that during the entire running time of *Special Effects*, there isn't one special effect; there isn't a fade in or a fade out; there aren't any opticals or any other kind of effects whatsoever in the picture. I was very careful to ensure that we never had any kind of special effects in a movie called *Special Effects*.

Did you consider adopting a vérité aesthetic [creating what appears to be candid realism] in shooting *Special Effects*?

No, that would have been too obvious and literal. The blurring of fantasy and reality was already inherent in the movie, so there was no need to overstate things by presenting the film as a documentary. It's a movie about movies, not documentaries.

What's the importance of Neville asking Mary-Jean [Zoë Tamerlis], "Ever had an experience and then realized you only saw it in the movies?"

Well, there are things you see in the movies that do get into your mind. There are also things that you dream, an event that didn't really happen but it seems very real to you. Perhaps after several years have passed you will think back and say, "Did that actually happen to me? Was it a dream I had or was it something that I saw in a movie one time?" You may come upon a familiar street on a trip and think, *Have I been here before? No, I saw this in a movie once. What movie did I see it in?* You think you've been there before, but it all happened in a film. That is exactly what Neville is driving at there. What I also find interesting is when you enter a theater and see people sitting there in the dark; they are always immobile and silent. They are completely without motion and are staring blankly at the screen—utterly lost in whatever is playing. It really is a strange experience to watch an audience watching a movie. It's a show in itself, observing all these people who look as if they have been taken out of their own reality. They are asleep and, at the same time, are awake. They have now entered somebody else's dream. A movie is really somebody else's dream, only you are allowed to be in it. When people enter a movie theater, they are putting themselves into a dreamlike state or reverie; a mind-fix in which they are opening their minds up to accept somebody else's fantasy.

Neville often employs film terminology and self-reflexive jargon to express himself. For instance, when he propositions Mary-Jean he announces, "I think we should dissolve to the bedroom." He then later says, "I'll call you when it's time for your entrance."

That dialogue merely illustrates the way Neville thinks. He thinks in movie terms, but it is also indicative of the way that movie terminology has infiltrated our everyday speech. We often hear expressions like "That's a wrap," "Cut to the chase," and "Let's fade out." All those expressions have been picked up from movies.

I like the idea that Neville is finally motivated to kill Mary-Jean when she begins regurgitating some of the bad reviews he has received from critics.

Yeah, she incites him. She realizes that he is trying to exploit her and photograph her having sex. In response, Mary-Jean uses the only weapon that she has—her mouth—because she's not physically strong. That's what women often use as their primary weapon—their mouth. They may not be able to physically overpower their husband or boyfriend, but they can desperately hurt him by saying things that they know will cut very deeply emotionally. Women will do that quite often. Mary-Jean was using her weapon against Neville and he reacted violently.

I also like the fact that Neville is a killer with enough sense to scrape his own incriminating skin cells from under his victim's fingernails.

Originally, that was not in the script. I made that up as we were going along, particularly as there was this fabulous Jacuzzi at the end of Lowell Nesbitt's bed. When I saw that, I immediately said, "Oh, this is great! After he kills the girl he can bathe her; and after he bathes her, he can dry her; and after he dries her he can give her a manicure!" I thought that would be a nice touch in a thriller and it was also something that I hadn't seen before in anybody else's movie. I think it was a perfectly logical and methodical thing for Neville to do, because when they were struggling in bed she probably did have his DNA under her fingernails.

How did you come to cast Eric Bogosian as the demented Chris Neville?

Eric had done a successful off-Broadway one-man show called *The Bogosian Explosion*, which I saw in Greenwich Village. Eric wrote all of his own material and played seventeen or eighteen characters during that performance. I was very impressed with him, and he was already a very well-known figure in the underground culture of New York City, both as a writer and actor. He went on to write another off-Broadway show called *Talk Radio*[4] that was performed all around the country and was then made into a high-profile movie by Oliver Stone. Stone hired Eric to play the lead part of the controversial radio host he had originated onstage, and all of this happened to him after we'd made *Special Effects*. Eric had never appeared in a movie before doing my film. As with *Perfect Strangers*, I was looking for actors who were not members of the Screen Actors Guild because I had to make this picture very cheaply. I couldn't afford to hire SAG actors and pay them the overtime, the penalties and all the other things that are stipulated. Eric was a stage performer, so he didn't have membership of SAG. Eric and I had a great relationship, except for something that occurred on the first day of shooting: he came to work and was behaving very strangely. As the day went on, Eric became extremely difficult, irritable, and hostile. I finally said, "What's the matter with you?" Eric suddenly started yelling at me and eventually I said, "Look, I can't continue on with you and this type of behavior. Why don't you just go ahead and leave. I'll find somebody else to play your part." So, I more or less fired him and he left. Everybody was just standing around in shock. My cameraman, Paul Glickman, then came over to me and asked, "What are you going to do?" I said, "Don't worry, he'll be back." An hour later, Eric did indeed come back and he apologized. He said, "Look, I'm hypoglycaemic and if I don't eat every two hours I go crazy." I said "What do you need to eat?" He said, "Well, I have to have nuts and fruit, stuff like that." I said, "We're going to get you a whole table laden with nuts and fruit, so you don't have to worry about that anymore. Everything will be fine." And everything was fine after that. Eric was always co-operative, generous, and did everything he was asked to do. I think Eric had a good time making *Special Effects*. I've seen him several times over the years and he often says, "I only wish we'd made the movie a few years later when I was more experienced as an actor. I could have been so much better in the part." I always tell him he did just fine. Eric really captured the same quality a lot of those kinds of directors have.

Which is what exactly? How would you articulate that quality?

Well, a lot of directors are social misfits. They are not very comfortable with themselves. They are not at ease within their own bodies and personalities. Directors are not always the most well-groomed and affable of people during a conversation. In fact, they are often uncommunicative in their speech. If you walk onto the set of a movie and you look for the nerdiest person there, usually that individual is the director. I've run into a lot of directors like that, including Michael Cimino. We were once at a film festival together in Avoriaz, France, and Cimino was terribly obnoxious and unpleasant to people. I mean, everybody hated him! I thought that Cimino really disliked me but when I ran into him again back in Los Angeles, he threw his arms around me and said, "Let's have dinner!" I never thought that he would actually call me, but a couple of days later he did. Cimino asked, "Where are we going to have that dinner?" I said, "Where do you want to eat?" He said, "I know, I'm taking you to dinner at the Hamburger Hamlet!" [Chuckles] Well, the Hamburger Hamlet is a nice little restaurant if you want to go for a hamburger, but it's not a fancy restaurant by any stretch of the imagination. Of all the nice restaurants in L.A., Cimino wanted to have dinner in this little hamburger joint. So, that's where we went. We had a very pleasant dinner together—him, my wife, and I—and then I never saw or heard from Cimino again. What can you say? He's had a strange life, but Cimino certainly reached the highest heights that any filmmaker can aspire to. What I find fascinating is he passed from that into nothing. When this happens to a director, you find that the phone never rings again and people cross the street when they see you coming. It's like the scene in *Special Effects* where Neville encounters his ex-agent, who is now a studio executive, and the guy more or less blows him off. Neville is now considered poison and that can happen to you very quickly in the movie business.

Bogosian's co-star, Zoë Tamerlis, plays the dual roles of the murdered Mary-Jean and her substitute, Elaine. Tamerlis is an actress of considerable cult status, but how did you first become aware of her?

I first saw Zoë in Abel Ferrara's *Ms. 45* in which she played a mute woman, who goes out on a killing spree to avenge her brutal rape. It was one of the first films that Ferrara made, and I thought Zoë had this vulnerable and peculiarly exotic quality. She didn't do much after *Ms. 45*, but when her name came up for the two parts in *Special Effects*, I grabbed her right away as she was a good actress. She was also very good-looking—although a little on the thin side—and was willing to do the nudity. Zoë was easily able to play both of those characters, but she was an extremely strange girl.

Strange in what way?

Well, firstly, nobody knew where she lived or what her phone number was. The production people came to me one day and said, "Larry, we don't know what to do. Zoë won't give us her address or phone number and we don't know how to handle this. What do we do if we need to communicate with her?" I said, "Has she ever been late to the set?" They said, "No." I said, "In that case, leave her alone. She obviously has her reasons." They actually tried to follow her home one day, but Zoë changed taxi cabs twice to throw them off her trail. Can you believe that? She did not want anybody knowing where she lived. I'm convinced she was a drug addict. Another odd thing was Zoë always kept a leather satchel with her that contained a script—not my script, a different one. I once asked her, "Zoë, why do you always carry that script about with you?" She said, "I can't leave it at home. Suppose somebody breaks in and steals it?" I said, "Why don't you just make a Xerox-copy of it?" She said, "No, somebody at the copy store could steal a copy of it and then where would I be?" I said, "Nobody is looking to steal a copy of your script," but she wasn't willing to take that chance. There's no question, she was totally obsessive about it. Everywhere Zoë went, that script went with her. That screenplay turned out to be *Bad Lieutenant*[5], which was later made into a successful movie by Abel Ferrara, starring Harvey Keitel. Zoë is credited as the screenwriter on that picture and, years later, it was remade very badly. Subsequently, Zoë moved to Europe, got married, and became Zoë Lund. She ended up dying of a drug overdose several years ago, which was very sad.[6]

Is Tamerlis's voice dubbed in her guise as Mary-Jean?

No, that was her. I think we did re-record some of Zoë's dialogue and it may seem like it is a little out of synch or something, but that was her voice in both parts.

Aspects of *Special Effects* seem to have definite echoes of *Vertigo*.

Yes, of course. Anytime you are dealing with a character who is obsessed with re-creating the personality and image of a dead person you are getting back to *Vertigo*. Brian de Palma certainly did that with his film, *Obsession*. Actually, de Palma is another example of a director who was extremely hot at one time. In fact, he couldn't have been hotter when he did pictures like *Carrie* and *Scarface*, but now you don't hear about him at all. Then there's Bob Rafelson who directed *Five Easy Pieces*. He hasn't done anything in twenty years or more! So, these are contemporaries of mine, who reached incredible heights that I never achieved, but then kind of evaporated. It's very tough to remain part of the A List, or the A-Plus List, and then fall out of that elite group. Usually, these directors don't go back and do low-budget pictures like I do. They just don't do anything. They seem unable to cope with the reality that they could continue making movies if they only made them cheaply. If they would make low-budget pictures, they could still make movies for the simple pleasure of making movies. They are not going to be making $80 million or $100 million movies anymore; they just have to make films for $1 million. Unfortunately, I don't think certain directors can quite wrap their minds around that thought. They just resist it and withdraw. The next thing you know they are doing nothing. Inevitably, what follows is their agents then dump them and they become undesirables. It's a sad case of people who have great talent and a great potential to keep working, but they won't deal with the cold hard fact that they can't make big-budget pictures anymore. That period has now passed them by. But there are plenty of pictures they could be making if they could just accept their situation and deal with it. Fortunately, I never rose out of the ranks of low-budget cinema, so I didn't have very far to fall! [Laughs] I could always get back on my feet and make another picture, no matter what happened.

The characters in *Special Effects* are very film savvy. Detective Delroy seems to harbor ambitions to become involved in movies and at one point informs Keefe [Brad Rijn] that Neville "made a bomb with about $30 million worth of special effects." Even taxi drivers seem aware of the current health of Neville's career.

Well, audiences are now more film savvy than they've ever been. Ever since television shows like *Entertainment Tonight,* and all the other daily programmes which deal with show business news, have come on the air, people now know every detail of a movie's production history, personnel, and performance. There are also things like the Internet and the special features on DVDs that inform people about how a movie was made and by whom, and also gives them a platform to criticize films. It used to be that when a movie came out and it played in theaters and was reviewed, people would go see the picture whether it was good or bad. Today, they not only put the reviews of the movie out, they also tell you how much the picture made at the box office. They inform you exactly what the grosses are so that by Friday, Saturday, Sunday, and the beginning of the following week, you immediately know whether the picture is a hit or a flop. If the movie is a box office bomb, nobody wants to see it because nobody wants to spend their money watching a movie that's a flop. So, they basically destroy the film before it has a chance to get back on its feet again. Very few movies can survive that kind of publicity and they are merciless in releasing this data. The availability of—and concentration on—this information has effectively changed the entire landscape of cinema. This stuff was never revealed in the old days of Hollywood, when the studios not only made the movies but also owned the theaters. They controlled everything, and audiences never really knew whether a picture was profitable or not. Nowadays, they advertise the grosses almost as loudly as they advertise anything else about the movie. When you go to a film festival and kids stand up to ask you a question, the first two things they want to know is how much did the movie cost and how much did it gross. They rarely ask you about the specifics of making the film, or its artistic intent, or the collaboration with the actors. No, it's an entirely different mind-fix on movies these days.

Keefe seems to be the only character in *Special Effects* who is not film-literate. He is even unable to operate a standard projector.

Sure, and that was intentional. He was just a kid from the Midwest, who came to New York and had no background in the movies at all. He didn't know who Chris Neville was, or who anybody else in the business was. Keefe simply wanted to retrieve his wife and take her back to the hometown with him. In the end, he gets his wish, but of course it's not his wife he's reclaiming, it's her double. He's going to bring this crazed woman back home with him to live the life of his dead wife and be a mother to his child. Her mind has more or less snapped, so she goes along with this illusion. It's actually a very bizarre ending. Then, to finish it all, Detective Delroy, who really didn't have any involvement in movies before he got assigned to this case, has more or less become stage-struck and is now sitting in on casting sessions and script conferences, making changes and offering suggestions. Suddenly, Delroy is taking over the movie after Neville dies and even gets the credit at the end instead of me! [Laughs] It reads "A Philip Delroy Movie." He receives the credit that I should have gotten, but I gave it to him. That's a further blurring of the boundaries between truth and illusion. Fantasy and reality has been bridged even within the movie itself. The part of Detective Delroy is a comedic take on Sonny Grosso, a New York detective who was the technical advisor on *The French Connection* and later became a movie and television producer himself. Grosso was hired by William Friedkin to advise on the film, but then he learned the business and enjoyed quite a long career.

Detective Delroy is essayed by Kevin O'Connor, whose work I've enjoyed in films such as *Let's Scare Jessica to Death* and *The Brink's Job*.

Kevin was a great actor, who had won several awards for his theater work. He was also an acting teacher in New York and had played Humphrey Bogart in the well-received TV movie, *Bogie*, so I knew he was a formidable talent. For some reason, Kevin was not in the Screen Actors Guild, or maybe he decided that he just didn't care and would do a non-union picture. Either way, I was extremely lucky to have him in *Special Effects*. We built up the part of Detective Delroy in the movie because Kevin was playing the role. I added new lines and other pieces of business for him and a lot of his stuff was made up on the set as we were shooting. I actually had to tell Kevin to bring his performance down because he was slightly over-playing it at first. I kept signalling to him, waving my hand for him to bring it down. He got the message and played the scenes a little less theatrically. That character needed to be a little more understated. Kevin took direction well and I liked him very much. He also appeared in a couple of my subsequent movies. He played the taxi driver at the beginning of *Island of the Alive*, who discovers that a woman is giving birth to a monster baby in his cab. He also had a small part in *The Ambulance* playing a panhandler on the street. Unfortunately, most of Kevin's part was later cut out of the picture. But he was in three of my movies and I wish I'd had him in more of them. He was a wonderful, affable guy who always delivered as an actor. Sadly, Kevin has also passed away.[7]

***Special Effects* plays like a cautionary tale of the pitfalls of pursuing fame and the manner in which show-business "chews beautiful girls up." You illustrate the sheer number of hopeful starlets and their indifferent treatment with the high-shot of Neville walking over the photographs of all the young actresses.**

Yeah, that image really sums it up: the cynicism and indifference of the business. We obtained the 8x10 headshots of every girl we could find in New York City and just covered the entire floor of the soundstage with all their photographs. You don't really know what that image is until Neville suddenly steps into the frame and you realize that it's an overhead shot and he is walking all over their faces. It's not a particularly subtle visual metaphor, but it does convey the amount of respect some movie people have for aspiring young actresses.

An unexpected moment is when the headshot of Dustin Hoffman as Dorothy Michaels in *Tootsie* is seen amongst the photographs Delroy is inspecting.

I didn't know if anybody would notice that. I just did it as a gag. Like I said, they have photographs of every available actress in New York and there she—or he—is!

Neville's soliloquy about the culture of stardom is savage: "This is the age of the non-entity. The glorification of the nobody, as long as they are victims. Look at the virtually non-existent careers of Dorothy Stratten or Frances Farmer. What makes them worthy of a $10 million eulogy on film? Murder, madness, suicide—that's what stars are made of today." Do you really believe that?

Absolutely. I don't believe that any director wants to make a movie about the life story of a movie star unless that person has suffered some kind of a tragic ending. Jessica Lange played Frances Farmer in a movie, but the question remains was Farmer really deserving of having a movie made about her?[8] The cold, hard reality is hardly anyone knew who she was. Farmer's enduring celebrity arose not from her modest achievements as an actress, but from the fact she went insane and was committed to a mental institution. It's the same thing with other actresses and models who have met with tragic endings: their very public misfortunes and deaths were sensationalized and then formed their lasting claims to fame. I mean, what's the point of making a picture about somebody's continued success? Where does that go? It's really not much of a story. Movies are only interesting if characters go through a terrible crisis. By that rationale, showing somebody who just becomes a star and rises to the top and nothing ever happens to them is just a linear story of success. So what? Who gives a shit? Of course, if somebody comes along and then murders you, or you murder somebody else; or if some other violent act or catastrophe occurs like you perish in a plane crash or you get paralysed in car accident and have to learn to walk again; or somebody kidnaps you; or you become an alcoholic or a drug addict; or you contract some terrible disease, then, and only then, is the movie worth making.

Considering our overloaded diet of reality television, Internet websites, and twenty-four-hour news channels that are dedicated to covering celebrity culture, do we now live in the true age of "the glorification of the nobody"?

Oh, yeah. You can't deny it. I mean, how many non-entities are now celebrities with their own TV shows? What makes these wannabes so special? Certainly not the fact that we get to see their boring domestic routines. It's not reality; it's a carefully manipulated representation of somebody's reality. Also, we constantly see celebrities and personalities getting arrested for drug addiction, for shoplifting, for getting into a fight in a nightclub, or for some other indiscretion. They get thrown in jail, then they get out, then they are eventually thrown back in jail again. The tabloid magazines, TV shows, and websites just eat all of this up and glorify them. The personal miseries of celebrities are then reduced to some quick newsflash or soundbite, and they cease to become real people in some bizarre way. Various media outlets will pay thousands of dollars for video footage and photographs of celebrities. The paparazzi follow them everywhere around town, haunting them, climbing trees next to their homes so they can document their every move. There is no privacy or decency. It's just a predatory stalking to feed people's unceasing fascination with them. If somebody has done something quite naughty it makes them interesting. Nobody is interesting if they live a normal, peaceful, ordinary life. They have to be all fucked-up.

As I mentioned, you name-drop Dorothy Stratten in the film. Were you tapping into the then recent tragedy of her murder as Bob Fosse had done with *Star 80*?

In the case of Dorothy Stratten, she was murdered by her own husband, who then killed himself. She was a Playboy Playmate, who perhaps had some potential as an actress, but I don't think Stratten would have been remembered by anybody if she hadn't have been murdered. Her true claim to fame was being a victim, it's very sad to say, and I feel the fact they've made movies about her supports that.[9] I don't think Stratten would have made it as a true movie star, but she certainly made it as a victim. I wrote my script many years before her murder, so it wasn't influenced by that unfortunate event. Actually, *The Cutting Room* was conceived long before Stratten was ever a model or a starlet, but they do say that life sometimes imitates art.

An interesting touch is when the movie pauses for a moment to illustrate the forthcoming scenes from script-to-screen using white titles on black.

I thought that since we were talking about a script and the making of a movie, it would be interesting to use some of the movie terminology and artefacts as chapters to move the film along, giving it a look and style that had not been done before. I don't think anybody had previously illustrated a screenplay onscreen using those kinds of titles during a movie as a means of advancing the story. There are a lot of interesting touches in *Special Effects* that I'm proud of, like the idea of Neville wearing editor's gloves to strangle the guy who is blackmailing him. I thought that was another methodical thing he would do in order to not leave any fingerprints. And what kind of gloves would be available to him? Editor's gloves, obviously!

Watching *Special Effects* again recently, I thought it was one of your most visually accomplished films.

I agree. I think *Special Effects* is very underrated. It's one of my best movies and should be more widely seen. Again, we were fortunate that we had Lowell Nesbitt's house, which gave us a beautiful locale to shoot in and made the film look very rich and elegant. We elected to do the movie in very bright vibrant colors and make it look decorous like a real Hollywood movie. I thought Paul Glickman did a very good job of shooting the picture. It looked really great and *Special Effects* is certainly one of the best-looking movies that I've done. *Perfect Strangers*, which Paul also shot for me, has this deliberate fuzziness to the image as we put filters on the lens to give the picture a certain kind of look. Did you like that look?

Yes, I did, but *Perfect Strangers* has that distinctive '80s haze to it, whereas *Special Effects* looks very sharp, clean, and controlled.

Yeah, it is a little more regimented than some of my pictures. *Special Effects* looks like it cost far more than it did. We got a lot up on screen for the money we spent. Having that access to Nesbitt's house added so much production value to the movie. We didn't have to build anything, because it was all there for us. Wherever we pointed the camera there was always something interesting to shoot. That enabled us to make the film look really good. For example, the sequence at the end where Neville is electrocuted in the swimming pool—all that came about because there was an indoor pool in the house. You don't find that in New York City very much. Frankly, it was a miracle that we did. I then did what I always do—I simply wrote the pool into the script and revised the sequences so we could make use of it. It was too good to waste.

Neville remarks, "I'm a maniac when I do a picture." Having listened to some of your crazy exploits and daring risks, it's safe to assume that you, too, are also a maniac when you do a picture.

[Laughs] Look, anybody who would do the crazy things I've done throughout my career would have to be a maniac! I've done so many wild things I can't count them all. One example: when I was doing *The Private Files of J. Edgar Hoover*, I once sneaked into the office of the Attorney General—the chief legal officer of the United States of America—to shoot a scene without his knowledge! Who else would try getting away with that kind of insanity? So, yeah, when I was making movies, I did stuff that I would never dream of doing in real life. You get into a rhythm when you are directing, or at least I do, where it seems like nothing can go wrong. Everything you say is going to happen and nobody is going to say no. Everything occurs just as you want it to and it's supposed to, and you will it that way. I must also say that during that time, as far as girls go, I never struck out. I was in this mind-fix where I couldn't lose and every woman I saw and approached would hop right into bed immediately. It was magic time! I can't explain why it would happen, but this aura suddenly surrounds you and everybody does everything you tell them to do. That's exactly the way it was for me. It was crazy and went way beyond normal behavior. You start taking bigger and bigger chances because you feel invincible and totally in control. I'm sure that is what Neville thought, only he committed murder instead of shooting without permits. But yeah, I'll admit it. I was crazy when I was making some of these movies, but I was always in control.

I guess a director must at least maintain the illusion of being in control.

Oh, when you are directing you must first convince yourself that you *are* in control. Once you succeed in doing that then ninety percent of the battle is already won. When you begin to believe that you can't do anything wrong, other people believe it, too, and just fall in line. It's incredible how that happens, but it very often does.

The Stuff (1985)

***The Stuff* marked your swift return—quite literally—to biting satirical horror. How did the project get started?**

Oh, I just wrote the script in the usual way: I sit down and write these scripts out of the clear blue sky. I get an idea then just go ahead and concoct the damn thing. That's what happened with *The Stuff*. There were no meetings or development deals. It was completely done as an independent project of mine. I simply came up with the idea of this white substance that is discovered coming out of the ground one day, which turns out to taste wonderful. It's then quickly packaged, marketed, and sold to the masses as an ice-cream dessert called The Stuff, but its soon apparent that this hugely popular food is actually a monstrous, living thing that does great harm to humans. After dreaming up this wacky concept, I took the project around various places in town. Eventually, I found a home for it at the new version of New World, which had formerly been Roger Corman's company but was no longer involved with him. New World had been bought by other people at this time, and they put *The Stuff* out. They provided the entire budget for the picture and more or less just let me go off and make my movie.

Can you identify some of the inspirations that led to the writing of the script?

My main inspiration was the consumerism and corporate greed found in our country and the damaging products that were being sold. I was constantly reading in the newspapers about various goods and materials being recalled because they were harming people. For example, you had foods being pulled off the market because they were hazardous to people's health. I don't know what the situation is elsewhere, but here in the U.S. we still have this problem. There are products always being recalled, whether its spinach, beats, or bananas, that are poisonous. There are other foods such as hamburger meat, cured meats, and sausages that are in some cases actually killing people and must be quickly withdrawn from sale. And of course, there are always the cigarettes, which, along with alcohol, have killed more people than anything else that can be bought legally. Back in the 1930s and '40s, there were a number of ad campaigns issued by cigarette companies which featured all the great radio stars like Bob Hope, Jack Benny, Edgar Bergen, Charlie McCarthy, and Abbott and Costello. All of these people were sponsored by cigarettes. In fact, I believe that cigarettes were the biggest sponsors on radio at that time. Of course, cigarette advertising isn't even legal anymore, but back in those days all the big movie stars were lighting up onscreen. Bette Davis and Humphrey Bogart all had cigarettes dangling from their mouths, and these images were being projected to people that smoking was a sexy thing. For kids, smoking was a sign of maturity, a rite of passage. These dangerous products were, and still are, deeply embedded into our way of life. I mean, look at the sheer volume of junk food we consume every day. We continue to eat these foods despite the fact some of them are killing us. That's when I started thinking that *The Stuff* could be an imaginary product—in this case an ice cream dessert—that is being consumed by millions and is doing irreparable damage to humanity. Everybody is gobbling down this yummy food, so how can it possibly be wrong for us?

There's this idea that is continually being reinforced in the western world that if you don't drink Coca Cola or own a television, you do not conform and are incapable of living a rich and meaningful existence.

Oh, absolutely. That's the projected image that is constantly being sold to us: happiness is a product that can be purchased and consumed and will make you part of something greater than yourself. It's a way to make you whole and content. In the movie, you see the young kid's family trying to cajole him and then force him to eat The Stuff, so that he can be exactly like them and have what they apparently have. That's an extreme example, but there are different kinds of external pressures that we all face to conform. It's something we see and experience every day in subtle and not so subtle ways, and it always looks very easy and fulfilling and obtainable. All of this was in my mind when I was making the picture.[1]

Some have speculated that the exploration of conformity in *The Stuff* was directly influenced by *Invasion of the Body Snatchers* and that the monster itself is a variation on *The Blob*. Were those films in any way influential on you?

Not really. *The Stuff* does have certain similarities with those movies, but they are mostly superficial. Once I decided that The Stuff was an ice cream dessert, and, of course, became an amorphous gooey substance, naturally some would assume that *The Blob* had something to do with it. The Blob was an alien organism from outer space that was crawling around dissolving people. In *The Stuff*, we were dealing with something that was a food that people actually ate and it lived inside them, taking possession of their mind, body and soul. It was an entirely different idea. Here, the victims were inviting, or at least contributing, to their own destruction, and, again, that can be a metaphor for whatever you like: alcohol, drugs, cigarettes, or junk food.

That has to be one of the most innovative concepts in the history of horror movies, that the victims eat the monster rather than the monster eating the victims.

Yeah, and that's what the whole ad campaign really focused on: "Are you eating it or is it eating you?" That's exactly how I originally sold the project to New World—as sort of a fresh twist or new take on the traditional monster movie.

What is your definition of a monster and by extension a monster movie?

My definition of a monster and a monster movie is something that involves a person or creature that is abnormal. *It's Alive* is clearly a monster movie. The monster is a human being but qualifies as an aberration—a threatening perversion of a normal child. Monsters can take on many forms, but they are always something outside of the normalcy of human experience. Sometimes they are recognizable; sometimes they are not. The Monster in *Frankenstein* is made up of human body parts stitched together and is a monster, but then a character like Dracula looks more recognizably human but is endowed with certain supernatural abilities that distinguish him from us. Then, you have monsters like the Alien in *Alien*, which is a creature from another planet, and the shark in *Jaws*, which is, of course, a real animal. I mean, it's a super-shark, but it's still a shark. *Jaws* is considered a horror movie, but I've always thought of it as an adventure film. The music is certainly the music of an adventure film. Of the great monster movies in the modern genre, I would say that *Alien* is the very best because it follows my theory of not revealing the monster in any great detail. That film only shows you suggestions of the monster without dwelling too much on the Alien's physical layout. That way, the audience always wants to see the monster and never gets tired of it. To me, that's what a good monster movie does: it makes you almost struggle to make sense of the monster allowing the mystery and threat to be sustained.

Do you believe that this patient, elusive quality has been lost in modern horror and science fiction cinema?

Yes, I do, and there are several reasons for that. Let me put it this way, the problem I have with CGI, and the great digital special effects we are capable of today, is that we can now create anything we want onscreen. At first you say, "Wow, look how well that's done! Isn't that a beautifully designed and rendered creature?" Well, it may look fantastic, but after a few minutes you get tired of it. You certainly aren't afraid of it anymore, not when it's been revealed so explicitly. Your fear and fascination diminishes as you become more familiar with the monster's appearance. So, I think that advancements in technology have really damaged the audience's ability to be afraid. They are no longer scared of what they are going to see, because the seemingly limitless ability of CGI is doing all their imagining for them. The audience are robbed of any opportunity to conceive what this thing could possibly be.

But surely the temptation to use CGI on *The Stuff* would have been strong, if it had been available and affordable at the time you were shooting the movie?

I would have still used it sparingly, if at all. CGI would have certainly given The Stuff a smoother, more fluid action, but I think it would have looked too slick and cartoony. I instead used miniatures, mattes, and stop-motion animation to realize the monster as I had done on *Q*. I thought stop-motion would give The Stuff a more tactile, realistic quality in its movements, and that's why I hired Dave Allen again. Dave went from realizing a giant bird flying around New York to making an ice cream crawl around, but the work was no less challenging in its own way. The serious problem with stop-motion was that it was such a painfully slow and time-consuming process. I'd check in with Dave every once in a while to see how the work was going, and discover he'd only executed about five or six seconds of completed animation at a time. It was frustrating, but I had to be patient because that's simply what you got with stop-motion techniques. We also had another accomplished artist working on *The Stuff* in Jim Danforth who is one of the masters of stop-motion and miniatures.[2] Jim worked on the sequence where the factory blows up at the end and he did some great work.

What materials did you use to realize The Stuff itself in the various sequences?

There were a number of things we used. For the scenes where The Stuff was moving around rooms, we occasionally utilized the same fire-fighting foam that the fire department uses to put out fires. That material was mainly made out of ground-up fish bones, so it smelled terrible! I remember we used the foam during one scene, and, immediately after I yelled cut, several of the cast who had gotten the foam on their costumes ran off to the nearby Hudson River and jumped in the water. They couldn't endure that awful smell a moment longer. For the scenes where the actors had to actually eat The Stuff on camera, we used something a little more palatable—ice cream and whipped cream, which certainly smelled better than the foam. For the miniature shots, I believe we used some kind of liquid plastic, and in some cases the sets—the miniature rooms—were tilted so that the material could flow about. This gave the impression that The Stuff was moving independently, pouring through doors and windows, and climbing up walls. In reality, we were actually using gravity to manoeuvre it around, but it worked out great.

Tell me about staging one of the most impressive scenes in the film: The Stuff attacking Michael Moriarty and Andrea Marcovicci in their motel room.

That scene was quite a difficult and complex operation. It begins with The Stuff starting to seep out of the mattress and pillow as Michael and Andrea are lying in bed. As they attempt to fend it off, the scene continues with The Stuff literally picking up a guy before climbing up the wall with him and leaping onto the ceiling as it is set on fire. To successfully pull off that gag, we had to employ a series of special effects, mechanical effects, and practical effects. We constructed a full-size rotating room, much in the same way it had been done in the old Fred Astaire picture, *Royal Wedding*. In that movie, the room turned upside down as Astaire started dancing and singing on the walls and ceiling. That was great, but the main difference between that scene and ours was that our room would be turned upside down while it was on fire! Nobody had ever attempted that before. Anytime you are working with fire it can be extremely dangerous, so I did have some reservations about doing the scene.

Where did you shoot the revolving motel room?

We shot it over at the former Mary Pickford Studios in Hollywood. I remember that the cameraman had to be strapped securely in a seat, so that he wouldn't fall out as the room went topsy-turvy. The special effects people who worked with me on that sequence had devised some of the gags in *A Nightmare on Elm Street*. There was one sequence where a kid is suddenly sucked into his own bed by Freddy Krueger and a torrent of blood explodes out and hits the ceiling. These guys had built that set for Wes Craven and claimed that they still had the original materials and could use them again. I guess they did have the mechanical portion of it but they didn't have the room itself, so that had to be built all over again. Interestingly, the room did not turn over with the aid of a motor, as you might think, but was actually operated manually. This meant they had three guys on each side of the room jumping up and down as hard as they could until they got the set spinning. Finally, the room turned over, but it was all done with manpower. In fact, showing that sequence being shot would have been more fascinating than watching the sequence itself. Seeing these six guys bouncing up and down in an effort to get this room upside down was quite a feat of physical labor. It really scared the hell out of me because you had this thing turning upside down and there were flames and people were locked inside it. I was lucky that nobody got hurt, but the scene looks great and is one of the film's highlights.

The character of Mo Rutherford, the industrial saboteur who is investigating the manufacturers of The Stuff, is beautifully played by Moriarty.

Yeah, it's another great performance. I think New World were reluctant to have me cast Moriarty in the part at first because he was not your typical, traditional hero. They were looking for somebody who was a more conventional, handsome leading man, but I wanted Moriarty. I may have gone around making one or two offers to various actors, but Moriarty was always my first and only choice. He played that character so well with his rambling Southern charm. Rutherford plays the fool, and at one point even says, "No one is as stupid as I appear to be." That's the act he puts on—pretending to be dumb when he's really the smartest guy in the room. When we started shooting, Moriarty's character was not called Mo Rutherford. He had a different name, a different personality, and attitude, and was much straighter. Then Moriarty said, "I have to get a handle on this guy. Give me something musical. I like to think in terms of music." He was looking for a sound or feeling, something he could hang his hat on. I said, "Why don't we make him a Southern boy? We've never done that before." So, I changed the character's name to Mo Rutherford, and Moriarty immediately liked the sound of that name. We both thought it was funny, so we stuck with it. Then, bit-by-bit, this character emerged. I mean, he was always an ex-FBI agent who'd been kicked out of the Bureau and was now working as an independent industrial spy. That never changed. I can remember thinking if a movie about an industrial saboteur had been made before as I was aware that such people existed. Over the course of an afternoon, Moriarty and I came up with the idea that this man was a Southern wise-guy with a different agenda. On the surface, he is apparently one thing, but underneath there is a lot more going on with this man. Once we got those details in place, we really had something for Moriarty to have fun with.

Moriarty is supported in the film by one of your most interesting and eclectic casts. How did you go about assembling the major players?

Andrea Marcovicci had played opposite Woody Allen in *The Front*, and I liked that film and Andrea's performance in it. I was happy about getting her onboard for the female lead as I thought she would play well alongside Moriarty. Paul Sorvino was cast as The Colonel after I ran into him at a restaurant in New York called Columbus, which was on Columbus Avenue over on the West Side. That place used to be a big hangout for actors and people in the film business, like Robert De Niro and Kevin Spacey. It was a wonderful watering hole where everybody could just mingle. You could go there and actually recruit people to work on your movies without having to go through their agents and have these long and occasionally painful negotiations. You'd just walk into Columbus for a drink or some dinner, and meet people who did your movies simply because they wanted to do them. I don't think there's any place left in New York, or even out here in Los Angeles, that quite has the same charm that Columbus had back in those days. You could literally put your whole movie together in there, and that's how I got Sorvino involved. He was actually one of my favorite actors and I was very pleased to get him. Sorvino brought a strong comedic aspect to *The Stuff*, which I always liked, as the Colonel was this larger than life character. Off-camera, Paul loved to sing opera. Every day at lunchtime, he would entertain the cast and crew by performing a few arias whilst we were all eating. Moriarty finally couldn't stand him anymore because Sorvino was hogging the spotlight. Moriarty didn't like it because he didn't have a piano to play, so he couldn't compete. That allowed Sorvino to stroll around bellowing his songs, unchallenged.

Another recognizable face is Garret Morris, who plays Chocolate Chip Charlie. Prior to appearing in *The Stuff*, Morris was of course a regular on *Saturday Night Live* alongside John Belushi and Dan Aykroyd.

That's right. *Saturday Night Live* was a hugely popular and influential TV show and Garrett was sharing the limelight each week with not only Belushi and Aykroyd, but Bill Murray and Chevy Chase—the cream of American comedy. Garret was the Black comedian in that group and he was a fairly big name at the time. I wrote Chocolate Chip Charlie as a deliberate take-off on a product in America called Famous Amos Cookies. Famous Amos was a Black gentleman, who had started this brand of cookies that had made a fortune and become nationally famous. I thought I'd take Famous Amos, call him Chocolate Chip Charlie, and make him a character in the movie. I had interviewed several Black comedians for that part including Arsenio Hall. New World didn't know who Arsenio was at the time, but shortly after the release of *The Stuff*, he had a successful self-titled TV talk show and co-starred with Eddie Murphy in *Coming to America*. Anyway, we went with Garret and he was a good actor who fitted the role nicely. Garret was also a lot of fun to work with. I very kindly gave him a nice death scene where The Stuff devours him from the inside out and his face begins to swell and stretch horribly. In fact, for many years I had Garret's replica head from his death scene at home. Each time I looked at it, I would think of the good time I had with him doing *The Stuff*. [Pause] Who else do we have in there?

Patrick O'Neal, Alexander Scourby, Danny Aiello . . . .

Patrick O'Neal had played the villainous commandant in *El Condor*, so I'd had some previous experience with him. Patrick was always very good at playing bad guys. I thought he would be great as this smooth, unfeeling corporate villain alongside Alexander Scourby. Actually, Scourby was an idol of mine. He had a wonderful speaking voice and was famous for providing voiceovers. Scourby had narrated Richard Rodgers' acclaimed documentary about World War II in the Pacific, *Victory at Sea*, and he was a consummate actor. I always loved him. When his name came up, I jumped at the chance of working with him. They say that it can be dangerous to meet your heroes, but it was personally very thrilling for me. Scourby could not have been nicer, and I love his performance in the film. Danny Aiello was another guy from the Columbus restaurant that I was friendly with. I remember Danny came to the set after learning the scene he had with Moriarty overnight. We rehearsed it for the first time and Danny knew all of his dialogue perfectly. Then, Danny suddenly asked if he could use cue-cards, and it was at this point that he started messing up his lines on the next couple of takes. He kept referring to the cue-cards constantly, but we eventually got through the scene. Of course, that sequence culminates with Danny's character getting attacked and eaten by his dog after it gets possessed by The Stuff. I don't think Danny was particularly happy to be working with that dog, which was a big, intimidating animal. The dog had to get physically close to him, and I think Danny found that very unnerving. In fact, every time I see Danny he kids me about his death scene. He always says, "Hey, this is the guy who once fed me to a dog! It was the most humiliating moment in my whole career!" [Laughs] Yeah, there was a distinguished actor that I reduced to the level of dog food!

Do you have any anecdotes regarding *The Stuff* that pertain to your own unmistakable brand of guerrilla filmmaking?

[Chuckles] Here's one: an assistant came to me one day and said, "I've found this great location where you can shoot the scene with the fashion show. There's this furrier showroom in New Jersey and the owner will give us the place for free. He'll also supply us with a dozen models, as long as the girls wear his fur coats." That sounded great and I immediately had this image in my mind of the models parading up and down the catwalk in bathing suits and fur coats, eating The Stuff. The prospect of shooting the scene there without it costing us a dime made me very happy, so I quickly said, "Okay, let's do it!" I didn't even bother to view the place. My production people showed me some photographs and it looked fabulous. How could we possibly go wrong there? So, we all got in our trucks and drove out to New Jersey. When we arrived at the building, we discovered that there were, in fact, two tenants there. The first was indeed the furrier showroom, but, unfortunately, the second occupants were the New Jersey offices of the Teamsters. Needless to say, *The Stuff* was a non-union movie and we weren't using any Teamsters on the production. Now, as many people know, the Teamsters are a highly unionized organization that is often considered to be allied with mobsters. As a result, people are often scared and intimidated of them.

But not you, right?

Being scared and intimidated is one thing, but showing people that you are is another thing entirely. Generally, the Teamsters close pictures down if you don't hire Teamster drivers to drive all the vehicles and keep them on salary. If you don't employ them and pay them huge amounts of money, the Teamsters often picket and sometimes block the movement of trucks and the transportation of equipment. They have an unpleasant history of being able to force companies to hire members of their own organization on various productions. Anyway, when we arrived there and realized this location was actually the Teamsters headquarters, oh, god! I mean, we weren't just shooting in New Jersey—we were shooting right under their noses! Right in their own building! I said to the crew, "We're not going home without shooting this scene today. Let's just unload all the equipment and see what happens." My thinking was that despite their fearsome reputation, the worst case scenario would be that the Teamsters would close us down. They'd make us pack everything up again and we'd have to scuttle back to Manhattan. I felt we should just seize the day because we had nothing to lose. We were already there and the entire day was ruined if we turned back. We had all these models and actors, so we went right ahead and set up. We started shooting the scene and, naturally, here come the Teamsters! They came swarming downstairs to see what was going on and couldn't quite believe that somebody possessed the guts to shoot a non-union movie in their headquarters. It was like a scene out of *On the Waterfront*. They were these big, surly, tough-looking guys in short-sleeve shirts. Their shirts weren't tucked-in and you could see the little bulge in their back pocket where they usually kept their guns. Everybody on the crew froze and said, "Larry, what are you going to do?" I then turned around, calmly walked towards the Teamsters and started singing "If I Was a Richman" from *Fiddler on the Roof*—only I changed the lyrics to "If I Was a Teamster." [Singing] "If I was a Teamster; all day long I really wouldn't have to work so hard; all day long I'd sit there in the truck; if I was a Teamster." And this went on and on . . . .

[Laughs] And what was their reaction?

These guys just stared at me as if I was fucking insane! I don't think they could quite believe what was happening. They thought I was completely crazy because I didn't show them any fear. I just kept singing and finally they cracked and started laughing. When they thought it was all over, one of them patted me on the back and said, "This guy has got the biggest pair of balls I've ever seen!" Then, they turned around, went back upstairs, and we finished shooting our scene. So, I got away with it yet again.

You earlier mentioned the use of slick advertising to push potentially hazardous products. You satirize that idea mercilessly in the film with your own fake commercials for The Stuff. Tell me about the creation of those adverts.

I always knew that the commercials would be an important element of the picture. We devised and shot a number of commercials and TV spots, and tried to make them as seductive and appealing as possible. We got some dancers and choreographed routines for them. We also had somebody come up with some memorable jingles as jingles are such an important element of commercials.[3] We then hired a few actors and celebrities to appear in the commercials as if they were representing a real product. One was Clara Peller, who was very recognizable on American television at the time. She'd featured in this famous commercial for Wendy's fast food restaurant, playing a little old woman who would repeatedly say, "Where's the beef?" It was one of the most inexplicably popular things on TV and everybody was doing takeoffs and jokes about it. We actually paid Clara

Peller quite a bit of dough to come in and shoot a fake commercial. Basically, she sat at a table with Abe Vigoda[4] and said, "Where's The Stuff?" And that was it. To be honest with you, it was a complete waste of money. It added little to the film, but it did end up costing an awful lot. We had been assured by the publicists that if we used Peller it would generate a tremendous amount of publicity for *The Stuff*. As it turned out, we hardly got any publicity at all based on her involvement. So, it was an entirely unnecessary expenditure. I could have spent that money on more special effects and less Clara Peller, or no Clara Peller! [Laughs] I mean, she was a nice little old lady who was more than eighty years old, and I don't begrudge her the money, but it was a pointless addition.

The use of spoof commercials was later popularised by *Robocop* and *The Running Man*, but *The Stuff* was one of the first movies to play with that idea.

I never realized that, but you may be right. Actually, we didn't even use some of the best ones we shot because there just wasn't any place for them in the movie. I think the commercials definitely slowed things down; that was certainly the feeling with the executives at New World. I was originally going to have a series of commercials squeezed in between the prologue where the two guys first discover The Stuff and the scene where the little boy wakes up at night and goes downstairs to the refrigerator. I thought the commercials acted as a nice bridge and showed how that substance in the snow had suddenly established itself as a national phenomenon. The opinion at New World was that we needed to move the story forward much quicker and instead sprinkle the commercials throughout the picture. I felt it would have been a nice transition to have included them in the beginning. It would have set the premise up nicely, but it just wasn't to be. Laurene Landon was in one of the commercials we ended up cutting, but her name is still in the credits. Brooke Adams' commercial was relegated to the end credits because I didn't know where else to put it. Paul Kurta, who was the production manager on a lot of my pictures, was doing a movie with Brooke and I asked him if he would approach her about doing a commercial. She agreed but, again, it was a waste of money. I'm not sure how many people would have recognized her, but Brooke had appeared in a lot of big movies, like *Invasion of the Body Snatchers*.[5] By the time the credits had finished rolling and Brooke appeared, I think most of the audience had left the theater. Tammy Grimes, the Tony-Award winning actress, also did one, which is still in the movie. I called Tammy up and asked if she would do a cameo as a favor to me and she did. We paid Abe Vigoda to come in for just the one day to shoot with Clara Peller. You'll find these people are all very employable. You pay them and they happily show up.

Can you tell me who designed the distinctive product packaging for The Stuff?

That was done by Larry Lurin, a friend of mine, who is a talented designer and art director. Larry had done some nice ad campaigns for my stage plays in New York and was also very experienced at doing motion picture posters. I asked him if he would design me some packaging for a new imaginary dessert. He agreed and I paid him a fee. I thought Larry came up with a very slick, seductive-looking product. It looks exactly like something you would see sold in stores. As a matter of fact, I suggested to New World that we could manufacture and sell packages of The Stuff as a real product—a frozen dessert or yogurt housed in Larry's container. My idea was that we could have placed this product in the lobbies of all the theaters where the film played, so people could buy The Stuff at the concession stand. Unfortunately, New World did not embrace my idea as it was obviously too complicated for them. They said, "Suppose somebody gets sick and they decide to sue us? We don't even have insurance to cover the distribution of food, so it just won't work." You must understand something about the movie business: generally, people don't want to do anything that may cause them any additional effort or problems. If you want to do something that is perceived as being out of the norm, or is going to complicate someone's life in some small way and add to the working hours in their day, they do not want to do get involved. I care about my movies a great deal. They are something special to me and I'll put in that extra time and effort to make them better or more successful. But for those individuals in distribution and advertising, it's merely a job. They want to go home at five o'clock and just forget about everything. So, New World didn't go for my suggestion, but it would have been a great idea.

It's still a great idea.

I certainly think so. I had some very definite ideas about what approach we should take in marketing *The Stuff*. I always thought that the best way to advertise the movie would have been to take commercials out on TV for The Stuff as if it was a real product. We could have run those commercials for a week and people would have gone to the supermarket to buy The Stuff and would be told that no such product existed. We could have even devised some form of coupon system or given away free tickets to customers at stores as a prize and tied it in with the release of the picture. Then, after a week of playing these realistic TV spots, we could have had a different commercial on the following week informing people that *The Stuff* was actually a new horror movie about a food product that could kill you. It would have been an elaborate campaign, but I think we could have earned some serious attention that way. Again, New World did not want to do anything that was out of the norm. They also didn't want to spend additional money on new commercials. So, they advertised *The Stuff* as they would any other ordinary picture. They didn't really have a good hook on it in order to sell the film. *The Stuff* could have been a huge success if they had just gone with my ideas. When we were selling *It's Alive*, we devised a commercial that fooled the audience into believing that it was selling an actual baby product. You hear some tinkling bells as the camera dollies over to a crib and a very pleasant voice announces: "There's only one thing wrong with the Davis baby . . . ."—then the camera moved to the other side of the crib and you suddenly saw this little claw reaching out as the narrator concludes—"*It's Alive!*" It was at that moment the audience realized the commercial was for a horror movie, not some baby product. We should have applied that same approach to *The Stuff*, but we didn't. It was a great idea, but a great idea is only great if it's welcomed and used by people. Otherwise, it's utterly redundant.

How was your second collaboration with Michael Moriarty? I understand that at one point he threatened to walk off the picture.

Yes, at the very beginning, on the first or second day. We were shooting in upstate New York and I had berated a member of the crew for some reason that seemed important at the time. Moriarty felt that I had been too hard on the guy and I don't recall exactly what happened, but it eventually culminated with Michael deciding to quit the film. It was obviously a delicate situation, but I calmly told him, "Okay, Michael, leave if you want to. I promise I won't sue you. Just go ahead and walk if you're not happy. I won't do anything to penalise you or harm you in any way. I know that we are going to lose a lot of money if you walk off the picture, but don't worry about it. Just go ahead and leave if you feel you have to."

Fortunately, Moriarty didn't feel like he had to. When he heard what I had to say, he calmed down a little, reconsidered his position, and decided to stay. Moriarty is a mercurial and often self-destructive personality, but I was very glad he decided to stick around.

Did you occasionally feel that you had to walk a careful line with Moriarty as not to upset him?

No, you just have to understand Michael. I knew he wasn't going to walk off the picture, but instead of being adversarial I played along. There was one unfortunate incident that happened which did upset him a little. There was originally a scene in the movie that took place after Moriarty and Andrea flee the motel. Moriarty was to open the trunk of his car and be shocked to discover that The Stuff had infiltrated his vehicle. We were about to shoot Moriarty's reaction shot when an idea came to me: I approached Michael's son, Matthew, who was just a kid at the time, and said, "Why don't we sneak you into the trunk for this next shot? We'll cover you with fake blood, so that when your father opens it up he'll see you lying there looking dead." Matthew agreed and we covered him in blood, placed him in the trunk, and shut it down. We then started shooting the scene, but soon realized that the guy who had the keys to the car had gone into town to get something. He was gone and here was Moriarty's kid stuck in the trunk and we couldn't get him out. Well, Moriarty had to be told what had happened and he wasn't too happy when he found out that his twelve-year-old son had been locked in a car. Some members of our crew started dismantling the vehicle, pulling out the back seat and everything, trying to get Matthew out of there. Fortunately, the guy with the keys came back and we got the kid out of the trunk without completely destroying the car. I was just trying to pull a little gag on Moriarty to see what his reaction shot would be when he suddenly saw his child lying there with all this blood over him. It wasn't exactly the smartest idea I've ever had and, naturally, it backfired. As it turned out, they should have had a camera on me when I found out that the guy with the keys to the car had left. It was not a happy moment.

Was the shoot a fairly smooth one?

Well, you always encounter problems and challenges on any movie, but I guess it went okay. You can always do with a little more money. I do remember that when we were shooting the prologue where the old man, who is played by Harry Bellaver, one of the stars of *Naked City*, finds the Stuff coming out of the ground, we had a problem. We went out to New Jersey to shoot the scene and it was a beautiful day with no sign of rain or snow. But when we got there it suddenly started snowing and there wasn't meant to be any snow in the scene. Then the snow quickly became a blizzard and I said, "Oh, my god! Look at the production value we are getting here! It would take twenty-five snow machines to reproduce this and we get it all for free! It's going to look great on film!" My cameraman, Paul Glickman, then said, "Yeah, Larry, it's going to look wonderful, but the equipment is not set up for a snowstorm. We aren't prepared for this weather." Pretty soon after those words left Paul's lips, all of the lights started exploding and our electrical equipment blew up. The cables were not insulated and were left exposed in the snow. What eventually happened was we kept on shooting and as went along we kept on losing equipment. Everything kept blowing up, but we got the sequence done and it does indeed look good on film.

I like the brief exchange Colonel Spears has with the young boy shortly before they battle The Stuff: "America has never lost a war," Spears contests. The boy then asks, "What about Vietnam, sir?" only for Spears to reply, "We lost that war at home, sonny."

I put that in there to add a little political flavor to the mix. It also tells you something about the Colonel and his attitude to the Vietnam War. A soldier always does his or her best, but it's our governments that have their own reasons for starting and ending any conflicts that we engage in with other countries. Of course, there's also the strength of public opinion and feeling. I liked the idea of this guy having his own private army that was just waiting to go to war with the commies. Instead the Colonel's forces go to war against The Stuff! Something amused me about the idea that the only man capable of defeating this monster is something of a monster himself—a half-crazed racist with his own highly-armed militia. Again, I must say, I love Paul Sorvino's performance as the Colonel. I think he's very, very funny.

It's obvious that Sorvino clearly relished the role.

Oh, he did. During filming Sorvino said to me, "You're the second best comedy director I've ever worked with." I asked, "Thank you, but who's the first?" He said, "Carl Reiner."[6] I certainly didn't mind being second best to Carl Reiner, who is a great comedy director and a wonderful performer.

That was a great compliment. Actually, we have two members of the Sorvino family in *The Stuff*. Paul's teenage daughter came by the set to visit one day when we were shooting the sequence where the army storms the factory where The Stuff is manufactured. As I was filming the scene where our heroes are chasing all these "stuffies"—that's what we called the factory workers in the yellow uniforms—I said to the young Sorvino girl, "Hey, do you want to be in the movie? Put on one of those yellow uniforms and you can be in the picture." She then got into a costume, and I put her in as an extra. Apparently, she's in the shot where you see all the stuffies lying dead on the factory floor. That was actually Mira Sorvino's first screen appearance. She's lying there somewhere amongst all those corpses. Of course, several years later, Mira went on to win an Academy Award for a Woody Allen picture[7] and has since enjoyed a good career. I'd forgotten all about her cameo, but when I met Mira several years later with her then boyfriend, Quentin Tarantino, she reminded me that *The Stuff* was her first acting role.

O'Neal and Scourby, who play the two corporate bigwigs, are eventually forced by Mo Rutherford to eat *The Stuff* at gunpoint. Talk about just desserts!

I love that scene. If only real life was like that. Unfortunately, it isn't. I remember Patrick O'Neal and Alexander Scourby were gorging on whipped cream—take after take after take—and they really did feel sick by the end of it. I think some members of the cast put on a little weight due to the sheer amount of ice cream and whipped cream they'd consumed during shooting. We originally closed that scene with Moriarty saying to the kid as they walk away, "Okay, son, let's go get a hamburger." Sadly, that line got lost in the sound-mix somehow, but I always liked it. I also think the last scene, which reveals that The Stuff is now being sold to addicts on the black market, makes perfect sense. Realistically, that is exactly what would happen if this product suddenly became illegal. Various criminal organizations would peddle The Stuff on the black market to meet the demand. It would naturally go underground. I mean, where else could it go? That's pretty much where it came from—underground!

When you were editing the picture, you cut a fairly sizable amount out of the finished film. I believe that some of this deleted material can be glimpsed in the theatrical trailer. What scenes hit the cutting room floor?

I don't remember all the scenes that were cut. I don't think any of them were crucial to the narrative, but we did lose a few funny scenes that I wanted to keep. When I showed New World my original cut, they felt strongly that the film should move a lot faster. I realized that I'd made a picture that was a little too dense and sophisticated, so we increased the pacing. I know that along with some of the commercials, we did lose a romantic scene between Moriarty and Andrea that took place in a hotel room. It was perhaps a wise decision to cut some of those scenes out, because I don't think they played well in the totality of the film. The story needed to drive forward at certain points and not be slowed down with extraneous material, although it can be painful cutting scenes out that you like. Sometimes the small scenes that cement the characters' relationships and romantic interests are the first things people want you to cut. They want you to get to the meat of the action and scares as quickly as possible.

You just mentioned the romantic scene in the hotel. I've seen stills of Moriarty and Marcovicci cuddling up in bed.

That's right. We actually shot that scene in a suite at the Sherry-Netherlands Hotel and Andrea's mother came to visit us on the set that day. As we were talking together, she looked around the room and said, "You know, Andrea's father was a well-known doctor in New York. One night, many years ago, he was called to the Sherry-Netherlands because Judy Garland had overdosed on sleeping pills. He actually saved her life and it all took place in this very room where you are shooting." I couldn't believe it! It was such a remarkable coincidence. To think that all those years later, we should be shooting that scene in not only the same hotel, but in the same room in the same hotel! It was pretty incredible.

You once indicated to me that New World were somewhat disappointed with *The Stuff* when you finally showed it to them. What prompted the negative reaction?

New World wanted a straight-up horror film, and, in retrospect, *The Stuff* had more comedic aspects to it than the executives were perhaps expecting. They thought they were going to get a flat-out horror movie with a lot of gore and scares, and we made a film that was more satirical and had a lot of humour and commentary in it. We played the characters for laughs in many cases and that greatly diluted the horror element. It made *The Stuff* more of what I would consider "A Larry Cohen Movie" but less of a conventional, commercial horror film. I think New World were disappointed that *The Stuff* wasn't more horrific and nasty—more of a balls-out monster movie. I knew before the film even hit theaters *The Stuff* would appeal to a different audience than the one we were trying to get. I mean, people who go to see a horror movie want to see the horror. They want to be scared and have some visceral thrills and chills. I think *The Stuff* was far too relaxed, too pointed, and too cerebral for them.

Are you suggesting that the horror audience is less literate than the general movie audience? I certainly don't think that's the case.

No, I'm not saying that, because I think those kinds of generalisations are dangerous. But there is a chunk of that audience—any audience really—who have no patience for something that makes small demands of their intellect and imagination. A lot of people like everything to be reassuringly predictable and undemanding. I think what ultimately harmed *The Stuff* was the fact that the audience were unsure about exactly what kind of movie it was. Was it a horror film or was it a comedy? They seemed to have trouble making that distinction and we suffered for it. In that regard, the only substantial fault with *The Stuff* was that it wasn't overtly horrific enough as a horror movie. Yes, there are moments when people's heads explode or their mouths stretch open grotesquely as The Stuff erupts out of their bodies, but the picture was still essentially a comedy. The audience did not respond to the comedic approach because they came to the theater to see a horror film and be shocked. They wanted to scream and cringe and shudder, and we gave them laughter instead. Unfortunately, that's not what they bought when they laid down their bucks for a movie ticket.

I think some of the critics also felt that there was an uneven and erratic quality to *The Stuff*—a criticism that some of your films have been labored with.

I don't understand that. The reviews I read were all good, actually. In fact, I have a big poster of great reviews for *The Stuff* hanging on a wall. Now that I think about it, I got really wonderful notices on that picture. This may be hard for you to believe, but the day *The Stuff* opened in New York a hurricane hit and the newspapers were not delivered. Of course, we had received all these great reviews, but it didn't matter because nobody ever got to read a single word of them. Even if they had been delivered, the newspapers would have probably been reduced to piles of wet shreds and mush. Nobody would have been able to decipher a word of them. That hurricane practically wiped us out and caused all sorts of problems. The windstorms were so powerful they actually blew the title of the movie off the marquee of the theater. What can you say? I should have taken that as a sign! It was one of those untimely things that sometimes happen. I just wish it had happened to somebody else.

Screenplays: Part II (1987–1997)

In the mid-1980s, it was announced that you planned to write and direct a film called *The Apparatus*. What exactly was this unmade project?

You know, it's incredible, but after all these years, somebody actually called me up just last week to talk about *The Apparatus*. It's another one of those scripts from the past that has suddenly re-emerged in the present. A producer called me and said, "What about *The Apparatus*? I'd really love to make it." I said, "Well, see if you can clear the rights to it." I then told him where to look. The problem with these long dormant projects is that when you sell something or option it to somebody, and then that company goes out of business, which most of these little companies have over the years, many of the people involved who were principals have died. Also, the chances are their widows and children don't know anything about the rights situation. So, having to trace back who owns these pieces of material is an arduous process, but you can't make a picture without clearing the rights first. You don't want somebody to come out of the woodwork after the film is made who claims they own it. I certainly don't want to get in the middle of a potential lawsuit. So, I told this enquiring producer, "Go out and find who owns the damn thing and I'll be glad to rewrite *The Apparatus*, or do whatever is necessary to get it made."

The screenplay for *The Apparatus* has gained a strong reputation over the decades, but very little is known about it. What is it actually about?

The Apparatus is a thriller about a man who goes on a trip to Europe and meets a beautiful girl. He takes her back to his hotel and goes to bed with her. He wakes up in the morning and discovers that the girl is gone and he now has this peculiar apparatus strapped to his chest. It has a leather band on it and when he tries to remove it, the apparatus starts to get hot and burns him. He then receives a phone call and a voice warns him not to attempt to remove the apparatus from his body. If he does, it will explode and kill him. The voice then instructs him to go to a certain location in the city and more will be explained to him. So, he arrives at this place and a stranger approaches him and says, "If you try to take this thing off it will blow you to pieces." The stranger then opens his shirt and reveals that he too has an apparatus strapped to his chest. The stranger then walks a few feet away and his apparatus explodes, blowing him apart. Our guy immediately realizes that this situation he finds himself in is no joke. It then becomes apparent that he is now a slave and must do whatever the dark forces behind the apparatus instruct him to do. The apparatus now controls him and he is informed that he must assassinate someone. That's basically the story.

It sounds a rather intriguing concept for a thriller.

Oh, it's a terrific story and a really great script. Twice we were close to making *The Apparatus,* once over in Italy and once over in France. On both occasions, various things conspired against us that meant the picture didn't quite work out. The first time we tried to do *The Apparatus*, the company that was going to make the picture got into some trouble and was bankrupted. The second time there was a rights clearance problem that prevented the film from being shot. Despite these disappointments, I did get a couple of nice trips to Italy and France out of it. Actually, in the French version of *The Apparatus*, my second wife, Cynthia, and I were in Paris for three or four months, all expenses paid, and had a beautiful apartment, a driver, and a weekly salary. Unfortunately, when the rights couldn't be cleared, the movie didn't happen. Now the damn thing has resurfaced again, so maybe someday it will get made.

Has your second wife, Cynthia Costas Cohen, been an important force in your writing career?

Cynthia has been instrumental in my success as a writer. We've been together for twenty-five years and she is directly responsible for my getting the work on *NYPD Blue* through her personal connections; as well as for the storyline of *Guilty as Sin*, which came about from a friend of hers who is a trial lawyer. Cynthia has been an invaluable companion who has made me extremely happy. We met on *Wicked Stepmother* when she came to work as my assistant, and was soon doing all the casting and set decoration for the film. Since that time she has been a successful sculptress and attended Antioch University where she gained a Masters in Clinical Psychology. I'm proud of her success with her practice in Beverly Hills and she has become an expert in hypnosis. She hypnotises almost all of her patients. Cynthia has twice travelled to Guatemala to train young workers in a successful attempt to influence young women there to stay in school past the fourth grade. She also travelled to the Philippines after the Tsunami, and recently went to Nepal following the earthquake to train young therapists in dealing with trauma. She has been a second mother to my children, who adore her, and in keeping with *Wicked Stepmother*, they nicknamed her "Wickedy." Cynthia is the author of two books: the first, *The 7 Day Energy Surge*, appeared on *The New York Times* Best Seller list; the second, *The Glass Enclosure*, is currently being published. She looks forward to writing more books on the subject of hypnosis and trauma therapy, of which I consider her to be one of the leading authorities in her field. Cynthia hypnotised me twenty-five years ago and I haven't woken up since.

You continued in the thriller genre with your next produced screenplay, the 1987 film *Best Seller*. Do you like that picture?

Uh, yes and no. I thought it was partially successful as a movie. *Best Seller* took about seven or eight years to finally get made. The project kept moving from one company to another without getting produced, which was very frustrating as I thought it was a good script. Then, Orion Pictures eventually bought it and made the film. *Best Seller* was an idea I had about a police detective, who writes a book that becomes hugely successful. Unfortunately, he is afflicted with writer's block and can't follow up his initial success with another book. He is desperate to find something to write about and satisfy his publishers when he is approached by a professional killer who wants his life-story as a paid assassin to be written. The cop and the hitman then form an uneasy alliance, and in that regard, I thought *Best Seller* shared certain similarities with Hitchcock's *Strangers on a Train*. In both of those movies you have two men who come to some kind of dangerous arrangement. I initially thought that *Best Seller* would make a terrific project for Burt Lancaster and Kirk Douglas, that's who I really had in mind when I first wrote it. Despite that, we ended up with a good cast anyway. Brian Dennehy played the cop and James Woods played the hitman, and I thought they were both good. I certainly had no complaints about those guys. The picture itself turned out to be pretty good with one glaring exception: the ending. Everything was going along great but then, in the last five minutes, they fucked up the whole movie. That is what I mean when I say it was only partially successful.

What was your problem with the ending, specifically?

It was unbelievable, simply unbelievable! In my screenplay, the finale of *Best Seller* originally took place on a yacht but—due to budgetary concerns—they relocated all the action to a beach-house. At the climax, there is the big shootout involving Woods, Dennehy, and the guy they are targeting with their book. In the middle of all this violence, you see Dennehy's daughter come running down the stairs towards a dangerous man who is shooting guns at her. That does not make any sense whatsoever! She should be running away from this person, not racing directly into his arms! I actually told them what they had done. I said, "Look, there is absolutely no reason why she would do such an illogical thing. If you keep this ending as it is, it will be terrible. You have to re-cut the scene." So, I explained to them how they could fix it without having to re-shoot anything, but the producer wouldn't listen to me. Of course, when *Best Seller* opened in New York I went to see it downtown at the Loews Theatre. Everything was going along great, but then, as the climax arrived, I saw that nothing had been changed. Just as before, the girl came running down the stairs and into the arms of the gunman. At that moment, the audience started screaming, "Kill that bitch! Kill that stupid little bitch!" They couldn't believe that any human being would be stupid enough to do what she did. That one moment ruined the film, and, unfortunately, it came at the end of the picture. That meant the sense of frustration and disappointment the audience felt was what they finally took away with them. That's all people ever really remember about a movie—the ending. You can have a great picture for an hour and forty minutes, but if the final ten minutes are bad, people will come walking out of the theater saying, "What a stinker that was!" *Best Seller* lost its audience completely in that final scene. They just blew it. What's most depressing of all is that I warned them ahead of time about how to fix it, but they wouldn't listen. I mean, the film has its moments, but it could have been really great.

An extraordinary moment in *Best Seller* occurs when Cleve the hitman murders the taxi driver in a photo booth. The photo strip is then ejected from the machine revealing a sequence of images that show Cleve cutting the man's throat.

Yeah, that was very good. That moment was in my script, too.

Were any interesting scenes excised from *Best Seller*?

They cut out a lot of stuff concerning the developing romance between Brian Dennehy's character and the female agent who represents his interests as a writer. I think they removed most of those scenes because they felt that Dennehy was too big and too heavy to enjoy a romance. So, they cut out all the moments that showed them doing anything even remotely romantic. They thought he looked grotesque—a big guy like him and a pretty girl like her—so all of that material is now gone. They also cut a really interesting scene that I think would have given the film a little more depth and shading. The hitman takes the cop to his family home so that he can see the environment he grew up in and meet his parents and sister. We learn that James Woods likes to send his mom postcards from all the places he has assassinated people. This becomes an interesting detail as the hitman uses the corresponding dates on the postcards to authenticate his life story. But at one point, Woods goes into his mother's room and talks to her about money and it becomes obvious that she knows exactly what he does for a living. She is well aware of the fact that he murders people, but this element was deemed to be too strange and unsettling. I didn't agree with the decision to lose that scene. It was an intimate little moment and keeping it in would have only enhanced Woods' character and given the audience more insight into the hitman's family life and background. Those are the only scenes that I know for sure that were cut from the picture. As I said, Dennehy and Woods were very good actors, but it wasn't the same as if we had used real stars. If *Best Seller* had starred Burt Lancaster and Kirk Douglas in those roles, it would have been a blockbuster. It certainly would have been a much better movie. Both Lancaster and Douglas were very intelligent and creative actors, who always had a lot of input into the movies they appeared in. They would never have allowed that stupidity at the end to have been included in the film.

How did *Best Seller* fare? I understand that it had a fairly short release.

It didn't do that well, even though—as I keep saying—it was a good picture all the way up to the climax. I don't want to go on about it, but they killed the movie with that conclusion and it's amazing how you can do that. If they had made that one little cut I suggested, maybe the word of mouth would have been a little better and *Best Seller* could have made some money. People are always so resilient about keeping their position; they never want to listen to what you have to say. It simply has to be their way and they are not interested in hearing any suggestions that might conflict with their own ideas and opinions. If you tell them they did something wrong, and even if that mistake can be easily rectified, they still can't accept it. They just can't. I keep telling you, that's the recurring problem with the business. The trouble has nothing to do with the creativity and everything to do with the egos.

Did this lack of understanding also extend to your relationship with the film's director, John Flynn?

I didn't work much with Flynn. I hardly knew him and we had no communication. In the movie business—the way they run it out here—the writers very seldom have anything to do with the directors. The producer deliberately keeps them apart in order for him or her to maintain some kind of power and control. Also, directors often feel threatened by the writers because half of them don't even understand what the hell they are shooting in the first place. All they know is where to put the cameras. They have no idea about the characterisations, or any understanding of what they should say to the actors. Some directors even make a concerted effort not to discuss the script with the actors that much. They just want to position the cameras in the right place, point them at something and shoot. When a pivotal character point or plot point does suddenly arise, they don't know what the fuck to do about it.

I was surprised to learn that you once scripted a film version of *Doctor Strange*, based on the Marvel Comics superhero created by Stan Lee and artist Steve Ditko. How did that opportunity come about?

I can't remember his name now, but I was hired by a producer to write a movie of *Doctor Strange*. I also met with Stan Lee quite a number of times and we became very good friends. We had many dinners, many afternoons and days together, and Stan and I are still friends. I did write the script, but then the production company went under and the guy who was producing died. That was the end of the whole project and the option eventually ran out and went back to Marvel. At the time, Stan had been running around Hollywood for ten years trying to sell these Marvel superhero characters for movies and television, without any success. He just couldn't get anything off the ground involving properties such as Spider-Man, The Hulk, Captain America, and The Fantastic Four. Roger Corman bought the rights to The Fantastic Four and made a real low-budget picture that was never released, just so that he would be able to hang onto the rights.[1] At the time, I remember Stan asked me, "Is there any way I can stop Corman?" I said, "I don't think so. If you sold it to him, he has the right to make the picture." But *The Fantastic Four* movie was so bad and cheaply made, it never saw the light of day. As I say, back then, Stan was having a terrible time getting anything made, and I realize that sounds rather incredible now considering Marvel's incredible recent success. The company eventually changed hands and new management took over. Stan then became kind of an emeritus figure. They paid him for the use of his identity, but he didn't really have anything to do with the organization anymore. So, Stan did not put all those huge deals together for the *Spider-Man*, *Fantastic Four,* and *Captain America* movies that have been made in recent years. They were done by the new management. The success of the first *Spider-Man*[2] movie changed everything and turned Marvel into an absolute goldmine. That film made all of those Marvel characters popular and viable again. Before that, it seemed audiences just weren't that interested in superhero movies anymore.

Was your *Doctor Strange* script an original or did it derive from the storylines in the comic books?

It was an origin story, so it told a little of the beginnings of Doctor Strange that had been detailed in the comic books. It was similar to *Batman Begins*, where he goes off to Tibet to train and gain knowledge and eventually becomes wise and powerful. I don't think I have a copy of my *Doctor Strange* script anymore. It's now lost.

Did you have any affinity or affection for the character itself?

No, absolutely not. It was just an assignment, but I thought I did a good job.

So, you weren't too disappointed that it didn't happen?

There are always a lot of scripts and projects I'm either writing, developing, or thinking about, so I always just keep moving forward. There have been interesting projects, like *The Apparatus* and *Doctor Strange*, that have fallen by the wayside over the years but I don't get too down about them. I just move on to the next one and the next one. Yeah, some of these things would have been fun to do but you have to be philosophical about them. I mean, I once thought about doing a new version of *The Invisible Man* with Marlon Brando playing the lead. The opportunity to have worked with Brando would have been wonderful, but it simply wasn't to be. So, you move on.

Can you tell me a little more about your unmade *Invisible Man* project?

Well, I'd always liked the old Universal version with Claude Rains and I thought we could do something great with it. There had been other updates of *The Invisible Man* made since, but I felt the idea still had a lot of potential. So, I talked to Elliott Kastner about doing *The Invisible Man* with Brando as the lead. Elliott was a close friend of Marlon's, and a successful producer, so I felt reasonably confident that we could work something out.[3] Brando was notorious for being paid millions of dollars to only make fleeting appearances in movies. He'd played memorable characters in films like *Superman* and *Apocalypse Now*, but he wasn't onscreen for very long and would only show up in a few scenes. But he was such a powerful and magnetic presence, Brando would dominate the screen and compel you to watch. You just couldn't take your eyes off him, which sounds a little ironic as I wanted him to be mostly invisible in my movie! [Chuckles] The basic idea was that if Marlon didn't have the energy or interest to shoot an entire movie, we'd only use his voice in the part. So, we'd see the invisible man moving objects, opening doors, and everything as Brando delivered the dialogue. That way, Brando could limit his direct involvement and would only be required to appear in the final scene. Then, and only then, the audience could finally get a look at him. Of course, the movie didn't happen and I later tried to get the idea started over at Paramount in a 3D version, but that didn't work out either. It could have been really great but, again, I didn't get too down about it. I just moved on to the next idea.

What was *Desperado: Avalanche at Devil's Ridge*, which you wrote in 1988?

Actually, that was just on television over here the other day. That was a two-hour TV movie I wrote that co-starred Rod Steiger. There was a mini-series called *Desperado* that was created by Elmore Leonard and produced by Walter Mirisch. It was about the adventures of a cowboy on the frontier. Walter called me and asked me if I would like to write a two-hour film for this series of feature-length TV movies they were planning. I liked the series and the central character, so I wrote *Avalanche at Devil's Ridge* and it turned out to be pretty good, too, I must say. When I watched it again, I couldn't find any fault with it. I thought Rod Steiger was particularly good in it.

What was the extent of your involvement with Abel Ferrara's *Body Snatchers*?

It was this: I was the first writer on the picture and the basic story of the pod people from *Invasion of the Body Snatchers* taking over an American military base was mine. That idea seemed to make good dramatic sense to me because military people are very similar in their behavior and look. So, in a way, they are already pod people to begin with. They are kind of unemotional and form part of a collective organization or consciousness. That was my starting point, conceptually. You can't tell who the humans are and who the aliens are because they all conform. I thought that was an interesting and scary approach to take with the material. People are pretty much behaving like aliens even before they become aliens, so who can you trust? That aspect of the story—the paranoia, fear, and uncertainty—was always a major element of those movies; from the original movie that was made in the 1950s through to the excellent Philip Kaufman version, to the not so excellent version which recently starred Nicole Kidman. I thought that last *Body Snatchers* movie was awful, frankly.

In what ways were the themes and ideas you introduced in your draft of *Body Snatchers* modified or altered in subsequent drafts by the other writers?

They pretty much built upon or reworked my existing ideas and characters. In my script, the little boy was the lead character. He discovers that his mother has turned into a pod person and that humanity is now in peril. I wanted to tell the story from the point-of-view of a child, but Warner Bros. were more interested in centering the film around teenagers. They felt that approach would hold more appeal. You see, *Body Snatchers* was a studio picture and, as is often the case, the studio then proceeded to hire several other writers to work on the screenplay after I'd delivered my draft. When Abel Ferrara came in as director, he brought another writer in with him and they rewrote my script, particularly the dialogue. They still retained a lot of the elements I'd devised for it: obviously the military base setting, but also the stuff about the pills keeping you awake and all the business concerning the child. That all came from me and was what got *Body Snatchers* made in the first place.

Were there any interesting scenes that were discarded in later drafts that you felt worked particularly well in yours?

There was a nice scene in my script where the little boy attends the school on the military base. All the children have to lie down for their afternoon nap and then the teachers bring out the pods. The boy suddenly wakes up and realizes that all the kids are now aliens. That was very good, a very disturbing scene. I think they deleted that from the finished film. If they didn't delete it entirely, it wasn't in there to the extent that it was in was my original script.

Interestingly, Stuart Gordon and his writing partner Dennis Paoli are also credited as co-writers on *Body Snatchers*.

Stuart is a friend of mine, but I've never actually discussed that with him. It never occurred to me that he had a credit on *Body Snatchers*. Oh well, god bless him! The more, the merrier! [Chuckles] Let all writers get a job out of it, I don't care. The most important thing is that I got the movie made. I went to Warner Bros., I pitched the idea, and I got the picture made. All the other people came in later.

Did you ever meet Abel Ferrara?

I met him once—very briefly—at a party some twenty years ago. I had done *Special Effects* with Zoë Lund, and so Ferrara and I had something in common there as they had also worked closely together on several projects. Apparently, the studio complained on *Body Snatchers* that Ferrara was under the influence of drugs the entire time he was shooting the picture and that he went way over budget. They were really pissed off at him and they penalized the producer. They held the producer responsible for letting it happen and took away his producer's salary and producer's points. He then quit the business as a direct result of that movie.[4] At any rate, he had a very bad reputation over at Warner Bros. for that particular picture.

Why didn't you direct *Body Snatchers*?

Nobody asked me to. By the time it got in front of the cameras, *Body Snatchers* had been through many, many phases and many, many writers, and I was no longer associated with the project. Like the situation with *Doctor Strange* and *The Invisible Man*, I had already moved on to something else. But when something like *Body Snatchers* occurs, I just take my money and immediately push forward to the next project. I have too many ideas, and too many original scripts, and too much to do, to waste my time worrying about some movie that a bunch of studio executives have decided to screw up. I am still credited on the picture along with those other writers and I do like the film. I thought Ferrara made a pretty good movie.

In 1993, you returned to the familiar surroundings of the courtroom drama with *Guilty as Sin* which was directed by the unrivalled master of the genre, Sidney Lumet. How did Lumet become attached as director?

Well, Sidney's involvement began with my sending the script for *Guilty as Sin* to the producer Martin Ransohoff.[5] I think it's well-known that Sidney had been making some pretty bad movies around this stage of his career. His previous film, *A Stranger Among Us*, had been about a female undercover cop who infiltrates the Hasidic Jewish community in Brooklyn to investigate a murder. Melanie Griffith played the cop and she was absolutely the wrong choice for that part. I mean, you had this squeaky-voiced, air-headed ditz playing a female detective getting involved with Hasidic Jews. It was ludicrous! A terrible movie in every way. At that time, Sidney had not had a successful picture in many years. The last major success he had enjoyed was *The Verdict*, which was wonderful. Before that,

Sidney had made some great films like *Twelve Angry Men*, *Serpico*, and *Dog Day Afternoon*. He also made several good pictures after *Guilty as Sin*, but none of them ever caught on. As it turns out, *Guilty as Sin* was the most successful movie he'd made in twenty-five years. It was probably the most successful movie of the last phase of his career. That success allowed him to make a bunch of other pictures afterwards, including a wonderful film he did towards the end of his life about the robbery of a jewellery store by two brothers who end up killing their own mother by accident. I forget the name of it.

Before the Devil Knows Your Dead.

Yeah, that's the one. Now that was a wonderful picture. Unfortunately, it didn't do any business. The only movie that Sidney had later on that did any business was *Guilty as Sin*. It actually became the highest-earning video in the video stores in America for about six weeks. So, it was good for Sidney and it was good for me. I got about five or six writing jobs over at Disney out of *Guilty as Sin*. They were a variety of different pictures that I can't really remember much about. Disney kept calling me up and asking me if I would come in and take over a project and I just couldn't turn them down. They were so enthusiastic about my doing everything, but they never made *any* of the pictures! Anyway, I did make a lot of money. So, *Guilty as Sin* was a fairly satisfying and profitable venture for all concerned.

Tell me about collaborating with Lumet. What was he like?

Sidney was very friendly at the beginning, very nice. I think he became less than enamoured with me as we went to New York and worked on the final script. Sidney liked to think of himself as being very democratic and respectful towards writers but, just like everybody else, he started putting his own two cents in when I wasn't around. He began rewriting dialogue and changing stuff, and I didn't think that was necessary. I could have made any and all of the changes he wanted overnight, if only he'd called me up on the phone and asked for them. Sidney didn't rewrite much, but the fact that he rewrote anything annoyed me because he had all this pretension about honouring the writer's integrity. Naturally, I was a little disappointed when I discovered he was fussing around with my script. Most of the time what he was putting in didn't make any sense, but we got by. Equally disappointing was the cast he assembled for the film. It was certainly not what I'd hoped for. It was really a second string cast. Sidney had originally tried to get Paul Newman and Sean Connery for the lead, but they both felt they were now too old for the part. That was too bad.

Lumet eventually cast Don Johnson in the lead role as the scheming wife-killer and Rebecca De Mornay as the doubting attorney assigned to defend him.

That's right, and I thought those actors were merely adequate. I do remember that Sidney was trying to shoot a love scene between the female lawyer and her boyfriend in an office at night. They were supposed to have a tryst up there and what Sidney shot was so inadequate and awkward, they couldn't use any of it. They pretty much had to cut the entire scene out of the picture. I couldn't imagine why Sidney was unable to shoot a love scene. I couldn't understand it at all. Sidney also had certain little oddities. For instance, he once told me, "I will not shoot a scene in a moving car." I said, "But Sidney, many years ago you once shot a whole movie inside a moving car, remember? It starred George Segal and was about a bunch of guys going to a funeral."⁶ He said, "Well, maybe that's why I won't ever shoot a scene in a moving car again." I said, "Okay, so we won't put these characters in a car. They'll be outside the club waiting for the car to be brought over by the parking attendants. We can do the dialogue with them standing in the street." And, as easily as that, I fixed it. I later thought to myself, "What is the problem if we have a scene in a moving car? People do ride in cars and they do conduct conversations inside them. What's the big deal here?" But if that was what Sidney wanted, it was fine by me.

***Guilty as Sin* was met with mixed reviews from critics. Most agreed that the battle between the debonair lady killer and his beautiful female attorney began rather cleverly, but devolved into little more than a series of melodramatic clichés involving a victimised woman. Is this criticism fair in your view?**

No, I don't think so. The picture got some very good reviews from other reviewers. Even the woman critic in the *New York Times* gave it a very good review. She said *Guilty as Sin* moved into Hitchcock territory and was actually one of Lumet's better pictures. The guy in *The National Re-*

view said *Guilty as Sin* was a fitting bookend to *Twelve Angry Men*, and *The Verdict*, so I was happy for the movie to be considered in that same illustrious category. So, you can't worry about what all the critics say. If you collect enough reviews, naturally you are going to receive a few bad ones.

Whilst reading most of the contemporary reviews, I stumbled upon Roger Ebert's notice in the *Chicago Sun-Times*. Ebert attacked the plot as "preposterous," describing the story's logic as "faulty." He also claimed that Rebecca De Mornay had an "inescapable resemblance" to the then-President's wife, Hillary Clinton, adding an intriguing tone to the movie that was perhaps not intentional. What is your response to those criticisms?

Oh yeah, sure, I intentionally made her look like Bill Clinton's wife! I have the power to do that with an actress, remold her face and hair so that she looks like somebody else entirely. What kind of comment is that? I mean, okay, Ebert might be correct, maybe Rebecca De Mornay did look like Hilary Clinton—when Hilary Clinton was better looking—but that certainly had nothing to do with me. It just happened to be that she resembled Hilary Clinton and that's all it was. There was no underlying theme, tone, or message intended from that. If there was some kind of political subversion going on there, it was certainly nothing I knew about.

Before we move on, do you have any final thoughts about Lumet?

Only that I'm glad I worked with him. Sidney had always been one of my heroes. I was such a big fan of his, it was a big thrill to get the opportunity to work with him. We had some nice times together on *Guilty as Sin*, but I shouldn't have. . . well, I criticized something in *The Verdict*, and I think Sidney took exception to it.

What was that criticism exactly?

In *The Verdict*, Paul Newman plays this alcoholic lawyer who is trying a big case. One day, this female lawyer, played by Charlotte Rampling, comes along and they begin a love affair. It turns out that this woman is secretly working for James Mason who is the opposing attorney in the case. Mason gives her a big cheque to pay her off and she puts the cheque into her purse. Later on, Jack Warden, who is assisting Newman in the proceedings, opens the purse to look for some matches, finds the cheque and realizes that she is, in fact, spying on them for Mason. Sidney and I were discussing logic in the script for *Guilty as Sin* and I said to him: "Look, logic means nothing because nobody ever pays any attention to it. For example, in your picture *The Verdict*, James Mason gives Charlotte Rampling a cheque. Do you know that in real life if Rampling had received a cheque from Mason, she could have had him disbarred? Mason is supposed to be playing one of the most ruthlessly brilliant, cunning, and experienced attorneys in the city, and yet he is stupid enough to give this bimbo a cheque—signed by him—that she could then use to either blackmail or destroy him. He could have lost his entire career, his whole firm would crumble, from that one action. It would not only be the end of the lawsuit, it would be the end of him! He could have even gone to jail for bribery and the unlawful subordination of a case. Mason would never have given her a cheque. Nobody in their right mind would give somebody a cheque for bribery and then let them walk around with it. More than that, it's certainly convenient that the cheque is in her purse and Jack Warden finds it. It's absurd and doesn't make any sense at all. It would have been easier to have come up with some other device rather than that." [Exhales] Well, after I'd finished my speech, Lumet looked at me like I had just stabbed him in the heart. After that, things were never the same again between us.

I can understand Lumet's reaction, but the logic of your argument is faultless.

Oh, absolutely. I even talked to Martin Ransohoff about logic. I remember telling him: "You once made a picture called *Jagged Edge* in which Jeff Bridges plays the murderer. In the first scene of the movie, Bridges' wife is tied to a bed and the maid lies dead on the floor. He is alone in the room and is about to kill her, but he's wearing a mask. If the maid is dead and the wife is tied up and is about to be slaughtered, why does Bridges need to wear a mask? What is the point of him doing that? Of course, the only reason is because the camera is there and the audience are watching, and you want to place doubt in their minds as to the identity of the killer. Okay, fine, but then at the end of the picture when he comes back to kill the female lawyer who has defended him in his murder trail, he puts the mask on again! Bridges is coming into the house to kill her and she knows beyond reasonable doubt that he is the killer, so why does he have to wear a mask?" It didn't make any sense to me, but Ransohoff was looking at me like I was crazy! [Laughs] But you know something? Both *The Verdict* and *Jagged Edge* were very successful and nobody ever mentioned these points that I've raised. I was merely telling Lumet and Ransohoff that logic doesn't always apply in movies. If the picture is playing successfully, the audience never seems to ask these important questions. I can never understand why they don't.

Digging up a director's past lapses in logic during conversation is certainly an effective way of alienating you from them. Believe me, I know!

I've done it on several occasions. I can remember once having a very pleasant lunch with Hitchcock. As we were talking, I said, "I saw *Strangers on a Train* forty times, but I had a problem with the ending." Hitchcock asked, "And what problem was that?" I said, "Well, Farley Granger has got to finish a tennis match so that he can get to the fairground and retrieve the cigarette lighter that will incriminate him in his wife's murder. Okay, now what is the quickest way to end a tennis match? Of course, you throw the game and lose. But Granger is compelled to win the tennis match first before leaving to get the cigarette lighter. That doesn't make any sense at all. What does this tennis match really matter when his life and liberty are at stake? Any sane person would just lose the tennis match as quickly and discreetly as possible. But, no, Granger has to win the match!" Hitchcock listened patiently as I said all this and when I'd finished he looked at me for a moment and said: [does an unerring impersonation of Hitchcock] "Yes, indeed, but that wouldn't be a very interesting scene now would it?" [Laughs] I swear that's exactly what he said! It just goes to show you, I meet these fabulously famous filmmakers and just insult them.

Two years after the release of *Guilty as Sin*, you did an uncredited polish on the script for the 1995 serial killer thriller, *The Expert*. Did you do much work on it?

I only did a little work on *The Expert*. My daughter, Jill Gatsby, wrote that movie. I just got the job for her, that's all. I really had nothing to do with the film, so I couldn't comment on it. I saw *The Expert*, but I don't remember much. I thought it was passable. The movie was supposed to be a remake of *Brute Force*[7] but it wasn't very good. Once again, somebody fucked around with the script.

Later that same year, you wrote the horror film *Uncle Sam* for William Lustig. Did you have any interest in helming that movie yourself?

No. *Uncle Sam* was a spec script that I wrote and then gave to Bill Lustig. I don't recall the exact year I wrote that script because some of these events just telescope together, but I do remember that we put the project together very quickly. True to his usual form, Bill called me and said, "I've got the financing to make the picture—if I can direct it." I said, "Well, you've got a deal as long as I get paid." So, I got paid my money and Bill got to direct the film. I did actually shoot some scenes for *Uncle Sam* previously—at a July 4th parade I attended—then gave them the footage. They did incorporate that footage into the picture, but Bill directed the entire movie.

***Uncle Sam* shares several similarities with Bob Clark's excellent 1972 film, *Deathdream*. It's the story of a young soldier killed in Vietnam, who is wished back to life by his distraught mother only to return as a blood-drinking zombie. Has anyone ever remarked to you about the similarity between those films?**

No, only you, but that movie sounds very much like the famous old horror story *The Monkey's Paw*.[8] That short story has the very same idea of the parents wishing their son back to life after he has been killed suddenly in a war or some kind of accident, and threatens to return as a decayed monster. So, I would say that both of these pictures bare more than a strong resemblance to *The Monkey's Paw*. I don't deny that.

The character of Uncle Sam was first drawn in 1812 as a larger than life figure, but what does he represent in your mind and the minds of the American people?

Uncle Sam symbolises strength, patriotism, loyalty, and a sense of purpose and pride. He symbolises the U.S. Government and the people it serves, and is this colorful embodiment and exaggeration of American values. I mean, he almost looks like a superhero in the red, white, and blue uniform, only in our movie, he's bad! [Chuckles] We subverted Uncle Sam, which is the way I always like to do it. When you corrupt any agency, person, or product and turn it into something evil, it's more interesting dramatically. It's very much like *God Told Me To* where I turned something that was considered irredeemably good like God into something irredeemably evil.

Uncle Sam is clearly an anti-war tract.

[Interrupting] Well, yeah, but then who is really pro-war?

There certainly have been films made that were pro-war and pro-military, like *The Green Berets*[9] for instance, that come off like government propaganda.

Of course, but usually those movies are saying, "Oh, we're fighting this war for peace." That's the excuse that is often given. For some unknown reason, peace always requires that you go to war and some Hollywood films do reflect that hypocrisy.

Well, who can forget the climax of *The Green Berets* when John Wayne famously tells the little Vietnamese orphan, "You're what this [war] is all about."

It's sickening, really. I mean, when you look back at some of the wars the United States have been involved in, all the way down to the War of 1812, when we tried to take Canada and got our asses kicked by the British that time, it's a rather shameful history. You can then move on to the Mexican-American War, which is one of the great crimes that have ever been committed by any government. We stole half the territory of Mexico for absolutely no reason whatsoever except greed. We got away with that one, except for the heavy American casualties, of course. Then we can move on to the Spanish-American War, a completely trumped-up war that was only initiated so we could seize even more territory. Then, we can move on to World War I, a conflict we had no business being in at all. What the hell did the Archduke of Serbia getting assassinated have to do with us? It makes no sense that we had anything to do with that war. Of course, World War I then predicated World War II, which wouldn't have happened had we not gotten involved in the First World War. Then you have the Korean War and I don't know if that conflict was entirely necessary either. They ended up right back where they started at the 48th parallel. Then you get to the Vietnam War, which was a complete farce, and more recently this domical in the Middle East, which is just idiotic! The fact that our forces are still over in Afghanistan, supporting drug lords who are growing poppies and making fortunes off of us, it's crazy! People are stealing the money and equipment we are sending and show no gratitude whatsoever. More than that, we are getting all of our poor guys killed over there. So, as you can see, it's just a long and depressing history of lunacy, misery and death. That's why I wanted to write an anti-war film like *Uncle Sam*, to touch upon some of the absolute chaos, madness and destructiveness of war.

Despite its cheesy violence and broad characterisations, *Uncle Sam* is ripe with commentary. It explores the dangers of blind patriotism and sweeping national pride and how destructive they can be. Are those themes important to you?

Yes, and that follows on directly from what I just told you: every one of those wars I mentioned was promoted as some kind of celebration or re-affirmation of patriotism. All of these conflicts are commemorated with songs, marches, and music like "Send the Boys off to War," "Hang a Star in your Window," "God Bless Us," and "Put a Flag on Your Porch." But what does all this patriotism do? Terrible things happen on account of all that flag waving, because we are being encouraged to pronounce our differences rather than our shared similarities. As a nation, America has committed an awful lot of bad things over the years in the name of patriotism. Most of those wars were unnecessary and unjust. They were fraught with greed and were ruthless attempts to expand the power of the country and seize other peoples' lands. You know, when I see all this fuss about illegal immigrants from Mexico, I just look around the city and see the names on every street—names like El Camino and Santa Monica. I mean, everything has got a Spanish name. Why, you may ask? Because this was their land, their country, and we stole it. Now we are prosecuting them for sneaking back into their own country?

Are you a proud American?

I love America. I love living here. I love the cities, the mountains, the ocean, all of the beautiful lands we live in, but I'm not in love with the politicians.

Did the finished film adhere closely to your screenplay?

Yeah, pretty much. *Uncle Sam* just wasn't very good, that's all. I didn't like the film particularly, not compared to what it could have been. It didn't have a really great Uncle Sam in terms of the character's makeup and appearance. It wasn't exactly state of the art. They failed to create a memorable character. You could have taken Uncle Sam and really transformed him into this fabulously scary figure like Freddy Krueger. He had that potential, but they didn't do that. Instead, he became this rather mundane villain wearing a bland-looking mask. I actually gave them a much better mask that I'd had made, but Bill had his own way. He wanted to make his own movie and he did. That's okay. Again, Bill got the money so he made the movie.

In 1996, you penned *Invasion of Privacy*, the story of a mentally disturbed man, who kidnaps the woman who is carrying his child in order to prevent her from having an abortion. Did you perhaps draw inspiration for that script from some real-life episode or news story?

No, I just made it all up. I thought the story of a man kidnapping the mother of his unborn child, and keeping her prisoner until such time as it would be illegal for her to have an abortion, was a highly original idea. In the script, the man finally releases her and she immediately has him arrested and he is put on trial. They eventually acquit him because he claims that the drastic action he took was done in order to save the life of their baby. So, he gets off, but then his psychopathic tendencies resurface again. *Invasion of Privacy* worked very nicely up to that point but, unfortunately, the ending of the picture is terrible.

The filmmakers tampered with your screenplay?

They rewrote the climax. They restaged it and seriously fucked it all up. They got mixed up with their own inane ideas and really made a mess of it. The best analogy I can think of right now about situations like *Invasion of Privacy* is this: it always seems to me that as a screenwriter, you are the guy that is taking the director through the jungle. You are leading him through some potentially treacherous territory but, just before you reach the destination, he suddenly decides to venture off blindly on his own and sinks right into a quicksand pit. That's what happened on this picture and so they got what they deserved. They followed my script almost ninety percent of the way and just when they arrived at the ending, which, as I told you, is the most important part of a movie, they deviated. Again, if the movie is good and the ending is bad that's all people remember. The audience will not give you credit for the early part of the film. They'll just think it's lousy, because they only judge you by how it works in the end. *Invasion of Privacy* had a very messed-up, disappointing ending that was very badly staged. A guy named Anthony Hickox directed it. His father was a very well-regarded director but, unfortunately, the father's talents did not descend to his son.[10] His mother was also a very famous editor who edited *Lawrence of Arabia* for David Lean and many other great pictures.[11] She is a very fine editor indeed. I've actually met her, but I never met Hickox himself.

What was the ending that you originally envisioned for *Invasion of Privacy*?

Oh, I don't remember now, but they basically took it and twisted it all around. They tried to put in other characters that had no business being there. They tried to build up the part of a supporting actress who was a famous Black model,[12] but she didn't belong in the ending of the picture at all. They were trying to find some way to insert her into the movie and they stuck her into the ending. That confused everything as she had no logical reason for being there. So, it all became a shambles in the end.

What did you think of the multi-screen technique that Hickox employed in several scenes?

That was interesting. As I say, the main body of the picture was okay because Hickox followed the script. I must also add that I thought the casting wasn't extraordinarily good either. The lead actress playing the mother was passable and the leading man was equally adequate.[13] That's about the best you could say about it, although I do see a through-line in *Invasion of Privacy* to a lot of my earlier films. A lot of my movies deal with pregnancy and abortion, most obviously the three *It's Alive* pictures and *God Told Me To*. Then there's *Daddy's Gone A-Hunting* in which a young woman has to resist being terrorised into killing her own child by her former lover—just as she willingly killed his child before. So, I have visited these themes and issues in my previous work, mostly because they are so potent and dramatically charged.

Invasion of Privacy clearly sympathizes with the mother, which is interesting as the issue of men's rights has become a big one in recent years. In the U.K., there have been instances where disgruntled fathers have chained themselves to rooftops and various public places in order to protest their lack of rights and access to their children. The courts often seem to favor the mothers.

Well, it's the mother who has to carry the baby and go through nine months of pain and discomfort followed by the agony of birth. The father's job is over after a couple of minutes of pleasure, then he gets to walk away. Some fathers want to claim their rights, but when they do obtain them, what happens then? Do they really want to spend the time and energy it takes to nurture a child and deal with all the problems that raising a child entails? Some men fight for their rights, but when they have their rights they don't want to exercise them. It's like those fathers who get their visitation rights then don't show up on the weekends when they are supposed to take the kids. The kids are waiting for them, all packed and ready to go. Sadly, for some reason or excuse, the old man doesn't show. This goes on all the time. The father spends so much time fighting for his child, but it's often their anger against the mother that is driving them not love for their kids. They want to punish the mother by taking away what she loves most. You know, some of the most profoundly destructive hatred that exists between people is often born out of love. That's always worth writing about.

Intermission: *Deadly Illusion* (1987)

The same year that you made *It's Alive III: Island of the Alive* and *A Return to Salem's Lot*, you wrote and began directing a picture for Pound Ridge Films that was eventually produced and released as *Deadly Illusion*.

Yes. *Deadly Illusion* was originally called *I Love You to Death*, but then somebody else made a movie with that title so I couldn't use it.[1] My script was a thriller about a private detective, who is approached by a man who wants to hire him to murder his wife in Long Island and make it look like somebody has invaded their home. The private detective takes an advance on the job and then goes out to the house in Southampton and warns the wife that her husband is trying to have her killed. He then makes love to the wife before leaving the house. The very next day the wife turns up dead and, of course, the private detective is the one accused of doing it. He goes to view the body at the morgue and discovers that the corpse is that of an entirely different woman. The woman that he approached and was intimate with was not really the man's wife, but an impostor. So, people now think that he is the murderer and the private detective must find out who actually committed this crime and framed him for it. That was basically the story.

That sounds like a relatively simple story, but you have attacked the completed film, accusing it of being incoherent and patchy.

That's because it made absolutely no sense at all. There were various aspects of it that weren't entirely coherent. There were numerous loose ends that weren't successfully tied up and so it was something of a mess. It's been a long time since I've seen the movie, but one example involves the private detective meeting the woman and making love to her. Pretty soon afterwards, he sees her again and doesn't recognize her! The question is why? Why didn't he know her? This guy should have realized exactly who she is. I mean, he was supposed to be a private detective after all, but his powers of observation certainly failed him on that occasion. He'd just slept with her and there is no way that he wouldn't know who she was. So, there were things like that which needed to be better explained because they were coming across as preposterous. It made the guy look stupid; it made the entire movie stupid, too! And if the movie looks stupid, we all look stupid.

What was missing that would have made the narrative more logical?

Oh, I don't know. I'm sure there are some other things that I didn't think were right, but what can you do? Again, I haven't seen the movie in a long time and I have no desire to reacquaint myself with it. But it was all there in my original screenplay—all the necessary elements that would have allowed the story to make perfect sense. They were just ignored, that's all. I mean, all the stuff about the little green bottles and their significance to Morgan Fairchild's character. Fairchild plays a top New York model, whose career is now well behind her. She is middle-aged and battling the ravages of age, and I thought that gave the film an interesting layer. In the script, she has endured a series of unsuccessful operations that have compromised her stunning looks, so by day she wears an artificial face that has been fabricated for her. The material in these little green bottles was supposed to be the lubricant that she smears on her face so that the artificial mask will attach to her own. That was the basic idea. That's why Billy Dee Williams, who played the private detective, doesn't recognize her later on. All of this was extracted from the picture by the producers. It didn't matter that it was interesting and rich and necessary—it just had to go!

***Deadly Illusion* was a troubled production, and you were famously fired for the second time in your career during the course of shooting. What happened?**

I was about halfway through shooting the picture when I got fired. I did receive co-directing credit, but it was a very poorly operated company. Once again, I wasn't in charge of the entire operation and I don't seem to do too well if I don't have complete control of everything. I tried to do things my way, but certain people were coming up with stupid suggestions and stupid objections and got in the way of everything. These producers were extremely obstructive, but I just ignored them and did what I wanted to do. Finally, they lost patience with me and I was fired. I mean, they were really fools, as the picture went way over budget and the company went into bankruptcy.

Were you suddenly getting a sense of déjà vu here?

Well, it was the same situation that had happened several years earlier on *I, the Jury*, almost a repetition of that same scenario. Certain people didn't know what they were doing and they were spending way too much money. I remember that at one point we were about to start shooting a scene when I said to them, "We don't need a hundred people here. We can't get more than twenty people into this location and you have seventy more people standing in the street. Can't you send them over to another location and prepare for tomorrow? That way, we can have everything cabled in and ready to go. We won't have to wait when we arrive at the set tomorrow. These people are clearly not doing anything. Send them over there!" They then replied, "Oh, but we don't do things that way." Obviously, they had their own way of doing everything, which was a good reason for why they eventually went over-budget. Again, I was trying to do things my way, and, of course, I couldn't. What can you say?

What problems occurred during shooting?

Billy Dee Williams was giving a very slow performance without much energy. I then found out that he was drinking, and was actually drunk for most of the time. He didn't have the look of an alcoholic, but he was drinking from morning till night. When I went into his trailer one day, the bottles came rolling out from under the couch and I realized exactly what was going on. Another unfortunate incident concerned the leading girl in the film, who was played by Vanity, a beautiful Black actress. She had done some movies before and later appeared in *Action Jackson*.[2] From what I understand, she has now quit the business and become a minister. Anyway, Vanity was lovely in her part, but then one day I turned up and she suddenly wasn't there anymore. I asked the producers, "Hey, where's Vanity?" They said, "Oh, we sent her back to Los Angeles. Her job was over." I said, "Wait a minute, she has two or three more scenes to shoot! What am I supposed to do here? You sent her home without telling me?" I called Vanity and she agreed to work for scale and complete the scenes we needed to do. That was very good of her, but the producers weren't interested. They felt her work was done and we had everything we needed. The truth was they didn't want to give Vanity any more money, even if it was just scale. At that point—this was a couple of weeks into shooting—I simply decided that I was going to make these producers as miserable as possible. I did this so they would have no other alternative but to fire me. Please understand, you can't just quit a movie otherwise they can sue you. You simply have to make things so miserable and difficult for them that they want—they *have*—to fire you. So, I began directly disobeying any requests and instructions they gave me. I just continued to do what I wanted to do until the end eventually came. As a matter of fact, I kind of forced them to fire me.

That must have been a deeply unpleasant situation to find yourself in?

It didn't bother me at all, to tell you the truth. Believe me, I was just delighted to get the hell out of there. I'd sold them the script and had received most of the money for it, as well as half of the directing salary. I was alright, not that the money made any difference. I just let them do what they wanted to do with the film. I didn't care anymore. If I'm not doing the things that I want to do, and I'm not fulfilling my needs and desires as a filmmaker, there's no sense in going to work everyday. You can't blindly do what people tell you to do, not when you know that what they are saying is wrong. All these individuals involved in the picture didn't know anything about making a movie. As if to confirm that fact, they have all just drifted into oblivion now.

William Tannen[3] replaced you as director. Did you ever meet him?

No, I never met him.

During my research, I was amused to discover that the Staten Island Ferry got caught on a sandbar during the filming of one sequence, the first time in the passenger service's history that this had ever happened.

Yeah, but it wasn't too amusing being stuck in the middle of that situation. That was quite a thing that happened and it could have very easily turned disastrous—even fatal—for all those involved.

Can you explain exactly what went down?

It occurred around Christmas when the temperatures in New York were freezing. I don't know if you have ever spent a winter in New York, but you can really feel that kind of cold deep in your bones. We were shooting a chase sequence on the Staten Island Ferry. This sequence was intended to be my original climax, not the one you now see in the picture. We ran aground of a sandbar in the middle of New York Harbor. As soon as the impact occurred, I knew we were in trouble. I just knew it. We had so many vehicles and equipment trucks and trailers on the ferry I think it was inevitable that we would encounter some difficulties. I actually complained that I didn't have enough room to shoot the chase on the boat, but there was nothing I could do about it. When the ferry got stuck, we were marooned for something like fourteen or fifteen hours, and there were helicopters, tugboats and the Coast Guard all out there. It suddenly became this huge media event with all the news stations covering the story. They had choppers flying above us and we were on every news show on TV and all the front pages of the newspapers. Somebody onboard had a video camera and he filmed the entire disaster as it was unfolding. Thankfully, it had a happy ending and we all reached the pier, cold and shivering, but safe and sound. I actually shiver sometimes just thinking about that day.

You did succeed in generating some free publicity for *Deadly Illusion*.

Well, it was really only a fleeting moment as far as making the news was concerned. By the time the movie came out, it didn't really matter anymore. Of course, it was a big deal for me because we could have all been dead. Seriously, if that ferry had capsized and we had all tumbled into the icy waters of the New York Harbor, we would have all been dead. We would not have lasted three minutes in those temperatures, there's no question about it. You do hear of boats capsizing all the time and people being drowned. There was a cruise ship that recently capsized and sank in Europe, wasn't there?[4] You may have read about it. A lot of people were killed. So, these tragedies do occur, and it makes you stop and think about what could have happened that day if things had turned sour. On top of everything, I didn't even get my chase sequence out of it. That was gone, too.

The climactic chase sequence was eventually relocated to Shea Stadium.

Yeah, but I didn't shoot that. I'm not responsible for any of that. That was entirely the work of the other guy and I take no credit for it. It's a pretty awful climax, very flat and uninspired. My original chase on the Staten Island Ferry would have been much better and a lot more exciting. Unfortunately, the producers were more interested in cheaping out. Oh well, who cares about that now? I certainly don't.

Did you draw any positives from the experience of making *Deadly Illusion*?

No, not really, but in this particular instance, I liked getting fired. Again, who cares? I must repeat it, if you are not doing what you want to do, what's the point? You are getting up early every morning and working for fourteen hours a day, and doing something that you don't want to do. Honestly, I would rather go home. We had a fairly decent cast on *Deadly Illusion*, but, as I say, the finished film was rather disjointed by the time they got through with it. They didn't shoot all the scenes that were in the script, so it quickly became something of a mess. The only positive I can think of is that *Deadly Illusion* actually opened here at Grauman's Chinese Theater, which is the biggest theater in town. For some incredible reason it actually got booked in there. Naturally, nobody went to see it, but *Deadly Illusion* was the only movie of mine ever to open at Grauman's Chinese. It certainly holds that distinction. Frankly, I was amazed. I actually went down there and took some photographs in front of the theater. [Laughs] It just amused me to no end that this awful movie would be the one that opened at Grauman's Chinese!

It's Alive III: Island of the Alive (1987)

It was only a matter of time before you concluded the saga of the mutant babies with *It's Alive III: Island of the Alive*. Why did the movie happen at this juncture of your career, nearly a decade after the release of *It Lives Again*?

Well, I had initially approached Warner Bros. about the possibility of doing a remake of *House of Wax*.[1] I was still friendly with Andre de Toth, the director of the original *House of Wax*, and talked to him about us doing it together with Andre as producer. I actually took Andre over to Warner Bros. and together we pitched them the idea. Our story was about this great sculptor, who creates these astonishing wax dummies of Hollywood stars like Marilyn Monroe and Humphrey Bogart. They are wonderful works of art, but, one day, these street kids break into the wax museum and destroy all of the sculptor's magnificent creations—also destroying his hands in the process. The police do nothing about this terrible crime, even though these thugs have basically ruined this man's life. In his despair, the sculptor soon loses his sanity and murders all of the kids responsible for his misfortune. He then has to restock his wax museum with models of famous people and—since he can no longer sculpt—he kills lookalikes, who resemble famous Hollywood celebrities, and puts them in his museum as replacements. It would have been a good, scary picture and a nice tribute to the original, but Warner Bros. was reluctant to do it. Then, subsequently, I learned that the studio was interested in me doing a movie for their video division. At the time, they were going to try and make pictures directly for home video, so I suggested that we do another *It's Alive* movie. They liked that idea, but I couldn't do it for the prices they wanted to pay unless they offered me a two-picture deal. That way, just as I had done with *Perfect Strangers* and *Special Effects*, I could make two pictures back-to-back and utilize the same crew and a lot of the same actors to save costs. I again suggested to Warner Bros. that the second movie could be a remake of *House of Wax*, but they still weren't going for it. They said, "No, we can't give you *House of Wax*, but you can have one of our other horror titles like *Salem's Lot*. We bought that property and have the sequel rights to it. Would you be interested in working on that instead?" I said, "Okay, but I can do whatever I like with it, right?" They said, "Yes, do anything you please." So, we made the two-picture deal and agreed that the two movies would be *Island of the Alive* and a sequel to *Salem's Lot*.

In an interview with *Fangoria* in 1987, you mentioned pitching Warner Bros. the idea of doing another direct-to-video sequel in the form of *The Exorcist III*.

I don't remember that. It's certainly possible that it may have come up in conversation as something we could have done, but I don't recall my ideas for it exactly.

I believe your story would have involved the child of a now grown-up Linda Blair becoming possessed by the Devil.

Really? That's interesting, because I don't have any recollection of that plot-line. I really don't. I do remember that at one time I was thinking of doing a picture set in Harlem with an all-Black cast that was about a Black exorcist. I had some very definite ideas about how I was going to do that movie. It would have had a lot to do with voodoo and black magic, all that stuff, but this was way back.

William Girdler[2] then beat you to the punch with his own blaxploitation *Exorcist* rip-off, *Abby*.[3]

He did, but I never saw Girdler's movie. You know, so many times you come up with various projects and when they don't come to fruition you just put them out of your mind. Then another idea pops up, then another one, and you just go with them. That's what must have happened with *Exorcist III* because that idea escapes me right now.

The business of creating low-budget direct-to-video sequels to theatrical films has proved to be popular with studios, hasn't it?

Yes, and of course, both *Island of the Alive* and *A Return to Salem's Lot* had a pre-sold value and were sequels to recognized titles that audiences and video store owners were familiar with. That's usually a very important consideration for the studios. *It's Alive, It Lives Again,* and *Salem's Lot* had all been popular rentals and it made sense to make the sequels. Today, there are people making direct-to-video pictures that are sequels to successful movies, particularly successful animated movies. Sometimes they'll have a hit cartoon film and they'll make a cheap version of it as a sequel in order to cash in. Disney has done that with a number of their titles. They managed to make some money on the basis that they were basically making these low-budget animated movies for kids—and parents do buy them for their children. I don't know if any of these pictures have become break-out hits, but they do the same thing with horror movies, too. They'll make a quick direct-to-video sequel to a film that has played theatrically, but most of these titles you don't even hear much about. Sometimes they'll turn up on HBO and Showtime, and you see them on cable. You often ask, "Hey, where have these pictures come from?" Some of these movies have pretty distinguished casts, too, but they have never received any theatrical release.

Island of the Alive begins with a particularly vicious pre-credit prologue: we see a young woman giving birth to a mutant baby in a taxi cab, only for the taxi driver to die in his attempts to execute it.

I wanted to put some horror in the movie and that was probably the only truly horrific thing in *Island of the Alive*.

The film is more explicit than *It's Alive* and *It Lives Again*.

That introductory scene certainly is. What else do we have in there that is explicit?

One character does have his arm torn off leaving a bleeding, ragged stump.

Yeah, but you don't really see the arm being torn off. You just see the guy falling down and staggering into shot with his arm missing. You don't actually see anything happen to him. It all occurs off-camera and is left to your imagination.

In the ten years between *Island of the Alive* and *It Lives Again*, horror films had become far more explicit. Was it perhaps a commercial consideration on your part to integrate more gore and violence into the third instalment?

Horror films were very gory at the time, but I didn't feel any commercial pressure to do the gore in *Island of the Alive*. If I had felt that pressure, I would have probably made a far more violent and bloody picture. For instance, that scene with the guy getting his arm bitten off—if I had bowed to people's thirst for gore, I would have shown that in great detail rather than taking a more restrained approach as I did.

Do you have a problem with gore in movies?

I much prefer to imply violence in my films rather than show it. I don't like slasher movies like *Friday the 13th* and the seemingly endless sequels it has given birth to. Those pictures always had some kind of masked psychopath killing a bunch of teenagers, pinning their bodies to walls with knives or driving sharp objects through their eyeballs. There are some filmmakers who seem to get excited if they can capture a decapitation or some other sadistic action on-camera. Personally, I've never been moved by that approach myself. The temptation to do that can be very strong for some directors, even good directors. Just before we made *Island of the Alive*, John Carpenter did his big-budget remake of *The Thing* and that movie showed you a lot of gore, blood, and monsters. It was a strong movie—it's still a strong movie—but Carpenter made a conscious choice to display that stuff. Of course, he could afford to spend a lot of money creating those gruesome special effects, but I prefer the original version of *The Thing*, which basically shows you nothing and is all the more effective for it. There have been instances on other pictures I've made, like *God Told Me To*, *It Lives Again*, and *The Stuff*, where I could have shown the gore in a very explicit way, but I chose not to. Gore will occasionally make an audience look away and I prefer it if the viewer doesn't turn away from the screen. If they avert their eyes for a moment they may miss something important or interesting. That's my feeling on it.

The opening courtroom sequence of *Island of the Alive* plays like a takeoff on the abortion debate as Steven Jarvis [Michael Moriarty] is forced to confront his monstrous offspring by the prosecutor. Why did

you decide to open the film with such a dramatic discussion of a highly controversial subject?

That scene was really what the picture was about: whether or not society was going to permit these creatures to live or if it would destroy them. Such an important question would have to be decided by a jury's prudence and so the idea of beginning our story with a courtroom trial made perfect sense to me. I liked the idea of commencing the film with a direct moral question. I thought it was a legitimate and challenging opening as the monsters' very existence was at stake. The monsters are eventually removed from society and quarantined on an island where they will come of age in isolation. In that regard, *Island of the Alive* is different from *It's Alive* and *It Lives Again,* as I wanted to try something that had a contrasting tone and thrust to the whole story. You'll no doubt notice that there is much more humour in the third film than in the previous two pictures.

Jarvis becomes a media star due to the notoriety of the court case and his being the father of one of the monsters. He then allows himself to be exploited on the talk show circuit in order to sell more books. Once again, you seem to be satirising tabloid culture and our irrepressible hunger for dirt and controversy.

Well, that's exactly what happens in our current society: every tragedy, no matter how desperately sad and despicable the event may be, is exploited to its utmost by every form of media whore you can possibly find. Each detail is dissected for the home audience and I don't know why people agree to appear on these programs to air their miseries. What is the point of it? Why subject yourself to public scrutiny and opinion? It would be better if you kept these matters private within your own family. Unfortunately, people insist on parading themselves. And, yeah, the public eats it up, too. They tune into all these shows every week and buy all these periodicals. Everybody wants to know everybody else's personal business. I think it's rather sad and depressing, and that was what I was trying to point out.

Jarvis bitterly acknowledges his own celebrity status by signing an autograph as "Steven Jarvis—the father of the monster." Do you think his wacky behavior is a means of facilitating a retreat from the grim reality of his situation?

It could be. I mean, Jarvis does develop a manic personality as a result of all this happening to him. He is getting crazier and crazier and is mocking himself mercilessly. I think it is probably a coping mechanism for him. Making everything seem like an absurd, twisted joke protects him like a shield. His craziness allows Jarvis to detach himself. In a way, he's confronting his predicament and he's also ignoring it at the same time. Is that what you're saying?

Yes, exactly. He's hiding in plain sight.

Well, when you think about it, there are really only two ways for him to respond to the horrific situation he finds himself in: one of them is to descend into a total depression from which he may never return. The other is to enter a manic state and ridicule the whole situation. Jarvis chooses to embrace the latter.

Even by his own standards, Moriarty's brilliant performance is particularly eccentric. Did you encourage him to play Jarvis quite so demented?

Oh, absolutely. The small-time crook he played in *Q* was a wacky guy, and even Mo Rutherford in *The Stuff* was pretty amped-up, so I thought we'd take the character of Jarvis in a similar direction. Jarvis is an entirely different person from Jimmy Quinn and Mo Rutherford, but I always like to make use of Moriarty's bravery and his willingness to give a way-out, individualistic performance. Your average actor will just give you a straight down-the-line performance, but Moriarty takes big chances. You'll find that when you are adventurous as an actor and take big chances, you often get good results. When I worked with Moriarty on *The Stuff* I got him a hairpiece, which he absolutely hated wearing! When we did *Island of the Alive* and *A Return Salem's Lot*, he refused to wear the same toupee twice, so he would always force me to buy him a new hairpiece for each new picture. I think his reasoning was, "Well, if I have to wear this stupid thing on my head, I'm going to make you pay for it every time!" [Chuckles] Moriarty is not the kind of actor who needs to dress up to inhabit a character. He has such great instincts and abilities, it just all comes out. I thought the character of Jarvis in *Island of the Alive* and Moriarty's performance was terrific. He had a controlled insanity about him, but that character is not without humanity and courage. The way Jarvis comes out and makes fun of himself, and everybody else around him, makes the entire situation seem insane. Obviously, in reality, it would be an insane situation if you and your wife had given birth to this monster child.

Why did you decide to make Jarvis a struggling actor?

I thought that his career would be completely destroyed by his involvement with this monster birth. No one is ever going to hire him to do commercials for their products; no one is ever going to cast him in a movie or a play or a television show because he's got this image attached to him. Jarvis is seen exclusively and completely as the father of the monster and that's it. That's all he can ever be and that's the role he must play for the rest of his life. So, he ends up being a shoe salesman in a shoe store and, of course, a lot of unemployed actors are in fact shoe salesman or waiters in restaurants.

Karen Black[4] plays Jarvis' estranged wife, Ellen, and gives a solid performance.

Karen is always good. I believe she's had a couple of Oscar nominations, and I particularly enjoyed the fact that she had starred in Alfred Hitchcock's last movie, *Family Plot*. I used to get a kick out of tormenting and teasing her all the time. I once said to her, "After working with Karen Black, Hitchcock never directed another picture again!" I even used to do these Hitchcock impersonations for her. I'd say, [impersonates Hitchcock] "Oh yes, the exquisite Karen Black! After doing *Family Plot* with her, I never wanted to direct another actor ever again!" Karen would always laugh at that and have a good time.

Where exactly was the island located that you used in the film?

It was the island of Kauai in Hawaii. After we finished shooting the picture, we went back to Kauai six months later and actually ran the picture for the people who'd helped us make it. They seemed to enjoy it.

What can you reveal about the rigors of shooting on Kauai?

Well, we had a lot of enjoyable situations! [Chuckles] I remember one day we were shooting at the foot of a waterfall in the jungle. It was a pleasant little place, but then halfway through the day we suddenly heard this tremendous *crack* fill the air. It sounded like a giant tree had been knocked down. It was in fact a log-jam further up the river that had broke, releasing these huge torrents of water. The water came rushing through, transforming this little waterfall into something that resembled Niagara Falls inside of thirty seconds. Massive gushes of water were coming down and quickly flooded the entire area where we were working. I started running up the side of the hill with the camera and the tripods, trying to save everything from being destroyed. People were running for their lives, as the whole place was filling up with water. At a certain point, somebody remembered that Art Lund, who was acting in the picture, was actually trapped up a tree. We had been shooting the discovery of his character's body hanging up there and Art had been wired into the branches. Now, in the middle of all this chaos, we couldn't get him back down. Cascades of water and debris were coming down all around us and there was no way we could reach him. Art was just sitting there in the middle of this huge flood, which didn't appear to be easing at all, calmly saying, "Don't worry, guys, I'm fine. I've really got a great view from up here!" [Laughs] It was a very shocking experience and nobody seemed to know quite what to do. We eventually had to swim out there, climb up the tree and get Art out. It was quite an operation.

Did anything else interesting occur on location?

That was just one incident in that particular area. On another day, we were shooting the scene where Moriarty is yelling into the jungle for the monster to come out and show itself. Michael was shouting, "Don't be afraid! Come on out!" As if in response, this huge wild boar suddenly charged out of the bushes. It went berserk and started running amongst the crew, zigzagging in, out and around the equipment. Nobody knew what to do, except to get out of the way of this rampaging animal. I kept yelling for the cameraman, Daniel Pearl, to get a shot of this boar that we could use, but he was too busy trying to save his own ass! [Laughs] Finally, the boar took off into the woods and that was the last we saw of it.

You enjoy subjecting yourself and your crew to these difficult and challenging environments, don't you?

Oh, sure. I mean, you always have to keep things interesting. When we were shooting on Kauai, there was always something dangerous or exciting happening. At one time, the equipment truck got mired in mud and was going to turn over on its side. It was leaning three-quarters of the way over and everyone was afraid to go inside and take the equipment out. This meant we couldn't shoot because the crew were terrified that if they ventured inside the vehicle it would capsize. Finally, I climbed into the back of the truck myself and retrieved the equipment. I didn't want anybody else to take the chance. I managed to do it without the vehicle tumbling over, and we then started shooting. There were other trials we endured involving the boat we rented for the movie. In the story, the expedition arrives on the island in a boat. The vessel we hired looked beautiful, but it was very unstable and had what they call a concrete hull. As we were shooting, the seas were very rough and the ship was rocking violently from side-to-side. It looked great on film, but for the people onboard it was just awful. Everybody was getting seasick except for me, Moriarty and Daniel Pearl. Even the stuntmen, who were accustomed to shooting movies on water, were turning color. People were leaning over the sides, heaving and throwing up. They were begging me, "Please take us back to shore! Get us off this boat!" I just couldn't do that because we only had the boat for a limited time. During the shoot, we had a helicopter coming out in order to get an aerial shot where it was flying over the boat. At this point, Moriarty's character was supposed to be alone on the ship and so this meant that everybody else had to go below decks out of sight. Now, asking a bunch of seasick people to venture down into the lower decks on a rough boat like that was virtually impossible. There was simply no way they could or would agree to it. So we decided to lay everybody down on the upper decks and cover them over with tarpaulin. This meant they were hidden from view and the helicopter camera wouldn't see them. But everybody was happy when that day was over, I can tell you! It was a long, long day.

So, nobody threw themselves overboard in desperation?

No, and I don't think anybody would have preferred to take their chances in that sea. It was pretty harsh. I do remember for one shot we actually put Moriarty on a raft in the water, just off the boat. I'm telling you, within ten seconds, he was gone! The ocean had immediately carried him away in just ten seconds! It was incredible. Fortunately, we had a little motor-boat so we chased after Moriarty, caught him, and got him off the raft. I mean, he was literally heading out to the Pacific somewhere and we might never have seen him again. [Chuckles] We had a good time, actually.

Didn't the crew continually play a trick on you during shooting that involved a rubber chicken?

Uh-huh. Nearly every scene we set up on every day, unbeknownst to me, they would hide a rubber chicken in the set somewhere. They would hang it here or there, and I wouldn't see it until after we had shot the scene a couple of times. Then, I would discover that there was this rubber chicken in the shot. The crew thought it was funny. I thought it was a waste of film, frankly. As if I didn't already have a million things on my mind, I had to search the set before we started filming each scene to make sure they hadn't planted this rubber chicken. Eventually, on this one occasion, I missed it and the rubber chicken can actually be glimpsed in the movie.

Island of the Alive presents the mutant offspring in their adult form, also revealing that they are now mating and can reproduce after a period of five years. Why did you decide to focus on this stage of their development?

Because nothing ever remains the same. All living creatures develop and evolve, and obviously these monster babies were eventually going to grow up. I was wondering what they would become when that happened. I thought if I was going to make a third movie, I had to follow this story through to some kind of new and satisfying resolution. So, I asked myself some questions: what are these babies like as adults? What is the monster going to look like when it physically develops and ages? I thought those were important questions to answer and deal with. Otherwise, there was no point in making the movie if I was just going to have a load of monster babies running around again, killing people. The second film was, to a degree, different from the first because the protagonists were trying to save the monsters. In the third film, we got all of the monster birth stuff out of the way in the prologue and gave the audience their horror. The rest of the movie was more of an exploration of Jarvis' character and the progress of the monster children. I thought that differentiation from the events of the previous pictures made *Island of the Alive* a worthwhile project.

The film also suggests that the mutant adults have developed human emotions; they hold hands, for example, and display affection for each other.

Remember, these creatures are partly human. Even animals in the animal world display affection for each other. They have rituals of behavior that are not unlike human behavior in terms of the mating process and nurturing their young. There is a touch of humanity, or human aspects, evident in animals and there is a touch of the animal evident in human beings.

Who played the adult monsters?

We put out a casting call for little people, and so the adult monsters were usually played by diminutive people: midgets or dwarves, and in some cases body-builders, who preferred to call themselves "little people." They were built very sturdily even though their stature was very small. I think in total we constructed about four or five monster suits for the performers to wear and each of them were fairly detailed with claws, musculature, and the large dome-like heads. It can sometimes be difficult and even dangerous to perform in a monster suit, as they can be quite cumbersome. I remember we were shooting a scene featuring Neal Israel, who is himself a director of some note having made *Bachelor Party* with Tom Hanks. Neal was playing one of the scientists, and, at one point, his character was supposed to be taking a bath in a pond. Unbeknownst to him, one of the monsters was to rise up out of the water behind Neal and attack him. We had the monster there and we had Neal there, and I said to the guy in the suit, "Okay, submerge yourself, count to ten, and then rise up behind Neal and grab him." So, we rolled the camera and the monster sank out of sight under the water. Ten seconds passed and the monster did not come back up. Then thirty seconds passed . . . then forty seconds . . . then a minute . . . and all this time Neal kept soaping himself, waiting for the monster to suddenly rise. We were still waiting for the creature to appear when I said, "Hey Neal, you better dive down there and get the monster!" Neal plunged down under the water and the next thing we knew he was dragging the monster out of the pond. What had happened was the monster's rubber suit had quickly filled up with water and had become extremely heavy. The performer couldn't make it back to the surface again and was quietly drowning. So, Neal had in effect saved the life of the very monster that was about to take his.

I know that you have kept some of the models and props from your movies including the monster babies from *It's Alive* and *It Lives Again*.

Yeah, I do have a closet here full of models and props. I like to look at them and even talk to them on occasion. I like to express my gratitude for all the joy and success they have brought me. Over the years, some of this stuff has deteriorated and has not held up well at all. Some of it falls apart and you have to throw it out, but most of the monsters are incredibly sturdy and still look remarkably fresh, even after all this time. I do have everything here and I figure that some day my family will sell all of these items off on the Internet to fans and collectors.

In your experience, it is true that some special effects artists are sensitive about relinquishing possession of their work after a film has been completed?

I've never had that problem with any of the makeup artists I've worked with, not that I can recall. In fact, when we were doing *It's Alive*, Rick Baker knew very well that I would be keeping the original monster baby elements. Rick had no issues with that. Coincidentally, I actually ran into Rick just a few weeks ago at the Academy of Science Fiction and Horror Awards dinner and he was interested to know how the monster baby model was holding up. He asked me if it was still viewable and I told him that it looks almost exactly as it did when he first made it back in the early 1970s. Back then, Rick knew I would be keeping the baby and that it was part of the arrangement, as was the arrangement with all of the special effects people on each of the three movies. If any of them were unhappy about it, they certainly never expressed that view to me.

Did you use everything you shot for *Island of the Alive*?

I believe so. I don't think there is anything we shot that is deleted from the final cut. The whole picture is right up there on the screen. There were probably ideas and scenes that I wasn't able to do in *It's Alive* and *It Lives Again* that I included in *Island of the Alive*, simply because I could. It was interesting to see the monsters as adults and also have the courtroom debate about whether or not they should continue to exist. Those were always ideas that interested me and seemed to be a perfectly logical extension of the first two movies.

All three *It's Alive* films are studies in familial stress and conflict, and how any deviation from the norms of society is viewed as both destruc-

tive and perverse. Why are you so intent on continually exposing our pieties and prejudices?

I guess my movies allow me to comment on some of the injustices and hypocrisies of life as I see them. The way in which we are quick to condemn people for living their lives as they would like—as long as it isn't harmful to others—is abhorrent to me. A lot of it also has to do with the sick fear people have of themselves and each other. As you know, I'm always interested in writing scenes that act as allegories for other things. In *Island of the Alive*, Moriarty is the father of the monster and is ostracized because of that. He meets a girl played by Laurene Landon, who is a hooker and goes to bed with her. The hooker remains interested until she recognizes her latest client from the newspapers and television, and realizes that she has in fact slept with the father of one of these creatures. She is immediately horrified that somehow this awful taint might rub off on her. That was intended as an allegory for the then-newly discovered AIDS virus, which, at that time, was becoming an epidemic that was earning enormous press attention. People were terrified of this disease and as a result did not want to get close to those who were suffering with it. They didn't understand what it was and they didn't want to know. All they wanted was for as much distance as was humanly possible to be put between them and the victims of AIDS. Compassion was very far from their minds. They only felt terror, revulsion, and a hysterical sense of self-preservation. That attitude is exactly the same as society's reaction to the monster babies and the parents that produced them. If this situation was to actually occur, people would probably want these children to be isolated or destroyed as soon as they were being born and their parents to be locked away. It's that cold, unreasoning fear and sense of outrage we have of anything that's different that is the most destructive aspect of human life. But hey, that's who we are.

The climax of *Island of the Alive* is far more upbeat than the conclusions of *It's Alive* and *It Lives Again*. Indeed, the final image is of the family united, hinting at a better understanding and a brighter future for the mutant species. Why did you decide to end the series on such an optimistic note?

I thought it brought a touch of hope that maybe the humans and the monsters could learn to get along. I felt this baby could be developed with love and affection and grow into something that could be dealt with and wouldn't be a killer after all. Who knows what it could become? Who knows what its intelligence potential could be? Of course, that's another movie entirely. *It's Alive* and *It Lives Again* do have rather bleak endings as we always killed the monsters at the climax and left the families in despair. Those endings were real downers, but for this particular movie (yes, we did kill a lot of the monsters) but we see that this one baby survives. Then Moriarty and Karen Black come together again as man and wife and ride off in the car with their grandchild. As you say, the family is reunited. This time the unit survives the horror intact and probably not before time.

Some critics felt that this third entry was the most muddled and unfocused of the trilogy. How do you respond to those assessments?

I don't agree with them. I don't think that's the case at all. I don't understand what is "muddled and unfocused" about the picture. It's a very, very clear story. I thought the character development of the father was actually more interesting than what was featured in the other pictures, because Jarvis went in a direction that was highly unusual but not untrue. Many people go nuts when they go through a traumatic situation like that, and so for me it felt particularly authentic. There is a lot of emotional truth in *Island of the Alive,* and everything makes perfect sense to me.

Don't you think there are too many disparate elements in the story as well as some unnecessary diversions? For example, at one point Jarvis unexpectedly floats off in his makeshift raft to Cuba and falls in with some of the militia there.

Well, he had to be rescued somehow after drifting from the boat. I also thought it would be interesting for Jarvis to be saved by the enemies of America rather than by our sympathetic friends. I liked the idea that he would be rescued by a group of people who were supposedly dangerous and then safely returned to American shores. I thought that would be something different, rather than having him being picked up by a boat or something. I didn't think that would be particularly interesting.

It also ties in with the film's themes of tolerance and acceptance.

That's right. It deals with the whole concept of sitting in judgment of people and deciding who our enemies are, who is bad, and who is good. Because human beings like to deal in absolutes. The entire film is about the fact that these babies are different and different is seen as being bad and threatening. If you are different then you have got to be destroyed. Naturally, this idea is allied with the Cubans, who are also perceived as being bad and dangerous. We are constantly being told that these are our enemies. They couldn't possibly do anything good because they are so irredeemably evil. Well, that's just not true. As it shows you in *Island of the Alive*, they are capable of sympathy and humanity, too, and they save this man's life. Why do Cubans have to be bad merely because we think they are going to be bad? So, that scene in particular deals with the suppositions of everyone's insistence on prejudging someone else's morality, character, and sense of decency. Again, it reinforces what the whole picture is concerned with. It's about reassessing who somebody is, not by virtue of the fact that they look and sound different, but by their actions and how they behave.

How do you rate the third film against the first two?

I happen to like the third picture a lot. I liked the fun we had making it. I also liked the fact that we got to venture off somewhere different to shoot the movie; and that we came back and took over the Santa Monica pier to shoot the scene where there is the rumble—the big gang-fight. That was all great production value and it added to the picture. I knew that making *Island of the Alive* would be an entirely new experience for me and I embraced that experience. I think the third picture holds up really well against the first two. *It's Alive* was almost totally concerned with the monster baby's father and mother. We then opened up the story a little bit more with *It Lives Again* with the three monster babies being rescued and taken to a place of sanctuary. *Island of the Alive* goes even further by dealing with the fate of an entire generation of adult monsters, expanding the moral discussion in a more profound way. So, I think all three films offer the audience something new and they fit together nicely as a trilogy and as a continuing story. I'm very glad I made all three movies.

Do you feel you have concluded the series satisfactorily or will there be a fourth *Alive* film?

Well, you never can tell. I have had some thoughts and ideas, but we would have to see if there is any interest from studios or producers for the financing of a fourth film. We could certainly make one.

In which direction would you take a fourth instalment?

Oh, I'm not going to tell.

Can't you give me a little hint? What ideas have you got?

No, I couldn't possibly tell.

Do you think that ultimately *It's Alive*—the film that started it all—will be the movie that you will be most remembered for?

It's certainly possible, but I'll probably be most remembered for *Phone Booth*.

Do you really think so?

Yeah, I do, if only because *Phone Booth* was a more recent movie and a percentage of the modern audience tend to have short memories. Actually, I'll probably be remembered for both *It's Alive* and *Phone Booth*. They will possibly be mentioned together. But I would have no complaints if people only remembered me for the *It's Alive* pictures. I mean, some directors would have given their right arm to taste that kind of success, so I'm very proud to be associated with them.

What would you sacrifice in order to achieve immortality for your art?

Well, I'm sure you're familiar with the story of Peg Entwistle, the actress who famously jumped to her death from the letter "H" on the Hollywood sign back in the 1930s. Nobody had ever heard of this young woman until she committed suicide in such a memorable manner. That incident recently got me thinking: in an effort to publicize my work and immortalise my own name for the ages, I plan on going to the Academy Awards next year and sitting up in the balcony. Then, as the ceremony unfolds and is being telecast live to an audience of millions, I will leap off the balcony and plummet to my death below. This will of course interrupt the Academy Awards and immortalise me in the history of Hollywood. A note will later be discovered in my pocket that will read: "I just wanted to get a better seat." That should do it.

A Return to Salem's Lot (1987)

After agreeing that *A Return to Salem's Lot* would become the second film of your two-picture deal with Warner Bros., did you have any reservations about creating a sequel to the well-received 1979 miniseries?

No, none at all. My take on the sequel didn't have much to do with Tobe Hooper's miniseries or Stephen King's original novel upon which it was based. When I was given the freedom by Warner Bros. to do what I wanted with their property, I quickly decided that the best way to go was to create a new set of characters and a new story. *Salem's Lot* concerned only one rather monstrous-looking vampire who is infecting a whole town, but my film was about a whole community of vampires that had been established for hundreds of years. Not only that, I think that my vampires were a little more human and didn't reveal their true monstrousness until quite late in the picture when it became necessary. So, it was an entirely different approach to what Tobe had taken. Actually, in many ways, I think of *A Return to Salem's Lot* as more of an original film rather than a direct sequel.

I understand that you worked on your own cinematic adaptation of Stephen King's novel back in the late 1970s. Is that right?

Yeah, I wrote a screenplay of *Salem's Lot* for Warner Bros. It was around 140 pages long and followed King's novel quite closely. Unfortunately, I believe they thought my script was too long and too expensive for a theatrical feature, so they abandoned it. Warner Bros. later hired Tobe to direct from an entirely new script and that became the two-part miniseries. I only saw a segment of *Salem's Lot* on TV, but I thought it was okay. From what I did see, I didn't think it really captured the sense of a town and its inhabitants being devastated by this evil presence in their midst.

In King's novel, the vampire was kind of rotting the town out from the inside and there was a tragic element to it. I don't think that was fully exploited as it could have been in the mini-series. Despite that, I do seem to recall that it had one or two scary sequences in it. The only idea they retained from my script was to make the lead vampire look demonic like Max Schreck in *Nosferatu*, which I always thought would be terrifying. Actually, I don't know for sure if they got that notion from my script or whether Tobe and the writer[1] came up with that approach independently, but it was an idea that I'd conceived before them. Apart from that, I don't think there was anything in the miniseries that wasn't taken directly from King's book.

Did you limit the ambitions of your script in any way knowing that the finished film was destined for the shelves of a video store rather than the projection room of a movie theater?

No. I wrote and directed the film the same way I would have if I'd shot it under any circumstances—based on budget. I couldn't do any more with the money I had to spend, but we did the best we could. My hope was that if we made a good enough movie, Warner Bros. would play it in theaters. After we finished the picture and I delivered it to them, I prevailed on the studio to distribute the film theatrically. They opened it up in Massachusetts or some other place in New England—maybe it was Cape Cod—and it did quite well. I think we did about $75,000 a theater. When I came back to discuss this with Warner Bros., they said, "Well, the film only did that business because it played up in New England, which is Stephen King country. It couldn't possibly do that well anyplace else." I said, "Okay, but can't you at least try it out someplace else?" The head of distribution really didn't want this picture in his schedule and there was some word coming down that the studio wanted to cancel the video division. In fact, after *Island of the Alive* and *A Return to Salem's Lot* came in, they fired the guy who had hired me and did indeed terminate the video division. The theatrical division did not want to be competing with movies being made for home video which might turn out to be better than the pictures they were making for a theatrical audience at ten times the money.

So, there were internal conflicts over the video division?

Well, politically, it just wasn't a sound choice to make those pictures as it irritated the theatrical people. They didn't even want to play my two movies theatrically, even though they had both tested well. So, when I asked Warner Bros. to give *A Return to Salem's Lot* another test, they took it down to some Midwest college town and opened it during the first week of the college semester. The picture did no business whatsoever because in a college town—after the first week of registration—nobody is going to the movies. So, *A Return to Salem's Lot* more or less bombed down there and that was the end of the theatrical distribution of the film. I guess it was what they call in the movie business "a self-fulfilling prophecy." When the distribution people don't believe in a picture, they can make it work so that the film won't do any business. By doing that, it allows them to ensure that their prediction comes true. All they have to do is make certain that there is a lack of advertising and put the movie into areas and theaters where they know there won't be any activity. And that's exactly what they did. They deliberately killed the picture.

***A Return to Salem's Lot* begins with Michael Moriarty's anthropologist filming a tribal sacrifice and justifying it by saying, "It's their society, their rules." Do you think he applies that same dispassionate logic and study to the vampire society?**

I think he does to some degree, but then he stays there and involves himself in chronicling the vampire's way of life by agreeing to write their "Bible." He doesn't leave or try to flee right away. He's fascinated with this secret society that exists and learns that it's just as vicious and bizarre as the people in the jungle he was filming. I was trying to say that there are all kinds of societies and cultures in the world that perform actions that we might consider horrendous, but are perfectly normal for them. They may appear to do terrible things by our own standards, but that is simply the way they live. For example, the manner in which they treat women or animals might seem horrific to us but is perfectly acceptable behavior to them. I always find the idea that we sometimes sit in judgment of other cultures and measure them by our own morals and ideals, quite fascinating. But in truth, I would imagine that a vampire society would be no worse than a lot of other societies, including our own.

My point is he gets actively and emotionally involved with the vampires, whereas he coolly surveys the tribe.

He has a personal reason to become involved with the vampires. He has an emotional, historical, almost blood connection to the town and its people. And, of course, he also has his son with him, too. As an anthropologist, he cannot help but be captivated with this society. It's so unique, he feels compelled to become this tool of theirs. He becomes deeply involved with the vampires and they are also greatly invested in him. The concept of an anthropologist visiting a vampire society came to me because I thought this character seemed like the perfect guy to be caught up in this situation. It would be the one opportunity for him to observe the behavior of such an exotic species—vampires! It makes sense that he'd be seduced into remaining in this town and writing about such a bizarre sect that has existed for so long. The vampire society has evolved to a point where they don't perform acts of violence on human beings except on special occasions. They are civilised creatures. See, the idea was to kind of affectionately satirize American values. I mean, these vampires are not entirely disagreeable. They aren't bloodthirsty killers right off the bat. They are pleasant and congenial and don't feed on human beings unless they absolutely have to.

The legendary director Sam Fuller plays Dr. Van Meer, the half-Dutch, half-Romanian vampire-hunter and Nazi-killer. How did he become involved?

Sam was a very good friend of mine. In fact, the house I have here in Coldwater Canyon, Beverly Hills, used to be Sam's house. He lived here during his most successful days as a director, when he was making movies like *The Steel Helmet*. I only found this out by coincidence, when John Ireland came here to read for the part of the villain in *Black Caesar*. We didn't use John in that film because we ended up shooting it in New York, but when we met he told me, "I've been in this house before, back when Sam Fuller owned it." I was amazed and had no idea about this as I had bought the house from Clint Walker.[2] When I eventually met Sam at a party, I said, "I own the house you used to live in." Sam was all excited about this as he had lost the house in a divorce. He then wanted to bring his new wife, Christa, up here and show it to her. After that, Sam and I got to be great friends and started seeing a lot of each other. He lived in France and we would spend some time in Paris with him. Actually, when my daughter was living in Paris, he helped look after her for a while. I enjoyed being with Sam because he was such a unique character. I wanted to spend even more time with him, so I wrote the part of the Nazi-hunter especially for him. I figured that all the previous directors who had given him cameos in their movies, where he was in and out in a single day, wasn't quite good enough.[3] I wanted to give him a role where he was around for four weeks and that's exactly what I did. He would also be receiving $40,000 for all his efforts which was good for him.

Did Fuller appreciate the fact that you had given him a meatier role to play?

I think Sam was expecting another small part. When I sent him the script, the first thing he said was, "Boy, there's an awful lot of dialogue for me to learn!" I said, "Don't worry, Sam, you'll have plenty of time do it. If you don't remember what you have to say, I'll tell you." We then brought Sam over to New England, and he did have some trouble remembering his lines. Of course, he was an old man by this time, but he was a real trooper. He never once complained about the hours or the conditions, and we had a lot of fun together. I remember Sam would slip away from the set unnoticed and go back to the hotel where he was staying nearby. He would take a shower, have a shave, and then quietly arrive back. He would suddenly look and feel tremendously refreshed and would be ready to work again. Everybody would say, "Hey, this guy is as cool as a cucumber. He looks great!" The crew would all be working for twelve hours straight and would be looking a little weary, but Sam always looked fabulous. Of course, they didn't know that he was sneaking off to smarten himself up. [Laughs] But Sam's work ethic kind of forced everybody else on the show to all jump in and follow suit. I mean, here was this old man who was clearly capable of handling the long shooting hours, so why couldn't anybody else? Nobody could have any excuses. Sam was a tremendous example to us all.

I very much enjoyed Fuller's rather quirky performance.

Oh, Sam stole every scene he was in! He just had a charm to him that always shined through. I remember Sam had this cigar that he wanted to be smoking all the time, but that caused me some continuity problems. In one take, the cigar would be long and in the other take the cigar had been smoked halfway down; then in the next take it was long again and in the take after that it was down again. When that happens you are now editing a movie based on the length of a cigar rather than the quality of a performance. But I think we really created Sam's performance in editing. We carefully cut his lines together, putting some of his dialogue over shots of other actors and giving it more rhythm and fluidity. Whatever I had to do to get a performance out of Sam, it was well worth it, but what I found most surprising of all was Sam had a complete ignorance of direction on the set. This was a man who had directed twenty-something movies—some of them outright classics—but when it came time for me to say, "Cheat camera left" or "Cheat camera right," he didn't know what I was talking about. At one point he had to get out of a car and move to his left, but he didn't know which direction he had to go in. I said, "Sam, cheat a little bit to the left because you're putting a shadow on the other actor's face." He'd then step out of the car and freeze because he wouldn't be able to do it. After a couple of takes, he still couldn't do it, so I finally decided to help him out. I literally got down on the ground below the level of the camera and as Sam got out of the car, I grabbed his legs and physically turned his body so that he would move in the direction I wanted him to go.

How did Fuller respond to you literally manipulating his body in that manner?

Sam put up with it because it made things simpler for him, but he wasn't going to accomplish the action any other way. Sam just couldn't compute the information in his head. You would have thought that he'd never set foot on a movie set in his entire life, but this man had more experience than anybody on that movie. It was very strange. Again, I must say that Sam was very good in the film, so it didn't matter whether or not his performance was technically perfect. Yes, I would occasionally have to be there moving him around like a puppet, but that was half the fun! Sam enjoyed himself and it was the best acting part he ever had. Here he was playing a memorable character that had a serious involvement in the whole body of the picture. He may not have known how to cheat left or right, but he did everything I asked him to do. What's also interesting is despite the fact he was a great director, he never once tried to direct my picture himself. He only made one small suggestion when we were shooting, and I happily took it. It was during the scene when his character shoots himself and then falls to the floor. It was Sam's idea to have the low camera angle on the floor when he falls into the frame. That suggestion was very much appreciated.

The film satirizes the vampire myth in some interesting ways: Evelyn Keyes acknowledging her "drinking problem"; vampires pledging the Oath of Allegiance; the wedding of the two undead children.

The intention was always to bring a sense of humour to the picture in playing with the established elements of vampire movies. Audiences recognize aspects of the mythology and know what they mean, but I don't like vampire movies particularly. In fact, I find them very tedious. With *A Return to Salem's Lot*, I tried to revamp the legend by making vampires the most persecuted race in Europe. The idea was they were like immigrants who had fled to America to seek freedom just like many other races, sects and religions once did. The vampires had travelled in their own boat, the Speedwell, which was a ship that was similar to the Mayflower which carried the pilgrims. They eventually settled in New England and prospered on the pretence that if you are going to live for 300 years you could become incredibly wealthy and successful simply by buying real estate as, over time, your investments would really pay off. All of this was my attempt at taking the mythology and fashioning it into something different than what it was. I thought that idea was fresh. Besides, the picture wasn't meant to be taken entirely seriously. All the characters are a little bit bigger than life and I thought the actors did a good job for me in realizing that.

Do you think your focus on the background details of the vampire town, its practices and people, came at the cost of the film's structure, plot, and pacing?

No, because only by fully realizing the minutia of the vampire milieu, their traditions and history, can you fashion a rich and interesting story. The little things are what it's all about, really. They allow you to bring this environment and its people to life. So I don't think the periphery details negate the pacing and structure. It's all good stuff.

You dismiss some components of the vampire myth such as bloodsuckers turning into bats and casting reflections in mirrors, but retain others such as the destructive power of sunlight and stakes. Why use some and not others?

My reasoning was that every society and generation has rules and beliefs and fallacies that get built up over time. There are some things you believe and other things that you don't believe. There are all kinds of lies that are passed-off as truths in every race and religion. It then becomes a question of selecting or discovering what you accept as the truth and what you dismiss as fictitious. So, when things become legend over a long period of time, they can change and a lot of falsehoods take hold. I was simply trying to say, "Hey, here is the *real* story of vampires. This is not the old Bela Lugosi vampires you think you know. These are the true facts of their existence."

Where did you shoot *A Return to Salem's Lot*? It looks a pleasant location.

We shot at this small town called Peacham in Vermont. It was a nice town and, naturally, since this was a story about vampires we were often shooting at night. We would begin work late in the afternoon and shoot all through the hours of darkness until dawn. I remember that we had half of the town staying awake all night with us, because all the local people played the residents of the vampires' town. Of course, we also needed children, and so all the local kids played the little vampires. That meant we had these kids up all night long and we didn't know exactly when we would be calling them onto the set. We had to have them all there, so we took over an empty church and put sleeping bags in there. All these children would be sleeping on the floor until we were ready for them. Then, at about four o'clock in the morning, we would wake the kids up, drag them into a car, take them to the school, and shoot the scenes. Their parents allowed them to be basically carted off and stored away all night long until it was time to shoot. These kids would wake up, pale-faced and bleary-eyed, and come shuffling into the classroom. They kind of looked like little vampires anyway, so it worked out fine. I do remember the people in the town said to me, "You know, we were really glad when you came and we'll be really glad when you leave!" [Chuckles] The experience turned out to be a little too much for them as we really took control of that entire town. We had our lighting equipment everywhere—lights in their homes and in their backyards. Occasionally, there would be rain or a thunderstorm and the lightning would come crashing down. Everybody was terrified that lightning was going to strike one of the tall electrical towers we had erected to illuminate the streets, so there was a little tension there.

Did any other mishaps occur during shooting?

The only other thing I can remember was that all through the picture we were experiencing problems with the sound. Sam was wearing a radio microphone and we were constantly getting these crackling static noises on the soundtrack. I had the sound man replace the microphone, but we were still getting this loud crackling. I was getting fed up with this sound man's faulty equipment and I eventually replaced him and brought somebody else up from New York. We then continued shooting only to discover that we still had the same problem, but only on Sam. We were trying to figure out what the hell was going on. All of this time, Sam had been sitting there listening to us debate the defective sound and had not uttered a single word about it. I walked over to him and said, "Sam, have you got anything in your pocket?" He said, "No, just my cigars." He actually had two or three cigars in each inside pocket which were wrapped in cellophane and every time he moved, the cellophane would crackle, and that was the noise we were hearing! Sam had been quietly observing all of these problems that were going on, but never once did he think that maybe he was the cause of them. Remember, this wasn't just anybody; this was Sam Fuller! This was the man who'd directed *Shock Corridor, The Steel Helmet,* and a lot of other great movies over the years, but it never once dawned on him to check his own pockets and that he may have been responsible! I had fired the sound man because of this, and now felt terrible about it. I quickly sent him a week's pay and a sincere apology.

How did you get on with Hollywood legend, Evelyn Keyes, who plays Mrs. Axel?

Oh, Evelyn was a lovely woman. I had a wonderful time working with her. She was certainly one of the brightest people I've ever met. I'm sure that when she was a young woman, she must have been extremely alluring. Even though Evelyn was in her seventies when we were shooting *A Return to Salem's Lot*, I could immediately see why she had attracted the attentions of men like John Huston, Mike Todd, and Artie Shaw. If you spent just an hour in her company, you'd understand why some of the most eligible bachelors in Hollywood fell under her thrall. Evelyn had also married Charles Vidor, who'd directed *Gilda* and a number of other good pictures, and I'm sure he was just as fascinated with her mind as her good looks. I mean, she truly was an intelligent and erudite woman. You could have extensive conversations with Evelyn about absolutely every subject. She actually wrote a screenplay and gave it to me to read. It was about Old Hollywood and although it never got produced the writing was excellent. Evelyn actually wrote a couple of books, as well as a very nice article about me which I reproduced in *Variety*. It was just wonderful. She basically said, "If you want to learn about making movies just follow Larry Cohen and you'll make a movie." Then she talked about her experiences with me and how much fun she'd had. I was incredibly flattered. This was an actress who had starred in some of the biggest movies ever made like *Gone with the Wind, Here Comes Mr. Jordan, The Jolson Story,* and so many other great films. She had done pictures with people like Clark Gable, Dick Powell, and Robert Montgomery. She had worked with everybody and hobnobbed with Hollywood royalty. Being married to the likes of John Huston, she was very friendly with Bogart and Bacall, and everybody else in that group. Evelyn had been part of the magical world of Old Hollywood. I was always fascinated with that period because those were the pictures I had grown up with as a kid when I was dreaming of someday making my own movies. So, I was thrilled to have her in *A Return to Salem's Lot* and she was always very nice to me. I kept making up new dialogue for her, giving her new things to do, and she was always receptive to my suggestions. I promised Evelyn that I'd build-up her part and I did. I used her again in *Wicked Stepmother* just because I wanted to see her again. Obviously, if I had met her at a different time in a different place, I would have been very attracted to her and something may have come of it. She was just a fascinating woman.

June Havoc, who plays Moriarty's elderly Aunt Clara, was another actress with an interesting history.

Yeah. June was actually the sister of the famous entertainer Gypsy Rose Lee and was the real-life basis for the character of "Baby June" in the famous musical, *Gypsy*.[4] She'd also appeared in a number of great movies, like *Gentleman's Agreement* with Gregory Peck. She had a lot of experience on Broadway and had written several books, so again, this was another extremely intelligent woman. I had used June in *The Private Files of J. Edgar Hoover* in which she had played Hoover's mother. I really enjoyed working with her and thought she would be great for the part of Moriarty's aunt. June was great to be around and I wanted to get her back so I could spend more time with her. For me, a big part of making these pictures involves socialising with the cast. I particularly enjoy socialising with people who have been in the business a long time and have great résumés. I love being around actors and technicians who've done great pictures and worked with great people. I really just want to hear all their stories and memories. At the other end of the spectrum from June and Evelyn in terms of age and experience was Tara Reid[5] who played the little vampire girl. *A Return to Salem's Lot* was the first film Tara ever did.

I interviewed her along with a lot of other children but she was by far the cutest and read the best, so we put her in the picture. She became a big fan of mine and for years after we made the movie, her mother would bring her to New York City to occasionally have lunch with me. I don't see her anymore, but I have run into her once or twice. She was always very friendly and polite, but the infatuation was certainly over! [Chuckles] But we did have a nice time together making the movie and she was good in it.

The actress who plays Moriarty's love interest, Kathy, appears to be dubbed.

Yeah, she is. Laurene Landon dubbed her voice. That actress didn't have much experience, but she looked right for the part. She also had these teeth that I kind of liked. I thought she had good teeth for a vampire.

Andrew Duggan, in his final role before his death on May 15, 1988, essays the part of Judge Axel, the leader of the vampire society. Was he your first choice for the part?

Originally, I had tried to get Richard Widmark for the Judge. Widmark had worked with Sam Fuller on a number of movies at 20th Century Fox, like *Pick Up on South Street* and the submarine picture *Hell and High Water*. I already had Sam in the movie and I thought it would be fun to reunite them together. Widmark actually resided in New England at that time and I felt there was a chance I could get him to be in the film because he was living nearby. I thought he could just drop by and do it, but by then Widmark had retired and expressed no desire to come out of retirement for me. I was pleased that Andy could then take the part because he was a dear friend and that marked the last time we worked together. I don't think Andy liked performing under all that rubber and greasepaint when the Judge transformed into the monster at the end, but I tried not to keep him in the makeup for too long. For his sake, we shot those scenes in the minimum amount of time and efficiency that was possible.

Judge Axel expresses his distaste for human blood that is tainted with "drugs, alcohol, hepatitis, and that AIDS thing." Interestingly, this is one of the first acknowledgements of the AIDS virus in a horror film, if not the very first.

Yes, I believe so. That was a time in our history when AIDS was still this mysterious and terrifying thing. People were somewhat reluctant to acknowledge it, but I thought that moment was apropos. It seemed perfectly logical that vampires would be appalled at having such impurities in their food. Blood is their thing. They want and need blood, but now they suddenly have to be concerned about catching some fatal disease. So, in spite of their longevity, they must now be careful in their dealings with humanity. No wonder they are turning to cows for their nourishment!

Which brings me to my next question: am I right in assuming that you drugged the cattle for those feeding scenes?

Yeah, we did. We had a veterinarian come in and put them to sleep. Unfortunately, he put one of these animals to sleep in the wrong place. We then had to have nearly the entire crew drag this unconscious cow across to the proper place so we could shoot the scene. I must say that moving an unconscious cow took quite a considerable effort. I think it took as many as fourteen people just to slide this animal across the ground from one area to another in a pouring rainstorm. Despite the inconvenience, it was rather hilarious to observe.

The idea of the "drones"—the human workers and protectors of vampires during the daylight hours—is, of course, an old one in vampire movies.

Didn't Bela Lugosi have Renfield do that job for him in *Dracula*? Renfield was basically Dracula's human helper, and I've always liked the idea of subservient humans working for the vampire cause. In this case, they are being bred specifically for that purpose. It was another effort on my part to create the new legend of vampires—the new Bible of rules. Everybody else seems to be doing it in movies and books, and often in disappointing and uninteresting ways, so I figured I was also entitled to contribute to this evolving mythology. If Bram Stoker could create his own rules for the vampire, and people like Stephen King could play off them, then why couldn't I? Also, the idea of vampires breeding human beings simply to be their life-long servants seemed pretty creepy to me. It's like being born into captivity.

What vampire movies have worked for you? Which ones have you enjoyed?

I liked the original *Dracula,* if only for Bela Lugosi's iconic performance. Today, it's easy for people to forget just how incredibly menacing and provocative he was in that part. Lugosi defined the way a vampire should be played on screen for generations to come. I also think some of the Hammer films with Christopher Lee as Dracula are good, although if you only saw one of them that would be enough. I've always felt that a lot of the sequels Hammer later made were derivative of their first *Dracula* film.[6] I've seen the original versions of *Nosferatu,* which was good, and *Fright Night,* which was okay. I also thought that *Interview with the Vampire* with Tom Cruise was enjoyable. But I'm not the kind of person who runs out to see every vampire movie as I find the repetition of ideas and elements tiresome. As I told you, I didn't even sit through the whole of *Salem's Lot*—and I made the sequel!

What about vampire fiction? Did you read anything for research?

I've never read any vampire fiction. Oh, I did once read an annotated version of *Dracula.*[7] It had notes and pictures in it, but even then I don't believe I finished the whole book. I did listen to the original radio production of *Dracula* that Orson Welles did with The Mercury Theater, which was very good, but nothing else really.

An interesting twist is having Judge Axel threatening to pound a stake through a human child's heart to demonstrate how terribly inhuman and painful it is.

I don't think I've seen that in any vampire film before. That really was new. Again, I tried to put things in there which were original, rather than adhering to the same old conventions of vampire movies that audiences had already seen. But there are some ideas in there that draw from other kinds of pictures I like. For instance, the Nazi-hunter that Sam plays was based on the same character that Edward G. Robinson played in *The Stranger.* In that film, Robinson is a Nazi-hunter who arrives in this New England village looking for a Nazi fugitive. He finds Orson Welles, who is in fact the war criminal he has been searching for and has now assumed a new identity. I always enjoyed that movie and decided to take Robinson's character and do a little variation on it. Sam then became a Nazi-killer rather than a Nazi-hunter, which is a different beast altogether. What's interesting is that Sam's character is not really that different from the vampires. He's not operating under the morays of society either. He is simply going to hunt down Nazis and execute them in cold blood. There will be no trial or appeal. If he finds a Nazi he is going to kill them, so he exists outside the rules and regulations of civilisation, just as the vampires do.

In response to a question about who will believe that vampires ever existed, Van Meer declares, "In 500 years who will believe there were Nazis?"

That's right. If you look at the enormity of what the Nazis did and their whole philosophy and syndrome, it moves so far beyond the scope of normal behavior that it approaches Biblical proportions. You can easily imagine that hundreds of years from now people might look back and think that those terrible events must have been embellished or were even made-up. Surely nobody could have possibly been that demonic and destructive? How could one individual like Hitler have inspired a whole nation of people with such an extreme sense of evil? It really is like something out of the Bible, it's so huge and excessive! If all the historical documents and film footage of the Nazis was destroyed and there was no evidence or witnesses to talk about their atrocities, and you only heard this story from legend, people would think that it was entirely fictionalised. They would assume that it's like Nebuchadnezzar or something, you know, it's that *big*! It's just not feasible that this could have happened in the recent history of human behavior, but of course, we know that it did.

What is the significance of having Judge Axel impaled on the Stars and Stripes at the climax?

Oh, I just thought that was a Larry Cohen touch. After all, it was a pole with a point on the end of it so why not? The American flag seems to work better than just having an ordinary stake go through his heart. The Judge is obsessed with his patriotism and is proud that he came to a country where vampires have had the freedom to flourish without persecution. They came to America for survival, and using the very symbol of Americanism as the instrument of his destruction seemed a very fitting and perverse end. I just felt that things had now come full circle, as in a way these vampires considered themselves to be the original Americans.

Am I right in thinking you imported several shots of a burning house from the original *Salem's Lot* miniseries for the sequel's fiery climax?

I don't think so. I might have got those shots from the Warner Bros. stock library. Unless, of course, Tobe Hooper acquired the footage from the same place. It may be that Tobe didn't originate that footage himself either and borrowed it from the library. I don't know. They were both Warner Bros. productions, so we both had access to it.

Do you have any final thoughts about *A Return to Salem's Lot*?

Only that I was—and still am—very pleased with the picture and glad that I made it. I had a good time working with Moriarty, Sam, Evelyn, June and everybody else in that cast. Once again, I would have liked a little more money for the special effects, but I still think we did a good job. I remember that when Sam finally saw the finished film, he remarked that it was "very well put together." Coming from the great man himself as those words did, I considered that quite some compliment.

When was the last time you saw Sam?

I last saw him after he gave up his place in Paris and came back to California. Sam had suffered a stroke and wasn't able to speak coherently. Of course, that still didn't prevent him from talking non-stop! Nobody could understand a word of what he was saying, but he would just babble on, constantly telling stories and relaying anecdotes. One evening, they organized a little tribute to Sam at the Raleigh Studios in Hollywood, and a lot of people who were old Sam Fuller veterans, friends, and family, came out to pay homage to him. One of the attendees that night owed Sam an interesting debt of gratitude. Back in the 1950s, Sam had been making the Western, *Run of the Arrow,* which starred Rod Steiger. Steiger's leading lady in that film was the Mexican actress Sara Montiel, but her voice was not usable and Sam needed to dub her. Sam had found this young secretary, whose voice he liked. He asked this girl if she thought she could dub the dialogue and she came in to give it a try. She dubbed Montiel's voice, and Sam liked what she had done. This secretary was also very beautiful, and so Sam decided to cast her in his next picture, *China Gate.* That young girl was Angie Dickinson. That was how Angie got her start in the business, and she went on to make some great pictures and have a successful career.[8] Of course, Angie showed up for this event and sat with Sam to show her appreciation. Sam talked and talked and talked, and nobody could understand him, but we all just sat there and listened. Then we ran Sam's Western, *I Shot Jesse James*, and I talked a little about the influence the movie had had on me, since I'd basically acquired elements of it for *Branded*. In *I Shot Jesse James*, John Ireland is branded a coward for having shot Jesse James in the back and a song is sung commemorating this deed: "The dirty little coward that shot Mr. Howard." We had a similar song in *Branded*: "Branded, marked with a coward's shame." As you know, that song is what people remember most about the show and I got that from Sam's picture. That night, I also talked about making *A Return to Salem's Lot* with Sam and the wonderful time we spent together in New England. Afterwards, when the tribute was over, we walked to Sam's car so he could go home with his wife and daughter. I kissed him goodnight and watched the car drive away and that was the last time I ever saw him. [Cohen becomes emotional] Anyway, he… he was a dear, dear fellow, and, when you talked to Sam, he'd always tell you his stories. He'd grab you by the arm, dig his nails into your wrist, and wouldn't release you until he was finished telling his tale. It was as if he thought you were going to run away, and that if he didn't hold onto you, you were never going to hear the end of his story. What a great old guy he was! I loved him, and I'm very happy to be living in his house. For me, this will always be Sam Fuller's house, and I'm right here now, in his bedroom, talking to you on the phone. So, there you go.

Maniac Cop Trilogy (1988–1993)

How did the idea for *Maniac Cop* first come to be?

I was attending the Los Angeles Film Festival—one of the very earliest ones that were held—and I met William Lustig there. Bill said that he was a big fan of my movies, and we ended up having lunch together. As we were talking, Bill mentioned that he was looking for something to do as his next picture. I think he was having a little trouble coming up with a good idea. I knew that Bill had directed a horror film called *Maniac*,[1] which I hadn't seen and still haven't. For some reason, I then said, "Well, you've already done a movie called *Maniac*. What if you do another movie about a maniac that is a combination of a horror film and a police thriller? Only this time the maniac isn't some sleazy psychopath; he's actually a uniformed cop. Think how interesting that could be. We could even call it *Maniac Cop*." Then, we both laughed, but Lustig immediately responded to that title. I was clearly on a roll that day because the very next words out of my mouth were, "Hey, I even have the ad campaign we could use: 'You have the right to remain silent . . . forever!'" I could see how excited Bill was getting over this. He thought the idea was great. He said, "Would you do that with me?" I said, "Sure," and then I forgot all about it. I never thought I'd ever hear from him again, but then a few weeks later, he called me. Bill said that he'd raised the money to make the picture and he hoped—and expected—that I would keep my word and write the screenplay. I didn't want to let him down, so I wrote *Maniac Cop*, and very shortly afterwards the picture got made. And that was it. I probably wouldn't have got myself involved with the project if I thought it was going to go forward. I wrote it simply as a courtesy to Bill. I was being nice to somebody.

What did you make of the cast that Lustig pulled together for the film?

I was very impressed with the casting. There were some excellent actors in there, such as Tom Atkins,[2] who is always very good, and Richard Roundtree, with whom I'd worked with previously. Then there was Sheree North, who played the Maniac Cop's crippled girlfriend. I was very pleased to see her in the film as she had once been a very big contract star at 20th Century Fox. In fact, back in the mid-1950s, she was being groomed by the studio as a potential threat to Marilyn Monroe's status as Hollywood's blonde bombshell. It didn't quite work out that way, but Sheree had done a number of big movies in which she'd played the lead. She was a solid actress and continued to work throughout her career up until her death.[3] I must say, I didn't know Bruce Campbell[4] very well but he was certainly very good in the part of the heroic young cop. I only ever met Bruce once, when we were recording the commentary narration for the release of *Maniac Cop* on home video. We met at the recording studio, and he seemed to be a very humorous fellow.

You've never been particularly reticent in expressing your displeasure at the choice of Robert Z'Dar for Matt Cordell, the Maniac Cop. Why exactly?

Oh, I never liked him for the part. I've always been very clear about that. I thought the casting of Robert Z'Dar was a mistake. He was basically this big lug with a thick neck and a large head. Frankly, when they put the makeup on him, he looked ridiculous. He just resembled this big, cumbersome float that was coming down a parade. Z'Dar moved rather awkwardly and I always thought that since the Maniac Cop didn't speak, he should move with considerable physical expression and menace in order to compensate. They should have hired a stuntman for the role, someone who possessed a great deal of agility and flexibility. Unfortunately, Bill would never listen to me and my suggestions. He kept using Z'Dar in picture after picture. He should have hired somebody for the part that allowed the makeup artists to build an impressive makeup on. Of course, the makeup changed from one movie to the next, but at least it got a little better in *Maniac Cop 2* and *Maniac Cop 3* as Cordell got progressively more decayed and monstrous-looking. There's no question about it, the makeup was dreadful in the first film. Lustig had a pretty good movie, up until the moment the Maniac Cop's face was revealed on screen in close-up. As soon as I saw that, I went, "Oh, no! Please, no!" I mean, the ridiculous expressions that Z'Dar was making in those final scenes! It was just bad! That upset me to some degree, I must say. I thought they blew the whole movie just by having that one awful makeup job.

Were you hoping that the Maniac Cop would become an iconic horror character?

I always thought he had that potential, certainly. When you create a monster for a movie, you hope to come up with some kind of iconic look. The Maniac Cop was obviously dressed in a police uniform and had the nightstick-knife, but every monster still needs to have a great look, like Karloff as Frankenstein's Monster and Lugosi as Dracula. In the horror movies that were around at the time of *Maniac Cop*, there was Freddy Krueger with his burned face and razor glove, and there was also Jason in the *Friday the 13th* movies whose hockey mask became iconic. As soon as the audience saw the visual aspects of those characters, they immediately knew exactly who and what they were. That level of recognition also means that these characters become extremely marketable. Masks and costumes are manufactured for the fans to wear; parodies appear on television and cartoon illustrations appear in newspapers. Suddenly, an iconic monster is born that has some kind of cultural impact, but the Maniac Cop never achieved that. That's why the three pictures never crossed over as some of the other horror movies have. They were always held back somehow. Even though some of the *Maniac Cop* movies were fairly well done, they never really caught on like *A Nightmare on Elm Street* or *Halloween*. The reason is that our monster was a disappointment. When you finally saw Cordell, you just said, "Geez, look at his face! It looks like a bunch of school kids did it over the weekend for an 8mm film in their backyard!" I mean, it looked amateurish, when it should have been frightening and powerful.

As both writer and producer on all three films, surely you could have supervised or consulted on the final look of the Maniac Cop?

Well, Bill is a very nice fellow, but he is extremely sensitive to any criticisms that are made or suggestions that are offered. I did not want him to think that I was trying to take over his movie. You know, when we were making *Phone Booth*, I suggested to the director, Joel Schumacher, that he replace the original actor who was providing the voice of the sniper.[5] Schumacher then went out and got Kiefer Sutherland for the role. He actually listened to my suggestion and it improved the picture immeasurably. Schumacher wasn't averse to hearing a suggestion and then acting upon it, but to Bill Lustig any suggestions were taken as an assault. Unfortunately, he just can't handle it.

Lustig did act upon your suggestion to cast Laurene Landon in the role of Theresa Mallory, didn't he?

Sure, he did hire Laurene for the movie and she also appeared in the second film, too. Her character was supposed to appear in *Maniac Cop 3* also, but once again, Lustig got up on his high horse and decided he was going to overrule me and not use Laurene again. I think they might have had some problems with each other on the set. I mean, she has a great sense of humour and he doesn't, so Laurene may have said something to Bill that might have offended him. I don't know. When he was doing *Maniac Cop 3*, Bill went out and hired an actress who looked exactly like Laurene.[6] He then had to alter the story to make her an entirely different character. So, he ended up getting a girl who was a former basketball player and also the girlfriend of Martin Landau. It's funny, because Landau actually called me up and thanked me for getting her the part but I didn't have anything to do with it.

How actively involved in the productions were you?

I tried to be as active as I could—without stepping on Bill's toes. On *Maniac Cop*, I was allowed to re-cut the picture. The editor, David Kern, and I sat down and spent a week carefully re-cutting *Maniac Cop*. I actually think we improved the film quite a bit. I also had some input on the first sequel, as well. On *Maniac Cop 2*, Bill called me up and said that he didn't know how to end the picture and required some assistance. He had finally reached out for help, so I went down to the location of the prison set that was in downtown Los Angeles. The stunt director, Spiro Razatos, and I worked out the climactic scenes where the Maniac Cop catches fire. Spiro is an extremely gifted second unit and stunt director. Together, we devised all the action where Cordell throws the other convicts around and catches fire. We also had the convicts catch fire, too, before Cordell tosses their flaming bodies up onto the second platform of the prison. I can remember asking Spiro, "Okay, how long can you keep these people burning for?" Spiro then figured out exactly how we could do it and it did look rather good on film. In fact, everything that is good in *Maniac Cop* and *Maniac Cop 2* is Spiro's work. He directed all the action sequences. That whole climactic fire sequence in *Maniac Cop 2* wasn't in my original script. That stuff wasn't anything that Bill could handle himself, so he called me up and I did it for him. As for *Maniac Cop 3*, I had virtually no input whatsoever as the third movie was taken away from us by First Look, the production company. They put their own people on it; rewrote my script and fired Bill. First Look basically did what they wanted to do, and so *Maniac Cop 3* bares very little resemblance to anything I wanted. However, the first two pictures followed my scripts almost completely, and I did enjoy some input.

The critical reaction towards the first *Maniac Cop* was mostly negative.

I didn't know there was any critical reaction. I didn't think anybody cared.

The first film does contain a terrific opening sequence that in some ways the rest of *Maniac Cop* fails to match: we see a young girl fleeing from some street muggers towards the apparent safety of a police officer, only for the cop to suddenly break her neck and toss her body away.

Yeah, that was a strong opening and a good way to introduce the Maniac Cop. Actually, my daughter, Jill, played the part of the doomed young girl. She wanted to be in films, and I suggested to Lustig that he use her for the part and he agreed.

The world of the *Maniac Cop* trilogy is filled with violent criminals, scheming officials, and dirty cops—the cops often being the worst of a bad bunch. It seems apropos to ask you what the present view of the police is in America.

People in America are generally scared of cops, particularly minority people. The police have always been a rather racist organization. Even the Black cops don't treat Black citizens too well. I mean, once they get themselves over into the establishment, they have an intimidating role in the community. Now maybe it's because there is so much crime, but the biggest victims of Black crime are Black people in the Black community. They suffer the most, but they are also very much afraid of the police. Of course, the police have earned that animosity by their behavior. A lot of cops are basically small-time people, who only achieve some degree of authority by joining the police department. Then they have to prove that they are tough guys. They have to show everybody that they are the boss and that they should command respect. They don't earn that respect; they merely demand it because they are now wearing a uniform. They can be extremely abusive and push people around. It's not too pleasant to be on the other end of their abuse. So, yeah, people generally do not like cops.

Have you ever been on the wrong end of abuse from police officers?

As a matter of fact, I just came from the Academy Awards last week and they had all these off-duty policemen in tuxedos working the red carpet. These cops were telling people to move along in the most obnoxious and disrespectful fashion. I very seldom come into contact with police officers, but when you go to the Oscars ceremony there are all these off-duty cops acting like they are really somebody important. They are pushing you around and you don't attend the Oscars to get pushed around. I'm a member of the Academy and I wish to be treated with dignity. They don't know how to treat anybody with dignity. They are just cops, that's all. Many times when you are dealing with cops, you would just like to sock them right in the face! Of course, you don't want to go to jail, and so you put up with their ignorant behavior. But they are really nothing. They are nothing guys. They probably go home, get drunk every night, and beat up their wives. They are not the most pleasant people to deal with and are usually rather stupid, to tell you the truth.

Guilt, culpability, and corruption are themes present in all three *Maniac Cop* films, would you agree?

I guess. Guilt is a powerful and destructive emotion and a great element to a story. The whole notion of guilt has been in several of my movies, actually. As a theme, it gives any dramatic writer a considerable weapon to wield. Characters afflicted with feelings of guilt, remorse, anger and vengeance can be interesting to write.

How does that relate to the character of Matt Cordell?

Well, I see Cordell as a tragic figure. A lot of the iconic monsters in movies, such as Frankenstein's Monster and King Kong, have a desperately sad and tragic element to them. I view Cordell as being the same. He was a man who tried his best to be a good and honest cop, but people were conspiring against him. He has been taken advantage of by the dishonest politicians and the compliant cops within his own force who've sought to frame him. He has been discredited, incarcerated, and violated, and the poor treatment he's received has turned him into something truly monstrous. The Maniac Cop has been born out of the corruption and deceit of the state that has betrayed him, transforming Cordell from a good man into a bad man. I've often said that the most terrifying bad guys are the ones who were formerly good guys. They have a bitterness and destructiveness to them that makes them even more dangerous. It's that fall from grace which gives their tragedy an added dimension, I think. Of course, last year, *Maniac Cop* really came true out here in Los Angeles. We had a renegade cop actually running around shooting and killing people. Do you know about this?

You mentioned this case to me several months ago and I did read up on it. The police officer's name was Christopher Jordan Dormer, but I believe that one or two media outlets actually referred to Dormer as the "Maniac Cop."

That's right. It's another case of art imitating life, not that *Maniac Cop* is art, but you know what I'm saying. This officer had been fired off the force and decided that he was going to kill as many policemen—and relatives of policemen—as he could. He claimed that he was forced out because he had informed on some fellow officers, who had committed acts of violence against people. He had turned them all in, but the result of his actions was that the LAPD punished him by firing him. This ex-cop then decided to get his revenge, and started off by killing the daughter of one of the police executives, as well as the daughter's boyfriend. After that, he then went on a rampage and killed a couple of cops and wounded several others, resulting in every policeman in L.A. being on alert. They were hunting him all over the city and finally tracked him down up in Big Bear, California, which is a ski resort. The police would never have caught him if certain civilians had not given them information on this guy's whereabouts. He was actually holed up right across the street from them—just a few feet away. Finally, some people the cop had spared and didn't kill—

he'd tied them up but they got loose—warned the police that he was there. They eventually ended up cornering the killer and burning him to death in a cabin. Apparently, he had already committed suicide, but he certainly was a maniac cop. So, there you go. One of my movies has come true again. It's remarkable how your films can occasionally anticipate real-life events. The same thing happened with the Washington Sniper attacks occurring around the release of *Phone Booth*—art imitating life. In the case of the maniac cop, it was disturbing for people to have a police officer go crazy like that, but it was also terrifying for the cops. For a while there, it really created an atmosphere of fear and paranoia.

Interestingly, there's a scene in *Maniac Cop* where a paranoid woman shoots a police officer who has pulled her over, mistakenly believing he is Cordell.

Yeah, and you know what? The events with this crazy cop resulted in police officers actually opening fire on a vehicle with two women inside it. They must have believed that this guy was inside. The cops fired countless shots at these two women, without even first identifying who was in the vehicle, and could have very easily killed them. It turns out that these women were simply delivering newspapers early one morning in a neighbourhood where the police thought this maniac cop might show up. The women weren't even in a car that matched the vehicle that the suspect was in, but the cops were so scared they opened fire with all kinds of weapons. That tells you just how terrified they were of this guy. So, with all this murder and mayhem and paranoia, it really was like a scene right out of one of my movies.

Let's move on to *Maniac Cop 2*, which personally I think is an underrated movie. What led to the decision to make a sequel?

I have no idea. For some reason, Bill found somebody in England who was willing to provide the dough required to make a sequel. They put up about $3.5 million, which was way more than the original picture cost—in fact, over three times as much. Unfortunately, the financer later went bankrupt and as a result never paid the residuals. They ended up owing me about $60,000 that I never received. We got a judgment against them from the Writer's Guild, but we could never collect the money because the company went bankrupt over in England. So, even though *Maniac Cop 2* continues to play, I'm getting cheated out of my residuals.

Lustig once pitched *Maniac Cop 2* as being "*The French Connection* meets *Frankenstein* with Robert Davi as Popeye Doyle." Is that how you viewed your script when you were writing it?

Absolutely not. How would he know what it's about? He doesn't know anything.

So, Lustig had no input into the screenplay?

Absolutely none. I wouldn't say that was true of the third *Maniac Cop* film, because I don't know exactly what he did after I submitted my screenplay. That was all done behind my back.

I believe Lustig wanted the characters of Jack Forrest [Bruce Campbell] and Theresa Mallory to be killed fairly early on in the sequel. Why exactly?

I don't know.

Did you think it seemed somewhat cruel and arbitrary that the heroes of *Maniac Cop* should receive such violent treatment? I mean, Forrest gets a nightstick blade callously rammed through the back of his neck as he is reading a newspaper and Mallory gets her neck broken.

Yeah, but Laurene's character doesn't get killed right away. She doesn't die until two thirds of the way through the picture—at least half way through. She is more of a supporting character in *Maniac Cop 2,* and, as I say, she would have also been in the third movie. Her character would not have died as a result of having her neck broken by Cordell. Originally, she was going to be stuck in a coma in the hospital as a result of that attack. Laurene would have played the unconscious, brain-dead woman in the third film that the Maniac Cop steals from the hospital and claims as his mate. Basically, he goes after someone he sees as being like himself—the living dead. This person is effectively dead, but like him is also very much alive. Cordell connects with her for that very reason.

The spectre of *Frankenstein* falls over several of your films and all three *Maniac Cop* movies bear traces of its influence. In the third instalment, there are definite echoes of *The Bride of Frankenstein*.

Oh, sure. In *The Bride of Frankenstein*, Karloff's Monster is seeking a mate and receives one in the form of Elsa Lanchester's Bride. It was the same idea in *Maniac Cop 3*. I think the addition of Laurene's character in the third film would have been an interesting continuation of *Maniac Cop 2*, but they decided to make that person somebody else entirely. What can I tell you? I sometimes think that a decision is made not on the basis of what benefits the overall quality of a movie, but is simply founded on someone's personal agenda. Bill knew that Laurene was a friend of mine, so he couldn't use her in the picture, that's all. It was an act of aggression, I think. He was going to prove that he didn't have to do what I wanted him to do. That was the beginning of the end for him also as he was eventually kicked off *Maniac Cop 3*, too. So, justice ultimately prevailed and he got what he deserved.

Getting back to *Maniac Cop 2*, the addition of Robert Davi's Lt. McKinney is obviously as a replacement hero for Jack Forrest.

Yeah, pretty much. I liked Robert Davi's performance in *Maniac Cop 2*. His character was that world-weary type of cop and it fit him well. I mean, Davi also has a great Film Noir face. He's not your usual handsome leading man type, but he certainly looks good in those kinds of dark crime movies, and he is a good actor. I know that Davi is now actually trying to be a singer. He thinks he's Frank Sinatra! The last time I saw Davi, he dragged me outside to his car and played me a tape of himself singing. I must admit, it was pretty good, too.

The first sequel sees Cordell teaming up with the vicious serial killer, Turkell [Leo Rossi], who is on "a crusade against the whores of the world." I've always—

[Interrupting] Don't ask me where the inspiration for that came from! I just sat there and wrote the damn thing. I was making it all up as I was going along.

I was about to say that the film seems to draw on *Son of Frankenstein*, and the relationship between Igor, as played by Bela Lugosi, and Karloff's Monster.

Yes, that's true. I guess there is a history in horror films of one monster teaming up with another monster. I just thought it was a cute idea to have these two characters cross paths. I particularly like the scene where the Maniac Cop and the serial killer both show their weapons to each other. [Chuckles]

Maniac Cop 2 features a remarkable stunt at the climax, where Cordell and Turkell fall from the prison and tumble down into the bus whilst on fire.

Uh-huh, and that was all Spiro Razatos. Everything from riding the cars without the wheels and driving the car down the street with Claudia Christian handcuffed to the wheel—that was all Spiro. I could write those sequences, but Spiro could certainly bring them to life. In my opinion, he is the real hero of the *Maniac Cop* movies. I actually got Spiro a job directing a picture called *Fast Getaway* as a reward for all his efforts on *Maniac Cop* and *The Ambulance*, which he also did for me. I felt I should do something nice for him in return, so I came up with a storyline for a movie. The first script was written by Jim Dixon, who also acts in a lot of my pictures. I got Jim the job as writer on the film and Spiro the job as director. I didn't take any money for it and *Fast Getaway* became a pretty good movie. Then the company made a sequel and, as usual, they stabbed the people who made the original in the back. They didn't hire Spiro to direct the sequel, which wasn't good, by the way, but they did have to pay me a substantial amount of money. My deal with them was that I wouldn't take any money on the first picture but I had to be paid if there was a sequel. Spiro eventually went back to stunt directing and he works on a lot of high-budget movies.

Leo Rossi gives a sickeningly convincing performance as the psychopathic Turkell. He is barely recognizable in the role.

Yeah, I thought Rossi was very good. He brought a sleazy intensity and energy to that character, which was exactly what was required. In fact, Leo played the lead role in *Fast Getaway*. He got that part in Spiro's film because of his excellent work on *Maniac Cop 2*. Rossi made a very memorable psychopath, but there were some other good people in *Maniac Cop 2*. You also had Michael Lerner, who is another solid actor. Around this same time, Michael had earned a considerable amount of acclaim for his role as a studio executive in The Coen Brothers film *Barton Fink*. I actually thought his was a rather clichéd performance. He was certainly good in the part, but there was nothing particularly fresh or inventive about it. That character was just the usual portrayal of a dim, boorish studio executive.

In *Maniac Cop 2*, Lerner plays the corrupt Deputy Commissioner Edward Doyle. I've heard that Richard Crenna was originally set to play that role, but dropped out of the film shortly before shooting commenced. Is this true?

No, I don't believe that. I have no knowledge of that. I don't believe that Richard Crenna—even at the lowest point of his career—would have done that.

What is your final estimation of *Maniac Cop 2*?

Maniac Cop 2 is certainly a lot better than the first film, in production value anyway. *Maniac Cop* had some good scenes and some pretty interesting ideas, but it was marred by poor direction and some cheaping out. For instance, there are moments where the Maniac Cop breaks down some doors and it looks like the doors are made of cardboard. I mean, you would have thought that Ed Wood had directed the picture! I couldn't stand how poorly some of the things were set up and how cheap some of the sets looked. I was like, "Gee, you could have done better than that!" But again, criticizing Bill Lustig can be very painful because anything you say to him—even the smallest criticism—is taken as an agonizing experience. He just can't stand it. The problem with Bill is that he doesn't enjoy directing pictures. He wants to be a director and he gets these pictures started by raising the money, but once the movie begins shooting he doesn't like the actors and he doesn't enjoy the experience. He's miserable on the set. He's a very big fellow, way overweight, and has trouble standing up. It must be physically painful for him to direct a film and he looks like he's in pain. He doesn't have a good time. I like to have a circus when I'm making a movie. I'm having a great time kidding around with the crew, putting on acts and tap dancing and driving them for fourteen hours a day. I enjoy every minute of it. But Bill looks like he can't wait for it to all be over. He just hates the experience of directing and that's too bad because he's so good at putting these projects together.

What did you make of the "Maniac Cop Rap" that is heard during the end credits of *Maniac Cop 2*?

Frankly, I've never stayed around long enough to hear it. I always walk out of the theater after a movie is over. I don't sit around to watch the credits. I hate endless credits that go on and on—all these names that just roll on forever—because nobody really looks at them. Everyone who works on a film, from the person who cleans the toilets to the people who serve the food, has to be credited. It's simply exhausting. Anybody and everybody who works on a particular special effect, miniature, or matte must have their name on the picture. Well, god bless 'em! I guess it makes them feel good, but who really cares? On my movies, we don't have those kinds of interminable credits.

Maniac Cop 3: Badge of Silence was released in 1993, three years after the second film. Out of curiosity, were you responsible for the Badge of Silence imprimatur?

Yeah, that was my idea.

How were you coerced into writing a third film after experiencing problems with your residuals on Maniac Cop 2?

After Bill called me up and said he had performed his magic once again and secured the money to make a third movie, there was no question that I had to write it. So, I did write it and I thought I wrote a good script, actually. Unfortunately, Bill—being the way he is—decided that he wanted to be the big cheese and kind of aced me out of the project. He sided with the production company and that was a mistake. Once he broke up the team, he became vulnerable and then they got rid of him, too. So, it ended up that the both of us were kicked off the picture. I was happy to be kicked off *Maniac Cop 3*. It wasn't really anything that was done to me personally. I had just written the script and they decided that they would do their own script, and that was it. I did get paid in full, so I was pleased. I didn't really want anything to do with the movie anyway, frankly. I didn't want anything to do with any of the *Maniac Cop* pictures. But instead of working with me as he had done before, even begrudgingly, as he always does, Bill decided that he would undermine my authority and have the script changed. That was his mistake.

Has Lustig ever acknowledged that mistake?

No, he isn't capable of acknowledging something like that. I don't dislike Bill. Honestly, I thank heaven that he came along. I've made quite a lot of money from my association with him, and we later did *Uncle Sam* together. I've done quite a number of pictures with him and, in fact, as I once told Bill, "We are batting a thousand." I've never ever worked on a project with him that did not get made. Every single movie has been made! In most cases, when you write a screenplay and are in development, you are lucky if fifty percent of them ever get made, but with Bill everything got made. He is certainly a lot better at raising money for movies than I am.

Of course, that is a great talent in itself.

Oh, absolutely. It's an extremely difficult thing trying to get money to make a film. I mean, god bless Bill, because he got the money to make the *Maniac Cop* movies and *Uncle Sam*. I don't know how he does it. I don't know why people would give him any money—certainly after the *Maniac Cop* pictures—but they always do.

There are reports that Lustig dropped out of *Maniac Cop 3* after apparently delivering a 51-minute rough cut of the film. He was then replaced at the helm by producer Joel Soisson. Are these reports accurate?

I really don't know the internal politics of *Maniac Cop 3*. I only know that Bill was replaced. I don't think he bowed out, I think he was replaced.

Do you remember any of the substantial changes that were made to your script?

I do remember there was something I had written where the policewoman in a coma is pregnant with the Maniac Cop's child. Cordell had basically inseminated her as she was lying there in a catatonic state. I thought that brought an interesting element into the story, because it raised the question of whether or not the authorities should terminate her life—and the life of her unborn baby—by switching off the life support system. I don't think the producers appreciated that aspect of the script. Maybe they thought it was a little too much. I don't know. What I do know is they simply wanted Cordell to be killing people left and right like he always did. Anything that deviated from that objective was frowned upon, I'm sure. I can't think of anything else that was cut or changed. To be totally honest with you, all of that has been completely blanked out of my mind because I just didn't care. In cases like *Maniac Cop 3*, I don't brood over these things. I simply erase them from my memory and quickly move on. Usually, the people who do those kinds of things to your script end up suffering for it themselves. They end up with a bad movie and a bad rep, and so what? I still get to keep the money no matter what happens. Honestly, I don't really care. If you want the opportunity to tamper with my script, you are going to have to pay for it. Then you can go ahead and make whatever changes you want. Just be prepared to also deal with the inevitable consequences.

There is a repetition of footage in *Maniac Cop 3*, as indeed there was in *Maniac Cop 2*. Was this done in order to pad out the running time or did you specifically write those flashbacks into the script?

I thought we needed some re-establishment of the story and situation in the sequels. I felt the flashbacks would be helpful in case people hadn't seen the previous films.

Yet again, Lustig comes through with an eclectic array of interesting players in his cast: Robert Forster, Paul Gleason, Julius W. Harris, and Jackie Earl Harley. Harley in particular has recently enjoyed a career revival after his Oscar-nominated performance in *Little Children*.

Yeah, that's right. Jackie Earl Harley is in the first scene where the gunman goes crazy in the store. I actually wrote that scene and it's still in the picture. Although Julius Harris and I had worked together previously, I frankly had nothing to do with him being hired for the part of the witch doctor. It came as a complete surprise to me when I saw him in *Maniac Cop 3*. Maybe the fact that Julius had been in a couple of my movies influenced whoever cast him. I don't know. I actually thought that Robert Forster's scene was rather embarrassing. It was just unfortunate, but he did an equally embarrassing scene in *Uncle Sam* for Bill. I mean, the fact of the matter is that Bob was down on his luck at the time and would take any job.

Did you write that scene where Forster's character is x-rayed to death?

I think I might have written that, yes, but I certainly didn't expect them to hire an actor of Bob's stature to play that part. It was a nothing part.

Maniac Cop 3 culminates with an extraordinary chase sequence in which Cordell drives a car down a highway whilst on fire. When you wrote the script, did you think that sequence would be difficult to realize?

I don't think about things like that. My job is to create the idea, and their job is to execute it.

You've delivered a withering assessment of the Maniac Cop trilogy, but which instalment do you think succeeds best?

I guess the second one.

It was recently announced that Nicolas Winding Refn, the acclaimed Danish director of Valhalla Rising, Drive, and Only God Forgives, is mounting a remake or prequel to Maniac Cop. Is this accurate?

Yeah, it is. There is going to be a remake of Maniac Cop, but it's not going to be too much like the original. It will be executive produced by Nicolas Winding Refn, and Bill Lustig is one of the producers. I'm the creator of the characters; that's my main role in the project. I did supply them with half a dozen scenes that they could use in the script and they did include them. So, I do have some contributions to the screenplay. Actually, the script is not bad, and it looks like the movie is going to move forward and will get made. It's being financed by Wild Bunch, but, presently, I have no idea who the director will be.

Are you an admirer of Nicolas Winding Refn's work?

Not particularly, but he's been to my house a couple of times. He came over here and gave me the old story about how much he admires my movies and all that stuff. He came over twice, sat around and drank and ate hors d'oeuvres. We treated him very nicely, but if you ask Nicolas Winding Refn for anything, you never hear back from him. It's the same old story again, you know?

What did you ask of him?

I asked him to read something that I had written, and he claimed he was just too busy. What can you say? You know, he's just not very pleasant. He asked me to write a scene for *Drive*, which was the picture he was directing at the time we met, but he didn't use the scene. He said that he didn't have time to shoot it. I can't go into details about what the scene was about, but it was rather superfluous. I'm sure it's true; he probably didn't have the time to do it. What I don't understand is why he was bothering me to write it for him in the first place. I was gracious enough to create something for him—for nothing! That's just the way it usually is with people in this business. They want something from you, but they offer you nothing in return.

It's my understanding that Winding Refn is indeed a big fan of your work.

Well, maybe he is. I can't stop him from being a fan. I don't judge people and tell them they can or can't be a fan of my movies. It's just the way they behave when they meet you that concerns me. Somebody may be a big admirer of your work, but that doesn't guarantee that they will always treat you with courtesy. But I really do want him to make the picture. I have no problem with them doing the remake. I'm glad they are doing it and I'm glad they have raised the money. I hope they make a good film.

In a recent interview, you indicated that if you were going to mount a remake of the film yourself, you would explore more of Cordell's life and background before he became the Maniac Cop.

I wouldn't direct a remake of *Maniac Cop*. I've already written that script and I have no desire to go back and explore the character more deeply. Back then, I wrote what I wrote and that was enough. As I say, I did come up with half a dozen new gags that could be inserted into the new movie and they did incorporate them into the script. As a matter of fact, everything I suggested was incorporated into the remake. On my own films, I never had to deal with anybody else, but that wasn't the case on the *Maniac Cop* movies. That's why dealing with somebody like Bill Lustig was an anomaly. It was an occasion when I had to work directly with somebody whose talent I did not respect. Again, I must say it, every suggestion I offered was an agonizing experience for Bill because the poor guy just wanted to make a movie, but he didn't know how. Unfortunately, anything you said to him was like a slap in the face. I would try to be helpful, but any help that I volunteered was rejected. He would just push me away. It was like putting your arm around somebody and having them just shrug you off. No matter what you tried to do for him—to make the picture better or to assist him—he just couldn't accept it. I really had no ulterior motive other than to try and help him make a good movie, but he couldn't and wouldn't allow it. Everything was an insult. What can you do?

Other than the forthcoming remake of *Maniac Cop*, I assume that you won't be collaborating with Lustig again anytime soon?

Oh, you never can tell. I mean, he may come up with the money for another picture at any time and, if that happens, I'll certainly write it for him. I have absolutely no problem with doing that. If Bill secures the finance for a project and he wants me involved, I will be right there. I don't care. Listen, I make my own pictures my own way but then I also write scripts and sell them to other people. Of course, I can't control what they are going to do with those scripts once I sell them, but I'm not averse to taking people's money.

Finally, you must concede that despite your feelings about the *Maniac Cop* trilogy they still continue to enjoy a considerable cult following.

Oh, absolutely, and I think I have acknowledged that. Look, I believe that when I wrote the three *Maniac Cop* scripts, it took just under a week to complete each one. Each one took three or four days to write—dictated—and I don't ever think for one moment that these movies represent the best of my work. But, yes, of course, I do realize that some people really do love these pictures. The *Maniac Cop* movies are quite popular and are still being embraced and enjoyed by audiences on DVD and Blu-ray. They are cited by other filmmakers as inspirational and favorite works, and I can't give you an answer for why that is. I really can't.

Wicked Stepmother (1989)

The story of *Wicked Stepmother*—the real story behind the making of the film—is in many ways more eventful and fascinating than the end product itself.

I guess there's some truth to that. *Wicked Stepmother* is usually considered to be a disaster because Bette Davis famously walked off the picture. It was a highly unfortunate situation and a lot of untruths have been written and spoken about it. The whole project really began with my desire to work with Bette. I'd always loved her performances, and, like most people during the 1980s, I had seen Bette as a guest on various TV chat shows, discussing her life and career. The most noticeable thing from those interviews was her shocking physical appearance, because she looked incredibly old and fragile. Listening to her conversations, I quickly realized that despite her health this woman was desperate to work. She was really putting herself out there on the circuit in the hope that somebody—anybody—would give her a part in a movie. I guess when you get to a certain age in Hollywood you begin to receive awards, honors, and dinners, celebrating your long and successful career. That's a perfectly fine and welcome thing, but when that's all you are getting and the employment dries up, it's no fun at all for an actor. Bette now found herself in that position, and I felt she deserved more. I then decided I was going to write something for her because clearly nobody else was interested in hiring her. I mean, the respect was still there for her achievements, but she was now seen as being too old and delicate to work. So, I wrote *Wicked Stepmother* for her and came up with the story of this wicked old witch who marries an elderly widower. He brings the witch back to the home of his daughter and her husband, causing all kinds of magic and mayhem in their lives. My basic idea was, "What would you do if Bette Davis suddenly came to stay and had married your father?" So, in a way, the whole picture was a takeoff of Bette's screen persona.

What was Davis' initial reaction to your screenplay when she read it?

Well, just getting the script to her proved to be difficult. When I first sent it out, it was rejected by Bette's agent, whom I doubt very much even took the trouble to read it. The second time I submitted it, Bette herself rejected the script without reading it. She thought *Wicked Stepmother* was a straight-up horror film and she had no desire to do a horror film. I was determined to secure her services, so, on my third attempt, I gave the script to Robert Osborne, who later became the host of Turner Classic Movies. Osborne was a friend of Bette's, and he rather generously got it into her hands. On this occasion, she actually read it. I remember I was in the kitchen of my house one day when the phone rang. I picked it up, and Bette's unmistakable voice said, "Hello, is this Mr. Cohen? I read your script last night and it certainly made me laugh. I liked it very much. Did you write this for me?" I told her I had indeed, and couldn't imagine anyone else possibly playing the part. We then arranged to meet, and I went over to Bette's house on Havenhurst in Hollywood to meet her. That's when I saw up close just how terribly frail she looked. Despite that, I really wanted her to do the movie. When that looked like it was going to be a real possibility, I immediately took out a full-page ad in *Variety* and commissioned a poster to be made that had the words "Bette is Bad Again!" emblazoned on it. We also had a picture of Bette smoking a cigarette and looking suitably evil. The agent and producer Robert Littman then approached his friends at MGM, and we managed to get the studio to give us $2.5 million to make *Wicked Stepmother*. $250,000 of that money would go to Bette.

How was the experience of working, however briefly, with a Hollywood legend?

Oh, I had a wonderful time with Bette, even though you might not think that from the way our association ended. Yes, Bette left the picture, but it wasn't because of any problems between her and me. We had a great time during pre-production, and even during the week that we shot, we had some fun together. I had bought Bette a little charm bracelet for her birthday, and every day she would come to the set wearing it. She'd always raise her wrist up and jingle the bracelet at me to make sure that I saw it. She liked me a lot and was always hanging onto me. She was constantly either holding my hand or hugging me or giving me a kiss. In fact, Bette wouldn't leave the set at the end of each day unless I gave her a kiss goodbye. The production assistant would come to me and say, "Miss Davis is ready to go home." I'd say, "Okay, fine. Please tell Miss Davis I'll see her tomorrow." They would then say, "No, she won't leave until she says goodnight to you." I would then have to go to wherever Bette was, and she would grab me with both hands—digging her fingernails into my skin—and give me a big wet kiss on the cheek. She would then make a point of telling me how much she had enjoyed the day's shooting. Then, and only then, would she go home. Of course, I never dreamed that anything was the matter with Bette because she was going out of her way to be nice. Bette was "an old pro" in the truest sense of the term. At the beginning of shooting, she came to me and said, "I arrived on the set this morning at seven o'clock and nobody was here." I said, "Bette, the call was for eight o'clock. You got here a half an hour before everybody else did. No wonder nobody was here. If you arrive on set tomorrow at seven o'clock, no one will be here then either." Bette just had to get there before anybody else, but then she'd get annoyed because nobody was there to welcome her. She just had to do things her way.

How did you persuade her to do things your way?

I tried to establish a good relationship with her very early on. During pre-production, Bette came to my house, and we spent some time together discussing the script and her character. She actually put a few cigarette burns into my furniture, but I didn't mind. In fact, I never got anything repaired and would proudly point them out to people and say that Bette Davis was responsible for those holes! [Laughs] Bette would also have certain ideas, like her character having red hair. She'd call me up, tell me her idea, and then immediately hang up—just like that! There was no small talk; she'd state her opinion and was gone. Even though we were comfortable with each other, Bette still could get irascible. The closest we ever came to a fight was when we had the fashion show over at the Western Costume Company. Bette was trying on all the various outfits that our costume designer, Julie Weiss, had prepared for her to wear in the picture. Like a model, Bette came tottering out dressed in each outfit. She would do her little turns whilst trying her best not to fall down, which she somehow managed. When Bette had finished parading, she asked, "Well, what do you think?" I said, "I don't know. Everything is fine, but it all looks the same. Every outfit is black. Why don't we put some color into it? Maybe some scarves, a handkerchief, or even a belt or sash." Suddenly, Bette got furious and said, "Right, everything has got to go! We have to start from scratch and do it all over again!" I said, "No, we don't have to do that. We just have to dress it up a little bit." I remember she was staring intensely at me with those flashing eyes. I said, "Bette, you asked me to give you my opinion. Well, I'm giving you my opinion." She then softened slightly and said, "Okay, fine." I mean, you just had to be firm with her. You certainly couldn't back down because if you did she would smell blood and start running the whole show. As I said, she liked to do things her way, but after a while she conformed and did things my way. I paid no attention whenever she started something.

So, Davis was relaxed on set when you started shooting?

She seemed to be. When we were making the film, we had a beautiful dressing room prepared for Bette and I'd put flowers in there every day. I had taken a guesthouse behind the house that we were shooting in, and fashioned it into a very elaborate area for her. It was gorgeous and had plenty of space for her to lounge around in. I would occasionally visit Bette there and discover that she'd vanished. She would get a chair and sit in the middle of the set when the crew were up on ladders, fastening lights to the ceiling. Cables and lights would be hanging down all around her and she'd just sit calmly beneath them. I'd say, "Bette, if these lights fall they are going to kill you. Why can't you stay in your lovely dressing room?" She said, "Oh, I like to see what's going on." And there she would remain, sitting in the middle of everything, smoking continuously like a chimney. This may sound hard to believe, but Bette would smoke Vantage cigarettes and we would have to get her about ten packs a day. She'd go through them all, and we're talking about 200 cigarettes here! It seems impossible that anyone could smoke that much in a day, but she did. We had a production assistant that would take the cigarettes out of the boxes and put them in ashtrays and glasses. There would be twenty cigarettes in one glass and twenty cigarettes in another glass, positioned all around the set so that Bette wouldn't have to reach into the packet to get one out as she hated fumbling for her cigarettes. She'd smoke one and would immediately segue into the next one, and the next one, and so on. Bette could smoke all day long, constantly, without stopping. Understand, this was a woman who'd had cancer and mastectomies and strokes, but she was still smoking a prodigious amount of cigarettes. I'd say, "Bette, you are doing yourself serious harm. Can't you stop smoking?" She'd say, "Larry, I wouldn't know what to do with myself if I didn't have a cigarette in my hand." If you look at *Wicked Stepmother* now, Bette is basically killing herself before your very eyes. Watching that movie is almost like watching the perfect anti-smoking commercial.

That must have been very distressing to witness.

It was, but you know what? Bette was always on time and she always tried her best. Unfortunately, on top of it all, she also had serious dental problems. Now, anybody could have had dental problems, but she had them before the picture started and didn't tell us about it. Bette didn't confide in me because she didn't want to delay the production. I would have been happy to have delayed the picture so that she could have gotten her teeth fixed. Bette actually had a broken bridge in her mouth. She had a terrible time trying to get the lines out without stopping to readjust her teeth. We were wondering why her performance was so eccentric because she would often stop in the middle of a speech. Of course, she was merely trying to get her teeth back in place. I mean, you can't act if your teeth are falling out. It's hard to say the lines if they are continually being dislodged. Finally, her teeth had disintegrated to such a degree that she couldn't work anymore. So, Bette left, and the situation only became clear to me when I received a letter from her dentist, explaining that she'd gone to New York and her prognosis was not good. Bette not only needed a new bridge to be built but also needed six teeth extracted. This meant she would not be available for work for between ninety and 120 days. Then, I received another letter stating that Bette was down to just 70 lbs and had lost all the weight because she was unable to eat during her treatment. Again, she knew this was a problem before she came to work but had kept it to herself. This caused a disaster later on. But if Bette had just told me about these problems, I would have postponed the picture for a time. However, being Bette, she would not admit that anything was the matter. She was afraid of anything that made her look old, vulnerable, or incapacitated. She thought such perceptions of her would mean she'd be unable to get any insurance and would never work again. By keeping her dental problems to herself, she only compounded them, because when it finally came down to it, Bette simply couldn't get the dialogue out of her mouth. Naturally, that is a serious issue for any actor. So, we had to make a decision. We'd talked several times about re-shooting the whole picture and recasting the part of the witch with somebody like Lucille Ball.[1] When we contacted Ball's agent about the possibility of her replacing Bette, we discovered that she was in the hospital in critical condition. In fact, Ball actually died shortly thereafter. We then briefly considered Carol Burnett[2] for the role. Finally, I said, "Look, we have fifteen minutes of Bette Davis in the can and I think we should keep this material. We are not going to do anything theatrically with this movie, but every video store in America has a Bette Davis section and the chances are we'll sell thousands and thousands of videos. A lot of people are Bette Davis fans and they will want to see this picture. I think this is virtually the only way we can make the money back. Let me rewrite the script and turn Bette's character into Barbara Carrera. I mean, she is a witch after all. She could very easily turn herself into somebody else entirely." So, that's exactly what we did. I didn't throw the footage away and we kept Bette in the picture.

Despite her truncated role as Miranda, Davis still featured largely in the film's advertising and had prominent billing. Were you in any way embarrassed or concerned about trading on her name and image after all that had gone on?

No, not at all. I mean, yes, I did have some thoughts about it, but there were other considerations, too. What's interesting is Bette had been in movies, like *Phone Call from a Stranger*,[3] in which she had played even smaller parts than she did in *Wicked Stepmother*. So, I wasn't ashamed to put the film out with her name on it. Bette had done several cameo roles in various movies before, and her involvement in my picture was now effectively reduced to an extended cameo due to these events. Ultimately, the weakest parts of *Wicked Stepmother* are the scenes that feature Bette because she looked so terrible. It's a shame, but we actually ended up using a lot less of Bette than we could have for that reason. You'd have thought we would have wanted to use every single frame of Bette Davis, but we simply couldn't. It was better if we minimised her role and just got on with the story. The unused material only amounts to a couple of minutes here and there, and is probably sitting somewhere over in the MGM vaults, if somebody hasn't already thrown it out.

Even though Davis is clearly vulnerable and ravaged by illness, she is still a fascinating presence that seems to permeate *Wicked Stepmother*.

Oh, absolutely. Her presence seems to linger over the film even when she isn't on screen. Despite her age and poor health, when she started talking she was still Bette Davis. She still retained that special something that all the true Hollywood greats have. Bette always had incredible anecdotes to tell. She knew I loved to hear about the old days at Warner Bros., so she kept regaling me with these wonderful stories about her career and experiences with the studio. She told me several times how much she liked me, which I can't emphasise enough because Bette didn't have a good thing to say about any of her other directors. She once told me that she thought all of the directors at Warner Bros. were useless, with the exception of William Wyler. Bette claimed that she always had to direct herself and that most of the directors were afraid of her. She actually once said to me, "Larry, I don't want you to be afraid of me because I think you're a great guy." I said, "Don't worry, Bette, I'm not afraid of you. I've directed a lot of your contemporaries, like Celeste Home, Evelyn Keyes, and Sylvia Sidney, and I got along with all of them. I'm just enjoying the opportunity to work with you." And that was the truth. Bette was delightful and was very affectionate towards me. Sadly, it just developed into a sorry situation.

Surely you met with some opposition to casting Davis before shooting started?

Oh, sure. Bette looked so frightening and fragile people actually said to me, "How are you going to make a movie with this woman?" When I first visited her at Havenhurst, my agent accompanied me. Bette was recovering from several strokes and cancer operations at the time, and had lost a lot of weight and was walking with a limp. At one point, my agent took me outside and said, "You cannot make a picture with her in that condition. Are you crazy?" I don't know, maybe I was crazy, but I really believed that I could make the movie with Bette. So, I just persevered with the project, as I had done when people told me I couldn't make a movie about J. Edgar Hoover. But I must also say that if we had not secured Bette for the picture, we would never have gotten *Wicked Stepmother* made in the first place. Having her in it was what convinced MGM to put up the money, but I was able to get the dough we needed without them ever seeing her, not once. I'm thinking that if they had seen her beforehand, MGM probably wouldn't have handed over the $2.5 million.

At what point did the MGM executives see her?

They didn't get a look at Bette until after we began shooting. They started viewing the dailies and as soon as they saw her they were in complete shock: "Oh my god, look at her! She's so frail and old!" What can you say? It was very sad. I mean, this project was a triumph of will power. I wanted to make a movie with Bette, and I insisted I was going to do it, and I did do it. Even though she eventually left, I still made a picture with Bette Davis. Whatever the circumstances were, there are a lot of great directors who can never make that claim. I remember that Bette was later quoted in *The New York Times* as saying, "I have dealt with many directors in my career, but in Larry Cohen I have finally met my Waterloo!" [Laughs] I thought that was cute. I found out that Bette was appearing at the New York Film Festival at Lincoln Center, so I sent a bouquet of flowers to her hotel with a card saying: "From your Waterloo."

How did the rest of the cast react to Davis' departure?

At first, nobody knew why Bette had left, as the cast weren't privy to her dental problems, and neither was I. Many excuses were given as to the reasons why she left, some suggesting she'd been badly treated on set and had suffered a fall and got hurt. All of this was complete nonsense. Bette later admitted this herself when she did the deposition, a sworn statement she had to give for the insurance company. She testified under oath and finally told the truth: her dentures had broken before the movie began and she thought she could get through it and make do with the situation. Being a perfectionist, Bette was mortified that her teeth kept slipping out. She was proud and it drove her crazy that she wasn't able to deliver a performance that met her own high standards. So, Bette had to leave, but she didn't want to admit it to anybody. At first, her lawyers came in and claimed she had been mistreated. Bette also made some unfortunate statements that painted the wrong picture. The cast didn't know anything about this until later. They all thought that the film was going to shutdown and they would receive their walking papers. They had their contracts, so they would have been paid, meaning the insurance company and the completion bond company would have had to eat the entire cost of the picture. I was able to save everybody that money by rewriting the script and changing the premise around: Miranda was now able to use her powers as a witch to transform herself into a beautiful young woman named Priscilla. That way, we were able to finish the movie. Oddly enough, *Wicked Stepmother* actually went into profits and the completion people and the insurance company got their money back, as well as a substantial profit.

Was Priscilla always a separate character in the story? I know that shortly before vanishing from the film, Miranda announces her daughter's arrival.

Yes, Priscilla was always in there and Barbara Carrera was always going to play her. In the original script, Bette had a daughter, who comes to visit her, and the two of them were to feature in the story together. Again, in the revised version, it was a way out for me to have Bette turn into her daughter. So, it really wasn't that much of a change other than taking Bette out of the picture and giving her scenes to somebody else. That was for the best. When Bette later heard we were keeping some of her footage in the film, she was rather upset about it. She hadn't seen *Wicked Stepmother*, but she decided to speak out against the movie anyway. I guess Bette felt like she was trapped in a film that she didn't want to be in. She went on *Entertainment Tonight*, and also spoke to *The New York Times*, and made some disparaging remarks. Later, she came back on TV again and said some things that were not so bad and were rather complimentary to me, actually. She had calmed down a bit at this point and had accepted the fact that we were going to use the footage.

Davis obviously did not want to look ridiculous.

And I understood that. I knew Bette did not like the way she looked in the film. It was bad enough that she looked emaciated and ill, but that might have been acceptable to an audience because she was playing this wicked old witch. Although Bette was having trouble speaking and moving, I shot and edited the picture as best I could to make her look as good as possible. I tried to carefully choreograph her movements around the set and paid close attention to how I was shooting her. I'd walk her from one position to the other, moving the camera at the same time to disguise the limp she had. In some instances where you see Miranda moving rather quickly, we used a double and later inserted shots of Bette to make it appear as if she was more mobile. So, I tried to minimise the negative aspects of her performance, but there was only so much I could do. As we were working during that first week, Bette knew her performance was poor and at one point she asked to see the dailies. I was reluctant to agree to that as I did not want to show her the dailies at all. Finally, we both went into one of the rooms and closed the door behind us. Bette then sat down on the bed and started to cry. I couldn't believe it. Here I was, alone in a room with Bette Davis, and she was crying. It was a sad and surreal experience. She looked up at me and said, "I have to see the dailies, Larry. I have to see what I look like." I now realize she wanted to see what was going on with her teeth, but at the time I had no idea what was troubling her. At that moment, I only saw she was feeling very vulnerable. So, I said, "Okay, Bette, on Saturday I'll run the dailies for you." That weekend, we viewed the dailies together, and when she saw what was going on, Bette never came back again.

How did the younger actors in the cast like Colleen Camp and David Rasche behave around Davis?

Colleen and David wanted to be in the picture because Bette was going to be in it. Let's not forget, whatever state Bette was in, she was still Hollywood royalty. I'm sure they both enjoyed meeting Bette and hanging out with her, although I don't think Bette really had much to do with anybody on the movie except me. She wasn't unfriendly to anybody, but she did spend a little time in her dressing room. If anybody brought friends or relatives to the set to meet her, Bette was always cordial and pleasant. She would sit down with any visitors and chat with them and exchange anecdotes. I wouldn't say that Bette was aloof with the cast members, but she wasn't that chummy with them either. I do recall that one day David Rasche, who was playing the young husband, made the mistake of interfering in a discussion Bette and I were having about blocking a scene. We were having a disagreement about whether she should be standing up or sitting down for the shot when David interrupted us and said, "I think Bette is right about this." As soon as he spoke, Bette turned around and for a moment there was the familiar, strong Bette Davis with the flashing eyes. She suddenly barked at him, "You keep out of this! He is directing this picture! I don't want to hear another sound from you!" I turned to look at David, but he was already gone. Literally, all I saw of him was the last of his heels crossing the door as he exited the room! [Laughs] All it took was a few sharp words from Bette, but she could do that. She wasn't going to tolerate interference from anybody, certainly not from an actor who was telling me how to direct my movie. David was playing sides with Bette, but she was definitely on my team all the way. I should add that Bette chose Colleen Camp for the role of the housewife. We had a casting session, but Bette selected Colleen because she liked her, and I liked her, too. Bette also requested Lionel Stander to play the part of the widower she marries. So, I went out and got Lionel and put him in the picture. That also made me happy because I was always a big fan of Lionel's work. I must also say that one of the many things that fascinated me about Bette was her amazing ability to zero-in on other people's deficiencies.

Can you give me an example of that ability?

[Chuckles] Well, I remember we had the first reading of the script over at my house. Afterwards, Bette took me aside and said that Lionel was deaf. I said, "That's okay, Bette, he's still a wonderful actor. Don't worry about it." I mean, there she was, barely able to stand up without hanging on my arm, and she was telling me that Lionel had a severe deficiency! Later on, I suggested that we hire Paul Henreid to do a cameo in the movie. The idea was that he could appear as the ghost of the witch's ex-husband. I thought Henreid could've had two cigarettes dangling from his mouth as a takeoff on the famous scene he and Bette shared together in *Now, Voyager*.[4] I thought it would be fun to reunite them on screen, but Bette suddenly said, "Oh, have you seen him lately? Paul can't be photographed! He's in terrible condition!" I couldn't believe what I was hearing. There was Bette swaying in front of me, looking like she'd just crawled out of a coffin, and she was telling me I couldn't hire Paul Henreid because his appearance was so awful! Another time, I asked Bette about Lillian Gish, with whom she had just co-starred in *The Whales of August*.[5] Bette said, "They complained that I deliberately lowered my voice so that Lillian couldn't hear her cues. She's so deaf I could have shouted my lines out of a bullhorn and she would never have heard me!" So, as you can see, Bette was merciless about other people's weaknesses but completely oblivious of her own.

Speaking of ghosts, a neat touch is having the photograph of Jenny's mother on the dresser which of course is a picture of Davis' great rival, Joan Crawford.

Actually, that was not in the original script, and when Bette saw that shot in the dailies, she was very upset. She thought I was trying to put something over on her and I don't know why. I suspect it probably had something to do with *Mommie Dearest*,[6] a book that had been written by Joan Crawford's daughter saying what a terrible person Crawford had been. Bette's own daughter, B.D.,[7] then went and wrote a scathing book about her saying what a terrible mother Bette had been. Somehow, a connection had been formed in Bette's mind between the criticism of her own motherhood and the shot of Crawford's photograph. She thought I was making some kind of personal comment on the raising of her child and, of course, I wasn't. Bette wasn't even on speaking terms with her daughter anymore, but that book was very damaging. I don't think Bette ever really recovered from the hurt of it. Although I must say, long after that book had been published and even though the two had been estranged for some years, Bette still had pictures of B.D. on the mantelpiece in her apartment. I guess Bette still harbored hopes of reconciling with her daughter someday.

How confident were you during shooting that you would be able to cobble together a workable film?

Oh, I always believed that *Wicked Stepmother* would come out alright after Bette had gone, because I still had a reasonably coherent story to tell. But if I had known that Bette was going to drop out of the picture I would have shot more of her scenes during the first week. I now regret that I shot other people's scenes while Bette was sitting in the dressing room, doing nothing but smoking. I could have had as much as twenty-five minutes of Bette if I'd only shot nothing but her scenes all week long. As it was, I believe we only had around fifteen to twenty minutes of her—perhaps a little less—but I could not have anticipated what was going to happen. I wish I could have received some kind of clue. I thought she was going to be on the picture for the entire four-week shoot, so I continued with the schedule as I ordinarily would have done.

After Miranda vanishes, you tie up the loose end by having the Witch Instructor reveal that two witches can't occupy the same body at the same time.

I tried to fashion some logic out of the whole situation by having Evelyn Keyes come in as this witch expert. If you watch any movies about witches, like *Bell, Book and Candle* and *I Married a Witch*, there is always a lot of nonsense about the rules of witchcraft. My feeling is that the rules of witchcraft are pretty much anything you want to make them. Witches are flexible creatures and can be altered and reconfigured in order to fit the story you want to tell. I tried to do a takeoff on *The Wizard of Oz* in the scene where the housewife throws a bucket of water over Priscilla, only for Priscilla to say, "This is reality not MGM, Dorothy!" I wanted to make fun of the regulations and rituals of witchcraft, but also recognize the fact that movies have impacted on the way witches are portrayed in works of fiction. Even though legends and tales of witches have existed for thousands of years, movies have also contributed to their mythology in some amusing and interesting ways. I mean, our picture even has a black cat smoking a cigarette! [Laughs] That's got to be a first, right?

Why, immediately before Davis makes her first appearance in *Wicked Stepmother*, did you insert explicit references to two of horror cinema's most recognizable boogeymen, Freddy Krueger and Jason Voorhees?

That was one of several tricks I used. That scene was supposed to be from the point of view of the housewife after she discovers that this horrible old woman has married her father and moved into her home. In her mind it's exactly like having Freddy or Jason in her midst. The other purpose of doing that was to juice the scene up a little since Bette's appearance was so shocking. I felt there had to be some kind of transition or diversion that would soften that shock for the audience. I thought the sight of her would be particularly alarming for those viewers who hadn't seen Bette onscreen for a while and remembered her somewhat differently. I thought if I cut in those shots of Freddy and Jason, maybe we'd get a laugh and the audience would relax a little and accept Bette's appearance. It really was disturbing to first see her, even for me. I can recall seeing Bette at the Golden Globes ceremony a couple of months before I wrote the script. She came on stage to present an award and was literally dragging her leg behind her. Bette was still suffering the facial paralysis from her stroke and she looked dreadful. Frankly, the audience were stunned that night and just couldn't believe what they were seeing. I mean, you could really feel it in the room. In fact, sitting at the next table to mine was Barbara Stanwyck. I glanced over at Stanwyck and noticed that she'd clasped a hand over her mouth and was visibly gasping. Stanwyck wasn't in the best of health herself at this point and actually died pretty soon afterwards of emphysema, but she still looked rather good. But Bette looked frightening and, oddly enough, Stanwyck was a star before Bette had even made any movies. However, Stanwyck never reached Bette's iconic standing and level of acceptance. Bette Davis was, unequivocally, the queen of Hollywood.

You just mentioned that you employed "several tricks" to soften Davis' first appearance in the film. Exactly what were they?

I tried to cram a lot of stuff in at the beginning of the movie to build up the witch's character and reputation before you saw her, making her almost this legendary figure. I did this because, again, I knew everybody would be disturbed by the sight of Bette. During the prologue, Tom Bosley plays a detective, who arrives at this house to investigate the disappearance of a family who were previously associated with the witch. I put in several lines of dialogue where characters are saying things like, "She's a horrible-looking old woman," and "She could be a hundred years old." All of this was designed to anticipate Bette's first appearance onscreen. I know all of this might sound a little extreme, but the strong reactions I had witnessed to Bette's appearance convinced me that I had to do something. I also wrote the scene where there is a police line-up of old women who've been brought in by the cops to apprehend this witch. I figured that these old women looked pretty bad themselves. My reasoning was that Bette might not look so bad herself after the audience had seen this parade of elderly ladies. Honestly, these were all considerations that we made. I was trying everything to lessen the impact of Bette's first appearance, but I guess I failed in that respect because everybody still kept endlessly talking about the way Bette looked.

Did you encourage the actors to go all out in their performances?

In a comedy, everything is always heightened and a bit of an exaggeration, so the genre invites that kind of colorful performance. There's always the danger that an actor will push it too far, but I thought all the performances in *Wicked Stepmother* were nicely measured and in keeping with the tone and mood. The fascinating thing about comedy is that when you encourage actors to go a little crazy and be inventive, you can achieve a real spontaneity and freshness. You can still achieve those improvisational effects when everything is tightly scripted and choreographed, but it isn't as much fun to do. I'd always intended to surround Bette with accomplished comedic actors because I thought that environment would bring out the best in her. The entire supporting cast did do a fine job and I still think that *Wicked Stepmother* is the best part Colleen Camp has ever played in a movie. David Rasche and Tom Bosley had done a lot of comedy before *Wicked Stepmother* and were very adept at it. As for Lionel Stander, it was all pretty effortless for him. I mean, Lionel had worked with some of the greats like Carole Lombard, Katherine Hepburn and Gene Arthur. He'd enjoyed a long and successful career. Lionel was even in *A Star is Born* with Janet Gaynor! I have these old newspapers from the day I was born and as it happens Lionel was actually appearing in a movie that was playing on Broadway at the Capital Theater the very day I came into the world. I know Lionel also enjoyed working with Laurene Landon, who played the game-show hostess. He was very taken with Laurene and her comedic abilities. Lionel actually told me that he thought Laurene had the potential to be a huge star, and he'd know because he'd worked with most of them.

How much of the budget was spent on the special effects for the climactic showdown between Jenny [Colleen Camp] and Priscilla?

It wasn't a great deal of the money as we didn't have a huge effects budget. In fact, it was the kind of budget where you only got to make everything once! We didn't get an opportunity to go back and do things over and over again like on big Hollywood films. Whatever we got on the first pass, that was what we had to live with as there was no time or money to finesse things. I think the special effects in the movie are not too bad. Yes, they are a bit hokey and ropey, but *Wicked Stepmother* is a comedy. It's not a realistic, literal production, and, in those terms, the effects fitted the wackiness of the whole film in a rather loose, self-conscious way. What I mean is, on one level, the effects needed to be a little cheesy. And I don't say that to hide the incompetence of some special effects people, who can often seriously fuck up your movie.

Were you generally sympathetic to the demands you placed on special effects artists toiling under the constraints of your low-budget productions?

Firstly, let me just say that it's amazing how much incompetence there is in the special effects business in terms of the quality of the work that sometimes comes in. I've had experiences where the effects are delivered and they are neither good nor suitable. What would always annoy me was when an artist would come in with a particular makeup or an effect and say, "I know this isn't quite right, but I wanted you to see it." I would then inevitably reply, "If you knew it wasn't right, why did you do it in the first place? Why bring me something that you know is not good? Are you doing this to intentionally get me upset? Go away and fix it!" Then certain individuals would approach me and say, "Larry, you are mistreating the special effects people. You were so nasty to that guy." In my defence I would argue, "How can I not be nasty to him when he brings me something that he already knows is deficient?" When you are making a low-budget movie, you can ill afford to waste time and money looking at something that is clearly wrong. Fix it, make it right, and then bring it in! That level of incompetence amazes me, but that's the way some people are. When you are fighting a tight schedule, and have little money, you'd prefer it if the artists brought you stuff that they know is done to the best of their ability. Why would anybody want my observations on something they've already acknowledged is a failure? It's crazy!

Were you happy with the shot of the miniaturised people in the shoebox?

There are a number of things I like about *Wicked Stepmother*, but that shot isn't one of them. I wanted the movie to open with somebody discovering a shoebox full of these tiny people—all of them victims of this witch—calling for help. I thought it would be an interesting scene, but that's another thing that could have been done better. We built an oversized shoebox set and put a big shoe in it along with some actors and shot it from overhead, high up on a crane. It wasn't entirely successful, but for the money we had to spend it looked okay. That was the first big effects shot of the movie and I wanted it to look good. Unfortunately, we didn't have the money to matte Tom Bosley's hands into the shot, so that it looked as if a huge pair of hands were holding the shoebox. That would have certainly added more value to the shot.

The film ends with the detective and his vehicle shrinking as they drive along a highway. He then looks into camera and says, "I suppose this

means there's a sequel." Judging by the reviews, most critics hoped there wouldn't be one.

I'm sure that's true. I really expected the entire audience to yell back at the screen, "That's what you think!" [Chuckles] To be honest, I hardly saw any reviews of the picture. If you have any reviews please send them to me because I didn't read any of them. I'm sure that a lot of the people who lambasted *Wicked Stepmother* didn't even see the movie. They probably thought that because Bette left the picture, there must have been something seriously wrong with it. If they'd actually watched the film, they might have found it enjoyable. Many of the contemporary articles were more concerned with Bette's departure and not the picture's overall quality. I certainly read a lot of that stuff. Everybody seemed to have an opinion that *Wicked Stepmother* was not up to her usual standards and that she had been mishandled. There was never much published about Bette's dental problems, because I chose not to respond in public to any of her remarks or those made by other people. I didn't want to attack Bette or do anything that might prevent her from making another movie. Perhaps somebody else would have hired Bette after her teeth were fixed and I didn't want to say anything bad. I liked Bette, and even our last conversation on the phone before she left, was very friendly. She actually apologized and never accused me of anything. She said, "Larry, I've made a terrible mistake and I can't continue." If only she had come to me before and told me about them. I would not have fired her. I would have listened and tried to find a resolution to this situation that satisfied everybody. That would have been better than Bette basically trying to deceive me. Bette prided herself on being a totally frank and honest individual. She was from New England and had that New England attitude of, "Hey, I'm right up front. I'm a straight-shooter and I always tell it the way it is." Unfortunately, she didn't always tell it the way it is. She misled me into thinking she could do the part when she knew that she couldn't. She tried to get through it and then, when that proved impossible, she tried to get out of it by blaming me in public. Of course, some journalists knew the facts and reported her version, as well as the truth. I just kept my mouth shut. All I said was: "A lot of people give Bette Davis testimonials and awards and honors, but I gave her a job."

Some critics have suggested that Davis' final performance should have been in Lindsay Anderson's *The Whales of August* rather than *Wicked Stepmother*.

I agree, *The Whales of August* should have been her final film, even though Bette looked pretty bad in that one, too. She played a blind woman who was mostly confined to a chair, so she didn't have to walk around and do very much. *The Whales of August* was a quality picture, but I think *Wicked Stepmother* is far from the worst movie Bette ever made. If you look at the films she made over the years, Bette was involved in some real stinkers. I remember one awful movie she did with Ernest Borgnine where they played two elderly folks dressed as hippies who basically just rode around on a motorcycle.[8] So, Bette made quite a number of bad pictures that she wasn't proud of. She was always looking around for employment and did several television pilots that never got on, including one shot in England called *Madame Sin* in which she played an evil Chinese woman. Let's face it, even though Bette had been one of the biggest stars in the history of motion pictures, at this late stage of her career she desperately needed a job. In fact, Bette didn't have a great deal of money when she died. She left around $1 million, which included her apartment and that was probably worth $750,000. So Bette only had something like $250,000 in the whole world, which she left to her stepson and to her secretary, Kathryn Sermak. A lot of people in Hollywood have accumulated vast fortunes over the years—some people are even billionaires—but Bette had fairly little to show for her career, except for all those wonderful movies she'd made at Warner Bros. She was more than happy about the $250,000 she was getting for *Wicked Stepmother*. But there's no getting away from the fact she had accepted a lot of very poor roles over the years. I guess *Wicked Stepmother* is historically significant because it was the last picture Bette ever made. She died the following year in Paris after attending a film festival.

Is it safe to assume you have no regrets about making *Wicked Stepmother*?

None whatsoever. I'm glad I made the film, despite all the chaos and subterfuge that went on. If I had to do it all again I would, because I enjoyed having Bette as an acquaintance and having her at least appear to like me. I certainly liked her. I guess that, ultimately, it was my fault because I was the one who hired her. I was the one who insisted on going ahead and making *Wicked Stepmother* with Bette despite certain people advising me against it. I've thought a lot about this over the years and I now realize that on one level I simply couldn't accept the fact that Bette Davis could no longer be in movies. I was such a big fan of hers, maybe I just wanted to prove all those people wrong. I wanted to bring some of that old magic back to the movies.

Cohen poses with Anne Carlisle on the set of *Perfect Strangers*. Photo courtesy of Larry Cohen.

Cohen gives the cameraman the hairy eyeball during the filming of *Special Effects* in New York. Photo courtesy of Larry Cohen.

The late, great stop-motion animator, David Allen, readies a shot on the manually-operated revolving set of *The Stuff*. Photo courtesy of Steve Neil.

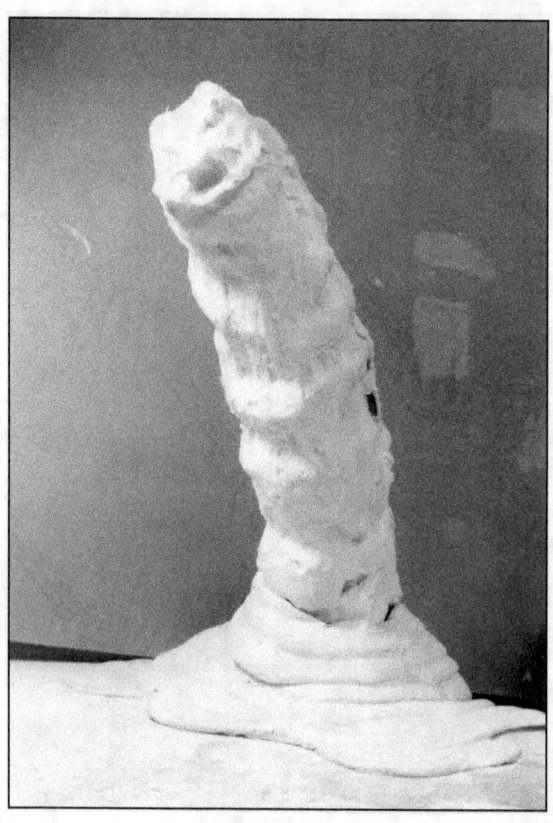

The Stuff—poised to strike!
Photo courtesy of Steve Neill.

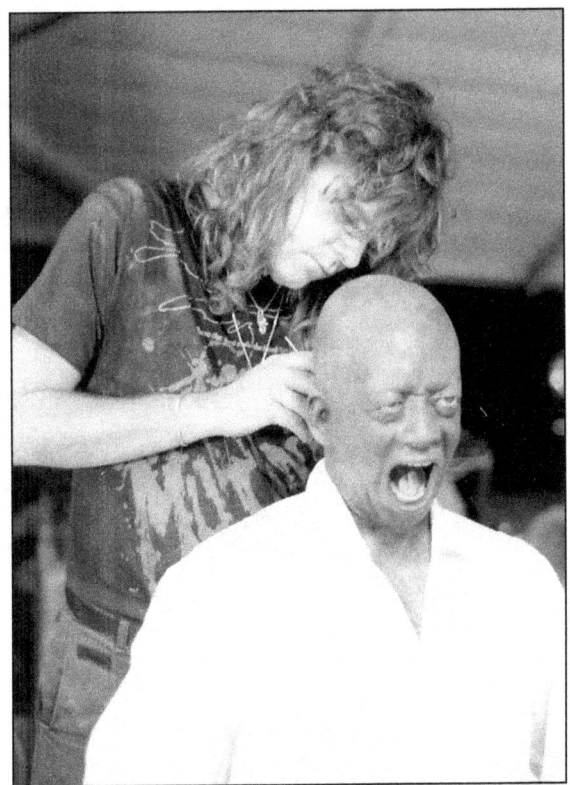

The FX crew prepare Garrett Morris's fake head and body for the gruesome death of "Chocolate Chip" Charlie in *The Stuff*. Photo courtesy of Steve Neill.

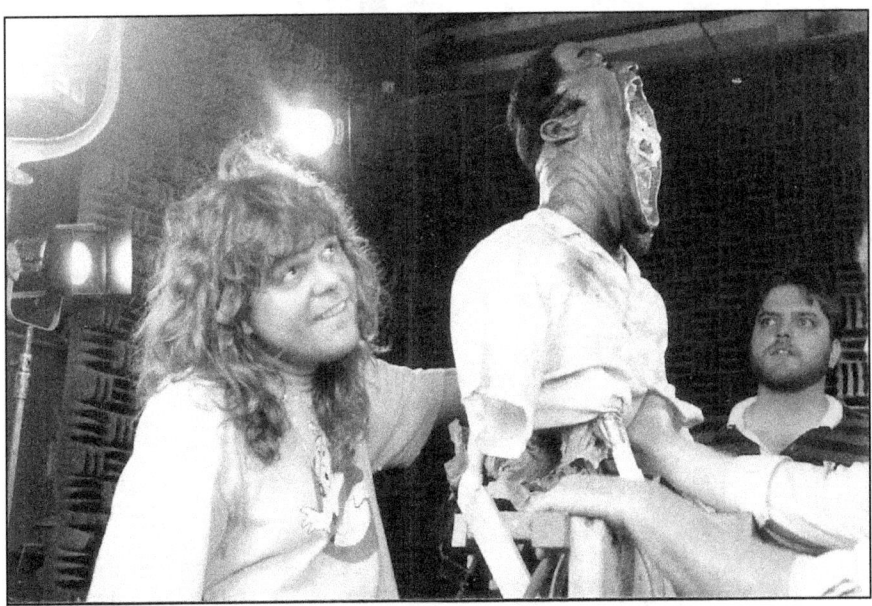

FX technicians operate the fake head and body on the set of *The Stuff*. Photo courtesy of Steve Neill.

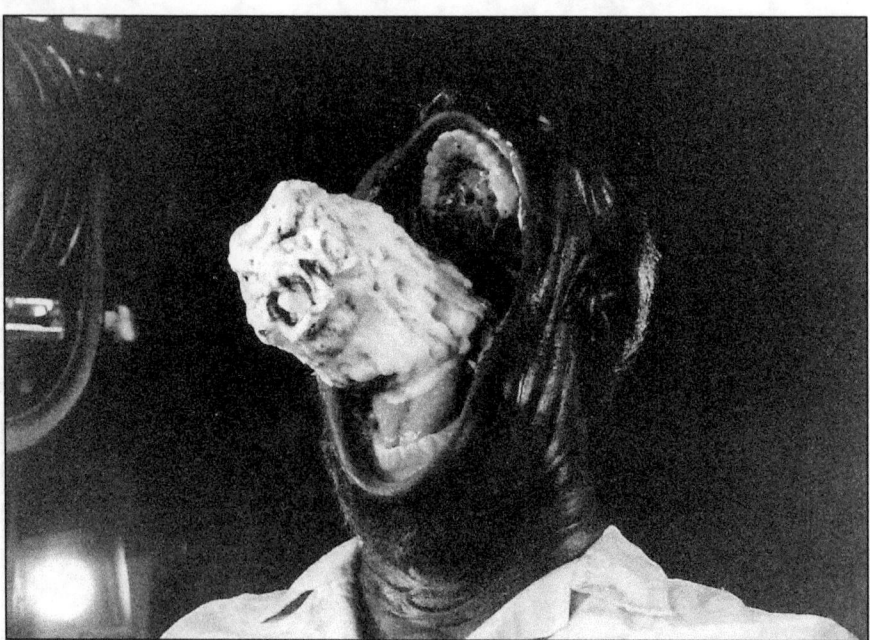

The Stuff emerges from Charlie's mouth. Photo courtesy of Steve Neill.

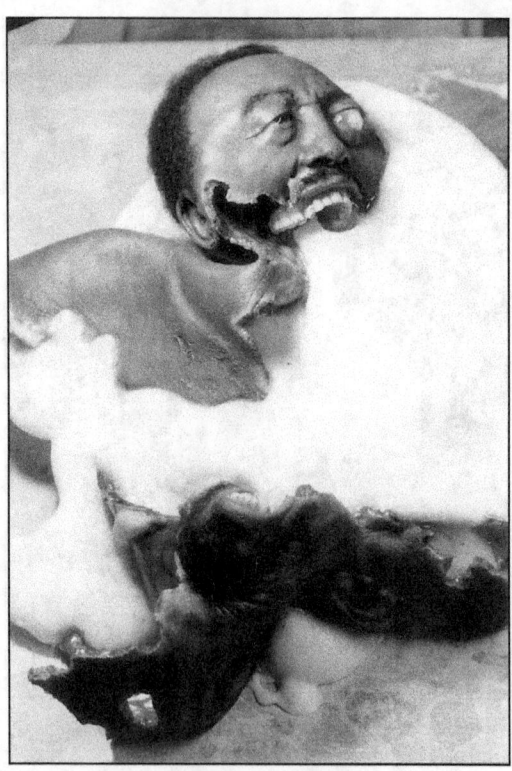

"Are you eating it or is it eating you?" Charlie's shattered remains after he is consumed by *The Stuff*. Photo courtesy of Steve Neill.

An "awful movie": Cohen and Billy Dee Williams during happier times on the troubled set of *Deadly Illusion*. Photo courtesy of Larry Cohen.

Cohen, Laurene Landon and Michael Moriarty in bed together on the set of *It's Alive III: Island of the Alive*. Photo courtesy of Larry Cohen.

Cohen directs Sam Fuller in Peacham, Vermont, during the shooting of *A Return to Salem's Lot*. Photo courtesy of Larry Cohen.

The fully-transformed Judge Axel shows his true face in *A Return to Salem's Lot*. Photo courtesy of Steve Neill.

Cohen takes a call in his office. Photo courtesy of Larry Cohen.

"Bette is Bad Again": The poster for *Wicked Stepmother* featuring Bette Davis and Barbara Carrera. Photo courtesy of Larry Cohen.

Cohen and Bette Davis on the set of *Wicked Stepmother*. The air of calm and delectation would soon come to an abrupt end. Photo courtesy of Larry Cohen.

A delighted Cohen with Bette Davis and Lionel Stander shortly before Davis' sudden departure from *Wicked Stepmother*. Photo courtesy of Larry Cohen.

Cohen with Eric Roberts during the shooting of *The Ambulance* on the streets of New York. Photo courtesy of Larry Cohen.

Cohen and James Earl Jones lying in the gutters of Lower Manhattan, trying to cool off between set-ups on *The Ambulance*. Photo courtesy of Larry Cohen.

Cohen with his second wife, Cynthia Costas Cohen, a successful therapist in Beverly Hills. Photo courtesy of Larry Cohen.

Cohen with his friend, the immortal Vincent Price. Photo courtesy of Larry Cohen.

Cohen nestled comfortably amongst the iconic monsters that have crawled, creeped, and killed in his movies. Photo courtesy of Larry Cohen.

Promotional poster art for *The Man Who Loved Hitchcock* featuring Sir Peter Ustinov, who was set to play the legendary director. Photo courtesy of Larry Cohen.

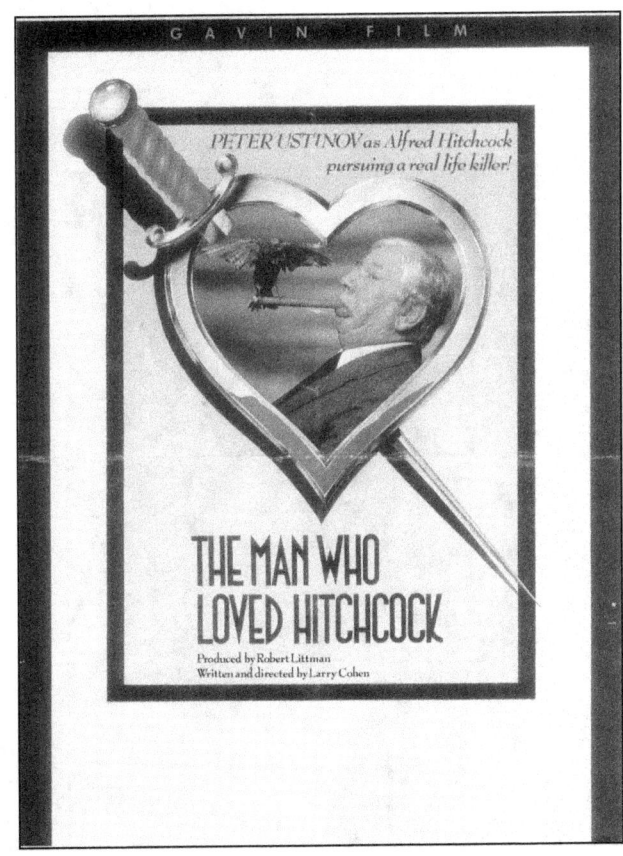

A promo shot of Cohen from the 1990s. Photo courtesy of Larry Cohen.

Cohen with Sanford Meisner. The Sanford Meisner Center later mounted Cohen's stageplay, *Fallen Eagle*. Photo courtesy of Larry Cohen.

Cohen with Oscar-winners Robert Benigni and Red Buttons.
Photo courtesy of Larry Cohen.

Cohen with movie mogul Samuel Z. Arkoff, co-founder of American International Pictures. "I have usurped Sam's trademark cigar," Cohen remarks of this picture.
Photo courtesy of Larry Cohen.

Cohen on the set of *Phone Booth* with director Joel Schumacher and producer Gil Netter. Photo courtesy of Larry Cohen.

Cohen on the set of *Phone Booth* with Colin Farrell. Photo courtesy of Larry Cohen.

Cohen in front of 20th Century Fox studios shortly before the release of *Phone Booth*. Photo courtesy of Larry Cohen.

Cohen hangs out with legendary Italian director Dario Argento during one of the *Masters of Horror* dinners held periodically in a "reasonably priced restaurant" somewhere in Los Angeles. Photo courtesy of Larry Cohen.

Cohen with filmmakers Adam Rifkin, Mick Garris, Katt Shea, Mary Lambert, Si Litvinoff, Ken Russell, and Russell's wife, Lisa Tribble, during a *Masters of Horror* gathering in 2010. Photo courtesy of Mick Garris.

Cohen at another *Masters of Horror* dinner. Amongst those pictured with him are Paul Thomas Anderson, Quentin Tarantino, Joe Dante, Frank Darabont, Mick Garris, Don Coscarelli, Stuart Gordon, Tom Holland, Adam Wingard, Ernest Dickerson, Adam Green, Axelle Carolyn, David Arquette, Ti West, and Laurene Landon. Photo courtesy of Mick Garris.

Intermission: *The Heavy* (1990)

When we discussed *Q - The Winged Serpent*, you briefly alluded to a film called *The Heavy*, which you started shooting in October 1990 but then shutdown. Can you reveal more about what this movie was or might have been?

The Heavy was a script that I wrote especially for David Carradine. It was basically a tribute to all the great movie heavies, you know, all those mean-looking actors that you've seen in hundreds of films. You know their faces, but you can never remember their names. These actors are always playing the bad guys, and you see them on screen all the time, and you get used to them. You say, "Oh look, there's that same guy again! Who the hell is he?" These nameless faces usually have long careers in the movie business. They've never made much money, but they appear in lots of pictures. They are the men who are constantly getting killed by every major star, because heroes always need villains to dispatch. In this particular film, David was playing a character, who is a long-time movie heavy, not unlike his father, John Carradine, who was a famous movie heavy.[1] This guy's career is going nowhere, and so he decides to leave Hollywood and go back to New Jersey where his family lives. As he is driving across country, he gets mixed up in a real-life crime that occurs in this small town. People recognize his distinctive face, as he is this mean-looking guy. The townsfolk are sure they have seen him somewhere before although he is a perfect stranger. Anyway, this actor becomes embroiled in a dangerous situation and ends up having to play the hero and solve the crime. The heavy wins the first fight he's ever had where he didn't have to lose, because every villain must lose a fistfight or get killed in a gunfight. That's the general law of movies, it seems. But on this occasion, the heavy gets to win the girl, save the day, and turn everything around in these strange set of circumstances he finds himself in while en route across the United States.

Were you excited and enthused to be making the movie?

Oh, yeah. *The Heavy* was a very good script and it would have made a very good movie. Of course, the story doesn't work so well anymore because of the advent of the Internet. The fact of the matter is that the heavy would probably be able to very quickly identify himself to the townspeople using a computer or one of these new-fangled cell phones. If I was going to make *The Heavy* now, I would set the story back around 1970. Back in those days, there were great movie heavies and there were great movie heroes. It's like I told you before—and it's very true—today, there are no great movie heroes anymore. Now everybody is an anti-hero.

Several articles published in November 1990 reported that "differences between Cohen and Carradine came to a head during an arm-waving and shouting match on Halloween evening."[2] You indicated to me in an earlier interview that *The Heavy* fell apart due to Carradine's behavior.

Yeah, he was drunk. That's the simplest way of putting it. I hate to speak ill of the dead, but David arrived drunk and he stayed drunk. He just became very difficult to deal with. I told David that I had written the script especially for him as a gesture of our long friendship. I thought his behavior on *The Heavy* was inexcusable, particularly since I'd gone to all the trouble to do this for him. I quickly realized that the biggest favor I could possibly do for David was to fire him, so he could then go into rehab and wouldn't be drinking all the time. So, after just two days of shooting, I'd had enough. I just closed the film down.

What were the immediate consequences of your hastily terminating the production after two days of shooting?

Well, I managed to get the insurance company to pay off most of the losses by claiming that alcoholism was an illness as defined by the American Medical Association. I basically argued that I had to close the production down for medical reasons, because David's drunkenness was indeed a medical problem. In order to keep from going to court on this situation and setting a precedent, this was obviously a delicate matter. I mean, it might have cost the insurance companies an absolute fortune if every drunken actor could be fired, because there are plenty of them around in Hollywood. The insurance company eventually did pay off the majority of the losses on the picture and I got out of *The Heavy* alright in the end. In fact, when I left the production in New Mexico, I travelled to Tucson, Arizona, which was fairly close by. There was a convention of criminal attorneys congregating there, and, after we got talking, they kindly invited me to dinner. So, I sat with all these lawyers and we started discussing various legal matters. It was fascinating, and I actually got the idea for *Guilty as Sin* from those conversations. It's certainly true that I would never have gotten the inspiration for that screenplay, or had the opportunity to later work with Sydney Lumet, had I not fired Carradine and closed down *The Heavy*. So, it all worked out spectacularly well in the end because I ended up selling *Guilty as Sin* for a lot of money.

You may have survived the termination of *The Heavy* intact, but certain members of the cast and crew were reportedly "gloomy and crying" upon learning that the film was being shutdown, as was the manager of the local Palomino Hotel where the company were staying during the shoot. He was expecting his rooms to be occupied for the next three or four weeks.

What can I say? It was a highly unfortunate situation and I was also very upset about it at the time. It certainly wasn't a decision I made lightly, but it was an entirely necessary one. There was no other alternative, really. I'm sorry that certain people were upset about what happened, but I don't have any regrets about it. I did what I thought was the right thing to do. Honestly, I simply could not do my best work under those conditions. I would not have been able to deliver a good movie, that's for sure.

Who co-starred with Carradine in *The Heavy*?

Uh, I don't really remember. Let me think. [Pause] Oh, there was Robert Carradine, David's brother, and then there was Keith Carradine, David's other brother.[3] So, all three Carradine brothers were going to be in the picture.

Had the other Carradine brothers arrived on set by the time you closed the film?

Bobby Carradine was there when it all happened, but Keith had not yet arrived. As a matter of fact, I had to pay Bobby his entire fee because he would not relinquish it. After we closed *The Heavy* down, he wanted to be paid and I had to pay him his whole salary.

How did Robert Carradine feel about the whole situation? Was he allied with his brother?

Well, Bobby certainly knew what was going on. He knew David was drunk all the time but, naturally, he wouldn't admit it. Bobby just said that he wanted to be paid in full for his services, even though we had only shot for two days. So, we paid him.

As you revealed to me previously, David Carradine later tried to make amends by offering you the chance to direct an episode of *Kung Fu: The Legend Continues*. That series ran between 1993 and 1997, so it was a few years before you and he patched up your differences.

Yeah, it took a little while. After I did the firing on *The Heavy*, and the dust from all the recriminations that inevitably followed had settled, we were able to talk again. It was a few years later, when David wrote me the apology letter saying he was sorry. That's when he stopped by my house a couple of times, rang the doorbell, and came in. We settled our differences and were on friendly terms again—that was until the final encounter we had at Paramount studios, when David was inexplicably obnoxious again. I guess that was the parting of the ways for us because the next thing I heard he was dead over in Thailand. Frankly, I think David was murdered by a pimp or a prostitute. There was no way he committed suicide. I mean, that was just complete nonsense. There is no way that he hung himself in a closet, particularly whilst wearing women's clothes. I'm almost certain he was murdered.

What makes you believe that?

They have these prostitutes over in Thailand, who appear to be beautiful women, but they are actually men. What these people sometimes do is they accompany you back to your hotel room and then beat you up and rob you. Of course, afterwards you are too ashamed to go to the police because you have brought a man up to your room who you mistakenly believed was a woman. Sometimes, these individuals come in pairs, and I suspect what probably happened that night is David fought back against his attackers and was killed. David was physically capable but if he was drunk or doped-up or drugged, he would not have been able to put up as good a fight as he might have done. I think somebody tried to rob him and he was murdered as a result. That's just my opinion. I have no proof, but there is no way that Carradine was going to kill himself. He was doing a movie over there and was working. I mean, nothing ever bothered the guy, at least not the things that sweat most people. When the tax people were following David around everywhere and were heavily on his back, it never mattered to him. He couldn't have given a fuck! He just moved on to a different house or a different apartment and everything always rolled right off him. There is simply no way that a guy like that would have ever killed himself.

The Ambulance (1991)

There have been several horror films and thrillers such as *Duel*, *The Car*, *The Hearse* and *Christine* that have centred on murderous vehicles. Were you consciously steering into this familiar territory with *The Ambulance* or were you drawing inspiration from someplace else?

I was coming from somewhere else. As with *It's Alive* and *The Stuff*, *The Ambulance* began with the concept of taking something that is thought of as being benign or benevolent, such as a baby, or ice cream, or anything else that has a safe and wholesome image, and turning it into an object of terror. I was again taking a positive and turning it into a negative, as I had also done in my script for *Maniac Cop*. A police officer is a symbol of justice that is meant to protect and save you from criminals, but in *Maniac Cop* the police officer turns out to be evil and kills you. I realized that when you hear or see an ambulance on the street, it's usually considered to be something that is going to rescue you and take care of you, a vehicle of mercy. In this story, it's actually a vehicle of murder. The whole idea of an ambulance that suddenly arrives from nowhere, picks people up, and takes them away to some dark place where they are never seen or heard of again was completely original and creepy. That was the basic idea of the movie, rather than a revisiting of the other car pictures you mentioned which were more concerned with the supernatural in some way. Those vehicles were possessed by some kind of spirit or entity and were driving around on their own. That was not what my movie was about. Personally, I didn't like *The Car* at all, but I thought *Christine* was very good, although a little ridiculous. Of course, Steven Spielberg's *Duel* was excellent.

I understand that your script was at one time titled *Into Thin Air*.

That's right. The producers were of the opinion that *The Ambulance* was not a particularly classy and sophisticated title for a movie, so they wanted something else. I then came up with *Into Thin Air*, which I didn't think was quite as strong but we needed something in there. The producers thought that a different title would attract a higher caliber of actor to the project, which could only be a good thing. They were concerned that a picture called *The Ambulance* would be perceived as an exploitation movie and nothing more. Ultimately, good sense prevailed and we went back to our original title. I thought that was the right thing to do, as *The Ambulance* was a more direct and intriguing title. Also, the image of the vehicle itself would be an effective one to use in the ads.

Like *It's Alive*, *The Stuff*, and *Maniac Cop*, *The Ambulance* also reasserts your suspicion of authorities and institutions, in this case the medical profession.

Well, you must know that there are a lot of mistakes made in the name of medicine. People frequently enter hospitals, which are scary places at the best of times, and never come out alive. In America, there is a very high rate of patients going to the hospital for one thing and inadvertently catching some other disease whilst there due to the failure to exercise proper sanitary precautions. I mean, these patients are dying! There are also the operations that go wrong. Some surgeons are so busy—and are so committed to making money—they are performing three or four surgeries a day, perhaps more, one after the other. After a while, they must get physically tired and a little careless and that's when mistakes are made. There is so much money to be made by putting somebody into surgery, what with the insurance in America and the overpricing of medical care. An operation here will cost you $500,000, more money than anybody's got. Of course, the U.S. Government is paying for it through medical insurance, and so they rip everybody off. And yet people still come here from all over the world for their surgeries and procedures because American medicine is considered to be the best. So, yeah, I do have a suspicion of the medical profession. I've always said the reason that doctors wear masks is to prevent you from identifying them after the operation. They only wear gloves because they don't want to leave any fingerprints behind! [Laughs] It's true, you just don't know who the hell is in there with you! When I was a kid, I remember seeing a British movie called *Green for Danger*. It starred Alistair Sim as a detective, who is investigating a murder that has taken place in an English hospital during the bombings of World War II. The killer was dressed in medical clothes and had a mask on, and I remember being terrified when I saw that figure standing in the corridor wearing the mask. I'm sure I carried the disturbing memory of that image with me when I was making *The Ambulance*.

Did you specify a certain model of ambulance in the script?

Yeah, I always wanted it to be an old-fashioned ambulance. The new ambulances are all square and resemble boxes on wheels. They didn't look sleek or interesting and I was looking for something that was more photogenic and scary. Of course, I realized that was wholly inaccurate as those kinds of ambulances were no longer on the road anymore, but that's what we used. There might have been one or two private ambulance services that were still using them, but that type of vehicle was probably in service during the 1960s and into the early 1970s.

I suspect that—in your time-honored tradition—you stole more unauthorized shots on the New York streets for the opening sequence, where comic book artist Josh Baker [Eric Roberts] makes a play for Janine Turner's character?

Oh yeah, we stole a lot of shots on Fifth Avenue in front of large crowds of thousands of people during the lunch hour. We actually built a twenty-foot platform above the street that resembled some kind of construction site. We then put the camera up on the platform and covered it up with tarpaulin so that people couldn't see it. We poked the camera out through the covering and used a long lens. We were then able to photograph right down the street and this allowed us to get some good shots without anybody realizing there was a camera crew up there. The actors just performed their dialogue and actions out on the street and it was a fun way to do the scene. We also shot the moments where Janine Turner collapses in the street in front of everybody and the ambulance pulls up at the side of the road and takes her away. This operation was not particularly difficult to co-ordinate, not for me anyway, as I was used to shooting that way. As a matter of fact, that is the same street corner where I filmed Fred Williamson getting shot and falling down in *Black Caesar*—right at that very same corner. For me, it was like revisiting one of my old locations again, the scene of the crime! [Chuckles] That whole sequence in

The Ambulance only took a day to shoot. It would have probably taken a regular movie company a week to get.

Why did you decide to make Josh a comic book artist?

I thought it was the kind of occupation people tend not to take seriously. I mean, there are those who might react with incredulity to this guy's claims—that he witnessed these strange and disturbing events. They may even say, "Oh, you are making this whole thing up in your head because you've got a comic book mentality. All this stuff about a girl disappearing and an old-fashioned ambulance prowling the streets isn't real." I thought that by making him a comic book artist we would also give him the ability to draw pictures of this missing girl that he could show people. On top of all that, there are several references to the Archie Andrews comic book series in the film.[1] There's a running gag about Jim Dixon's character resembling Jughead, the jerky-looking guy who is Archie's best friend in the comics. We also had the idea of having a girl in the story that looked like Veronica, another character from the *Archie* comics. We found an actress in Janine Turner, who did look something like Veronica. I was sitting in the Columbus Restaurant in New York, and Janine walked in with the ballet dancer Mikhail Baryshnikov, whom she was dating at the time. As soon as I saw her I said, "That's the girl I want to play this part! She looks just like Veronica." So, I had the manager of the restaurant call Baryshnikov and get her name. We then invited her to come in and gave her the job. Janine later starred with Sylvester Stallone in his mountain-climbing thriller, *Cliffhanger*, and had a TV series for a while.[2] So, she enjoyed some success afterwards. I also found another good actress in Megan Gallagher, who played the policewoman who befriends Joshua. Megan had played the lead in the Broadway production of *A Few Good Men*. That play was later made into a movie with Demi Moore playing the part that Megan had originated on stage. Megan was very good. That whole cast was good, as a matter of fact.

Again, as exemplified in earlier films, one of your consistent strengths is the casting. You almost never fail to assemble an eclectic and accomplished group of actors and *The Ambulance* is no exception.

It's such an important aspect of making a movie, but it's something I occasionally do out of instinct. You just get a feeling for a particular actor.

My approach to casting movies has always been about wanting to get the best possible actors that I've seen somewhere else, either on stage or in another film. The odd thing about *The Ambulance* is that when we were looking for a lead actor to play the comic book artist, I first considered John Travolta. At that time, Travolta was not enjoying a good moment in his career. He had dramatically fallen by the wayside as far as being a major movie star was concerned, but I still wanted him for the lead. The production company refused to let me hire Travolta and insisted that he'd made too many flops and unreleased pictures. They certainly did not want to make another failed John Travolta movie, so we ended up going with Eric Roberts. I was happy with that choice, as Eric is tremendously good in the part and was wonderful to work with. We did have a big bust-up before shooting began. Eric stormed out in a fury one day, and I half expected to get fired by the producers. Of course, he came back an hour later, apologized, and was just fabulous to work with after we'd cleared the air. But if it wasn't for the objections of the company, Epic Pictures, who were making the film, we could have had Travolta playing Eric's character. Just two years after *The Ambulance* was released, Travolta landed the starring role in *Pulp Fiction* and was suddenly a huge star again.

Eric Roberts has had a varied career, but did you ever think he had the same potential as Travolta to become a major movie star?

Oh, I've always believed that. I saw Eric just a few weeks ago at an Academy Awards luncheon and I actually told him then that I thought he was a great actor. I suggested he go back to Broadway and do a play and try to jumpstart his career. The only way to rejuvenate your career in Hollywood is to get out of Hollywood. You have to go back to New York and make a big hit on Broadway. The next thing you know, everybody wants you again. Unfortunately, Eric has been in so many straight-to-video pictures, and C-movies and D-movies, he has tarnished his career somewhat. People don't think of him as an A-movie actor, but any film that Eric is in where he has a decent part he steals every scene. He was wonderful in movies like *The Pope of Greenwich Village, Star 80, The Specialist,* and *The Dark Knight*. There is never a scene that Eric is in where he doesn't dominate it. He's a very powerful actor with a commanding voice and presence. He really should be a star. Actually, he started out pretty close to being a star when he did *The Pope of Greenwich Village* and *Star 80*. Eric told me that the audience "never forgave him for killing a centerfold." Those were his exact words. In *Star 80*, he played the psychopathic husband and murderer of Dorothy Stratton. He was so good in that part, so electrifying and authentic; people actually believed that character was really him. They thought he was some kind of crazy guy. Eric felt that after that film was released, people always had a certain image of him, meaning the only parts he was then offered were crazy people. He firmly believed that *Star 80* had worked against his career and he may have been right.

Another dominating presence in *The Ambulance* is James Earl Jones, who plays Lt. Frank Spencer, the cop Josh tries to convince of the young woman's disappearance. How did you secure his services?

James came to me through Eric, as they were both good friends. One day I asked Eric, "What do you think about James Earl Jones playing the part of the cop?" Eric said, "Well, why don't I call him up and ask him." So, Eric got James to read the script, and James said he would do the film. He then came in and we both hit it off immediately. We had a great time together and I just loved working with him. James is one of my favorite actors of all time. I saw him in *The Great White Hope*[3] when it first opened on Broadway. I also saw him in *Fences*[4], which is a play he did just before *The Ambulance*. I actually saw *Fences* three or four times, he was so fabulous in it. James is such a brilliant actor, and I was thrilled to get him in our picture. One of the things his character is always doing in the film is chewing gum, so he and I improvised a little moment after the cop is run over by the ambulance. When the cop falls into the street, he keeps chewing his gum until the moment he dies. I remember saying to James as he lay on the sidewalk, dying, "Just keep chewing and when you stop working your jaw, we'll know that you're dead!" So, James just lay there, staring up and quietly chewing his gum into oblivion. When James was later in a Broadway production of *On Golden Pond*, I went backstage to see him after the performance. He knew I was coming, and when I stepped into the stage door, this booming voice suddenly came swirling down the stairs from above. It was the voice of Darth Vader himself, calling out: "Larry Cohen, have you brought me some chewing gum?" [Laughs] I just thought that was great. I hadn't seen James in a couple of years at this point, but the memory of shooting his death scene was still endearing to him. I went back to see James again when he was playing Big Daddy in *Cat on a Hot Tin Roof*—again on Broadway—and this time I remembered to bring him a bag of chewing gum.

However amusing it may have seemed, do you think that moment with the dying cop chewing his gum robs some of the tension and pathos from the scene?

No, I don't think so. I mean, yes, it could have, but this was a Larry Cohen movie! Nothing is ever too much!

Red Buttons, who plays the elderly wisecracking reporter Elias Zacharias, also provides a humorous, lighter touch to the proceedings.

Yeah. I felt that character was exactly what the picture needed to balance it out. Red had appeared in a number of big movies such as *The Poseidon Adventure* and had won an Academy Award playing opposite Marlon Brando in *Sayonara*. I felt Red would fit the role of the newspaper reporter perfectly. I didn't write that part for him, but I thought he was as good a choice as we could find. Eric wasn't acquainted with Red and he was actually pushing for Mickey Rooney to play that part. Eric was complaining to me about my choice, and I said, "Look, just get hold of a video of *Sayonara* and watch Red performing with Brando." The very next day, Eric called me up and said, "You are absolutely right. He's a wonderful actor and I'd love to work with him." Red's performance in *The Ambulance* seemed to really embody the fast-talking, wisecracking reporter, particularly those that came out of the old newspaper movies that were made in the 1930s and '40s with Edward G. Robinson, Lee Tracy, and Pat O'Brien. Those films were all based on the famous play, *The Front Page,* by Ben Hecht and Charles MacArthur. It was made into a movie and formed the prototype for all those newspaper pictures that featured the rapid-fire reporter or newspaper editor. If Lee Tracy or Pat O'Brien, who starred in the first theater play and movie adaptations of *The Front Page* respectively, had been around when I was making my film, it certainly would have been nice to have had one of them take a shot at Red's part. Unfortunately, by that time, I don't think either of them was alive.

Did you get on well with Buttons?

Oh, we got on great. In fact, Red became one of my best friends. Many years earlier, when I was trying to break into television as a kid, I tried to get a job writing for Red's TV show on NBC. I didn't succeed, but I found it rather ironic that, all these years later, we were working together on a movie. Red was good during the improvisations we did. We would improvise various jokes and ideas that gave his character a little more meat on his bones. Each and every day, Red and I would make up some new piece of business, and I think we had a mutual respect and appreciation for how easy our working relationship was. At one point, Red said, "Larry, I wish you had been around when I was doing my TV show.[5] I could have done with a guy like you." I said, "Red, I was around when you were doing your TV show but I couldn't get a job!" [Chuckles] It's funny how life sometimes throws up these odd little coincidences. I just felt fortunate to get a chance to work with Red Buttons, even if it was nearly thirty years after I first went looking for it.

Did Stan Lee's cameo in *The Ambulance* come about as a result of your working on the unmade *Doctor Strange* project?

By the time the *Doctor Strange* movie died, Stan and I had already cemented our friendship. One day, we were hanging out and I said, "Stan, one of these days I'm going to write a part for you in one of my movies." When I decided to make Eric's character a comic book artist, the natural thing was to have Stan Lee come in and play himself in the film. So, he did, and Stan did a very nice job for me. Usually Stan is only given a walk-on in the *Spider-Man* and *Hulk* movies. He gets to utter one line, or appears briefly onscreen, and is gone. In *The Ambulance*, at least he had some dialogue and could perform a little. I must say that I don't think he was very believable as Stan Lee. Personally, I felt he was all wrong for the part!

Was the studio Josh works in supposed to be the famous Marvel Bullpen?

Yeah, that's where we wanted you to think it was. We didn't actually shoot it in the actual place where all those great comic books were drawn. We created that set in an office building in Manhattan, but Stan told me that in reality there isn't actually much of a "Bullpen." The artists mostly did the work at home and brought it in, but in *The Ambulance* I wanted to have some place which was a focal point. A lot of the guys sitting at the tables in those scenes are the actual artists who drew the Marvel comics. They came in and did it, but I couldn't identify which one is which for you. I do know that a lot of fans call me up or write me, and tell me that the people working at the various tables in that scene are actual Marvel artists.

Eric Braeden plays "The Doctor," the villain of the piece. What was he like?

Well, I had originally hired Wesley Addy[6] to play that part, but I didn't think he was suitably scary and menacing enough. He was a pretty good actor, but he was a little too old and wasn't quite right for The Doctor. I managed to secure some additional shooting time, and we got Eric Braeden to come in and perform all of his stuff in just one ten-hour shooting day. It was a little tough, but sometimes a film is only as good as its villain and Eric made a very good villain. Actually, Eric was a German-born actor formerly known as Hans Gudegast when he first started out in the business. In the 1960s, he played one of the Nazi officers in *The Rat Patrol*. Braeden was also in a couple of other television shows that I did, too, again billed as Hans Gudegast, but he later took the name Eric Braeden and became hugely popular in America as the lead on the daytime soap opera, *The Young and the Restless*. In fact, when I was casting the villain in *The Ambulance*, I asked my mother who I should hire to play The Doctor. She immediately said, "Eric Braeden." So, naturally, I went out and got Eric Braeden. It was entirely my mother's idea, simply because she watched *The Young and the Restless* every day.

There is a wonderfully creepy moment early in the film, when The Doctor touches Janine Turner's character with rubber gloves.

Yeah, and he says, "I love the feel of human flesh through surgical gloves!" [Chuckles] I think I made that up on the spot when we were shooting the scene. I thought Braeden played that moment very well.

Tell me about your approach to creating moments of suspense. Do you subscribe to Hitchcock's "showing the bomb" theory?

There are various approaches you can use in creating suspense that follow Hitchcock's theory. Of course, it's true, you can't deny it, there is more suspense generated when the audience is ahead of the characters in the movie. If the audience knows that danger is lurking nearby, they are waiting on edge to see if the hero will walk around the corner and meet his fate. Your choice as a filmmaker is to either use that approach or have the hero simply walk around the corner and suddenly discover that the villain is waiting for him. So, as Hitchcock understood, you have a moment of shock as opposed to having maybe two or three moments of prolonged tension. There are very few moments of genuine suspense in movies today. Everything is thrown at you and its all pyrotechnics and second unit and special effects. There is no build-up for the audience to get edgy and concerned. They immediately want to give you everything right away. A perfect example of a patient escalation of suspense is *North by Northwest*. Cary Grant gets off a bus in the middle of a quiet cornfield and is standing at the side of the road. He is just waiting there and nothing happens. Then a bus stops and an old man gets off and in the background we see a crop duster plane flying over the cornfield. There is a lot of waiting—a gradual developing of suspense—and then, finally, the plane approaches and starts shooting at him. By the time that happens, you are really hanging on the edge of your seat because you've been waiting for something to happen. Hitchcock allows you the time to get fully immersed in the scene as the tension builds and builds. If a modern director was going to stage that sequence today, the actor playing Cary Grant would step off the bus and bam! The plane would immediately start shooting at him. There would be no time for the audience to get involved with the scene. Today, there is no editorial sense of setting scenes up, establishing suspense, and letting it play out. Actually, I don't see much in the way of suspense in anybody's movies lately, certainly nobody who approaches Hitchcock's intelligence as a filmmaker. Everything is cut very quickly and every movie looks just the same now. When you look at the trailers in the cinema, five trailers come on and each one looks like the same movie. A lot of directors don't seem to have any individuality or personality anymore. Modern cinema is homogenised and bereft of originality. Nothing around now interests me very much.

You decided to reveal that Josh's potential love interest is alive shortly after she has been abducted. Obviously, you don't think that was a mistake.

No, because I wanted the audience to know that she was alive. I wanted it to seem like there was something clearly at stake. Our hero is desperately trying to save this young woman and we only know that there is somebody worth saving because I've shown you that she is alive.

You also disclose the source of the evil behind the ambulance early on in the film, rather than hiding the identity of the villain and preserving a sense of mystery.

Yes, but you wouldn't have cared if you simply had an anonymous figure lurking around. The audience needed to specify in their minds exactly who this person was and what he wanted. Otherwise there basically wouldn't have been any villain. *The Ambulance* wasn't structured like a mystery, where there are a bunch of suspects and you have to guess which one is the killer. If we had not shown you The Doctor, the hero would have been chasing after nobody. We did have these two big ambulance attendants that would appear occasionally in the picture and chase him around, but there was no shadowy villain that was the equivalent of Professor Moriarty or somebody. You need to quickly set up a formidable adversary and I thought by putting The Doctor in there early enough and giving him some really evil, diabolical dialogue we could establish an adversary that the audience would be interested to see more of. They would be waiting to see exactly how our hero would fare when he eventually crossed paths with the bad guy. I think *The Ambulance* worked just the way I wanted it to work.

A tense scene occurs when Josh is drugged in his apartment and struggles to remain conscious long enough to convince his fellow tenants that the ambulance attendants are about to whisk him away to his death.

I thought that scene functioned as an effective red herring. It was a fun twist, having a real ambulance show up to collect him, but he struggles and fights against the attendants. He believes that the moment he loses consciousness he will be taken away to his demise. Of course, it turns out that it's actually a legitimate ambulance and he's made a fool of himself. That misunderstanding now reinforces the idea that nobody believes his story. He has totally discredited himself by going into this rage and I felt that development worked well. The same idea was used by Hitchcock in pictures like *The 39 Steps*, *Saboteur*, and *North by Northwest*. Hitchcock often had the hero embroiled in a mystery and nobody ever believes him. Something terrible is going to happen and the hero is trying to find the true spy, or the true ringleader, and stop him, but the police usually think that the hero is the bad guy and are pursuing him instead. Hitchcock's heroes are always railing against more than the villain because the authorities doubt their integrity. In *North by Northwest*, Cary Grant tries to tell his story after he's been picked up as a drunk driver. He tries to say that he's been kidnapped by spies but nobody believes him. That was the same thing I tried to do in *The Ambulance*. I wanted to discredit our hero in the eyes of everybody, but the audience knows he really is onto something and they are rooting for him. We stack these obstacles against our hero because these obstacles create the drama.

A neat reversal on the scene where Josh is drugged occurs when he incites the street gang that have just mugged him into attacking the ambulance attendants.

Yeah, and of course, this time it really is the evil ambulance men coming to claim him. Again, that scene feels very Hitchcockian. Whenever I do these kinds of offbeat suspenseful scenes in pictures I always ask myself, "Okay, what would Hitchcock do in this situation? How would he have handled this scene?" I then try to create something that approaches what Hitchcock would have done, or at least what I imagine he might have done.

Were any sequences particularly difficult or demanding to shoot?

When it came time to shoot the last sequence where the ambulance crashed into the huge excavation and blew up, the New York Film Commission would not allow us to do it in New York. They said it was too dangerous to blow up a vehicle in downtown Manhattan, so we had to shoot that stunt in downtown Los Angeles. I remember we spent the entire night carefully setting the sequence up. We had this catapult that was going to propel the ambulance way down into the pit where it would crash at the bottom and explode in flames. In the meantime, a stuntman was going to be hanging on a fence and dangling above the explosion. Now when it comes to working with explosives, you have to put yourself and your movie in the hands of experts because you don't want to get someone killed. An unfortunate result of this is that you no longer have control as a director anymore. The shot is in some ways somebody else's responsibility and I don't like surrendering control. But it's entirely necessary in instances like this because no movie is worth dying for. The stunt director and the special effects people on *The Ambulance* didn't get along and they were arguing all night long about how this sequence was going to work. I kept saying to them, "Look guys, the sun is going to be coming up shortly. We are not going to get this scene at all if you keep fighting like this. I don't need to remind you that once the sun rises, it's not night anymore and the footage is not going to match with any of the other stuff we've shot. C'mon, we've got to shoot this now!" Eventually they got the ambulance completely rigged with explosives and positioned the stuntman above it on the fence. By now, it was literally minutes before sunrise and I was getting nervous. Finally, they propelled the ambulance through the air and it plunged down into the pit and—wouldn't you just know it—the fucking thing didn't explode! I couldn't believe it. Everybody just stood there like statues, not knowing what to do next. People weren't sure if they should approach the vehicle because it could still obviously explode at any moment. We were all just looking at each other, saying, "The sun is going to rise any second now! What are we gonna do?" Then someone suggested that we obtain a can of gasoline and hurl it down into the pit in the hope that it would slide underneath the ambulance. The idea involved possibly attaching a wire to the can and detonating it so that the igniting gasoline would set off the other explosives. That sounded fairly plausible to me, so I agreed to it. Some guy was quickly assigned to creep half way down, toss the can of gasoline under the ambulance before scrambling away to safety. He managed to accomplish this and we swiftly pushed the button on the detonator. Mercifully, all of the explosives went off and the ambulance exploded. Boom! Almost immediately, it seemed as if by magic, the sun came up and illuminated the pit. It was quite remarkable, really. We had just about got the shot we needed by the skin of our teeth. It was incredible, racing against time like that. Of course, all filmmaking is essentially a race against time, but this was too literal for my comfort! It was a very close situation. If we hadn't have got that shot—at that exact moment in time—we would've had to come back another night and go through all the work of setting this complicated stunt up again. That would have been at a tremendous expense of time and money that we could ill afford to squander.

I get the impression that *The Ambulance* was something of a family affair for you as your daughter, ex-wife, and current wife all have parts in the film.

I know my ex-wife played a nurse in the movie, and my daughter, Jill, played the young girl who gets abducted at the horse stables. I don't think my other daughter, Melissa, appeared in the film, but she was the still photographer on *The Ambulance*. [Pause] Yeah, just the one daughter and one ex-wife was in it. Actually, I don't think my second wife is in there.

Yes, she is. I believe she is credited as "Cynthia from Chicago".

Oh, right! She appeared at the disco scene and was wearing a red dress. She didn't have any dialogue, she just did a walk-on. I told her that everybody was wearing black in that scene, so she showed up in a red dress!

A charge levelled against *The Ambulance*—and some of your other pictures—is that you often create an interesting and compelling premise, but frustratingly fail to develop or maximise its dramatic potential. Is that criticism fair in your view?

No, I don't agree with it. I don't know what the critics mean by that. I thought there was considerable tension and suspense in *The Ambulance* and that the ending really paid off. In fact, I thought the film contained a couple of endings. The first one occurs in the nightclub when the ambulance completely decimates the place; we then have a second ending afterwards when the ambulance crashes into the excavation pit and explodes. I thought those were good scenes that resolved the story in an intriguing and satisfying way. I don't think we had any opportunity to do any more than that. I don't know what the critics mean when they claim I don't "maximise" the dramatic potential. I always fully explore every story's dramatic possibilities to the utmost. I thought *The Ambulance* contained an especially nice touch that occurs after the hero finds the girl and liberates her: the first thing she does is to ask him to call her boyfriend. I thought that was a lovely and painfully ironic moment in the picture, because of everything the hero has gone through. He's continually risked his life and reputation to save this girl and when he finally finds her, he realizes that she has no romantic interest in him whatsoever. That was something I'd never seen in anybody else's movie before.

After the complications you faced on *Wicked Stepmother* and *The Heavy*, it sounds like *The Ambulance* was a reasonably smooth shoot.

I had a nice time on *The Ambulance*. It was a fun movie to make. I enjoyed working with the cast, particularly Eric, James, and Red. For once, I also had a good working relationship with my producers. *The Ambulance* was a well-organized picture and was one of the few movies I've made where I had some producers who were competent and actually helped me. Contrary to what you might think, that is not always the case on a picture. As you know, I usually had to produce these movies myself but on *The Ambulance* I had some people who did a decent job. They were supportive and didn't get in my way. They let me do my thing the way I wanted to do it, which is important to me. The producers understood that there was a way I liked to work and, if they allowed me certain freedoms, the final result would be good.

Did you share a good understanding with your crew, also?

For the most part, but I do remember some things that got me crazy. We had an office set up in downtown Manhattan and there were a lot of people in there who had gone to film school and had worked on other pictures. Everybody was trying to be efficient, but they weren't really helping at all. In fact, their efficiency was making everything worse. Being who I am, everyday I would be changing the script around and coming up with new scenes and new dialogue. Every time I turned around, somebody would then be mimeographing fifty copies of the script. The next day, I would change the script around again, and they would be out there mimeographing another fifty copies. I said, "Please stop mimeographing everything! Wait until the end of the week and we finally get the script locked up. Every single day we are throwing fifty copies of the script in the garbage because the next day's changes supersede it again. There is no reason to have fifty copies of the script. It's completely unnecessary, so just stop!" These people had been instructed in film school to do it that way and were simply following their training. Despite what I'd told them, the next thing I knew they were out there mimeographing fifty copies of the script again! I couldn't believe it. It was the same thing when we were shooting: I would walk onto the set and notice that twelve people were standing around holding walkie-talkies. I'd say, "Who are all these people with walkie-talkies? What are they there for?" I never really did get an answer to that question. You know, the one piece of equipment that is most often stolen from a movie set is a walkie-talkie. Honestly, it's true. If you start out with twelve walkie-talkies, by the end of the day you only have eight of them as somebody has stolen four. It's the company that always ends up paying for this and it's another totally unnecessary expenditure. My theory is that everybody on a film set suddenly feels important if they have a walkie-talkie in their hands. No doubt, this is another unfortunate result of film school training. I would constantly be asking people, "Why do they need these walkie-talkies? What are they actually saying into them? If anybody wants to know anything, come and ask me. I'm the only one in authority and nobody else can make any decisions. So, put away your damn walkie-talkies!"

Did *The Ambulance* go straight to video?

It played in some theaters but not in the major markets. Epic Pictures was, like many companies, on the verge of collapse, so they didn't have a lot of money to spend on advertising. As always, if you don't have a lot of money to spend then a theatrical release is futile. One of the people who ran Epic, who also happened to be one of the producers, said to me, "*The Ambulance* is the best picture we've ever made, but that's not saying much." I was actually pleased by that comment because he knew the kinds of films turned out by that company were not very good. But as satisfied as they were with *The Ambulance*, Epic still didn't give it much of a theatrical release. To tell you the truth, I was very disappointed by that. I felt I'd made a good movie that could have done very good business. I know that *The Ambulance* did very well in France, as I was over there when it played. I went to three French theaters it was playing at, and it was doing good business. It also earned some good reviews, so what can you do? You can control every aspect of a movie when you are making it, from the scripting to the casting to the shooting to the editing, but you can't control distribution. Once your movie falls into the hands of other people, they are not going to listen to you. It then becomes a matter of how much money they are willing to spend, and it's not my money, it's their money. They are always going to do exactly what they want with it. You certainly can't tell them what to do. In the end, it all comes down to dollars and cents. If you don't spend the money, you can't make the money.

What else comes to mind when you think of *The Ambulance*?

One of the funniest things that happened was when we were shooting down by the *New York Post* building. *The Ambulance* was a non-union movie and the unions turned up to harass us and prevent us from shooting. They were situated across the street from us and were holding horns and pots and pans. They suddenly started blowing these horns and banging on the pots and pans, and were making this incredible noise. As this was all going on we were just setting up the scene and hadn't actually started filming anything at this point. When we were finally ready to shoot, the picket line had already exhausted themselves from all their efforts and had stopped their racket. So, we just shot our scene with no clamour or complaints. Despite that, they were still parading around with these signs and everything, and they certainly weren't going anywhere. So,

I approached my daughter, Melissa, and said, "I'm going across the street to join the picket line. I want you to take a picture of me on the picket line, picketing my own movie." I then walked across the street, picked up a picket sign, and at that moment a bunch of these union guys came striding over towards me. They were giving me the evil eye and said, "Who the hell are you? What are you doing?" I said, "Well, gentlemen, I'm the director of this motion picture and I want you to know that I do sympathize. I think this movie should be shut down, too. Unfortunately, I can't do it because I'll get sued. I thought I'd just come over here and demonstrate my support." I then started marching on the picket line, waving my sign about and shouting. It was a crazy thing to do, but I got a couple of great photographs out of it. It's amazing to think that I actually got out of there without getting beaten up. I thought, "If this stunt doesn't work out and they realize I'm putting them on, they might knock me out; or at the very least punch me in the stomach." Anyway, I just marched back and forth a few times, picketing my own movie, before calmly putting down my sign. I then walked back across the street and continued shooting. You know, my feeling is anything can happen when you are making a picture, and, when it does, you should just embrace it and have fun.

That means a lot to you, doesn't it—having fun on a movie set, creating memories and lasting friendships?

Oh, that's very important to me. It's what making movies is all about really, the friendships and associations you form. Another wonderful memory has just come back to me that occurred when we were shooting James' death scene: it was an incredibly hot summer night in New York City and the heat and humidity was intense. We had already shot part of the scene where James is left to die in the street by the evil ambulance attendants. James was still lying down on the ground and looked very comfortable and content. I asked him, "Hey, what's it like down there?" He said, "It's really rather nice. It feels so cool and refreshing; I think I'll just continue to lie here until they get the next shot set up." That sounded very appealing to me and so I said, "Okay, move over!" I then lay down beside James in the street and it did feel rather cool and refreshing. We were both laying horizontal in the gutter, in New York City, gazing up at the stars shining in the night sky above us. Then James said, "Well, Larry, here we are, back to our original beginnings!" [Laughs] I then asked our still photographer to take a nice picture of me and James lying in the gutter together. It was wonderful. Those kinds of moments endear you to an actor and endear them to you, because you never forget the small things. They somehow magically transform the experience of making a movie into something more meaningful and worthwhile.

As Good As Dead (1995)

Four years after the release of *The Ambulance*, you briefly returned to making television movies again, writing and directing the thriller, *As Good as Dead*. Who produced the film and what was it about?

I made *As Good as Dead* for The USA Channel, which is a cable channel in the United States owned by Paramount Pictures. The story concerns two girls who become friends. One of them is sick and goes to the emergency room of a hospital, but she hasn't got insurance. The other girl lets her use her medical insurance card, and so they temporarily swap identities. However, it then turns out that the sick girl's condition is something very serious and the doctors have to perform a surgery. The sick girl unexpectedly dies after her operation, and now—according to the authorities and official records—the girl who lent her the insurance card is officially dead. She is suddenly scared because she has committed a crime. Obviously, she cannot return to her own place, as all the tenants in her building believe she has died, so she goes back to her dead friend's apartment. The dead girl's clothes are there and she has to wear them, which alters her own appearance somewhat. Then it turns out, as the story progresses, that the dead girl was actually murdered in the hospital. Somebody deliberately changed her blood type so that she received the wrong blood and that's what killed her. That was the premise of the film.

The two girls, Susan [Crystal Bernard] and Nicole [Traci Lords[1]], meet in a nightclub and become instant friends. Do you think you were stretching credulity somewhat by having Susan willingly commit insurance fraud for somebody she has only just met?

No, not really. I don't think the one girl lending the other her insurance card stretches credulity. They go to the hospital emergency room and the girl obviously needs attention because she doesn't have insurance. They hear the hospital staff turning other people away who don't have insurance, so she just gives her the card. Susan figures that it will only be a temporary thing and the sick girl will be out of there in just a couple of hours. She doesn't realize that the situation is going to quickly deteriorate into something far graver. I'd be willing to believe that this kind of thing has happened many times before. I'm sure people have been using other people's identities for insurance purposes, for medical care and dental care, for years.

The film was shot in San Diego, correct?

All of The USA Channel's movies were shot in San Diego. I don't know why, but that was their deal. They had an arrangement in San Diego and it wasn't up to me where they did the picture. We shot the movie in about two and a half weeks, which was the allotted time in which all of these films were shot. I have to be clear on this: *As Good as Dead* was not a Larry Cohen production. I was just working for a company that was producing movies for cable, one after the other on a regular weekly basis. So, I had to go along with their production people, their cameraman, their editors, and their producers. I didn't have the prerogative to do what I wanted to do, and I did the best I could under those circumstances. It was a very unpleasant experience, actually. Any picture that I make where I don't have control of every aspect is an unpleasant experience—with the notable exception of *The Ambulance*, where the producers were totally supportive.

Did you enjoy good relations with the cast?

I didn't care for Crystal Bernard very much. She was the star of a TV series called *Wings*[2] and the company that were doing these movies wanted a television name in there. So, they settled on her, but that particular casting choice was not up to me. I had nothing against Crystal; she just didn't bring anything special to the part. She was merely a competent actress and that was about it. However, I did choose Judge Reinhold to play the murderer. He was a very charming and capable actor, but certainly not in the class of Michael Moriarty. As a matter of fact, I tried some of the same improvisational stuff with him as I had with Moriarty, but Reinhold just fell apart. He simply couldn't handle it. If you interrupted him during a scene and gave him some new piece of business to do or a new line to say, he got completely flustered. He didn't have the focus and creativity that Moriarty had. I actually gave Reinhold some tapes of my movies and he was very impressed with Moriarty's performance in *Q* and with Eric Roberts' performance in *The Ambulance*, but when we tried to experiment a little, as I had done previously with those actors, he couldn't do it. So, I gave up trying, but Judge was a nice enough fellow. He actually told me he was manic depressive and that on certain days he had bad mood swings. He would apologize for it, but I never noticed anything really negative about him.

Before *As Good as Dead*, Reinhold was mostly known for playing comedy roles in films like *Beverly Hills Cop*, *Ruthless People*, and *Vice Versa*. Were you deliberately playing with his benign, goofy image so that the later reveal of his character being a murderous psychopath would have more impact?

Yes, that's absolutely correct. We cast him against type.

Did Traci Lords' notorious history as a former porn star deter the production company from hiring her in any way?

Well, time and time again, Traci had been up for various parts in these Movies of the Week at The USA Channel. She always did a great job at the auditions and was often acknowledged as probably being the best one at many of them. Unfortunately, the company never gave her the part due to her previous association with porno movies. They actually told me, "Oh yeah, she's great, but we would never hire her because she's done porno." I said, "Well, she did the best reading, so I'm giving her the part." Before they could do anything, I told Traci she had the role. Naturally, the company were furious with me. They did not like the fact that I had overstepped them and made my choice, but by that time they couldn't do anything about it. Traci had already talked to her agent, and I had talked to her agent, and she had been hired. That was it. After all the auditions she had done without any positive results, Traci finally got to do a part—simply because I told her she had the job. I didn't like the idea that they kept constantly bringing Traci back to do readings with the intention of never hiring her. To me, that seemed utterly futile and a little cruel. Traci did a good job on *As Good As Dead* and I had a nice time working with her. She was a good little actress, very attractive, friendly, and easy to direct. We had a couple of dinners together and she was an intelligent, professional young woman. There was nothing social about it, or anything between her and me, but I enjoyed her work. I'm glad she was in the film.

Did the casting of Lords gain any unwanted or negative attention?

No, not really, but we did have some idiot show up on location one day saying he wanted to meet her. He claimed to have seen every one of Traci's porno movies. I quickly got him thrown off the set.

A lot of directors have complained about not always getting an opportunity to supervise and approve the final editing of the TV movies they have shot. Was that also true of your experience on *As Dead as Dead*?

I was present in the editing room, but the editor was an extremely obnoxious fellow. He was not my editor; he was the editor that The USA Channel had on the picture.[3] He wasn't very pleasant at all and certainly wasn't receptive to any suggestions I made. It seemed to me that he was irritated that I was even there. Of course, there was nothing he could do about it because under the Director's Guild contract the director gets to make the first cut. So, I was there and I made the first cut. That was pretty much the cut that they then telecast. Again, all in all, *As Good A Dead* was a deeply disagreeable experience. The producer of the film—whatever his name is—was not particularly pleasant to deal with either.

In your mind, what sparked this animosity between you and the company?

Well, one thing was the fact that they were constantly bothering me about shooting schedules: "You have to shoot this! You have to be finished here by twelve o'clock! You have to be finished here by four o'clock!" I didn't like that kind of thing, because I always finish on schedule or under schedule. All you have to do is leave me alone and I'll give you a finished picture. I'll probably even end up saving you some money. But these idiots kept badgering me all the time. *As Good as Dead* was another example of having a production manager looking over your shoulder and behaving like they are herding cattle. It wasn't the same thing as being able to make my own movie at my own pace. It was unfortunate that I wasn't always permitted an opportunity to do the little touches and nuances that dress a picture up and make it a Larry Cohen movie. But you can't argue with people when they keep hustling you around all the time. You just can't. If I wanted to do something that was clever or cinematic, they simply wouldn't go for it. They were only interested in shooting an establishing medium shot, then a couple of over-the-shoulder shots of both actors, and then maybe a close-up, and that was it! You then quickly moved on to the next scene and the next scene, and so on. The USA Channel didn't need a director to direct these films; they could have been done by a machine. That is not the way I work. I like to work in modified masters; I've got moving shots and innovative stuff, and I really get into the scene and have some fun with it. They didn't want you to do anything but the most basic television coverage. So, I was constantly in conflict with them and half the time I felt like quitting. I mean, things were always just stupidly done.

Can you give me some examples?

One example concerns the casting of the girl's father, which was the top supporting role in the film. The agent called me up and said, "We can get Rod Taylor for this." Of course, Taylor had been the star of *The Birds* and several other great features, like *The Time Machine*. I thought to myself, *Oh, I'll have some fun with him! We can talk about Hitchcock*. So, I said to the company, "I'd like to have Rod Taylor for the father." They said, "Oh no, he wants $10,000 and we don't want to spend that amount." I said, "Okay, what kind of money do you want to pay for the actor who plays this part?" They said, "$5,000." I said, "I tell you what, we'll get Rod Taylor and you pay him $5,000 and then deduct $5,000 from my salary and pay it to him. It won't cost you any more money and I'll cover the difference." They said, "Oh no, we can't do that!" "Why can't you do that?" "No reason, we just can't do that." I then said, "Fine, I'll pay the whole $10,000 for Rod Taylor." "Oh no, we can't do that!" Finally I just said, "Okay, if that's the way it's got to be, but I don't understand why you can't do it." [Sighs] Once you have a few experiences of dealing with people like that you just say to yourself, "Oh, to hell with it! I'll just shoot the damn picture the best I can and then get out of there!" I did not want to get fired on another job, and the money was decent, so I decided to just go through it and endure it.

Did you have to lose a particular shot or scene in *As Good As Dead* that was especially galling for you?

Oh, there were some wonderful little touches I'd planned to do. One was to occur when the girl who dies first comes to visit Susan at her home. She rings the doorbell, and it's a glass door. When Susan comes to answer the door, the girl on the outside plants a kiss on the glass, leaving a big lipstick mark. Later on in the picture, after that girl is dead, Susan briefly returns to the apartment to get some stuff and when she reaches the door she sees the lipstick stain. They are the lips of her dead friend and she reaches up with her finger and traces the lipstick on the glass. It was a very nice piece of business, but they wouldn't let me do it. Apparently, that would have taken up too much time. I mean, any time I came up with anything clever they didn't want me to do it. So, what the hell! I just drifted through it as best I could.

Were you able to sneak in at least one Larry Cohen moment?

I did come up with a clever ending that was not featured in the original script. Susan has come to a mortuary which is located on a cliff overlooking the ocean. She is going to dispose of the ashes of her dead friend by throwing them into the water. Judge Reinhold then shows up and tries to attack her. She suddenly throws the ashes into his face and he is blinded by the remains of the very girl he murdered. He then stumbles backward and falls over the cliff. So, in effect, the dead girl has brought about her own killer's death from beyond the grave. I thought that was a clever piece of business and I was able to incorporate that into the movie. So I did have a little fun with it.

Despite the tensions that surfaced during pre-production, production, and post-production were The USA Channel happy with the finished film?

I have no idea. *As Good as Dead* did get some good reviews. I think *Variety* said it was one of the best of The USA Channel movies that had been made, but that wasn't saying much. Most of them were stinkers.

I'm assuming there was no offer to come back and helm another movie for them?

I wouldn't have come back to do another one. The company considered me to be a most disagreeable fellow anyway, not like the usual television directors they had employed. These films were usually directed by TV directors, or what they call "journeymen." These are the directors who always finish on time and on budget, but don't bring anything special to the production. They merely shoot the regular routine coverage with no creative deviations. I've had friends who've directed hundreds of episodes of shows like *Barnaby Jones* and *Murder, She Wrote* and they have not added one unique directorial flourish to any of the work they've done. It's all completely homogenised and uninspired. These directors simply shoot the stuff and finish on time. That is what TV directing was in those days. It isn't today, of course. Now there is a lot more creativity in episodic television and in Movies of the Week, particularly ones that are done for cable companies like HBO and Showtime. It's become a whole different business, but back then, television was merely perfunctory.

A lot of television shows, like *The Sopranos, Breaking Bad*, and *Game of Thrones*, have the production values of movies, and contain convoluted and complex storylines that often surpass those found in cinema.

Yes, but there is a difference: when you go to work on a show like any of those you just mentioned, the cast is already in place. You don't get to cast anybody and the sets are already constructed. Also, the visual style has to match the look and feel of every other episode in the series. So, there is very little chance to bring anything unique—like I have in my films—to these projects. They want everything to look uniform from one episode to the next, and you can't tell which particular director has directed which episode. I like to think that when anybody sees my movies, after a couple of minutes they instantly recognize it as a Larry Cohen movie. I like to have the feeling that I'm doing something that is uniquely me when I'm working. You can't do something that has your own personality, identity, and stamp on any of these shows because everything has to look just like everybody else's work.

For the reasons you've stated, I imagine you are neither particularly proud nor pleased with *As Good as Dead*, as it, too, is mostly unvarying and featureless.

Basically, I think it had a good story and there was a clever twist to the film. Again, I did enjoy working with Judge Reinhold and Traci Lords, and some of the supporting players. I did not like the production guys. I did not like the editor, and I did not like the cameraman, whatever the hell his name was. He was just used to shooting the regular TV coverage, and when you asked them for anything different—ugh! I once asked them for a crane, and when I arrived on the day, the crane wasn't there. I said, "Hey, you promised me a crane." They said, "Yeah, well, what are you going to do about it?" So, again, I had a choice: either walk off the set and quit or just shoot the scene without the crane. I decided to shoot the scene without the crane. I moved on, because I realized that this was just a couple of weeks and it would all be over soon and I could go home. I now look back on *As Good as Dead* as just another experience, but once was certainly enough. [Pause] At least I didn't get fired.

Original Gangstas (1996)

How exactly did you come to be involved with *Original Gangstas*, as I understand that the project did not originate with you?

That's right. Fred Williamson was not only starring in the film, he was putting *Original Gangstas* together as the producer. He called me up and said that he was going to reunite all the original stars from the blaxploitation pictures of the 1970s—people like Richard Roundtree, Pam Grier, Ron O'Neal, Jim Brown, and himself of course—and make a big all-star movie. He then asked me if I would consider directing the film. I said, "Sure, I'll do it, but why don't you get a Black director to make the film?" My reasoning was that when we had made *Black Caesar* and *Hell up in Harlem* back in the early 1970s, there were very few Black directors working in the industry. By the mid-1990s, there were quite a number of notable Black directors who had been very successful and had made good movies. I suggested to Fred that he hire one of them to do the picture, but he suddenly said, "I don't like taking orders from Black people." I said, "Well, Fred, that's just about the most racist thing I've ever heard, but if you truly feel that way then I'll direct the picture." Of course, I didn't ever think for one moment that he was going to come up with the necessary financing, so I agreed to do it. This project wasn't going to be one of Fred's ultra-low budget movies. In fact, *Original Gangstas* was going to cost something approaching $4 million. I thought that figure was way beyond what Fred could bring and I never dreamed that he would raise that kind of dough.

But, of course, he did.

He did, yeah. Fred suddenly came back and said he'd secured the money to make the film and that we would be shooting it in Gary, Indiana. Gary was Fred's hometown—actually, his mother still lived there—but that news greatly concerned me. I mean, Gary, Indiana, was the gang capital of America. There were more murders occurring there than in any other place in the United States. Every day, there was a shooting or a violent act of gang warfare, so I wasn't too happy about having to go down there to make a movie. At this point, I had serious second thoughts about committing to the picture but I couldn't really back out. I didn't want to suddenly leave Fred in the lurch and screw up his project. Also, he was my friend and we'd enjoyed such a good time doing *Black Caesar* and *Hell Up in Harlem* together. So, despite my trepidation and being afraid for my own personal safety and the safety of my crew, we ventured off to Gary to make *Original Gangstas*. I just gritted my teeth and hoped that we wouldn't be caught in the crossfire.

What steps or precautions did you take to ensure your safety?

We had 101 gang members employed on the picture as crew members and actors, and also as staff and back-up people. Every one of them behaved perfectly well on the set and everybody showed up on time. In fact, there was very little crime and very little violence in Gary whilst we were shooting the movie. That's because mostly everybody affiliated with the gangs was working for us.

Did Williamson make *Original Gangstas* for purely altruistic reasons? I believe he wanted to set the film in Gary to demonstrate that a neighbourhood "conversion" into gangland could happen anywhere, but he also wanted to create jobs and keep the city thriving.

Yeah, that's what he said, but it didn't help Gary very much. In fact, after we finished the picture and left the city, within two weeks there was so much violence, murder, and chaos they had to bring in the National Guard to establish some order. Everybody literally went nuts after we had gone because they had nothing else to do anymore. They had invested a lot of hope in our project and there was a lot of activity to occupy them during the time that we were there. But once the movie company had gone, there was nothing for anybody to do except kill each other again. So, the shooting of the movie was all over in a month and everything went back to the way it was before. Maybe you could say that Fred helped the city for a month, but it didn't really do any lasting good in the overall scheme of things, I believe.

In an interview to promote the film, Williamson stated that it was "payback time" and that he had hired you to direct *Original Gangstas* in order to "clear his obligation" to you. What exactly did he mean by that?

I have no idea. I've never felt that Fred had any obligation to me, although I guess *Black Caesar* and *Hell up in Harlem* were two of his most successful movies. We did go into profits on those pictures and I've been sending Fred cheques over the years. Every quarter, whenever I receive my profits from those movies, I always send my money onto him faithfully. I always fulfil my contractual obligations, which is rather unusual. Generally, people in the movie business do not pay off profits to other people. They usually steal the money and it's a very dishonest profession. I don't operate that way. I always paid Fred the money that was due him on a regular basis and I think he's always appreciated it. Fred had also been directing pictures himself for several years after watching me direct. He thought he knew how to direct, but he didn't. Most of the pictures Fred has directed are pretty bad. They were very sloppily made and I think that *Original Gangstas* was a bigger project than he thought he could handle. Fred wanted somebody to come in who could give him a quality movie. That's why he asked me to do it. We hoped that the fun and laughs we'd shared on our earlier pictures would continue on *Original Gangstas*.

And did it?

No, it didn't. As I mentioned earlier, Fred was the producer and therefore he was accountable for the money. Suddenly, he was wearing two hats: he was the actor in the picture but he was also the financially responsible person and that did not make him happy. Of course, that did not make me happy either because Fred didn't know what he was doing in terms of producing a picture. All kinds of problems would occur that were difficult and I would have to work my way out of them. For example, we had a car in one scene where a guy was firing a machine gun out of the vehicle's window. The next day when we had to shoot the additional coverage, Fred suddenly didn't have the car anymore. He had gotten into a fight with the guy who owned it and this gentleman did not want to lend him the car back. So, now we had a completely different car. I said, "Fred, we can't shoot this way. It's not going to match." He just looked at me like I was crazy. I said, "Look, I mean it. You have got to go back and apologize. You have to get the original car back or otherwise I'm not going to shoot it." Situations like that put Fred and I at odds with each other, which had never occurred before. He was worried about expending the budget and about the fact that the contingency money would be spent and he wouldn't be able to keep it. On most movies they have a budget and then the budget has a ten percent contingency that's for the side. Apparently, in some cases, if you don't spend that contingency money the producer can then keep it. So, Fred didn't want to spend the contingency money, but of course, we had to spend it to get the picture made. Naturally, Fred didn't like that because it was coming out of his pocket.

Did you have to tighten up on certain basics or extravagances on the production?

Oh sure, but that depends on your definition of what is an extravagance and what is a necessity. For example, another problem came when Fred would not spend the necessary money for air conditioning. The temperature down in Gary was something like 106° and the actors were nearly dying of the heat. It was very difficult to shoot them because they were perspiring so heavily. Also, a couple of the actors were having respiratory problems, and we had to bring in oxygen and put them on it. Despite this, Fred would still not spring for the air conditioning. Usually you bring in these huge portable air conditioning units with gigantic hoses and feed them through the windows to push in the cold air. That's how it's done on most movies, but Fred would not spend the money to get them. This really slowed things down, because we had to keep mopping the sweat off the actors and changing their wet clothes. It was very unpleasant and tiring working in that kind of intense heat. Anyway, those were some of the things I found difficult to deal with but this was a movie that I wasn't in complete control of. I was in control of the creative aspects of directing the picture, but I wasn't in control of the financial aspects. Fred was becoming more and more upset all the time with each expenditure, and this meant that certain tensions arose between us. So, *Original Gangstas* did not provide the same kind of fun we had enjoyed together previously. Since that time, Fred and I have patched up our differences and we are very friendly now. Actually, last year my wife and I spent the Christmas holidays with Fred down in Palm Springs. He and his wife were very cordial and we had a great time. So, our problems on *Original Gangstas* are all firmly in the past but, at the time, it was very difficult for me.

Were you enthused to be returning to the blaxploitation genre more than two decades after doing *Black Caesar* and *Hell up in Harlem*?

To me, *Original Gangstas* was just a gangster movie—Black or White—and I enjoyed that aspect of it. I saw the film as a crime story and social drama as much as an action or blaxploitation movie. What defined it as a blaxploitation film was, of course, the cast and I enjoyed the actors very much. There were a lot of good people in there, like Pam Grier, who was quite good in her part. In fact, *Original Gangstas* was the movie that got Pam *Jackie Brown* with Quentin Tarantino. Tarantino once told me that he went to see *Original Gangstas* in a Magic Johnson Theater with a predominantly Black audience in a predominantly Black section of Los Angeles. I said, "Why did you go to see it all the way over there?" He said, "I wanted to see it with the audience for which it was intended." I think Tarantino came away from seeing *Original Gangstas* with an increased respect for Pam Grier and ended up hiring her for his next picture. Robert Forster was also in *Original Gangstas* playing a cop, and Tarantino ended up hiring Bob for *Jackie Brown,* as well. So, a lot of good things came out of *Original Gangstas* for some people, and I was very happy about that.

Despite your history with blaxploitation movies, did you receive any static from certain quarters over the fact that you were a White director making what was perceived to be a Black picture? I know that Tarantino and Michael Mann received similar criticisms after making *Jackie Brown* and *Ali*, respectively.

No, I never had any problems, not from anyone. The only criticisms or doubts came from me, when I first suggested to Fred at the beginning that he should hire a Black director for the project. Other than that, nobody ever said anything, at least not directly to me. I did not anticipate that there would ever be any problems about the fact I was White and the cast was predominately Black.

Had you seen any of the films that had been made about Black gang life, such as *Boyz n the Hood* and *Menace 2 Society* before embarking on *Original Gangstas*?

Oh yeah, absolutely. I saw them all and those two movies in particular were very good. They succeeded in crossing over into the general audience by virtue of the fact that they were very well written and directed films. In fact, some of the initial reviews we got of *Original Gangstas* likened our picture to *Boyz n the Hood*. *The New York Times* review actually commented that we had covered some of the same areas and issues as *Boyz n the Hood* and with the same degree of insight and sensitivity. They saw some quality to *Original Gangstas*—other than it merely being some kind of knuckle-headed action movie about people shooting each other.

Did you do a polish on Aubrey Rattan's screenplay?

I rewrote Rattan's script extensively. It's funny, but I always thought that Aubrey Rattan was a Black man. In fact, I was very hesitant to rewrite his script because I didn't want to take anything away from a Black writer. I was happy that a Black writer was getting his work produced and I didn't want to put in for any credit, even though I firmly believe that I would have received co-screenplay credit if I had applied for arbitration. I figured, "No, I won't do that. Let this Black writer get his credit in full." Then, at the premiere of the movie and the party afterwards, I was introduced to Rattan and he was a White guy! [Chuckles] I was flabbergasted by that, actually.

What specific things did you revise in the script?

Oh, I changed a lot of it, including the whole thrust of the story. I also rewrote almost all of the dialogue. I came up with the whole business about rigging the weapons so that they would explode and I also devised the big fight at the end. All of the father's dialogue in the hospital, when he spoke about his life and sleeping in a cardboard box and all that stuff, was all written by me. I didn't mind rewriting the script at all. Every morning, I'd climb into the trailer with a pad and write the scene for the day and distribute it to everybody. We would then go shoot it and that was it. I felt that none of the stuff really worked in the original script, because we didn't always have the same locations we were supposed to have. In some cases, even some of the cast members were not around when they were supposed to be around, which also necessitated some changes.

Why weren't certain actors available at certain times?

Well, the key moment came when somebody informed me that Jim Brown was leaving that very same day. I said, "Nobody told me that Jim was leaving. He still has several scenes to shoot. What's the story here?" I went to see Jim and he said, "Fred has known since the beginning that I had a stop date. I have to attend a political convention in New Jersey." I said, "Fred certainly never told me." So, I went to see Fred and said, "How can you let Jim leave? He hasn't finished his part. We'll be left hanging if he suddenly disappears from the movie." Naturally, Fred did not know what to tell me. I said, "We have got to get him back. There is simply no other way around this situation." I then went back to Jim and said, "Look, what if we flew you to New Jersey? What if you made your appearance at this rally, then we flew you back here to finish the picture? Would you do that?" Jim said, "Well, I can give you two days." So, we had Jim flown there and back again, and he gave us the two days. Fred had to cough up for the additional airfare—a round-trip on a private plane, which cost a lot of money—and he wasn't too happy about that. I was delighted because it meant I got to finish the movie. You know, as a matter of fact, I don't think Jim gave me two days, I think it was just one day. Yeah, that's right. It was only the one day. I had to shoot all the rest of his scenes in just one day.

Were any of blaxploitation's "Fab Five" at all reluctant to commit to *Original Gangstas* for any particular reason?

Not as I recall. Richard, Pam, Jim, and Ron were all in place, and I have to credit Fred entirely for that. He arranged the casting of all the lead parts and all the supporting roles, too: the mother and father, the gangsters, and Bob Forster, as well as Charles Napier[1] and Wings Hauser[2], who played the mayor and mayor's delegate respectively. Charles and Wings had been widely seen in other exploitation pictures over the years, and they were both excellent actors. I had nothing to do with securing them, but I was delighted to have them in the movie. In their own way, both of them were name actors in genre films. They had a lot of fans out there who appreciated their work, so I wrote new scenes for them, including the scene in the chapel where Wings shows up. I tried to give both Charles and Wings something that was a little meatier than what was originally there. The same goes for all the blaxploitation stars, I really wanted to give them something good. It was a lot of fun working with them all on one movie, and each one brought something to their part. There was certainly no reluctance from any of them to be involved. Pam Grier was very nice and co-operative, but I didn't get to know her very well. She was always pleasant on the set, but off the set we never had very much to do with each other. Pam was always very focused and professional, and always knew her lines. Richard Roundtree came in and did his job, and it was just a job for him. I hadn't worked with Richard since *Q* and he was only there for something like a week. He was pleasant enough, but all I remember about Richard on *Original Gangstas* is that he usually took his wardrobe with him when he left. The clothes you see him wearing in that picture? They went home with him! [Chuckles]

What about the late Ron O'Neal?[3] Did you enjoy working with him?

Yes, very much. Ron was a very accomplished actor. He had a great history of working off-Broadway in New York City, although a lot of people only seem to remember him for *Superfly*. That's rather unfortunate as this guy had a lot of talent. Besides doing *Superfly*, Ron had done a lot of serious and diverse work. Of all the cast members in *Original Gangstas*, he was by far the best actor in my opinion. As a matter of fact, I asked Ron to do the narration at the beginning of the picture because I liked his voice and the way he delivered dialogue. I like the opening of *Original Gangstas*, actually. I think Ron's narration and the shots of the city established the urban decay and the social plight of the town very concisely. I should also add that Gary itself was in very sad shape. There wasn't even a bank in the entire town. If you had a cheque and you wanted to cash it, you had to go to a cheque-cashing store, where they would charge you something like 10% of the value of the cheque just to cash it for you! So, if you had a cheque for $100 you had to pay $10 to cash it, if they would cash it for you at all. There were no banks, no economy, no employment, nothing. The whole town was just devoid of any hope or sense of optimism. There was no future for anybody living there except to engage in criminal activities.

Were there any ego problems or professional jealousies simmering amongst the principal members of the cast?

Fred Williamson and Jim Brown always had a little bit of a competitive edge to them. Both of them had been famous football players, but Jim was certainly the foremost football player of the two. Fred had enjoyed a secondary career in football and he never came anywhere close to the level of success Jim had achieved. Jim was the undoubted king, and so Fred was always a little bit jealous of him. But by the time we did *Original Gangstas*, Jim was in bad health. He was having a lot of physical problems due to the injuries he'd sustained playing professional football. Jim had a lot of trouble moving around, particularly when he was required to run. So, I tried to minimise the amount of running his character would have to do because he would be in such pain. The only time Jim ever got mad at me during the shoot was when I had him running down an alley in one scene. He asked me, "How far do I have to run?" I said, "Until I tell you to stop." Well, Jim did not like that at all! He turned to me and was suddenly furious. I calmed him down, quickly apologized, and said, "No, just run to the end of the alley." I thought I was being funny, but Jim didn't take it that way. That one altercation was our only run-in and must have lasted all of thirty seconds. I think Jim is in even worse physical shape today, as his old football injuries have really caught up with him. But back when we were shooting *Original Gangstas*, Jim was a good fellow and he tried his best at all times. He was a pretty good actor, too, although he had the strange habit of clicking his teeth as he delivered his dialogue. This clicking sound would be picked up on the soundtrack and we ended up having to carefully edit out all these clicks, as it was very distracting. I also wrote that scene for Jim and Pam—that long scene they have together—and they both did a beautiful job of playing it. Jim was very complimentary towards me and my work. He told me that *It's Alive* was his favorite horror movie. He claimed to have been more scared watching *It's Alive* than any other film he'd ever seen. I'm certainly proud of being the man who terrified big Jim Brown! [Laughs] Of course, Jim had co-starred in *El Condor*, and after I'd reminded him that I'd written that movie, we got to be quite friendly. However, as far as Fred and I were concerned, we were at each other's throats throughout the whole production—arguing over the locations and the money.

Aside from his casting, did Williamson have any other strengths as a producer?

Oh, sure. Fred had arranged for us to have an entire street of abandoned houses, which we eventually exploded for the film. These homes had been empty for years, and it was Fred that made it possible for us to actually blow up the entire street and burn it down. Let me tell you, that was no small feat. We had crew people come in and decorate the windows with curtains and furniture, and we placed bicycles and chairs outside on the front lawn. We made that derelict area look like it was an inhabitable neighbourhood before carefully mining the place with explosives. I had strategically positioned a bunch of cameras at various points and angles to cover the explosion. I was two blocks away when I finally shouted, "Action," and we literally blew the whole damn place up. It was an incredible thing to witness. We had put more explosives inside those houses than I—or anyone else, for that matter—were expecting. I'm telling you, the resulting blast looked like a nuclear bomb had gone off! We destroyed the entire city block at once. Although I was far away, I can distinctly remember that when the explosives detonated, the heat swept over me and actually gave me sunburn. It was simply enormous, and the stuntmen who were standing on the front lawn got blown through the air for real. They didn't need a catapult for that effect, as the force literally knocked them off their feet. That was a good sequence, and Fred was the one who engineered the whole thing. It was Fred who cleared everything with the city officials, and I didn't have anything to do with it. He should rightfully be credited for what he did contribute to *Original Gangstas* and, of course, there would not have even been a movie if it weren't for Fred.

In what ways do you think Black culture and society has changed since the days of the blaxploitation era?

Culturally, it's plain to see the influence of Black culture on White people in the last few decades in terms of music, fashion, and even everyday speech and language. Politically and socially, you would immediately think that Black culture had changed over the years due to the inroads that have been made in terms of education, opportunities for Black people, and the rise of the Black middle class. But you know what? I don't think it's really true. On the surface it may have seemed true, but when you got right down to it, the reality was very different. I think the perfect illustration of the recent divisions and ill-feeling that exists between White people and Black people was the O. J. Simpson trial. When we were shooting *Original Gangstas*, the Simpson trial was in progress, and you could plainly see the split between Whites and Blacks. White people believed that this guy had committed murder and he should be punished for it. Black people didn't seem to care less about whether or not Simpson had committed the murder; they just didn't want him to get convicted because he was their hero. It turned out that the jury assembled for the case was a mixed jury and there were a number of Black people in it. By having a Black jury, the likelihood of ever securing a conviction was remote, to say the least; because after the guilty verdict would have been announced, those Black jurors that had condemned him would then have to return to their communities and answer to their friends and neighbours for it. They would have been held accountable for sending their Black hero to jail for a murder he may or may not have committed.

Were these differing opinions and divisions also apparent on the set?

Incredibly, during the entire shooting of *Original Gangstas*, not one word was ever uttered about the O. J. Simpson trial. Remember, this case was a huge media event and was being televised. It seemed that the trial was being discussed and dissected in every home, every street, every city, and every state in America. Back in Hollywood, it was the only subject people were talking about. But down in Gary, Indiana, there was not one single murmur about it. Then, one day, I was riding on the back of a camera truck, and it was very cold. I looked around and said, "Has anybody got a pair of gloves?" Somebody found a pair of workmen's gloves and tossed them over to me. As a bit of a joke I held up my hand and said, "Hey, this glove doesn't fit!" Of course, that was in direct reference to Simpson's situation in court, where he had tried on the glove that had been found at the murder scene and it didn't fit him, or apparently didn't fit him. The attorney representing him then made this piece of evidence a big thing by saying to the jury, "If the glove don't fit, you must acquit." My little joke immediately got a huge laugh from all the gang members. They understood what it meant and they thought it was funny. It also showed that every person on that set knew exactly what was going on, but they never once mentioned the Simpson trial. Not a word, not a peep, not once. Isn't that remarkable?

It really is. How do you account for their reticence?

I have no idea. The trial just seemed to exist outside the realm of their conversation for whatever reason. The gang members never brought the subject up. They never asked me for my own thoughts on the case and I never offered them.

Fred Williamson's character, John Bookman, is an ex-football player and former gang-banger, who returns to his hometown in time to see it crumbling under his old gang's reign of terror. However, Bookman

initially urges residents to get up and leave, surrendering their community to these thugs.

At first, Bookman believes that people should just get out in order to save themselves, but then he comes to believe that the town is actually worth saving and fighting for. When he arrives back home, he wants to move his elderly parents out of there and avoid all the social problems. This is what many of us often do—we simply ignore the poverty and the inequity that surrounds us in order to insulate ourselves. But Bookman's mother does not want to abandon her town. She and her husband have their home and their store there, even though the fact that the father has been beaten up and shot would seem an obvious motivation to go. This terrible thing that has occurred makes Bookman want to pull out, but now that his mother won't leave; he has to stay, stand his ground, and fight. With the aid of his friends, he finally does something about the problems in the town. So, there was some character development and a story arc in *Original Gangstas* that was good, I think. The basic idea of Aubrey Rattan's screenplay was that Fred's character comes back and fights the gang, but in my revisions, I tried to get more inside Bookman's head. I wanted to explore his feelings and fears concerning his family and community.

For all his macho posturing and kung fu chop-socky, there is a nice sense of self-deprecation in the moment when Ron O'Neal's character suggests that Bookman "better suck that gut in, man".

Well, it would have been very easy for Fred—as both producer and star—to somehow make Bookman this impervious hero. But that moment was a nice acknowledgement that we were all now much older and we weren't young men anymore. The whole idea was to humanise the guys and let them play their real age instead of trying to hide it. Every character in there was already past middle-age, and the young gang members referred to them as "old guys" and pointed out their age periodically. The basic story of *Original Gangstas* is the pitting of old against young; experience and wisdom against vitality and strength.

The theme of social responsibility is also present in the narrative. Bookman and Trevor [Jim Brown] started the gang back in their youth, so they are in effect responsible for the current problems in the town.

I must admit, that idea was intrinsic in Rattan's original screenplay—responsibility and acceptance that something must be done. The fundamental core of *Original Gangstas* is that the old gang members must return and reform in order to take the town back from the new gang members. Over the years, the gang has changed its personality and motivations. Street life, or gang life, has basically escalated into something that is much more violent and dangerous than the old days.

An idea encapsulated by Slick [Richard Roundtree] when he tells Trevor: "It ain't about throwing bottles and stones anymore ... it ain't about breaking fingers anymore."

Exactly. The gang has now become something evil and abhorrent. It has evolved into this monstrous organization that is too violent, destructive, and cruel to be allowed to exist any longer. In effect, the older characters must slay the monster that they themselves created and I thought that was an interesting element. Also, it's a difference in values between the generations. There is no honor or loyalty anymore, and, as a result, no hope of reconciliation through peaceful means. When the gangs first started, they were there to offer their members a shield against the police, who were very racially prejudiced. The gang was always about protecting the streets and the people. Individuals joined the collective because they needed to feel safe and were no longer isolated, alone, and vulnerable. You wanted to be a member of a strong organization, who were looking after you, so you could walk the streets unafraid. If you were in a gang, nobody would attack you, because they knew that the gang would then immediately retaliate. What was originally created to ensure self-preservation and support then became something else entirely in the ensuing years. The gangs got into the drug business and things began to change as they were competing for customers, money, and territory. This inevitably resulted in violence, ruthlessness, and death. Various gangs devolved into criminal outfits that would murder anybody who got in the way and restricted their profits. The downward progression of the gang—not only in Gary but everywhere else—just became almost unbearable. This is the same situation you are now seeing in Los Angeles and Chicago. In fact, there is tremendous gang warfare going on in Chicago.[4] There have been more killings there this year than anybody could have ever imagined. It's because the two gangs are just at each other constantly and Chicago is not too far away from Gary, Indiana.

Were you happy with how the action scenes in *Original Gangstas* turned out?

Well, let me first say that I directed all the action in the picture. What was unfortunate was we only had a limited amount of stuntmen available to us, which was another problem that I had with Fred. Instead of giving me seven or eight stuntmen, I think we only had four. This meant that we had to constantly keep dressing the stuntmen up, changing their appearance, and using the same people over and over again. This was rather difficult, and we had to limit the action scenes in certain ways for that reason. Fred simply wasn't going to pay for more than four stuntmen, so that's what we had to work with. I had to do the best I could, but it did affect some of the bigger action scenes we had originally planned. I'd have liked to have had more production value in one or two sequences, but we couldn't do it because we didn't have enough stuntmen.

How actively involved were you in selecting the music and songs that were featured in the film?

I wasn't involved at all. I just let Fred take care of all that. He wanted to do the soundtrack and he seemed to know more about that genre of music than I did. The Chi-Lites[5] also make an appearance in the movie and, again, that was all Fred's doing. He brought them in for that one scene.

How hands-on was Williamson as producer? Did you receive final cut?

I edited *Original Gangstas*, yeah. There were almost no adjustments made afterwards and Fred left the film exactly the way I cut it. Fred trusted me and he seemed to be pleased with the movie. Orion Pictures, the company that released *Original Gangstas*, also seemed to be very satisfied with the film.

What kind of business did *Original Gangstas* do?

The movie did pretty well. Of all the independent films that were made that year—and I'm talking about independent films which are made outside the system—we were probably number six or number eight in terms of box office receipts. Of course, a sizable portion of the industry do not consider an independent film to be an independent film if the cast is Black.

For some strange reason, it falls outside the category of independent films if it's a blaxploitation movie. So, a lot of people did not give us credit for the success of *Original Gangstas*. If it had been strictly considered an independent film, then we would have been higher than the number six position in terms of box office for the year. We could have done much better business except Orion made the mistake of moving the opening date of the picture. There was another "Black picture" opening and they did not want to open on the same day as it. That other movie turned out to be a flop anyway and I forget what it was right now.[6] Anyway, they moved our picture ahead by two weeks but, unfortunately, *Original Gangstas* then opened on the very same day as *Twister,* which was a huge blockbuster that cost something like $200 million. That movie was actually moved back two weeks and landed on the same release date as us. *Twister* was probably the biggest opening of the year and it simply buried us. I mean, it was produced by Steven Spielberg and had a huge budget and outstanding special effects. It quickly became a huge hit, and we came in at second place. So, we still had the highest box office success of any film that week other than *Twister*. If we hadn't have had *Twister* on our ass, we would have done twice as good, but there was nothing we could do about that.

As is often the case with smaller movies, *Original Gangstas* opened in 400 theaters and was then reduced to 200 prints after two weeks in release.

Yeah, that's usually the way it happens. The business is in the first two weeks when there is money for advertising. After the first two weeks, they cut the advertising budget to almost nothing and so you lose a lot of theaters. Of course, it also depends on what is coming in next. The theaters will naturally move your film out if a big picture is coming in that they think will do better. After a couple of weeks, you lose a lot of theaters, but then every film does, particularly when there is this parade of blockbusters coming in, one after the other. For example, if there was a twelve-plex theater that has twelve screens, four of those twelve screens would be playing *Twister*. No matter what time you went to the theater, *Twister* was always playing. If you arrived at eleven o'clock, it was on; if you arrived at twelve o'clock, it was on; if you arrived at three o'clock or six o'clock, it was on. Naturally, if *Twister* was only playing in just one theater, we might have caught the overflow if they had sold out that screening. Some people would have said, "Oh well, let's go next door and see *Original Gangstas* instead." Unfortunately, when a movie is being shown in four theaters, it doesn't matter what time the audience walk in. *Twister* will always be available to them. Ultimately, *Original Gangstas* just didn't get the chance that it should have had. I mean, you just get devoured by these blockbusters because they release them in 3,000 theaters at the same time and they spend $25 million to open the picture. Something like *Original Gangstas* could not afford to pay that kind of money, so we got 400 theaters right across the country and maybe they were spending $10 million on advertising—if that! You get swamped by the other advertising and the array of theaters the competition is playing in. That more or less drowns you in terms of being able to compete. It's not a fair playing field at all. In addition to all that, the television stations and the newspapers charge you the same amount of money for advertising if you have a $200 million movie as they would if you have a $4 million movie. So, you are in a difficult situation because they have the means to destroy you.

Can good reviews help a picture when the playing field is that uneven?

Well, we got some very good reviews on *Original Gangstas*. In fact, I have a poster on the wall that has wonderful reviews from *The New York Times*, the *New York Post*, *The Washington Post*, the *San Francisco Chronicle*, and the *Los Angeles Times*. Everybody liked the movie and some critics even said it was one of the most entertaining pictures of the year. I was very pleased with the reviews, but as I always say, good reviews don't mean anything unless the company is willing to spend the money to run the quotes in the newspapers—in big enough ads so that the audience actually sees it. They have to buy a full-page ad in those papers and run those quotes, but a full-page ad costs $25,000—just for one day! To put in a full-page ad with good quotes on *Original Gangstas*, they would've had to have spent $25,000 for just one day. For a weekend, they would've had to have spent $75,000. That's one city and one newspaper. So, the prices of advertising are so expensive that even if you receive good reviews on a small picture, the companies have to spend a lot of money to get the general audience to actually see those reviews.

Not all the reviews from the time of the film's release were positive. Some critics felt that the message was overstated and confused, robbing *Original Gangstas* of its power and effectiveness. Do you think it was slightly contradictory sending out an anti-violent message in a violent film?

You had to have some violence depicted in the movie in order to address the subject of violence. It's also important to consider that there is no way to fight violent gangs without fighting them violently. You can't gently persuade gang members to disband and willingly retire themselves out of existence. They have to be forcefully quelled. As it was, we tried to have a compassionate approach to the violence and killing. I mean, the characters played by Fred and Jim did not want to kill these kids. They tried to stop them in other ways but, finally, there was no other option available to them except to retaliate with violence. The kid that Jim's character kills at the end actually tells him: "You created me and now you want to kill me?" And it was true—Jim had created him and was now destroying him. It was very much like *It's Alive* in a way: here is the father facing the monster he has created and he has the choice of letting it live or die. But yes, I can certainly understand why some critics were saying, "Look at these old guys viciously killing these kids!" Sadly enough, history has repeatedly shown us that violence can only be halted by further acts of violence. That's why we seem to be going to war all the time. It's the only way of stopping the bad guys, because you can't just talk them out of being bad. The bad guy's ability to be ruthless and cruel is the source of their power and you can't remove that power simply by talking to them. You have to crush them and keep telling yourself that what you have done is right. Ultimately, good and evil are merely different points of view. In reality, there are no absolutes in terms of what is good and what is evil.

Did you think there was an audience out there that could have embraced the nostalgia and sense of celebration *Original Gangstas* was offering?

Oh, absolutely. I think *Original Gangstas* was recognizable to some members of the audience as a revisiting of an older genre—an older type of movie experience—but one that embraced modern movies, as well. There is an audience out there that are tuned in to nostalgia and are very knowledgeable about cinema history. Each year, we see the success of movies that are remakes, or are based on an old TV show, a comic book, or a celebrated novel, whatever it may be. Each of these films has a brand name and a built-in interest and reputation. Perhaps the blaxploitation genre was a little too obscure and far-reaching than some other things to have had a real mass appeal, but as you know Tarantino was chasing a similar audience with *Jackie Brown*, which came afterwards. *Original*

Gangstas didn't break out into the public consciousness and do business like a mainstream movie would. That mostly occurred for the reasons I stated earlier: *Twister* and the reluctance of Orion to supply revenue for advertising. Actually, Orion was very close to going out of business as this point, and within six months of releasing my picture, they ceased to exist and was sold to MGM. I think *Original Gangstas* was a pretty good movie and I still do. In my mind, it more or less finishes the cycle of those Golden Age blaxploitation films and it's a rather fitting end.

Screenplays: Part III (1996–2011)

After nearly three decades, you revisited the works of Ed McBain by writing the teleplay for *Ed McBain's 87th Precinct: Ice*, a TV movie that aired on NBC in February, 1996. What did that feel like?

I found it amusing because, as you know, the very first show I ever wrote in live television—back when I was a kid—was adapted from an *87th Precinct* book. All those years later, I was suddenly invited to return to that material again. *Ice* was based on a novel by Evan Hunter, who of course writes all of those *87th Precinct* books under the name Ed McBain. It was about a dancer, who is found dead in a snow-covered street, and the detectives have to solve the case, which becomes increasingly more complex and deeper as it goes on. I don't think I strayed very far from the book, but I did try to have some fun with it. I mean, *Ice* was an assignment and the opportunity to do it only came my way because I'd written the well-received episode of *NYPD Blue*. That show was very popular and widely watched, and soon after it was broadcast, I got a call from these people at NBC offering me the job. I didn't tell the executives that I had written an Ed McBain story many years before. I don't know why. Maybe I didn't think it was important. Besides, I didn't want to prejudice myself in any way, because you can't always tell what people are thinking when they hear something like that. Maybe I wanted them to think I was entirely fresh to the material because that takes some of the pressure off—not that there was much pressure. My involvement with "The Eighty-Seventh Precinct" was a long time before when I was just starting out, and so I just took the job. *Ice* was relatively successful, and so they quickly asked me to write a second movie, which then became *Heatwave*.

Did *Heatwave* turn out as well as *Ice*?

I thought *Ice* was better, actually. *Ice* was set during an incredibly cold and bleak winter in the city, and, naturally, *Heatwave* was set during a blisteringly hot summer in the city. So, both movies were set in opposing extreme weather conditions. The films were okay, and I liked some of the moments between the detective and his mute wife who communicate with each other by sign language. That was pretty good, but once again the leads were not particularly interesting actors. If those movies had been better cast, *87th Precinct* might have been turned into a series. Unfortunately, it didn't happen that way and it isn't very difficult to see why.

I agree that the casting wasn't inspired. Dale Midkiff played McBain's famous Detective Steve Carella and he is a rather limited performer in my view.

He was adequate, that's all. If they had hired better directors as well as better actors, NBC would have probably been able to do something with it. In *Heatwave*, Erika Eleniak was cast as a woman detective, and I thought she was very good in the part. I had no complaints about her. She played a female cop, who is raped by the very rapist she is pursuing. She doesn't want to admit that it has happened because she doesn't want her career in the police department to be ruined. She allowed the rapist to get control of her and have sex with her, so she lies about it and is wracked with guilt. Of course, the rapist knows what he has done to this female detective and is kind of blackmailing her. Actually, the second movie was pretty good. The problem was that they shot both *Ice* and *Heatwave* in Canada and neither movie had the distinctive flavor and feeling of New York City to them. They didn't have any trace of the grittiness of the New York metropolis, which I felt was extremely important and integral. The atmosphere of both films was just too bland and insipid.

That same year, you adapted John Lutz's novel, *The Ex*, into a screenplay, which was directed by Mark L. Lester.[1] Were you satisfied with his direction?

I thought, up to a certain point, *The Ex* was pretty good. I just used the basic idea of Lutz's book: the mentally unstable ex-wife comes back after several years in an asylum to hound the husband and his new wife and child. She's just completely nuts and has the capacity to kill people. Pretty much everything else in the movie was original. Unlike *Ice* and *Heatwave*,

I thought the cast for *The Ex* was much stronger. Nick Mancuso was good as the husband, and I thought Yancy Butler was excellent in the part of the psychotic ex-wife. The second wife was played by an actress who has since married James Cameron.[2] With that cast and my script, everything was in place to make a really good movie. Unfortunately, Mark Lester is not a very good director and he seriously limited our chances of delivering something great. Again, as in the case of *Best Seller* and *Invasion of Privacy*, Lester followed the script all the way up to the end. Of course, then, at the climax, somehow or other that same demon that possesses some directors also possessed him. Mark suddenly had to do something "creative" and he screwed up the ending. It was a real shame.

The Ex concludes with the architect's young son setting fire to the ex-wife as she terrorises the family in their home. Was that your ending?

Yeah, that's the way it was in my script, too. She is consumed by flames. The manner in which Lester staged that scene was so awkward and poorly directed; it destroyed any sense of tension and suspense. The rest of *The Ex* was okay, but that ending really exposed Mark's directorial inabilities. It was rather sloppily put together, when it could have had real power. Lester succeeded in losing the whole subtext of the climax: that the child has now become psychopathic due to the events of the story. In effect, one psychopath has been destroyed by fire, and another one has been born in fire. That was the idea, anyway. It would have been nice if Mark had retained that element, but I don't think he understood the script. He clumsily inserted a few things into the story that were contrary to good logic, which led me to believe that he didn't fully comprehend what he was directing. This was also evident when I wrote another movie for him afterwards called *Misbegotten*. Incredibly, he screwed up the ending of that picture, also! I mean, once is unfortunate, but twice?

Let's talk about *Misbegotten*. You seemed to be a natural candidate to adapt James Gabriel Berman's novel with its story of a deranged man, who fathers a child through artificial insemination and then tracks down the family and terrorizes them.

Yeah, there we have the same thing again—it's birth again! It's the same subject that just keeps popping up in my work. I guess Berman's book and its concentration on the darker aspects of parenthood made a nice fit for me, but I couldn't tell you exactly what it is about that particular theme that continually fascinates me. The subject of parenthood and birth—of bringing a new life into the world—is often celebrated and reaffirmed in movies, but in my films that experience often shades over into horror and fear and death. In real life, I do think the idea of killing children or killing babies is unfortunate, but I am not against abortion necessarily. However, I am against abortion as a means of birth control. I'm not against abortion as a means of preserving somebody's sanity if they have been raped or incestually attacked by someone; or if the mother's health and life is threatened. But people who practice birth control by having one abortion after another just seem to be unthinking and cold-blooded.

How exactly did Lester succeed in ruining the climax of *Misbegotten*?

Mark unfortunately went haywire again, just as he had done on *The Ex*. He turned the climax of *Misbegotten* into a huge gunfight in which the villain killed about a dozen cops. That shooting spree had people dropping left and right, and it had nothing to do with the story and the characters. I suppose Mark thought he needed a lot of action in the picture in order to sell it to foreign markets. Apparently, by his rationale, overseas audiences are only interested in seeing people getting blown away because there seemed to be no other reason for having all that violence at the end. *Misbegotten* was a psychological thriller and Lester seemed to lose the whole tone and thread of the picture. Instead of dealing with the characters and bringing the proceedings to a logical conclusion, he denigrated the whole film into a stupid shoot-up, where people were dying in such succession it became ludicrous. But again, Mark is an incompetent director and nothing is going to make him any better. When he followed the script, it was alright. I was pleased with half of *Misbegotten*. Half of it worked well when they stuck to the screenplay. When he went off on his own and got lost in the wilderness for a second time, naturally, it wasn't.

In 1998, Showtime commissioned a series of films based on *The Defenders* TV series and even had E. G. Marshall reprising his role as Lawrence Preston. What was the extent of your involvement as I believe Andy Wolk adapted your original story for his script, *Choice of Evils*?

What happened was this: my mother called me up and said, "I was watching TV and I saw this movie on Showtime. It was called *The Defenders* and it was the first *Defenders* script that you wrote, back in the old days when you were a kid." It turned out it was actually my teleplay for "Kill or Be Killed," the episode that had been directed by Sidney Pollack. My mother informed me that Showtime had taken my script and turned it into a two-hour television movie—without giving me any credit at all! I then contacted the producer, and he said, "Yeah, we took your script, but call so-and-so and you'll get paid." He just said it like that, as if it didn't mean anything. I was rather annoyed that they thought they could just get away with doing something like that and not suffer for it. So, I contacted the studio. Paramount had made the TV movie and also owned all of the old *Defenders* shows, and I asked them, "What are you going to do about this?" I then went to the Writer's Guild and they arbitrated the situation. Paramount eventually had to give me $110,000, which is much more than I would have received had I actually written the script for them. When they later put the DVD out on the market, they forgot to put my name on it again! That meant they had to pay me an additional $15,000. It just goes to show that the studios are so ruthless and uncaring towards people, they will try just about anything if they think they can get away with it. This happens all the time. They probably thought I was dead—I'm quite serious—because this show was written so many years ago. They figured whoever authored the script was gone by now. They didn't realize that I was just a young kid when I wrote "Kill or Be Killed" and I was still very much around. I was fortunate that my mother happened to be watching television that night and told me about it. I thanked her for her vigilance. In fact, I believe I gave her $5,000.

Now we'll move on to one of your most famous screenplays for the 2002 film *Phone Booth*. I know this project has a convoluted history but I was wondering how you first arrived at such a unique concept?

Well, the concept for *Phone Booth* had originally come to me many years earlier during one of my meetings with Alfred Hitchcock. Hitchcock and I had talked about various ideas and projects, and I kept thinking of things that could possibly appeal to him and his sensibilities. I then realized that he'd once directed a film called *Lifeboat* that was set entirely on a lifeboat and concerned the survivors of a ship that had been torpedoed. I thought Hitchcock would be interested in stories that could be done in similarly limited situations and environments. I then suddenly thought, *Hey, what can be more restricted and confining than a telephone booth?* It was such a ridiculous idea—making a movie in the smallest possible space—but Hitchcock was immediately sold on it. "Oh, that's marvellous!" he said. We then knocked the idea around for a while, but we never quite figured out how to do it. The central question was always, "How can we sustain a story that is set entirely in a phone booth for ninety minutes?" It was such a difficult notion and we never really came up with anything concrete. When I met Hitchcock again on the opening night of *Family Plot*, he introduced me to his wife, Alma, by saying, "This is the young man I told you about who wants to make a film in a telephone booth." He then asked me how the idea was coming along and I told him, "It hasn't." By this time, I don't think Hitchcock was seriously considering doing it anymore, and a few years later he died.

How did you eventually make a breakthrough with the concept?

This is the interesting thing: it suddenly occurred to me one day that I already knew exactly how to do *Phone Booth* as I had written the character of the sniper shooting people on the roof in *God Told Me To*. I realized that if I inserted the sniper from *God Told Me To* into the phone booth concept, I would not only have a plot that I could follow, I would also have a good reason for why the protagonist could not leave the booth. After this epiphany, I became aware that if I could have a communication going back and forth between the guy in the booth and the sniper, I would have a movie. That was the breakthrough I'd been searching for. Once I figured out how to do *Phone Booth*, it only took me one week to write the script.

You then sold the screenplay to 20th Century Fox in December 1998 for a reported mid-six-figure sum.

Uh-huh. Just a couple of months after I wrote it, I got $750,000 for the script. Since then, I've earned millions of dollars from *Phone Booth* on residuals and extras.

What were the initial reactions in Hollywood to the screenplay?

Well, many people in Hollywood loved the script, but the general consensus was that it wouldn't work and would be impossible to pull off.

Is it true that during the search for a director, the first thing Michael Bay[3] said during his meeting with you and the 20th Century Fox executives was, "How can we get him out of the phone booth?"

"How can we get him out of the *fucking* phone booth." That's what he said, actually. That sentence virtually marked the end of the meeting, because the Fox executives and I exchanged a glance and we realized that we had the wrong director in Michael Bay. We then quickly moved on to somebody else and the studio passed it by several different directors. Unfortunately, when *Phone Booth* was sent over to Steven Spielberg's company, his executive over there passed on the script. Spielberg subsequently got hold of *Phone Booth*, read it, and wanted to do it, but by that time it had already been bought by Fox. I later met Steven at an Oscar party and he told me how he was kicking himself around the block because he'd missed out on getting that particular piece of material. It was too bad, because *Phone Booth* would have been a great Spielberg production. But I must say that Joel Schumacher did a good job as director. I mean, he shot the entire movie in just eleven days.

Who were some of the people being considered for *Phone Booth* before Joel Schumacher signed on?

Previous to Schumacher's involvement, I'd worked for a week with Mel Gibson. Mel wanted to direct *Phone Booth*, as well as star in it. That didn't work out, but a lot of the changes and improvements in the script came from Mel. He did a lot of research and brought in an expert from the FBI on surveillance techniques and wiretapping. Mel also had somebody go to New York and photograph the locales and make a diorama out of it. He did a lot of prep before we met, and I thought we had him, but it just didn't happen. Mel had his own company that would have taken over the entire project. He would have put his own producer on *Phone Booth*, but Fox didn't want to give away the whole picture. Besides, at this point, they thought that Will Smith wanted to play the lead role, so they blew Mel Gibson off. Then, Will Smith backed out, and Jim Carrey stepped forward and said he would do the film. Then, Jim Carrey backed out, when he discovered that Schumacher wanted to complete the movie in a two-week shooting schedule. Finally, after Carrey was gone, we ended up with Colin Farrell, who had nothing to lose because he wasn't yet a star. There was no downside to the project for him, only an upside. To this very day, *Phone*

Booth remains Farrell's most high-profile movie. Most of the movies he's made since have been flops. He's had a succession of failures including, *Alexander*, a disastrous historical picture he did with Oliver Stone about Alexander the Great. In fact, Farrell's latest movie opened in America just two weeks ago to absolutely dismal box office.[4] I forget what it's called, but it just went down the drain. So, he's had no luck since *Phone Booth*. At any rate, I think we would have done greater box office with Will Smith or Jim Carrey playing the lead, as they are both very charismatic actors with box office appeal. Despite that, the picture was successful and it constantly plays on cable and on TV. There isn't a week that goes by that *Phone Booth* isn't on two or three times.

Is it true you also considered Tony Curtis for the central role of Stu Shepherd?

Well, the character of the publicist trapped in the phone booth is really Sidney Falco, the same character that Tony Curtis played in *Sweet Smell of Success*.[5] When I first wrote *Phone Booth*, my intention was to direct it myself and I knew I wasn't going to be able to afford a high-budget actor for the lead. Tony Curtis was no longer a box office star and did not command a lot of money, so I thought I could get him for very little. If I was going to direct *Phone Booth*, I thought Tony could play the same character he had played so well in *Sweet Smell of Success*. It would have been interesting to see Curtis reprise the best performance he ever gave in his career. So, I sent him the script and he loved it. He thought it was the best opportunity that had come his way in years and was thrilled at the prospect of doing it. Then his agent called me up and said, "There's a lot of dialogue in your screenplay. Tony would need a teleprompter or cue cards." As soon as I heard that, it was the end of the negotiations. I knew that if I was going to direct *Phone Booth*, there was going to be plenty of improvisation and a lot of dialogue changes. I couldn't have my lead actor trying to read teleprompters or cue cards in that situation. But when I bypassed Tony, he was a real gentleman about it. He understood that I just couldn't work that way.

What do you see the phone booth itself standing for?

I always thought the booth kind of symbolised a confessional like in church, where Stu Shepard is forced to confess his sins.

Considering the torments and terrors that Shepherd is put through in the film, one might suspect you have a problem with publicists.

I don't have any problem with publicists. I certainly don't feel they should experience situations of extreme fear and jeopardy for any sins they may commit.

According to some sources, the word "fuck" is used 143 times throughout the course of the film. Are you responsible for that?

No, not at all. I might have had one or two profanities in there, but the rest of them came courtesy of Colin Farrell. I believe he was the one responsible for inserting so many in there. Frankly, I can live without them. Most of the greatest pictures ever made don't have any profanities in them. There seems to be no benefit to having quite so many in a movie as far as I can see.

How would you have shot *Phone Booth*? Would your version have been darker and edgier than Schumacher's film?

Probably, and it would have also been more chaotic and disordered. I wanted to shoot *Phone Booth* in New York City on a real street, on 44th Street and 8th Avenue, with real traffic, buses, sirens, police cars, and hundreds of people present. I wanted to shoot it partially with hidden cameras. I wanted to have one man trapped in the midst of all this madness that is downtown New York. Of course, that was lacking in Schumacher's film, as the location was a fabricated set in downtown Los Angeles posing as New York. It might have been worse if *Phone Booth* had been directed by Mel Gibson, because Mel wanted to shoot it out on the back lot at Warner Bros. I kept telling Mel that we shouldn't do that. I said, "This film is not going to work on the back lot because it looks phoney. We need the real intensity and vibrancy of a metropolis." Mel thought he could bring it off, but I didn't think so. Also, at the point in the story where the police arrived and shut down the street, I would have turned the proceedings into nighttime. We could have shot in darkness, because at night we would have been able to close down the streets and control them. We could have had police cars and searchlights and things like that, which would have given it a more threatening atmosphere. You could never have done that during the daytime because the authorities would never have shut down a metropolitan area for a movie shoot, at least not for a low-budget movie shoot. I would have had to switch to night. I'd have the story start later in the day, then have the transition into darkness. By doing that, I would have been able to get the streets closed and we could have shot the last half of the picture. But I don't think even I could have shot *Phone Booth* in eleven days as Schumacher did. I've never shot a movie in less than eighteen days, but Schumacher beat me by a week.

In order to combat the problem of shooting at mostly one location and with the events supposedly unfolding in real time, Schumacher deploys the multi-camera technique, shooting scenes on the street from a variety of angles and using split-screen and cutaways to generate a more energetic, fast-paced feel. What did you make of his visual style?

I thought it was pretty good. Of course, Schumacher used five camera crews that were shooting simultaneously and all the actors were present on the location. They were all performing their parts in concert and Schumacher was covering everybody like it was an actual news event. So, the cameras were shooting all the different actors from various angles and they were all behaving like it was basically a stage play. It was as if they were performing the play and were being photographed at the same time. It was an interesting approach to take with the material and it created its own unique energy. I was impressed that Schumacher was able to pull it off. I don't think any director has ever shot a movie quite like that.

You have received a lot of attention as the "creator" of *Phone Booth*, perhaps more than Schumacher has enjoyed. Do you think that's fair and have you actively encouraged it?

No, I haven't encouraged it, but I don't think it's unfair. I feel the true creator of a movie—particularly an original screenplay—is the writer, and then the director comes in second. Something like *Phone Booth*, which is quite an original concept, is basically a writer's movie, although, again, Schumacher did a good job in bringing the script to life. I don't take anything away from him. I must tell you though, he did resent the fact that I was getting so much attention. When we had the New York premiere, I remember we held a party afterwards. As Schumacher walked into the room, he looked at me and the very first thing he said was, "I've just spent the entire day talking about you." Obviously, during all the interviews and press he'd been doing with the newspapers and critics, all they wanted to ask him about was Larry Cohen. I don't think he liked that very much. When we had the premiere for *Phone Booth* at the Toronto Film Festival, at first I wasn't invited. So, I called Schumacher up and said, "Can you please get me invited? I'd really like to be there." He showed absolutely no inclination in being helpful at all. Despite that, I did manage to get myself invited through some Fox executives. When I showed up in Toronto, Schumacher was clearly surprised and rather disappointed to see me there. In fact, his very words were, "What are *you* doing here?" Later that day, they held a press conference at the hotel for all the attending journalists. Schumacher, Colin Farrell, Kiefer Sutherland, and everybody else were there, everybody except me. I was not invited to be on the platform, but everybody else was sitting there answering questions. I found myself a spot in the audience amongst the reporters and watched it. When they asked Schumacher about me he said, "Fox bought a script from Larry Cohen, but I changed everything." He didn't identify me as being in the audience or acknowledge my presence at all. I just thought, "Oh well, that's a shame." I felt it just went to show how insecure Schumacher was, that he would do something like that. He was afraid that somebody would steal some of the credit away from him.

Did your relations with Schumacher thaw at all?

Well, the very next night we screened *Phone Booth* in a 2400-seat theater in Toronto. Myself, Schumacher, and the cast and crew, were all backstage when, in front of everybody who was present, he put his arm around me and declared, "None of us would be here tonight if it wasn't for Larry Cohen." I guess that was his way of apologizing. I then walked out on stage with the rest of them to take a bow before the audience. I suppose Schumacher was ashamed of himself to some degree, and rightly so. It was too bad that he was so uncomfortable with the truth, which is that he was the director of this film but somebody else wrote it. We sometimes say that the writer is the father of the movie and the director is the mother. The director has to see the whole project through and endure all the pains of shooting on location, dealing with the actors and bad weather, and the problems with the schedule, all the same kinds of agonies a mother goes through in bringing a baby into the world. However, the father, who is there only at the inception, has an equal amount of input and occasionally more. Sometimes the baby comes out looking like the father after all the pain and effort the mother has suffered. I can imagine at those times the mother thinks, "What the hell did I have to do all this for?" But that's the way it is with a movie, also. The worst thing any director can assume is that somebody is going to give credit to the writer.

When we talked about *Maniac Cop* and the tragedies of art imitating life, you mentioned that the release of *Phone Booth* coincided with the Beltway Sniper Attacks in October 2002.[6] How did those violent events affect the film?

The immediate result was we postponed the movie. After those attacks happened, there were some questions raised about releasing the film. I was called up by the press—*The New York Times* and some other periodicals—and asked about it. I said, "I think *Phone Booth* should be postponed because a movie about a sniper threatening and killing people might be extremely painful for the relatives of the victims to watch. I certainly don't want to add to their grief, so I think we should delay the release for a while." Well, 20th Century Fox were rather furious with me for my comments but that was the way I felt and I expressed it.

The release date was pushed back from November 15, 2002, to April 4, 2003.

Uh-huh, but I don't think the postponement really hurt the business *Phone Booth* did. Of course, I don't know whether or not the picture would have done more business if it was released in the midst of the killings. I certainly hope not. I also hope that the trailer for the film, which emphasised the sniper and had played for several weeks in theatres, wasn't seen by the Beltway snipers. I certainly hope they didn't get the idea for the attacks from it, because that trailer was out before the killings began. It's very possible that the snipers could have seen the trailer and it put them in mind to do what they did. I hope not because that's a rather terrible and troubling thought.

I understand that *Phone Booth* was turned into a 2009 stage play in Japan, which ran successfully for several months.

Yes, that's true. They came to me and said they wanted to do a stage production of *Phone Booth* and I let them do it. It did very well and I made quite a bit of money from it. Of course, I never attended any performances because it was in Japanese and I had no intention of flying to Tokyo to see something I wouldn't understand. Despite that, I did cash the cheques. Actually, there was some talk recently of doing a British stage production of *Phone Booth*, but nothing ever came of it.

It's interesting that the year after selling *Phone Booth*, you sold another telephone-themed screenplay in *Cellular*—again for $750,000.

Yeah, I sold *Cellular* directly afterwards. 20th Century Fox felt that *Cellular* was too much like *Phone Booth* and they were rather annoyed with me for doing another movie that was a telephone related story. Of course, there was nothing they could do about it and I don't agree that *Cellular* was the same movie in any way. In my view, it was like the abortion scripts that I wrote: there was a similarity in theme between things like *It's Alive* and *Invasion of Privacy* in the same way there was some similarity between *Cellular* and *Phone Booth*. But then *Cellular* and *Phone Booth* are both similar to *Sorry, Wrong Number,* which was a story about a bedridden woman, who overhears a murder plot when her telephone connection is crossed. That story had been done many times on radio starring Agnes Moorhead back in the 1940s, and there was also a film adaptation starring Barbara Stanwyck. Even though *Sorry, Wrong Number* anticipates both *Phone Booth* and *Cellular* in its use of a telephone as a major element of the story, you would not say they were all the same film.

In what ways did you attempt to riff on the idea of using a phone again as a focal component of the narrative that was different from *Phone Booth*?

As you know, *Phone Booth* is about a man who is trapped on the phone in a booth. *Cellular* is concerned with a female victim being held captive, who manages to get a stranger on the phone and he becomes her lifeline. Throughout the whole picture, he stays on the line with her and attempts to find her and stop her child from being kidnapped. Finally, he is responsible for saving her and—in the last shot of the movie—he at last gets to meet her face to face. So, it was a rather clever screenplay, much different to *Phone Booth*, although they definitely make good companion pieces. *Cellular* was actually remade by Warner Bros. China as *Connected*.

Or *Bo chi tung wah* to give the film its Chinese title.

Right. I believe that basically translates as "*Connected*" in English. As a matter of fact, the Chinese version of *Cellular* is in some ways superior to the American version. I urge people to see it if they can.

Your script for *Cellular* was rewritten by Chris Morgan. What did you make of his contributions?

I thought Chris did a good job and I told him that. I felt he actually improved my script. Basically, what he did was to make the characters younger and he also wrote a lot of the small talk between the lead character and his girlfriend, and his friends on the pier. It was a lot of superfluous material that doesn't really matter that much, but it was good stuff. I find these dialogue changes rather amusing because in the Chinese version of *Cellular,* these alterations don't really matter. Naturally, the dialogue was all changed into Chinese in *Connected,* but the story, the structure, the twists, and all the action remained the same. So, it hardly makes a difference. Although Chris rewrote my dialogue, he did also add a few touches that were good. I was very complimentary to him and when we had the premiere of *Cellular* here in Hollywood, we both walked down the red carpet together and did all the interviews together. We said some nice things about one another and I tried to treat him the way I would have liked to have been treated if I'd come in to do a rewrite on somebody's else's script. He did a great job and I wanted to acknowledge that, and I continue to do so. Chris made the script better than it was, so I have no complaints.

Around the same time *Cellular* was purchased, you also sold a screenplay entitled *Cast of Characters*. This project proved to be rather controversial and resulted in a lawsuit. What can you tell me about it?

Cast of Characters was optioned, but it wasn't produced. It was a big, sprawling epic featuring some of the most celebrated public domain characters in literature. There were different versions of it, including one that had Sherlock Holmes, Doctor Watson, and Jack the Ripper. Then we had Dorian Gray from Oscar Wilde's *The Picture of Dorian Gray*, Mowgli from Rudyard Kipling's *The Jungle Book*, along with Dracula and Frankenstein. Everybody was in the movie and the unique thing about it was all these characters were in there for a reason. It wasn't like they were all just slopped together without any thought or consideration. Everything paid off and there was a definite logic to the story and a plot twist that integrated all of these literary creations. *Cast of Characters* was a lot of fun. We actually optioned it a number of times and then, basically, the whole thing—we claimed—was stolen and turned into a movie at 20th Century Fox called *The League of Extraordinary Gentlemen*.[7] We sued them for plagiarism and it was settled. Amicably settled. I'm not allowed to say what the settlement was, but I must say that we were very pleased with it.

***The League of Extraordinary Gentlemen* was released in 2003 and is based on Alan Moore's 1999 graphic novel. How could it be claimed that Moore had got the original idea for his graphic novel from your unproduced screenplay?**

Well, the producer of *The League of Extraordinary Gentlemen* was the same person who had earlier produced *From Hell*, which was a movie about Jack the Ripper that was based on another graphic novel by Alan Moore. It was our contention that this same producer, who had read *Cast of Characters* over at Fox, must have mentioned the idea to Moore and convinced him to write a graphic novel based on this concept of mixing all these public domain characters together. So, that was our contention and the facts supported it, too. That's why we had an amicable settlement. I don't think Alan Moore realized that the idea that was being given to him was stolen from somebody else's script. Moore acted in good faith and nobody was thinking that he willingly went out and pirated my idea. However, even Moore stated in his testimony—he gave a deposition— that in writing comic books and graphic novels there is a great deal of borrowing of ideas by the writers.

When I first read about the lawsuit, I was wondering what the connection was between yourself and Alan Moore, the world's pre-eminent comic book writer, who lives and works in Northampton, England.

I never met Alan Moore, and he never knew that I, or the screenplay of *Cast of Characters*, ever existed. All he knew what that this producer, who had worked on a previous Alan Moore project had, as I say, put the idea in his head of taking the public domain characters and putting them together in a graphic novel. So, he went ahead and did, that's all. That's what came out and it wasn't Moore's fault. He certainly wasn't a thief or anything—nobody was accusing him of that. When 20th Century Fox realized what had happened, they immediately settled the case. I don't think Fox knew what was happening, but the producer knew what he was doing. He had read the script and was familiar with its contents. After putting the idea into Alan Moore's head to copy this idea as a graphic novel, he took this property to Fox. The studio then bought it and made it into a feature. That is what happened, and it wasn't Fox's fault, really. It was an employee of Fox that did it, but the studio had to take responsibility for what he had done. I don't think they consciously stole my material. I think they were unfortunately a party to it without knowing. But, on the other hand, Fox were also aware of my script because *Cast of Characters* had been submitted over there. Meetings had been taken and there were several script analyses written by development people at Fox. When the idea for *The League of Extraordinary Gentlemen* came across their desk, it would have been proper for them to call me up on the phone. They could have said, "Larry, we're working with you on *Phone Booth* and have a great relationship, but we've just started to develop an idea which is similar to something you submitted to us. We wanted you to know that this isn't your idea, it came from Alan Moore over in England." If they had said that to me up front, I would have probably understood and would never have known how the idea was put into Moore's head by this producer. But Fox knew about the conflict and they should have advised me of it and come clean at the beginning. When you try to hide things, you make it appear that you are somehow complicit.

Let's discuss the 2007 film, *Captivity*, which is based on your script. I already know that you are no great admirer of it.

That's an understatement! [Sighs] Oh, what a fucking disaster that was. *Captivity* was a really good script, a lovely script. It was brimming with my style of writing, humanity, and humour. My original screenplay was about the same thing as the finished film, but it didn't involve all of that torture and brutality. It was supposed to be about two people—a man and a woman—who are mysteriously imprisoned together in a cellar. They eventually fall in love, but we later discover that it's all an elaborate set-up as this guy and his brother are actually the ones behind the kidnapping and imprisonment in the first place. They have done this before with other females they have murdered and that was the big twist, and it was a good one, too. The first half hour of my script had a gentle, comical aspect to it and was a lot of fun. It was not humourless and disgusting and the final picture they made was certainly humourless and disgusting.

What do you think happened to *Captivity*?

What happened was the filmmakers just went out of their way to make the movie repellent and nauseating. It wasn't even entirely the fault of the director, because *Captivity* was taken away from him.[8] There were other scenes shot that the director had nothing to do with and were not part of the original story. These scenes were then arbitrarily inserted into the film to make it more overtly horrific. That was all done by some very, very second-rate talent. I'm talking about truly amateurish people here, who consider themselves to be filmmakers, but really aren't. They should be out of the business. They don't deserve to be making pictures as they are simply garbage-makers. They made a concerted effort to continually and systematically ruin the picture and they succeeded. Actually, I must say that *Captivity* wasn't really that good when it was originally finished either, before the movie was tampered with.

The film was shot in Russia, right?

That's right. Can you believe that? I mean, the story takes place in New York and it was somebody's great idea to shoot the picture in Russia, and that's what they did! They spent fifty days or more shooting something that all takes place in this cellar. I would have been able to shoot *Captivity* in two or three weeks, but it took them fifty days! Of all the people to have shot the movie, the director of photography was Daniel Pearl, the cameraman on many of my films. He said that the crew was drunk half of the time and were very, very slow. I don't know if Daniel ever voiced his opinions or not, but one day somebody dropped a pipe on his head from a catwalk that was above him. Maybe this person didn't like Daniel very much and was trying to inflict some damage on him. I don't know. Daniel was incapacitated for a few days after this incident, but he did manage to finish the picture. That just makes the whole movie seem even more sickening to me. *Captivity* took forever to make and it really wasn't great. I should also add that the casting was second-rate, too.

Some critics have grouped *Captivity* with other "torture porn"⁹ films such as *Saw, Hostel,* and *The Devil's Rejects* that depict the most heinous and explicit acts of physical violence onscreen.

I haven't seen any of those pictures and I wouldn't—even if I was warmly invited to. I don't go to see "torture porn" movies that parade these countless acts of brutal torture and then pass them off as entertainment. In the case of *Captivity*, I thought it was a shame to take this rather clever script that was a lot of fun and transform it into an irredeemable piece of sadistic garbage. At one time, we actually did a one-off stage-play of *Captivity* back here in Los Angeles—just for fun. This was before the picture was made and was done at a theater belonging to The Milton Katselas Acting School. I must say that production was a far more satisfying experience for me. As a matter of fact, it hurts my head just thinking about that movie. Let's move on.

Your next produced screenplay was the 2009 TV movie, *The Gambler, the Girl, and the Gunslinger*. This production marked your return to the Western genre that you had served so well in previous years.

Oh, that was another awful picture! It was made up in Canada for The Hallmark Channel. Apparently, Hallmark have made a lot of movies up in Canada. Unfortunately, the film was miserably cast and was made by a woman director.¹⁰ She didn't know what she was doing, frankly. All I can say is that I'm glad somebody finally bought that screenplay after thirty-six years! Honestly, that script had been around for more than three and a half decades before it was finally purchased. *The Gambler, the Girl and the Gunslinger* was originally entitled *The Hostiles* and was written by myself and a friend of mine named Bob Barbash.¹¹ After completing it, we sent *The Hostiles* out to Clint Eastwood and he optioned it. Actually, Clint optioned it twice: once over at Universal and then later on he optioned it again at Warner Bros. through his own company, Malpaso. Clint was going to direct the picture and he wanted to make it with John Wayne starring opposite him.

That could have potentially been quite some project, bringing together the two most popular and iconic Western stars.

It could have been. *The Hostiles* was a Western about two guys, an older cowboy and a younger cowboy, so Clint sent it to John Wayne, thinking they could both play the leads. But Wayne rejected it, and so Clint then sent it to him a second time, only for Wayne to reject it once again. Clint was very disappointed that Wayne did not want to do the picture. He did not want to make *The Hostiles* with anybody else but The Duke. Clint's option eventually ran out, and Michael Wayne, who was John Wayne's son, approached me about optioning the property. I said, "Michael, if I do that Clint will have a fit! You guys have been obstructing this project for years and now you suddenly want to option it?" Michael said, "Let me just show the script to my father. We are going out on the boat at Newport for the weekend. He'll have nothing to do and I'll get him to read it again." The following week, I got Michael on the phone and asked him what had happened. He said, "Well, Dad was sitting on the boat and I handed him the script. He looked at it for a few minutes and then said, 'This piece of shit again!' And then he threw it overboard." I quietly thought to myself, "Oh, there goes my beautiful script, slowly sinking beneath the blue Pacific along with the hopes and dreams of Clint Eastwood and Bob Barbash!" A few years later, I ran into Clint and said, "Hey, what about *The Hostiles*? Why don't we still do it?" Clint said, "I guess I'd have to play the old guy now, wouldn't I?" We both laughed and that was it.

What was Eastwood and Wayne's relationship like? Were they friends?

There was no relationship. They had no friendship. But Clint really did want to work with John Wayne. Apparently, John Wayne was not that anxious to work with Clint Eastwood.

How did *The Hostiles* eventually devolve into *The Gambler, the Girl and the Gunslinger*?

Well, I had been wanting to get it made for several years, and at one point Elliot Kastner was trying to do it with Marlon Brando playing John Wayne's part. Of course, that never came off, but I was still hopeful that it one day would. Then, the phone rang one day and this producer said, "You know that script you gave me nine years ago? Well, I think I've actually got it sold over at Hallmark." So, we took $200,000 for it, but by this time Bob Barbash had died. I really only sold the script so I could send $100,000 to Bob's widow and family. They certainly weren't expecting that money.

That was a very nice gesture.

It was but, unfortunately, they didn't ever once say thank you or anything. It's funny, but you do something nice for people and sometimes you don't receive any kind of acknowledgement or response at all. If somebody called me up and said they were sending me $100,000, I would be very much grateful for it. I mean, that would be the equivalent of money falling out of the sky.

I must say it again: it certainly would have been wonderful to have seen Wayne and Eastwood together in a Western.

Oh, are you kidding me? It was one of the great disappointments of my career! My two biggest career disappointments were *Daddy's Gone A-Hunting*, when Universal told me that Hitchcock had suddenly changed his mind about doing the picture, and *The Hostiles* falling apart with Eastwood and Wayne playing the leads. I mean, we already had Clint and, okay, suppose he didn't do the picture with John Wayne: what if he did it with say George C. Scott or Burt Lancaster or some other big actor? It could have still been great. But again, Clint did not want to do *The Hostiles* with anyone else except John Wayne. The failure of those two projects to happen in their early incarnations were both heartbreakers for me—huge heartbreakers.

I understand that another heartbreaker for you was the recent thriller, *Messages Deleted*, which was released—illegally—in 2010. How are you recovering from that disappointment?

Well, that was another blow. The producer was looking for distribution on *Messages Deleted* but, in the meantime, somebody stole the picture and put it out on the Internet for free. That ruined all opportunities for us to get the movie out there, and, inevitably, the company went bankrupt. It was just a devastating situation to find yourself in, but what can you say? This is the kind of despicable thing that happens in our business. You just have to accept these things when they happen and there's very little you can do about it. *Messages Deleted* was shot in Canada and was the third part of my "telephone trilogy" along with *Phone Booth* and *Cellular*. Again, we have a telephone as a central element of the story, but each one uses the device in a new and interesting way. That was the idea anyway. *Messages Deleted* was a thriller about a screenwriting teacher, who is implicated in a series of mysterious murders that resemble those described in his screenplays. It was another clever script with some interesting moments in it, but the whole movie has been stolen. *Messages Deleted* was not a great film—it was awful compared to my script—but that's not the point. The poor producer lost a fortune, but I still got paid for my script. That doesn't mean I'm not sour about the whole thing. I am. In fact, that's another movie that really hurts my head when I think about it. Let's not talk about it anymore, okay?

Masters of Horror: Pick Me Up (2005)

It's safe to assume that you were one of the original attendees of the infamous *Masters of Horror* dinners that have been held in Los Angeles since 2002.

Oh, I've been to almost every one of them. I actually attended a dinner just two weeks ago. They are one of the most pleasant events you could possibly imagine. Usually most of the guys are there—John Landis, Joe Dante, Tobe Hooper, and of course Mick Garris, who actually arranges these meetings. Then, you have people like John Carpenter, David Cronenberg, Quentin Tarantino, Guillermo Del Toro, and others, who come by and we always have a great time. I mean, collectively, we may all be responsible for some of the scariest horror films ever made, but you couldn't find a nicer, more civilised bunch of guys anywhere. Basically, all of us directors get together at a reasonably priced restaurant, where we are usually given a private room. Everybody then moves around the table and talks to everybody else. We ask each other what projects we are currently working on and what's going on in our lives and careers. We relay all our problems and disappointments about trying to get movies made, and discuss the trepidations and tragedies of distribution. For example, John Landis made *Burke & Hare* in England, a comedy-horror film about the two famous body snatchers, and he's been unable to get distribution for it here in the United States. Joe Dante also shot a movie in 3D recently and he can't get it distributed[1], and these are two guys with great track records who have made very successful movies. Of course, I have my own nightmare stories to share, too, like the unfortunate situation we had with *Messages Deleted*. So, everybody has their tales of woe and despair. Even the guys who have made successful pictures have their tales to tell. During one dinner, we all got to hear Tarantino tell some of his stories from

Inglorious Basterds, the movie he made over in Germany, and that was great fun.

It sounds like these events are deeply cathartic for you all.

Each of us respectfully listens to what the others have to say and you realize that you relate to many of their experiences. It's really a fascinating group of people because you have directors like Guillermo Del Toro, who are very hot right now, sitting next to somebody who hasn't been able to get a picture made in fifteen years, but they are there, too, god bless us! So, it's very democratic and everybody is treated well and has a good time. We couldn't possibly be nicer to each other and everybody is always very open and honest about everything. The truth is, we love to do it and we all genuinely like each other. Oddly enough, one of the most interesting things is that everybody insists on taking photographs of one another. Honestly, you have all these directors and all they want to do is take photographs of themselves with other directors! [Chuckles] Dario Argento was at one dinner and everybody took pictures with him. I mean, *everybody* takes pictures with everybody else and they are all running around the table like crazy, constantly posing and clicking away. You would think they were all members of some fan club rather than famous filmmakers.

At what point did the *Masters of Horror* series for Showtime evolve out of these dinners?

Well, as the dinners went on, everybody started talking about the possibility of us doing something together. Mick Garris was really the instigator of the project and he was the one who took it to the company that financed it. Mick is a great guy, and is rightfully credited with creating *Masters of Horror*. It was Mick's perseverance that put the project together and he made the deal. All the guys were enthusiastic about doing *Masters of Horror* and even some of the directors who were living and working overseas, like Dario, wanted to be involved.

Considering the fact that you mostly work from your own original material, you declined the opportunity to write a script and instead selected *Pick Me Up* by the acclaimed horror author David J. Schow.[2] Why exactly?

I was sent a couple of scripts they had from various writers, but I saw something in *Pick Me Up* that I immediately liked. I was intrigued by the premise of these two isolated serial killers—one a truck driver, the other a hitchhiker—roaming around like lone wolves and preying on people without conscience. These men eventually end up crossing each other's paths in pursuit of their next victim, a young woman, which leads to this amusingly dark climax. I thought *Pick Me Up* took a rather unique and unexpected approach with the serial killer theme. It also had the prominent part of the truck driver that I knew I could give to Michael Moriarty. Of course, in choosing David's script, I saved myself the trouble of having to write something. The money portion of *Masters of Horror* was very small compared to features, so I was more than happy to find a good story that I liked and wanted to do. Although David's script was very good, I was able to rework a little of it and change some of the dialogue. I invited David to be on the set in Vancouver, Canada, and he was up there every day with us. I kept him apprised of everything we were doing. I wanted to treat David as I would want to be treated if I was the writer on a picture. I've been through experiences on movies, where the writer was not welcome on the set, and I'd always felt bad about it. A lot of directors feel uncomfortable when a writer is present, as they feel the writer is looking over their shoulder. I don't feel that way. If I was going to direct this script, which had been written by somebody else, I wanted to give this person the respect he deserved. So, I made sure that David was involved in every decision we made.

Were there any other scripts produced for the series that you were considering?

I have no recollection whatsoever of the scripts I rejected, or my reasons for doing so. To tell you the truth, I don't even remember most of the films that were done by the other directors. I wasn't too excited about most of the ones that were made. I thought *Pick Me Up* was very good, but many of the others were below the high standards of the people who were directing them. I felt that *Masters of Horror* wasn't as good as *Tales from the Crypt*[3], which was a previous horror series that had been done on HBO. I thought the level of quality on that show was much higher than on ours. I also felt that many of the guys didn't do a good job on their pictures and selected very poor material to begin with. I won't specify which ones I'm talking about because I don't want to insult anybody. I just felt that the series as a whole really wasn't great. I'm sure that is one of the reasons why *Masters of Horror* didn't go on any longer than two seasons. What about you? Which films did you like?

Personally, I liked Joe Dante's *Homecoming*, John Carpenter's *Cigarette Burns*, and Stuart Gordon's *Dreams in the Witch-House*.

Joe Dante did the one about the war veterans, who came back from the dead to vote. Yeah, I liked that picture and thought it was clever. It was very well-directed by Joe. Let me see, which other ones were pretty good? [Pause] Oh, I don't know. I don't even want to speculate. I think a couple of the other films were also good, but I must be honest and say that I didn't watch them all. I caught a couple of them and when I saw they weren't very good, I didn't watch the rest. I can't really recall which film was John Carpenter's. I do recall he did one about a monster baby being born.

Yes, *Pro-Life*, which featured in the second season.[4]

I looked at that one with a great deal of curiosity because the idea was so obviously stolen from *It's Alive*. I couldn't understand why John would do such a thing, but I never said anything to him about it. I didn't think that film was very good either, but on the whole, John has done tremendous work. I just don't think that is one of his better efforts. I really wished they hadn't done something that was such an obvious takeoff on *It's Alive*, particularly when I was involved in the series.

In fairness, I think the writers of *Pro-Life* were mostly referencing Carpenter's previous body of work, particularly *Assault on Precinct 13* and *The Thing*.

I really don't remember much about it. I saw the film once and I was just a little repelled about the whole experience, frankly. I had my questions about why that material was selected in the first place. There were so many other stories that could have been done; so many other choices that could have been made.

There were few restrictions on the content of the films that the directors could make. I know that you are no great lover of excessive

violence, but were you at all tempted to do something outrageous as Dario Argento did with *Jenifer* and Takashi Miike did with *Imprint*?

No. The prospect of doing extreme violence didn't appeal to me at all. As you know, the blood and gore is just not my kind of movie. I believe I did see Dario's film, which was about a flesh-eating monster-girl. It was very explicit, but it was also pretty good, too. If I remember correctly, at one point she is performing oral sex on some guy and then eats his penis up! [Laughs] That was pretty disgusting, and I don't go in for the disgusting stuff. I wanted my film to work from a good premise and contain some good suspense and dark humour. I know that a lot of the horror fans love that kind of explicit violence and were perhaps expecting it.

You did shoot the scene where Walker [Warren Cole] partially skins and tortures the young woman in the motel room.

Yeah, but that sequence didn't go on for too long. I believe I cut that torture scene back a little. In fact, we never shot that much of it anyway. The producers demanded that some moments of horror be included in each film. They didn't have any input, but they more or less told you that the film had to contain some gruesome and scary aspects. Otherwise *Pick Me Up* would have just been a suspense story, not a horror film. I didn't dwell on the torture for too long, but a very creepy little touch in that scene is when Warren Cole puts tape over the young girl's mouth and paints lipstick on it to simulate a mouth. I actually came up with that idea on the set. That did not appear in David's script. I thought that was something that had never been done before. It was a little detail that was perverse and disturbing, but not explicitly violent. You don't see any knives penetrating flesh or anything like that. You simply see this sadistic guy putting lipstick on somebody's face while they have a bandage over their mouth. It's weird. It's very weird, but it isn't gory.

What was it like returning to directing after nearly a ten year absence?

Well, on *Masters of Horror* there was a staff that was producing the series in Vancouver, and they shot every film there for John Carpenter, for Dario Argento, for John Landis, for me, for everybody. They had everything pretty much worked out in terms of the sets, the transportation, the equipment, and the crew. All we had to do was show up and direct the picture, whereas on most of my movies I've had to hire the crew and set up the entire production myself. Here, I could literally just walk in and direct the film, and that's probably why I did it. We shot for about ten days and were working thirteen or fourteen hours each day. Unfortunately, they booked us in there at the worst time of the year. It was freezing cold and it rained every damn day! We were working under the worst possible conditions, and so it became a very difficult shoot. The whole thing worked out okay, but I must tell you that I was glad when it was all over. *Pick Me Up* was the only movie I've ever made where I spent all my time inside the trailer. On all the pictures I've done, I've never even had a trailer because I always want to stay on the set with the actors and crew. On this particular film the cold weather and constant rain was so punishing, I would retreat into the trailer at every opportunity. I'd sit in there and wait until somebody informed me that the camera and lighting was ready. Then—and only then—would I venture out and direct the scene. I can honestly say that is the only time I've done that in my career.

Did you miss being on a set in spite of the conditions?

Not on that picture! No, the unpleasantness of the location was more than I could bear and greatly affected my ability to enjoy the experience. It was a pretty miserable shoot. I mean, we were basically out in the wilderness. At one point, some of the crew went up on a hill above the road in these cherry pickers to put up these big 10K lights that we were using to illuminate the exteriors. They suddenly radioed us and said, "Hey, we can't get back down! There are two bears roaming around up here!" They were trapped and afraid they were going to get eaten. I said, "Okay, I'll send a couple of guys up there to get rid of the bears." Of course, I had no idea exactly how they were going to do this, but these guys went up there and succeeded in driving the bears away. As soon as they were gone, we proceeded onward. So, we were not only fighting the rain, the cold, and the rigors of this wilderness area, we were also fighting off bears, too!

Like a lot of serial killer movies, *Pick Me Up* flirts with the idea of fate and the fear of inexplicably random violence. Is that something you relate to personally?

I think most of us can relate to that fear. People who have been victimized will often say, "Why me? Why hasn't this awful thing happened to somebody else?" Well, the fact is it's always got to happen to somebody. That's not a pleasant thought but it's true. Somebody always has to suffer in this world. Somebody's misfortune and pain always has to make the newspapers that we read and the television that we watch. It's always somebody's mother, father, daughter, son, brother, sister, friend. It's always somebody. The two serial killers in *Pick Me Up* are out there somewhere and it is Fairuza Balk's great misfortune that she happens to stumble into their universe.

Interestingly, Stephen King once claimed that the fundamental root of all horror stories is that "bad things happen to good people."

I'm sure that's true. Again, how many people live their lives without a thought for the bad things that can occur? I would think very few. Most of us are conscious of the horrors of life—the accidents and unfortunate coincidences that can destroy you. One morning you can be kissing your child goodbye and sending them to school, and in the back of your mind you are thinking, *Will they return home safely?* We see news stories of kids being murdered in their schools. You believe they are safe there, but maybe an intruder or another kid has brought a gun to school and gone on a killing spree. You can wave goodbye to your wife as she gets in the car and never see her again. She can be involved in an automobile accident or breakdown at the side of the road and be murdered by some passing maniac. You can go to the doctor's office and get some bad news—it's cancer or some other terminal disease. These are all very disturbing thoughts, but these are the realities of life. Bad things can and do suddenly happen, and yeah, all of these fears inform our horror stories to some extent.

How much thought and effort went into selecting the truck that Wheeler, Michael Moriarty's character, drives?

I told the production people exactly what kind of truck I wanted, and they told me they couldn't get it. I then told them they had to get it. When they finally did get it, I told them that I wanted the truck painted red. They did this, and I was happy. I mean, these things can sometimes be important. Although the truck is just a truck, if it looks right it can be an interesting and menacing presence, even a supporting character in some ways. The first truck they brought me was this ridiculously small truck. It was like a pickup truck or something, and I immediately sent it away. I insisted, "No, you've got to get me a great big truck," and they did. Sometimes, in filmmaking, it's just a matter of having to reject the first notion that people come up with in order to get what you want. People will always take the easiest course for themselves at first, so you just keep sending them back until you get exactly what you require.

Were there any conflicts on set?

I did have my differences with the crew up there on location. When we were shooting the picture, they had their way of doing things and I had my way of doing things. The crew had been shooting these *Masters of Horror* films for months and they were used to working together a certain way. My approach was somewhat different from theirs, so I had to quickly get them accustomed to my way of working, at least for the duration of making *Pick Me Up*. For example, the motel you see in the film: we took over that entire establishment for our purposes. At one point, I asked somebody, "Hey, where's the makeup people and the wardrobe people?" This person replied, "Oh, they are at the holding area." I said, "Where's the holding area? Take me there." We then got into a car and drove for fifteen minutes to a vacant lot, and there were all these trucks parked there. Somebody said, "This is the wardrobe department; this is the makeup and hair department; and over there is everything else." I said, "Why do you have everybody stationed all the way out here? Every time we need to do something you have to drive for fifteen minutes going and fifteen minutes coming back. That's thirty minutes of production time! We have an entire motel at our disposal with all these empty rooms. Get your stuff together and move over to the motel." They said, "That's not how we do things." I said, "It's the way you do things on this production." So, they did eventually move everything over to the motel and there were plenty of rooms available to house the various departments and their equipment. I mean, it was ludicrous! That one decision must have saved us several hours every single day, but that was the way they worked. If you leave things to production managers and production people, they always do things the wrong way.

That was your considerable low-budget experience coming into play there.

It was common sense, that's all. They had all these trucks and they felt like they just had to use them. They didn't need them at all because there was maybe one wardrobe change in the whole film. I mean, the actors all wore the same clothes and the action all happened in consecutive time. We didn't need a lot of costume changes, so why the hell did we need a whole wardrobe department and wardrobe truck when we could hang the one costume up in a closet? That would never have happened on one of my other pictures, but I had to deal with the way these people operated. If you tried to change things they would give you this strange look because that was not their established procedure. People then think you are a difficult person. They say, "Oh that Larry Cohen, he likes to push everybody around!" What can you say? All I was interested in was making a good movie. It's all I really care about. I'm not concerned about anything else except what goes up on the screen. Actually, I have no idea what the exact figure for the budget was. I wasn't the producer and I never asked them because, frankly, I didn't care. I wasn't paying for it. But I do know that the budget wasn't that much.[5]

One of the most self-consciously impressive shots in *Pick Me Up* is the bird's eye-view tracking shot over Walker, Wheeler and Stacia [Fairuza Balk] as they rest in their respective motel rooms.

Well, I wanted to execute some shots that were ambitious, but still very simple. So I came up with the idea for that shot and we built the set accordingly. We used an electronic crane that was operated by remote control and gave the camera a nice fluid movement. Since the set had the three motel rooms positioned directly next to each other, we simply raised the camera up from the first room, moved it slowly across the second room, and dropped it into the third room. That way, we could see the various activities of the three characters without having to cut between them. It worked out fine and we only did two takes and both of them were good.

Moriarty gets another opportunity to play the piano, as he did in *Q – The Winged Serpent*, performing his song "Snakes in the Snow."

Yeah, I told him he could. We put a piano outside the café as if there was a garage sale or something going on, and his character could just sit down for a few moments and play something. Moriarty was then able to perform his song and he was happy about that. It also made me happy that Michael was happy. We actually shot that on the very first day and got it over with. I must confess that I don't exactly know what "Snakes in the Snow" means. You'd have to ask Michael.

How was it reuniting with Moriarty again after an eighteen-year break?

Gosh! Was it really that long?

Yes, it was, stretching all the way back to *A Return to Salem's Lot* in 1987.

I can't believe it was that long. It felt as if we'd been working together only a year or two before. That's quite incredible. You know, in the time that had elapsed between those two films, Michael had been through a lot of physical problems. First of all, he had left the U.S. and moved to Canada. He swore he would never come back to America again and developed some imagined fixation that the Justice Department was out to get him. Michael was convinced that Janet Reno, the attorney general, had it in for him because he had gone to Washington with Dick Wolf, the creator and producer of *Law & Order*, to talk to the Justice Department about violence on television. Moriarty had gotten into an argument with Reno and just went nuts. Afterwards, he came back and eventually quit *Law & Order*, even though he had been the star and backbone of the show for four years and was making a fortune. Michael had been nominated for the Emmy Award for television every year, but he just walked away from it all. Personally, I feel that Michael always wanted to do everything he could to destroy himself, or at the very least make life difficult for himself. When things are going well for him, he has to do something to screw it all up. Unfortunately, that is what he has done throughout his whole career. He's a truly wonderful actor, but every time things are going great he creates this situation of absolute chaos. After leaving *Law & Order*, he then went to Canada and started drinking like a lunatic and getting into fist-fights in bars. On one occasion, he got beaten to a pulp by a bunch of guys in a bar who basically crippled him. Michael was in a wheelchair and on crutches, and he never fully recovered from the beating he took.

Was this before you made *Pick Me Up*?

Yes. In fact, the word quickly got to me that Moriarty couldn't do the film because he was now basically an invalid. I said, "Don't make any decisions until I see him first. Let me meet with him and figure out what we can or can't do." When I arrived in Canada and met with Michael, I immediately saw that he was walking with a cane and had a significant limp. I thought

I could double him and found an actor that looked a lot like Michael from the side and the rear. I used the double for certain shots where his character was required to run around or fight. Moriarty still plays the part in ninety-five percent of *Pick Me Up*, it's just a few instances where the action is very physical. So, we did get him in the film, even though there was some resistance from the producers, who believed he was physically incapacitated. The fact was they had to let me do what I wanted, and I wanted Moriarty for that part. He was my first and only choice. So, I hired him and, of course, he was fabulous. I actually think that Michael gave one of his greatest performances in *Pick Me Up*. At various times he is incredibly charming and then incredibly menacing, and sometimes he's both at once! You can't take your eyes off him. In fact, I was more than satisfied with all the actors we had on that film including Fairuza Balk and Warren Cole.

Let's talk about Fairuza Balk, who plays the object of the serial killers attentions. How did she come to be cast?

Frankly, I was surprised we got Fairuza. I didn't think we'd be able to get somebody as good as her for the part of the girl, although Fairuza had appeared in a few horror movies before *Pick Me Up*.[6] I was very happy to have her in the film, and she had a wonderful sense of humour. I kept Fairuza happy, and was fooling around with her all the time. She was a pleasure to work with and we never had a moment's conflict. I also enjoyed working with Warren Cole. I'd seen Warren in a television miniseries and thought he would play well against Moriarty, which he did. It was important that these two male characters be equally threatening. I must say that for the money we had to spend, and the fact you had to make these films quickly, it all worked out. I mean, you literally arrived there and went into pre-production, but sometimes these things are not cast until two or three days before you start shooting. There is not a lot of lead time and you can get down to a point where you have to select somebody and get them to Canada to shoot the damn film. I already had Moriarty and Fairuza, but Warren was the last minute choice. Fortunately, he turned out to be good.

How did you stage the climactic truck crash?

Even though I am averse to storyboarding, I had a storyboard artist come in to help work out what that sequence was going to be. Another reason I storyboarded the truck crash was because we had a wonderful stunt director on *Pick Me Up* and I was going to delegate a great deal of that sequence to him.[7] As I keep saying, it was always pouring with rain and freezing cold and, to be perfectly honest with you, I didn't want to stand out in that weather and choreograph the stunt. That process takes hours and hours. You are not only preparing the area where the stunt is going to take place, you are readying the catapults, putting in the safety equipment, and supervising all the other small details which have to be done. I might have supervised that sequence if the weather was fine, but it was awful. I also had the actors to deal with and we were shooting a dramatic scene elsewhere at the same time as the stunt director was preparing the truck crash. He called me when everything was ready, and I went up there to observe the stunt. I would then say if it was okay or if we needed to do it again. So, the stunt director deserves the credit for shooting that crash, but I did come up with the way it should play and I did supervise the drawing of the storyboards.

You clearly seem happy with how *Pick Me Up* turned out.

I thought it was very good, actually. *Pick Me Up* was better than I expected it to be. It was entertaining and the performances were better than those found in some of the other films. In fact, I thought Moriarty's performance was by far the best of any found in the entire series. That's only my opinion, but then he's just a better actor than everybody else so I suppose it was to be expected. We had a lot of fun together but, sadly, towards the end of shoot, Michael got a little irritable. Part of the reason for this was we had to film some other stuff ahead of him and he didn't like waiting around for his scenes to be shot. We had built a version of Moriarty's truck on a soundstage that was on a winch. This enabled us to turn the entire vehicle over onto its side with Fairuza strapped down inside of it. That took a lot of preparation and we had to keep Moriarty waiting for a very long time and he got annoyed. So, towards the end, things did get a little tense between us, and by the last day we weren't even on speaking terms. Afterwards, we did patch it up over the telephone and it was all okay.

When did you last see Moriarty?

Uh, I'm trying to remember. [Pause] Actually, I think that was the last time I saw him in person. Michael is a man who thinks about things deeply, perhaps too deeply. He is an incredibly intelligent and creative person but, unfortunately, he has these paranoid conspiracy theories and some other crazy ideas and opinions about life. But when it comes down to acting and playing a part, he has the ability to bring characters to life and invest them with an energy and believability that most actors can only ever dream of approaching.

Stella Adler, the legendary acting teacher, once hailed Moriarty as "one of the great actors in the Western world."

And she's absolutely right. He is one of the very best. Michael is a highly honored performer, who has won almost every major award in acting, including the Tony Award.[8] He's won the Emmy Award three times: firstly for *The Glass Menagerie* in which he starred alongside Katherine Hepburn, and, secondly for *Holocaust*, a role which also won him a Golden Globe. *Holocaust* was a very successful six-hour miniseries in which he played a despicably cruel Nazi officer. Michael was so deeply affected by that character, he vowed never to play a villain again, at least not until *Pick Me Up* came along. He won his third Emmy a few years ago for *James Dean*, in which he played Dean's father. The only major acting award that has eluded him is the Oscar, so he really is an exceptional talent.

Along with Takashi Miike, Don Coscarelli, and John McNaughton you were the only director who failed to return for the second season of *Masters of Horror*. Why was that? Surely it wasn't solely due to the weather conditions?

To tell you the truth, my last experience on *Masters of Horror* was not the most pleasant shoot. It wasn't only because the weather was horrendous and the money negligible, I simply had no desire to go back there again. I mean, you got paid very little for the amount of time and energy you put into the work. I felt that I had done my duty towards *Masters of Horror*. We all said that we would do one film and I did one film, just as I said I would. I didn't then feel obliged to go back and direct another film in the second season. Again, I don't think *Masters of Horror* was that good considering all the incredible talent involved. Frankly, I didn't think it was going to last, and the second season was worst than the first!

As of this conversation, *Pick Me Up* is your last credit as a director. John Carpenter told me he felt reinvigorated by working on *Masters of*

Horror, saying it re-ignited his love for making movies and led him to direct *The Ward*, his first theatrical feature in almost a decade. The experience obviously did not arouse that same feeling in you, but do you harbor any ambitions of one day returning to warm a director's chair?

Oh sure, I would love to direct again. I don't think I have the energy to do the insane eighteen to twenty-hour working days I used to do! [Chuckles] I'm not that crazy madman anymore—driving everyone forward—although those days were a lot of fun. The only problem these days, and it's rather a big one, is being able to get distribution on the pictures. Nowadays, lower-budgeted movies have a very difficult time getting any kind of distribution or advertising budget from the distributors. They want to sell you directly to DVD, or directly to Netflix, or directly to cable. There is no backend, no profits, and the exhibition of the picture is minimal. Nobody really sees your film, so what's the point of working so hard to make something if nobody is going to see it? I wish I could say that things were different now, but, ever increasingly, there are a couple of big movies that do all the business and every other movie does no business. A significant number of pictures never get played theatrically at all and you see them on DVD and say, "Look at the stars in this movie?" You'll find there are big name people associated with it, but the film was never in theaters. I was fortunate in my day that most of my pictures got theatrical distribution, or at least received very favorable video distribution. Today, you can work extremely hard on a movie and find yourself left totally frustrated. That situation greatly lessens my enthusiasm to return to directing.

What if somebody approached you with an offer you couldn't refuse?

Well, I've found that you can never say never in this business. I try not to make any definitive statements, just in case I later change my mind! [Chuckles] But as far as the directing goes, I will say that if somebody ever came to me and said, "Yeah, we'll make your picture. I would love to have you direct the film and here's when we can start," I wouldn't immediately turn them down. I would listen to what they have to say and seriously weigh the situation up. But to go out there now at my age and beat the bushes, trying to get these things put together like I used to do, I just can't do that anymore. It requires too much effort for too little reward. I don't want to struggle and work hard on a picture only for it not to ever be seen by anybody after I make it. No, that's just too traumatic and tragic for me.

Despite these hardships, you've already noted that both John Landis and Joe Dante are still out there in the trenches, making movies.

Yeah, and John Landis is a particularly good example. As I said, a few years after doing *Masters of Horror*, John went to England to make *Burke & Hare* and put together a very good cast with two excellent British actors in the leads.⁹ The picture was made, but then John couldn't secure distribution in the United States. One day, I was watching cable on Showtime and, suddenly, there was *Burke & Hare*. I ran into John a couple of days later and said, "Hey, John, I really enjoyed your movie." He asked, "Where did you see it?" I said, "It was on Showtime." He was like, "Oh, my god! I did not know that!" So, there you go. You struggle and sweat to make a whole movie and you don't even know what has happened to it. You have no idea where it is eventually going to show up, or indeed if it will ever be seen. This news was a total surprise to John because nobody ever told him about it. Those who were in control of *Burke & Hare* didn't feel they had an obligation to inform John that his movie was going to be on Showtime. That's the kind of treatment that you don't like to receive. It's incredibly depressing and disheartening. I mean, you would really love it if the people you are working with would be honest enough with you to tell you what the hell is going on.

There is obviously a collision of values here.

I would say it's more of a collapse than a collision. Sometimes there are no values in this business—at least none that you can recognize—and it becomes an adversarial situation. That's another problem with the business of making motion pictures: when you are on the set directing a film, it's about dealing with the producers and the associate producers and the studio executives and the other people on the picture, like the production managers. Sometimes, the production managers are not working in your interests, but are really working for the producers and the backers of the studio. A production manager is basically an informer, that's all. You sometimes hear them say, "Hey, he shot two hours over yesterday! He's wasting too much time on this scene!" There are too many people coming back, giving you complaints and arguments and discussions. Naturally, as a director, many people can come between you and a single decision or request you may make. That's just the way it is, but if I'm making a movie like *Pick Me Up* and I want to write a new scene where Michael Moriarty plays the piano, I don't have to ask for anybody's permission. I have the freedom to do what I want. I just say, "Put a piano in here, we're going to do a scene," and we just do it. If you are doing a regular picture, like most directors have to, you must obtain permission from the studio, the production executives, and other people. Almost immediately, somebody will say, "Hey, if you do that you are going to throw the picture over-budget and over-time!" With me, on my movies, I do what I damn well please. That's the way I want to make my pictures. If I can't make them my way, I don't ever want to make movies at all. I must be in absolute control of a film. I must have the freedom to improvise and make up new material and have some fun with it. If that is taken away from me, I simply can't work. I don't want to get up at five o'clock every morning to shoot these damn things, only to find that I'm dancing to somebody else's tune. I will never direct another movie again if I can't have complete autonomy.

On Writing

There seems to be a consensus amongst some critics that you are a better writer than you are a director. Do you agree with this view?

Yeah, I suppose, but then I don't really know if that's true. I mean, the movies I've made would not have been made the way they were if I had not directed them. There was so much of films like *God Told Me To*, *Q*, and *The Stuff* that was made up on the set, as opposed to being tightly scripted; material that was actually created with the actors as we were shooting. I would often send my pictures off in different and interesting directions that were not down on the page, but certainly felt a part of the continuing story. I often deviated from the scripts when I was shooting, but I did more than most directors did with the scripts that I wrote. I went off like a jazz musician, using the basic material as a theme and doing various riffs on the theme, occasionally returning to the theme. Did my ability to riff on my own stories make me a better writer? Or did my ability to implement these new ideas and communicate them successfully to the cast and crew make me a better director? So, I suppose the question of whether I'm a better writer or a better director is still open for discussion.

When you are writing a script, do you ever think about your audience?

No, I think about me.

Do you write at a particular time of day? Do you work set hours?

I don't write at any specific time of day. I more or less write in my spare time. I write when I have the chance, but I don't write to a regular schedule. I've never written to set hours. Back when I was first married and had kids, I used to write late at night after everybody went to sleep. I would wait for my wife and children to go to bed and then I would sneak downstairs and work from midnight until about four o'clock. I would then go to sleep, wake up in the morning and read the pages that I'd written the night before. I usually couldn't remember exactly what I had written and I used to find that fascinating, actually. It was almost like I was reading the scenes for the first time. It was like the work was totally subconscious and was coming from a different place—the depths of my subconscious mind. I would read this stuff as I was rubbing the sleep out of my eyes and be amazed at how good it often was. I'd go, "Wow! A little gremlin must have come in here last night and done all this!" [Laughs]

How conscious are you of theme and subtext before or during the writing? Or do you impose meaning onto some of these narratives postmortem?

I don't impose any meaning; it's just there to be interpreted by people. I don't consciously cook up a pre-emptive theme or allegory and then start writing it. Sometimes, a moral emerges during the writing; other times, it only becomes apparent to me after I've finished the script. So, it's not a conscious thing.

Some critics have detected themes and motifs in your work that they claim relate to Judaism and Jewish-ness. I know you've been asked about this previously and have insisted that you are not conscious of it. Were you being completely honest?

Oh, absolutely. It's not something I consciously think about when I'm writing. If you are analysing my pictures and you want to fix a Jewish angle on all the work, well, okay. God bless you! But you shouldn't ignore other things that are in there, too, as there are a lot of different themes and motifs in my movies. There's stuff about family, social issues, politics, sexuality. A lot of things. It's not only the religious aspects.

What things encourage these religious readings in your opinion?

Well, there are characters in my movies that are gods or are god-like, but I think all of that is seen from a very human perspective. Do you know what I mean? There's always that sense of fallibility and mystery, because

I don't know all the answers. Nobody does. I just write these things and, again, it all comes out of my subconscious. Yeah, some people do see Jewishness in my work, but I always say the same thing over and over again: I don't know where it comes from. I once went to a question and answer session with Robin Wood, and one kid claimed he'd found a lot of Jewish things in my movies. He started pointing to various scenes that supported his argument and it was all very cogent and eloquent. I just didn't agree with it!

Specifically, what scenes did this person refer to?

Oh, I don't know. One was the scene in *It's Alive* where the milkman is killed and the bottles shatter and the milkman's blood mingles with the milk. This kid felt that moment was an explicit reference to the dietary decrees of Jewish law, in that you cannot eat a meal that mixes meat and milk. What he said was very well thought-out, but it couldn't have been further from my intentions. It was just an idea I had, that's all. All the meanings he read into it were the product of his imagination, not mine.

As a writer, do you often sympathize with your characters, or do you prefer to maintain a distant objectivity?

I do sympathise with some of them. I try to get inside a character's head. Sometimes, you sympathise and empathise with characters when you are writing them because they are feeling moments of pain, fear, doubt, and shame. You can relate to those negative emotions as a human being. As a parent, you can sympathise with the parents of the monster babies in the *It's Alive* films and imagine how you would feel and behave if that was your child; if you were suddenly responsible for bringing this despised and feared creature into the world. Contrary to that, anyone who has ever felt alone or abandoned or rejected, can sympathise with the plight of the monster baby. You may not have maliciously killed anyone in cold blood, or maybe you have, I don't know, but it's still relatable to your own life, your own experiences, your own thoughts and feelings. If you can inhabit a character when you are creating them, never mind how despicable or undesirable they may be, I think that can only help you as a writer. Of course, if you haven't got any personal experience of something, in the end it all comes down to instinct and imagination.

One source of strength for your characters is the family unit and its central importance in life, but it's also the source of the horror in your films, isn't it?

Yes. Horror comes from the home as surely as love does. Those you love can often do you serious harm—even kill you—and the family experience can be painful and destructive. In *Bone*, you have a seemingly prosperous American family, but then the underside of it is the husband and wife hate each other and their son is locked up on a drug wrap. The entire idealized version of the American family is turned inside out. In *It's Alive, It Lives Again,* and *God Told Me To*, there are families mired in guilt, confusion, and violence, and it all grows out of the blood relations. All of the great plays that have been written by the likes of Eugene O'Neil and Arthur Miller deal directly with the family. The family seems to be the beginning of everything, and that's where all the trouble lies. The family is the sanctuary and the battleground. It's actually true that you are more likely to be killed by a member of your own family than a complete stranger. They say that most murders happen amongst acquaintances, and so people will kill other people that they know quite well, like a family member, a friend, or a business partner. People are always worried about somebody breaking into their homes and doing them harm, but they are often in more danger from the people they live with—and love—than any external threat.

A stick that has been used to beat horror and science fiction cinema is the lack of characters that are consistently well-developed, layered, and articulate. Is that something you always strive to establish in your writing?

Yes, totally, and I think it's true—a lot of horror and science fiction films are shallow. Historically in horror movies, particularly those made during the 1950s and '60s, the characters were mostly cardboard figures, who would utter this incredibly stupid dialogue. Developing characters and giving them something important to say was secondary. The casting was often highly ridiculous, too. They would have some beautiful girl with big breasts and glasses, stumbling through her dialogue, and we'd have to simply accept that she was a nuclear physicist. You'd see the movie and say, "Sure, of course Raquel Welch is a scientist!" It was absurd. The characters in horror movies were often completely inane. They wouldn't have any true conflicts between them except that they would be running around trying to kill the monster. If you go back to the films that were done at Universal in the 1930s, there were some solid characterisations and wonderful casts. The studio would employ fine British actors, like Claude Rains in *The Invisible Man*, Sir Cedric Hardwicke in *The Invisible Man Returns,* and Boris Karloff in *Frankenstein*. Those films had strong performances and they meant something. Karloff's portrayal of the Monster is one of the great film performances of all time and certainly one of the most iconic. Later on, when you got into the 1950s and pictures like *The Creature from the Black Lagoon* were made, the actors were less accomplished. Those films were mostly populated with B-movie actors, who weren't very good, playing underwritten characters in seriously undernourished stories. By the 1970s, when they started making pictures like *Jaws* and *Alien*, the acting obviously got a lot of better, as horror and science fiction were embraced by the big studios and awarded higher budgets. As a result, those movies attracted a higher caliber of actor. Even though my pictures had low-budgets, they still have some of the best acting that you will find in any horror and science fiction movies. The parts that Tony Lo Bianco played in *God Told Me To*, Michael Moriarty played in *Q*, and John P. Ryan in *It's Alive*, are all remarkable, regardless of budget or genre. They are at a much higher level of quality than what you usually see.

Would it be prudent to say that the emphasis on character in genre films is often sacrificed in favor of a concentration on scares and violence?

Sure, but it all starts with the script: discovering who your characters are; the world they inhabit, what happens to them, and how they react to what has occurred. A lot of writers will consciously punctuate a horror script with a scare or a messy kill every few pages, probably because they don't have enough confidence in their material. I never work that way because it's too restrictive. I think that some of my movies were not as scary as they perhaps could have been. They might have been more successful if they were less literate, less intelligent, and concentrated on being just plain frightening. At the box office, horror movies are basically more successful in direct relation to their scare ratio. In other words, the number of times the audience jumps in the theater throughout the film's running time. If a horror movie has two or three good jump-scares, you probably have a hit regardless of the picture's overall quality. I think my horror movies mostly contained one great jump-scare, a lot of good dialogue, sophisticated characters, and strong performances. That's not always what makes for a big box office hit, but it does create a movie that has some kind of longevity to it. People do appreciate these pictures over a period of time and still talk about my films. In the case of *It's Alive*, I think it even brings a tear to your eye at the end when Frank Davis finds the monster baby in the storm drains, picks it up in his arms, and tries to save it. That is not the typical climax of your standard horror movie, which aims for scares and violence as opposed to having an emotional impact on the audience. You don't have a strong emotional dimension in many horror movies.

You have complained of being left frustrated and angered by the tampering of your screenplays by various directors and producers. Did you exhibit that same sense of ruthlessness when you were adapting novels like *I, the Jury* and *The Ex*, or did your own experiences compel you to be true to the source material?

No. I would just read the book, get the basic idea of the story, and then I wrote the script without ever once looking back. As a matter of fact, I may have only read those particular books you mentioned once and then that was it. Anyway, I was not only translating those books into a different medium, I was also doing my own version of somebody else's story. I certainly never felt guilty or concerned about making any changes that I felt were necessary. I've never had one sleepless night about it.

Some authors and screenwriters have complained about the destructive aspects of writing; how the process can deplete, damage, or destroy you. Is that something you can connect with?

No, not at all. I very much enjoy writing—all kinds of writing. It's such a kick to write a script, finish it, and send it out into the world. I find the whole process to be very easy, so I don't find the act of creating to be destructive. Quite the reverse, actually; it's exhilarating and stimulating. I mean, sure, writing can sometimes be a lonely business. You are often just sitting there alone in a room, scribbling like crazy or pounding away on a computer. That can feel isolating for some writers, but I find the actual writing, creating new characters, stories, and scenes to be a lot of fun. I see it more as a voyage of discovery, not something that can destroy you. Frustration and bitterness at not getting your books published or your screenplays produced—now that can certainly destroy you! Of course, frustration and bitterness can also come from having your scripts produced and they in no way resemble what you originally wrote. That can be almost as bad, except for the money.

Have you ever experienced writer's block?

No, never.

Is there a secret to your immense productivity?

If there was a secret to my being so prolific I would certainly tell you. I just find it very easy to write and I tend not to examine why that is. You are only truly a writer when you are writing. Maybe that's why I keep on doing it. If I could point to one thing it would probably be the fact that when I am writing, I'm excited to see where the story is heading. I don't know where it's going and I'm anxious to find out. That keeps me energised and working hard every day. Maybe that's the secret.

Do you do much in the way of rewriting?

No, not a great deal. I really only do a small amount of rewriting. Some scripts need a little polish and a few loose ends tidied up, but once it's done it's done.

I once read an interview in which you revealed that you actually write your screenplays with the aid of a pen and paper.

Yes, lately, I do. I used to write all of my earlier scripts by dictation. I used to dictate into a tape recorder. Before that, I used to dictate the words to a secretary, but I eventually wore all the secretaries down. They would quite literally collapse, so I purchased a tape recorder. After that, I then started writing in longhand.

Was there any particular reason for why you didn't use a typewriter, a word processor, or a computer?

I just enjoyed the process of writing more by doing it that way. Actually, and this is going way back, I once got a staple stuck in my finger. It seemed pretty innocuous at the time, but the wound just wouldn't heal itself. Eventually, I had to have an operation and the surgeons had to graft some skin from my arm and put my hand in a cast. This forced me into dictating my scripts, but I quickly realized that I could get a lot of work done. So, out of that misfortune came something good. It was so easy and I found it very comfortable and productive to work that way.

Didn't you find it difficult not actually seeing the words appear or emerge on the page in front of you?

I don't like to see anything on a screen. I like to write the whole script and then look at it afterwards. I don't like to read it while I'm writing it. I don't like to judge what I'm writing. I like to get fully involved with a story and then just speed on ahead.

Do you think the process you use directly affects the number of pages you write, the length and structure of the script, and the duration of certain scenes?

That's a good question, but I never think about things like that. I don't like to write to any particular form at all. I just write the screenplay as I see the movie unfolding in my imagination. I certainly don't follow any kind of formula, procedure, or structure that you might read about in a book on screenwriting or might hear in a class about screenwriting. I mean, you have that famous guy who apparently teaches the rules of screenwriting . . . uh, what's his name?

Robert McKee.

That's him. I hate McKee's writing class and everything he stands for. The fact that he is telling everybody where everything has to be in order for a script to be considered a good one, it just seems ridiculous to me. Far too many people have read his books or attended his classes, and this is viewed as some kind of proof or endorsement of McKee's methods and suggestions. To me, it just seems stupid. Here is a man who has never sold a script and never had a picture produced, and yet he has the audacity to tell everyone else how to write screenplays. What the hell does he know about screenwriting? The man is a fool—or perhaps he isn't. I mean, people actually pay him to be told about *Casablanca*! What amazes me is the fact that *Casablanca* is the most atypical screenplay ever written. First of all, it's a stage play adapted into a movie. Secondly, it mostly all happens at Rick's Café on the one set. Thirdly, the ending was written at the last minute. That's not the way screenplays are written. McKee doesn't know anything about anything, except for taking people's money.

Do you detect McKee's influence on how screenplays are being written?

I think several things have happened in the wake of McKee's success: firstly, studio executives, who have taken his class or read his books, now believe that McKee's model is the law. If a script comes in that doesn't follow McKee's form, they immediately assume that it's bad because they don't know any better. Studio executives have no creative ability anyway. Most of them are a bunch of pretentious fools. They can't really do anything. They can't write, they can't produce, they can't direct, they can't compose. All they can do is sit there telling everybody else what they should or should not be doing. They have no credentials whatsoever, no knowledge that gives them any kind of insight, and yet they can still come in with their little notepads and tell everybody what to do. They are a bunch of idiots, frankly, but you have to put up with them. Of course, I don't have to put up with them too much because I usually write screenplays on spec. I just sell them the script when it's finished, so I don't always have to endure their wisdoms.

If you don't subscribe to any particular structure or method of screenwriting, what about the actual layout of your scripts?

I don't follow any layout. I just write the scripts. I start telling the story as I'm watching the movie in my head and I just lay it out. Again, it's like I'm freely drawing everything out of my subconscious. I speak into the tape recorder, or I write on a piece of paper, what the scene is I'm imagining. I don't know what's coming next and I don't know where it's going. I just make it up as I go along. I'm not working from a step outline, as I'm just taking an idea and letting it evolve naturally. It's almost like automatic writing, really. That's the only way I can explain it that makes any sense.

I think you've misunderstood me. I'm referring to the industry standard in which a script is physically laid out on the page.

Oh, I see. When I give the script to the typist, she has a program in her computer that makes the script come out in its finished form. I don't do it. I send it out to a typist.

Screenwriters are often treated with disdain, aren't they? They provide the blueprint for the movie, but their work is routinely rewritten by other screenwriters. Then a director is attached to the project and brings his or her own writer onboard, who then proceeds to deliver yet another draft or polish.

Screenwriters are never treated with the respect they deserve. It's hard for any writer to maintain his or her dignity and enthusiasm when you are faced with such ruthlessness and duplicity. Writers are often shut out of the production—when their input can not only be valuable but crucial to the success of a movie. It's always the final film that ends up suffering in terms of the overall quality and consistency. A lot of times, these movies turn out to be absolute pieces of junk! I mean, look at the pictures I've written that have been made in the last ten years. One has been worse than the other. Oh, they are just absolutely awful! *Messages Deleted* turned out to be terrible; *Captivity* was a nightmare it was so bad; the ones that were directed by Mark Lester, *The Ex* and *Misbegotten*, were also very poor. All of those scripts were infinitely superior to what was eventually realized on screen. And, of course, your name is on the film as the writer. You are then associated with them in perpetuity and you are blamed for these things: "Yeah, it's his fault this is a shallow, irredeemable piece of trash!" You know, I almost feel sorry for these guys—the Mark Lesters of the world—because they get a good piece of material and they simply don't have the ability to bring it to the screen without fucking it up. Nearly every single picture has just been a total subversion and perversion of my original script. On every project, they took a great screenplay and systemically made a lousy movie out of it. What can you do? You write these things—and I can be perfectly honest with you and say I did them all for the money. As soon as I sell these scripts, I know that my authority and control over them is finished. I can then only hope and pray that they will make a good movie out of it. Unfortunately, in most cases, that's yet to really happen.

Is the secret to completely disassociate emotionally as a means of protecting yourself? To understand that this is simply the way the machinery works?

I don't know. It can be extremely painful watching something you've created be transformed into a steaming turd. When you have a whole succession of movies that have been ruined—like I have—it can be tough. Knowing how the business works certainly doesn't lessen that anguish. In fact, it only increases it. But you know what? I don't get dispirited. I just keep cashing the cheques, one after the other, and I try to forget about it. If perchance the picture gets made, then I can lament how poorly it was done. I do have the freedom to condemn them. Things like *Captivity*, which, as I keep telling you, is a piece of shit, have been totally ruined. You just have to try and put that disappointment in its place. It's not always easy, but you do it.

One thing that has been most welcome is the publishing of screenplays as books for readers to enjoy. This can sometimes allow people to see what a script was in its original form, particularly if it's been greatly altered for better or for worse.

Yes, that is something I like very much—the fact that people can read an original screenplay and still get a lot of enjoyment out of it. In fact, some of my unpublished screenplays, like *The Man Who Loved Hitchcock*, are available on my website, larrycohenfilmmaker.com. There is something on there I call "Movies for Your Imagination." I have this idea that movies are basically dreaming with your eyes open, and I invite people to share in my dreams. "Movies For Your Imagination" basically informs people that there are ten wonderful screenplays available on the website for free that they can enjoy. You can read them and imagine your favorite actors playing the characters. You can even play your favorite movie music as you go through the scenes. You can read the pages aloud with your friends playing the various characters and have a lot of fun imagining the locations and special effects. In fact, you can do everything with these scripts but publish and produce them! But those ten screenplays are works that I'm extremely proud of. I would even say that the scripts featured on my website are far better than any movie you will currently see in the theater.

Do you think by making those screenplays available on the Internet you've made it difficult for them to ever get made?

I don't understand why it would be harder to get them made. I mean, there's a big difference between reading a script and going to the theater to see a movie. Those are two entirely different experiences. It's like saying that if a book is published, you wouldn't be able to make a movie out of it later on. Of course, publishing a book very often incites interest in making the movie. People already know the story, but they want to see it realized on the big screen. How many times have you heard the words: "You've read the book—now see the movie!" That was the old saying they used to have emblazoned on the advertisements. In my case, maybe it should be: "You've read the script—now why wouldn't you want to go see the movie?"

Earlier, you said that you enjoy "all kinds of writing." I suppose this is as good a time as any to discuss the theater plays that you have written throughout your career. What was the first play you had performed on stage?

The first play I did was in 1970 and that was *The Nature of the Crime*. It had Tony Lo Bianco, Robert F. Simon, and a lot of other very good actors in it and was directed by Lonny Chapman, who wasn't a very good director. It was about a nuclear physicist, who refuses to give up his ideas and discoveries to the government. The government then puts him on trial, claiming that his mind is government property. That was the one I told you about which was based on an earlier television show I had written called "The Secret." The play was adapted directly from that episode after I had bought the rights back from Herbert Brodkin. It's interesting but when I was casting *The Nature of the Crime*, I originally tried to get a young actor named Al Pack-i-no for the role. When I called Mr. Pack-i-no up to discuss it, he actually corrected me and said his name was Al Pacino! Anyway, he was doing *Panic in Needle Park* at the time and couldn't commit, so my next choice was Tony Lo Bianco. *The Nature of the Crime* then became the second-longest off-Broadway play—serious play—of the year, but it didn't do that well. It played something like eight weeks, but even then it was still the second-longest off-Broadway play. I do recall that the first-longest off-Broadway play that year was *[The Effect of Gamma Rays on] Man-in-the-Moon Marigolds*.[1]

Was *Motive* then your second play?

Yes, I believe it was. I wrote *Motive* after *The Nature of the Crime*. That play was mounted over in England during the time I lived there in the mid-1970s. It starred Honor Blackman, George Cole, and Ian Hendry. *Motive* was first performed at Guilford's Yvonne Arnaud Theatre. We then went on tour with it around England and it played at a number of different theaters. That production had an excellent cast, but I do remember that Ian Hendry was drinking all the time. He was a nice fellow, but he always had a bottle in his pocket. George Cole was also nice. At the beginning of the show, the actors weren't too friendly. They were all being directed by Val May, who was the manager of the Guildford Theater. When the play went out on tour, Val remained in Guilford and didn't go with us. So, I said to the actors, "Would you mind if I redirected some of the scenes?" They said they didn't mind at all. I then came in and started having rehearsals and began redirecting the play. The cast all responded favorably, and *Motive* got better as we toured around with it. Later on, Honor Blackman didn't perform the play in Ireland and some other areas, and her part was done by Carroll Baker. Carroll had famously appeared in *Baby Doll*.[2] She'd been a Hollywood star, playing Jean Harlow and things like that. Then, we toured the United States with *Motive* and once again had a very nice cast. The American version starred Craig Stevens, who had played *Peter Gun* in the popular television series, Elizabeth Allen, and John Randolph. Another excellent group of people.

Was the American incarnation of *Motive* more successful than the British one?

No, it was about the same. It toured for a few months before closing.

You then did *Motive* on Broadway as *Trick*, which I understand was performed in February 1979.

Trick was a thriller that starred Tammy Grimes. Tammy was quite a formidable lady—very intelligent and dedicated—and a wonderful actress. She had a very studious and meticulous approach to her work, which I respected. The overriding memory I have of Tammy from those days is the amount of questions she would constantly ask me. She seemed to have a question for every page we turned and every piece of dialogue. I remember on the first day of rehearsals, she was stopping on every line and asking me a question about this and that. I wasn't exactly used to that level of scrutiny, but I answered every single question she threw at me. By the time that first day was over, Tammy had a fix on her character and the story and she never once asked me another question. She was incredibly attentive and co-operative, and I never had a single problem with her.

What Tammy had been doing that first day was probing me and testing me. She wanted to know if I was as smart as I thought I was. What she didn't realize is that whenever I was incapable of answering one of her questions, I simply made an answer up! [Chuckles] But that was another good cast right there.

Trick co-starred Donald Madden and Lee Richardson and you famously joined a performance of the play one night after Richardson took ill. You must have often been asked about that night?

Well, it's one of those incredible evenings in my life. It was Tammy's idea that I should play Lee Richardson's part. I would never have dreamed of such a thing happening, but there I was, making my Broadway debut. If I'd have gotten a chance to think about it, I probably wouldn't have done it. As it was, I had the script in my hand as I performed, but I didn't look at it all that much. I knew the lines because I had written and rehearsed them. I managed to struggle my way through the performance and even got a few laughs, but I had no desire to repeat the experience. I do remember that at one point my character was killed by Donald Madden's character and I accidentally dropped the script on the stage. As we played the scene, Donald then had to drag my corpse behind the couch so Tammy's character wouldn't see it. As he did this, I whispered, "Donald, get the script! Get the script!" So, he went back, scooped up the script, and hid it behind the couch. Well, the audience saw all this and just roared with laughter. It was a wonderful moment, actually. It could have been disastrous, but it turned out to be the highlight of the evening. *Trick* got some pretty good reviews, I must say. It was all set to have a decent run but, unfortunately, we then we ran into the winter—heavy snowing and vicious blizzards every single day. It was very hard for the audience to get to the theater, so we eventually decided that we'd had enough, and *Trick* closed. I then went back to Hollywood because I had other things to do. I wanted to make some real money.

Washington Heights was your next play, which was first performed in 1987.

Yeah, that was several years after *Motive*. *Washington Heights* played in New York at what they call The Jewish Repertory Theater. That was a semi-autobiographical play about growing up during World War II in

Washington Heights. That played for about eight weeks and got a good audience because they sold the production out in advance to subscribers. The Jewish Repertory was a subscription theater and whenever *Washington Heights* was playing, they came to see it because they had bought group tickets, things like that. We did very well with that play. Although I don't really have a favorite of the plays I've written—as I think all the plays had something good in them—I do feel *Washington Heights* is the closest to my heart because it was about me as a child. It was a nice play, and I wish we had gotten more performances of it. There was some talk of doing it out here in Los Angeles. We'll see what happens.

More recently, you wrote a play called *Fallen Eagle*. Is that the Charles Lindbergh project you once planned to do as a movie?

Yeah. We did *Fallen Eagle* at The Sanford Meisner Theater in Burbank around 2009, I think, after also doing the stage play of *Captivity* here in Los Angeles. It was a biographical play about Charles Lindbergh, the famous American aviator and explorer. *Fallen Eagle* was received alright and ran for about five weeks, but I had to cast it out of The Sanford Meisner Acting School. As a result of that, some of the casting wasn't very good, so it wasn't the best possible production. I did direct *Fallen Eagle*, but I wasn't happy with many of the performances. I'm afraid we kind of just went through the motions on that one, but I am happy that we did it. I once talked to Oliver Stone about the possibility of his directing the Lindbergh movie, but nothing ever came of it. Of course, it would have been a period film, and they can be difficult to make—and very expensive! It could be done now by recreating the backgrounds digitally with digital effects, but it's not quite the same as photographing the real environment. You just don't get that tactile reality when you use digital effects. But *Fallen Eagle* is another script that is available to read on my website.

Can you talk about the differences, challenges, and benefits of writing theater plays as opposed to writing teleplays and screenplays?

Well, one of the rewards of the theater is you can go there and see the audience reaction every night, and then, afterwards, make revisions and adjustments to the play. You can write new scenes, makes cuts, and change the dialogue, so the play is essentially a living, breathing, functioning entity. A play allows you to gauge the audience reaction directly and intimately; and by integrating that reaction into the actual production you are doing something that is nearly impossible in movies—not unless you make a sequel. That's kind of fun and uniquely challenging in its own way, because the theater offers a writer a continuous and evolving process. I should also say that directing a play is much easier than directing a film because you don't have to deal with the camera, the lighting, the microphones, and all the other technical problems you encounter. You don't have to deal with planes flying overhead and other disruptive background noise; the actors all know their lines as you go through it and the only difficult time for me on a play is the tech day. That's the day when you first put the lighting in and the scene changes, etc. On a two-hour play, it probably takes twelve hours to do that day because the technical requirements have to be done. You have to stop and go, stop and go, stop and go, so the tech day is very much like working on a movie. A movie literally consists of eighteen or twenty or thirty days of tech days, which are even more exhausting. So, making a play is a lot easier.

Do you plan on writing any more plays in the near future?

You never know. Actually, that's not a bad idea. There's not much money in doing these plays, so writing them is really just a matter of personal satisfaction.

As opposed to the big bucks you can earn writing screenplays.

Absolutely. I mean, it's an entirely different ballgame. Right now, I'm writing scripts that people pay me a million dollars for. So, if you can get somebody to give you a million dollars for a script, I'd say you might as well sell it to them and go ahead and write another one, and another one, and another one. It's a much easier and profitable life being a screenwriter than it is being a playwright. Actually, it's a much easier life being a writer than it is being a director—or a writer-director. The rewards are better and your stress levels are not quite so high. After I wrote *Phone Booth*, I got a great number of screenplay assignments and sold a great number of scripts. Some of them have been made and some of them were bought, but they never made the picture because they ran out of money. I'm hoping that some of these scripts I've written recently do eventually get made because they are very good scripts. I just keep on writing more and more of them. I actually sold two scripts last year, and neither of them has been made, but they sold, and I was paid, and the money is in the bank. So far this year, I've turned out at least three new scripts. They are out there in the marketplace and we're still only in May. I think we'll sell one or two of them, so there's a certain satisfaction in selling your scripts and knowing that people are still buying my material. I will continue to write screenplays, and if something else arouses my interest, like a play, then I'll write a new play. It's as simple as that.

Methodology, Movies & Madness

You are a fiercely independent director, but do you see yourself as belonging to or coming from any particular tradition or movement of American filmmaking?

I don't really understand what that means. Yes, there was an era back in the late 1960s and early '70s, when a lot of young filmmakers were coming up and they were the so-called "Movie Brats." I don't include myself with them because they did a lot of big studio work. I suppose that would be the likes of Spielberg, Scorsese, Coppola, and Lucas, some of whom went to film school and were familiar with the history of movies both in Hollywood and in Europe. Then there are the "horror guys"—another group I'm sometimes included with by some people. You know, directors like John Carpenter and Tobe Hooper, all the usual suspects. Speaking for myself, I've never been part of any movement whatsoever. I am my own movement. I just did my own thing and that was it. That's probably the best thing about me. I never once thought that I belonged to any tradition or school of filmmaking.

Can you identify your own individual style as a director, and, if so, how would you describe it?

Gosh! [Pause] I always leave that kind of analysis for other people to attempt. I don't like to be too self-conscious about what I do in terms of saying this is my particular style or that is. What has developed over the years, as the films have progressed, is more humor has been introduced into the mix than was maybe evident in the movies I made earlier in my career. So, I suppose that if you have to put a label on what I do, I make suspense-thrillers with a humorous undertone. I also try to do pictures that have a rich thematic subject and some kind of serious connotation. I try to make something that has a definite political or subversive context of some kind. The horror films I've made, and the science fiction and fantasy films, are all engaged in some kind of social or political commentary. It's more pronounced in some pictures than it is in others but it's always there. I'm not interested in making some kind of infantile horror movie that is devoid of intelligent discussion. That isn't my kind of picture.

As you've implied, you have used horror and fantasy as a means of addressing contentious issues such as pollution and abortion. So, is there a certain freedom in masquerading social commentaries as genre films?

Usually you can't get movies made that deal directly with serious subjects like pollution or abortion, so that would suggest that genre films do offer you more freedom to explore serious issues. Otherwise, you would have a hard time getting the pictures made and distributed because those kinds of difficult subjects are not considered commercial. But if you put them in the context of a horror film or a thriller or an entertainment movie, then you can address controversial issues head-on and get the message you want to make out there. I've used horror, science fiction, and fantasy as a vehicle to provide a commentary on certain thoughts and concerns I've had about the world. Some will understand what you are attempting to say and will receive the message and others won't, but you do have the fun of making a picture that has audience potential. That's really the way to get these movies made.

Would you agree that one of your primary strengths as a filmmaker is your ability to make the most ludicrous premise seem intelligent and dynamic?

Yeah, I think that's probably true. I mean a monster baby, or an ice cream that kills people, or a flying dinosaur terrorising New York City, are all outrageous ideas, but we made them believable, at least for the hour and a half that you were watching the movie. So, yes, I'd agree, but that only works if you approach the material in a certain way that doesn't insult the audience's intelligence. You must take the subject matter seriously even when you dress it up with fantastical elements. What I like is when people say, "We watched a movie last night on cable and we came in about fifteen minutes into the picture. We didn't know who made the film, but after we were watching it for about ten minutes we said, 'Oh, this must be a Larry Cohen movie!'" I like it when people can clearly recognize the film as being mine from just viewing the picture itself without seeing the credits. I consider that a great compliment, because it means they have noticed and recognized different elements in my work.

One element I've noticed about your movies is your continued insistence on placing characters up on tall buildings. It's certainly evident in *Hell up in Harlem, God Told Me To, Full Moon High,* and *Q – The Winged Serpent.* Where do you think this fascination with great heights comes from?

I don't know. I've never really considered it. In *Full Moon High*, there's the scene where the guy is going to jump off the building, and I always think it's funny if a person is about to leap off a great height and somebody else is telling them to go ahead and do it! [Chuckles] In fact, there exists an entire school of psychology where they insult, berate, and even assault the patients for coming in with their problems. It's a form of treatment that follows the route of attacking the patient. That particular scene was an exaggeration of that practice, so it had some truth to it. When I was doing *Daddy's Gone A-Hunting*, I had to climb to the top of the Mark Hopkins Hotel in San Francisco because the climax took place on the roof. When we did *El Condor* in Spain, they built the fort and I simply had to climb to the top of it. When we were doing *Q*, I had to climb to the eighty-eighth floor of the Chrysler Building on a little ladder and, as I told you, there was nothing up there to keep you from falling. I guess I'm constantly climbing on top of things. There's no question about it. When we were scouting locations in France for *The Apparatus*, I was climbing on top of things like the Paris Opera House. Believe me I would not ordinarily do that if I wasn't making a movie. I would not scale these high places, but I always seem to end up climbing up something. I can't explain it, other than to say there is the inherent dramatic potential in staging scenes like that as a lot of people are afraid of heights. I would imagine that it's one of the most common fears we have. So, if you are going to do a scary and suspenseful movie like *God Told Me To* or *Q*, you should use some height. Hitchcock understood that and made excellent use of heights to create moments of suspense. He had characters climbing on top of the Statute of Liberty in *Saboteur,* and climbing on Mount Rushmore in *North by*

Northwest. There is also the scene in *Foreign Correspondent*, where Edmund Gwenn tries to push Joel McCrea off the Bell Tower of Westminster Cathedral, and, of course, in *Vertigo*, the entire movie is about heights.

You've spoken of collaborating and developing scenes with actors as they are being shot. Do you consider yourself an actor's director?

I'll say this: there are a lot of things that I don't think of until I see the scene being played out as the cameras are rolling. I don't direct my films from behind a monitor half a block away from the set like a lot of directors do. Some directors are not looking directly at the actors and are viewing the performances on television screens that keep them separated from the action. I like to be right behind the camera in direct communication with the actors—both visually and vocally—so I can talk to them while they are doing the scenes. I can't work unless I'm right on top of the actors and I'm watching the proceedings carefully and feeding them new information. I think the actors like it that way and find it creatively stimulating. They like to see that something new is developing all the time.

Did that technique evolve over time or have you always been interested in actors and their various processes?

It's just the way I like to work, but a lot of directors don't like actors. They are afraid of actors and try to keep their distance from them. A lot of directors try to create a position of authority, so they can seize the first opportunity that presents itself to announce, "Hey, I'm the boss here! I'm the dictator of the show and everybody has to do exactly what I tell them!" Those kinds of directors don't want to be questioned or second-guessed by the performers. To me, the real fun of making a movie is to hire really good, inventive actors and work with them. I don't mind it when actors ask me a question. In fact, I've always found that the better the actor is, the more questions he or she is going to ask. When you're dealing with actors who don't ask any questions, then they are probably not going to give you much of a performance. In my mind, they don't care enough about exploring their characters. The more queries an actor asks, the more creative ideas they can come up with. That in turn inspires me as a writer to come up with other ways to enrich the character. So, I'm never threatened by actors. I enjoy the process of adding new material and writing new scenes for them. If you sit down in front of an actor with a pencil and paper, and you write a new scene right there in front of them, and then you pass it over, it's wonderful. There is only one handwritten copy of that scene in existence and the actor has it right there in their hands. Then we just walk out onto the set and do it. I've always found that you more or less own the actor after doing that. They are made to feel special and involved. They often say, "Wow! This guy just created that scene for me right there—out of nothing!" Once you've done that, the actor just wants you to do it more and more. When we were making *The Ambulance*, Eric Roberts would often say to me, "Give me a Larry Cohen line for this! Give me a Larry Cohen line for that!" And I would just do it for him. I'd write the line down, pass it along, and Eric would incorporate it into the scene. That kind of creative interaction really turns an actor on.

It seems counterproductive to the success of any film that a director would attempt to alienate or restrict his or her actors.

Oh absolutely, but some directors will take an adversarial approach because they think it will somehow strengthen their position. I don't think that way. What I like is when some of the actors will occasionally turn up at the set on the days when they are not supposed to be working. I'll say to them, "Hey, what are you doing here? You're not on the call sheet today." They will invariably say, "I just came in to see what was happening." This only occurs because they seem to be interested in the project and the working environment I've tried to create. They feel compelled to show up just to see what's going on. They don't want to miss a thing. That's great because you realize that these people are really into the process of making the movie. I mean, the actors work tremendously long hours—particularly on these low-budget movies—and nobody complains about it. They are so hyped-up about everything that's going on, like I am, nobody asks for overtime or makes a big deal about the fact that they've had to work late and didn't get their meal on time. They are committed and excited and involved in what we're doing and they're having fun. I really love that because I know these people will basically do anything for me, and that's wonderful.

Why do you often employ the same actors? Some of your regulars, like James Dixon and Andrew Duggan, have been labeled "Larry Cohen's Irish Players."

I often use the same actors over and over again because I enjoy the sense of familiarity and camaraderie you get from a stock company of players. It's always been my thinking that if the actors can tolerate me, and perhaps understand me, then they'll be willing to come back and work with me for a second, a third, maybe even a fourth time. They also know exactly what to expect. Of course, not everybody is going to enjoy you or the atmosphere you are trying to create on the set. Some actors either do not or can not respond to you for whatever reason. Some people get with it and enjoy it and others simply don't. That's okay. It's probably not for everybody. But I think those who can relish the experience (at least this is the feedback that I've received from certain actors) will get a lot from it. I encourage the performers to improvise and be inventive, and that's a very seductive working environment for an actor. They know that as the director you are relying on them to be creative and bring their own ideas to how a scene is going to play. That can be irresistible.

Do you adjust your working methods to accommodate an actor?

It depends on the actor as not everybody responds to the improvisational approach. Some actors require more attention and direction, or have their own methods and approach to performance. On some of the pictures I made with Michael Moriarty, we would shoot scenes that would include two or three actors, but Moriarty would occasionally insist that I shoot his close-ups last without any of the other actors being present. In my experience that is highly unusual. I'd say, "Michael, are you sure about this?" He'd say, "Yeah, let the other actors go home and shoot my close-ups just with me. I want to do this scene all by myself." Of course, that approach would concern me somewhat. I'd suggest to Moriarty that the script girl read the other actors' dialogue to him, but he would refuse: "No, I don't want anybody to read the lines to me. I know everybody's lines. I'll say them to myself in my head as we are going along." I'd say, "What about the pauses? What about the looks to the other actors off-camera?" Moriarty would just shake his head and say, "I know when to pause and where to look. Let's just do it." So, we'd shoot the scene and, sure enough, he would know exactly when to pause and could follow the movements of the other actors with his eyes as if they were standing right in front of him, reciting their lines. It was a completely unorthodox technique, but when I would finally cut the scene together there wouldn't be one false move or word; it was always absolutely perfect! There aren't many actors who possess that kind of awareness and control. In fact, Moriarty would say to me that he could play the other actors' parts better than they could, but that gives you some indication of the strength of his concentration. It really was a remarkable thing to witness. Moriarty's approach was not exclusive to our working relationship. I spoke with one of the directors on *Law & Order*, who told me that Michael had done the same thing on that show, shot some of his close-ups alone without the other actors, and the high quality of his performance was unaffected.

For you, what is the most vitally important aspect of being a director?

Most directors would probably say it's the ability to communicate. I like to do as much as I can on my movies: I write, produce, direct, and edit them; I hire the composer and do it all my way but—try as I might—I still need other people to make a film happen. That's just the way it is. So, if you can't communicate your ideas, thoughts, and instructions to the cast and crew, and they might be simple or complex, you threaten the stability and success of your movie. If you haven't explained something properly and been understood, and it could be related to a scene or a character or something technical that you demand of the cameraman, the costume designer, or the makeup artist, it can all come out wrong. You can end up with something you don't want or need. Now, on the other hand, I often find that the more crew people know the more questions they ask. The more questions they ask, the more time is wasted explaining everything to them. On top of that, they don't always understand what you are telling them anyway, so it's sometimes better not to tell anybody anything. Just tell them where to stand and what to do and just shoot it. This gets back to my not using boards and shot lists when I shoot, which confounds some crew-people. They can't seem to understand that I have the entire movie locked inside my head and I know exactly where everything will fit. Nobody else needs to know where all the shots and action is going to fit, because they'll never figure it out anyway. You just communicate the information people need to know, when it is important they know it. As long as I know what's happening and where it's all going to go, everything is alright. It's as simple and as difficult as it sounds.

What about when you are composing your shots? I don't imagine that you always strive for the poetic image, something that looks aesthetically beautiful.

I do like pretty-looking and innovative shots, but some directors can be too self-conscious about them. I like the spontaneity of arriving on set and finding the best coverage, blocking that doesn't intimidate or dictate to the actors. But when you preoccupy yourself only with creating beautiful images and complex shots, you often ignore other important aspects of a movie. I mean, fancy shots often draw attention to themselves and that can be distracting. It can take the audience out of the reality and intimacy of a moment. Also you are really just showing off, you know? Of course, showing off worked great for Hitchcock and Welles, but I'm mostly interested in finding the shot that captures the best performance and advances the story. There are a few shots in *Special Effects* that are pretty fancy, but they are always conveying information and emotion to the viewer.

How authoritative are you when working with a director of photography?

I must say that on a lot of my pictures all the visual ideas mostly come from me. I simply tell the DP where to put the camera, how to frame it and when to move it. I block the scenes—exclusively—so there is never too much creative input from the cameraman in that regard as there might be on some other directors' movies. I mean, I don't tell the cameramen how to light the set or where to place the lights. I don't very often tell them what lens to use either, but I will tell them exactly how I want the scene covered. I leave only the strictly technical aspects to my cameramen.

Let's talk about editing. Some directors allow the editor to create an assembly of the film. The director then comes in, views the assembly, discusses it, and together they make any refinements or adjustments they feel are necessary.

Yeah, but I can't work that way. I've never worked that way. I'm the one in the editing room telling the editor exactly where to make the cuts. Back in the days when I made *Hell up in Harlem* and *It's Alive*, we worked on Moviolas. The editor would be sat at the machine and had a little yellow pencil and I would be hovering right over him. I would tell him where to mark the film and that would be where the first cut goes; then the next cut and the cut after that. We would then go out, have lunch, before coming back to see what it looked like when the footage was all put together. That would be the way it worked. I always designated all of the cutting in my movies, and the editors did exactly as I instructed. Every cut was exactly the way I wanted it. I mean, editing is really the final stage of control you enjoy as a director and is perhaps the most important phase. Through the editing, you can sharpen the focus of a scene, improve it, and twist it in ways you perhaps didn't see when you were writing or shooting the picture. You can also place a different emphasis on the scene where something small suddenly becomes very big and important. That's the wonderful thing about editing: it gives you the most amounts of freedom and authority.

What is the most valuable advice you have ever imparted to a fledgling editor?

The most valuable advice I've ever given to an editor is to forget about matching the shots as the important thing is, again, always the performance. Most editors will use the takes that match the best, but I always urge them to use the takes in which the actors' performance is the best. You can always make the footage match if you devise some cutaways or experiment with various things, but the performance must always be at the level you are aspiring to. The most accomplished editors must be able to use their own judgments about maintaining the continued quality of a performance, particularly if for some reason the director is not present, which was never the case with me. As I say, I always supervised every cut.

Some of your contemporaries, who made independent horror and science fiction films in the 1970s, readily embraced the studio system in the 1980s. Occasionally, these directors made studio films that have no discernable personality when compared to the distinctiveness and innovation of their independent work.

Yeah, but that's what you get. That's the bargain you make when you agree to become part of the studio machine. You sometimes compromise yourself and the instincts that have served you so well on the smaller independent films. Your hands are basically tied and you have to follow the studio's rules, whereas before there were no rules, or perhaps you were just ignorant of them. Unlike some directors who got involved with studio filmmaking, I wanted to maintain my independence. I wanted to make the kinds of pictures I wanted to make, and say the kinds of things I wanted to say. Studio interference and politics are not things I can tolerate, but

I can understand why some directors do it. It's easy to be enticed by money and big budgets, and the glamour of working with movie stars. Maybe that's what some people want to do with their careers. I don't know, you'd have to ask them. That's always a difficult thing to turn down for the sake of personal integrity, but any interference would poison that situation for me. As for keeping my own personal voice, I think I was a better writer than most of the other directors who worked in the genre. I actually had something meaningful to say. I never made a horror movie with the typical things you always find in them. I wasn't lured by the big studios like some of the other guys were, so I never made pictures that might have been dissected by committee. You see some directors succumb to the system, and their originality and creativity is destroyed or damaged. You start making movies that look and feel just like everybody else's movies and there are no surprises for the audience.

One of the things that has afflicted genre cinema is the fact that both studio and independent films are guilty of producing deeply homogenised fodder that, as you suggest, lack originality. Look at the way slasher movies were popularised in the wake of the success of *Halloween*. To this day, they still stubbornly refuse to choke on their own blood and survive in one form or another.

Well, this is the fundamental problem with horror movies: if everybody's ideas are coming from the same place then you are not going to get anything that is new and innovative. Some members of the audience derive pleasure from the repetition and familiarity of horror movies. I certainly don't, but then I don't run out every week to watch them. Some people get their kicks from knowing where all the beats are, but that's no fun for me. *Halloween* was a scary and suspenseful movie that enjoyed great success, but everybody wanted to repeat the formula that John Carpenter used. Okay, fine, but then *Halloween* and *Friday the 13th* became the models for many untalented filmmakers to follow and were the definition of horror for many years. Even when some new ingredients are introduced into the mix, slasher films are still predictable. Audiences may get nervous when they see a teenager wandering through the woods in their underwear, waiting for the killer to appear from behind a tree; we may get a shock when the killer leaps out and chops somebody's head off, but how scary is something like that when you know exactly what is going to happen? There is nothing substantial to a scene like that. But if you can fashion a strong idea, some kind of metaphor or deeper significance that goes beyond mere sadism, then you can really hit people where it hurts. They will remember what they thought as much as what they felt. I think ideas can provoke big reactions from the audience and can *really* scare them. When people leave the theater, they will think about the film and consider its wider implications. That kind of fear often lasts longer than some quick jolt.

Do you feel you have credibility and respect as a filmmaker?

I don't know. When I ran my movies at the Vienna Film Festival, we sold out every single show. The theater held 800 or 900 seats, and every screening was completely packed out. The audience really seemed to enjoy my work. Frankly, I was surprised that people in Austria would even know my films, but they did. That's mostly been the case all over the world when I attend film festivals: people are very familiar with my movies. When we hold screenings of my pictures here in the United States, we usually get a big, enthusiastic crowd. I find those situations very gratifying, but credibility? Honestly, I really don't know. Aside from the screenings, there is always interest in my work and every week somebody calls up to do an interview. I've always said that if you keep making movies for long enough, people will eventually discover you. Maybe that's the best you can hope for.

You and John Carpenter have been somewhat neglected and dismissed by some high-brow critics—with the notable exception of Robin Wood—whereas others such as David Cronenberg have been critically feted. Why do you think that is?

I really don't know. I think David has made some fabulous pictures over the years and not all of them have been horror films. Whatever attention David has received I think he deserves, because he's done some very good work. John Carpenter has also done some good work, but I can't speak for him. I believe that whatever it is you are doing as a filmmaker, you can't live your life for the critical acceptance of others. If you do, you can never be true to yourself. You just have to make your movies, get them out there and see what happens. You simply hope that people will like and enjoy them, that's all. Above everything, what you try to do is just keep on working and creating—if you can survive! Survival is far more important to me than any critical appreciation and I'd imagine that both Carpenter and Cronenberg feel the same way.

You've mentioned the popularity of the screenings and festivals you have attended, but can you talk about your relationship with your fans? On average, what kind of attention does a cult film director receive from the general public?

Its okay, I guess. I have about as much attention as I can tolerate. I do get recognized on the street occasionally, but not so much that it disrupts my life. I also get calls and letters from some people telling me how much they admire my work. Being a movie director is not like being a movie star or a rock star. You can still get around and have a normal life without being chased by girls, not that that would be such a bad thing! [Chuckles] But when I go to the theater and attend screenings, festivals, and conventions, I do enjoy meeting a lot of the fans. It's always wonderful when people tell you that they love your work and that it means something to them. I mean, I'm not entirely invulnerable to flattery and compliments. I'll take whatever I can get these days. [Pause] Speaking of fans, did I ever tell you my Frank Capra story?[1]

No.

Two years ago, I got a letter from a man in Palm Desert, California, who said that he used to live next door to—of all people—Frank Capra. He wrote: "I wanted you to know that Frank Capra was a huge fan of yours. He loved your movies and also loved your TV series, *Branded*." This gentleman said that Capra had seen *The Big Country*, a movie in which Chuck Connors had played the villain, and he thought Connors was a terrific actor. After that, Capra became a big fan of *Branded*, and it was through that show that he became a fan of my work. Apparently, Capra then started going to the theater with this neighbour and they would watch all of my movies together whenever they came out. The letter also mentioned that Capra had once tried to contact me, that he'd actually called me. Incredibly, I remembered that one day many years earlier I had walked into an office and somebody said, "Larry, you got a phone call from Frank Capra." I just laughed and said, "Yeah, sure. I wonder who the hell that is playing a joke on me." I never returned the call because I thought it was a gag. I didn't even recall that incident until after I'd received this letter. Then it suddenly hit me again. *Pow!* And I remembered that phone call. Amazing! I mean, who would have ever imagined that Frank Capra would be calling me? So, I never got to meet the great man. But this gentleman had thought that, somehow or other, I should find this out and wrote me a nice, long letter. I couldn't believe it! *Frank Capra!* Oh, what I would have given to have spent an afternoon with him.

You hear of some filmmakers, who seem to revel in the desperate struggle of financing their projects and realizing their personal vision against all the odds. Are you one that savors the rigors of independent filmmaking?

On most of the movies I've made, I've secured distribution before I started shooting. I always had somebody who was going to buy the picture, pay for the picture and play the picture in theatres, putting out the prints and making the film visible. I've not been forced to run around with my thumbs in hand, begging and pleading with somebody to distribute my pictures. I've always managed to find somebody, so the fight has not been as hard or as desperate as it might have been. These days, everything is different. Trying to find a home for your movie in a marketplace that doesn't want to buy pictures anymore—and certainly doesn't want to pay for them—is tough. There are people who will take a picture, but they won't pay any money for it. They'll just pay for prints and advertising, but then if the film opens and doesn't do well in one market that's the end of the prints and advertising. If you want to get your picture back you probably have to sue them in court, and that could take three or four years and a fortune in expenses for lawyers. So, you just get yourself into a terrible situation and you are going to get angry at people and miserable. To be honest with you, I've made a lot of money in my career. I have a beautiful mansion and a bunch of acres up here in Beverly Hills, and plenty of dough in the bank, so the fight just isn't worth it. I'm not going to get myself worked up and angry and run into conflicts with people when I don't have to do it anymore.

That's a rather depressing indictment of the moviemaking business.

Maybe, but it's an accurate one. It's a terrible business to be in at the present time. It used to be that if there was a film festival, the organisers would receive 500 applications from filmmakers. Today, they are getting 10,000! I mean, everybody who owns a video camera is making a movie and trying to submit it to a film festival. Ninety-nine percent of these movies are awful and will never get distributed. That puts the distributors in a tremendously advantaged position because there is so much stuff being thrown at them. People are more than happy to give their work to them for free—just to get it out there—as getting distributors to pay for something isn't easy.

What advice would you give to new filmmakers about to embark on a career?

If you want to make movies, you just have to go out there and make them. You have to make your film and, hopefully, somebody will see it. There are a lot of people who are going to film school now. When I was going to college, there were only a couple of schools in the entire country that had film classes. At that time, you could walk into a book store or a library and literally count the number of books on filmmaking on one hand. There were only two or three, namely *The Liveliest Art* by Arthur Knight[2] and a couple of well-regarded books on editing. That was it, basically. Today, there are hundreds and hundreds of books on moviemaking, and hundreds and hundreds of people who are supposedly teaching screenwriting and filmmaking classes in colleges all over the country. There simply isn't room enough for all these people to get jobs in the industry. Thank god there is television and cable, because they now have a plethora of these new channels that have to be supplied with material for broadcast. The documentary area has really blossomed in the wake of reality television and other documentary channels. There is now a chance for young filmmakers to work in television, but there also seems to be more opportunities for documentary filmmakers today than there ever was. There were comparatively few documentaries that were distributed theatrically back in the old days.

So, the gist of your counsel is to follow your dream, regardless?

You have to. If you don't give it a shot, you obviously have no chance of succeeding. But I will say this: the big advice I have for people is that if you want a career in the motion picture business you have got to give it at least eight to ten years. You can't expect to just walk in and be successful in six months, a year, or even two or three years. You've got to give it a long time and if you stick with it, you've always got a chance. If you walk away from it after two or three years, you'll be walking away in disappointment. The people that are willing to tough it out, and suffer all the rejections and disappointments over a long period of time, can realize their ambitions. Usually it helps to have another job at the same time so you can make a living. Some scripts get bought and they don't get made for six or seven years. Other scripts get written but don't get bought for six or seven years. I've sold scripts that were nine or ten years old, so you just have to keep submitting them. You have to keep trying and trying and trying and then, eventually, you'll find someone who likes your work. They may think it's the greatest thing that has ever been written, but these same people might have been turning down the very same script for years. Suddenly, you may get a director like Sidney Lumet, who says he'll do the picture, and the very next day you've got a deal. That's the peculiar thing about the business: good writing and talent usually finds its way to somebody. You've just got to keep persevering and not believe in the negative comments you are hearing. There will be the inevitable knock-backs along the way, but if you believe in your work, you've got to maintain that belief and continue on. You can't listen to all the contrary opinions because it takes a long time to get things done. Remember, it isn't always the most talented people who succeed; it's the people with the most perseverance. Sometimes the most capable and original artists are the ones that never get the break. Their confidence may be more fragile and they quickly get disheartened and throw in the towel. If you are going to make it in the movie business, you've got to be prepared to put the time in.

How would you gauge the true success of a film?

In my opinion, the true success of any film is not determined until twenty years or more after it's made. The real difference between an A-movie and a B-movie is that you have to wait two or three decades to discover its true worth. If you look at the history of the motion picture business, there have been B-movies which have enjoyed a much longer life than the more illustrious A-movies that were made during the same year. Oddly enough, if you went out on the streets today and gave people the names of 230 movie stars of the 1930s, '40s, and '50s, and asked them who these people were, you'd be surprised at the reaction. I always say that the vast majority of them wouldn't have a clue who those actors were—particularly the A-movie stars like Robert Taylor and Greer Garson, people like that. But if you showed them a photograph of Boris Karloff or Bela Lugosi, people would instantly recognize them. If you asked people who Abbot and Costello and The Three Stooges were, they would probably know them, too. It's funny how, over time, fame can fade. Some of the people who have remained most famous are those who made B-movies and didn't make A-movies at all. It's the low-budget horror and comedy pictures that audiences remember. They have endured and lasted longer than many of the A-movies have. So, you can't properly evaluate which movies are going to be considered true classics until a little time has passed.

If you could program your own film festival what movies would you include?

Of my own films? All of them. Of other people's films? I wouldn't be interested.

If you were given *carte blanch* in terms of time, money, and creative freedom, would you make your films any differently?

Do you mean how I'd make my movies, or the kinds of movies I'd want to make?

I'm talking about your actual process.

No, I don't think so. I have a way of working that I'm comfortable with and it has proved rewarding, creatively and financially. I can't be expected to just change my spots, certainly not after all these years. Even if I had unlimited resources and control, my process would still be the same. That's not to say you don't make certain modifications as a director when you're dealing with various egos and personalities. Every situation is different. Sometimes you have to surrender yourself a little and let certain things go. I've enjoyed having the control on my movies, but it's sometimes been tough trying to work under the same circumstances every time. If I had all the freedom, time, and money to do what I wanted, I'd still do things my own way because I can only be me. Only I can make the kinds of pictures that I make.

One of the things I've gleaned from our many conversations is how proud you are of your body of work.

Oh, I'm immensely proud of the work. None of my pictures are perfect, but they are all mine. I've found a lot of joy in making movies. I've always loved going to work every day on a set, even though I had to get up early in the morning and there were some challenging and difficult days. My own concentration and focus were so intense when I was directing, I often wouldn't allow myself to get sick during shooting. I'm being serious! I'd refuse to be ill! As soon as we'd wrap the picture and it was all over, I would invariably be sick for a week. Usually I would come down with a cold or the flu, but when we would be shooting the picture, no matter how miserable the weather was, be it rain or snow, I would be right out there. Sometimes, in order to encourage the crew, I would take off my coat and work in my shirtsleeves or something, even though it may have been freezing. I did this just to shame the crew and they couldn't complain about how cold it was. Despite doing this, I never got sick during production. It's a very peculiar thing. I mean, you may notice that I actually have a cold as I'm talking to you right now! [Chuckles] But on a film set, it hardly ever seemed to happen. Maybe it's because of the power of my will, or maybe its pure luck, but I simply refused to go down until the movie was made.

A continuing theme of our conversations has been your repeated determination to always be in control of every aspect of a film. You've suggested that this resolve has its pathological roots in your experiences working in television.

Well, it's something I've always been conscious of. Many writers and directors are obsessed with having control because it's so important. The lack of control and the question of true authorship can become the thing that destroys you. It can destroy you in your heart. *Is this thing really mine? Why do they want to take it away from me? Why do they want to claim credit for my work?* These thoughts can rot you out from the inside. Again, I didn't want any input or help from anybody. I always wanted to do it all myself. I didn't want anybody else receiving or claiming credit for my movies and scripts. I mean, I work in an empty room. You can come in and search the room because you won't find anybody hiding in there. I've got the pages I wrote and that's it. Nobody else could have written them. It was the same thing when I was directing: I was in charge of every element of the film and that is what has given me satisfaction throughout my life and career. I've turned out twenty movies that are more or less all me. Whatever anybody thinks of their faults and virtues nobody can deny that.

Finally, I must ask, how have you felt about spilling your guts for this book and recounting the minutiae of your career in such exhaustive detail?

It hasn't been too painful. Let's hope your readers feel the same way when they read it! [Chuckles] I think the difference between me and most directors is when people usually direct a movie, they go to the studio every morning and the process becomes like factory work. The filmmakers are merely going through the motions. If you read the biographies of most directors, they may pontificate about the meanings, metaphors, and methods of their work, but they have little to say about the actual production of their movies. This is because they have nothing particularly interesting to write about. Basically, the actors show up at the studio, put on their costumes, and do their makeup; walk out on set, say the lines, perform the action, and then they go home. The next day, everybody comes back and this machine-like process is repeated with little or no variations. They simply do the same thing over and over again for forty or fifty days until they eventually grind out the picture. There's no story to tell because nothing ever happens. People just go to work. You could never say that about my movies. Nearly every working day, we were shooting out at some crazy location. We'd do something risky or insane, venturing into places we had no business going: shooting action scenes on a bustling New York City street and driving taxis on the sidewalk; sneaking into the Justice Department Building and the Attorney General's office and closing down Pennsylvania Avenue; shooting a non-union movie in the headquarters of the Teamsters and making a picture in a dangerous city with 105 gang members. Directors don't ordinarily encourage this kind of madness, certainly not today. In this troubled age we live in, half of the things we did would be impossible to repeat without getting shot in the head. But we were always overcoming terrible adversity and daunting situations with courage and creativity. On most movies, people simply sit around between takes, read magazines and books, or sleep in their trailers, only coming out to do a scene. They have nothing to talk about when the film is completed. On my pictures, people were always running around, going crazy, and having fun. That's the stuff that is really worth reading about. The only reason there have been so many stories to tell is because we had so many adventures making these movies.

Notes

CHAPTER 1: YOUTH (1941-1958)

1. Joseph Stalin died on March 5, 1953, at the age of seventy-four.
2. Cohen is probably thinking of *Winter Carnival* (1939), directed by Charles F. Reisner.
3. Max Steiner (1888-1971) was an Austrian composer for theatre, film and television who worked in America from 1924. His film scores include *King Kong* (1933), *Little Women* (1933), *Jezebel* (1938), *Gone With the Wind* (1939), *Casablanca* (1942), *Mildred Pierce* (1945) and *The Big Sleep* (1946). He was nominated for twenty-four Academy Awards, winning on three occasions for *The Informer* (1935), *Now, Voyager* (1942) and *Since You Went Away* (1944).
4. Boston Blackie is a fictional character created by author Jack Lloyd (1881-1928). Originally a safecracker, jewel thief and confidence man, Blackie reformed his criminal ways and became a private investigator. Although there had been silent film adaptations made from 1918 to 1927, beginning with E. Mason Hopper's *Boston Blackie's Little Pal*, which featured Bert Lytell as Blackie, Colombia Pictures revived interest in the character with Robert Florey's *Meet Boston Blackie* (1941) which starred Chester Morris in the titular role. This 58-minute "quickie" inaugurated a series of fourteen B-pictures, that all starred Morris, culminating with *Boston Blackie's Chinese Surprise* (1949).
5. Michael Curtiz (1886-1962) was a Hungarian-American director, credited early in his career as both Mihály Kertész and Michael Kertéze. He moved to Hollywood in the 1920s to work for Warner Bros. where he developed a reputation for "arrogance and ruthlessness." His final film, *The Comancheros*, was released six months before his death from cancer aged seventy-five.

6. Jimmy Durante (1893-1980) was an American actor, singer, and entertainer renowned for his trademark gravelly voice and heavy New York accent ("Everybody wants to get into de act!") Known affectionately as "Schnozzle," the mighty-nosed comedian enjoyed a long and successful career performing in Vaudeville, nightclubs, radio, and television. His film work began with the gangster picture *Roadhouse Nights* (1930) and ended with the animated feature *Frosty the Snowman* (1969), which has become a staple of seasonal entertainment for Americans. In between, Durante appeared in *Hollywood Party* (1934), *Melody Ranch* (1940), *The Man Who Came to Dinner* (1942), *It Happened in Brooklyn* (1947) and *It's a Mad, Mad, Mad, Mad World* (1962).

7. Tito Puente (1923-2000) was an American salsa musician and Latin jazz composer known to his many admirers as "The Musical Pope." His compositions include "Oy Como Va," "Ran Kan Kan," "Salsa y sibor" and "Mambo Gozon." Puente appeared in such films as *Armed and Dangerous* (1986), *Radio Days* (1987) and *The Mambo Kings* (1992), often playing himself. He made a memorable suspect in the two-part episode of *The Simpsons*, "Who Shot Mr. Burns?"

8. Hans Richter (1888-1976) was a German artist, author and experimental filmmaker. Born in Berlin, he moved to the United States in 1940 and became an American citizen. Richter later directed the films *Dreams That Money Can Buy* (1947), *8x8: A Chess Sonata in 8 Movements* (1957) and *Dadascope* (1961) in collaboration with such luminaries as Jean Cocteau, Max Ernst, Paul Bowles, Marcel Duchamp, and others.

9. Otto Preminger (1906-1986) was an Austrian-American director. Beginning his career in his native Austria with *Die große Liebe* (1931), he arrived in Hollywood four years later as part of the "European exodus" which included Fritz Lang, Michael Curtiz and Billy Wilder. Preminger then began a tumultuous relationship with 20th Century Fox, helming such films as *Laura* (1944), *Fallen Angel* (1945), *Daisy Kenyon* (1947), and *Whirlpool* (1949). The following decade saw him make a series of taboo-breaking pictures that dealt with such difficult subjects as drug addiction (*The Man With the Golden Arm*, 1955), rape (*Anatomy of a Murder*, 1959), and homosexuality (*Advice & Consent*, 1962). His legendary reputation as a "tyrant" on set was perhaps encouraged by his memorable turn as a Nazi prison camp commandant in Wilder's *Stalag 17* (1950).

10. Dominick Dunne (1925-2009) was an American writer and investigative journalist. After working in television, he contributed to such publications as *Vanity Fair* (covering his daughter Dominique's murder trial in 1983) and went on to chronicle the "celebrity trials" of O.J. Simpson, Claus Von Bülow and William Kennedy Smith.
11. This NBC television version of *Brief Encounter* was filmed under its original title, "Still Life", as a segment of Noel Coward's *Tonight at 8:30*. First aired on October 18, 1954, as part of *Producers' Showcase*, it featured Trevor Howard revisiting the part of Dr. Alec Harvey that he had originated in David Lean's 1945 film.
12. *Li'l Abner* was a satirical American comic strip written and drawn by Al Capp (Alfred Gerald Caplin, 1909-1979). It ran from August 13, 1934, through to November 13, 1977, and centred on the adventures of a naive country boy named Li'l Abner Yokum and the clan of hillbillies that inhabited the fictional mountain backwater of Dogpatch, Kentucky. Hugely popular with readers, the cartoon unfortunately assisted in cementing some of the Appalachian stereotypes often associated with the entire American South by popular media, namely impoverished, inbred, culturally ignorant mountain folk with no teeth or common sense. *Li'l Abner* was first adapted for radio in 1948 and was followed by the Broadway musical in 1956 and a film in 1959.
13. Stuart Gordon (b.1947) is an American writer, producer and director. He was co-founder and artistic director of Chicago's Organic Theatre where his directing credits included the world premiere of David Mamet's *Sexual Perversity in Chicago* (1974). Gordon made his outrageous cinematic debut with *Re-Animator* (1985), a gloriously gory adaptation of H.P. Lovecraft's 1922 short story. His subsequent films include *Dolls* (1986), *From Beyond* (1986), *Robot Jox* (1988), *The Pit and the Pendulum* (1991), *Castle Freak* (1995), *Space Truckers* (1997), *The Wonderful Ice Cream Suit* (1998), *Dagon* (2001), *King of the Ants* (2003), *Stuck* (2007), and *Edmund* (2008). Gordon also directed two episodes of Showtime's *Masters of Horrors – Dreams in the Witch-House* (2005) and *The Black Cat* (2006)—and an episode of *Fear Itself* titled *Eater* (2008).
14. *Lolita* (1962) opened in New York on June 12, 1962.

CHAPTER 2: THE TELEVISION YEARS

1. *Where the Sidewalk Ends* (1950) was Otto Preminger's final film for 20th Century Fox under contract as a director-for-hire. The radio adaptation of "Night Cry" was first broadcast on *Suspense* on July 10, 1948. *Lux Radio Theater* then broadcast a second sixty-minute radio adaptation of William L. Stuart's novel on April 2, 1951, in which Dana Andrews resumed the role of Det. Sgt. Mark Dixon he had originated on screen.
2. Cohen is in fact referring to the television movie *The Million Dollar Incident*, which was broadcast on April 21, 1961. Directed by Norman Jewison, this comedy-drama stars Jackie Gleason (1916-1987) playing himself, and concerns the legendary American comedian, actor and musician being kidnapped by two bungling crooks.
3. Brendan Behan (1923-1964) was an Irish playwright, poet and author. The son of a house painter, he came from a well-read family with Republican sympathies living in the slums of Dublin. He left Catholic school at the age of fourteen and was arrested in 1939 for his involvement with the IRA as a messenger boy. Sentenced to three years in Borstal for attempting to blow up a battleship in Liverpool harbor, Behan later drew on this period in his autobiographical novel *Borstal Boy* (1958). After his release he returned to Ireland, but in 1942 was sentenced to fourteen years for the attempted murder of two detectives. Behan started to write whilst incarcerated and, after his release in 1946 under a general amnesty, produced such works as his debut play *The Quare Fellow* (1954) which is set in an Irish prison on the eve of a hanging. His other pieces include *The Big House* (1957), a radio drama for the BBC, and *An Giall* (*The Hostage*, 1958), a sprawling tragi-comedy written in Gaelic about an English soldier, who is kidnapped and held hostage in an Irish brothel. Alcoholism ended his career and life in a Dublin hospital in March 1964 and his funeral (reportedly the biggest since that of Michael Collins in 1922) was awarded an IRA guard of honor. His third play, *Richard Cork's Leg*, was nearly complete at the time of his death and was edited and directed by Alan Simpson in 1972 for the Dublin Theater Festival.
4. Sydney Pollack (1934-2008) was an American film director, producer, screenwriter, and actor. His films include *They Shoot Horses Don't They* (1969), *Jeremiah Johnson* (1972), *The Way We Were* (1973), *The Yakuza* (1975), *Three Days of the Condor* (1975), *Ab-*

sence of Malice (1981), Tootsie (1982), Havana (1990), The Firm (1993), Sabrina (1995), and The Interpreter (2005). He won Academy Awards for directing and producing the romantic drama, Out of Africa (1985).
5. Gordon Douglas (1909-1993) began his career as a child actor. Moving to Hollywood in 1930, he began working for Hal Roach as a gag writer, producer and director. Douglas directed thirty Our Gang shorts, including Bored of Education, which won an Academy Award for Best Short Subject One Reel in 1937, before helming his first feature film, the Laurel and Hardy comedy Saps at Sea (1940). Proficient at most genres, Douglas' uneven career includes Them! (1954), Up Periscope (1959), Follow That Dream (1962), Robin and the Seven Hoods (1964), In Like Flint (1967), Tony Rome (1968), and Skulduggery (1970).
6. J. Peverell Marley (1901-1964) is one of only six cinematographers to have a star on the Hollywood Walk of Fame. His first film was Cecil B. De Mille's silent epic The Ten Commandments (1923), and he continued his association with the director on Feet of Clay (1924), The Golden Bed (1925), The Volga Boatman (1926), and The King of Kings (1927). Marley received Academy Award nominations for Suez (1938) and Life With Father (1948), later winning a Golden Globe for Best Cinematography (Color) for The Greatest Show on Earth (1952). His other films include House of Wax (1953), The Spirit of St. Louis (1957), and The Left-Handed Gun (1958). The Sins of Rachel Cade (1961) was his final production before his death of a heart attack.
7. The writer of "Killer Instinct" was Elliot West.
8. In an interview conducted with Tony Williams for the book Larry Cohen: The Radical Allegories of an Independent Filmmaker (1997), Cohen reveals that he once submitted several story ideas to the producers of Alfred Hitchcock Presents without success.
9. The cast of "Medal for a Turned Coat" was rounded out by such seasoned British actors as Nigel Stock, Sylvia Kay and Catherine Lacey.
10. The sitcom that replaced Branded was Hey, Landlord. Created by Garry Marshall and Jerry Belson, it starred Will Hutchins as Woody Banner, a young man who inherits a New York Brownstone from his deceased uncle. Hey, Landlord ran on NBC for one season and thirty-one episodes from January 11, 1966, to April 23, 1967, before being cancelled.

11. Cohen is billed in the credits of *Spies Like Us* as "Ace Tomato Agent." He appears briefly as an armed guard patrolling a secret operations bunker located beneath a disused drive-in.
12. *The Americans* is a television period drama created by Joe Weisberg which (as of this writing) has been renewed by FX for a third season. Set during the Cold War of the 1980s, it revolves around Phillip (Matthew Rhys) and Elizabeth Jennings (Keri Russell), two KGB Agents posing as a married middle-class American couple in the suburbs of Washington DC, who live with their unsuspecting children Paige (Holly Taylor) and Henry (Keidrich Sellati).
13. Custer was essayed by Canadian actor Wayne Maunder (b.1937). Maunder also played Scott Lancer in the Western television series *Lancer* (alongside Andrew Duggan) and made appearances in TV shows such as *The Monroes*, *Kung Fu*, *The F.B.I.*, *The Rookies*, *Police Story*, *The Streets of San Francisco*, *Barnaby Jones*, and the films *The Seven Minutes* (1971) and *Porky's* (1982).
14. Alan A. Armer (1922-2010) produced such television series as *My Friend Flicka* (1956), *Broken Arrow* (1956-1958), *Man without a Gun* (1957-1959), and *The Untouchables* (1961-1963). He then joined Quinn Martin Productions to work on *The Fugitive* (1963-1966), for which he won an Emmy, and then later *The Invaders* (1967-1968). Subsequent shows he produced were *Lancer* (1968-1970) and *Cannon* (1971-1972), as well as the TV Movies *Along Came a Spider* (1970), *Birds of Prey* (1973), and *The Stranger* (1973). His last involvement with television came with *The Magician* (1973-1974), which starred Bill Bixby as a wealthy illusionist who uses his skills to help people in trouble. After retiring, Armer taught at the Department of Cinema and Television Arts at Cal State Northridge, becoming a part-time faculty member in 1980. He retired from teaching in 1999, eleven years before his death from colon cancer.
15. Robin Wood (1931-2009) was a British-born film critic and theorist who spent much of his working life in Canada. His first book, *Alfred Hitchcock*, was published in 1965, at a time when few volumes on cinema were available in the English language never mind one devoted to the work of an individual filmmaker. Wood subsequently wrote (or co-wrote) books on Howard Hawks, Ingmar Bergman, Claude Chabrol, Michelangelo Antonioni, Satyajit Ray and Arthur Penn. In 1979, he co-edited a small publication with Richard Lippe for the Festival of Festivals in Toronto titled *The American Nightmare*. One

of the first serious academic publications focused entirely on horror films, it included a glowing overview of Larry Cohen's oeuvre, as well as articulating Wood's theory of the "Return of the Repressed." Wood advanced that American family life is the product of the repression of natural instincts and the contemporary American horror film routinely presents monsters that function as images of what has been repressed that are returning to claim its own. Wood's argument that horror dramatises this process of repression and its dissolution in ideological terms has proved influential in horror film criticism.

16. The "*American Bandstand* kind of show" that Cohen recalls here might be *Where The Action Is*, which aired on ABC from June 27, 1965, to March 31, 1967.

17. "Murder by the Book" concerns two bestselling authors who've formed a long and profitable association writing a series of mystery novels together. When one member wishes to dissolve the partnership in order to pursue a solo writing career, the less-talented partner murders him.

18. Steven Bochco received an Emmy nomination for his "Murder by the Book" teleplay, but did not in fact win. The winner that year (1972) for Outstanding Writing for a Drama Series was another *Columbo* episode from season one, "Death Lends a Hand," written by Richard Levinson and William Link.

19. James Farentino (1938-2012) was a dashing American leading man. His career was mostly sustained on television roles in the likes of *Naked City*, *Ben Casey*, *The Virginian*, *The Bold Ones*, *Night Gallery*, *Police Story*, *Dynasty*, and *Jesus of Nazareth* (the latter earning him an Emmy nomination for his role as Simon Peter). Farentino's film appearances include *Me, Natalie* (1968), *The Final Countdown* (1980), *Dead & Buried* (1981), *Her Alibi* (1988), and *Bulletproof* (1996).

20. *Barnaby Jones* was developed by Edward Hume and ran on CBS from January 28, 1973, to April 3, 1980. The series is renowned for being on the air for longer than any other Quinn Martin show, with the exception of *The F.B.I*, which ran for nine seasons (although the final two seasons were produced in association with Philip Saltzman and Woodruff Productions).

21. The actor playing the lead role of Jess Sparrow in *Sparrow* was Randy Hermann. His few film credits include *Rolling Thunder* (1977), *Close Encounters of the Third Kind* (1977), *Our Winning Season* (1978), and *Little Miss Marker* (1980).

22. The character Cohen created on *NYPD Blue* was John Irvin, a gay administrative aide played by Bill Brochtrup (b.1963). Brochtrup would go on to become a series regular appearing in 156 episodes, including the final episode of the show, "Moving Day," broadcast on March 1, 2005.

CHAPTER 3: SCREENPLAYS PART I (1966-1986)

1. Walter Mirisch (b.1921) is an American producer who started his career producing low-budget B-movies at Monogram Pictures before forming The Mirisch Company in August 1957 with brothers Harold (1907-1968) and Marvin (1918-2002). After signing a twelve-picture deal with United Artists, which was extended to a twenty-picture deal within two years, the company delivered such classic films as *Some Like it Hot* (1959), *The Apartment* (1960), *The Magnificent Seven* (1960), *West Side Story* (1961), *The Great Escape* (1963), *The Pink Panther* (1963), *A Shot in the Dark* (1964), *In the Heat of the Night* (1967), *The Thomas Crown Affair* (1968), and *Fiddler on the Roof* (1971). His films have earned eighty-seven Oscar nominations, securing twenty-eight wins. Mirisch was also president of the Academy of Motion Picture Arts and Sciences from 1973 to 1977. His memoir, *I Thought We Were Making Movies, Not History*, was published in 2008.
2. Burt Kennedy (1922-2001) was an American screenwriter and director. Originally a radio writer, Kennedy penned the screenplays for such Westerns as *Seven Men from Now* (1956), *The Tall T* (1957), *Ride Lonesome* (1959), and *Comanche Station* (1960), before helming his own as director with *The Canadians* (1961). For the next thirty years, Kennedy enjoyed a variable career which included such films as *Six Black Horses* (1962), *Mail Order Bride* (1964), *Welcome to Hard Times* (1967), *The War Wagon* (1967), *Support Your Local Sheriff* (1969), *Young Billy Young* (1969), *Support Your Local Gunfighter* (1971), *Hannie Caulder* (1971), *The Train Robbers* (1973), *Escape from the Dark* (1976) and the Hulk Hogan vehicle *Suburban Commando* (1991).
3. Andrew V. McLaglen (1920-2014) was an English-American director. The son of actor Victor McLaglen (1886-1959), he began his career with the revenge Western, *Gun the Man Down* (1956),

followed by the Film Noir *Man in the Vault* (1956) and the crime drama *The Abductors* (1957). McLaglen also directed a prodigious amount of television, helming multiple episodes of *Perry Mason*, *Gunslinger*, *Rawhide* and *Have Gun – Will Travel*. Amongst his best-known works—which often star John Wayne or James Stewart—are *McLintock!* (1963), *Shenandoah* (1965), *The Rare Breed* (1966), *The Way West* (1967), *Hellfighters* (1968), *The Undefeated* (1969), *Chisum* (1970), *Cahill U.S. Marshall* (1973), *The Wild Geese* (1978) and *The Sea Wolves* (1980). A journeyman director, McLaglen's Westerns were often derivative of John Ford in their scale, sentimentality and machismo but lacked the master's delicate poetry and élan.

4. Cohen is not be mistaken for Lawrence D. Cohen, screenwriter of *Carrie* (1976), *Ghost Story* (1981), *It* (1990), and *The Tommyknockers* (1993); or Lawrence J. Cohen, screenwriter of *Start the Revolution Without Me* (1969), *S*P*Y*S* (1974), *The Big Bus* (1976), and *Delirious* (1991).

5. Lorenzo Semple, Jr. (1928-2014) was an American screenwriter. His screenplays include *Papillion* (1970), co-written with Dalton Trumbo, *The Parallax View* (1974), co-written with David Giler, *The Drowning Pool* (1975), *Three Days of the Condor* (1975), co-written with David Rayfiel, *King Kong* (1976), *Flash Gordon* (1980), and *Never Say Never Again* (1983). Semple once maintained that his work on the much-maligned 1960s TV series *Batman* (he was responsible for the first four teleplays and consulted on all 120 episodes) was the best thing he ever wrote.

6. Carol White (1943-1991) was an English actress notable for her early work with Ken Loach on the acclaimed television plays *Up the Junction* (1965) and the groundbreaking *Cathy Comes Home* (1966), the latter still considered one of the finest and most socially impacting single television dramas ever made. White continued her association with Loach on the feature film *Poor Cow* (1967) before leaving for Hollywood and appearing in such movies as *The Fixer* (1968), *Daddy's Gone A-Hunting* (1969), and *Something Big* (1971). She died in Florida at the age of 48.

7. The male lead in *Daddy's Gone A-Hunting* was Scott Hylands (b.1943), a Canadian actor, whose credits include *Earthquake* (1974), *The Boys In Company "C"* (1978) and *Death Hunt* (1981).

8. Lew Wasserman (1913-2002) was a powerful American talent agent and motion picture executive. Born in Cleveland, Ohio, to Russian

immigrant parents, Wasserman's first involvement with movies was as an usher at a Cleveland theater when he was seventeen. He later worked as a booking agent for the Chicago-based MCA, becoming the head of the corporation in 1946 when he was just thirty-three and building it into a successful outfit. Following the damaging impact of television on movie studios after World War II, Wasserman acquired Universal and Decca Records, merging them with MCA in 1962. This combined company dominated Hollywood for the next thirty years until it was eventually sold off to Seagram by its then Japanese owners, Matsushita, who had purchased the organization in 1990 for $6.6 billion. Wasserman continued to serve on the board of directors until 1998, three years after being awarded the Presidential Medal of Freedom by President Clinton.

9. John Michael Hayes (1919-2008) wrote four consecutive screenplays for Hitchcock: *Rear Window* (1954), *To Catch a Thief* (1955), *The Trouble with Harry* (1955), and *The Man Who Knew Too Much* (1956). Their association was swiftly terminated after Hayes challenged Hitchcock over a credit dispute, although the two men had been discussing a potential new project tentatively titled *The Man in Lincoln's Nose*. This idea would eventually become the basis for *North by Northwest* (1959). Steven DeRosa's book, *Writing with Hitchcock: The Collaboration of Alfred Hitchcock and John Michael Hayes* (Faber & Faber, 2001), explores their working relationship.

10. The biographical drama, *Hitchcock* (2012), which stars Anthony Hopkins as the filmmaker, is based on Stephen Rebello's fascinating book, *Alfred Hitchcock and the Making of Psycho*. First published in 1990, Rebello interviewed every surviving member of the film's cast and crew, and was granted access to Hitchcock's personal archives. Directed by Sacha Gervasi, *Hitchcock* co-stars Helen Mirren as Alma Hitchcock, Scarlet Johansen as Janet Leigh, Jessica Biel as Vera Miles, James D'Arcy as Anthony Perkins, and Toni Collette as Peggy Robertson.

11. Park Chan-wook is a South Korean screenwriter, producer, director, and former film critic, whose violent and impeccably crafted films include *Sympathy for Mr. Vengeance* (2002), *Oldboy* (2003), *Sympathy for Lady Vengeance* (2005), *I'm a Cyborg, But That's OK* (2006), and *Thirst* (2009). The excellent psychological thriller, *Stoker* (2013), was the movie Chan-wook was making in America at the time he met with Cohen, and is his first in the English language.

12. André de Toth (1912-2002) was a prolific Hungarian-American maverick, whose movies embraced a variety of genres: war films *None Shall Escape* (1944), *Play Dirty* (1969); Film Noir *Dark Waters* (1944), *Pitfall* (1948), *Crime Wave* (1954); romance *The Other Love* (1947); adventure films *Tanganyika* (1954), *Morgan, the Pirate* (1960); spy thrillers *The Two-Headed Spy* (1958); horror *House of Wax* (1953) and, most notably, the Western, *Ramrod* (1947), *Man in the Saddle* (1951), *Carson City* (1952), *The Stranger Wore a Gun* (1953), *Riding Shotgun* (1955), *The Indian Fighter* (1956), and *Day of the Outlaw* (1959). De Toth also worked as a second unit director for Alexander Korda on *The Thief of Baghdad* (1940), David Lean on *Lawrence of Arabia* (1963) and Richard Donner on *Superman* (1978). He was married seven times, most famously to actress Veronica Lake (1922-1973) with whom he had two of his nineteen children and stepchildren. His candid memoirs, *Fragments: Portraits from the Inside*, were published in 1994.
13. Although he appeared in a variety of different films and television shows, Jack Elam (1920-2003) is indeed mostly celebrated for his appearances in Westerns. These include *High Noon* (1952), *Wichita* (1955), *Jubal* (1956), *Gunfight at the O.K. Corral* (1957), *The Comancheros* (1961), *The Rare Breed* (1966), *Once Upon a Time in the West* (1968), *Support Your Local Sheriff* (1969), *The Cockeyed Cowboys of Calico County* (1970), *Hannie Caulder, Pat Garret and Billy the Kid* (1973), *Grayeagle* (1977), and *Bonanza: The Return* (1993).
14. Elam's co-stars in *Shootout in a One-Dog Town* included Dub Taylor (1907-1994), John Pickard (1913-1993), Arthur O'Connell (1908-1981), and Henry Wills (1921-1994), all conspicuous for their myriad appearances in countless Westerns.
15. William Richert's girlfriend was Belinda Bauer (b.1950), who plays the role of Sarah in *The American Success Company*.
16. The play Cohen touches upon here is *Motive*.
17. A recent production that portrays Hitchcock as a manipulative and vindictive sexual predator is *The Girl* (2012), a BBC television movie based on Donald Spotto's book, *Spellbound by Beauty: Alfred Hitchcock and His Leading Ladies* (2009). Both works enact Hitchcock's alleged obsession with actress and model Tippi Hedren, who starred in the director's films *The Birds* (1963) and *Marnie* (1964). Written by Gwyneth Hughes, and starring Toby Jones as Hitchcock and Sienna Miller as Hedren, *The Girl* garnered a mixed reception, draw-

ing criticism from some quarters for its unflattering portrayal of the filmmaker and praise from others who regard it as a balanced and sensitive depiction of a complex relationship.

18. Robert Morley (1908-1992) was a rotund, bushy-browed British character actor, who specialized in essaying pompous upper-class English gentlemen. Morley began his career on the stage in a 1928 production of *Dr. Syn*. His film career commenced a decade later, when he portrayed King Louis XVI in *Marie Antoinette* (1938), a performance that earned him an Academy Award nomination. Notable roles followed in *The African Queen* (1951), *Beat the Devil* (1953), *Around the World in Eighty Days* (1956), *Oscar Wilde* (1960), *Cromwell* (1970), and *Theatre of Blood* (1973). His turn as a food critic in Ted Kotcheff's crime comedy *Who Is Killing the Great Chefs of Europe?* (1978) won Morley both the Los Angeles Film Critics Association Award and National Society of Film Critics (U.S.A.) Award for Best Supporting Actor.

CHAPTER 4: BONE (1971)

1. *The Liberation of L.B. Jones* (1970) is a racial drama based on the novel by Jesse Hill Ford. The story of a well-to-do Black undertaker (Roscoe Lee Brown) living and working in the fictional town of Somerset, Tennessee, whose wife (Lola Falana) is having an illicit affair with one of the town's racist police officers (Anthony Zerbe). Upon hearing that the undertaker is seeking a divorce from his philandering spouse, the cop fears the resulting scandal will damage him if the case is ever heard in a court of law, so takes matters into his own hands. Met with mixed reviews (*Variety* labeled it "not much more than an interracial sexploitation film"), Wyler's swansong is a violent and intense film.
2. Pippa Scott (b.1935) is the daughter of screenwriter Alan Scott (1906-1995). Her film roles include *The Searchers* (1956), *As Young We Were* (1958), *Auntie Mame* (1958), *My Six Loves* (1963), *The Confession* (1964), *Petulia* (1966), *Some Kind of Nut* (1969), *Cold Turkey* (1971), and *Footprints* (2009). Her many TV appearances include *The Twilight Zone*, *The Waltons*, *Dallas*, *Falcon Crest*, and *Knots Landing*.
3. Elaine May (b.1932) is an American screenwriter, filmmaker, actress, and comedienne. Her initial success came as one half of Nich-

ols & May, an influential improvisational comedy duo she formed with Mike Nichols (1931-2014). After the act was disbanded in 1961, May wrote several plays, including *Adaptation, Not Enough Rope*, and *Mr. Gogol and Mr. Preen*, before making her movie debut as director with *A New Leaf* (1971), a screwball comedy that had an initial cut of 180 minutes before the studio hacked it down to a more acceptable 102 minutes. She followed this with the critically lauded comedy, *The Heartbreak Kid* (1972) and the troubled crime drama *Mickey and Nicky* (1976), which was delayed in release and damaged her reputation in Hollywood. More than a decade later, May returned with *Ishtar* (1987), considered one of the most notorious turkeys in the history of cinema, ending her directing career. May's screenplays include *Heaven Can Wait* (1978), for which she earned the first of two Academy Award nominations, as well as *The Birdcage* (1996) and *Primary Colors* (1996) for her old partner, Nichols.
4. *Sheila Levine is Dead and Living in New York* (1975) was directed by Sidney J. Furie and adapted from Gail Parent's 1972 novel by screenwriter Kenny Solms. Anticipating the rom-com likes of *Bridget Jones Diary*, it is the story of an awkward, introverted Jewish-American girl from Harrisburg, Pennsylvania, who arrives in The Big Apple in search of love. Although Furie's movie (and to a certain extent, Parent's book) now seem rather dated, it is not as bad as Cohen or the film's reputation will have you believe.
5. The picture Cohen was shooting at the time was *Q – The Winged Serpent*.
6. At various turns amusing, excruciating, and disturbing, Martin Scorsese's *The King of Comedy* (1983) is the story of celebrity stalker/wannabe comedian Rupert Pupkin (Robert De Niro), an obsessive fantasist, who harbors dreams of becoming a superstar stand-up comedian. Pupkin graduates from rehearsing imagined TV appearances with cardboard cut-outs at home to kidnapping chat-show host Jerry Langford (Jerry Lewis) in the hope of securing his shot at stardom. A box office failure upon release, the film is a stunningly prescient meditation on celebrity and media culture, and is perhaps more relevant now than it has ever been.
7. The young Parisian girl in *Last Tango in Paris* (1971) is played by French actress Maria Schneider (1952-2011).
8. On February 4, 2013, after the interview on *Bone* was conducted, Larry Cohen spoke at the Hollywood Walk of Fame ceremony for

Jack H. Harris, during which the producer and distributor was awarded the 2,717th star. In his speech, Cohen generously remarked: "Jack's had a wonderful career and he's really a pioneer of the business and one of the great showmen—not just a picture-maker but a showman—who knows how to advertise a movie, how to promote a movie, sell the tickets; he goes out and sells the popcorn. He's out there, working the whole place!"

CHAPTER 5: BLACK CAESAR (1972)

1. Samuel Z. Arkoff (1918-2001) was a highly influential producer and distributor. Often credited as the inventor of the beach party and outlaw biker genres, he was once hailed by critic Roger Ebert as the man "who in some ways invented modern Hollywood." In April 1954, Zarkoff and his associate James H. Nicholson (1916-1972), the former sales manager of Realart Pictures, founded the American Releasing Company, which later became American International Pictures. Their first film, *The Fast and the Furious* (1955), starring John Ireland and Dorothy Malone, would be followed by many other low-budget pictures released during the summer and aimed ostensibly at the teenage drive-in market. AIP and a number of other independent companies were able to exploit the lack of seasonal competition and their monopoly continued until June 1975 and the release of *Jaws*. The unprecedented success of Steven Spielberg's film convinced the majors that they should release their movies in the summer months, and thus the age of the blockbuster was born. After Nicholson resigned from AIP in 1972, Arkoff assumed full control until the company merged with Filmways seven years later. After leaving Filmways in 1980, he then formed Arkoff International Pictures. During an appearance on television in the 1980s, he famously revealed his "A.R.K.O.F.F. Formula" for making a successful movie: apparently, a movie should include Action (excitement and drama), Revolution (controversial or revolutionary ideas), Killing (a degree of violence), Oratory (memorable speeches and dialogue), Fantasy (popular dreams and wishes acted out), and Fornication (sex appeal to both sexes). His amusing autobiography, *Flying through Hollywood by the Seat of My Pants*, co-written by Richard Trubo, was published in 1993.

2. *The Legend of Nigger Charley* (1972) is a blaxploitation Western directed by Martin Goldman. Set in pre-Civil War America, three escaped Virginia slaves (Fred Williamson, D'Urville Martin and Don Pedro Colley) seek their freedom in the West. Their arduous journey is made even more treacherous when they discover a gang of Whites led by their sadistic slave-owner are in pursuit of them. Although the film was met with mostly negative reviews upon its release, it was successful enough to generate two sequels, *The Soul of Nigger Charley* (1973) and *Boss Nigger* (1974).
3. *Across 110th Street* (1972) is an American crime drama directed by Barry Shear and starring Anthony Quinn and Yaphet Kotto. Two New York City cops, (one an aging, crooked Italian-American, the other a young, honest African-American) are assigned to track down three Harlem racketeers involved in the murder of seven gangsters and the robbery of $300,000 from a Mafia-owned bank. Featuring a memorable title song by Bobby Womack, this violent thriller benefits from its authentic locations and committed performances but at times is too self-consciously tough and gritty for its own good.
4. *Nigger*, the autobiography of comedian, author, and political activist Dick Gregory (b.1932) was co-written with sports journalist Robert Lipsyte during the American Civil Rights Movement. First published in 1964 by E.P. Dutton, it has since sold over a million copies and been reprinted many times. Gregory famously addressed his controversial use of the pejorative term as a title for the memoir in his dedication: "Dear Momma—Wherever you are, if ever you hear the word 'nigger' again, just remember they are advertising my book."
5. *The Molly Maguires* (1970) is an evocative adaptation of Arthur H. Lewis' 1969 historical novel set amidst the coalfields of Pennsylvania in 1876. After an ineffectual strike engineered to improve conditions, Irish-American coalminers form a covert organization dedicated to committing acts of terrorism and sabotage against the exploitative mine owners. Refusing to submit, the mining company hire Pinkerton Detective James McParlan (Richard Harris) to secretly infiltrate the "Mollies" and identify the perpetrators. Adopting the name "McKenna", McParlan begins an uneasy friendship with "Black Jack" Kehoe (Sean Connery), the leader of the secret society and a man willing to commit murder to meet his objectives. Denounced by some critics as humourless and preachy, *The Molly*

Maguires nevertheless bristles with a textured grittiness and boasts a career-best performance by Harris as the conflicted *agent provocateur*.

6. The Tottenham Riots, or England Riots of 2011, occurred between Saturday August 6 and Thursday August 11, 2011, in several boroughs, cities, and towns across England. The disturbances began in protest at the death of Mark Duggan, a twenty-nine-year-old Tottenham resident, who was shot in the chest and killed by police on August 4. Duggan had been suspected of "planning an attack" and was thought to be in possession of a handgun. The upheaval that followed his death included acts of arson, looting, and damage to vehicles and property, as well as violent clashes between rioters and police. Initially concentrated around North London, rioting spread to other areas of London as well as to cities such as Birmingham, Bristol and Manchester in what was described as instances of "copycat violence." The disorder resulted in five deaths and an estimated £200 million of property damage, culminating with the local economy being severely affected. The family of Mark Duggan condemned the riots.
7. Directed by Gordon Douglas, *Slaughter's Big Rip-Off* (1973) is a sequel to the blaxploitation revenge/crime drama, *Slaughter* (1972). It features several actors, who would later work with Cohen such as Jim Brown, Gloria Hendry, and Ed McMahon.
8. *American Gangster* (2007) is a biographical crime drama directed by Ridley Scott and written by Steve Zaillian. Derived from the article "The Return of Superfly" by Mark Jacobson (which appeared in an issue of *New York* magazine in 2001), the film embellishes the nefarious exploits of Frank Lucas, a former Heroin dealer who operated in Harlem during the 1960s and 1970s.

CHAPTER 6: HELL UP IN HARLEM (1973)

1. Julius W. Harris died of heart failure on October 7, 2004. He was eighty-one years old. *Maniac Cop III: Badge of Silence* was one of his final films.
2. *That Man Bolt* (1973) is a violent blaxploitation/chop-socky action film directed by David Lowell Rich and Henry Levin. Fred Williamson plays Jefferson Bolt, a martial arts expert, who agrees to become

a courier and deliver a briefcase containing $1 million of syndicated money from Hong Kong to Mexico City via Los Angeles. Soon after arriving in Los Angeles, Bolt realizes he has been double-crossed and becomes embroiled in a series of fights, car chases, and torture by acupuncture. A tired and confused attempt to make a blaxploitation James Bond movie (it was marketed with the clumsy tagline "He's Bonded!") *That Man Bolt* is nonetheless enlivened by some good location filming and Williamson's brutish charm.

3. D'Urville Martin died of heart disease on May 28, 1984. He was forty-five.

4. Cohen is featured in Isaac Julien's blaxploitation documentary *Baadasss Cinema: A Bold Look at Blaxploitation Films* (2002) alongside such luminaries as Fred Williamson, Pam Grier, Melvin Van Peebles, Gloria Hendry, Quentin Tarantino, and others. Anybody who is seriously interested in exploring the subgenre should also track down Howard Johnson's excellent 1984 documentary, *Black Hollywood: Blaxploitation and Advancing an Independent Black Cinema*.

CHAPTER 7: IT'S ALIVE (1974)

1. Saul Bass (1920-1996) was an American graphic designer and director. In a career spanning more than forty years, he designed title sequences for Otto Preminger's *Carmen Jones* (1954), *The Man With the Golden Arm* (1955), *Saint Joan* (1957), *Exodus* (1960), and *The Cardinal* (1963); Billy Wilder's *The Seven Year Itch* (1955); Alfred Hitchcock's *Vertigo* (1958), *North By Northwest* (1959), and *Psycho* (1960); and John Frankenheimer's *Seconds* (1967) and *Grand Prix* (1968). Bass later worked on *Goodfellas* (1990), *Cape Fear* (1991), *The Age of Innocence* (1993), and *Casino* (1995) for Martin Scorsese in association with his wife, Elaine.

2. Rick Baker (b.1950) is an American makeup artist and the winner of eight Academy Awards, including the first ever competitive makeup Oscar for the startling illusions he designed and created for *An American Werewolf in London* (1981). Like many of his contemporaries, Baker was inspired by the pages of *Famous Monsters of Filmland* magazine and *Dick Smith's Monster Make-up Handbook* (1965), later becoming Smith's protégé and assisting him on *The Exorcist* (1973). After making the mutant babies for *It's Alive*, Baker

created and wore the ape suits for *King Kong* (1976), *The Kentucky Fried Movie* (1977), and *The Incredible Shrinking Woman* (1981). His other credits include the assorted "cantina scene" aliens of *Star Wars* (1977), the flesh-stretching hallucinations of *Videodrome* (1982), the realistic primates of *Greystoke: The Legend of Tarzan, Lord of the Apes* (1984), the benign Bigfoot of *Harry and the Hendersons* (1987), the fat-suit for Eddie Murphy in *The Nutty Professor* (1996), and the simians of *Planet of the Apes* (2001).

3. An irreverent homage to horror and science fiction movies, *Schlock* (1973) revolves around a thawed prehistoric creature known as the Schlockthropus (that just might be the missing link between simians and humans). Running amok in a small Californian town and leaving a trail of banana skins in its wake, "The Banana Killer"—as it is dubbed—falls in love with a blind girl, who believes the beast is a rather large dog. Shot for the paltry sum of $60,000, *Schlock* features an impressive ape-suit by a then twenty-year-old Rick Baker (writer/director/star John Landis was himself only twenty-one at the time) and cameos from Forest J. Ackerman and John Chambers.

4. Alongside Jack Nicholson and Daniel Day Lewis, Walter Brennan (1894-1974) is the only actor ever to win three Best Actor Academy Awards. Damaged vocal chords and false teeth meant he often played old, cackling, toothless southerners whilst still in his early thirties. Although a capable character actor, he remains best remembered for essaying dependable sidekicks to the rugged Western hero. His memorable turns in *My Darling Clementine* (1946), in which he played the villainous Old Man Clanton, *Red River* (1948), *Rio Bravo* (1959) and *How the West Was Won* (1963) ensured that he quickly became one of the most distinctive performers of his time.

5. The tragic helicopter crash involving John P. Ryan (1936-2007) occurred during the shooting of *Delta Force 2: The Columbian Connection* (1990). The accident happened on May 16, 1989, and claimed the lives of the pilot, Capt. Jojo Imperiale, and four crew people: Geoff Brewer (stuntman/Major Anderson), Gadi Danzig (cameraman), Mike Graham (key grip) and Don Marshall (gaffer). The film is dedicated to their memory.

6. *Them!* is considered one of the best monster movies of the 1950s and is a certified science fiction classic. After being exposed to massive doses of lingering atomic radiation in the New Mexican desert, ants mutate into an enormous size. They migrate to Los Angeles and

infest the sewer system, eventually revealing their nests to a startled city after draining a freight car of its cargo and leaving a trail of formic acid in their destructive wake. Gordon Douglas' suspenseful, intelligent and atmospheric film boasts a documentary style approach. The oversized, irradiated insects, replete with moving antennae, hardened black carapaces, and terrifying war cries, are also impressive for a low-budget film of this vintage. The affecting scene in which the military discover the queen ant's egg chamber was an obvious influence on a similar sequence near the climax of James Cameron's *Aliens* (1986).

7. François Truffaut (1932-1984) was a French filmmaker, actor, author and critic, who, along with his compatriots Jean-Luc Godard, Claude Chabrol, Eric Rohmer, and Agnès Varda, was one of the founders of the French New Wave. In 1954, he began writing for *Cahiers du cinéma* and quickly established himself as a ruthless and contentious critic. His highly controversial article, "Une Certaine Tendance du Cinéma Français" ("A Certain Trend of French Cinema"), famously denounced the French film industry and called for the director to be redefined as "the auteur," or individual author, of a motion picture. Throughout the 1950s, Truffaut supported Andre Bazin in the formulation and promotion of the auteur theory before making his first feature, *The 400 Blows* (1959), which won Truffaut the best director award at the Cannes Film Festival. His subsequent works include *Shoot the Piano Player* (1960), *Jules and Jim* (1962), *Fahrenheit 451* (1966), *The Wild Child* (1970), *Bed and Board* (1970), *Day for Night* (1973), *The Story of Adele H* (1975), *Love on the Run* (1979), and *The Last Metro* (1980). In 1967, Truffaut's book-length interview with Alfred Hitchcock, *Hitchcock: A Definitive Study of Alfred Hitchcock*, was published by Simon & Schuster to great acclaim. He died of a brain tumour in Paris.

8. *It's Alive* won the Special Jury Prize at the 1975 Avoriaz Film Festival.

CHAPTER 8: GOD TOLD ME TO (1976)

1. Erich von Däniken's *Chariots of the Gods?* is a best-selling book first published in Germany in 1968 under its original title *Erinnerungen an die Zukur ft: Ungeloste Ratsel der Verganggenheit* (*Memories of the Future; Unsolved Mysteries of the Past*). It introduced the theory

that an advanced alien race had visited Earth during ancient times and that certain ruins, structures and artefacts of antiquity point to an extraterrestrial intervention having occurred. More radically, von Däniken postulates that the human race itself are the descendants of these first "galactic pioneers" and that the religions and technologies of ancient civilisations were in fact bestowed to humanity by these alien astronauts. Viewed by some as a monumental and profoundly revelatory work, others regard it as nothing more than graspingly speculative, baseless fiction. Predictably, the book's phenomenal success led von Däniken to quickly spawn several sequels that exploited his theories including *Return to the Stars* (1970), *Gods from Outer Space* (1972), and *The Gold of the Gods* (1973). A German documentary based on von Däniken's book, also titled *Chariots of the Gods*, was produced in 1970 and directed by Dr. Harald Reinl.

2. Created by Chris Carter (b.1957), *The X-Files* was an American science fiction horror television series (filmed in Canada for the first five of its nine seasons) that ran on the Fox Network from 1993 until 2002. The show revolves around FBI Agents Fox Mulder (David Duchovny) and Dana Scully (Gillian Anderson) who are appointed to the X-Files, a division of the Bureau that tackles unsolved cases involving the paranormal. Mulder is a believer in the existence of aliens and other unexplained phenomena; whereas Scully is a sceptic assigned by her superiors to observe, analyse and ultimately disparage Mulder's investigations so that he can be returned to more conventional cases. *The X-Files* contained an expansive mythology that involved government conspiracies and encounters with extraterrestrials (a key back-story is that Mulder's sister was abducted by aliens). These central storylines were interspersed with "Monster-of-the-week" episodes that existed outside of the show's wider story arc and featured the pair confronting vampires, werewolves, ghosts and supernatural serial killers. At the time of this writing, there are plans to resurrect the series with its original stars and creative team.

3. *The Honeymoon Killers* (1969) is an American crime drama and the only film directed by Leonard Kastle (1929-2011), a respected composer, librettist, and teacher. Originally titled *Dear Martha*, Kastle's screenplay is based on the true story of Martha Beck and Raymond Fernandez, a serial killer couple dubbed "The Lonely Hearts Killers." Together, they murdered at least twenty women between 1947 and 1949 after luring them through personal ads placed in newspapers.

The homicidal pair was executed by electric chair at Sing Sing prison in 1951, shortly after pledging their love for each other to the assembled observers. Starring Shirley Stoler as Beck and Tony Lo Bianco as Fernandez, *The Honeymoon Killers* is a disturbing meditation on desire and death. One of the great one-shot efforts by a fledgling filmmaker in American independent cinema, it was greatly admired by Michelangelo Antonioni and Francois Truffaut. The film has been viewed by some critics as the antithesis of Arthur Penn's *Bonnie and Clyde* (1967), with Kastle portraying the couple's tumultuous relationship as a twisted, torrid love story and their unfortunate victims as poor White trash. It should also be noted that the original director hired to shoot *The Honeymoon Killers* was Martin Scorsese, who was fired after several clashes with producer Warren Steibel (apparently over the time Scorsese was taking to compose his shots).

4. *Taxi* is an award-winning American sitcom that ran on ABC from 1978 to 1982 and on NBC from 1982 to 1983. Created by James L. Brooks, Stan Daniels, David Davis and Edwin Weinberger, the show revolves around the staff of the Sunshine Cab Company and the firm's fleet garage in Manhattan. Andy Kauffman played immigrant mechanic Latka Gravas (derived from the comedian's "foreign man" character) in all five seasons of the series.

5. Richard Lynch (1940-2012) was a distinctive-looking American-Irish character actor famed for his many villainous roles in film, television and theater. The incident to which Cohen refers occurred behind the Metropolitan Museum of Art in Central Park in 1967. Under the influence of LSD, Lynch set himself on fire and sustained serious burns to seventy percent of his body. After spending more than a year recuperating from his injuries, Lynch made a memorable cinematic debut in *The Scarecrow* (1973). He later appeared in *The Seven-Ups* (1973), *The Premonition* (1976), *Vampire* (1979), *The Ninth Configuration* (1980), *The Sword and the Sorcerer* (1982), *Invasion USA* (1984), *Bad Dreams* (1988), *Little Nikita* (1988), *Necronomicon* (1993), *Scanner Cop* (1994), as well as Rob Zombie's remake of *Halloween* (2007). Lynch was scheduled to work with Zombie again on *The Lords of Salem* (2012), but dropped out through ill health and was replaced by Andrew Prine shortly before his death.

6. Les Bowie (1913-1979) was a Canadian-born special effects artist who worked primarily in Britain. A pioneer of the "glass shot," a method of painting additional scenery onto a pane of clear glass

which is then positioned in front of the camera, he began his career as a scenic artist for Rank Studios in 1946, working on films such as *Great Expectations* (1946), *Oliver Twist* (1948), and *The Red Shoes* (1948). In 1950, Bowie left Rank and toiled as a special effects artist creating a diverse number of mattes, miniatures and mechanical effects for a variety of productions. His vast array of credits includes *The Quatermass Xperiment* (1955), *X: The Unknown* (1956), *The Curse of Frankenstein* (1957), *The Crawling Eye* (1958), *The Brides of Dracula* (1960), *The Curse of the Werewolf* (1961), *The Day the Earth Caught Fire* (1961), *The Evil of Frankenstein* (1964), *Dracula: Prince of Darkness* (1966), *Fahrenheit 451* (1967), *Five Million Miles to Earth* (1967), *Frankenstein Created Woman* (1967), *One Million Years B.C.* (1966), *2001: A Space Odyssey* (1968), *Moon Zero Two* (1969), *Frankenstein and the Monster from Hell* (1974), *Star Wars* (1977), and *Superman* (1978). Bowie died shortly before he was to receive a well-deserved Special Achievement Academy Award for his work on *Superman*.

7. *Space: 1999* is a British science fiction TV series created by Gerry and Sylvia Anderson. It originally ran from 1975 to 1977 and was budgeted in its first season at £3.25 million, making it the most expensive show in the history of British broadcasting. A comparative cash-in on *Star Trek*, *Space: 1999* concerned the inhabitants of Moonbase Alpha, a scientific research station on the moon. A sudden explosion of humanity's vast nuclear waste (which has been deposited on the moon's dark side) causes Earth's only natural satellite to be blasted out of its orbit and the hapless humans cast adrift in the uncharted reaches of the cosmos. Despite a cast headlined by American actors Martin Landau and Barbara Bain (a failed attempt to appeal to U.S. markets), *Space: 1999* was derided by critics and sci-fi enthusiasts alike. Some of the show's core scientific ideas (such as a thermonuclear explosion displacing the moon from its orbit and parsecs being employed as a velocity of speed rather than a unit of distance) were criticized by sci-fi authors Isaac Asimov and John Brosnan. Although these inaccuracies were compounded by some limp teleplays and stiff performances, *Space: 1999* did boast lavish production values and accomplished visual effects and model work. Just ask Larry Cohen.

8. Gaspar Noé (b.1963) is a controversial Franco-Argentine director and screenwriter. His work, which has often polarized critics, has

been associated with the New French Extremity, a transgressive style of cinema which deals with violence, nihilism, perversion, and psychosis. The son of the Argentine painter Luis Felipe Noé, he fled his native country in 1976 with his parents and is now based in France. After making the forty-minute film, *Carne* (1991), which opens with a horse being killed and butchered onscreen, Noé achieved notoriety for the feature films *I Stand Alone* (1998), *Irreversible* (2002), and *Enter the Void* (2009), each distinguished as much by their intense sexual violence and misanthropy as they are by their technical brilliance and narrative ingenuity. Noé has also directed music videos for Bone Fiction (*Insanely Cheerful*, 1997), Placebo (*Protégé-Moi*, 2003), Sebastian (*Love in Motion*, 2011), Animal Collective (*Applesauce*, 2012), and Nick Cave and the Bad Seeds (*We No Who U R*, 2012). As of this writing, Noé's proposed remake of *God Told Me To* appears to be dead.

CHAPTER 9: THE PRIVATE FILES OF J. EDGAR HOOVER (1977)

1. Directed by Mervyn LeRoy and adapted for the screen by Richard L. Breen and John Twist from Don Whitehead's 1956 book, *The FBI Story* (1959) is indeed a select and sanitized history of the Bureau. Featuring a strong cast headed by James Stewart as diligent Federal Agent Chip Hardesty, the film recounts one man's colorful career spent confronting everyone from the Klu Klux Klan and machine-gun toting gangsters to the Nazi secret service. According to some sources, J. Edgar Hoover was a co-producer of the film and insisted that LeRoy re-shoot certain scenes that he felt depicted the FBI in a less than flattering light. Hoover also allegedly deployed two trusted FBI men to "supervise" the director on set.
2. *The House on 92nd Street* (1945), directed by Henry Hathaway, is a terrific semi-documentary espionage thriller lensed in New York. It concerns a young American college graduate (William Eythe) who is recruited and trained in Hamburg, Germany, to be a spy. However, in truth, he is actually working as a covert double agent for the FBI. The doom-laden narration, authentic locales and vérité approach (pioneered by producer Louis de Rochemont) proved highly influential on the post-war American crime film, inspiring the likes of Jules Dassin's *The Naked City* (1948).

3. *The Street with No Name* (1948), directed by William Keighley, features Richard Widmark as a psychotic, wife-beating, hypochondriac gangster (capitalizing on the actor's star-making turn in *Kiss Of Death* two years earlier) whose mob outfit is infiltrated by an FBI agent (Mark Stevens). Entertaining and richly atmospheric, the film is still a stilted affair and was not greatly improved upon when loosely remade by Samuel Fuller as *House of Bamboo* (1955). Lloyd Nolan reprised the role of Inspector George A. Briggs which he had originated in *The House on 92nd Street*.

4. *Walk East on Beacon* (1952), directed by Alfred L. Werker, is a "red scare" spy thriller concerning an FBI agent (George Murphy) who is assigned to apprehend a ruthless communist mastermind who threatens the free world. Based on a *Reader's Digest* article titled "The Crime of the Century"—penned by Hoover himself—the film registers as either a hysterical denouncement of Cold War communism or nothing more than a recruitment commercial for the Bureau.

5. Broderick Crawford (1911-1986) won an Academy Award for his role as politician Willie Stark in the political drama *All the King's Men* (1949). The film also won Oscars for Best Motion Picture and Best Supporting Actress for Mercedes McCambridge.

6. Albert Finney played Winston Churchill in *The Gathering Storm* (2002). A co-production between the BBC and HBO, it was directed by Richard Loncraine and written by Hugh Whitemore. The film begins in 1934 during Churchill's "wilderness years" and ends in 1939 as World War II erupts and he assumes command of the Royal Navy as First Lord of the Admiralty. An equally impressive sequel, *Into the Storm* (2009), directed by Thaddeus O'Sullivan, starred Brendan Gleeson as Churchill.

7. Walter Winchell (1897-1972) was a powerful and highly controversial newspaper and radio gossip columnist. After working in Vaudeville for a decade from the age of thirteen, he began his career in journalism at the *Evening Graphic*, a newly-founded tabloid, when he was twenty-seven. Penning a syndicated column titled "Your Broadway and Mine," Winchell invented the sensationalist gossip column with its tawdry titbits on celebrity activities when he joined the *New York Daily Mirror* in 1929. By the 1940s, he was at the height of his success with his column appearing in 2,000 newspapers and his radio show the top-rated program on the air. Often preferring salacious innuendo and idle talk to established facts, Winchell wielded considerable

influence and counted President Franklin D. Roosevelt and J. Edgar Hoover as supporters. After the *Daily Mirror* ceased publication in 1963, Winchell lost his column and his platform, and was beset with a catalogue of personal miseries and tragedies. He divorced his third wife, lost one daughter to pneumonia and a son to suicide, and became a virtual recluse. Held accountable by some for the decline in ethical standards and quality of the American press, Winchell died of cancer with only his surviving daughter, Walda, attending his funeral.

8. Cohen elaborates further on Hoover and his relationship with Tolson during an interview with Tony Williams in *The Radical Allegories of an Independent Filmmaker*: "They were just two bachelors who liked to watch prize fights, football, and horseraces together . . . . I think had he been openly homosexual, Hoover would have been a better person. He lived with such total repression that it made him an unhappy man and he made everyone around him unhappy. The most sad thing about him was that he was unable to express love openly. That was the tragedy of the man."

9. Hoover's long-time maid was Annie Fields, whom he left $3,000 in his will. Along with Hoover's current chauffeur, Tom Moton, and former chauffeur, James Crawford, it was Annie who discovered the FBI Director's body lying on his bedroom floor on May 2, 1972, after Hoover suffered a fatal heart attack.

10. *Down Three Dark Streets* (1954) is a suspenseful crime drama directed by Arnold Laven. Broderick Crawford stars as Ripley, an FBI agent who takes on the caseload of a deceased colleague and becomes mixed up in three investigations involving car theft, a gangster on the run and an extortion racket.

11. *Then Came Bronson* was an adventure drama series created by Denne Bart Petitclerc that ran on NBC for twenty-six episodes from 1969 to 1970. The show concerns James "Jim" Bronson, who quits his job as a journalist after his friend commits suicide, hops on a Harley-Davidson motorcycle and begins roaming the highways and byways of America in search of his soul. As the soft-spoken nomadic drifter atop his metal steed, Michael Parks cut a memorable figure as Bronson and the series remains a sensitive, understated and affecting paean to 1960s counterculture values.

12. The inspirational poem that Hoover recites to the waiter is "If–" by Rudyard Kipling. First published in *Rewards and Fairies* (1910), an historical fantasy book of verse and poetry, "If–" deftly captures

the essence of "stiff upper-lip" British stoicism and masculinity. Although the poem is addressed to Kipling's son, John, the author was moved to write it in honor of his friend, Leander Starr Jameson, the famous Scottish explorer and politician. Presented as a series of rules and motivational nuggets designed to impart wisdom and humility to the listener, "If–" remains one of the United Kingdom's most beloved poems.

13. After a unanimous decision by the thirty-nine-member board of the Academy of Motion Pictures and Sciences, Elia Kazan (1909-2003) was presented his honorary Oscar by Martin Scorsese and Robert De Niro at the 71st Academy Awards ceremony in 1999. The award was a highly controversial one due to the fact that Kazan was amongst the first to cooperate with the House of Un-American Activities Committee in 1952, which ended the Hollywood careers of many people and caused "irrevocable harm." Despite publicly stating that he deeply regretted his actions, the announcement of the award was met with opposition from the executive council of the Eastern unit of the Writer's Guild of America. On Oscar night, a few hundred demonstrators, as well as at least 100 supporters, congregated outside the theater. Inside the theater, several of the attendees at the ceremony remained seated and stony-faced during the presentation, including Nick Nolte, Ed Harris, and Amy Madigan. Those who stood and applauded included Karl Malden, Warren Beatty, Meryl Streep, Kurt Russell, Helen Hunt, Kathy Bates, and Lynn Redgrave. Steven Spielberg and his wife Kate Capshaw remained in their seats but applauded.

14. *Highway Patrol* was a syndicated crime series that debuted on October 3, 1955, and ran for four seasons and 156 half-hour episodes. Broderick Crawford was the only series regular, starring as Fedora-wearing Captain Dan Matthews, the tough and irascible head of a police force serving a nameless western state. When asked for the reasons why *Highway Patrol* came to an unwelcome end in September 1959, Crawford famously joked, "[Because] we ran out of crimes." In 1977, Crawford made an amusing uncredited cameo as Dan Matthews in a first season episode of the crime show *CHiPS* (titled "Hustle") when he is stopped for a traffic violation by motorcycle cops Ponch (Erik Estrada) and Jonathan (Larry Wilcox) of the California Highway Patrol.

15. The writer of *J. Edgar* (2011) is Dustin Lance Black (b.1974). Black also wrote *Pedro* (2008), the life story of the openly-gay Cuban activist and TV personality Pedro Pablo Zamora, who was one of the first men

with AIDS "to be portrayed in popular media," and *Milk* (2008), a biographical film about politician and gay rights advocate Harvey Milk. *Milk* won Black the Writer's Guild Award and Academy Award for his screenplay. He later wrote and directed *Virginia* (2010), which starred Jennifer Connelly as a mentally unstable woman, who conducts a twenty-year affair with a local married sheriff (played by Ed Harris). He also wrote *8* (2011), a Broadway play that dramatises the closing arguments of Perry vs. Schwarzenegger, a federal case that began in 2009 and led to the abolishment of Proposition 8, an amendment that eliminated the rights of same-sex couples to marry in the state of California. In the June/July 2009 issue of *The Advocate*, Black placed at number one on the "Forty Under 40" list of most influential gay people.

CHAPTER 10: IT LIVES AGAIN (1978)

1. *Cat People* (1942) is a horror film directed by Jacques Tourneur and is the first of Val Lewton's series of B horror and suspense movies in which the terrors are suggested rather than seen. It tells the story of Irena Dubrovna (Simone Simon), a fashion artist living in Manhattan, who fears that an ancient Serbian curse will transform her into a panther and she will kill those she loves. Tourneur's deft use of shadows and sound to impart an unnerving sense of a looming unseen threat is hair-raising. The swimming pool scene that Cohen cites, where a woman is trapped by a beast prowling the surrounding shadows, is only bettered by an atmospheric sequence in which a woman is chased through Central Park at night by a hidden snarling creature.
2. The mob movie that Cohen is referring to here is most likely Richard Fleischer's *The Don is Dead* (1973), which starred Anthony Quinn, Robert Forster and Frederic Forrest. It was released on November 14, 1973, more than a year and a half after *The Godfather* first hit theaters in March 1972. A hastily produced cash-in on Francis Ford Coppola's masterpiece, Fleischer's film arrived a year before *The Godfather: Part II*, which starred Robert De Niro as the young Vito Corleone.
3. *The Missouri Breaks* (1976) is a revisionist Western directed by Arthur Penn and written by Thomas McGuane. The meandering plot concerns an eccentric bounty hunter named Clayton (Marlon Brando), who is hired by a wealthy Montana cattle baron to kill a gang

of horse rustlers. The rabble is led by Tom Logan (Jack Nicholson), who is masquerading as an aspiring cattle-rancher on an adjacent property. Although dismissed by critics upon release, Penn achieves an authentic sense of time and place and the scenes between Brando and Nicholson hold a fascinating charge. The outstanding supporting cast includes Kathleen Lloyd, Harry Dean Stanton, John P. Ryan, as well as Lloyd's *It Lives Again* co-star Frederic Forrest.

4. Lemmy Caution is a fictional FBI Agent created by British author and ex-policeman Peter Cheyney. The character first appeared in the book *This Man is Dangerous* (1936) and was followed by a further ten novels in the ensuing decade, culminating with *I'll Say She Does!* (1945). Eddie Constantine (1917-1993) first appeared on screen as Lemmy Caution in *La môme vert de gris* (1953), but continued to play the role well into his seventies, his last turn in *Allemagne année 90 neuf zéro* (1991) coming just two years before his death.

5. Jean Luc-Godard's *Alphaville* (1965) is a dystopian science fiction film. By far the most celebrated work to feature the character of Lemmy Caution, it sees the world-weary, trenchcoat-wearing private eye searching the distant automated metropolis of Alpha 60 for scientist Henri Dickson (Akin Tamiroff). Adroitly combining elements of Film Noir, Greek mythology, pulp fiction, and comic books to create a thought-provoking hybrid, *Alphaville* remains a hypnotic and visceral experience that features the stunning cinematography of Raoul Coutard.

CHAPTER 11: FULL MOON HIGH (1981)

1. *Teen Wolf* (1985) is a comedy directed by Rod Daniel. Michael J. Fox plays a teenager who discovers he has inherited a family curse which transforms him into a werewolf. He then uses his newfound hirsuteness to secure a place on the school basketball team and improve his low social standing. A Xeroxed sequel followed in the form of *Teen Wolf Too* (1987) with Jason Bateman replacing Fox and boxing supplanting basketball.

2. *The Mummy* franchise is a series of American fantasy/adventure/period horror films that began with *The Mummy* (1999), an excessive if spirited special effects spectacle written and directed by Stephen Sommers. Owing more to Indiana Jones than Boris Karloff, the film

was a surprise hit, grossing $43 million in its opening weekend and $416 million worldwide, leading Sommers and Universal to make a sequel, *The Mummy Returns* (2001). Chuck Russell then contributed a spin-off, *The Scorpion King* (2004), before Rob Cohen restored some of the original characters to the weakest offering in the series, *The Mummy: Tomb of the Dragon Emperor* (2008).

3. The film appearances of Ed McMahon (1923-2009) include *The Incident* (1967), *Fun with Dick and Jane* (1977), *The Last Remake of Beau Geste* (1977), *Butterfly* (1982), *Mixed Blessings* (1998), *The Vegas Connection* (1999), *Bewitched* (2005), and *The Weather Man* (2005).

4. Paul Douglas (1907-1959) was a big and burly actor with an unexpected gift for playing comedy roles. His film appearances include *It Happens Every Spring* (1949), *Panic in the Streets* (1950), *Angels on the Outfield* (1951), *We're Not Married!* (1952), *When in Rome* (1953), *Green Fire* (1954), *The Solid Gold Cadillac* (1956), *This Could Be the Night* (1957), and *The Mating Game* (1959). Douglas died of a heart attack a day after production began on the *Twilight Zone* episode "The Mighty Casey." The role had been written especially for him by Rod Serling as a nod to Douglas' celebrated turn as an irascible baseball team manager in *Angels on the Outfield*. He was later replaced by Jack Warden.

5. Elizabeth Hartman (1943-1987) earned an Academy Award nomination as Best Actress for her role as the blind teenager Selina D'Arcey in *A Patch of Blue* (1965). However, that same year, she did win the Golden Globe for Most Promising Newcomer – Female and, in 1966, was nominated for the Golden Globe Best Actress Award in a Musical or Comedy for her performance in Francis Ford Coppola's *You're a Big Boy Now* (1966). Her other films include *The Group* (1966), *The Fixer* (1967), *Walking Tall* (1973), *Love, American Style* (1973), and *The Secret of NIMH* (1982).

6. Filmed in an antebellum plantation in Louisiana, *The Beguiled* (1971) is a psychological thriller/gothic Western directed by Don Siegel (1912-1991). Set during the closing days of the American Civil War, it is the story of John McBurney (Clint Eastwood), a wounded Unionist soldier, who arrives at a Southern all-ladies seminary school run by Martha Farnsworth (Geraldine Page) and chaste instructor Edwina (Elizabeth Hartman). Taking refuge there, the women nurse McBurney back to health, but when several of the

females show romantic inclinations towards him, suspicion, resentment and deceit rear their ugly heads, leading inexorably to his demise.

7. Bob Newhart (b.1929) is an American stand-up comedian and actor, renowned for his deadpan delivery and hangdog face. His first major success was an album of comic monologues entitled *The Button-Down Mind of Bob Newhart* (1960), which topped the Billboard charts and won Album of the Year at the 1961 Grammy Awards. He later starred in two hugely successful sitcoms, *The Bob Newhart Show* (1972-1978) and *Newhart* (1982-1990), before playing a fictional comic book writer in the short-lived but critically acclaimed vehicle *Bob* (1992-1993). His notable film roles include *Catch 22* (1970), *On A Clear Day You Can See Forever* (1970), *The Rescuers* (1977), *The Rescuers Down Under* (1990), *In and Out* (1997), and *Elf* (2003).

8. Don Rickles (b.1926) is a highly-regarded and influential practitioner of "insult comedy" and is known by the monikers "Mr. Warmth" and "The Merchant of Venom." His film roles include *Run Silent, Run Deep* (1958), *X: The Man With the X-Ray Eyes* (1963), *Kelly's Heroes* (1970), *Innocent Blood* (1993), *Casino* (1995), and *Toy Story* (1995). He was also the subject of a feature-length documentary by John Landis, *Mr. Warmth: The Don Rickles Project* (2007), which features appearances by Clint Eastwood, Martin Scorsese, Robert De Niro, Roger Corman, Robin Williams, Jay Leno, Debbie Reynolds, and Sidney Poitier.

9. The werewolf transformations in *The Howling* were created by Rob Bottin with Rick Baker serving as "special makeup effects consultant."

10. Mort Drucker (b.1929) is an American comic book artist and caricaturist. Born in Brooklyn, New York, he first began contributing to *MAD* magazine in 1956 and has continued parodying an unrivalled array of celebrities, politicians, and other assorted public figures in his unmistakable signature style ever since. Capable of capturing the persona and personality of his subject with unerring accuracy, Drucker's art has also appeared in *Newsweek* and *Time* (his covers for the latter publication currently reside in the National Portrait Gallery of the Smithsonian Institute).

11. Kenneth Mars died of pancreatic cancer on February 12, 2011, several months before this conversation took place. He was seventy-five years old.

12. Edmund Gwenn (1877-1959) was an English actor, who achieved his greatest fame and success in Hollywood during middle age. He is mostly remembered today for playing Kris Kringle in *Miracle on 34th Street* (1947), for which he won an Academy Award as Best Supporting Actor. His other credits include *Foreign Correspondent* (1940), *Louisa* (1950), *Mister 880* (1950, for which he received a second Oscar nomination), *Les Miserables* (1953), *Them!*, *The Student Prince* (1954), and *The Trouble with Harry*.
13. Edwin Thomas Booth (1833-1893) was a celebrated Shakespearean actor, regarded by some critics as the greatest American actor of the nineteenth century. He toured throughout the United States and Europe, and also founded his own theater in New York, Booth's Theater, which was one of the most modern of its age. He was a brother to John Wilkes Booth (1838-1865), the man who assassinated President Abraham Lincoln (of which Edwin was an enthusiastic and vocal supporter). Ironically, a year or two before the assassination, Edwin had saved the President's son, Robert Todd Lincoln, from serious injury—or perhaps even death—when he threatened to tumble off a platform and into the path of an oncoming train.

CHAPTER 12: SEE CHINA AND DIE (1981)

1. *Good Times* was an American sitcom that ran on CBS from February 8, 1974, until August 1, 1979. Developed by Norman Lear, it starred Ester Rolle and John Amos as Florida and James Evans, a couple whose devoted family are struggling to make ends meet in a Chicago housing project. *Good Times* was a spin-off from the series *Maude* (1972-1978), which itself was a spin-off from *All in the Family* (1971-1979), which in turn was derived from Johnny Speight's landmark British sitcom *Till Death Do Us Part* (1965-1975).
2. Paul Dooley (b.1928) has appeared in *Slap Shot* (1977), *A Wedding* (1978), *A Perfect Couple* (1979), *Breaking Away* (1979), *Popeye* (1980), *Endangered Species* (1982), *Sixteen Candles* (1984), *O.C. and Stiggs* (1985), *Flashback* (1990), *Shakes the Clown* (1991), *The Underneath* (1995), *Clockwatchers* (1997), *Runaway Bride* (1999), *Insomnia* (2002), *A Mighty Wind* (2003), *Cars* (2006), *Hairspray* (2007), *Cars II* (2011), and *Turbo* (2013). Dooley's wife is the dramatist, screenwriter and producer Winnie Holzman (b.1954). *Wicked*

(2003) marked Holzman's Broadway debut, winning her the Drama Desk Award for Outstanding Book of a Musical and a nomination for a Tony Award for Best Book of a Musical.

3. Despite Cohen not seeing him around, Kene Holiday (b.1949) has continued to appear in films and television since *See China and Die*. His movie credits include *No Small Affair* (1984), *The Philadelphia Experiment* (1984), *Bulworth* (1998), *The Immaculate Misconception* (2006), *The Human War* (2011), and *Handle Your Business* (2015). His TV appearances include *Kojak*, *The Incredible Hulk*, *Lou Grant*, *Quincy, ME*, *Hart to Hart*, *Hill Street Blues*, *Benson*, *The Fall Guy*, *Matlock*, *Doogie Howser M.D.*, *Jake and the Fatman*, *Diagnosis Murder*, and *The District*.

4. Miguel Pinero (1946-1988) is the Puerto Rican actor, poet, and playwright Cohen speaks of here. Pinero began his writing career whilst serving a prison sentence in Sing Sing for armed robbery. Deeply affected by the events he witnessed whilst incarcerated, he joined a prison workshop called "The Family" and wrote several short plays. *Short Eyes* is the most famous of these works and is the harrowing story of an imprisoned child molester who is put on trial, judged and then executed by his fellow convicts. In 1974, *Short Eyes* won the New York Drama Critics Circle Award for Best American Play of the Year and was soon followed by an Obie Award for Best Off-Broadway Play. Pinero also wrote the screenplay for Robert M. Young's film adaptation of *Short Eyes* in 1977 and played the supporting role of Go-Go. Aside from essaying "Gonzales" in *See China and Die*, Pinero also appeared in *The Jericho Mile* (1979), *Fort Apache The Bronx* (1981), *Breathless* (1983), *Deal of the Century* (1983), *Alphabet City* (1984), and *Almost You* (1985) before dying of liver disease. A biographical film about his life, *Pinero* (2001), was written and directed by Leon Ichaso and starred Benjamin Bratt in the title role.

5. *Marathon Man* (1976) is a flawed but compelling conspiracy thriller directed by John Schlesinger and adapted by William Goldman from his own 1974 novel. Dustin Hoffman plays a graduate history student and avid marathon runner who becomes inadvertently involved in the machinations of his rogue government agent brother (Roy Scheider) and an exiled Nazi war criminal (a terrifying Laurence Olivier) who is seeking to smuggle a priceless haul of Jewish diamonds out of America.

6. Agatha Christie's *Ten Little Indians* was first published in the U.K. in 1939 and in the U.S. the following year as *And Then There Were None*. The story concerns ten people who are invited to an isolated island under different pretexts, only to discover that an unseen killer is murdering them one by one for their respective past crimes and indiscretions. Often regarded as Christie's masterpiece it is also the best-selling mystery novel of all time, shifting over 100 million copies.
7. *Witness for the Prosecution* (1957) is a gripping courtroom drama directed by Billy Wilder and adapted for the screen by Wilder, Harry Kurnitz and Larry Marcus. Derived from Agatha Christie's short story (which was first published in 1925 as *The Witness For the Prosecution*), it boasts a masterful performance by Charles Laughton as Sir Wilfrid Robarts, a brilliant but ailing barrister, who agrees to defend Leonard Vole (Tyrone Power), an American war veteran arrested on suspicion of murdering an elderly acquaintance. Marlene Dietrich plays Christine Helm Vole, the wife who testifies against the accused as the prosecution's star witness. Apparently, Wilder's film was Christie's favorite of her works adapted for film and television.

INTERMISSION: I, THE JURY (1982)

1. Richard T. Heffron (1930-2007) began his career as a documentary filmmaker before branching out into cinema and television. His feature credits include *Fillmore* (1972), *The California Kid* (1974), *I Will Fight No More Forever* (1975), *Futureworld* (1976), *Outlaw Blues* (1977), *Foolin' Around* (1980), *Pancho Barnes* (1988), *Tagget* (1991), and *No Greater Love* (1996).
2. Mickey Spillane was a pseudonym of Frank Morrison Spillane (1981-2006).
3. Victor Saville (1895-1979) was an English director, who directed thirty-nine films between 1927 and 1954. He only produced the 1953 version of *I, the Jury*, which was actually directed by Harry Essex from his own adapted screenplay.
4. The full title of this American/Spanish co-production is *Yellow Hair and the Fortress of Gold* (1984). Directed by Matt Cimber, whose previous efforts include the blaxploitation movies *The Black 6* (1973) and *Lady Cocoa* (1975), and the horror film *The Witch Who Came from the Sea* (1976), it plays like a modestly-budgeted amalgamation

of the spaghetti Western and *Raiders of the Lost Ark* (1981). Laurene Landon stars as Yellow Hair, a White woman raised from childhood by an Apache tribe, who becomes mixed-up in a series of adventures with The Pecos Kid (Ken Roberson). Cimber also directed Landon in *Hundra* (1983).

5. *Moonlighting* is an American TV series created by Glenn Gordon Caron that aired for five seasons on ABC from March 3, 1985, until May 14, 1989. A deft mixture of comedy, drama, mystery, and romance, the show revolved around the working relationship (and underlying sexual tension) between Maddie Hayes (Cybil Shepherd) and David Addison Jr (Bruce Willis) of the Blue Moon Detective Agency. Invigorated by some sharp writing and the chemistry between its engaging leads, *Moonlighting* assisted in launching Willis on his way to stardom.

CHAPTER 13: Q – THE WINGED SERPENT (1982)

1. In an interview with the author published in *Rue Morgue* #137 (September 2013), conducted to publicize the release of Scream Factory's Blu-ray of *Q – The Winged Serpent*, Cohen commented on the Aztec influence in the film: "I liked the idea of making a horror film that had an Aztec flavor [to it] as opposed to the Catholic flavor of *The Exorcist* or *God Told Me To*."
2. Randall William Cook (b.1953) is an American animator, visual effects and makeup artist whose credits include *Caveman* (1981), *The Thing* (1982), *2010* (1984), *Ghostbusters* (1984), *Fright Night* (1985), *Poltergeist II: The Other Side* (1986), *The Gate* (1987), and *Dragonworld* (1994). Cook also co-wrote and directed the film *Demon in a Bottle* (1996) and played Malcolm Brand, the scar-faced psychopath in the horror film *Hardcover* (1989). Invited by Peter Jackson to serve as Animation Director on his *Lord of the Rings* trilogy, Cook won three Academy Awards and three BAFTAs for his efforts on *The Fellowship of the Ring* (2001), *The Two Towers* (2002), and *The Return of the King* (2003).
3. David Allen (1944-1999) was an American visual effects artist, considered by many to rival Ray Harryhausen and Jim Danforth as one of the best stop-motion animators to have ever lived. His extensive credits include *Equinox* (1970), *When Dinosaurs Ruled the*

Earth (1970), *Flesh Gordon* (1974), *The Crater Lake Monster* (1977), *Laserblast* (1978), *The Howling*, *The Hunger* (1983), *Twilight Zone: The Movie* (1983), *Trancers* (1984), *The Stuff*, *Young Sherlock Holmes* (1985), *Batteries Not Included* (1987), *Dolls*, *Willow* (1988), *Robot Jox*, *Honey, I Shrunk the Kids* (1989), *Ghostbusters II* (1989), *Bride of Re-Animator* (1989), and *Freaked* (1993). From the late 1970s up until his death from cancer, Allen had also been toiling on an unfinished feature titled *The Primevals*, "a tale about a secret Himalayan valley populated with giant yetis and an ancient race of alien lizard men." Hopes persist that it will one day be completed by other hands.

4. Ray Harryhausen (1920-2013) was an influential American visual effects artist, writer and producer who lived in London from 1960 until his death. Famed for creating a form of stop-motion animation known as "dynamation," Harryhausen served his apprenticeship under his mentor Willis H. O'Brien (1886-1982), who surrendered much of the animation duties on *Mighty Joe Young* (1949) to his gifted protégé. This assignment was later followed by Harryhausen's work on *The Beast from 20,000 Fathoms* (1953), *It Came from Beneath the Sea* (1955), *Earth Versus the Flying Saucers* (1956), and *20 Million Miles to Earth* (1957), for which he also co-authored the story. Harryhausen later created the animation for *The Seventh Voyage of Sinbad* (1958), *The Three Worlds of Gulliver* (1959), *Mysterious Island* (1961), *Jason and the Argonauts* (1963), *One Million Years BC* (1966), *The Valley of Gwangi* (1969), *The Golden Voyage of Sinbad* (1974), and *Sinbad and the Eye of the Tiger* (1977). His swansong was *Clash of the Titans* (1981) by which time his stop-motion animation techniques, although still brilliantly executed, were beginning to look increasingly dated in the wake of other technological developments.

5. Shortly after the furore caused by shooting this sequence Cohen took out a full page advertisement in *Variety* at his own expense which was published on Wednesday, July 1, 1981. It read: "Dear New York, Sorry If We Scared You: Last week, the headlines of the newspapers and national radio and TV told about the shock waves caused when a crack 75 man SWAT team invaded the pinnacle of the Chrysler Building and opened fire on the swooping forty foot flying SERPENT that had nested there. IT WAS ONLY A MOVIE—but thousands of New Yorkers saw and heard the scene in progress and thought it was real. Police even had calls reporting actual sightings of a giant bird

up on the Chrysler tower. To anyone who was frightened, our apology. To the NYPD and the New York City Motion Picture Division our thanks for making this spectacular scene possible. It's only one of many great sequences in this new thriller which stars MICHAEL MORIARTY, DAVID CARRADINE, CANDY CLARK, and RICHARD ROUNDTREE. Next time we scare you we hope it's in a movie theatre."

6. The artist who created the poster art for *Conan the Barbarian* was Renato Casaro (b.1935). Cohen is mistaken here as Boris Vallejo (b.1941) is responsible for the poster of *Q – The Winged Serpent*. An award-winning Peruvian painter and illustrator specialising in idealized images of fantasy and erotica, Vallejo has developed his own distinctive and sensual style which can be seen on the posters for *Barbarella* (1968), *The White Buffalo* (1977), *Knightriders* (1981), *Deathstalker* (1983), *National Lampoon's Vacation* (1983), and *National Lampoon's European Vacation* (1985).

7. On June 4, 2009, David Carradine was found dead in his room at the Swissôtel Nai Lert Park Hotel in central Bangkok, Thailand. He had been staying there whilst shooting the French film *Stretch*. Carradine was found hanging by a rope and naked in a closet. Initial reports in the media suggested that the actor had taken his own life. Two autopsies were conducted and the cause of death was later thought to be due to autoerotic asphyxiation.

8. *The Royal Hunt of the Sun* by Peter Shaffer concerns the Spanish explorer Francisco Pizarro whose expedition slaughters 3000 unarmed Incas and captures their deified (and supposedly immortal) chieftain, Atahualpa, on a ransom of 9000 pounds of gold. The play was first presented by The National Theatre at the Chichester Festival in 1964. It was subsequently performed at the Old Vic Theatre before transferring across the Atlantic to Broadway where it was staged at the ANTA Playhouse on October 26, 1965. The original Broadway cast featured Christopher Plummer as Pizarro and David Carradine as Atahualpa, and ran for 261 performances.

9. *Kung Fu* was an American martial-arts/adventure/Western drama series that initially ran on ABC for three seasons and sixty-three episodes from October 14, 1972, until April 16, 1975. Created by Ed Spielman, Jerry Thorpe and Hermann Miller, the show centred on Kwai Chang Caine, a Shaolin monk who traverses the Old American West in search of his brother. The show later sired a TV movie, *Kung*

Fu: The Movie (1986), and an unsuccessful pilot starring Brandon Lee, *Kung Fu: The Next Generation* (1987), before eventually being revived as *Kung Fu: The Legend Continues*. This syndicated series ran from January 27, 1993, until January 1, 1997.

10. Robert Carradine (b.1954) is an American actor and the youngest of the three actor sons of John Carradine. After making his debut opposite John Wayne in *The Cowboys* (1972), Robert went on to appear in *Mean Streets* (1973), *Massacre at Central High* (1976), *The Long Riders* (1980)—in which he co-starred with his brothers, David and Keith, *The Big Red One* (1980), *Revenge of the Nerds* (1984), *Revenge of the Nerds II: Nerds in Paradise* (1987), *Rude Awakening* (1989), *Buy and Cell* (1990), *Body Bags* (1993), *The Tommyknockers* (1993), *Escape from L.A.* (1996), *Ghosts of Mars* (2001), *The Lizzie McGuire Movie* (2003), and *Django Unchained* (2012).

CHAPTER 14: PERFECT STRANGERS (1984)

1. A riff on the age-old fable of the boy who cried wolf, *The Window* (1949) is an RKO thriller directed by Ted Tetzlaff. Adapted from a short story by Cornell Woolrich called "The Boy Who Cried Murder," it concerns a youngster (Bobby Driscoll), who sneaks out onto the fire escape of his grimy tenement building one hot summer night and witnesses the couple in the apartment above killing a drunken seaman. Since the child has a habit of telling tall tales neither his parents nor the police believe his story, but when the murderous neighbours learn that the boy knows the truth of their crime they decide to ensure his silence. An accomplished and suspenseful Film Noir, Driscoll was presented with a miniature Oscar for his superb performance.

2. *Liquid Sky* (1982) is a science fiction art film co-written and directed by Vladislav "Slava" Tsukerman (b.1940). An amusing and occasionally seedy effort, it concerns invisible aliens, who land on the roof of a Manhattan penthouse in a miniscule flying saucer. Observing the inhabitants of New York's sordid punk/new wave drug culture, they are attracted to the chemicals released by humans using heroin and/or achieving orgasm. Tsukerman's other works include the feature films *Poor Liza* (2000) and *Perestroika* (2008), and the documentary *Stalin's Wife* (2004).

3. Richard Hambleton (b.1954) is the artist Cohen invokes here. Born in Vancouver, Canada, he is regarded as "The Godfather of Street Art" and emerged in the early 1980s during the heyday of the New York art scene alongside his contemporaries Keith Haring (1958-1990) and Jean-Michel Basquiat (1960-1988). Hambleton's signature "shadowman" paintings are amongst his most famous works and depict a life-size silhouette on the wall of a New York building or structure (often described as a "splashy shadow figure"). Hambleton later painted similar figures on the streets of London, Paris, Rome and Berlin.

4. Janelle Webb Cohen has written or co-written several songs that have been heard in her former husband's films including "Big Poppa" for *Hell Up in Harlem*; "Sweet Momma, Sweetlove" for *God Told Me To*; "We Came So Close to Love" for *The Private Files of J. Edgar Hoover*; "Full Moon Anthem", "Tony, My Pet", "When the Sun Goes Down" and "Meet Me in the Moonlight" for *Full Moon High*; "Ride the Bull" for *See China and Die*; "Let's Fall Apart Together Tonight" for *Q - The Winged Serpent* and "Firing Line of Life" for *Perfect Strangers*. The song featured in *Perfect Strangers* during the sequence where Johnny spray-paints a shadowy figure is "I'm a Shadow (On the Walls of the City)", written and performed by Michael Minard.

5. After making *Special Effects*, Ann Magnuson went on to appear in such films as *Desperately Seeking Susan* (1985), *Sleepwalk* (1986), *Making Mr. Right* (1987), *Tequila Sunrise* (1988), *Clear and Present Danger* (1994), *Small Soldiers* (1998), *Glitter* (2001), and *Panic Room* (2002).

6. The actor who played the gangster, Maletti, is Zachary Hains. *Perfect Strangers* appears to be his only film credit as an actor.

7. The blond heavy that grabs Johnny in the cemetery is played by actor Bill Fagerbakke (b.1957). Fagerbakke is most famous for playing Michael "Dauber" Dybinski in the ABC sitcom *Coach* (which aired for nine seasons on ABC) and for voicing Patrick Star in the popular animated series *SpongeBob SquarePants* (1999-present).

8. John Daly (1937-2008) pulled off the remarkable achievement of producing back-to-back Academy Award winning films for Best Picture: *Platoon* in 1986 and *The Last Emperor* in 1987.

9. The film that Daly directed was *The Aryan Couple* (2004), an Anglo-American film starring Martin Landau as a wealthy Jewish tycoon, who must give up his considerable wealth in order to ensure that his family receive a safe passage from Nazi-dominated Hungary.

CHAPTER 15: SPECIAL EFFECTS (1984)

1. Lowell Blair Nesbitt (1933-1993) was an American painter, draughtsman, printmaker and sculptor celebrated for his notable floral works of art. During his career, Nesbitt had more than eighty one man shows since his first was mounted in 1957. His works are currently housed in several prestigious museums including the Metropolitan Museum of Fine Art in New York and the National Gallery of Fine Art in Washington DC.
2. Michael Cimino (b.1940) began his career producing commercials and industrial films for a company in New York. After shooting ads for clients such as Eastman Kodak, United Airlines and Pepsi, he moved to Los Angeles and co-wrote the screenplays for *Silent Running* (1972) and *Magnum Force* (1973) before helming his first feature as director, the crime drama *Thunderbolt and Lightfoot* (1974). After the notable success of *The Deer Hunter* (1978), for which Cimino won the Academy Award for Best Director, he then assisted in bankrupting United Artists with the notorious Western, *Heaven's Gate* (1980), the failure of which signalled the end of New Hollywood. Cimino's reputation has never recovered and the stink of this film has tainted his subsequent career, despite the unedited version of *Heaven's Gate* later being hailed by some critics as a masterpiece.
3. "The English Fellow" who directed *Chariots of Fire* (1981) is Hugh Hudson (b.1936). Aside from helming the multiple Oscar-winning historical sports drama, Hudson's other films include *Greystoke: The Legend of Tarzan* (1984) and the notorious period piece *Revolution* (1985), a critical and commercial failure which encouraged its star Al Pacino to take a four-year hiatus from movies.
4. Eric Bogosian and Tad Savinar's play *Talk Radio* was inspired by the 1984 assassination of attorney and talk show radio host Alan Berg. It premiered off-Broadway on May 28, 1987, at The Public Theatre and concerns the life and death of Barry Champlain, a controversial Jewish shock-jock whose Cleveland-based radio show is about to earn national syndication. Oliver Stone's film adaptation of *Talk Radio* (co-written and starring Bogosian) was released on December 21, 1988.
5. The remake of Abel Ferrara's controversial 1992 crime drama, now re-titled *Bad Lieutenant: Port of Call New Orleans* (2009), is a lighter and tamer affair than its unremitting predecessor. Directed by Werner Herzog, it stars Nicolas Cage as a police officer who develops a

serious drug problem after sustaining a back injury whilst on duty in post-Hurricane Katrina New Orleans.

6. Zoë Lund died on April 16, 1999, of heart failure in Paris, France, due to her extended drug use. She was just thirty-seven years old.
7. Kevin O'Connor died of cancer on June 22, 1991, at the age of fifty-three. *The Ambulance* was his final film.
8. Jessica Lange played Frances Farmer in *Frances* (*1982*), a highly sensationalized account of the actress's life and alleged mental illness that draws on erroneous details first perpetrated in William Arnold's largely fictionalised 1978 biography, *Shadowland*. Lange's sensitive performance earned her an Academy Award nomination for Best Actress.
9. Preceding the release of *Star 80* in 1983, an NBC television movie titled *Death of a Centerfold: The Dorothy Stratten Story* was broadcast on November 1, 1981 (nearly fifteen months after Stratten's murder on August 14, 1980). Accused by some critics of being "exploitive" and "insensitive," it is naturally a more restrained biopic than Bob Fosse's theatrical film but boasts an impressive performance from Bruce Weitz as Stratten's psychopathic husband, Paul Snider.

CHAPTER 16: THE STUFF (1985)

1. In an interview with Alan Jones for *Starburst* magazine to publicize the theatrical release of *The Stuff* in the United Kingdom, Cohen mentions a film he planned to do next (again with New World Pictures) that would have satirized another contemporary craze of the 1980s. *F.I.T. to Kill* would have concerned "the trendy fetishes of fitness, diet and health" and the potentially harmful fascination the public has with attaining "Arnold Schwarzeneggar [sic] type bodies." Cohen's story concerns The F.I.T. Institute, an aerobics/fitness center that offers its clients the chance to achieve an incredibly muscular physique in only a very short time. People acquire these heavenly bodies with the aid of an experimental steroid developed and administered by an evil Soviet scientist who has defected. An unfortunate side effect of this radical drug is that the fitness fanatics lose control of their own minds and bodies at the slightest provocation, suddenly becoming murderously psychotic. Cohen's concept for *F.I.T. to Kill* is clearly allied to the destructive properties and conforming allure of the malevolent dessert in *The Stuff*.

2. Jim Danforth (b.1940) is a legendary stop-motion animator whose extensive credits include matte work and model animation on a number of classic and cult films. These include *The Time Machine* (1960), *Jack the Giant Killer* (1962), *It's a Mad, Mad, Mad, Mad World, 7 Faces of Dr. Lao* (1964)—for which he received an Academy Award nomination, *When Dinosaurs Ruled the Earth, Dark Star* (1974), *Clash of the Titans, Caveman, The Thing, The Never Ending Story* (1984), *Prince of Darkness* (1987), *They Live* (1988), *Memoirs of an Invisible Man* (1992), *Body Bags*, and *Body Snatchers*.
3. All the advertising jingles for *The Stuff* commercials were written, composed and produced by Richard Seaman.
4. Abe Vigoda (b.1921) is an American actor. His most memorable roles remain his portrayal of doomed *capo* Salvatore "Sal" Tessio in *The Godfather* (1972) and the world-weary Jewish-American cop Sgt. Fish on the television sitcom *Barney Miller* (which originally aired on ABC from January 23, 1975, to May 20, 1982). Bizarrely, Vigoda is also famous for the premature reports of his death, firstly by *People* magazine in 1982 and then again in 1987 when a New Jersey news presenter referred to him as "the late Abe Vigoda."
5. Brooke Adams appeared in Philip Kaufman's *Invasion of the Body Snatchers* (1978), the second of four cinematic adaptations of Jack Finney's 1954 novel *The Body Snatchers*.
6. Carl Reiner (b.1922) is an American actor, stand-up comedian, writer, producer, director and singer. His films as director include *Where's Poppa?* (1970), *Oh, God!* (1977), *The Jerk* (1979), *Dead Men Don't Wear Plaid* (1982), *The Man with Two Brains* (1983), *All of Me* (1984), *Summer School* (1987), *Bert Rigby, You're a Fool* (1989), and *That Old Feeling* (1997).
7. The film that secured Mira Sorvino her Academy Award for Best Supporting Actress was *Mighty Aphrodite* (1994).

CHAPTER 17: SCREENPLAYS PART II (1987-1997)

1. Roger Corman executive produced this unreleased film of *The Fantastic Four* (1994) which was directed by Oley Sassone and written by Craig J. Nevius and Kevin Rock. It starred Alex Hyde-White as Reed Richards, Rebecca Staab as Susan Storm, Jay Underwood as

Johnny Storm and Michael Bailey Smith as Ben Grimm. Although (as Cohen states) the film was made in order to retain the rights, it was rushed into production and shot on a stringent budget. Apparently, none of the aforementioned cast members were aware that the movie was never intended for release.
2. After wallowing in development hell for a quarter of a century and at various junctures orbiting the likes of James Cameron, Roland Emmerich and Chris Columbus, *Spider-Man* (2002) was eventually directed by Sam Raimi. Released to critical acclaim, the film also became the highest-grossing movie based on a comic book and resulted in Raimi returning to direct two sequels, *Spider-Man 2* (2004) and *Spider-Man 3* (2007).
3. Elliott Kastner (1930-2010) produced *Where Eagles Dare* (1968), *The Long Goodbye* (1973), *Farewell My Lovely* (1975), *The Missouri Breaks*, *Equus* (1977), *The Big Sleep* (1978), *Garbo Talks* (1984), *Angel Heart* (1987), and *White of the Eye* (1987).
4. The producer of *Body Snatchers* was Robert H. Solo.
5. Born in 1926, Martin Ransohoff's credits as a producer include *The Cincinnati Kid* (1965), *The Loved One* (1965), *The Fearless Vampire Killers* (1967), *Ice Station Zebra* (1968), *10 Rillington Place* (1971), *Save the Tiger* (1973), *The White Dawn* (1974), *Silver Streak* (1977), *Nightwing* (1979), *The Wanderers* (1979), *Class* (1983), *Jagged Edge* (1985), and *Physical Evidence* (1989).
6. The film Cohen makes reference to here is *Bye, Bye Braverman* (1968). A meandering black comedy and character study set in Brooklyn, director Sidney Lumet apparently had mixed feelings about it himself, stressing that it had only partially met his objectives as a movie.
7. *Brute Force* (1947), directed by Jules Dassin from a screenplay by Richard Brooks, is a powerful prison drama that was considered exorbitantly violent for its time. Hume Cronyn plays a memorably sadistic prison warden, whose guards systematically brutalise the convicts until Burt Lancaster's rebellious prisoner leads them in a savage revolt. *The Expert* bears little relation to Dassin's film, which suggests whoever "fucked around" with the script did so without inhibition.
8. *The Monkey's Paw* was written by English author W.W. Jacobs and was first published in 1902. The story has proved hugely influential and has been adapted into stageplays, short films, feature-length movies, episodic television shows, comic books, and even an opera.

9. *The Green Berets* (1968) is a war drama directed by Ray Kellogg, the man responsible for such cult schlockers as *The Giant Gila Monster* (1959) and *The Killer Shrews* (1960). Co-director John Wayne stars as Colonel Mike Kirby, a solider who selects two crack teams to execute a dangerous mission in South Vietnam. Riddled with clichés and embarrassing in its unrepentant one-sidedness, *The Green Berets* is a jingoistic attempt to counter the protests, criticisms and unrest surrounding American involvement in the Vietnam War. A patriotic and occasionally offensive effort, Wayne's dedicated soldiers are portrayed as noble and courageous men—ready and willing to lay down their lives to protect the persecuted peasantry.
10. Douglas Hickox (1929-1988) was an English director. His films include *The Giant Behemoth* (1959), *Entertaining Mr. Sloane* (1970), *Theatre of Blood* (1973), *Brannigan* (1975), *Sky Riders* (1976), *Zulu Dawn* (1979), and *The Hound of the Baskervilles* (1983).
11. Anthony Hickox's mother is Anne V. Coates (b.1925). Aside from cutting *Lawrence of Arabia* (1962), for which she won an Academy Award, her credits include *Tunes of Glory* (1960), *Becket* (1964), *The Public Eye* (1972), *Murder on the Orient Express* (1974), *The Eagle Has Landed* (1976), *The Elephant Man* (1980), *Farewell to the King* (1987), *Chaplin* (1992), *In the Line of Fire* (1993), *Out of Sight* (1998), *Erin Brockovich* (1999), *Unfaithful* (2002), *The Golden Compass* (2007), and *Fifty Shades of Grey* (2015).
12. The "famous Black model" to which Cohen refers is Naomi Campbell.
13. The lead girl in *Invasion of Privacy* is Mili Avital, an Israeli-American actress who has appeared in films such as *Stargate* (1994), *Dead Man* (1995) and *Arabian Nights* (2000). The leading man is played by Johnathon Schaech whose credits include *That Thing You Do* (1996), *The Doom Generation* (1995), *Quarantine* (2008), and *Takers* (2010).

INTERMISSION: DEADLY ILLUSION (1987)

1. The film Cohen is probably thinking about is *Love You to Death* (1990), Lawrence Kasdan's black comedy about a scheming wife (Tracey Ullman), who repeatedly tries to murder her womanizing husband (Kevin Kline). It was actually released three years after *Deadly Illusion*.

2. *Action Jackson* (1987) is an action thriller directed by Craig R. Baxley. It stars Carl Weathers as the eponymous hero, a Detroit cop with a Harvard law degree, who is attempting to apprehend an evil businessman played by Craig T. Nelson. Vanity was nominated for a Golden Raspberry for her stilted performance as a sultry lounge singer combating a heroin addiction.
3. Born in New York City in 1942, William Tannen began his career directing commercials before moving to Hollywood in the early 1970s. His credits include the thrillers *Flashpoint* (1984), *Hero and the Terror* (1988), *Inside Edge* (1992), and *The Cutter* (2008), and the historical drama *Love Lies Bleeding* (1998). Tannen has also directed music videos for artists such as Aretha Franklin, The Commodores, The Temptations, and Tangerine Dream.
4. Cohen is almost certainly referring to the *Costa Concordia* disaster that occurred on the night of January 13, 2012. Only hours after leaving the port of Civitavecchia, the Italian cruise ship ran aground with more than 4,000 people onboard (3,206 passengers and 1,032 crew). After striking a reef on her portside the vessel capsized and sank, killing thirty-two people.

CHAPTER 18: IT'S ALIVE III - ISLAND OF THE ALIVE (1987)

1. With the advent of television luring moviegoers away in their droves, Hollywood devised 3D as a means of offering audiences something they couldn't get at home. *House of Wax* (1953) is one of the superior 3D pictures of the early 1950s and is Warner Bros.' first effort at adopting the format. Although not as accomplished as Michael Curtiz' *Mystery of the Wax Museum* (1933), Andre De Toth's remake is a resplendent effort with several effective moments. The story concerns Henry Jarrod (Vincent Price), an insane sculptor whose body has been disfigured by a fire at his museum that was started by his greedy partner (Roy Roberts). Jarrod decides to repopulate his destroyed museum by dipping human corpses in boiling wax so that he can display them in his chamber of horrors. Ironically, having only one eye, De Toth could not see the 3D effect onscreen.
2. William Girdler (1947-1978) was an American director, producer, and screenwriter. He made nine films in six years before his sudden death in a helicopter accident at the age of thirty whilst scouting

locations in the Philippines for his next project *The Overlords* (a science fiction movie designed to capitalise on the phenomenal success of *Star Wars*). His spirited oeuvre includes *Asylum of Satan* (1972), *Three on a Meathook* (1973), *Abby* (1974), *Grizzly* (1976), *Day of the Animals* (1977), and *The Manitou* (1978).

3. To illustrate the extent of the debt *Abby* owes to *The Exorcist*, consider the fact that Warner Bros. launched a lawsuit against the filmmakers for copyright violation and succeeded in winning their case. This resulted in William Girdler's film being withdrawn from theaters but, according to williamgirdler.com, a website dedicated to the late director, this was not before *Abby* had earned a whopping $4 million at the box office.

4. Karen Black (1939-2013) was an American actress, screenwriter, singer, and songwriter, whose career peaked in the 1970s with a succession of impressive roles. After training under Lee Strasburg at the Actors Studio, Black made her debut in *You're a Big Boy Now* before going on to appear in *Easy Rider* (1969), *Five Easy Pieces* (1971), *The Great Gatsby* (1974), *The Day of the Locust* (1975), *Trilogy of Terror* (1975), *Nashville* (1975), *Burnt Offerings* (1976), *Capricorn One* (1978), *Invaders from Mars* (1986), and *House of 1000 Corpses* (2001). Twice the winner of the Golden Globe for Best Supporting Actress, she was also nominated for an Academy Award for her performance in *Five Easy Pieces*.

CHAPTER 19: A RETURN TO SALEM'S LOT (1987)

1. Paul Monash wrote the teleplay for *Salem's Lot* (1979).
2. Clint Walker (born Norman Eugene Walker in 1927) is a retired American actor, best known for his role as Cheyenne Bodie in the television series *Cheyenne*.
3. Amongst his credits as an actor, Sam Fuller appeared in *The Last Movie* (1971) for Dennis Hopper; *The American Friend* (1977), *Hammett* (1982), *The State of Things* (1982) and *The End of Violence* (1997) for Wim Wenders; *1941* (1979) for Steven Spielberg; *The Blood of Others* (1984) for Claude Chabrol; *Sons* (1990) and *Somebody To Love* (1994) for Alexandre Rockwell; and *Golem, le jardin pétrifié* (1993) and *Metamorphosis of a Melody* (1996) for Amos Gitai.

4. Gypsy Rose Lee (1911-1971) was a Burlesque entertainer famed for her striptease act. The musical *Gypsy: A Musical Fable* (first performed on Broadway in 1959) was derived from her 1957 memoir and featured lyrics by Jule Styne and music by Stephen Sondheim. Her sister, June Havoc (1912-2010), wrote her own memoirs, *Early Havoc* (1959) and *More Havoc* (1980), after being displeased with the manner in which she was portrayed in the musical. This led to the siblings becoming estranged for many years, but they finally reconciled in 1970, shortly before Lee's death of lung cancer at the age of fifty-nine.

5. Tara Reid (b.1975) is an American actress. She later appeared in *The Big Lebowski* (1998), *Urban Legend* (1998), *American Pie* (1999), *Dr. T & the Women* (2000), *Josie and the Pussycats* (2002), *Van Wilder* (2002), *My Boss's Daughter* (2003), *Alone in the Dark* (2005), *American Reunion* (2012), *Sharknado* (2013), and *Sharknado 2: The Second One* (2014).

6. Terence Fisher's *Dracula* (1958) was released in the United States as *Horror of Dracula*.

7. The annotated version of *Dracula* Cohen alludes to is most likely Leonard Wolf's *The Annotated Dracula* (1975), later published in a revised edition as *The Essential Dracula* (1994).

8. After her efforts on *Run of the Arrow* (1957) and *China Gate* (1957) for Sam Fuller, Angie Dickinson's subsequent career credits include *Rio Bravo, Ocean's 11* (1960), *The Sins of Rachel Cade, The Killers* (1964), *The Chase* (1966), *Point Blank* (1967), *Young Billy Young, Big Bad Mama* (1974), *Dressed To Kill* (1980), *Death Hunt, Even Cowgirls Get the Blues* (1994), *Sabrina, Pay It Forward* (1999), *Duets* (2000), and *Big Bad Love* (2001). Dickinson also starred in the successful television series *Police Woman*, which ran for five seasons on NBC from September 13, 1974, until March 29, 1978.

CHAPTER 20: THE MANIAC COP TRILOGY (1988-1993)

1. William Lustig's *Maniac* (1980) is a notorious grindhouse slasher film starring Joe Spinell as Frank Zito, a psychopathic serial killer who murders and scalps young women.

2. Tom Atkins (b.1935) has appeared in *The Fog* (1979), *The Ninth Configuration* (1980), *Escape from New York* (1981), *Halloween III:*

Season of the Witch (1982), *Creepshow* (1982), *Night of the Creeps* (1986), *Lethal Weapon* (1987), *Two Evil Eyes* (1990), *Bob Roberts* (1992), *Striking Distance* (1993), *Bruiser* (2001), *My Bloody Valentine* (2009), and *Drive Angry* (2012). His TV appearances include a recurring role in *The Rockford Files* (1974-77), as well as guest turns on *Rhoda, Hawaii Five-O, Lou Grant, M*A*S*H, Quincy M.E., Alfred Hitchcock Presents,* and *Oz.*

3. Sheree North died on November 4, 2005, during cancer surgery at Cedars-Sinai Medical Center in Los Angeles. She was seventy-three years old.
4. Bruce Campbell (b.1958) has achieved lasting cult status for his role as Ash in Sam Raimi's *The Evil Dead* (1982) and its sequels, *Evil Dead II* (1987) and *Army of Darkness* (1992). His other credits include *Crimewave* (1984), *Moontrap* (1989), *Darkman* (1990), *Sundown: The Vampire in Retreat* (1990), *Lunatics: A Love Story* (1991), *Waxwork II: Lost in Time* (1992), *Mindwarp* (1992), *Congo* (1995), *Escape from L.A., Fargo* (1996), *The Majestic* (2001), *Spider-Man, Bubba Ho-Tep* (2003), *Cloudy with a Chance of Meatballs* (2009), and *Cars 2.*
5. The actor originally hired to voice the sniper in *Phone Booth* was Ron Eldard.
6. Gretchen Becker plays the stricken cop Kate Sullivan in *Maniac Cop 3: Badge of Silence*. Her other credits include *The Doors* (1991), *Dream Lover* (1993), and *Ed Wood* (1994).

CHAPTER 21: WICKED STEPMOTHER (1989)

1. Lucille Ball (1911-1989) was an American actress, comedian, and studio executive, and the star of the phenomenally successful CBS sitcoms *I Love Lucy* (1951-1957), *The Lucy-Desi Comedy Hour* (1957-1960), *The Lucy Show* (1962-1968), and *Here's Lucy* (1968-1974). After the failure of *Life with Lucy* (1986), Ball never again committed to making another sitcom and died a month after presenting an award with Bob Hope at the 1989 Academy Awards ceremony.
2. Carol Burnett (b.1933) is an American actress, comedian and singer. She is best known for starring in the variety show *The Carol Burnett Show,* which ran on CBS for eleven seasons from September 11, 1967, until March 29, 1978. Burnett's film roles include *Pete 'n' Tillie*

(1972), *The Front Page* (1974), *A Wedding* (1978), *The Four Seasons* (1981), *Annie* (1982), *Noises Off* (1992), and *Horton Hears a Who!* (2008).

3. *Phone Call from a Stranger* (1952) is a portmanteau drama directed by Jean Negulesco that revolves around the survivor of a plane crash (essayed by Bette Davis' real-life fourth husband Gary Merrill) who calls the three families of the dead passengers with whom he became acquainted with on the doomed flight. Davis plays the relatively small supporting role of Maria Hoke, the bedridden wife of a deceased travelling salesman (played by Keenan Wynn).

4. *Now, Voyager* (1942), Bette Davis' most commercially successful film of the 1940s and the first of four collaborations with director Irving Rapper, is a romantic melodrama about a repressed young woman who is driven to an emotional breakdown by her tyrannical mother (Gladys Cooper). After recovering at a sanatorium, her psychiatrist (Claude Rains) recommends a cruise—during which she begins a bittersweet romance with an unhappily married architect (Paul Henreid). The classic "cigarette scene" resulted in Henreid receiving requests for many years afterwards from female fans to light their cigarettes for them in the manner he had for Davis.

5. Based on the play by David Berry, *The Whales of August* (1987) concerns Sarah, a former actress in silent films (played by ninety-one year-old Lillian Gish), and her disagreeable blind sister, Libby (Bette Davis), whom she cares for. Both reside at a seaside house in Maine, where the elderly widows reflect on their lives and the memories of past summers they shared in the company of their long-deceased husbands. A delicate change of pace for director Lindsay Anderson, the film is a beautifully restrained and contemplative drama that offers viewers a chance to see two Hollywood legends share the screen together (and also throws Vincent Price into the mix as a charming Russian exile who befriends the women).

6. *Mommie Dearest* is a notorious memoir and expose written by Christine Crawford, the adopted daughter of Joan Crawford (1904-1977). First published in November 1978 by William Marrow & Co, the book details the author's childhood and her troubled relationship with her mother. It contains allegations that Joan inflicted emotional and physical abuse on Christine and her brother, Christopher. Many friends such as Marlene Dietrich, Van Johnson, Katherine Hepburn, Myrna Loy, and Crawford's long-serving secretary,

Bette Barker, denounced the book; others such as Helen Hayes, Rex Reed, James McArthur, Betty Hutton, and June Allyson claimed to have witnessed acts of child cruelty. In 1981, *Mommie Dearest* was made into a campy biographical film of the same name that was met with mixed reviews but considerable box office success. Directed by Frank Perry, it starred Faye Dunaway as Crawford and Diana Scarwid as Christina.

7. B.D. Hyman (b.1947) is the adopted daughter of Bette Davis and her third husband, William Grant Sherry. She made brief appearances in her mother's films, *Payment on Demand* (1951) and *Whatever Happened to Baby Jane* (1962). Hyman actually wrote two books chronicling her difficult relationship with her mother, *My Mother's Keeper* (1985) and *Narrow is the Way* (1987).

8. The film Cohen brings up here is *Bunny O'Hare* (1971), directed by Gerd Oswald. An embarrassingly misjudged comedy that is about as subtle as a sledgehammer, the bizarre plot concerns an aging, penniless widow (Bette Davis), who blackmails an aging career criminal (Ernest Borgnine) into teaching her how to be a bank robber. Davis famously sued American International Pictures for their heavy-handed post-production tampering with the film.

INTERMISSION: THE HEAVY (1990)

1. John Carradine (1906-1988) was born Richmond Reed Carradine in New York, the son of an artist and a surgeon. A prolific character actor, he made his debut in the play *Camille*, which was staged in a New Orleans theatre in 1925. Arriving in Hollywood two years later, Carradine made his cinematic debut in *Tol'able David* (1930) under the name Peter Richmond. With his lanky frame, gaunt face, and rich baritone voice, Carradine cut a distinctive figure and capably maintained a successful stage career in classical Shakespearean roles whilst also appearing in movies such as *The Invisible Man* (1933) and *The Bride of Frankenstein* (1935) for James Whale. Carradine was also counted amongst "The John Ford Stock Company", working with the legendary director no less than ten times on *Mary of Scotland* (1936), *The Prisoner of Shark Island* (1936), *The Hurricane* (1937), *Drums Along the Mohawk* (1939), *Stagecoach* (1939), *The Grapes of Wrath* (1940), *The Last Hurrah* (1958), *The Man Who Shot Liberty Valance*

(1962), and *Cheyenne Autumn* (1964). Although he delivered a number of accomplished performances throughout the 1930s and 1940s, Carradine began appearing in an increasing number of horror films and quickly became associated with the genre. His résumé from this period includes *The Hound of the Baskervilles* (1939), *Captive Wild Women* (1943), *Revenge of the Zombies* (1943), *Voodoo Man* (1944), *The Mummy's Ghost* (1941), *House of Frankenstein* (1944), and *House of Dracula* (1945). His later genre credits include *The House of Seven Corpses* (1972), *The Sentinel* (1976), *Shock Waves* (1977), *Satan's Cheerleaders* (1977), *The Howling*, *House of Long Shadows* (1982) and *Evil Spawn* (1987). Married four times and the father of five sons (including actors David, Keith and Robert), Carradine once famously summed up his own career thusly: "I've made some of the greatest films ever made—and a lot of crap, too!"

2. Quotes taken from "Talk of the Town," John W. Wilson, *Los Angeles Times* (Nov. 11, 1990).

3. Keith Carradine (b.1949) can be seen in films such as *McCabe & Mrs. Miller* (1971), *Thieves Like Us* (1974), *Nashville* (1975), *The Duellists* (1977), *Pretty Baby* (1978), *The Long Riders* (1980), *Southern Comfort* (1981), *Choose Me* (1984), *Trouble in Mind* (1985), *Mrs. Parker and the Vicious Circle* (1994), *Wild Bill* (1995), *2 Days in the Valley* (1996), and *Cowboys and Aliens* (2010). He has also played recurring roles on television series such as *Deadwood*, *Complete Savages*, *Dexter*, *Damages*, *Missing*, and *Fargo*. Carradine's song "I'm Easy," which featured in *Nashville*, won him an Academy Award and Golden Globe Award for Best Original Song.

CHAPTER 22: THE AMBULANCE (1991)

1. Archibald "Archie" Andrews is a fictional comic book character created by Vic Bloom and Bob Montana who debuted in *Pep Comics* #22 in December, 1941. A clumsy, red-haired teenager living in the small town of Riverdale, his exploits and capers mostly revolve around his best friend, Jughead Jones, and the love triangle that exists between Archie and two beautiful local girls, Veronica Lodge and Betty Cooper. The adult Archie was dramatically killed off in the July 2014 issue of *Life with Archie*, fatally shot in the stomach whilst trying to protect his gay friend, Kevin Keller.

2. The TV series Cohen mentions here is *Northern Exposure*, an extended fish-out-of-water story that concerned a Jewish physician (Rob Morrow) from New York, who is sent to the remote Alaskan town of Cicely to repay a student loan. Whilst there, he encounters a parade of quirky residents and experiences a series of amusing culture shocks. The show ran on CBS for six seasons and 110 episodes from July 12, 1990, until July 26, 1995.

3. *The Great White Hope* is a play by Howard Sackler (1999-1982) that opened on Broadway on October 8, 1968 at The Alvin Theatre. Running for 546 performances, the production starred James Earl Jones as the fictional boxer Jack Jefferson (based on the former heavyweight world champion Jack Johnson), a man struggling against the constraints and inequities of society. It was adapted into a 1970 film by Martin Ritt, with Jones and co-star Jane Alexander resuming their stage roles. Both received Academy Award nominations for Best Actor and Best Actress, losing to George C. Scott for *Patton* and Glenda Jackson for *Women in Love*, respectively.

4. *Fences* by August Wilson (1945-2005) was the playwright's second play to go to Broadway and was first performed in 1983 at the Eugene O'Neill Theatre Center in Waterford, Connecticut. Seeking to write about African-American experiences in twentieth century America, *Fences* begins in 1957 after the Korean War and ends in 1965 with the advent of the Vietnam War and the Civil Rights Movement. The focus of the play is Troy Maxson, a talented baseball player in his youth, who was unable to play Major League Baseball due to being incarcerated for an accidental murder (and the fact that "color separation" still existed in the sport). Now an embittered, hard-headed garbage-man in his early fifties struggling to provide for his loved ones, his resentments threaten to destabilise his family. *Fences* won Wilson the 1987 Pulitzer Prize for Drama and the 1987 Tony Awards for Best Play, Best Actor (James Earl Jones) and Best Actress (Mary Alice).

5. The TV series Cohen hints at here is possibly *The Double Life of Henry Phyfe*, which ran for seventeen episodes on CBS in 1966, and starred Red Buttons in the titular role.

6. Wesley Addy (1913-1996) was an American actor. His film roles include *The Garment Jungle* (1957), *Seconds* (1966), *Mr. Buddwing* (1966), *Tora! Tora! Tora!* (1970), *Network* (1976), *The Verdict* (1982), *The Bostonians* (1984), *A Modern Affair* (1995), and *Before and After*

(1996). A favorite of Robert Aldrich's, Addy appeared in *Kiss Me Deadly* (1955), *The Big Knife* (1955), *Ten Seconds to Hell* (1959), *Whatever Happened to Baby Jane?* (1962), *4 For Texas* (1963), *Hush… Hush, Sweet Charlotte* (1964), and *The Grissom Gang* (1971) for the director.

CHAPTER 23: AS GOOD AS DEAD (1995)

1. Traci Lords (b.1968) is an American actress, model and singer. Born and raised in Ohio as Nora Louise Kuzma, Lords' initial notoriety came from her underage performances in pornographic films between 1984 and 1986. Her "legitimate" résumé includes *Not of This Earth* (1988), *Cry Baby* (1990), *The Tommyknockers, Serial Mom* (1994), *Virtuosity* (1995), *Blade* (1998), *Zack and Mira Make a Porno* (2008), and *Excision* (2012). Lords has also appeared in television shows, such as *MacGyver, Married…with Children, Melrose Place, Profiler, The Gilmore Girls,* and *Will & Grace.* Her autobiography, *Traci Lords: Underneath It All,* was published in 2003.
2. *Wings* is an American sitcom that ran on NBC for eight seasons and 172 episodes from April 19, 1990, until May 21, 1997. Created by David Angell, Peter Casey and David Lee, the show concerns the fictional Tom Nevers Field Airport in Nantucket, Massachusetts, where the Hackett brothers, Joe (Tim Daly) and Brian (Steven Weber), operate Sandpiper Air. Crystal Bernard played the brothers' friend, Helen, who eventually married Joe during the sixth season.
3. Please see the credits section for a rundown of the crew people on *As Good As Dead*.

CHAPTER 24: ORIGINAL GANGSTAS (1996)

1. Charles Napier (1936-2011) began his career by appearing in the Russ Meyer productions *Cherry, Harry & Raquel* (1970), *Beyond the Valley of the Dolls* (1970), *The Seven Minutes* (1971), and *Supervixens* (1975). His later credits include *The Blues Brothers* (1980), *Swing Shift* (1984), *Rambo: First Blood Part II* (1985), *Something Wild* (1986), *Married to the Mob* (1988), *Deep Space* (1988), *The Grifters* (1990), *The Silence of the Lambs* (1991), *Maniac Cop 2* (1990), *Phila-*

delphia (1993), *The Cable Guy* (1996), *Austin Powers: International Man of Mystery* (1997), *The Manchurian Candidate* (2004), *Lords of Dogtown* (2005), and *One-Eyed Monster* (2008).
2. Wings Hauser (b.1947) has appeared in *Who'll Stop the Rain* (1978), *Vice Squad* (1982), *Deadly Force* (1983), *Mutant* (1984), *A Soldier's Story* (1984), *Jo Jo Dancer, Your Life is Calling* (1986), *Tough Guys Don't Dance* (1987), *The Carpenter* (1988), *Dead Man Walking* (1988), *Beastmaster II: Through the Portal of Time* (1991), *Watchers 2* (1994), *Tales from the Hood* (1995), *The Insider* (1999) *Savage Season* (2001), *The Stone Angel* (2007), and *Rubber* (2010).
3. Ron O'Neal died of pancreatic cancer on January 14, 2004, at the age of sixty-six.
4. In 2012, the year before this particular interview with Cohen took place, the escalating homicide rate and instances of violence in Chicago garnered worldwide press attention as gangs fought wars over turf, drugs and money. It has been claimed that the majority of the resulting murders were gang-related vendettas and revenge attacks. According to the National Gang Intelligence Center, Chicago has one of the largest concentrations of gang members in the US. Seventy-three active street gangs have been identified by the Chicago Police Department, encompassing an estimated total of 68,000 members (although some sources put the figure as high as 150,000).
5. The Chi-Lites were a soul quartet who formed in Chicago in 1959. Their hits include "Have You Seen Her", "Oh, Girl", "Homely Girl," and "Too Good to Be Forgotten."
6. The film Cohen cites here is *The Great White Hype* (1996), a boxing comedy directed by Reginald Hudlin and starring Samuel L. Jackson, Damon Wayans, Jeff Goldblum, and Jamie Foxx. It was actually released on May 3, 1996, a week before *Original Gangstas*.

CHAPTER 25: SCREENPLAYS PART III (1997-2010)

1. Mark L. Lester (b.1946) began his career with such drive-in obscurantia as *Just Can't Reach* (1970), *Steel Arena* (1973), *Truck Stop Women* (1974), *White House Madness* (1975), and *Bobbie Joe and the Outlaw* (1976), before helming the disco movie *Roller Boogie* (1979) and the cult action-thriller *Class of 1984* (1982). His mainstream breakthrough came in the form of *Firestarter* (1984), a serviceable

2. adaptation of the Stephen King novel, and the Arnold Schwarzenegger vehicle *Commando* (1985). Lester's subsequent efforts include the John Candy action-comedy *Armed and Dangerous* (1986) and the martial arts film *Showdown in Little Tokyo* (1990).
2. The name of the actress Cohen speaks of here is Suzy Amis (b.1962).
3. Michael Bay (b.1965) is an American director and producer who began his career making music videos and award-winning commercials. He is noted for making loud, brash, mega-budget spectacles littered with fast cuts, ferocious action and fantastic special effects. His movies include *Bad Boys* (1995), *The Rock* (1996), *Armageddon* (1998), *Pearl Harbor* (2001), *Bad Boys II* (2003), *The Island* (2005), *Transformers* (2007), *Transformers: Revenge of the Fallen* (2009), *Transformers: Dark of the Moon* (2011), and *Transformers: Age of Extinction* (2014).
4. Cohen is talking about the supernatural fable *Winter's Tale* (2013), which received generally negative reviews. The movie earned just $7.3 million in its first weekend and scraped a total gross of $30 million worldwide, only half of its $60 million budget.
5. *Sweet Smell of Success* (1957) is a superlative Film Noir directed by Alexander Mackendrick, famed for his nine-year association with Ealing Studios in which he made the classic comedies *Whiskey Galore* (1949), *The Man in the White Suit* (1951) and *The Ladykillers* (1955). Mackendrick's first American film after departing England for Hollywood in 1955, *Sweet Smell of Success* concerns a scheming Manhattan press agent (Tony Curtis), who becomes involved with a powerful newspaper columnist (Burt Lancaster) intent on destroying his younger sister's romance with a jazz musician. Written by Ernest Lehman and Clifford Odets (who based Lancaster's villainous character, J.J. Hunsecker, on Walter Winchell), this dark and cynical picture was a box office failure upon its release but is now regarded as one of the best American films of its time.
6. The Beltway Sniper Attacks were a series of coordinated shootings that occurred in the Washington Metropolitan Area over a three-week period in October 2002. A blue 1990 Chevy Caprice was used as a rolling sniper's nest by John Allen Muhammad and Lee Boyd Malvo as they gunned down ten people and seriously wounded a further three using a Bushmaster .223-caliber rifle with a scope and tripod. The backseat of their vehicle had the metal sheet removed between the passenger compartment and the trunk, allowing the

shooter to access the trunk from inside the car. Malvo, who was seventeen at the time of the killing spree, was given multiple life sentences and is currently incarcerated at the Red Onion State Prison in Virginia. Muhammad was executed by lethal injection at the Greensville Correctional Center on November 10, 2009.

7. Directed by Stephen Norrington from a screenplay by James Dale Robinson, the film adaptation of Alan Moore's *The League of Extraordinary Gentlemen* (2003) sees seven fictional figures of literature coming together to battle a villain known as the "Fantom" in an alternate Victorian Age world. They include Alan Quatermain of *King Solomon's Mines*, Mina Harker from *Dracula*, and Captain Nemo from *Twenty Thousand Leagues Under the Sea*, as well as The Invisible Man, Tom Sawyer, Dorian Gray, and Dr. Jekyll (and Mr. Hyde). Impressive special effects and the presence of Sean Connery as Quatermain are not enough to rescue this illogical effort from costly mediocrity.

8. Incredibly, the perpetrator of *Captivity* is Roland Joffé, whose films *The Killing Fields* (1984) and *The Mission* (1986) both earned him Academy Award nominations for Best Director.

9. "Torture Porn" is the term coined by critics to describe a horror film that concentrates heavily on graphic violence and sexually suggestive imagery. Examples of this subgenre (which are often promoted with lurid and salacious ad campaigns) include *Saw* (2004) and its six sequels, *Hostel* (2005), *Wolf Creek* (2005), *The Devil's Rejects* (2005), *Turistas* (2006), *Hostel Part II* (2007), *Borderland* (2007), *WΔZ* (2007), and *Captivity* (2007). In Europe, Lars Von Trier's *Antichrist* (2009) and a wave of French horror films, sometimes referred to as the New French Extremity, have also been grouped with their American, Australian and British brethren; these include *Switchblade Romance* (2003), *Inside* (2007), *Frontiers* (2007), and *Martyrs* (2008).

10. *The Gambler, the Girl, and the Gunslinger* was directed by Anne Wheeler (b.1946). A Canadian director, writer, and producer, Wheeler's filmography includes the docudrama *A War Story* (1981), which told the story of her father's capture by Japanese soldiers during World War II, and the features *Loyalties* (1986), *Bye Bye Blues* (1989), *Angel Square* (1990), and *Knockout* (2011). She has also directed episodes of the TV shows *The Ray Bradbury Theater*, *Jake and the Kid*, *Mysterious Ways*, and *This is Wonderland*.

11. Bob Barbash (1919-1995) wrote the screenplays for the features *The Plunderers* (1960), *Tarzan and the Great River* (1967), and *How To Make It* (1969), and furnished the story for the Disney science fiction epic *The Black Hole* (1979). He also worked as a television story editor and producer, penning episodes of *Playhouse 90*, *Maverick*, *The Zane Grey Theatre*, *The Dick Powell Theatre*, *Wagon Train*, *Stoney Burke*, *The Wild Wild West*, *Gunsmoke*, *Starsky and Hutch*, and *The Adventures of Superboy*. He died in Los Angeles of cancer.

CHAPTER 26: MASTERS OF HORROR: PICK ME UP (2005)

1. The 3D film directed by Joe Dante that Cohen mentions here is *The Hole* (2010).
2. David J. Schow (b.1955) is an American author and screenwriter. His novels include *The Kill Riff* (1988), *The Shaft* (1990), *Bullets of Rain* (2003), *Gun Work* (2008), the non-fiction book *The Outer Limits: The Official Companion* (1986)—which he co-authored with Jeffrey Frentzen—and the short story collections *Seeing Red* (1990), *Lost Angels* (1990), and *Black Leather Required* (1994). His screenplays include *A Nightmare on Elm Street 5: The Dream Child* (1989), *Leatherface: The Texas Chainsaw Massacre 3* (1989), *The Crow* (1994), *The Texas Chainsaw Massacre: The Beginning* (2006), and *The Hills Run Red* (2009). Schow also adapted the John Farris story "We All Scream for Ice Cream," which was directed by Tom Holland in the second season of *Masters of Horror*.
3. *Tales from the Crypt* (1989-1996) was an American anthology show based on the William M. Gaines/EC Comics series of the same name. The episodes were also derived from stories originally published in the six other EC titles: *The Crypt of Terror*, *The Vault of Horror*, *Haunt of Fear*, *Crime SuspenStories*, *Shock SuspenStories*, and *Two-Fisted Tales*. Free from the censorship imposed by network standards and practices, *Tales from the Crypt* was able to attract high-caliber talent behind the camera, including directors Richard Donner, Robert Zemeckis, Walter Hill, William Friedkin, Tobe Hooper, Peter Medak, John Frankenheimer, Russell Mulcahy, Howard Deutch, and Freddie Francis (who also directed the 1972 Amicus film adaptation).
4. John Carpenter's *Pro-Life* was the fifth film to be screened (on March 20, 2007) during the second season of *Masters of Horror*. Written by

Drew McWeeny and Scott Swan, it is the violent and gruesome tale of a teenage girl (Caitlin Wachs), who arrives at a secluded abortion clinic claiming her accelerating pregnancy is the result of being raped by a demon. Meanwhile her Bible-thumping, gun-toting father (Ron Perlman) shows up with her three equally fanatical brothers (all armed-to-the-teeth) to rescue the foetus from destruction. Then, to compound matters, the unborn child's Daddy shows up…

5. The budget allotted to each *Masters of Horror* film was $1.5 million.
6. Fairuza Balk (b.1974) had previously appeared in the horror films *The Craft* (1996) and *The Island of Dr. Moreau* (1996). Her other credits include *Return to Oz* (1985), *Valmont* (1989), *Things To Do in Denver When You're Dead* (1996), *The Waterboy* (1998), *American History X* (1999), *Almost Famous* (2000), and *Bad Lieutenant: Port of Call New Orleans*.
7. The stunt co-ordinator on *Pick Me Up* was Jim Dunn. The stunt driving double for Michael Moriarty was Ian Thompson.
8. Michael Moriarty won the Tony Award in 1974 for *Find Your Way Home*, a play written by John Hopkins (1931-1998).
9. *Burke & Hare* are played by Simon Pegg and Andy Serkis respectively.

CHAPTER 27: ON WRITING

1. *The Effect of Gamma Rays on Man-in-the-Moon Marigolds* is a Pulitzer Prize-winning play by Paul Zindel first performed at The Mercer-O'Casey Theatre, New York City, in 1970. The drama revolves around a dysfunctional family consisting of an abusive mother and her two daughters (one an introverted loner with a passion for science, the other a confused extrovert teetering on madness). A fine film adaptation directed by Paul Newman was released in 1972, starring his wife, Joanne Woodward, who was named Best Actress at the Cannes Film Festival in 1973 for her performance.
2. *Baby Doll* (1956) is a controversial melodrama/black comedy directed by Elia Kazan. Adapted for the screen by Tennessee Williams from his own one-act play, *27 Wagons Full of Cotton*, it concerns a Sicilian businessman (Eli Wallach) in the Deep South who initiates a bizarre love triangle with a boorish rival (Karl Malden) and his flirtatious nymphet wife (Carroll Baker). At the time of its release,

the film aroused a scandal due to its risqué sexual themes, earning a "C" for "Condemned" from the Catholic Legion of Decency, who labeled it "grievously offensive to Christian and traditional standards of morality and decency".

CHAPTER 28: METHODOLOGY, MOVIES & MADNESS

1. Frank Capra (1897-1991) was a hugely influential American director, producer and screenwriter, whose sentimental cinematic "fantasies of goodwill" assisted in defining and aggrandising the myth of ordinary Americana. His laundry list of masterful films includes *It Happened One Night* (1934), *Mr. Deeds Goes to Town* (1936), *Lost Horizon* (1937), *You Can't Take It with You* (1938), *Mr. Smith Goes to Washington* (1939), *Meet John Doe* (1941), and the perennial seasonal classic *It's a Wonderful Life* (1946). The winner of five Academy Awards (three for Best Director), Capra even inspired his own adjective, "Capraesque". This relates to a style of film that promotes the positive social effects of individual acts of courage and determination, and how these qualities enable the underdog to triumph. His autobiography, *The Name Above the Title*, was published in 1971.
2. *The Liveliest Art: A Panoramic History of the Movies* was written by the eminent film critic, historian and instructor Arthur Knight (1916-1991). First published by New American Library in 1957, the book offers a pioneering history of American cinema from its technological beginnings with Thomas Edison to the important contributions of such key players as D.W. Griffith, Mack Sennett, Charlie Chaplin, John Ford, Rene Clair, Orson Welles, and others. *The Liveliest Art* has long been a staple textbook in colleges and universities throughout the world.

Credits

FILMOGRAPHY

BONE (1971)

Production Company: Jack H. Harris Enterprises, Larry Cohen Productions. Directed by Larry Cohen. Produced by Larry Cohen. Written by Larry Cohen. Co-producer: Janelle Cohen. Associate Producer: Peter Vizer. Executive Producer: Peter Sabiston. Cinematography by George Folsey, Sr. Edited by George Folsey, Jr. Music by Gil Melle. Post-Production Supervisor: Michael D. Corey. Special Make-up Effects by Rick Baker. **Cast:** Yaphet Kotto (Bone), Andrew Duggan (Bill), Joyce Van Patten (Bernadette), Jeannie Berlin (The Girl), Casey King (The Boy), Brett Somers (X-Ray Lady), James Lee (Woody), Rosanna Huffman (Secretary), Ida Berlin (Lady on Bus).

BLACK CAESAR (1972)

Production Company: American International Pictures. Directed by Larry Cohen. Produced by Larry Cohen. Written by Larry Cohen. Associate Producer: James Dixon. Executive Producer: Samuel Z. Arkoff. Executive Producer: Peter Sabiston. Co-producer: Janelle Cohen. Cinematography by Fenton Hamilton, James Signorelli. Edited by George Folsey, Jr. Music by James Brown. Production Designer: Larry Lurin. Special Make-up Effects by Rick Baker. **Cast:** Fred Williamson (Tommy Gibbs), Gloria Hendry (Helen), Art Lund (McKinney), D'Urville Martin (Reverend Rufus), Julius W. Harris (Mr. Gibbs), Val Avery (Cardoza), Minnie Gentry (Momma Gibbs), Philip Roye (Joe Washington), William Wellman, Jr. (Alfred

Coleman), James Dixon (Bryant), Patrick McAllister (Grossfield), Don Pedro Colley (Crawdaddy), Myrna Hansen (Virginia Coleman), Omer Jeffrey (Tommy as a Boy), Michael Jeffrey (Joe as a Boy).

HELL UP IN HARLEM (1973)

Production Company: American International Pictures. Directed by Larry Cohen. Produced by Larry Cohen. Written by Larry Cohen. Associate Producer: James Dixon. Executive Producer: Peter Sabiston. Co-producer: Janelle Cohen. Cinematography by Fenton Hamilton. Edited by Peter Honess. Music by Fonce Mizell and Freddie Perren. Production Designer: Larry Lurin. Special Make-up Effects by Rick Baker. **Cast:** Fred Williamson (Tommy Gibbs), Julius W. Harris (Papa Gibbs), Gloria Hendry (Helen), Margaret Avery (Sister Jennifer), D'Urville Martin (Reverend Rufus), Tony King (Zach), Gerald Gordon (Mr. DiAngelo), Bobby Ramsen (Joe Frankfurter), James Dixon (Irish), Ester Sutherland (The Cook), Charles MacGuire (Hap).

IT'S ALIVE (1974)

Production Company: Warner Bros. Directed by Larry Cohen. Produced by Larry Cohen. Written by Larry Cohen. Executive Producer: Peter Sabiston. Co-producer: Janelle Cohen. Cinematography by Fenton Hamilton. Edited by Peter Honess. Music by Bernard Herrmann. Production Designers: Bob Briggart and Pat Somerset. Special Make-up Effects by Rick Baker. **Cast:** John P. Ryan (Frank Davis), Sharon Farrell (Lenore Davis), James Dixon (Lt. Perkins), William Wellman Jr. (Charley), Shamus Locke (The Doctor), Andrew Duggan (The Professor), Guy Stockwell (Bob Clayton), Daniel Holzman (Chris Davis), Michael Ansara (The Captain), Robert Emhardt (The Executive), Mary Nancy Burnett (The Nurse), Diana Hale (Secretary), Patrick McAllister, Gerald York, Jerry Taft, Gwil Richards, W. Allen York (Expectant Fathers).

GOD TOLD ME TO (1976)

Production Company: New World Pictures. Directed by Larry Cohen. Produced by Larry Cohen. Written by Larry Cohen. Cinematography by

Paul Glickman. Edited by Mike Corey, Arthur Mandelberg and William J. Waters. Music by Frank Cordell. Special Make-up Effects by Steve Neill. **Cast:** Tony Lo Bianco (Dt. Peter J. Nicholas), Deborah Raffin (Casey Forster), Sandy Dennis (Martha Nicholas), Sylvia Sidney (Elizabeth Mullin), Sam Levene (Everett Lukas), Robert Drivas (David Morten), Mike Kellin (Deputy Commissioner), Richard Lynch (Bernard Phillips), Sammy Williams (Harold Gorman), Jo Flores Chase (Mrs. Gorman), William Roerick (Richards), Lester Rawlins (Board Chairman), Harry Bellaver (Cookie), George Patterson (Zero), Walter Steele (Junkie), John Heffernan (Bramwell), Alan Cauldwell (Bramwell as a Youth), Robert Nichols (Fletcher), Andy Kaufman (Police Assassin).

THE PRIVATE FILES OF J. EDGAR HOOVER (1977)

Production Company: Larco Productions. Directed by Larry Cohen. Produced by Larry Cohen. Written by Larry Cohen. Associate Producer: Arthur Mandelberg. Co-producer: Janelle Cohen. Cinematography by Paul Glickman. Edited by Chris Lebenzon. Music by Miklós Rózsa. Production Designer: Cathy Davis. Costume Designers: Lewis Freedman and Carolyn Loewenstein. Make-up by Steve Neill, Ve Neill, Rivka Gold and Josephine Cianelli. **Cast:** Broderick Crawford (J. Edgar Hoover), Michael Parks (Robert F. Kennedy), Jose Ferrer (Lionel McCoy), Celeste Holm (Florence Hollister), Rip Torn (Dwight Webb, Jr.), Dan Dailey (Clyde Tolson), Ronee Blakely (Carrie DeWitt), Howard Da Silva (Franklin D. Roosevelt), John Marley (Dave Hindley), Michael Sacks (Melvin Purvis), Raymond St. Jacques (Martin Luther King), June Havoc (Hoover's Mother), James Wainwright (Young Hoover), Lloyd Nolan (Attorney General Harlan Stone), Andrew Duggan (Lyndon B. Johnson), Jack Cassidy (Damon Runyon), George Plimpton (Quentin Reynolds), Lloyd Gough (Walter Winchell), William Jordan (John F. Kennedy), Brad Dexter (Alvin Karpis), George D. Wallace (Senator Joseph McCarthy), Henderson Forsythe (Harry Suydam), Fred J. Scollay (Putnam), William Wellman, Jr. (Dwight Webb, Sr.), Ellen Barber (Janice Harper), Art Lund (Benchley), Mary Alice Moore (Miss Bryant), Jim Antonio (Senator Kenneth McKellar), Gregg Abels (President's Aide), Dan Resin (President's Advisor), James Dixon (Reilly), Penny DuPont (Newscaster), Alvin Miles (Valet), John Bay (Heywood Brown), Brooks Morton (Earl Warren), Richard Dixon (The President), James Dukas (Frank).

IT LIVES AGAIN (1978)

Production Company: Warner Bros., Larco Productions. Directed by Larry Cohen. Produced by Larry Cohen. Written by Larry Cohen. Associate Producer: Wiliam Wellman, Jr. Cinematography by Fenton Hamilton. Additional Photography by Daniel Pearl. Edited by Curtis Burch, Louis G. Friedman and Carol O'Blath. Music by Bernard Herrmann and Laurie Johnson. Special Make-up Effects by Rick Baker. **Cast:** Frederic Forrest (Eugene Scott), Kathleen Lloyd (Jody Scott), John P. Ryan (Frank Davis), John Marley (Mr. Mallory), Andrew Duggan (Dr. Perry), Eddie Constantine (Dr. Forrest), James Dixon (Det. Lt. Perkins), Dennis O'Flaherty (Dr. Peters), Melissa Inger Cohen (Valerie), Victoria Jill Cohen (Cindy), Lynn Wood (Jody's Mother).

FULL MOON HIGH (1981)

Production Company: Filmways Pictures, Larco Productions. Directed by Larry Cohen. Produced by Larry Cohen. Written by Larry Cohen. Cinematography by Daniel Pearl. Edited by Armond Lebowitz. Music by Gary William Friedman. Art Direction: Robert A. Burns. Special Make-up Effects by Steve Neill. Additional Make-up: Christine Boyer. **Cast:** Adam Arkin (Tony Walker), Roz Kelly (Jane), Ed McMahon (Col. Walker), Alan Arkin (Dr. Jacob Brand), Joanne Nail (Ricky), Elizabeth Hartman (Miss Montgomery), Bill Kirchenbauer (Flynn), Kenneth Mars (The Coach), Louis Nye (Reverend), Desmond Wilson (Cabbie), Jim Bullock (Eddie), James Dixon (Deputy Jack), Tom Clancy (Priest), Pat Morita (Silversmith), Tom Aldredge (The Jailor), Laurene Landon (Blondie).

SEE CHINA AND DIE (1981)

Production Company: CBS, Big Hit Productions. Directed by Larry Cohen. Produced by Larry Cohen. Written by Larry Cohen. Executive Producer: Hal Schaffel. Cinematography by Paul Glickman. Second Assistant Cameraman: Frederick Iannone. Music by Joey Levine, Chris Palmaro. Orchestrations by Michael Abene. Production Assistant: Anthony Baldasare. **Cast:** Ester Rolle (Momma Sykes), Kene Holliday (Sgt. Alvin Sykes), Frank Converse (Tom Hackman), Paul Dooley (Ames Prescott),

Andrew Duggan (Edwin Forbes), Laurence Luckinbill (Dr. Glickman), Jean Marsh (Sally Hackman), Fritz Weaver (Poston), Jane Hitchcock (Ruth), Claude Brooks (Jessie Sykes), William Walker II (Andy Sykes), Miguel Pinero (Gonzalez), Jack Straw (Norman), James Dixon (Sweeney).

Q – THE WINGED SERPENT (1982)

Production Company: United Film Distribution Company, Larco Productions. Directed by Larry Cohen. Produced by Larry Cohen. Written by Larry Cohen. Executive Producer: Samuel Z. Arkoff. Executive Producer: Dick Di Bona. Executive Producer: Peter Sabiston. Executive Producer: Don Sandburg. Associate Producer: Paul Kurta. Line Producer: Salah M. Hassanein. Cinematography by Fred Murphy. Edited by Armond Lebowitz. Music by Robert O. Ragland. Special Make-up Effects by Dennis Eger, Steve Neill and Rick Stratton. Special Visual Effects by Randall William Cook, David Allen and Peter Kuran. **Cast:** Michael Moriarty (Jimmy Quinn), Candy Clark (Joan), David Carradine (Det. Shepard), Richard Roundtree (Powell), James Dixon (Lt. Murray), Malachy McCourt (Commissioner), Fred J. Scollay (Capt. Fletcher), Peter Hock (Det. Clifford), Ron Cey (Det. Hoberman), Mary Louis Weller (Mrs. Pauley), Bruce Carradine (Victim), John Capodice (Doyle).

PERFECT STRANGERS (1984)

Production Company: Hemdale Film Corporation, Larco Productions. Directed by Larry Cohen. Produced by Paul Kurta. Written by Larry Cohen. Executive Producer: Carter DeHaven. Associate Producer: Barry Shils. Associate Producer: Kato Wittich. Cinematography by Paul Glickman. Edited by Armond Lebowitz. Music by Dwight Dixon. Set Decoration by Paula Longendyke. **Cast:** Anne Carlisle (Sally), Brad Rijn (Johnny), John Woehrle (Fred), Matthew Stockley (Matthew), Stephen Lack (Lt. Burns), Ann Magnuson (Malda), Zachary Hains (Moletti), Otto von Wernherr (Private Detective), Kitty Summerall (Joanna), Steven Pudenz (Man in Cemetery), Bill Fagerbakke (Carl), Bruce Jerreau (Manny).

SPECIAL EFFECTS (1984)

Production Company: Hemdale Film Corporation, Larco Productions. Directed by Larry Cohen. Produced by Paul Kurta. Written by Larry Cohen. Executive Producer: Carter DeHaven. Associate Producer: Barry Shils. Cinematography by Paul Glickman. Edited by Armond Lebowitz. Music by Michael Minard. Production Design by Teri Kane. Costume Designer: Joanne Malkanthene. **Cast:** Zoë Lund (Andrea Wilcox/Elaine Bernstein), Eric Bogosian (Chris Neville), Brad Rijn (Keefe Waterman), Kevin O'Connor (Det. Lt. Delroy), Bill Oland (Det. Vickers), Richard Greene (Gruskin), Steven Pudenz (Wiesanthal), Heidi Bassett (Neville's Assistant Director), John Woehrle (Studio Executive), Kitty Summerall (Andrea's Roommate), Mike Alpert (Taxi Driver), Kris Evans (Cosmetician).

THE STUFF (1985)

Production Company: New World Pictures. Directed by Larry Cohen. Produced by Paul Kurta. Written by Larry Cohen. Executive Producer: Larry Cohen. Associate Producer: Barry Shils. Cinematography by Paul Glickman. Edited by Armond Lebowitz. Music by Anthony Guefen. Art Direction by Marlena Marta and George Stoll. Costume Designer: Tim D'Arcy. Special Make-up Effects by Steve Neill, Ed French and Rick Stratton. Visual Effects by David Allen, Jim Danforth, Paul Gentry, John Lambert, David Stipes and Jim Doyle. **Cast:** Michael Moriarty (David 'Mo' Rutherford), Andrea Marcovicci (Nicole), Garrett Morris ('Chocolate Chip' Charlie Hobbs), Paul Sorvino (Col. Spears), Scott Bloom (Jason), Danny Aiello (Vickers), Patrick O'Neal (Fletcher), Alexander Scourby (Evans), James Dixon (Postman), Russell Nype (Richards), Gene O'Neill (Scientist), Colette Blonigan (Jason's Mother), Frank Telfer (Jason's Father), Brian Bloom (Jason's Brother), Harry Bellaver (Miner).

DEADLY ILLUSION (1987)

Production Company: Columbia, Pound Ridge Films. Directed by Larry Cohen and William Tannen. Produced by Irwin Meyer. Written by Larry Cohen. Executive Producers: Michael Shapiro, Rodney Sheldon. Associate Producers: Bill Elliott, Steve Mirkovich, Michael Tadross. Cinematography by Daniel Pearl. Edited by Steve Mirkovich, Ronald Sprang. Music by Patrick Gleeson. Art Direction by Ruth Ozeki Lounsbury, Marina Zurkow. **Cast:** Billy Dee Willaims (Hamberger), Vanity (Rina), Morgan Fairchild (Jane Mallory/Sharon Burton), John Beck (Alex Burton), Joseph Cortese (Det. Paul Lefferts), Michael Wilding, Jr. (Costillion), Dennis Hallahan (Burton Inspector), Jenny Cornuelle (Gloria Reed), Allison Woodward (Nancy Costillion), Joe Spinell (Crazy Man in Gun Bureau), Harriet Rogers (Mrs. Bains), George Loros (Levante), John Woehrle (Boardroom Executive).

IT'S ALIVE III: ISLAND OF THE ALIVE (1987)

Production Company: Warner Bros., Larco Productions. Directed by Larry Cohen. Produced by Paul Stader. Written by Larry Cohen. Executive Producer: Larry Cohen. Associate Producers: Barry Shils, Barbara Zitwar. Supervising Producer: Paul Kurta. Cinematography by Daniel Pearl. Edited by David Kern. Music by Laurie Johnson. Art Direction by George Stoll. Costume Designer: Tim D'Arcy. Special Make-up Effects by Steve Neill, Mark Williams and Dan Frye. Original Creature Designer: Rick Baker. Model Effects by Bill Hedge. Effects Assistant: Terry McGreal. **Cast:** Michael Moriarty (Steven Jarvis), Karen Black (Ellen Jarvis), Laurene Landon (Sally), James Dixon (Lt. Perkins), Gerrit Graham (Ralston), Macdonald Carey (Judge Watson), Neal Israel (Dr. Brewster), Art Lund (Dr. Swenson), Anne Dane (Dr. Morrell), William Watson (Cabot), C.L. Sussex (Hunter), Bobby Ramsen (TV Host).

A RETURN TO SALEM'S LOT (1987)

Production Company: Warner Bros., Larco Productions. Directed by Larry Cohen. Produced by Paul Kurta. Story by Larry Cohen. Screenplay by Larry Cohen and James Dixon. Executive Producer: Larry Cohen. Associate Producers: Barry Shils, Janelle Cohen. Cinematography by Daniel Pearl. Edited by Armond Lebowitz. Music by Michael Minard. Art Direction by Richard A. Frisch. Costume Designer: Catherine Zuber. Special Make-up Effects by Steve Neill, Mark Williams, Carl Sorensen and Dan Frye. **Cast:** Michael Moriarty (Joe Weber), Ricky Addison Reed (Jeremy

Weber), Samuel Fuller (Dr. Van Meer), Andrew Duggan (Judge Axel), Evelyn Keyes (Mrs. Axel), Jill Gatsby (Sherry), June Havoc (Aunt Clara), Ronee Blakely (Sally), James Dixon (Rains), Katja Crosby (Cathy), Tara Reid (Amanda), David Holbrook (Deputy), Brad Rijn (Clarence), Georgia Janelle Webb (Sarah), Robert Burr (Dr. Fenton), Bobby Ramsen (Guide).

WICKED STEPMOTHER (1989)

Production Company: Larco Productions, Metro-Golden-Mayer. Directed by Larry Cohen. Produced by Robert Littman. Written by Larry Cohen. Executive Producer: Larry Cohen. Associate Producer: Kathryn Sermak. Cinematography by Bryan England. Edited by David Kern. Music by Robert Folk. Production Designer: Gene Abel. Costume Designer: Julie Weiss. Animatronic Cat Effects by Lisa Rocco. Special Effects by Mark Williams. Stop Motion Animation by Larry Arpin. **Cast:** Bette Davis (Miranda), Barbara Carrera (Priscilla), Colleen Camp (Jenny Fisher), Lionel Stander (Sam), David Rasche (Steve Fisher), Shawn Donahue (Mike), Tom Bosley (Lt. MacIntosh), Richard Moll (Nathan Pringle), Evelyn Keyes (Witch Instructor), James Dixon (Det. Flynn), Seymour Cassel (Feldshine), Susie Garrett (Mandy), Laurene Landon (Vanilla), Bob Goen (Game Show Host).

THE AMBULANCE (1991)

Production Company: Epic Productions, Esparza/Katz Productions. Directed by Larry Cohen. Produced by Moctesuma Esparza, Robert Katz. Written by Larry Cohen. Associate Producer: Barbara Zitwer. Cinematography by Jacques Haitkin. Edited by Claudia Finkle, Armond Lebowitz. Music by Jay Chattaway. Production Designer: Lester Cohen. Art Direction by Nancy Dreen. Set Decoration by Jessica Lanier. Costume Designer: Sylvia Vega-Vasquez. Special Make-up Effects by Rob Benevides. **Cast:** Eric Roberts (Josh Baker), James Earl Jones (Dt. Lt. Spencer), Megan Gallagher (Sandra Malloy), Red Buttons (Elias Zacharai), Janine Turner (Cheryl), Eric Braeden (The Doctor), James Dixon (Det. 'Jughead' Ryan), Jill Gatsby (Jerilyn), Martin Barter (Street Gang Leader), Laurene Landon (Patty), Nicholas Chinlund (Hugo), Deborah Headwell (Nurse Feinstein), Janelle Webb (Nurse Carter).

AS GOOD AS DEAD (1995)

Production Company: Paramount Television. Directed by Larry Cohen. Produced by Larry Cohen. Written by Larry Cohen. Executive Producer: Artie Mandelberg. Cinematography by Billy Dickson. Edited by Neil Mandelberg. Music by Patrick O'Hearn. Production Designer: Bryan Ryman. Set Decorator: Christopher R. DeMuri. Costume Designer: Tami Mor. **Cast:** Crystal Bernard (Susan Warfield), Judge Reinhold (Ron Holden), Traci Lords (Nicole Grace), Carlos Carrasco (Eddie Garcia), George Dickerson (Edgar Warfield), Daniel MacDonald (Thomas A. Rutherford), Scott Williamson (Dr. Sullivan), Jerry Bernard (Funeral Director).

ORIGINAL GANGSTAS (1996)

Production Company: Orion, Po' Boy Productions. Directed by Larry Cohen. Produced by Fred Williamson. Written by Aubrey Rattan. Executive Producer: Wolf Schmidt. Line Producer: Linda Williamson. Cinematography by Carlos González. Edited by Peter B. Ellis and David Kern. Music by Vladimir Horunzhy. Production Designer: Elayne Barbara Ceder. Set Decorator: Aaron Holden. Costume Designer: Lisa Moffie. **Cast:** Fred Williamson (John Bookman), Jim Brown (Jake Trevor), Pam Grier (Laurie Thompson), Paul Winfield (Reverend Dorsey), Isabel Sanford (Gracie Bookman), Oscar Brown, Jr. (Marvin Bookman), Richard Roundtree (Slick), Ron O'Neal (Bubba), Christopher B. Duncan (Spyro), Eddie Bo Smith, Jr. (Damien), Dru Down (Kayo), Shyheim Franklin (Dink), Robert Forster (Dt. Slatten), Charles Napier (Mayor Ritter), Wings Hauser (Michael Casey), Frank Pesce (Dt. Waits).

MASTERS OF HORROR: PICK ME UP (2005)

Production Companies: IDT Entertainment, Industry Entertainment, Nice Guy Productions, Reunion Pictures, British Colombia Tax Credit. Directed by Larry Cohen. *Masters of Horror* Created by Mick Garris. Written by David J. Schow. Based on the short story by David J. Schow. Executive Producers: Keith Addis, Morris Berger, Steve Brown, Andrew Deane, Mick Garris, John W. Hyde. Producers: Lisa Richardson, Tim Rowe. Co-producers: Ben Browning, Adam Goldwyn, Pascal Verschooris. Consulting Producer: Grant

Rosenberg. Cinematography by Brian Pearson. Edited by Marshall Harvey. Music by Jay Chattaway. Production Designer: David Fisher. Art Decoration by Don Macaulay. Set Decoration by Ide Foyle. Costume Designer: Lyn Kelly. Special Make-up Effects by K.N.B Effects Group. **Cast:** Fairuza Balk (Stacia), Michael Moriarty (Wheeler), Warren Kole (Walker), Laurene Landon (Birdy), Malcolm Kennard (Danny), Tom Pickett (Bus Driver), Peter Benson (Deuce), Kristie Marsden (Marie), Michael Eklund (Cashier), Paul Anthony (Stoney), Crystal Lowe (Lilly), Michael Petroni (Ambulance Attendant), Mar Andersons (Ambulance Driver), Danielle Rees (Pepper).

TELEVISION

AS WRITER AND/OR SERIES CREATOR

Kraft Mystery Theater: **"The Eighty Seventh Precinct"** (June 25, 1958)

Network: NBC. Directed by Paul Bogart. Produced by Alex March. Written by Larry Cohen. Based on characters created by Ed McBain. Cast: Robert Bray (Steve Carella), Martin Rudy (Meyer Meyer), Joseph Sullivan (Capt. Byrnes), Joan Copeland (Louise Carella), Pat Henning (Keetso), Salome Jens (Rita), Henderson Forsythe (Clavin).

Kraft Mystery Theater: **"Night Cry"** (August 13, 1958)

Network: NBC. Directed by Michael Dreyfuss. Produced by Alex March. Written by Larry Cohen. Based on the novel by William A. Stewart. Cast: Jack Klugman (Mark Deglan), Diana Van der Vlis (Morgan Taylor), Martin Roberts (Redfield), Peter Falk (Izzy), Ray Poole (Captain), John McQuade (Riley).

Zane Grey Theater: **"Killer Instinct"** (March 17, 1960)

Network: CBS. Directed by Murray Golden. Produced by Hal Hudson. Created by Luke Short and Charles A. Wallace. Story by Larry Cohen.

Written by Elliot West. Cast: Wendell Corey (Marshall Bigger), Marc Lawrence (Wade McGill), Robert Harland (Lee Phelps), Howard Petrie (Killegrew), Anne Barton (Ann Bigger), John Clarke (Frank Powers), John Newton (Barton), Dick Powell (Host).

The Witness: "Dillinger" (January 19, 1961)

Network: CBS. Directed by Marc Daniels. Produced by Nick Mayo. Created by Irve Tunick. Written by Larry Cohen and Irve Tunick. Cast: Warren Stevens (John Dillinger), Richard McMurray (Matthew Leach), Jack Collins (Seymour Compton), Richard Hamilton (Homer Van Meter), Carol Bruce (Mildred Hall), William Griffis (Clerk), Verne Collett (Reporter), Frank A. Milan, William Smithers, Charles Haydon (Committee Members), Paul McGrath (The Chairman).

Way Out: "False Face" (May 26, 1961)

Network: CBS. Directed by Henry Kaplan. Produced by Jacqueline Sassin. Written by Larry Cohen. Special Make-up Effects by Dick Smith. Cast: Alfred Ryder (Michael Drake), Martin Brooks (The Man), Gerry Jedd (Rita Singer), Dana Elcar (Flophouse Proprietor), Roald Dahl (Host).

The United States Steel Hour: "The Golden Thirty" (August 9, 1961)

Network: CBS. Directed by Tom Donovan. Produced by George Kondolf and Carol Irwin. Written by Larry Cohen. Cast: Henny Youngman (Buddy Parker), Keir Dullea (David March), Nancy Kovack (Fran Loring), Bibi Osterwald (Mrs. Ross), Don Di Leo (Harry Brock).

Surfside 6: "A Matter of Seconds" (November 27, 1961)

Network: ABC. Directed by George Waggoner. Produced by Tom McKnight. Created by William T. Orr and Hugh Benson. Written by Stephen Lord. Story by Larry Cohen. Cast: Claude Akins (Harry Lodge), Alan Baxter (Swenson), Steve Brodie (Sgt. Carter), Troy Donahue (Sandy Winfield

II), Anne McCrae (Maggie), William Schallert (Marty Kemp), Jack Shea (Officer Toomey), Abigail Shelton (Gita), Van Williams (Ken Madison).

Checkmate: **"Nice Guys Finish Last"** (December 13, 1961)

Network: CBS. Directed by Alan Crosland. Produced by Dick Berg. Created by Eric Ambler. Written by Larry Cohen. Cast: Anthony George (Don Corey), Sebastian Cabot (Dr. Hyatt), Doug McClure (Jed Sills), James Whitmore (Lt. Dave Harker), Diana Van der Vlis (Hope Riordan), Dennis Patrick (Nick Culley).

The Defenders: **"Kill or Be Killed"** (January 5, 1963)

Network: CBS. Directed by Sydney Pollack. Produced by Robert Markell. Created by Reginald Rose. Written by Larry Cohen. Cast: E.G. Marshall (Lawrence Preston), Robert Reed (Kenneth Preston), Gerald S. O'Laughlin (Bernard Jackman), Joanne Linville (Vera Jackman), Simon Oakland (District Attorney), Joanna Roos (Elsa Lundee).

The Nurses: **"Night Sounds"** (January 24, 1963)

Network: CBS. Directed by Don Richardson. Produced by Arthur Lewis. Written by Larry Cohen. Cast: Shirl Conway (Liz Thorpe), Zina Bethune (Gail Lucas), Donald Davis (Norman Ruskin), Noah Keen (Dr. Furst), Patricia Benoit (Edith Ruskin), Alan Alda (Dr. John Griffin).

The Defenders: **"The Traitor"** (February 16, 1963)

Network: CBS. Directed by David Greene. Produced by Robert Markell. Created by Reginald Rose. Written by Larry Cohen. Cast: E.G. Marshall (Lawrence Preston), Robert Reed (Kenneth Preston), Fritz Weaver (Vincent Kayle), Tom Clancy (Merv Erwin), Howard Weirum (Malcolm Standish), George Hall (Lew Bartlett).

Sam Benedict: "Accomplice" (March 9, 1963)

Network: NBC. Directed by Richard Donner. Produced by William Froug. Created by E. Jack Neumann. Written by Larry Cohen. Cast: Edmond O'Brien (Sam Benedict), Richard Rust (Henry Tabor), Eddie Albert (Lew Wiley), Brock Peters (Frank Elton), Roger Perry (Leonard Pittman), Phillip Pine (District Attorney), Ellen Holly (Melissa Ryan).

The Nurses: "Party Girl" (March 28, 1963)

Network: CBS. Directed by Stuart Rosenberg. Produced by Herbert Brodkin. Written by Larry Cohen. Story by Jay Roberts. Cast: Shirl Conway (Liz Thorpe), Zina Bethune (Gail Lucas), Inger Stevens (Clarissa Robin), Inga Swenson (Sandra Leonard), James Broderick (Dr. Tom Milford), Robert Gerringer (Hal Leonard), Tim O'Connor (Bert Handell), Vincent Gardenia (Mervyn Fowler), Arlene Golonka (Ronnie).

The Defenders: "The Colossus" (April 13, 1963)

Network: CBS. Directed by Paul Bogart. Produced by Robert Markell. Created by Reginald Rose. Written by Larry Cohen. Cast: E.G. Marshall (Lawrence Preston), Robert Reed (Kenneth Preston), Leo Genn (Dr. Morton Cheyney), Joe Mantell (District Attorney), Donald Moffat (Dr. Leo Elm), Frances Reid (Mary Cheyney), Tonio Selwart (Dr. Von Ecker), Jon Voight (Alan Link).

The Defenders: "The Noose" (April 27, 1963)

Network: CBS. Directed by Stuart Rosenberg. Produced by Robert Markell. Created by Reginald Rose. Written by Larry Cohen. Cast: E.G. Marshall (Lawrence Preston), Robert Reed (Kenneth Preston), Milton Seltzer (Constable Raymond Kimball), Bruce Gordon (Bennett Fletcher), Roy Poole (Lee Sanderson), Rochelle Oliver (Jean Lowell), Larry Hagman (Jim Lewton).

The Defenders: "The Captive" (October 12, 1963)

Network: CBS. Directed by Charles S. Dubin. Produced by Robert Markell. Created by Reginald Rose. Written by Larry Cohen. Cast: E.G. Marshall (Lawrence Preston), Robert Reed (Kenneth Preston), Ludwig Donath (I. Vorchek), Andrew Duggan (Franklin Rawlins), Mary Fickett (Joanne Rawlins), Robert Ellenstein (Anton Lazlov), Tim O'Connor (U.S. District Attorney Jim Evans), Dana Elcar (Rankin).

Arrest and Trial: "My Name is Martin Burnham" (October 13, 1963)

Network: ABC. Directed by Ralph Senensky. Produced by Frank P. Rosenberg. Written by Larry Cohen. Cast: Ben Gazzara (Sgt. Nick Anderson), Chuck Connors (John Egan), John Larch (Deputy District Attorney Miller), James Whitmore (Martin Burnham), Nina Foch (Ellen Burnham), Richard Eyer (Jerry Burnham), John Kerr (Barry Pine), Kenneth Tobey (Bill Latham), Noah Keen (Lt. Carl Bone), Don Galloway (Mitchell Harris).

The Nurses: "The Gift" (October 17, 1963)

Network: CBS. Directed by Alex March. Produced by Herbert Brodkin. Written by Larry Cohen. Cast: Shirl Conway (Liz Thorpe), Lee Grant (Doris Kelly), Robert Webber (Arthur Luskin), Edward Asner (Phil Granger), Robert Gerringer (Dr. Thorsen), Anne Meacham (Claire Luskin).

Espionage: "Medal for a Turned Coat" (January 15, 1964)

Network: NBC. Directed by David Greene. Produced by Herbert Brodkin. Written by Larry Cohen. Cast: Fritz Weaver (Richard Keller), Joseph Furst (Von Elm), Nigel Stock (Harry Forbes), Rosemary Rogers (Ilsa), Catherine Lacey (Mother), Richard Carpenter (Luber), Michael Wolf (Ernst), Sylvia Kay (Ellen), Gerard Heinz (Doctor).

The Defenders: "The Secret" (February 8, 1964)

Network: CBS. Directed by Paul Bogart. Produced by Robert Markell. Created by Reginald Rose. Written by Larry Cohen. Cast: E.G. Marshall (Lawrence Preston), Robert Reed (Kenneth Preston), Martin Landau (Daniel Orren), Georgann Johnson (Phyllis Orren), George Voskovec (Dr. Ladzlaw), Tim O'Connor (U.S. District Attorney Evans), Cec Linder (Dr. Bell).

The Defenders: "May Day! May Day!" (April 18, 1964)

Network: CBS. Directed by Stuart Rosenberg. Produced by Robert Markell. Created by Reginald Rose. Written by Larry Cohen. Cast: E.G. Marshall (Lawrence Preston), Robert Reed (Kenneth Preston), Torin Thathcer (Admiral Lucas J. Kiley), Skip Homeier (Commander Randall Kiley), Frances Sternhagen (Louise Kiley), Tim O'Connor (U.S. District Attorney Evans).

The Defenders: "The Go Between" (October 15, 1964)

Network: CBS. Directed by Paul Sylbert. Produced by Robert Markell. Created by Reginald Rose. Written by Larry Cohen. Cast: E.G. Marshall (Lawrence Preston), Robert Reed (Kenneth Preston), Arthur Hill (Matthew J. Ritter), Phyllis Thaxter (Dolores Ryder), Addison Powell (Harrison Alder), John Randolph (FBI Agent Slattery), Sally Gracie (Carolyn Harkness), Roberts Blossom (Riggs).

The Fugitive: "Escape Into Black" (November 17, 1964)

Network: ABC. Directed by Jerry Hopper. Produced by Alan A. Armer. Created by Roy Huggins. Written by Larry Cohen. Cast: David Janssen (Dr. Richard Kimble), Barry Morse (Lt. Gerard), Ivan Dixon (Dr. Towne), Betty Garrett (Margaret Ruskin), Paul Birch (Capt. Carpenter), Bill Raisch (One-Armed Man).

Branded: "**Survival**" (January 24, 1965)

Network: NBC. Directed by Richard Whorf. Produced by Cecil Barker. Created by Larry Cohen. Written by Larry Cohen. Cast: Chuck Connors (Jason McCord), Alex Cord (Jed Colbee), Robert Carricart (Navajo), Janet De Gore (Sally Colbee), Valerie Szabo (Jessie Colbee), Harry Harvey, Sr. (Stable Owner).

Branded: "**The Vindicators**" (January 31, 1965)

Network: NBC. Directed by Joseph H. Lewis. Produced by Cecil Barker. Created by Larry Cohen. Written by Larry Cohen. Cast: Chuck Connors (Jason McCord), June Lockhart (Mrs. Pritchett), Claude Akins (Ned Travis), Harry Carey, Jr. (Lt. John Pritchett), John Litel (General James Reid), Johnny Jensen (Johnny Pritchett), John Pickard (Sergeant).

The Defenders: "**The Unwritten Law**" (February 4, 1965)

Network: CBS. Directed by Robert Stevens. Produced by Robert Markell. Created by Reginald Rose. Written by Larry Cohen. Cast: E.G. Marshall (Lawrence Preston), Robert Reed (Kenneth Preston), David Opatoshu (Leo Rolf), Kim Hunter (Eileen Rolf), Jessica Walter (Sharon Ruskin).

Branded: "**Rules of the Game**" (February 14, 1965)

Network: NBC. Directed by Lawrence Dobkin. Created by Larry Cohen. Written by Larry Cohen. Cast: Chuck Connors (Jason McCord), Jeanne Cooper (Else Brown), Russ Conway (Sheriff Pollard), Brad Weston (Vance), L.Q. Jones (Miles), Harry Bartell (The Mayor), Kathy Garver (Ginny Pollard).

Branded: "**The Bounty**" (February 21, 1965)

Network: NBC. Directed by Harry Harris. Created by Larry Cohen. Written by Richard Carr, Jerry Ziegman and John Wilder. Story by Larry Cohen. Cast: Chuck Connors (Jason McCord), Pat Conway (Johnny Dolan), Gene Evans (Paxton), Michael Ansara (Thomas Frye), Juli Reding (Liz), Charles Maxwell (Andy Starrett), Reg Parton (Vince Starrett).

Branded: "Coward Step Aside" (March 7, 1965)

Network: NBC. Directed by Harry Harris. Created by Larry Cohen. Written by John Wilder and Jerry Ziegman. Story by Larry Cohen. Cast: Chuck Connors (Jason McCord), Johnny Crawford (Clay Holden), Richard Arlen (Hatton), G.V. Homeier (Garrett), Charles Doherty (Karin), Allen Jaffe (Topaz), Dennis Cross (Webb).

Branded: "The Mission: Part 1" (March 14, 1965)

Network: NBC. Directed by Bernard McEveety. Created by Larry Cohen. Written by James Brewer. Story by Larry Cohen. Cast: Chuck Connors (Jason McCord), Kamala Devi (Laurette Lansing), McDonald Carey (Senator Lansing), John Carradine (General Josh McCord), Robert Q. Lewis (Ray Hatch), Jon Lormer (Col. Harry S. Snow), William Bryant (President Ulysses S. Grant).

Branded: "The Mission: Part 2" (March 21, 1965)

Network: NBC. Directed by Bernard McEveety. Created by Larry Cohen. Written by James Brewer. Story by Larry Cohen. Cast: Chuck Connors (Jason McCord), Peter Breck (Crispo), John Carradine (General Josh McCord), Cesar Romero (General Arriola), H.M. Wynant (Brissac), Jon Lormer (Col. Harry S. Snow), William Bryant (President Ulysses S. Grant).

Branded: "The Mission: Part 3" (March 28, 1965)

Network: NBC. Directed by Bernard McEveety. Created by Larry Cohen. Written by James Brewer. Story by Larry Cohen. Cast: Chuck Connors (Jason McCord), Wendell Corey (Maj. Whitcomb), Peter Breck (Crispo),

Rochelle Hudson (Alice Whitcomb), Patrick Wayne (Corp. Dewey), H.M. Wynant (Brissac), Steven Marlo (Pte. Taylor).

Kraft Suspense Theater: "Kill No More" (April 29, 1965)

Network: NBC. Directed by Tom Gries. Produced by Arthur H. Nadel. Executive Produced by Frank P. Rosenberg. Written by Larry Cohen and William Wood. Story by Larry Cohen. Cast: Lew Ayres (Dr. Thomas Clay), Robert Webber (Robert Burke), Julie Adams (Joanne Clay), Robert F. Simon (Gen. 'Red' Brockman), Leonard Nimoy (Cowell), Morgan Jones (Chester), Garry Walberg (Dr. Martin Sorbin), Michael Fox (Howard Link), Ted Knight (Dr. Lessing).

Branded: "A Taste of Poison" (May 2, 1965)

Network: NBC. Directed by Ron Winston. Created by Larry Cohen. Written by William Putnam and Nicholas Rowe. Story by Larry Cohen. Cast: Chuck Connors (Jason McCord), Carol Rossen (Dr. Evelyn Cole), Walter Burke (Luke), Clarke Gordon (Howland), Stuart Margolin (Cavalry Officer), Eddie Little Sky (Indian).

Branded: "Price of a Name" (May 23, 1965)

Network: NBC. Directed by Leonard Horn. Created by Larry Cohen. Written by Nicholas Rowe. Story by Larry Cohen. Cast: Chuck Connors (Jason McCord), Marilyn Maxwell (Lucy Benson), Keith Andes (Roy Harris), Don Megowan (Carruthers), Jess Kirkpatrick (Pete), Don Douglas (Banker Lewis), Charles Fredericks (The Boss), Jay Sullivan (The Shopkeeper).

Blue Light: "The Last Man" (January 12, 1966)

Network: ABC. Directed by Walter Grauman. Produced by Buck Houghton. Created by Larry Cohen and Walter Grauman. Written by Larry Cohen. Cast: Robert Goulet (David March), Christine Carére (Suzanne Duchard), John van Dreelen (von Lindendorf), Donald Harron (Guy

Spaulding), Werner Peters (Elm), Christiane Schmidtmer (Erika von Lindendorf), John Alderson (Gorleck), Oscar Beregi, Jr. (Glauber).

Blue Light: "Target – David March" (January 19, 1966)

Network: ABC. Directed by Walter Grauman. Produced by Buck Houghton. Created by Larry Cohen and Walter Grauman. Written by Larry Cohen. Cast: Robert Goulet (David March), Christine Carére (Suzanne Duchard), Edward Binns (Major Traynor), Allan Cuthbertson (Col. Dennison), Geoffrey Fredrick (Eddie Fry), Hasns Reiser (Col. Richter), Margit Saad (The Baroness), John Alderson (Gorleck), Peter Capell (Professor Felix Eckhardt).

Blue Light: "The Fortress Below" (January 26, 1966)

Network: ABC. Directed by Walter Grauman. Produced by Buck Houghton. Created by Larry Cohen and Walter Grauman. Written by Larry Cohen. Cast: Robert Goulet (David March), Christine Carére (Suzanne Duchard), John van Dreelen (von Lindendorf), Eva Pflug (Gretchen Hoffmann), Peter Capell (Professor Felix Eckhardt), Horst Frank (Luber), Osman Ragheb (Dr. Brunner), Dieter Eppler (Dr. Stolnitz), Manfred Andrae (Dr. Zimmer), Dieter Kirchlechner (Becker), Paul Glawion (Submarine Pilot).

Blue Light: "The Weapon Within" (February 2, 1966)

Network: ABC. Directed by Walter Grauman. Produced by Buck Houghton. Created by Larry Cohen and Walter Grauman. Written by Larry Cohen. Cast: Robert Goulet (David March), Christine Carére (Suzanne Duchard), John van Dreelen (von Lindendorf), Eva Pflug (Gretchen Hoffmann), Horst Frank (Luber), Osman Ragheb (Dr. Brunner), Dieter Eppler (Dr. Stolnitz), Manfred Andrae (Dr. Zimmer).

Blue Light: "Traitor's Blood" (February 9, 1966)

Network: ABC. Directed by Walter Grauman. Produced by Buck Houghton. Created by Larry Cohen and Walter Grauman. Written by Larry

Cohen. Cast: Robert Goulet (David March), Christine Carére (Suzanne Duchard), Lyle Bettger (The Colonel), Henry Beckman (Schreiber), David Macklin (Brian March), William Wintersole (von Clausitz), Jerry Ayres (Hodges), James Dixon (Kelly).

Blue Light: "Agent of the East" (February 16, 1966)

Network: ABC. Directed by James Gladstone. Produced by Buck Houghton. Created by Larry Cohen and Walter Grauman. Written by Donald S. Sanford. Story by Larry Cohen. Cast: Robert Goulet (David March), Christine Carére (Suzanne Duchard), Jan Malmsjö (E.W. Vorchek), James Mitchell (Col. Freidank), Dick Davalos (Capt. Hegner).

Blue Light: "Sacrifice!" (February 23, 1966)

Network: ABC. Directed by William Graham. Produced by Buck Houghton. Created by Larry Cohen and Walter Grauman. Written by Dick Carr. Story by Larry Cohen. Cast: Robert Goulet (David March), Christine Carére (Suzanne Duchard), Larry Pennell (Nick Brady), John Ragin (Maj. Zimmer), Barry Ford (Capt. Klauss), Harry Davis (The Frenchman), Richard Bull (Maj. Kurtz), James Brolin (American Pilot), Barry Cahill (American Intelligence Officer), Brendan Dillon (Engineer).

Blue Light: "The Secret War" (March 2, 1966)

Network: ABC. Directed by Walter Grauman. Produced by Buck Houghton. Created by Larry Cohen and Walter Grauman. Written by Larry Cohen. Cast: Robert Goulet (David March), Christine Carére (Suzanne Duchard), Roger C. Carmel (Schuman), Gail Kobe (Elke Lublin), Kevin Hagen (Erik Kozlof), Gilbert Green (Helmut Kautner), Fred Holliday (Courier).

Blue Light: "Return of Elm" (March 23, 1966)

Network: ABC. Directed by Walter Grauman. Produced by Buck Houghton. Created by Larry Cohen and Walter Grauman. Written by Larry

Cohen. Cast: Robert Goulet (David March), Christine Carére (Suzanne Duchard), Werner Peters (Heinrich Elm), Malachi Throne (Krnaz), Susanne Cramer (Ilsa), Lawrence Montaigne (Gestapo Captain), Michael Hausserman (Dorshak), Hans Heyde (Max).

Blue Light: "How to Kill a Toy Soldier" (April 13, 1966)

Network: ABC. Directed by Leo Penn. Produced by Buck Houghton. Created by Larry Cohen and Walter Grauman. Written by Roger Swaybill and Merv Bloch. Story by Larry Cohen. Cast: Robert Goulet (David March), Christine Carére (Suzanne Duchard), Michael Shea (Klaus Werner), Todd Martin (Col. Werner), Donald Losby (Norwegian Boy), Peter Bourne (Fisherman).

The Rat Patrol: "The Blind Man's Bluff Raid" (October 24, 1966)

Network: ABC. Directed by Lee H. Katzin. Produced by Stanley Shpetner. Created by Tom Gries. Written by Larry Cohen. Cast: Christopher George (Sgt. Sam Troy), Larry Casey (Mark Hitchcock), Hans Gudegast (Capt. Hans Dietrich), Gary Raymond (Sgt. Jack Moffit), Justin Tarr (Private Tully Pettigrew), Salome Jens (Patricia Bauer), James Philbrook (Dr. Keller).

The Invaders (January 10, 1967 – March 26, 1968)

Network: ABC. Produced by Alan A. Armer. Executive Produced by Quinn Martin. Created by Larry Cohen. Regular Cast: Roy Thinnes (David Vincent), Kent Smith (Edgar Scoville).

Coronet Blue (May 29, 1967 – September 4, 1967)

Network: CBS. Produced by Edgar Lansbury. Executive Produced by Herbert Brodkin. Created by Larry Cohen. Regular Cast: Frank Converse (Michael Alden), Joe Silver (Max Spier).

Custer (September 6, 1967 – December 27, 1967)

Network: ABC. Produced by Frank Glicksman. Executive Produced by David Weisbart. Created by Samuel A. Peeples and David Weisbart. Series Suggested by Larry Cohen. Regular Cast: Wayne Maunder (Gen. George Armstrong Custer), Slim Pickens ('California' Joe Milner), Robert F. Simon (Gen. Alfred Terry), Peter Palmer (Sgt. James Bustard), Michael Dante (Crazy Horse).

Columbo: "Murder by the Book" (September 15, 1971)

Network: NBC. Directed by Steven Spielberg. Produced by Richard Levinson, William Link and Robert F. O'Neill. Created by Richard Levinson and William Link. Written by Steve Bochco. Story by Larry Cohen (uncredited). Cast: Peter Falk (Lt. Columbo), Jack Cassidy (Ken Franklin), Rosemary Forsythe (Joanna Ferris), Martin Milner (Jim Ferris), Barbara Colby (Lilly La Sanka), Lynette Mettey (Gloria), Bernie Kuby (Mike Tuicker), Hoke Howell (Sergeant), Marcia Wallace (Woman).

Cool Million: "The Mask of Marcella" (October 16, 1972)

Network: NBC. Directed by Gene Levitt. Produced by David J. O'Connell. Executive Produced by George Eckstein. Created by Larry Cohen. Written by Larry Cohen. Cast: James Farentino (Jefferson Keyes), John Vernon (Inspector Duprez), Barbara Bouchet (Carla Miles), Jackie Coogan (Merrill Cossack), Christine Belford (Adrienne Pascal), Lila Kedrova (Mme Martine), Patrick O'Neal (Dr. Emile Snow), Guido Alberti (Tomlin), John Karlsen (Werner), Mickey Hargitay (Frederick).

Columbo: "Any Old Port in a Storm" (October 7, 1973)

Network: NBC. Directed by Leo Penn. Produced by Robert F. O'Neill. Created by Richard Levinson and William Link. Written by Stanley Ralph Ross. Story by Larry Cohen. Cast: Peter Falk (Lt. Columbo), Donald Pleasence (Adrian Carsini), Joyce Jillson (Joan Stacey), Gary Conway (Enrico Giuseppe Carsini), Dana Elcar (Falcon), Julie Harris (Karen Fielding), Vito Scotti (Maitre D'), Robert Donner (The Drunk).

Columbo: **"Candidate for a Crime"** (November 4, 1973)

Network: NBC. Directed by Boris Sagal. Produced by Edward K. Dodds, Roland Kibbee and Dean Hargrove. Created by Richard Levinson and William Link. Written by Irving Pearlberg, Alvin R. Friedman, Roland Kibbee and Dean Hargrove. Story by Larry Cohen. Cast: Peter Falk (Lt. Columbo), Jackie Cooper (Nelson Hayward), Joanne Linville (Vickie Hayward), Tisha Sterling (Linda Johnson), Ken Swofford (Harry Stone), Robert Karnes (Sgt. Vernon), Jay Verela (Sgt. Rojas).

Columbo: **"An Exercise in Fatality"** (September 15, 1974)

Network: NBC. Directed by Bernard L. Kowalski. Produced by Edward K. Dodds, Roland Kibbee and Dean Hargrove. Created by Richard Levinson and William Link. Written by Peter S. Fischer. Story by Larry Cohen. Cast: Peter Falk (Lt. Columbo), Robert Conrad (Milo Janus), Gretchen Corbett (Jessica Conroy), Pat Harrington (Buddy Castle), Colin Wilcox (Ruth Stafford), Philip Bruns (Gene Stafford), Jude Farese (Al Murphy), Darrell Zwerling (Lewis Lacey).

NYPD Blue: **"Dirty Socks"** (March 21, 1995)

Network: ABC. Directed by Elodie Keene. Produced by Burton Armus, Chad Savage and Gardner Stern. Executive Produced by David Milch, Steven Bochco and Mark Tinker. Created by David Milch and Steven Bochco. Written by Larry Cohen. Cast: Jimmy Smits (Det. Bobby Simone), Dennis Franz (Det. Andy Sipowicz), James McDaniel (Lt. Arthur Fancy), Nicholas Turturro (Det. James Martinez), Sharon Lawrence (A.D.A. Sylvia Costas), Gordon Clapp (Det. Greg Medavoy), Gail O'Grady (Donna Abandando), Susanna Thompson (Joyce Novak).

SCREENPLAYS & TV MOVIE TELEPLAYS

RETURN OF THE MAGNIFICENT SEVEN (1966)

Production Companies: United Artists, Mirisch Production Company, C.B Films S.A. Directed by Burt Kennedy. Produced by Ted Richmond. Associate Producer: Robert Goodstein. Written by Larry Cohen. Cinematography by Paul Vogel. Edited by Bert Bates. Art Direction by José Alguero. Music by Elmer Bernstein. **Cast:** Yul Brynner (Chris), Robert Fuller (Vin), Julian Mateos (Chico), Warren Oates (Colbee), Claude Akins (Frank), Elisa Montes (Petra), Fernando Rey (Priest), Emilio Fernandez (Lorca), Virgilio Teixeira (Luis), Rudy Acosta (Lopez), Jordan Christopher (Manuel), Gracita Sacromonte (Flamenco Dancer), Carlos Casaravilla (First Peon).

I DEAL IN DANGER (1966)

Production Company: 20th Century Fox, Rojo Productions. Directed by Walter Grauman. Produced by Walter Grauman and Buck Houghton. Written by Larry Cohen. Cinematography by Kurt Grigoleit and Sam Leavitt. Edited by Jason H. Bernie and Dolph Rudeen. Art Direction by Jack T. Collis, Jack Martin Smith and Rolf Zehetbauer. Music by Joseph Mullendore and Lalo Schifrin. **Cast:** Robert Goulet (David March), Christine Carère (Suzanne Duchard), Donald Harron (Spauling), Horst Frank (Luber), Werner Peters (Elm), Eva Pflug (Gretchen Hoffmann), Christiane Schmidtmer (Erika von Lindendorf), John Van Dreelen (von Lindendorf), Hans Reiser (Richter), Margit Saad (Baroness), Peter Capell (Eckhardt).

BLADE RIDER, REVENGE OF THE INDIAN NATIONS (1966)

Production Company: Mark Goodson/Bill Todman Productions, Sentinel Productions. Directed by Harry Harris, Vincent McEveety and Allen Reisner. Produced by Andrew J. Fenady, Mark Goodson and Bill Todman. Written by Larry Cohen, Frederick Louis Fox, Ken Pettus, John Wilder and Jerry Ziegman. Cinematography by Lester Shorr. Edited by Melvin Shapiro. Art Direction by Stan Jolley and Hal Pereira. Music by Dominic Frontiere. **Cast:** Chuck Connors (Jason McCord), Burt Reynolds

(Red Hand), Greg Morris (Pvt. Johnny Macon), Lee Van Cleef (Charlie Yates), Noah Beery, Jr. (Maj. Lynch), David Brian (Gregory Hazla), Kathie Browne (Jennie Galvin), Michael Keep (Chief Watookah), Robert Lansing (Gen. George Armstrong Custer), Felix Locher (Chief Sitting Bull), Michael Pate (Crazy Horse).

THE LEGEND OF CUSTER (1968)

Production Company: 20th Century Fox. Directed by Norman Foster and Sam Wanamaker. Produced by Frank Glicksman and Robert L. Jacks. Suggested by Larry Cohen. Created by Samuel A. Peeples and David Weisbart. Written by Samuel A. Peeples and Shimon Wincelberg. Cinematography by William M. Spencer and Harold E. Stein. Edited by Jason H. Bernie, Ronald J. Fagan and George A. Gittens. Art Direction by Russell C. Menzer and Jack Martin Smith. Music by Richard Markowitz, Joseph Mullendore and Leith Stevens. **Cast:** Wayne Maunder (Lt. Col. George Armstrong Custer), Slim Pickens (California Joe Milner), Michael Dante (Crazy Horse), Robert F. Simon (Gen. Alfred Terry), Mary Ann Mobley (Ann Landry), Alex Davion (Capt. Marcus A. Reno), Grant Woods (Capt. Myles Keogh).

DADDY'S GONE A-HUNTING (1969)

Production Company: Warner Bros., Red Lion. Directed by Mark Robson. Produced by Mark Robson. Story by Larry Cohen. Screenplay by Larry Cohen and Lorenzo Semple, Jr. Cinematography by Ernest Laszlo. Edited by Dorothy Spencer. Art Direction by Stan Johnson and James Sullivan. Music by John Williams. **Cast:** Carol White (Cathy Palmer), Paul Burke (Jack Byrnes), Mala Powers (Meg Stone), Scott Hylands (Kenneth Daly), James Sikking (Joe Menchell), Walter Brooke (Jerry Wolfe), Matilda Calnan (Ilsa), Gene Lyons (Dr. Blanker), Dennis Patrick (Dr. Parkington), Barry Cahill (FBI Agent Crosley), Rachel Ames (Nurse).

EL CONDOR (1970)

Production Company: National General Pictures, Carthay Continental. Directed by John Guillermin. Produced by André De Toth. Story by Steven

Carabatsos. Screenplay by Larry Cohen and Steven Carabatsos. Cinematography by Henri Persin. Edited by Walter Hannemann and William M. Ziegler. Production Design by Julio Molina. Music by Maurice Jarre. **Cast:** Jim Brown (Luke), Lee Van Cleef (Jaroo), Patrick O'Neal (Chavez), Marianna Hill (Claudine), Iron Eyes Cody (Santana), Imogen Hassall (Dolores), Elisha Cook (Old Convict), Gustavo Rojo (Colonel Anguinaldo), Florencio Amarilla (Águila), Julio Peňa (Gen. Hernández), Angel del Pozo (Lieutenant), Patricio Santiago (Julio), John Clark (Prison Guard Captain).

IN BROAD DAYLIGHT (1971)

Production Companies: Aaron Spelling Productions, ABC. Directed by Robert Day. Produced by Robert Mirisch. Executive Producer: Aaron Spelling. Written by Larry Cohen. Cinematography by Archie R. Dalzell. Edited by Edward Mann. Art Direction by Paul Sylos. Music by Leonard Rosenman. **Cast:** Richard Boone (Tony Chappel), Suzanne Pleshette (Kate Todd), Stella Stevens (Elizabeth Chappel), John Marley (Lt. Bergman), Fred Beir (Alex Crawford), Whit Bissell (Capt. Moss), Paul Smith (Charles), Dan Spelling (Teenager), Barbara Dodd (Mother).

SHOOTOUT IN A ONE-DOG TOWN (1974)

Production Company: Hanna-Barbera Productions, ABC. Directed by Burt Kennedy. Produced by Richard E. Lyons. Written by Larry Cohen and Dick Nelson. Cinematography by Robert E. Hauser. Edited by Warner E. Leighton. Art Direction by Phillip Bennett. Music by Hoyt Curtin. **Cast:** Richard Crenna (Zack Wells), Stephanie Powers (Letty Crandell), Jack Elam (Handy), Arthur O'Connell (Henry Gills), Michael Ansara (Reynolds), Dub Taylor (Halsey), Michael Anderson (Billy Boy), Richard Egan (Petry), John Pickard (Preston), Jay Ripley (Little Edgar).

MAN ON THE OUTSIDE (1975)

Production Company: Universal, ABC. Directed by Boris Sagal. Produced by George Eckstein and David Victor. Written by Larry Cohen. Cinematography by Mario Tosi. Edited by Bud Hoffman and Douglas Stewart.

Art Direction by Arch Bacon. Music by Elliot Kaplan. **Cast:** Lorne Greene (Wade Griffin), James Olsen (Gerald Griffin), Lee H. Montgomery (Mark Griffin), Lorraine Gary (Nora Griffin), Brooke Bundy (Sandra Ames), Ken Swofford (Lt. Matthews), William Watson (Ames), Bruce Kirby (Scully), Charles Knox Robinson (Mr. Arnold), Garry Walberg (Benny).

SPARROW (1978)

Production Company: CBS. Directed by Stuart Hofmann (John Berry). Produced by Walter Bernstein. Written by Larry Cohen. Cinematography by Irving Lippman. Edited by Ed Forsyth. Set Decoration by Robert Gould. Music by Paul Williams. **Cast:** Randy Hermann (Jess Sparrow), Catherine Hicks (Valerie), Lillian Gish (Widow), Don Gordon (Charles Medwick), Beverly Sanders (Tammy), Karen Sedgley (Harriet), Dick Anthony Williams (Martin), Lou Gilbert (Guard).

THE AMERICAN SUCCESS COMPANY (1980)

Production Company: Columbia Pictures. Directed by William Richert. Produced by Daniel H. Blatt and Edgar J. Scherick. Story by Larry Cohen. Screenplay by Larry Cohen and William Richert. Cinematography by Anthony B. Richmond. Edited by Ralph E. Winters. Production Design by Rolf Zehetbauer. Music by Maurice Jarre. **Cast:** Jeff Bridges (Harry), Belinda Bauer (Sarah), Ned Beatty (Mr. Elliott), Steven Keats (Rick Duprez), Bianca Jagger (Corinne), John Glover (Ernst), Mascha Gonska (Greta), Michael Durrell (Herman), Eva Marie Meineke (Mrs. Heinemann).

I, THE JURY (1982)

Production Company: American Cinema Productions, Larco Productions, Pellepont and Solofilm. Directed by Richard T. Heffron. Produced by Robert H. Solo. Screenplay by Larry Cohen. Based on the novel by Mickey Spillane. Cinematography by Andrew Laszlo. Edited by Garth Craven. Production Design by Robert Gundlach. Music by Bill Conti. **Cast:** Armand Assante (Mike Hammer), Barbara Carrera (Dr. Charlotte Bennett), Laurene Landon (Velda), Alan King (Charles Kalecki), Geoffrey Lewis (Joe Butler), Paul Sorvino (Dt. Pat Chambers), Judson Scott (Charles Kendricks), Barry Snider (Romero), Julia Barr (Norma Childs), Jessica James (Hilda Kendricks), Frederic Downs (Jack Williams), Mary Margaret Amoto (Myrna Williams), F.J. O'Neil (Goodwin), William Schilling (Lundee), Robert Sevra (Breslin), Don Pike (Evans), Lee Anne Harris, Lynette Harris (Twins).

WOMEN OF SAN QUENTIN (1983)

Production Companies: David Gerber Productions, NBC, MGM/UA Television. Directed by William Graham. Produced by Stephen Cragg and R.W. Goodwin. Story by Larry Cohen and Mark Rodgers. Screenplay by Mark Rodgers. Cinematography by Robert Steadman. Edited by Ronald J. Fagan. Production Design by Stan Jolley. Music by John Cacavas. **Cast:** Stella Stevens (Lt. Janet Alexander), Debbie Allen (Carol Freeman), Amy Steel (Liz Larson), Hector Elizondo (Capt. Mike Reyes), Yaphet Kotto (Sgt. Therman Patterson), Gregg Henry (Williams), Rosanna DeSoto (Adela Reynosa), William Allen Young (Larry Jennings), Rockne Tarkington (Big William), Ernie Hudson (Charles Wilson), Jenny Gago (Gloria), William Sanderson (Countee) James Gammon (Officer), Francisco Lagueruela (Assistant D.A.).

SCANDALOUS (1984)

Production Companies: Orion Pictures, Angeles Cinema Investors, Raleigh Films, Lantana. Directed by Rob Cohen. Produced by Arlene Sellers and Alex Winitsky. Story by Larry Cohen, Rob Cohen and John Byrum. Screenplay by Rob Cohen and John Byrum. Cinematography by Jack Cardiff. Edited by Michael Bradsell. Production Design by Peter Mullins. Music by Dave Grusin. **Cast:** Robert Hays (Frank Swedlin), Ron Travis (Porno Director), M. Emmet Walsh (Simon Reynolds), John Gielgud (Uncle Willie), Ed Dolan (Purser), Paul Reeve (Flight Co-ordinator), Aleta Kennedy (Stewardess), Pamela Stephenson (Fiona Maxwell Sayle), Nancy Wood (Lindsay Morning), Kevin Elyot (Matt), Duncan Preston (Hal).

BEST SELLER (1987)

Production Company: Hemdale Film Corporation, Orion Pictures. Directed by John Flynn. Produced by Carter DeHaven. Written by Larry Cohen. Cinematography by Fred Murphy. Edited by David Rosenbloom. Production Design by Gene Rudolf. Music by Jay Ferguson. **Cast:** James Woods (Cleve), Brian Dennehy (Dennis Meechum), Victoria Tennant (Roberta Gillian), Allison Balson (Holly Meechum), Paul Shenar (David Madlock), George Coe (Graham), Anne Pitoniak (Mrs. Foster), Mary Carver (Cleve's Mother), Sully Boyar (Monks), Kathleen Lloyd (Annie), Charles Tyner (Cleve's Father), E. Brian Deane (Taxi Driver), Jeffrey Josephson (Pearlman), Edward Blackoff (Thorn).

DESPERADO: AVALANCHE AT DEVIL'S RIDGE (1988)

Production Companies: NBC, Walter Mirisch Productions, Charles E. Sellier Productions, Universal TV. Directed by Richard Compton. Produced by Lester Wm. Berke. Executive Producer: Andrew Mirisch. Supervising Producer: Charles E. Sellier, Jr. Created by Elmore Leonard. Written by Larry Cohen. Cinematography by Robert C. Jessup. Edited by Mark W. Rosenbaum. Art Direction by Bill Cornford. Music by Michael Colombier. **Cast:** Alex McArthur (Duell McCall), Rod Steiger (Silas Slaten), Lise Cutter (Nora), Lee Paul (Joshua Barrens), Alice Adair (Rachel Slaten), Hoyt Axton (Sheriff Ben Tree), Dwier Brown (Jim Buckner).

MANIAC COP (1988)

Production Company: Shapiro-Glickenhaus Entertainment. Directed by William Lustig. Produced by Larry Cohen. Written by Larry Cohen. Cinematography by James Lemmo and Vincent J. Rabe. Edited by David Kern. Production Design by Jonathon R. Hodges. Music by Jay Chattaway. **Cast:** Bruce Campbell (Jack Forrest), Laurene Landon (Teresa Mallory), Tom Atkins (Frank McCrae), Richard Roundtree (Commissioner Pike), William Smith (Capt. Ripley), Robert Z'Dar (Matt Cordell), Sheree North (Sally Noland), James Dixon (Clancy), Nina Aversen (Regina Sheperd), Nick Barbaro (Councilman), John F. Goff (Lawyer), Jake LaMotta

(Detective), Jill Gatsby (Cassie Phillips), Sam Raimi (Newscaster), William Lustig (Hotel Manager).

MANIAC COP 2 (1990)

Production Companies: Medusa Pictures, The Movie House Sales Company, Fadd Enterprises, Overseas FilmGroup. Directed by William Lustig. Produced by Larry Cohen. Written by Larry Cohen. Cinematography by James Lemmo. Edited by David Kern. Production Design by Gene Abel and Charles M. Lagola. Music by Jay Chattaway. **Cast:** Robert Davi (Dt. Sean McKinney), Claudia Christian (Susan Riley), Michael Lerner (Edward Doyle), Bruce Campbell (Jack Forrest), Laurene Landon (Teresa Mallory), Robert Z'Dar (Matt Cordell), Clarence Williams III (Blum), Leo Rossi (Turkell), Lou Bonacki (Dt. Lovejoy), Paula Trickey (Cheryl), Charles Napier (Lew Brady), Sam Raimi (Newscaster), James Dixon (Range Officer).

MANIAC COP 3: BADGE OF SILENCE (1993)

Production Companies: NEO Motion Pictures, First Look Pictures, Overseas FilmGroup. Directed by William Lustig. Produced by Michael Leahy and Joel Soisson. Written by Larry Cohen. Cinematography by Jacques Haitkin. Edited by Michael Eliot, David Kern and Rick Tuber. Production Design by Clark Hunter. Music by Joel Goldsmith. **Cast:** Robert Davi (Dt. Sean McKinney), Robert Z'Dar (Matt Cordell), Caitlin Dulany (Dr. Susan Fowler), Gretchen Becker (Katie Sullivan), Paul Gleason (Hank Cooney), Jackie Earle Haley (Frank Jessup), Julius Harris (Houngan), Grand Bush (Willie), Doug Savant (Dr. Peter Myerson), Robert Forster (Dr. Powell), Bobby Di Cicco (Bishop), Frank Pesce (Tribble) Ted Raimi (Reporter).

BODY SNATCHERS (1993)

Production Companies: Dorset Productions, Robert H. Solo Productions, Warner Bros. Directed by Abel Ferrara. Produced by Robert H. Solo. Screen Story by Larry Cohen and Raymond Cistheri. Screenplay by

Stuart Gordon, Dennis Paoli and Nicholas St. John. Based on the novel *The Body Snatchers* by Jack Finney. Cinematography by Bojan Bazelli. Edited by Anthony Redman. Production Design by Peter Jamison. Music by Joe Delia. **Cast:** Terry Kinney (Steve Malone), Meg Tilly (Carol Malone), Gabrielle Anwar (Marti Malone), Reilly Murphy (Andy Malone), Billy Wirth (Tim Young), Christine Elise (Jenn Platt), R. Lee Ermey (Gen. Platt), Kathleen Doyle (Mrs. Platt), Forest Whittaker (Maj. Collins), G. Elvis Phillips (Pete).

GUILTY AS SIN (1993)

Production Company: Buena Vista, Hollywood Pictures. Directed by Sidney Lumet. Produced by Martin Ransohoff. Written by Larry Cohen. Cinematography by Andrzej Bartkowiak. Edited by Evan A. Lottman. Production Design by Phillip Rosenberg. Music by Howard Shore. **Cast:** Rebecca De Mornay (Jennifer Haines), Don Johnson (David Greenhill), Stephen Lang (Phil Garson), Jack Warden (Moe Plimpton), Dana Ivey (Judge Tompkins), Ron White (Prosecutor DiAngelo), Norma Dell'Agnese (Emily), Sean McCann (Nolan), Luis Guzmán (Lt. Martinez), Robert Kennedy (Caniff), James Blendick (McMartin), Tom Butler (D.A. Heath), Brigit Wilson (Rita Greenhill), Christina Baren (Miriam Langford), Lynn Cormack (Ester Rothman).

INVASION OF PRIVACY (1996)

Production Company: HBO, Senator Film Produktion. Directed by Anthony Hickox. Produced by Hanno Huth and Carsten H.W. Lorenz. Written by Larry Cohen. Cinematography by Paul Wunstorf. Edited by Dana Congdon. Production Design by Jane Ann Stewart. Music by Anthony Marinelli. **Cast:** Mili Avital (Theresa Barnes), Johnathon Schaech (Josh Taylor), David Keith (Sgt. Rutherford), Tom Wright (Devereux), R.G. Armstrong (Sam Logan), Charlotte Rampling (Deidre Stiles), Naomi Campbell (Cindy Carmichael), Scott Wilkinson (Dr. Shuman), Susan Dolan Stevens (Lt. Gibbons), Tom Wright (Devereux), Anthony Hickox (Father Figure).

UNCLE SAM (1996)

Production Company: A-Pix Entertainment. Directed by William Lustig. Produced by George G. Braunstein. Written by Larry Cohen. Cinematography by James Lebovitz. Edited by Bob Murawski. Production Design by Charlotte Malmlöf. Music by Mark Governor. **Cast:** David 'Shark' Fralick (Sam Harper), Christopher Ogden (Jody Baker), Leslie Neale (Sally Baker), Bo Hopkins (Sgt. Twining), William Smith (Major), Matthew Flint (Phil), Anne Tremko (Louise Harper), Isaac Hayes (Jed Crowley), Timothy Bottoms (Mr. Crandell), Tim Grimm (Ralph), P.J. Soles (Madge Cronin), Thom McFadden (Mac Cronin), Zachary McLemore (Barry Cronin), Morgan Paul (Mayor), Richard Cummings Jr. (Dan), Robert Forster (Congressman Cummins).

ED McBAIN'S 87TH PRECINCT: ICE (1996)

Production Companies: NBC, Diana Kerew Productions, Hearst Entertainment Productions. Directed by Bradford May. Produced by Diana Kerew and Erik Storey. Teleplay by Larry Cohen. Based on the novel by Ed McBain. Cinematography by Bradford May. Edited by Bud Hayes. Art Direction by Alistair MacRae. Music by Joseph Conlan. **Cast:** Dale Midkiff (Dt. Steve Carella), Joe Pantoliano (Dt. Meyer Meyer), Paul Johansson (Dt. Bert Kling), Andrea Parker (Dt. Eileen Burke), Dean McDermott (Tim Moore), Andrea Ferrell (Teddy Carella), Diane Douglass (Emma Forbes), Nigel Bennett (Brother Anthony), Michael Gross (Lt. Peter Bynes), Lenore Zann (Angie), Philip Akin (Dt. Arthur Brown), Tim Koetting (Howard).

ED McBAIN'S 87TH PRECINCT: HEATWAVE (1997)

Production Companies: NBC, Diana Kerew Productions, Hearst Entertainment Productions. Directed by Douglas Barr. Produced by Diana Kerew and Erik Storey. Teleplay by Larry Cohen. Based on the novel by Ed McBain. Cinematography by Malcolm Cross. Edited by Raúl Dávalos. Production Design by Alistair MacRae. Music by Patrick Williams. **Cast:** Dale Midkiff (Dt. Steve Carella), Erika Eleniak (Dt. Eileen Burke), Paul Johansson (Dt. Bert Kling), Paul Ben Victor (Dt. Meyer), Ron Kuhlman (Alan Slocum), Marc Gomes (Dt. Brown), Andrea Ferrell (Teddy Carella), Michael

Gross (Lt. Peter Bynes), Louise Vallance (Margaret Grayson), Annie Kidder (Marian Piper), Ian D. Clark (Jerry Piper), Lynne Cormack (Karen Jensen).

THE EX (1997)

Production Companies: HBO, American World Pictures, Cinépix Film Properties, Lions Gate Films. Directed by Mark L. Lester. Produced by Dana Dubovsky and Mark L. Lester. Screenplay by Larry Cohen and John Lutz. Based on the novel by John Lutz. Cinematography by Richard Leiterman. Edited by David Berlatsky. Production Design by Paul Joyal. Music by Paul J. Zaza. **Cast:** Yancy Butler (Deidre Kenyon), Suzy Amis (Molly Kenyon), Nick Mancuso (David Kenyon), Hamish Tildesley (Michael Kenyon), Babs Chula (Dr. Lilian Jonas), Claire Riley (Dt. Lang), Barry W. Levy (Frank), Roger Brasnes (Sam Beltzer), Tom Pickett (Kenyon's Doorman), Barry 'Bear' Horton (Biker), Arlene Belcastro (Next Door Neighbour).

MISBEGOTTEN (1998)

Production Companies: American World Pictures, Cinépix Film Properties. Directed by Mark L. Lester. Produced by Dana Dubovsky and Mark L. Lester. Screenplay by Larry Cohen. Based on the novel by James Gabriel Berman. Cinematography by Mark Irwin. Edited by David Berlatsky. Production Design by Paul Joyal. Music by Paul J. Zaza. **Cast:** Kevin Dillon (Billy Crapshoot), Nick Mancuso (Paul Bourke), Lysette Anthony (Caitlin Bourke), Robert Lewis (Dt. Cross), Matthew Walker (Dr. Dotterweigh), Stefan Arngrim (Conan Cornelius), Megan Leitch (Serena), Jo Bates (Dr. Rory Sorensen), J.B. Bivens (Dt. Helfand), Claire Riley (Dt. Gandy), Mark Holden (Captain), Kate Luyben (Myrna Casey), Felicia Shulman (Instructor).

THE DEFENDERS: CHOICE OF EVILS (1998)

Production Companies: Paramount Network Television Productions, Showtime Networks, Stan Rogow Productions. Directed by Andy Wolk. Produced by Sy Fischer. Executive Producer: Stan Rogow. Teleplay by

Larry Cohen, Andy Wolk and Peter Wolk. Story by Larry Cohen. Cinematography by John Newby. Edited by Lauren A. Schaffer. Production Design by Anthony Cowley. Music by David Goldblatt and Mark Isham. **Cast:** Beau Bridges (Don Preston), E.G. Marshall (Lawrence Preston), Martha Plimpton (Mary Jane Preston), Jon Polito (D.A. Al Orsini), Lisa Gay Hamilton (Jeanne Baptiste), Melanie Nicholls-King (Sarah Casey).

PHONE BOOTH (2002)

Production Companies: Fox 2000 Pictures, Zucker/Netter Productions. Directed by Joel Schumacher. Produced by Gil Netter and David Zucker. Written by Larry Cohen. Cinematography by Matthew Libatique. Edited by Mark Stevens. Production Design by Andrew Laws. Music by Harry Gregson-Williams. **Cast:** Colin Farrell (Stu Shepard), Kiefer Sutherland (The Caller), Forest Whitaker (Capt. Ramey), Radha Mitchell (Kelly Shepard), Katie Holmes (Pamela McFadden), Paula Jai Parker (Felicia), Arian Ash (Corky), Tia Texada (Asia), John Enos III (Leon), Richard T. Jones (Sgt. Cole), Keith Nobbs (Adam), Dell Yount (Pizza Guy), James MacDonald (Negotiator), Josh Pais (Mario), Yorgo Constantine (ESU Commander), Colin Patrick Lynch (ESU Technician), Troy Gilbert (ESU Sniper), Richard Paradise (ESU Guy).

CELLULAR (2004)

Production Companies: New Line Cinema, Electric Entertainment, LFG Filmproduktions & Company. Directed by David R. Ellis. Produced by Dean Devlin and Lauren Lloyd. Story by Larry Cohen. Screenplay by Chris Morgan. Cinematography by Gary Capo. Edited by Eric A. Sears. Production Design by Jaymes Hinkle. Music by John Ottman. **Cast:** Kim Basinger (Jessica Martin), Chris Evans (Ryan Hewitt), Jason Statham (Ethan Greer), William H. Macy (Sgt. Bob Mooney), Eric Christian Olsen (Chad), Matt McColm (Deason), Noah Emmerich (Jack Tanner), Brendan Kelly (Mad Dog), Eric Etebari (Dimitri), Valerie Cruz (Dana Bayback), Richard Burgi (Craig Martin), Jessica Biel (Chloe), Adam Taylor Gordon (Ricky Martin), Ester 'Tita' Mercado (Rosario), Caroline Aaron (Marilyn Monroe).

Credits • 673

CAPTIVITY (2007)

Production Companies: Captivity Productions, Foresight Unlimited, Russian American Movie Company (RAMCO). Directed by Roland Joffé. Produced by Mark Damon, Gary Mehlman, Serge Konov and Leonid Minkovski. Story by Larry Cohen. Screenplay by Larry Cohen and Joseph Tura. Cinematography by Daniel Pearl. Edited by Richard Nord. Production Design by Addis Gadzhiyev. Music by Marco Beltrami. **Cast:** Elisha Cuthbert (Jennifer), Daniel Gillies (Gary Dexter), Pruitt Taylor Vince (Ben Dexter), Michael Harney (Dt. Bettiger), Laz Alonso (Dt. Ray Di Santos), Maggie Damon (Dt. Susan Luden), Carl Paoli (Victim #1), Trent Broin (Victim #2).

BO CHI TUNG WAH ("CONNECTED") (2008)

Production Companies: Emperor Motion Pictures, China Film Group, Warner China Film HG Corporation, Armor Entertainment, BNJArmor, Sirius Pictures International. Directed by Benny Chan. Produced by Benny Chan, Albert Lee, Jiang Toa and Kevin Yung. Original Story by Larry Cohen. Screenplay by Alan Yuen, Benny Chan and Bing Xu. Cinematography by Anthony Pun. Edited by Chi Wai Yau. Production Design by Chung Man Yee. Music by Nicolas Errèra. **Cast:** Louis Koo (Bob), Barbie Hsu (Grace Wong), Nick Cheung (Dt. Fai), Ye Liu (Senior Inspector Fok), Siu-Wong Fan (Tong), Siu-Fai Cheung (Dt. Cheung), Beibi Gong (Jen), Carlos Chan (Roy Wong), Flora Chan (Jeannie), Ankie Beilke (Michelle), Cheuk-lap Hung (Joe).

IT'S ALIVE (2008)

Production Companies: Millennium Films, Foresight Unlimited, Signature Pictures, Amicus Entertainment, IPW Productions, Aramid Entertainment Fund, Alive Productions. Directed by Josef Rusnak. Produced by Simon Fawcett, Robert Katz and Marc Toberoff. Original Story and Screenplay by Larry Cohen. Screenplay by Paul Sopocy and James Portolese. Cinematography by Wedigo von Schultzendorff. Edited by James Herbert and Patrick McMahon. Production Design by Pier Luigi Basile. Music by Nicholas Pike. **Cast:** Bijou Phillips (Lenore Harker), James Murray (Frank Davis), Raphaël Coleman (Chris Davis), Owen Teale (Sgt. Perkins), Ty Glaser (Marnie), Oliver Coopersmith (Mike), Ioan Karamfilov (Adam), Jack Ellis (Prof. Baldwin), Skye Bennett (Nicole), Arkie Reece (Perry), Todd Jensen (Dr. Orbinson).

THE GAMBLER, THE GIRL AND THE GUNSLINGER (2009)

Production Companies: The Hallmark Channel, Randolph Films, Blueprint Entertainment, Gary Hoffman Productions. Directed by Anne Wheeler. Produced by Randy Cheveldave. Written by Larry Cohen and Bob Barbash. Cinematography by Paul Mitchnick. Edited by Jana Fritsch. Production Design by Andrew Deskin. Music by Brian S. Carr and Terence Davis. **Cast:** Dean Cain (Shea McCall), James Tupper (BJ Stoker), Allison Hossack (Liz Calhoun), Keith MacKechnie (Cal Stoomey), Michael Eklund (Red), John DeSantis (Mule), Teach Grant (Joker), Serge Houde (Marshal), Alejandro Abellan (Diego), Garwin Sanford (The General).

MESSAGES DELETED (2010)

Production Companies: Waterfront Pictures, Main Street Productions. Directed by Rob Cowan. Produced by Rob Cowan and Jim O'Grady. Written by Larry Cohen. Cinematography by Stephen Jackson. Edited by Garry M.B. Smith. Production Design by Geoff Wallace. Music by Jim Guttridge. **Cast:** Matthew Lillard (Joel Brandt), Deborah Kara Unger (Dt. Lavery), Gina Holden (Millie), Serge Houde (Dt. Breedlove), Chiara Zanni (Claire), Michael Eklund (Adam Brickles), Xantha Radley (Nurse Bev), Ken Kramer (Ben Brandt), Brandon Jay McClaren (Dude Up Front), Woody Jeffreys (Patrick), Ildiko Ferenczi (Kathy), Paul Lazenby (Tractor).

Bibliogaphy

SELECT ARTICLES & INTERVIEWS

Burrell, James. "Baby Killer," *Rue Morgue* #93, (September, 2009)
Calcutt, Ian. "More Little Terrors," *Samhain* #13, (February/March, 1989)
Cohen, Larry. "I Killed Bette Davis," *Film Comment*, Vol. 48/No. 4, (July/August, 2012)
Collins, Max Allan & Traylor, James L. *Mickey Spillane On Screen: A Complete Study of the Television and Film Adapations* (2012), McFarland & Co.
Doyle, Michael. "*God Told Me To*," *Rue Morgue Magazine's 200 Alternate Horror Films You Need To See* (2012), Marrs Media
Doyle, Michael. "The Terror of '82," *Rue Morgue* #137, (September, 2013)
Doyle, Michael. "Larry Cohen on Alfred Hitchcock," *Rue Morgue Magazine's Horror Heroes* (2014), Marrs Media
Dretzka, Gary. "Reclaiming Their Turf," *Chicago Tribune*, (May 12, 1996)
Dutka, Elaine. "Fox Sued Over *Gentlemen*," *Los Angeles Times*, (September 26, 2003)
Ebert, Roger. "*Demon*," *Chicago Sun-Times*, (December 1, 1976)
Ebert, Roger. "*Q - The Winged Serpent*," *Chicago Sun-Times*, (October 29, 1982)
Eisenberg, Adam. "The Year of the Werewolf: *Full Moon High*," *Cinefantastique* Vol. 10/No. 3 (Winter, 1980)
Everitt, David. "The Arresting Saga of *Maniac Cop 2*," *Fangoria* #96 (September, 1990)
Fischer, Dennis. "Larry Cohen's *The Ambulance*," *Cinefantastique* Vol. 21/No. 5, (April, 1991)
Fischer, Dennis. *Horror Film Directors: 1931-1990* (1991), McFarland & Co.

Fischer, Dennis. "Directed, Written & Produced By Larry Cohen: From Monster Babies to Homicidal Messiahs," *Midnight Marquee* #34, (Fall 1985)

Garris, Mick. "Larry Cohen on *Demon*," *Cinefantastique* Vol. 6/No. 1, (Summer 1977)

Grant, Barry Keith (ed). *Planks of Reason: Essays on the Horror Film* (1996), The Scarecrow Press, Inc.

Howard, Josiah. *Blaxploitation Cinema: The Essential Reference Guide* (2008), FAB Press

Huber, Christopher. "Monstrous Satire: Larry Cohen's Low Budget Operations," *Cinema Scope* Vol. 13/No. 1 (Winter, 2011)

Humphries, Reynold. "*It's Alive*," *Cinefantastique* Vol.4/No.3, (Fall, 1975)

James, Darius. *That's Blaxploitation: Roots of the Badasssss 'Tude* (1995), St. Martin's Press

Johnson, Richard. "Horror Movie Stirs Up A Real Scare," *New York Post*, (June 11, 1981)

Jones, Alan. "Nasty Stuff," *Starburst* #83, Vol. 7/No. 5, (July, 1985)

Kerber, Fred. "A Nesty Scare," *Daily News*, (June 11, 1981)

Konow, David. "*Phone Booth*," *Creative Screenwriting*, Vol. 9/No. 6 (November/December, 2002)

Konow, David. "*Cellular*," *Creative Screenwriting*, Vol. 11/No. 5 (September/October, 2004)

Martin, Bob. "Larry Cohen & *Q*," *Fangoria* #24, (December, 1982)

McDonagh, Maitland. "Larry Cohen: Thriving Outside the Mainstream," *Film Journal* #88 (July, 1985)

McDonagh, Maitland. "Dispatches from the Cohen Zone," *Psychotronic* #11, (Fall, 1991)

McGilligan, Patrick. "Larry Cohen: Manic Energy," *Backstory 4: Interviews with Screenwriters of the 1970s and 1980s* (2006), University of California Press

Milne, Tom. "*It Lives Again*," *Monthly Film Bulletin* Vol. 45/No.539 (December, 1978)

Newman, Kim. *Nightmare Movies* (1988), Bloomsbury

Newman, Kim. "*Full Moon High*," *Monthly Film Bulletin*, Vol. 58/No.635 (December, 1986)

Nicholls, Peter. *Fantastic Cinema* (1984), Ebury Press

O'Brien, Geoffrey. "Lesser Evil: J. Edgar Hoover and the End of an Era," *Film Comment*, Vol. 47/No. 4 (July/August, 2011)

Parish, James Robert and Hill, George H. *Black Action Films* (1989), McFarland & Co.

Shapiro, Marc. "On the Beat with *Maniac Cop*," *Fangoria* #72, (March, 1988)

Swires, Steve. "The Mutant Master Cometh: Part One," *Fangoria* #67, (September, 1987)

Swires, Steve. "The Private Files of Larry Cohen: Part Two," *Fangoria* #68, (October, 1987)

Taylor, Paul. "Hitchcock, Hammer & Sit-Com Suicide," *Monthly Film Bulletin* Vol. 53/No. 627, (April, 1986)

Taylor, Paul. "*The Stuff*," *Monthly Film Bulletin* Vol. 53, No. 627, (April, 1986)

Vale, Vivian & Juno, Andrea (ed). *Incredibly Strange Films* (1986), Plexus

Welkos, Robert W. "Fox Postpones *Phone Booth* because of sniper attacks," *Los Angeles Times*, (October 16, 2002)

Wells, Jeffrey. "Larry Cohen: From Hip Pocket Movies to ACP's *I, the Jury*," *The Film Journal* Vol. 84/No. 8, (May 4, 1981)

Wells, Jeffrey. "Larry Cohen, Like a Cat: The Writer/Director of UFD'S *Q* on Life in the Jungle," *The Film Journal* Vol. 85/No. 20, (October 20, 1982)

Wiater, Stanley. *Dark Dreamers: Conversations with the Masters of Horror* (1990), Avon Books

Williams, Tony. *Larry Cohen: The Radical Allegories of an Independent Filmmaker* (1997), McFarland & Co.

Williams, Tony. "Cohen on Cohen," *Sight and Sound*, Vol. 53/No.1, (1983/1984)

Wilson, John M. "Talk of the Town," *Los Angeles Times*, (November 11, 1990)

Wood, Robin. "Gods and Monsters," *Film Comment* Vol. 14/No. 5, (September/October 1978)

Wood, Robin & Lippe, Richard (ed). *The American Nightmare*, Toronto: Festival of Festivals, (1979)

About the Author

Michael Doyle. Photo courtesy of Siân Doyle

MICHAEL DOYLE IS A JOURNALIST AND AUTHOR, whose words have appeared in such publications as *Rue Morgue*, *Fangoria*, and *Scream*. He has interviewed many celebrated filmmakers, including William Friedkin, John Carpenter, Philip Kaufman, David Cronenberg, Roger Corman, Guillermo Del Toro, Ivan Reitman, Joe Dante, Paul Verhoeven, Wes Craven, Sydney J. Furie, Michael Wadleigh, Peter Medak, Mick Garris, and Stuart Gordon. He currently lives in Wales with his wife, two children, and a Chinese Dwarf Hamster named Blossom II. *Larry Cohen: The Stuff of Gods and Monsters* is his first book.

Index

Numbers in **bold** indicate photographs

Abby 374, 625
"Accomplice" 55, 651
Across 110th Street 109, 595
Adams, Bette 246
Adams, Brooke 336, 621
Addy, Wesley 471, 631-632
Adler, Joseph 69
Adler, Stella 541
Aiello, Danny 333, 644
Albert, Eddie 55, 651
Allen, David 282, 283, 328-329, **442**, 614-615, 643, 644
Allen, Woody 310, 331, 341
Ambulance, The xii, 320, 415, **449**, 463-480, 481, 482, 483, 567, 620, 630-632, 646
American Gangster 121, 596
Americans, The 50, 586
American Success Company, The 84-86, 87, 591, 665
American Werewolf in London, An ii, 94, 243-244, 249, 597
Amis, Suzy 509, 634, 671
Apparatus, The 345-346, 352, 565
Argento, Dario **455**, 530, 533
Arkin, Adam 242, 247, 248, 642
Arkin, Alan **222**, 247-248, 642
Arkoff, Samuel 107, 113, 137, 173, 180, 181, 200, 247, 280, 288-289, 291-292, **453**, 594, 639, 643
Armer, Alan A. 53, 586, 653, 659
Arrest and Trial 33, 64, 652
As Good As Dead 481-488, 632, 647
Ashley, Ted 236-237
Assante, Armand 265, 272, 273, 274, 280, 665
Atkins, Tom 406, 626-627, 667
Aubrey, Jim 50
Avery, Margaret 131, 640

Bad Lieutenant 317
Bad Lieutenant: Port of Call New Orleans 619, 637
Baker, Rick 1, 142-144, 228-229, 248, 249, 384, 597-598, 610, 639, 640, 642, 645
Balk, Fairuza 535, 537, 539, 540, 637, 648
Ball, Lucille 428, 627
Balsam, Martin 31
Barbash, Bob 524, 525-526, 636, 674
Barnaby Jones 60-61, 487, 586, 587
Barton Fink 415-416
Bass, Saul 141, 597
Batman 25, 47-48, 589
Bauer, Belinda 85, 591, 665
Bay, Michael 513, 634
Behan, Brendan 31, 584
Belushi, John 201, 202, 332
Benigni, Robert **453**
Bergman, Ingrid 72, 73
Berlin, Jeannie 95-97, 639
Berman, James Gabriel 509-510, 671
Bernard, Crystal 481, 482, 632, 647
Bernhard, Sandra 97
Bernstein, Elmer 69, 662
Best Seller 306, 347-350, 509, 667
Big Lebowski, The 46-47, 626
Black Caesar 3, 12, 105, 107-121, 123, 124, 125, 126, 127, 130, 131, 133, 134, 135, 136, 137, 143, 155, **212**, **213**, 246, 260, 273, 392, 465, 489, 490, 491, 493, 594-596, 639-640
Black, Karen 379, 386, 625, 645
Blackman, Honor 556-557
Blatt, Daniel 159-160, 174, 665
Blind Alleys see *Perfect Strangers*
"Blind Man's Bluff Raid, The" 49, 659
Blue Light 46, 47-48, **211**, 656-659
Bobbitt, Charles 119
Bocelli, Andrea 82
Bochco, Steven 58-59, 587, 660, 661
Bo chi tung wah 519-520, 673

Body Snatchers 353-355, 621, 622, 668-669
Bogosian, Eric 311, 314-315, 316, 619, 644
Bone 1, 91-106, 112, 113, 116, 143, 170, 176, **211, 212**, 309, 548, 592-594, 639
Boone, Richard 82, 664
Booth, Edwin 255, 611
Bosley, Tom 436, 437, 438, 646
Bourne Identity, The 50
Boyz n the Hood 493-494
Braeden, Eric 471, 646
Branded 1, 40-47, 48-49, 52, 56, 86, **210**, 404, 574, 585, 654-656
Brando, Marlon 101, 200, 231, 237, 352, 469, 525, 607-608
Bride of Frankenstein, The 4, 413-414, 629
Bridges, Jeff 46, 84-85, 86, 359, 665
Brodkin, Herbert 34, 38, 49, 51, 64, 556, 651, 652, 659
Broken Sabre 48
Brooks, Mel 31, 168, 253-254
Brown, David 102
Brown, James 117-119, 134, 639
Brown, Jim 77, 78, 489, 495, 496-497, 500, 505, 596, 647, 664
Brute Force 360, 622
Brynner, Yul 67, 69, 662
Burke & Hare 529, 543, 637
Butler, Yancy 509, 671
Buttons, Red **453**, 469-470, 476, 631, 646

Caine, Michael 80, 85
Call Holme 59
Campbell, Bruce 406, 413, 627, 667, 668
Camp, Colleen 432, 433, 437, 646
Capra, Frank 42, 574-575, 638
"Captive, The" 95, 652
Captivity 522-524, 554, 555, 559, 635, 673
Carlisle, Anne 296-297, 298, 303, 304, **441**, 643
Carpenter, John 14, 248, 376, 529, 532, 533, 541-542, 563, 572, 573-574, 636-637
Carradine, David 34-35, **223, 224, 225**, 232, 276, 278, 280, 281, 283, 293-294, 457, 458-461, 616, 617, 630, 643
Carradine, John 457, 617, 629-630, 655
Carradine, Keith 459-460, 617, 630
Carradine, Robert 459-460, 617, 630
Carrera, Barbara 265, 267, 428, 431, **447**, 646, 665
Carrey, Jim 513, 514
Carson, Jack 35-36
Casablanca 9, 552-553, 581

Cast of Characters see *League of Extraordinary Gentlemen, The*
Cat People 229, 607
Cellular 293, 519-520, 526, 672
Cerullo, Al 284
Chan-wook, Park 77, 590
Chariots of the Gods 160, 599-600
Checkmate 33, 650
Chi-Lites, The 502, 633
Christian, Claudia 415, 668
Christie, Agatha 263, 613
Cimino, Michael 311, 315-316, 619
Clark, Bob 361
Clark, Candy 276, 278, 616, 643
Clinton, Bill 186-187, 357, 590
Clinton, Hilary 358
Coates, Anne V. 364, 623
Coen Brothers 46, 47, 415
Cohen, Cynthia Costas 346-347, **450**, 475-476
Cohen, Janelle Webb 78, 149, **208, 216**, 298, 475, 618, 639, 640, 641, 645, 646
Cohen, Melissa Inger 475, 479, 642
Cole, Warren 533, 539, 648
Columbo 29, 58-59, 587, 660-661
Coney Never Closes 20
Connected see *Bo chi tung wah*
Connery, Sean 356, 595, 635
Connors, Chuck 1, 40-47, **210**, 574, 652, 654-656, 662
Constantine, Eddie 233, 608, 642
Converse, Frank 49, 260, 642, 659
Cook, Randy 282, 283, 614, 643
Cool Million 59-60, 660
Coppola, Francis Ford 231, 246, 563, 607, 609
Cordell, Frank 173-174, 641
Corey, Wendell 32, 649, 655
Corman, Roger 174-175, 325, 351, 610, 621
Coronet Blue 49-51, 52, 260, 659
Crack in the Mirror 87-88
Craven, Wes 155, 239, 240, 330
Crawford, Broderick 181, 187, 188, 189, 190, 191, 198, 201, 202, 204, **218, 219**, 604, 605, 606, 641
Crawford, Joan 434, 628-629
Crenna, Richard 83, 416, 664
Crewdson, John 181
Cronenberg, David 248, 299, 529, 573, 574
Crowther, Bosley 102, 271
Curtis, Tony 514, 634
Custer 51, 586, 660
Cutting Room, The see *Special Effects*

Daddy's Gone A-Hunting 70-72, 74-76, 77-78, 365, 565, 589, 663
Dahl, Roald 32-33, 649
Dailey, Dan 180-181, 187-188, 189, 190-191, 641
Daly, John 296, 306-307, 309, 618
Danforth, Jim 329, 614, 621, 644
Dante, Joe ii, 175, 248, **456**, 529, 532, 543, 636, 679
Davi, Robert 413, 414, 668
Davis, Bette 326, 423-440, **447**, **448**, 628, 629, 646
Davis, Jr., Sammy 107-108
Deadly Illusion 367-372, **445**, 623-624, 644-645
Deathdream 361
Defenders, The 1, 33, 34, 35, 37, 38-40, 50, 51, 64, 95, **210**, 510-511, 650, 651, 652, 653, 654, 671-672
Defenders, The: Choice of Evils 510-511, 671-672
De Mornay, Rebecca 357, 358, 669
De Niro, Robert 151, 152, 231, 331, 593, 606, 607, 610
Dennehy, Brian 348, 349, 667
Dennis, Sandy 2, 72, 165, 641
De Palma, Brian 148, 151, 152, 317
Desperado: Avalanche at Devil's Ridge 353, 667
De Toth, Andre 78, 80-81, 373, 591, 624, 663
Devlin, Dean 292-293, 672
Dial Rat for Terror see *Bone*
DiCaprio, Leonardo 186, 188
Dickinson, Angie 31, 403, 626
"Dirty Socks" 62-63, 661
Dixon, Jim 283, 415, 466, 567, 639, 640, 641, 642, 643, 644, 645, 646, 658, 667, 668
Doctor Strange 350-352, 355, 470
Dooley, Paul 260, 611, 642
Dormer, Christopher Jordan 411-412
Douglas, Gordon 31-32, 585, 586, 599
Douglas, Kirk 26, 72, 347, 349
Douglas, Paul 245, 609
Doumanian, Jean 202
Dracula 8, 400, 401, 407, 635
Drivas, Robert 162, 641
Drive 420, 421
Drucker, Mort 252, 610
Duggan, Andrew 95, 98, **211**, 260, 399, 567, 586, 639, 640, 641, 642, 643, 646, 652
Dullea, Keir 35, 649
Dunne, Dominick 21-22, 583

Eastwood, Clint 78, 153, 186, 188, 194, 197, 203, 204, 205, 246, 524, 525, 526, 609, 610
Ebert, Roger 272, 291, 292, 358, 594
Ebsen, Buddy 61
Ed McBain's 87th Precinct: Heatwave 507-508, 670-671
Ed McBain's 87th Precinct: Ice 507, 508, 670
"Eighty Seventh Precinct, The" 27, 507, 648
Elam, Jack 83, 591, 664
El Condor 77, 78-81, 82, 333, 497, 565, 663-664
Eleniak, Erika 508, 670
Empire Strikes Back, The 68
Erlichman, Marty 82
"Escape into Black" 36, 653
Espionage 33, 37-38, 652
E.T. the Extra Terrestrial 299-300
Exorcist, The 1, 140, 148, 239, 249, 597, 614, 625
Exorcist III, The 374
Expert, The 360, 622
Ex, The 508-509, 510, 550, 554, 671

Falk, Peter 28-29, 59, 648, 660, 661
Fallen Eagle **452**, 559-560
"False Face" 32-33, **209**, 649
Family Plot 71, 73, 76, 379, 512
Farentino, James 59, 60, 587, 660
Farmer, Frances 321, 620
Farrell, Colin **454**, 513-514, 515, 517, 672
Farrell, Sharon **215**, 230, 640
Fast Getaway 415
Felt, Mark 182-183, 184, 187
Ferrara, Abel 316, 317, 353-355, 619, 668
Finney, Albert 181, 604
Flynn, Errol 7, 8, 9, 58
Flynn, John 350, 667
Folsey, George 94, 98, 101, 143, 170, **212**, 639
Ford, Betty 187, 188
Forrest, Frederic 230, 231, 607, 608, 642
Forster, Robert 164-165, 232, 419-420, 493, 495, 607, 647, 668, 670
Foxy Brown 107, 120
Frankenstein 8, 143, 145-146, 327, 407, 411, 413-414, 520, 549
Frenzy 71, 73, 74
Friday the 13th 376, 407, 572
Friedkin, William 1, 148, 320, 636
From Hell 521

Fugitive, The 36-37, 51, 52, 586, 653
Fuller, Sam 392-394, 396-397, 399, 403-404, **446**, 604, 625, 626, 646
Full Moon High xi, 126, **221**, **222**, 241-255, 257, 307, 565, 608-611, 618, 642

Gallagher, Megan 466, 646
Gambler, the Girl and the Gunslinger, The 203, 524-526, 635, 674
Garland, Judy 30, 94, 342
Garris, Mick 1-3, **456**, 529, 530, 647
Gatsby, Jill 360, 409, 475, 646, 668
Gazzara, Ben 33, 652
Gibson, Mel 120, 513, 515
Gielgud, John 87, 666
Girdler, William 374, 624-625
Gish, Lillian 433, 628, 665
Glickman, Paul 163, 169, **218**, 315, 323, 340, 641, 642, 643, 644
"Go-Between, The" 39, 653
Godfather, The 119-120, 125, 231, 246, 607, 621
God Told Me To 2-3, 55, 141, 150, 155, 159-177, **217**, **218**, 282, 288, 301, 302, 361-362, 365, 376, 512, 545, 548, 549, 565, 599-603, 614, 618, 640-641
Godzilla (1998) 292
"Golden Thirty, The" 35-36, **209**, 649
Good Times 257, 259, 611
Gordon, Gerald 124, 131, 640
Gordon, Stuart 25, 354-355, **456**, 532, 583, 669
Goulet, Robert 47, **211**, 656-659, 662
Granger, Farley 74-75, 360
Grant, Cary 9, 60, 472, 473
Grauman, Walter 47, 656-659, 662
Green Berets, The 362, 623
Greene, David 38, 39, 650, 652
Greene, Lorne 60, 61, 665
Green for Danger 464-465
Gregory, Dick 110, 595
Grier, Pam 232, 489, 493, 495, 496, 597, 647
Griff 60-61
Griffith, Melanie 355
Grimaldi, Alberto 79
Grimes, Tammy 336-337, 557-558
Grosso, Sonny 319-320
Guillermin, John 78, 79-81, 663
Guilty as Sin 346, 355-360, 459, 669
Gwenn, Edmund 255, 566, 611

Hall, Arsenio 332
Harley, Jackie Earl 419, 668
Harris, Jack H. 103-104, 105, 594, 639
Harris, Julius W. 126, 131, 419, 596, 639, 640, 668
Harrison, Joan 71-72
Hartman, Elizabeth 246-247, 609, 642
Hauser, Wings 495, 633, 647
Havoc, June 398, 403, 626, 641, 646
Hayes, John Michael 75, 590
Heartbreak Kid, The 96, 159, 593
Heavy, The 293, 457-461, 476, 629-630
Heffron, Richard T. 265, 271, 613, 665
Hell up in Harlem 3, 12, 83, 105, 118-119, 123-137, 143, 155, 260, 489, 490, 491, 493, 565, 570, 596-597, 618, 640
Hemmings, David 307
Hendry, Gloria 115, 124, 131, 596, 597, 639, 640
Hendry, Ian 556, 557
Henreid, Paul 433, 628
Henry, Ed 71
Herrmann, Bernard 74, 88, 89, 141-142, 147-152, 169, 173, 174, **215**, **216**, 251, 640, 642
Herrmann, Norma 88, 149-151
Hickox, Anthony 365, 623, 669
Hickox, Douglas 365, 623
High Noon 84, 591
Hitchcock, Alfred 9, 31, 32-33, 55, 70-77, 88-89, 150, 151-152, 296, 347, 357, 359, 379, **451**, 471-472, 473, 474, 485, 511-512, 526, 555, 565-566, 570, 585, 586, 590, 591, 597, 599, 627
Holliday, Kene 260-261, 612, 642
Honess, Peter 129-130, 640
Hooper, Tobe 235, 389, 403, 529, 563, 636
Hoover, J. Edgar 2, 116, 173, 179-206, 238-239, 253, 307, 324, 398, 429, 603-607, 618, 641
Hope, Bob 7, 21, 326, 627
Hostiles, The see *Gambler, the Girl and the Gunslinger, The*
Houghton, Buck **211**, 656, 657, 658, 659, 662
House of Wax 373-374, 585, 591, 624
Housewife see *Bone*
Howard, John 42
Howling, The ii, 159, 243-244, 249-250, 610, 615, 630
Hudson, Hugh 619
Hudson, Rock 59, 85

Hunter, Evan see McBain, Ed
Huston, John 77, 193, 397, 398
Hylands, Scott 72, 589, 663
Hyman, B.D. 434, 629

I Deal in Danger 48, 662
In Broad Daylight 82-83, 664
Inglorious Basterds 204, 530
Into Thin Air see *Ambulance, The*
Invaders, The 1, 52-57, 161, 586, 659
Invasion of Privacy 364-366, 509, 519, 623, 669
Invasion of the Body Snatchers 52, 327, 336, 353, 621
Invisible Man, The 352, 355
Ireland, John 392, 404, 594
Iron Eyes Cody 81, 664
I Shot Jesse James 404
Israel, Neal 383, 645
I, the Jury xii, **223**, 265-274, 275, 276-277, 280, 369, 550, 613-614, 665-666
It Lives Again **221**, 227-240, 373, 375, 376, 377, 383, 384, 385, 386, 387, 548, 607-608, 642
It's Alive 1-2, 83, 126, 129, 139-157, 161, 169, 174, 179, **214, 215**, 227, 228, 229, 230, 234, 237, 238, 292, 301-302, 365, 375, 377, 383, 384, 385, 386, 387, 388, 463, 464, 497, 505, 519, 532, 547, 548, 549, 550, 570, 597-599, 640
It's Alive (2008) 156, 673-674
It's Alive III: Island of the Alive xii, 116, 367, 373-388, **445**, 624-625, 645
I Was a Teenage Werewolf 241-242

Jackie Brown 232, 493, 505
Jagged Edge 359-360, 622
J. Edgar 186, 188, 194, 197, 203, 204, 205, 606-607
Johnson, Arte 59
Johnson, Don 357, 669
Jones, James Earl **449**, 468, 476, 479-480, 631, 646

Kaleidoscope 73-74
Kastner, Elliott 352, 525, 622
Kaufman, Andy 3, 165-168, 641
Kazan, Elia 18, 199-200, 606, 637
Kennedy, Burt 68, 69, 588, 662, 664
Kennedy, Robert F. 116, 193-194, 197, 641
Kern, David 408, 645, 646, 647, 667, 668

Kershner, Irvin 67-68
Keyes, Evelyn 394, 397-398, 403, 429, 435, 646
Kilbride, Percy 31
Kill Bill 232
"Killer Instinct" 32, 585, 648-649
King, Martin Luther 116, 184-185, 641
King of Comedy, The 97, 593
King, Stephen 389-390, 400, 535, 634
King, Tony 128, 131, 640
Klugman, Jack 28-29, 648
Kotto, Yaphet 93-94, 101, 105, 107, **211**, 595, 639, 666
Kovack, Nancy 35, 649
Kraft Mystery Theater 27-29, 648
Kubrick, Stanley 25-26, 143
Kung Fu: The Legend Continues 293, 460, 617
Kurta, Paul 336, 643, 644, 645

Lack, Stephen 299, 643
Lancaster, Burt 347, 349, 526, 622, 634
Landau, Martin 39, 170, 408, 602, 618, 653
Landis, John ii, 47, 94, 143, 248, 529, 533, 543, 598, 610
Landon, Laurene xi-xii, **222**, 265, 272-273, 274, 336, 385, 399, 408, 413, 414, 437, **445, 456**, 614, 642, 645, 646, 648, 665, 667, 668
Last Tango in Paris 101-102, 593
Law & Order 538, 569
Law, John Phillip 72, 73
League of Extraordinary Gentlemen, The 520-522, 635
Lebenzon, Chris 130, 641
Lee, Stan 350-351, 470
Legend of Nigger Charley, The 108, 111, 595
Leno, Jay 242, 610
Leonard, Herbert B. 61-62
Lerner, Avi 156
Lerner, Michael 415-416, 668
Lester, Mark L. 508, 509, 510, 554, 633-634, 671
Levine, Joseph E. 102-103
Levinson, Richard 58-59, 587, 660, 661
Levy, Alfred 23
Lewton, Val 72, 229, 607
Lifeboat 511
Lindbergh, Charles 559
Link, William 58-59, 587, 660, 661
Liquid Sky 296, 617
Littman, Robert 424, 646

Lloyd, Kathleen 230, 231, 232, 608, 642, 667
Lloyd, Norman 88, 151
Lo Bianco, Tony 2, 164, 169, **217**, 549, 556, 601, 641
Lock, Stock and Two Smoking Barrels 119
Lords, Traci 481, 483-484, 487, 632, 647
Lucas, George 68, 171, 563
Ludlum, Robert 50
Ludmer, Mike 70, 71, 74
Lumet, Sidney 9, 310, 355-360, 459, 577, 622, 669
Lund, Art 115-116, 380, 639, 641, 645
Lund, Zoë see Tamerlis, Zoë
Lurin, Larry 337, 639, 640
Lustig, William 361, 363, 405-406, 407, 408, 409, 412, 413, 414, 416, 417-418, 419, 420, 421-422, 626, 667, 668, 670
Lutz, John 508, 671
Lynch, Richard 2, 168-169, 171, **217**, 601, 641

Madden, Donald 558
Magnuson, Ann 302, 303, 618, 643
Mancini, Henry 74
Mancuso, Nick 509, 671
Maniac Cop xii, 405-422, 463, 464, 518, 626-627, 667-668
Maniac Cop III: Badge of Silence 126, 405-422, 596, 626-627, 668
Maniac Cop 2 xii, 405-422, 626-627, 632, 668
Man on the Outside 60-61, 664-665
Man Who Loved Hitchcock, The 88-89, **451**, 555
Marathon Man 262, 612
Marcovicci, Andrea 329, 331, 339, 342, 644
Marley, Peverell 31-32, 585
Marshall, E. G. 22, 38, 510, 650, 651, 652, 653, 654, 672
Marsh, Jean 260, 261, 643
Mars, Kenneth 254, 610, 642
Martin, D'Urville 131, 595, 597, 639, 640
Martin, Quinn 36-37, 52, 53, 57, 61, 586, 587, 659
Marty 22, 268
"Mask of Marcella, The" 59, 660
Master of Suspense 87-88
Masters of Horror: Pick Me Up xii, 3, **455**, **456**, 529-544, 636-637, 647-648
"May Day! May Day!" 39, 653
May, Elaine 96, 592-593
McBain, Ed 27, 507-508, 648, 670

McDaniel, Hattie 259
McKee, Robert 552-553
McLaglen, Andrew 68, 588-589
McMahon, Ed 245, 596, 609, 642
"Medal for a Turned Coat" 37-38, 39, 585, 652
Meet Me in St. Louis 30, 94
Meisner, Sanford **452**, 559
"Member of the Posse" see "Killer Instinct"
Messages Deleted 526-527, 529, 554, 674
Midkiff, Dale 508, 670
Milch, David 62-63, 661
Milford, Gene 18
Miller, Mindy 124
Miracles in Brooklyn 168
Mirisch, Walter 67, 68, 69, 353, 588, 662, 667
Misbegotten 509-510, 554, 671
Mission, The 48, 655-656
Mod Squad 83
Momma the Detective see *See China and Die*
Mommie Dearest 434, 628-629
Monkey's Paw, The 361, 622
Montiel, Sara 403
Moore, Alan 521-522, 635
Moore, Roger 31, 60
Morgan, Chris 520, 672
Moriarty, Michael 2, **223**, **224**, 275-276, 278-279, 280, 290, 291, 329, 330-331, 332, 333, 338-339, 341, 342, 376, 378, 380, 381, 385, 386, 391, 398, 399, 403, **445**, 473, 482-483, 531, 535, 537-539, 540-541, 543-544, 549, 568-569, 616, 637, 643, 644, 645, 648
Morley, Robert 89, 592
Morris, Garrett 332-333, **443**, **444**, 644
Motive 556-557, 558
Ms. 45 316
"Murder by the Book" 58-59, 587, 660
Murder, She Wrote 258, 487
Murphy, Eddie 120, 280, 332, 598
Murphy, Fred 289, 643, 667

Naked City 61-62, 282, 340, 587
Napier, Charles 495, 632-633, 647, 668
Nature of the Crime, The 39, 164, 556
Neill, Steve **221**, **442**, **443**, **444**, **446**, 641, 642, 643, 644, 645
Nesbitt, Lowell 310, 314, 323-324, 619
Netter, Gil **454**, 672
Never Too Young 57-58
Newhart, Bob 247, 610
Newman, Paul 357, 358, 637

Newmar, Julie 24-25
Nichols, Mike 102, 105, 593
Nicholson, Jack 231, 280, 598, 608
"Night Cry" 27-29, 584, 648
"Night Sounds" 34, 650
Noé, Gaspar 175-176, 602-603
Nolan, Lloyd 181, 190, 604, 641
North By Northwest 9, 76, 148, 472, 473, 590, 597
North, Sheree 406, 627, 667
Nosferatu 390, 401
Nurses, The 33-34, 51, 64, 650, 651, 652
NYPD Blue 62-63, 507, 588, 661

O'Brien, Edmond 33, 55, 651
O'Connor, Kevin 312, 320, 620, 644
Once Upon a Mattress 35
O'Neal, Patrick 333, 341, 644, 660, 664
O'Neal, Ron 489, 495, 496, 500, 633, 647
Original Gangstas 12, 120, 232, 489-506, 632-633, 647
Osborne, Robert 424

Pacino, Al 168, 280, 556, 619
Paoli, Dennis 354, 669
Paris Holiday 21
Parks, Michael 193-194, 605, 641
"Party Girl" 34, 651
Payback, The 119
Pearl, Daniel 235, 380, 381, 523, 642, 645, 673
Peller, Clara 335-336, 337
Perfect Strangers 295-308, 309, 315, 323, 373, **441**, 617-618, 643
Phone Booth 388, 407-408, 412, **454, 455**, 511-519, 522, 526, 560, 627, 672
Pinero, Miguel 261, 612, 643
Play Dirty 80, 591
Poitier, Sidney 9, 99, 246, 610
Polanski, Roman 153, 309-310
Pollack, Sydney 31, 38-39, **210**, 511, 584-585, 650
Preminger, Otto 19, 27, 28, 582, 584, 597
Price, Vincent **450**, 624, 628
Private Files of J. Edgar Hoover, The 2, 116, 173, 179-206, **218, 219, 220**, 238-239, 253, 307, 324, 398, 603-607, 618, 641
Pro-Life 532, 636-637
Puzo, Eugene 124
Puzo, Mario 119-120, 124

Q – The Winged Serpent 2, 3, 97, **223, 224, 225**, 274, 275-294, 328, 378, 457, 483, 496, 537, 545, 549, 565, 593, 614-617, 618, 643

Rafelson, Bob 317
Raffin, Deborah 172, **217**, 641
Raimi, Sam 47, 622, 627, 668
Rambo: First Blood Part II 269-270, 632
Ransohoff, Martin 355, 359, 622, 669
Rasche, David 432-433, 437, 646
Rat Patrol, The 49, 471, 659
Rattan, Aubrey 494, 500, 501, 647
Razatos, Spiro 408-409, 415
Reed, Rex 291, 629
Reed, Robert 38, 650, 651, 652, 653, 654
Refn, Nicolas Winding 420-421
Rehme, Bob 291
Reid, Tara 398-399, 626, 646
Reiner, Carl 340, 621
Reinhold, Judge 482-483, 486, 487, 647
Reno, Janet 538
Reservoir Dogs 111
Return of the Magnificent Seven, The 67-69, 86, 271, 662
Return to Salem's Lot, A xii, 297, 301, 367, 374, 375, 378, 389-404, **446**, 538, 625-626, 645
Richardson, Lee 558
Richert, William 84, 85, 591, 665
Richter, Hans 18, 582
Rickles, Don 247, 610
Rief, Dennis 286
Rijn, Brad 297-298, 300, 303, 304, 305, 318, 643, 644, 646
Ringer, The see *American Success Company, The*
Ritt, Martin 9, 115, 631
Roberts, Eric **449**, 465, 467-468, 476, 483, 567, 646
Robertson, Peggy 75, 151-152, 590
Robinson, Edward G. 7, 107, 108, 111, 401, 469
Robson, Mark 72, 75, 663
Rolle, Esther 257, 259-260, 261-262, 611, 642
Romero, George A. 14, 155
Rooney, Mickey 469
Rose, Reginald 39, 650, 651, 652, 653, 654
Rossi, Leo 414, 415, 668
Roundtree, Richard **223**, 276, 284, 406, 489, 495, 496, 501, 616, 643, 647, 667

Rózsa, Miklós 173, 198, **220**, 251, 641
Run of the Arrow 403, 626
Ryan, John P. 144, 147, 230, 549, 598, 608, 640, 642

Sabiston, Peter 33, 124-125, 639, 640, 643
Salem's Lot 374, 375, 389-390, 401, 402-403
Sam Benedict 33, 55, 64, 651
Sarandon, Susan 95
Saturday Night Live 201-203, 332
Saville, Victor 266, 267, 613
Sayonara 469
Scandalous 87, 666
"Scapegoat" 36-37
Scherick, Edgar 159-160, 174, 665
Schow, David J. 3, 530-531, 533, 636, 647
Schumacher, Joel 407-408, **454**, 513, 515-518, 672
Scorsese, Martin 97, 150, 151, 152, 310, 563, 593, 597, 601, 606, 610
Scott, Pippa 95, 592
Scourby, Alexander 333, 341, 644
Scream, Baby, Scream 69-70
"Secret, The" 39, 556, 653
See China and Die 257-264, 611-613, 618, 642-643
Sellers, Peter 85
Semple Jr., Lorenzo 71, 72, 589, 663
Shaw, David 39
Shelia Levine is Dead and Living in New York 96, 593
Shoot-Out in a One-Dog Town 83-84, 86
Short Eyes 261, 612
Sidney, Sylvia 2, 170, **218**, 429, 641
Simpson, O. J. 106, 498-499, 583
Sins of Rachel Cade, The 31-32, 585, 626
Slaughter's Big Rip-Off 118, 119, 596
Smith, Dick 33, 248, 597, 649
Smith, Will 513, 514
Snoop Dog 136
Soisson, Joel 418, 668
Sorry, Wrong Number 519
Sorvino, Mira 341, 621
Sorvino, Paul 265, 331, 332, 340-341, 644, 666
Space: 1999 170-171, 602
Sparrow 61-62, 587, 665
Special Effects 296-297, 307, 308, 309-324, 354, 373-374, **441**, 570, 618, 619-620, 644
Spelling, Aaron 57, 83, 664

Spielberg, Steven 59, 88, 91, 131, 143, 278-279, 299-300, 463, 503, 513, 563, 594, 606, 625, 660
Spies Like Us 47, 586
Spillane, Mickey 265, 266, 267, 268, 271, 613, 665
Stander, Lionel 433, 437, **448**, 646
Stanwyck, Barbara 435-436, 519
Steel Helmet, The 392, 397
Steiger, Rod 22, 181, 353, 403, 667
Stockley, Mathew 297, 299, 300, 301, 303, 643
Stone, Oliver 176, 314-315, 514, 559, 619
Stranger Among Us, A 355
Strangers on a Train 347, 360
Stranger, The 401
Stratten, Dorothy 321, 322, 620
Stuart, William L. 27, 28, 584
Stuff, The xii, 2, 87, 97, 161, 297, 301, 325-344, 376, 378, **442**, **443**, **444**, 463, 464, 545, 615, 620-621, 644
Sullivan, William 184
Summers, Anthony 186
Superman 237-238, 284, 352, 591, 602
Sutherland, Kiefer 407, 517, 672
Sweet Smell of Success 514, 634

Talk Radio 314-315, 619
Tamerlis, Zoë 311, 313, 316-317, 354, 620, 644
Tannen, William 370, 624, 644
Tarantino, Quentin 111, 132, 193, 204, 232, 341, **456**, 493, 505, 529, 529-530, 597
Tate, Sharon 309-310
Taylor, Rod 485
Teen Wolf 244, 608
Texas Chainsaw Massacre, The 154, 235
That Man Bolt 126, 127, 128, 596-597
Them! 146-147, 585, 598-599, 611
Thing, The 376, 532, 614, 621
Thinnes, Roy 53, 56, 659
Tolson, Clyde 181, 183, 184, 185, 188, 189, 605, 641
Too Young to Go Steady 23
Topaz 70, 71, 75
Torn, Rip 191-193, 641
Torn, Tony 192-193
"Traitor, The" 39, 50, 650
Travolta, John 232, 467
Trick 557-558
Truffaut, François 151, 599, 601
Turner, Janine 465, 466, 471, 646
Twister 503-504, 506

Uncle Sam 361-364, 418, 419, 670
United States Steel Hour, The 35-36, **209**, 649
"Unwritten Law, The" 39, 654
Uris, Leon 75
Ustinov, Peter 88-89, **451**

Van Cleef, Lee 77, 78, 79, 663, 664
Vanity 369-370, 624, 645
Vanoff, Nick 93, 95
Van Patten, Joyce 95, 96, 98, 101, **211**, 639
Verdict, The 355, 358, 359, 360, 631
Vertigo 148, 317, 566, 597
Vigoda, Abe 336, 337, 621
Von Däniken, Erich 160, 599-600

Wallach, Eli 89, 637
Washington, Denzel 121
Washington Heights 13, 558-559
Wasserman, Lew 74, 128, 589-590
Wayne, John 203, 362, 524-526, 589, 617, 623
Wayne, Michael 525
Way Out 32-33, **209**, 649
Weaver, Fritz 38, 259, 260, 261, 643, 650, 652
Weiss, Julie 425, 646
Welles, Orson 20, 401, 570, 638
Whales of August, The 433, 439-440, 628
Where the Sidewalk Ends 27-28, 584
White, Carol 72, 589, 663
Wicked Stepmother xii, 192-193, 398, 423-440, **447**, **448**, 476, 627-629, 646
Widmark, Richard 111, 399, 604
Wilder, Billy 77, 198, 582, 597, 613
Williams, Billy Dee 368, 369, **445**, 645
Williamson, Fred 108, 110, 111, 114, 115, 116, 121, 124, 125, 126, 127, 128, 129, 130, 131, 143, **213**, 465, 489-492, 493, 495, 496-497, 498, 499-500, 502, 505, 595, 596, 597, 639, 640, 647
Willis, Bruce 273-274, 280, 614
Woehrle, John 302, 643, 644, 645
Wolfen 243-244
Wolk, Andy 510, 671, 672
Women of San Quentin 86-87, 666
Wonder, Stevie 117-118
Wood, Robin 55, 171, 204, 547, 573, 586-587
Woods, James 348-349, 667
Wymore, Patrice 58

X-Files, The 164, 600

Young and the Restless, The 471
Youngman, Henny 35-36, **209**, 649

Zane Grey Theater 32, 636, 648-649
Z'Dar, Robert 406-407, 667, 668

www.ingramcontent.com/pod-product-compliance
Lightning Source LLC
Chambersburg PA
CBHW071710300426
44115CB00010B/1376